Water Lilies

&

Flores del Agua

Water Lilies

Flores del agua

*An Anthology of
Spanish Women Writers
from the Fifteenth
through the
Nineteenth Century*

Amy Katz Kaminsky

EDITOR

University of Minnesota Press
Minneapolis
London

Published by the University of Minnesota Press
111 Third Avenue South, Suite 290, Minneapolis, MN 55401-2520
Printed in the United States of America on acid-free paper

Water lilies : an anthology of Spanish women writers from the
    fifteenth through the nineteenth century / Amy Katz Kaminsky, editor.
        p.   cm.
    Spanish and English.
    Includes bibliographical references.
    ISBN 0–8166–1944–1 (hardcover). — ISBN 0–8166–1946 –8 (pbk.)
    1. Spanish literature—Women authors.   2. Spanish literature—
    Women authors—Translations into English.   3. Spanish literature—
    Women authors—History and criticism.   I. Kaminsky, Amy K.
    PQ6173.W38   1996
    860.8'09287—dc20   95–604

The University of Minnesota is an equal-opportunity educator and employer

For my mother, Florence Katz,
and in memory of my father, David Katz

La flor del agua · Water lily

a Robustiana Armiño

¿Por qué tiembla? —No lo sabe.
¿Qué aguarda en el lago? —Nada.—
De las aguas enlazada
a los hilos su raíz,
el movimiento suave
de la linfa va siguiendo,
la cabeza sumergiendo
del agua, al menor desliz.

Así la halló la alborada,
así la encuentra el lucero,
siempre el esfuerzo postrero
haciendo para bogar;
Y en las olas la encallada,
vaga y frágil navecilla
sin poder la florecilla
impeler ni abandonar.

Movimiento que no cesa,
ansiedad que se dilata,
ni el agua que sus pies ata
sostiene a la débil flor,
ni deja, en sus olas presa,
que vaya libre flotando,
quiere que viva luchando
siempre en continuo temblor.

¡Ya se inunda!. . .¡Ya se eleva!. . .
¡Ya la corriente la traga!. . .
¡Ya navega. . . ya naufraga!
¡Ya se salva. . . ya venció!
¡Ya el agua otra vez la lleva
en sus urnas sepultada!. . .

to Robustiana Armiño

Why does she tremble?—she does not know.
What awaits her in the lake?—Nothing.
Bound by tender threads to her
Roots in the water,
Her blossom submerges,
Swaying with its lymph to
Every gentle ripple
Of the waters.

Thus did dawn find her
Thus the morning star did see her,
In ever desperate struggle
To sail free
And atop the waves the floundering,
ethereal and fragile little boat
Cannot push off,
The little flower cannot escape.

Unceasing movement,
Swelling anxiousness,
The water that binds her feet
Can neither support the frail flower
Imprisoned in its waves, nor let it
Float freely away.
It condemns instead her life to struggle,
Ever in constant flux.

Now she is drowning! Now she emerges!
Now the current swallows her!
Now she swims . . . Now she drowns!
Now she is saved . . . Now she prevails!
Now the water again pulls her down
Sinking her in its watery urns!

¡Ya de nuevo sobre-nada
en el agua que la hundió!....
    Flor del agua, ¡cuántas flores
viven en paz en la tierra!
Sola tú vives en guerra
en tu acuático jardín:
te da la lluvia temores,
el manso pez te estremece
y tu belleza perece
sin gozar descanso, al fin.

    Tú, poetisa, flor del lago,
por amante, por cantora,
has venido en mala hora
con tu lira y tu pasión;
que en el siglo extraño y vago
a quien vida y arpa debes,
donde quiera que le lleves
fluctuará tu corazón.

    Que las cantoras primeras
que a nuestra España venimos
por sólo cantar sufrimos,
penamos por sólo amar;
porque en la mente quimeras
de un bello siglo traemos
y cuando este siglo vemos
no sabemos dó bogar.

    Las primeras mariposas
que a la estación se adelantan
y su capullo quebrantan
sin aguardar al abril,
nunca saben temblorosas
adonde fijar las alas,
siempre temen que sus galas
destroce el aire sutil.

    Las ráfagas las combaten
las extrañan los insectos
y de giros imperfectos
si cansado el vuelo ya,
sobre las plantas lo abaten
buscando el capullo amigo
hallan que néctar ni abrigo
la flor en botón les da.

    Las orugas que encerradas
aun están en sus clausuras

Now again she floats
Atop the water that submerged her!
    Water lily, how many flowers
Live in peace on the earth!
While you live alone in constant struggle
In your aquatic garden:
The rain makes you tremble,
The gentle fish make you quiver
And yet your beauty fades
Without enjoying its final rest.

    Poetess, water lily,
Both as lover and singer
Your coming is ill-chosen
With your lyre and your passion;
For in this strange and vague time
To which you owe life and harp,
Wherever you lead it
Your heart will vacillate.

    For the first women singers
To grace this our Spain
Suffer just to sing,
Suffer just to love;
For we bear with us chimeras
Of a more harmonious time
And seeing only that lovely time,
We know not where to row.

    The first butterflies
To appear in spring,
Who break their cocoon
Without waiting for April,
Never know, trembling,
Where to affix their wings,
Ever fearing lest the
Subtle air destroy
Their beauty.

    The storm engulfs them,
Strange insects startle them,
And after wavering flights
They alight wearily
On some plant;
Hoping for the friendly blossom,
They find instead that the tender bud
Offers them neither nectar nor shelter.

mañana al campo seguras
podrán sus alas tender;
¡mas, aquellas desdichadas
que antes cruzan la pradera
morirán, la primavera
risueña, sin conocer!. . .

    ¿Cuál es tu barca? —Una lira.
—¿Qué traes en ella?— Sonidos.
—Vuélvete, que no hay oídos
para tus sones aquí;
vuélvete, joven, y mira
si en tu barca, más sonoro,
puedes trasportarnos oro
u otro cargamento así.

    ¿Quién te llama? ¿A qué nos vienes
con peregrinas canciones?
El trueno de los cañones
del siglo el concierto es,
y en vano sus anchas sienes
pretendes ceñir de flores,
¡ay! sus pies destrozadores
hollarán cuantas le des.

    ¿Vienes de nuevo, alma mía?
¿Qué traes en la barca? —Amores.—
Torna a otras tierras mejores,
torna el camino a emprender;
si es oro nuestra poesía
nuestros amores son. . . nada.
Ve si la nave cargada
de cetros puedes traer,

    que, si no de amor, tenemos
tan elevadas pasiones
que sentimos ambiciones
de un cetro garzón;
Y cada garzón podemos
con nuestros genios profundos
media docena de mundos
fundir en una nación.

    ¿Otra vez? ¿Qué traes ahora?. . .
siempre en el mismo camino
sobre el cauce cristalino
en su barquilla la flor:
así la dejó la aurora
así la encuentra el lucero

Caterpillars still enveloped
In their cocoons
Tomorrow may safely spread
Their wings to the sky;
But those unfortunate butterflies
Who before ever crossing a field
Will perish, never having
Known the sweet springtime! . . .

    What is your boat? —A lyre.
What does it carry? —Songs.
Go back, there is no haven
For your songs here;
Return, young poetess, and see
If in your boat, you can bring us
The resonant sound of gold
Or some other welcome cargo.

    Who has called you? Why do you come
To us with your strange songs?
The thunder of cannons
Is the concert of these times,
And in vain do you attempt
To garland its broad chest;
Alas, with destructive feet
It will trample all your flowers.

    Do you still come, my dear one?
What do you carry in your boat? —Love.
Return to better lands,
Retrace your route;
If gold is our poetry
Then love is for . . . naught.
See if instead you can fill
Your boat with scepters,

    For, though we love not, ours
Is such a great passion
That every lad desires
A scepter,
Yes, we lads are able
With our great genius
To forge one mighty nation
From a half-dozen worlds.

    Again? What do you offer us now? . . .
Still following the same route
Upon the crystalline river
The flower in her boat:

siempre en el afán primero,
siempre en el mismo temblor.
  Tú, poetisa, flor del lago,
por amante, por cantora
has venido en mala hora
con tu amor y tu cantar:
que en el siglo extraño y vago,
a quien vida y arpa debes,
donde quiera que la lleves
puede el alma naufragar.

  Mas escucha, no estás sola
flor del agua, en el riachuelo;
contigo en igual desvelo
hay florecillas también:
que reluchan contra el ola,
que vacilan, que se anegan,
que nunca libres navegan
ni en salvo su barca ven;

  Pero enlazan sus raíces
a la planta compañera
y viven en la ribera
sosteniéndose entre sí:
y cual ella más felices
desde hoy serán nuestras vidas
si con las almas unidas,
vivimos, las dos así.

Carolina Coronado

Thus did the dawn leave her
Thus the morning star did find her
Ever with her first desire,
Trembling still.
  Poetess and water lily
Both as lover and singer
Your coming is ill-chosen
With your lyre and your passion;
For in this strange and vague time
To which you owe harp and life,
Wherever you lead it,
Your soul may flounder.

  But take heart, you are not alone
Water lily, in the river;
With you in the same frightful state
Are other flowers
Who struggle against the current,
Who waver and who sink,
Who never swim free
Nor see their boat safe;
  But they entwine their roots
With their sister plants
And dwell on the river's bank
Sustaining one another:
And how much happier
Will we be from this day forward
If with our souls entwined
The two of us join together.

(Translated by Lou Charnon Deutsch)

Contents

xi

The Eighteenth Century

Preface

Delicate, lovely, and like other flowers fundamentally useless beyond its decorative function, the water lily appears, moreover, to be isolated, eccentric, and unnatural. In its fragility, a flower should hold to solid land; floating on the water is foolish and dangerous. But water lilies are not unnatural, nor are they frail or solitary. Like Carolina Coronado, from whom I borrow the felicitous metaphor of the woman writer as water lily, I hope in this anthology to illuminate the strong, intertwined, submerged stems and roots of these flowers that on the surface have seemed to exemplify isolated, extravagant fragility.

It is a commonplace of feminist criticism that traditional criticism has tended to confuse women writers with their texts, as if the latter were a bodily effluence of the former. For that reason, it is risky to use similar metaphors for the writer and her writing. Yet just as Carolina Coronado found the image of the water lily evocative of the woman writer, the flower has been taken to symbolize the literary text. The word "anthology" comes from the Greek for "bouquet of flowers." It is an apt metaphor, not only for the result but also for the process of preparing such a volume. Like any bouquet, the final product depends on the skill of the maker in choosing, cutting, and arranging the flowers, and of deciding what is a flower in the first place.

In Western culture, flower arranging is a domestic art; and like any women's art, it lacks prestige. Yet flower arranging is subtle and complex. The well-made bouquet is an artifice that provides a multiple view of the flowers that form it. It invites the contemplation and comprehension of each of its flowers individually, calling to mind the existence of others of its species, enjoyed at other moments. It also evokes the landscape from which the flowers were gathered. Finally, it offers a juxtaposition in which all the flowers gathered together compose a new whole, in which each individual bloom might be seen afresh.

The grouping of texts in this anthology — the flowers I have picked and arranged, and sometimes cut — represents another version of Spanish literary history. It is a version that puts into relief both women writers' resistance to, and their complicity with, a literary tradition that has tried to exclude them, in which the very act of refusing to obey the proscription against women's speech is a challenge. Some texts, like Rosalía de Castro's "The Bluestockings" and Teresa de Cartagena's *Wonder at the Work of God*, call into question the relationship between the woman writer and the

act of writing itself. Others represent strategies that open paths to women's literary
expression. Some of these overtly seek out a literary tradition — for example, Coronado's "The Twin Geniuses: Sappho and Saint Teresa of Jesus." Others, like Saint
Teresa's *Life* and Luisa Sigea's poems, are the touchstones for other women writers in
search of such a tradition. I have chosen texts that tell of the daily lives of women,
such as the poetry of Sor Marcela de San Félix and María Gertrudis Hore, and those
that propose new definitions for the experiences that many women share. Both
María de Zayas and Emilia Pardo Bazán, for example, tell new stories of love, friendship, and marriage. Some of the texts mark women's presence in fields long assumed
to be exclusively male territory, such as Beatriz Bernal's novel of chivalry and Ana
Caro's *comedia*. All represent the complex relationship between women's writing and
the male-centered canon of Spanish literature that serves as the ghostly backdrop for
this volume.

As varied as the texts in this book are, I have chosen them from a very particular
field. They are all written in Castilian Spanish and as such do not represent the other
languages of contemporary or historical Spain: Catalonian, Galician, Basque, Hebrew,
or Arabic. They are also all by peninsular Spanish writers. They include no Latin
Americans, even from the colonial period, since it seems to me that those writers be-
long to quite another tradition.

Flores del Agua was born of the women's movement, which made me question the
lack of women's names in my own education in Spanish literature. I had developed an
elaborate theory to explain the dearth of women writers in Spain, never guessing that
so many Spanish women had in fact written. My theory received its first blow when, in
1977, my colleague Aníbal Biglieri showed me Reinaldo Ayerbe-Chaux's edition of
Leonor López de Córdoba's autobiography. If Leonor López existed, I thought, so
must others, and I set out to find them. My second discovery was Manuel Serrano y
Sanz's bibliography of women writers, published at the beginning of this century.
This extraordinary piece of scholarship contains the names of over eleven hundred
women who wrote in Spain between 1401 and 1833, the titles of their works, whatever
biographical information Serrano could find, and even some literary texts. Serrano's
bibliography is the work of a man who admired these women, but whose very conventional views about gender, religion, and morality inevitably colored his scholarship. Serrano is not always entirely reliable, but he remains an invaluable source.

I have worked on this collection for a long time, and many people have helped
me along the way. Many, including Electa Arenal, Kenneth Brown, Alan Deyer-
mond, Monroe Hafter, Susan Kirkpatrick, Francisco López Estrada, and Constance
Sullivan, have, in the finest spirit of scholarly exchange, shared their work with me.
I am grateful for their generosity. I am also indebted to those who read, encouraged,
and criticized my work: Cristina Enríquez de Salamanca, Sara Evans, Ruth Ellen Jo-
eres, Elaine Dorough Johnson, David Kaminsky, Linda Gould Levine, Elaine Tyler
May, Joanna O'Connell, Riv Ellen Prell, Cheri Register, Elena Sánchez Mora, Naomi

Scheman, Constance Sullivan, and Denise Walen. I am grateful to both the State University of New York's Faculty Research Fund and the Graduate School of the University of Minnesota, which provided me with time and money to do some of the research for this volume. Biodun Iginla, Meg Aerol, Kerry Sarnowski, Elizabeth Knoll Stomberg, David Thorstad, Becky Manfredini, and Kathy Wolter at the University of Minnesota Press have helped in innumerable ways to make this book a reality. Finally, I am indebted to the translators, whose painstaking work has re-created these texts for an English-speaking audience.

Since I began my work on this anthology in the late 1970s, feminist scholars and literary historians have created the subfield of Spanish feminist literary studies. I am indebted to their work and hope that this volume will serve to advance knowledge in the field and bring it to a new audience.

Introduction

... porque inhumana cosa nos pareció de sofrir que tantas obras de virtud y ejemplos de bondad fallados en el linaje de las Mujeres fuessen callados y enterrados en las escuras tinieblas de la olvidanza.

Don Álvaro de Luna, *Libro de las virtuosas y claras mujeres*

For it seemed to us an inhuman thing to suffer that so many works of virtue and examples of goodness found in the lineage of Women should be silenced and buried in the dark shadows of oblivion.

Don Álvaro de Luna, *Book of Virtuous and Fair Women*

Women and Spanish History

Despite patriarchal prescription, the lives of Spanish women across the centuries have been diverse and various. The popular version of that prescription is particularly savage: *La mujer casada, pierna quebrada y en casa—y la mujer soltera pierna y media* (The married woman, at home with her leg broken—and the unmarried woman, a leg and a half). Yet the very brutality of the proverb suggests that real women resisted enclosure and passivity. Even in the gentler version of Fray Luis de León's "perfect wife," it is less a description of reality than a largely class-bound ideal that flesh-and-blood women were supposed to emulate. It does not represent the life of Catalina de Erauso, for example, who, in the sixteenth century, dressed as a man, ran away from the convent that had been her home since the age of four, and went off to participate in the conquest of the New World, and who, after many years, was revealed to be a woman and returned to Europe where she received papal permission to wear men's clothing and go back to America as a mule driver. It is not the model followed by passionate, daring Saint Teresa, "fémina inquieta y andariega" (a restless, wandering woman), crisscrossing Spain with her monastic reforms; nor is it the model of Leonor López de Córdoba, who as a child in the fourteenth century survived nine years in prison and the loss of all her possessions, to become, years later, counselor to a queen. Inés de Suárez, who served as soldier and nurse in the colonial conquest of Chile, and Rosario Weiss, a painter who was exiled for her liberal political activities in the nineteenth century, the women anarchists of Catalonia, and the conservative patriots of

1

the Napoleonic Wars who chose and fought for a political cause did not live the model life of the Spanish woman. Nor did the hundreds of thousands of anonymous women who, in order to survive, worked the land or earned their living in towns and cities.[1]

Still, women's participation in the history of Spain has not always been visible.[2] A grammar that hides women's presence in an all-encompassing masculine, and the organization of history from the point of view of certain powerful and politically successful men, have made it seem that "the" Spanish woman is a fundamentally ahistorical being. Relegated to a cyclic world of birth and death, where the great events barely graze her life, it is inconceivable that she might be an agent of history. But even so-called private life, that feminine province, is created in culture. The sphere of the family and its reproduction does not emerge from nature naked and untouched. It is, on the contrary, dressed in laws and adorned with custom, fashioned by historical processes. At the same time, the lines of demarcation that have structured modern notions of history function differently for men and women (as well as for individuals of different social classes and ethnicities). Although great military and political events affect both men and women, their impact is differentially felt and progress may be measured differently, depending on one's gender. The conquest of America, for example, was a fundamentally masculine enterprise. It gave many Spanish men the opportunity to risk their lives in a novelesque adventure, and to gain glory and riches in a New World. For the women in their families it meant greater personal and economic autonomy — and often hardship, no doubt — in the Old. What it meant for the indigenous men and women in what was, for them, not a new world at all but a familiar one that was to undergo irreparable change, was not much considered by the Spanish.

From the time of the Roman Empire, women in the Iberian Peninsula have lived in conditions of legal and social inferiority to men. Roman *patria potestas* (father right) that invests all the power of the family in the figure of the husband/father, reducing the free, adult woman to a state not unlike slavery, has left profound marks on Spanish legal and sociocultural systems. On this foundation Spain's laws were created, some of which have improved the condition of women, without ever abandoning the fundamental inequality between the sexes. In general, these laws conceded women certain economic rights and protected women physically in public spaces, but they strictly controlled women's sexuality. This control turns out to be sufficiently ample to subjugate women, since it derives from and exists in a system in which reproduction is woman's only legitimate function. Control that, and you control her.

In early Christian Spain, under the Germanic Ervigian Code of 681, the value of an individual's testimony in court depended on his or her economic status, rank, religion, and mental stability, not on gender. Women could participate directly in the judicial system, acting as their own defense counsel (though not in defense of others, which only men could do).[3] Before the reign of Ervig, the life of a woman was worth less, on a monetary scale, than the life of a man; but the new code stated that the fine

that had to be paid to satisfy a murder charge was the same whether the victim was male or female. Within marriage, the man retained his dominance, but the woman was granted some economic autonomy. During her married life she controlled the dowry her husband brought to the marriage (limited by law to no more than one-tenth his wealth), and she was empowered to inherit and will money, goods, and land. Upon the death of her husband, the widow assumed all familial rights.[4] Hundreds of years later, in the sixteenth century, women lost economic ground when the Laws of Toro consolidated hereditary laws favoring eldest sons and depriving wives of their inheritance; the Council of Trent put women's economic assets under their husbands' control.[5] Yet the legal history of women in Spain is complex, and far from unitary. It reflects the pull between regionalism and national consolidation, so that history and political geography both affect women's legal status. Early laws protecting women's rights in some regions survive legal consolidation; others do not.

The Ervigian Code protected women against kidnapping and rape, punishing those crimes severely.[6] In part, these laws functioned to solidify masculine control over female sexuality and reproduction, and the control of women's sexuality was not just a family or even a religious affair. It extended to the civil authorities, who could take over if the individual men charged with controlling women's sexuality did not fulfill their task. A single woman who eloped with a man or who had (hetero)sexual relations before marriage lost her rights of inheritance. Both husband and brothers had the right to kill an adulterous wife, and if they decided not to exercise that right, the civil authorities were empowered to whip or mutilate her.[7] Abortion was also a capital offense.[8]

Despite the differences between Muslim and Christian women during the Spanish Middle Ages, there are structural similarities between the two as well. Like their Christian counterparts, Muslim women enjoyed certain juridical rights. They could inherit or accept gifts, enter into agreements and sign contracts, litigate before the court, and serve as witnesses. They had control of their financial assets. Formal education was common for girls. Many women studied, and they were permitted to undertake advanced studies in theology, medicine, and law. They could occupy bureaucratic posts in the caliphate or enter into the professions of education, medicine, and literature. They had the right to transmit the sacred word to believers, earning their living copying the Koran. Nevertheless, very few women did these things. History records one woman doctor, a handful of theologians and teachers, a few hundred scribes, and some poets. The legal rights of Muslim women, like those of Christian women, were undercut by formal and informal laws that relegated their bodies to male domination. Polygyny, sexual slavery, legal suppression of women's will in marriage, and the enclosed life of the harem annulled, for the majority of women who were of a class that might otherwise have taken advantage of them, their legal and civil rights.

Toward the end of the twelfth century, Christian society in Spain was becoming urbanized. As a result, women were growing increasingly visible in the streets and

markets of the new towns. Due to the perpetual wars of the Reconquest, there were more women than men in Christian-held lands, and many women participated in manual labor not only in the countryside but also in the cities.[9] The towns recently reconquered from the Muslims, nevertheless, had a shortage of Christian women, at least from the victors' point of view. The presence of Christian women represented stability in the areas to be newly populated, and women's migration to these frontier towns was encouraged by economic and social incentives, as well as by greater legal protection. Christian women willing to accept the dangers of frontier life enjoyed opportunities to improve their state, above all as legitimate wives with extensive rights over their own and their jointly held property. These women coexisted with the women who served in their houses, some of whom were Muslim slaves. Others were also Christians, who had come to the frontier in search of domestic work and to escape the semislavery of rural feudalism.[10] Free Jewish and Muslim women lived in these areas as well.

The laws set down in the Fuero de Cuenca (1177-89), influential in the writing of subsequent legal codes, reflect the public presence of women in the sometimes rowdy frontier towns.[11] They call for fines for calling a woman a bad name, stealing her clothes while she bathes in the public baths, pulling her hair, or knocking her to the ground.[12] These laws, which protected honor perhaps more than safety and property, applied to women of all social classes, with the exception of those who by definition lacked honor: prostitutes and Muslim slaves. In terms of inheritance laws, power over children, access to goods and money during marriage, and the independent situation of widows, there was a certain level of equality between men and women.[13] Men, however, exercised complete control over their wives' sexuality. The early charter laws authorized husbands to kill adulterous wives. This right was reinscribed into Spanish law when the charter laws were largely superseded by the centralized national law of 1567, the Nueva Recopilación de las Leyes de España.

From earliest times, Christian women found respectable alternatives to marriage in religion, although Priscilianism, a fourth-century religious movement originating in Galicia and counting many women among its adherents, apparently went too far in this direction when it rejected marriage as unholy. Priscilianism was ultimately condemned as heresy. Still, Christian women could eschew marriage in favor of a religious life. Renouncing the exercise of their sexuality within the context of Catholicism, they might live free from the domination of a man who would have been empowered to keep that sexuality contained. There are many variations on the theme of independent Christian women. Women's religious communities are recorded as early as the third century, and the fourth-century travel book of the Galician woman Egeria relates how she journeyed to the Holy Land. Upper-class women might choose the cloister to retain some autonomy. The Convent of San Juan, founded in the ninth century by Wilfred the Hairy and his wife Vinilda for their daughter Emona, was governed for many years by women of the powerful families of Catalonia. Benedictine and Cistercian monasteries were home to many

upper-class women. The abbesses of the Huelgas de Burgos, who had jurisdiction over the Knightly Order of Calatrava, enjoyed almost episcopal power for centuries, until it was revoked by the pope in 1875. The Huelgas boast a long line of powerful abbesses, including one in the eighth century who refused to stop saying mass and was excommunicated.[14] In addition to the communities of professed nuns, there were groups of women who lived together and took vows of poverty and chastity, but not obedience. These *beatas* managed to escape much of the control to which nuns belonging to orders were subject. For many religious women, nuns and *beatas* alike, their communities fulfilled an important social function as a legitimate alternative to marriage.

In the secular world, as in the religious, women's lives were likely to be a somewhat uncomfortable reconciliation between the patriarchal ideal of the enclosed woman and the everyday reality of participation in the world. A key factor in this equation was a woman's social and economic class. Even among the nobility, women could rarely influence the great events of the day — few women had indirect, much less direct, access to power. Yet Spanish women have by no means remained silent.

The so-called feminist debate of the fifteenth century took place among men, with the participation of only one woman, Teresa de Cartagena. This dearth of female participation is not surprising, given the low level of literacy even among the women of the aristocracy. Women's education was almost nonexistent, and without access to the classical and ecclesiastical literatures that were the foundation of the intellectual life of the era, fifteenth-century women were in no position to show off their ideas in written form.

The rise of humanism in the sixteenth century brought a marked change in the attitude toward the education of women. The works of Erasmus, which were read in Spain during the first half of the sixteenth century, proposed and defended a wide, humanist education for women. At the end of the fifteenth century, with the first stirrings of humanism in Spain, two women were already teaching in the universities: Francisca de Nebrija in Alcalá and Lucía de Medrano in Salamanca. Isabel I studied Latin with Beatriz Galindo, who was to become the queen's adviser.

The study of classical texts reached women of the highest rank during the reign of the Catholic Monarchs, Isabel and Ferdinand, when the queen contracted two eminent Italian humanists, Antonio and Alessandro Geraldino, as tutors to her daughters. One of the illustrious students, Catherine of Aragon, later queen of England, inspired Juan Luis Vives, and perhaps Erasmus himself, in his writing on women's education. Vives's treatise, *De institutione feminae christianae* (1524-28), written at the behest of Isabel I, nevertheless reflects the writer's belief in women's inferiority to men and his purpose in educating them only enough so that they might carry out their familial tasks. Vives's work, which was not translated into Spanish until 1539, had less influence in Spain than Erasmus's, translated and widely read by an avid audience between 1527 and 1535. In contrast to Vives, Erasmus proposed an unrestricted classical education

for women. In effect, during the first decades of Spain's Golden Age, many women whose families could afford books and a preceptor enjoyed a classical education, and a number distinguished themselves in the intellectual world.

Like Francisca de Nebrija, who taught at the University of Alcalá, two of the most famous women humanists of the sixteenth century were daughters of humanist fathers. The father of Juliana Morell (c. 1595-1693) chronicled the story of his daughter's education, which he himself directed. According to his own testimony, Morell quickly discerned his daughter's talent, and he imposed a strict regime of learning on her when she was only four years old. By the time she was seventeen, Juliana Morell spoke fourteen languages. She studied philosophy, theology, law, and music, and was three times prioress in the Dominican convent where she professed at the age of fourteen.

Oliva Sabuco de Nantes (1562-1622?), celebrated in her own time for her learning, wrote on natural science. Sabuco's treatise *Nueva filosofía de la naturaleza del hombre* (New philosophy of the nature of man, 1587), has a curious history. After Oliva's mother died and her father, Manuel, remarried, father and daughter became estranged. Instigated, apparently, by his second wife, who was concerned about the inheritance of her own children, Manuel sued Oliva over her dowry. The issue was never resolved, but the last word was had by Manuel Sabuco, in his will, in which he claimed to have written the treatise attributed to his daughter. Most historians still accept Manuel Sabuco's version of events, on no more authority than his disputed word.[15]

Spanish literary history remembers Ana Girón as the dutiful widow of Juan Boscán who published her late husband's poems, together with those of his friend, thus bringing the new Italian verse forms to sixteenth-century Spain. But Girón was more than the conduit who brought Garcilaso and Boscán to the attention of the Spanish reading public. She was a highly educated woman, well versed in the classics. Luisa and Angela Sigea, Cecilia Morillas, and Isabel de Joya are others whose intellectual abilities were recognized and celebrated during the period. Many others, educated at home or by nuns, never gained the preeminence of these women, but they enjoyed the fruits of Renaissance humanism before the Counter-Reformation prohibited Erasmus's books and before the social conservatism that accompanied Spain's political decadence set in. With few exceptions, classical education for women disappeared in the seventeenth century. In 1647, María de Zayas y Sotomayor lamented this situation, criticizing men for refusing to educate their daughters, and women themselves for frivolously rejecting their humanist legacy.

Women in the sixteenth century cultivated the spiritual as well as the intellectual life. Illuminism, the Spanish version of a pietistic Christianity that did away with the need for elaborate ritual and a hierarchical clergy in its attempt to achieve direct access to God, attracted many women. Its spiritual leader, who organized centers for adherents in Alcalá and Toledo, was Isabel de la Cruz, a *beata* from a family that had converted from Judaism either prior to or in 1492, the year all Spanish Jews were forced to choose between conversion and exile. Accused of sexual excesses (not a surprising

charge to be leveled against a group that believed in the spiritual equality of the sexes and that rejected male hegemony in its avoidance of priests), Illuminism was condemned as a heresy, and Isabel de la Cruz was executed by burning in 1529.[16]

Orthodox mysticism counted many women among its practitioners, the greatest of whom was Saint Teresa, also from a once-Jewish family. Like her, other women of the period combined a diligent faith with practical ability and intelligence. Religion and politics often intertwined. Between 1643 and 1665, Sor María de Ágreda, prioress of the convent established by her family, sustained a correspondence with Philip IV. She drew on her religio-political dreams in advising him on affairs of state as well as of the soul. Lucrecia de León, on the other hand, was tried and punished by the Inquisition in 1594 for her antiestablishment religious and political visions.

The tribunals of the Inquisition affected many women. Large numbers were tried and burned as crypto-Jews, secret Muslims, or Protestants; but the witch-hunts that soiled the rest of Europe with the blood and ashes of thousands of women barely touched Spain and its colonies. Before about 1530, the Inquisition did try several hundred women as witches, but it was much more interested in the Protestant threat, and the great majority of women arrested by the Holy Office in this era were accused of Protestantism. Furthermore, after a number of witch trials in the Basque Country in the early part of the sixteenth century, the Inquisition stopped concerning itself with accused witches altogether. Although it maintained secret records about the matter, it seems to have been in agreement with its functionary, who saw the Basque trials and concluded that witchcraft did not really exist.[17] By the beginning of the following century, witchcraft had been reduced to a fashion among the ladies of Madrid, who played at "white magic" without anyone taking them seriously.

The life of a Spanish woman during the Golden Age varied according to her class, her civil status, her religion, and the place she lived. The social freedom of the women of the aristocracy stands in sharp contrast to the restricted life of middle-class women in provincial cities, and the discrepancy between the groups grew with the conservative provincial reaction to the growing liberty, and libertinism, of the court. Peasant women had their responsibilities in the home and in the fields. There were women, many of them widows, in commerce and in the military orders. At the beginning of the eighteenth century more than 20 percent of the landlordships of the religious/military Order of Calatrava in Castile and Aragon were under the titular control of women. The economic situation of women in eighteenth- and nineteenth-century Spain, however, is summed up in the Commercial Code of 1885, which held that an adult woman had the right to engage in commerce only with the permission of her husband, unless he was absent due to death, divorce, imprisonment, or desertion. Throughout the nineteenth century, husbands in most of Spain consolidated the control they exercised over property held jointly by the couple, and even over the property that was their wives' alone.[18] Only by surviving marriage and becoming widows could most Spanish women be assured of some economic independence.

The question of women's education in the eighteenth and nineteenth centuries recalls the feminist debates of the fifteenth and the subsequent brief surge of humanist education for some women in the sixteenth. One of the themes of the Spanish Enlightenment was women's education; but as in the debates of the fifteenth century, almost all the discussants were men. Enlightenment men, like ecclesiastics, saw in women the key to the formation of the next generation, and thereby of the future of the nation. They were therefore most interested in educating women to be good mothers. Charles III, convinced of the importance of women's education, commanded the establishment of schools for girls that taught catechism, personal hygiene, and sewing. This utilitarian education was far from intellectual development, but it established the foundation for the next century's implementation of an education more or less like the one boys received.

In the eighteenth century, the name of one woman, Josefa Amar y Borbón, stands out as a voice claiming a serious education for women. A century later, in 1868, the Escuela de Institutrices de Madrid (Madrid Teachers College for Women) was inaugurated, and in 1869 the Catalonian feminist Dolors Moncerdà de Macià published her first article on women's education.[19] At conferences on pedagogy in 1881 and 1882, women's education was proposed as a right; among the participants were approximately 450 women. The 1892 conference had over five hundred women in attendance, including social reformer Concepción Arenal, most of whose feminist work has been forgotten; writer and feminist Emilia Pardo Bazán; and the Colombian educator and novelist Soledad Acosta y Samper.[20]

The protofeminist posture of these conferences, which claimed women's right to equal education, is the posture—not always unambivalent—of the writers in this anthology. Like their compatriots who flourished in the absence of men, whether as medieval nuns who ran their own convents or nineteenth-century widows who ran their own businesses, they found their authority in the interstices of patriarchal culture. Rejecting a life dedicated only to reproduction, refusing to live the myth of the woman sheltered from the world but often without direct access to the world of ideas and literary creation, they sought and took advantage of what autonomy they could, and they wrote. Women's literary history, like women's history in general, was long unwritten. This book seeks to bring some of that history to light, both for its own sake and in order to participate in the process of the reconfiguration of a Spanish literature that includes, and is transformed by, women's words.

Toward a Women's Literary Tradition in Spain

The codification of Spanish literary history took place through the nineteenth century, an era in which the ideal of womanhood, propagated by a new bourgeoisie, was associated with the private world of family and a spirituality aimed at the well-being of the home. The public world of letters and the intellect was considered inappropriate for a

respectable woman. By this time, the guardians of Spanish culture had prohibited women entry into such institutions as the Spanish Royal Academy and the university professoriat. The new architects of literature—these same academicians and professors—relegated women to the cultural margin, categorizing as second-rate the few women-authored texts that they allowed into their histories and anthologies.

It is not that women stopped writing during the nineteenth century—far from it. Many of them, though, including Pilar de Sinués, Angela Grassi, and Faustina Sáez de Melgar, propagated an ideology of separate spheres to a primarily female readership, which, paradoxically, virtually ensured that their own writing would be forgotten. Among the women writers of the nineteenth century who wrote on other issues, and to an audience of both men and women, we find various survival strategies. At one extreme, Cecilia Böhl de Faber, masked by the pseudonym Fernán Caballero, protested that she created nothing, but only served as a conduit to transmit the reality she saw in front of her. Cecilia Böhl's chosen name associates her with the deepest roots of conservative Spanish, male-centered tradition. Fernán is an archaic man's name, associated with medieval ballads, and Caballero means "knight" or "gentleman." At the other extreme, Carolina Coronado claimed women needed to create a literary sisterhood and implored other women poets to join together in the enterprise of literary creation. Later in the century Emilia Pardo Bazán both exhorted women to claim their rights and responsibilities and insisted on her own right to participate in literary culture.

The nineteenth century also brought with it the notion of writing as a solitary activity, but the woman writer's solitude is more profound than the man's. The male writer, however isolated he might be, has always been in the company of others. He has written within a tradition of other solitary men, and his work has been received, classified, and preserved by a fraternity of critics, literary historians, and academics with whom he shares a culture and a language. It is man who has had the privilege of naming in the traditionally patriarchal monotheistic religions—Jewish, Christian, and Muslim—that have been crucial to the development of Spanish culture. His definitions of secular experience, as well as his explanations of the spiritual realm, have been considered not only normative but authorized. From the time of Eve, man has been wary of the word of woman. Indeed, it might well be said that one of the punishments God imposed on Eve's daughters was the appearance of silence. Neither Mary nor the women who followed her son have left their version of the Gospel.

All of which does not mean that women have not spoken during these millennia, but rather that, like Cassandra, they have not been attended to. This anthology, which contains but a small number of the many Spanish women who wrote before the twentieth century, demonstrates that there has been an ongoing production of literary texts by women in Spain. This is not to say that a women's literary tradition exists, for a tradition that is hidden from those who participate in it is a contradiction in terms. If tradition is a symphony of voices and countervoices in harmonious dialogue and

fruitful debate, it requires a medium in which each voice is sounded and sustained long enough to be joined by others.

The heroic feat of advancing into the world armed only with a pen (which may well be mightier than the sword, but only in the long run) is doubly heroic for women. Virtually all of those who have been of the social and economic class that provided them with the leisure and education to write have found that this very status also demanded that they maintain their modesty, or acknowledge their intellectual inferiority, or claim no further identity than that of obedient wife or nun. The world was to be men's territory, and the woman who went out into the street, without the knowledge that many preceded her (or, in many cases, that others were there with her), had to walk alone or seek out the company of those who belonged there. Going out alone is risky: a woman can get lost, or be attacked. It is, then, no surprise that many of the writers who fill these pages sought masculine protection and access to the world through connections to men. They did so in exchange for certain expressive freedom and at the cost of the suppression of part of their experience, which often asserted itself, transformed or sometimes deformed, in their texts.

That is to say that Spanish women writers have been seen, and have tended to see themselves, in relation to the masculine literary tradition. They incorporate in their work the language and preoccupations of the men of their time, though not always without submitting them to their scrutiny. In her *Novelas amorosas y ejemplares* (Enchantments of love), María de Zayas y Sotomayor addresses herself to men and women readers both, and her tales follow the model used by Cervantes and others. Florencia Pinar composes courtly poetry that has been confused with her brother's, so that it is still impossible to attribute certain poems to one or the other. Beatriz Bernal writes a novel about knights in shining armor that appeals to popular taste, and Ana Caro Mallén de Soto's plays follow the pattern of the drama of her day. Even cloistered women, like Sor María de la Antigua and Sor María de Santa Isabel, use their respective era's conventions of rhyme and meter.

Like Ana Caro, Luisa Sigea, Catalina Clara de Guzmán, and Carolina Coronado, women writers may be celebrated in their time only to be deprived of their place in literary history by the architects of official culture. Many "tenth muses" have disappeared, like so much invisible ink, requiring each generation to reinvent the category "woman writer," each of these a unique Athena cast into the world from the head of her father.

If there is a constant in women's literature, it is that of perpetual anomaly. The tension between the words "woman" and "writer" as categories that are simultaneously contradictory and complementary appears as a subtext in almost all the writers included in this book. Many of them, while fully participating in masculine literary discourse, also initiate conversations among women, in a not always fully conscious effort to create a literary history in which their participation might be taken for granted. From their apparent solitude, some seek out the company of other women. María de Zayas enjoys the friendship of Ana Caro, and Fernán Caballero

maintains a correspondence with the Cuban Gertrudis Gómez de Avellaneda, who visits her when she is in Spain. This search for community may be diachronic—the beginning of a tradition that starts to crystallize in the imaginative meeting of two or more writers from different eras. In the nineteenth century Carolina Coronado writes a novel about the Renaissance humanist Luisa Sigea, and Fernán Caballero bases a story on the life of the eighteenth-century poet María Hore. Saint Teresa inspires generations of nuns to write poems in her honor, and Emilia Pardo Bazán makes the writing of Sor María de Agreda and María de Zayas accessible to her contemporaries by reissuing them through her publishing company, Biblioteca de la Mujer (The Woman's Library). Many cloistered women cultivated and enjoyed the literary community offered by the convent.[21]

Despite the impulse toward a women's literary community, these writers do not wish to establish a separate literature, but rather to include women and the representation of their reality in the existing literary panorama. The question of audience also takes in this issue. For whom does the woman writer write? For the most part, she wants a broad readership, made up of men and women, but the "and women" part is crucial. It means that the woman reader does not disappear into an all-inclusive reader, tacitly gendered masculine. María de Zayas, for example, proposes two ways to respond to her *Desengaños amorosos* (Disabusals of love): men ought to improve their treatment of women, and women ought to avoid the perils of love. Other writers do not speak so directly to the effect they want their writing to have on their women readers, but they do often reveal their interest in that segment of their audience. Besides creating the Biblioteca de la Mujer, Emilia Pardo Bazán writes feminist essays. One of these, on the essayist and social reformer Concepción Arenal, laments the fact that the first thing history erases in a woman is her feminism.

A more literal variation on the theme of an apparently exclusively female literary community is the devotional and occasional literature written by nuns, particularly in the sixteenth and seventeenth centuries. Besides the personal spiritual poetry that expresses the relationship between the writer and God, there is a great body of poems that celebrate the solemn rituals of the cloister—holy feasts, professions, funerals. Also abundant are spiritual autobiographies, many times written at the behest of a confessor. These notable and devout lives were to serve as examples to the religious community. Some nuns wrote spiritual biographies, often about the founder of a convent or an abbess. These too were used to edify nuns and laywomen, but they also might be called upon as evidence in favor of beatification.

Secular women's writing also has its "just among us women" aspect. The fiction of personal communication between two women, in which the work is addressed to a friend or protector, as is the case with Teresa de Cartagena and María Hore, is not uncommon. Although it would be naive to believe that this pretext was to be taken literally, it does suggest that a woman—and therefore a sympathetic individual—is the prototypical reader of the text. Hore's epistolary poems, for example, mime personal letters to friends. Although the publication of these poems indicates that Hore wanted

a wide audience for them, their form and subject matter both suggest that the poet had her women readers particularly in mind.

At the beginning of the seventeenth century, Isabel de Liaño composed a poem completely inscribed in a feminine world. Its subject is Catherine of Siena, and it is dedicated to Queen Marguerite of Austria. The poet warns in her first canto that if some man should chance to read it, he should know that it was not intended for his eyes:

> And if you, sir, feel lukewarm,
> and ill perceive my verses,
> I beg you do not read them.
> My lines were written not for you;
> I wrote them but for women.
> For that which is devout
> do they best understand;
> and though it be unworthy
> they will esteem the rhyme
> that's writ by woman's hand.[22]

Here Liaño affirms that women readers particularly value the work of women writers and suggests that there is a female audience in search of a women's literary community that will privilege women as readers of the work of women writers. Liaño addresses herself to the woman reader who, like the woman writer, feels herself not fully included in male-centered literary discourse.

The creation of a women's literary tradition responds to a desire to resolve the paradox of the (woman) writer, but it is also a protective strategy against masculinist attack. Liaño knows that she cannot exclude the male reader, and it is unlikely that she really wants to. She admits that in her use of the too-familiar trope of feminine modesty, in which the writer begs forgiveness for the inferiority of her talent before the gentlemen who read her work do her the favor of pointing it out to her. But, by claiming to write only for women, Liaño's resistance to her potential male readers' disapproval is more sophisticated and has greater resonance. For Liaño to say that her poem ought to stay within a purely feminine world is to suggest that Paul's prohibition against women's public voice is not really broken. If the poet writes only for other women to read her, her voice never reaches the public sphere, in which, by definition, only men are present. Of course, this announcement that she intends to write exclusively for women makes sense only if the text reaches a male audience. To declare that she does not wish the male reader's participation is to affirm that his judgment is beside the point. If he wishes to read her, he then must take on the responsibility of approximating a woman reader's reception, which is founded, according to Liaño, on a moral superiority that includes a greater appreciation for devotional themes and a disdain for rhetorical ostentation, in favor of humility, when dealing with the sacred. For Liaño, simple language is feminine language:

The plainness of the poem, so free of the ornament that famous poets use, bears witness to the truth, for such homely language, without quotes from profane stories, Ovid's tales, Virgil's curiosities, stars, planets, Satyrs and Nymphs, very clearly shows itself to be the trace of woman's breast; though I confess that having read some I might know how to use them here if my inclination were not so averse to seeing holy stories poisoned with the profane ones poets often use, and the most mundane opinion says that any poetry that abjures this adornment is worth little.[23]

It is no coincidence that Liaño is responding here to the charge that was also made against her contemporary, Oliva Sabuco de Nantes, and against Teresa de Cartagena a century before them: that so erudite a work could not have been composed by a woman. Aside from its use in discrediting particular writers, this accusation perpetuates the vicious circle that excludes women from literature. Woman is incapable of writing, ergo any well-written text could not have been penned by a woman, thus such a work cannot be part of a women's literary tradition, the lack of which demonstrates that women are incapable of writing. As Liaño notes:

One of the things least admitted in human law is knowledge administered by women's judgment; it must have been advantageous, for as great a saint as Saint Paul is of the same opinion. Together with this we know that for the most part, among writers ancient and modern, our name has been annihilated.[24]

The annihilation of the name of the woman writer has two aspects, artistic and personal. The guardians of Truth, the prototype of whom might well be that "great saint," maintain both that women do not have the intellectual and creative ability of men, and therefore their poetry is inferior, and that any woman who speaks publicly is immodest. The charges that women did not write their own works (Teresa de Cartagena), that their works are in minor genres (Fernán Caballero), or that they do not fit into any literary movement (Rosalía de Castro) are variants on the first. The accusations that they have written pornography (María de Zayas and Luisa Sigea) or that they are ridiculous in their pretensions (Pardo Bazán) are examples of the second.

In today's world, where basic knowledge changes, is revised, and grows daily, we cannot permit ourselves the luxury of losing once again the story of women's writing in order to experience the pleasure, as I did when I began this work, of discovering it anew. Women need a history; women's writing needs its tradition. Feminist literary critics and historians have begun, in the words of María de Zayas, to "recover women's good name," so that it may be recovered for good. It is my hope that this anthology might serve as an indication of the ample, varied, and complex voices of Spanish women writers, the voices of the literary foremothers of this century's notable women writers and of those of the century about to begin.

1. Mary Elizabeth Perry's study *Gender and Disorder in Early Modern Seville* (Princeton, N.J.: Princeton University Press, 1990) explores the many ways in which women in sixteenth- and seventeenth-century Seville—nuns, uncloistered religious women, prostitutes, women who wanted to study or write, even wives and daughters—kept disrupting the bounds that lay and ecclesiastical authorities set for them, without ever getting rid of patriarchal authority altogether.

2. The Spain I speak of is not a singularity. It has been comprised of both warring and allied kingdoms, provinces, and regions, with different laws and languages. The need to be brief, however, requires simplification, and thus I am primarily concerned here with what today is Castilian-speaking Spain.

3. Paul David King, *Law and Society in the Visigothic Kingdom* (Cambridge: Cambridge University Press, 1972), 102, 103.

4. King, 261.

5. Joan Connelly de Ullman, "La protagonista ausente. La mujer como objeto y sujeto de la historia de España," in *La mujer en el mundo contemporáneo*, ed. María Ángeles Durán (Madrid: Universidad Autónoma de Madrid, n.d.), 37.

6. King, 432.

7. King, 234.

8. King, 238-39.

9. Jocelyn Nigel Hillgarth, *The Spanish Kingdoms 1250-1516*. Vol 1: 1250-1410 (Oxford: Clarendon Press, 1976), 83. Also R. Serra Ruiz, *Honor, honra e injuria en el derecho medieval español* (Murcia: Sucesores de Nogues, 1969), 65-67, 249.

10. Heath Dillard, *Daughters of the Reconquest: Women in Castilian Town Society, 1100-1300* (Cambridge: Cambridge University Press, 1984), 219.

11. The *fueros*, or charter laws, provided certain provincial juridical autonomy.

12. Hillgarth, 82.

13. Hillgarth, 82-83.

14. Sibylle Harksen, *Women in the Middle Ages* (New York: A. Schram, 1975), 29.

15. Not all do, however. Perry cites Oliva Sabuco as the author of the treatise.

16. J. H. Elliott, *Imperial Spain 1496-1716* (Harmondsworth: Penguin, 1963).

17. Gustav Henningsen, *The Witches' Advocate: Baroque Witchcraft and the Spanish Inquisition 1609-1614* (Reno: University of Nevada Press, 1980).

18. María Victoria López-Cordón Cortezo, "La situación de la mujer a finales del antiguo régimen (1760-1860)," in *Mujer y sociedad en España 1700-1795*, ed. Rosa María Capel Martínez (Madrid: Ministerio de Cultura, Dirección General de Juventud y Promoción Socio-Cultural, 1982), 89. Cristina Enríquez has pointed out to me, however, that even after the establishment of the 1889 national civil code, Catalonian women kept their property and administration rights thanks to the survival of preexisting charter laws.

19. María Aurelia Capmany, *De profesión: Mujer* (Barcelona: Plaza y Janés, 1975), 151.

20. Rosa María Capel Martínez, "La apertura del horizonte cultural femenino: Fernando de Castro y los congresos pedagógicos del siglo XIX," in Capel Martínez, ed., *Mujer y sociedad en España*, 111-45.

21. See Stacey Schlau and Electa Arenal, *Untold Sisters: Hispanic Nuns in Their Own Works* (Albuquerque: University of New Mexico Press, 1989).

22. Y tú, lector, si tibio te sintieres / Y mis versos en tí mal se perciben, / No los leas, te ruego, si quisieres, / Pues para tí los tales no se escriben; / Sólo los escribí para mujeres, / Que lo que es devoción mejor reciben, / Y aunque no lo merezca harán estima / Por ser de mano femenil la rima. (cited in Manuel Serrano y Sanz, *Apuntes para una biblioteca de escritoras españolas desde el año 1401 al 1833*, vol. 2, [Madrid: Real Academia Española, 1903-5; repr. 1975], 13). This and subsequent translations from Liaño are my own.

23. "La llaneza del verso, tan sin ornamento del que usan los famosos poetas, da testimonio de la verdad, pues un lenguaje tan casero, sin acotar con historias profanas, fábulas de Ovidio, curiosidades de Virgilio, astros, planetas, Sátyros y Ninfas, bien claro manifiesta ser traza de pecho femenil; aunque confiese de mí que por haber leído algunas dellas, quizá supiera engerillas aquí si mi inclinación no fuera tan enemiga de ver las historias divinas adulteradas con las profanas de que por la mayor parte usan los poetas, y las más opiniones mundanas dicen que cualquiera poesía que no vaya con este adorno, vale poco" (Isabel de Liaño, "Prólogo al lector," *Historia de la vida, muerte, y milagros de Santa Catalina de Siena*, cited in Serrano y Sanz, 2:13).

24. Una de las cosas menos admitida entre leyes humanas, es la ciencia administrada por femeniles juicios; debió de ser conviniente, pues un tan gran Santo como San Pablo aprueba la misma opinión. Junto con esto sabemos que por la mayor parte, entre escritores antiguos y modernos, anda nuestro nombre aniquilado" (Liaño cited in Serrano y Sanz, 2:12).

A Note on Spanish Verse Form

Unlike English poetry, whose basic unit is the foot, Spanish verse is measured by the number of syllables per line. Spanish rhyme is often assonant, that is, the vowels match but the consonants do not. Many Spanish poems are in forms that have no English equivalent. The following is a list of Spanish terms used in this volume.

canción	Literally, "song"; also, any of several Italianate verse forms combining lines of seven and eleven syllables.
décima	Stanza of ten lines, each with eight syllables, in consonant rhyme.
endecha	Multi-stanza poem, usually expressing sadness, in five, six, or seven syllable lines.
glosa	Gloss, or poetic commentary on a short poem. Each line of the original provides the lead-in for one stanza of the *glosa*.
lira	Stanza of five lines, patterned in seven and eleven syllables (7-11-7-7-11), with consonant rhyme.
loa	Poem of praise; dramatic monologue used as a prologue to a play.
octava	Stanza of eight lines.
quintilla	Stanza of five lines, each with eight or fewer syllables.
redondilla	Stanza of four eight-syllable lines, in consonant rhyme.
romance	Traditional stanza of indeterminate length, consisting of eight-syllable lines with assonant rhyme in the even lines.
seguidilla	Stanza of seven lines, patterned in five or seven syllables (7-5-7-5-5-7-5), with consonant rhyme.
villancico	Traditional song that usually begins with a two-to-four-line refrain, followed by stanzas that develop the theme set out in the refrain, in six- or eight-syllable lines with consonant rhyme. Today, *villancico* means Christmas carol.

The Fifteenth Century

Leonor López de Córdoba

Leonor López de Córdoba is not only Spain's first autobiographer, but also the first woman to sign her name to a piece of writing in Spanish. Her autobiography is a short but vivid account of a proud, strong-willed woman caught in the political upheavals of her time.

Daughter of Martín López de Córdoba and Doña Sancha Carrillo, Leonor López de Córdoba was born in December 1362 or January 1363. Her father was Grand Master of the military orders of Calatrava and Alcántara, and a supporter of Pedro I. Her mother, niece of King Alfonso XI, died when Leonor was still very young; in her autobiography Leonor claims to have no memory of her. When she was seven years old, Leonor's father married her to Ruy Gutiérrez de Henestrosa, who was also related to the royal family.

Leonor López's aristocratic lineage is the determining element in her autobiography, for her family ties are the source of her victimization as well as of her authority to write. Hers is the classic case of a woman who, not authoring the great events of her time, suffers their consequences. Her father had remained loyal to his king during the battle for the throne between Pedro and his half brother, Enrique de Trastámara — and he was on the losing side. As a result, eight-year-old Leonor was condemned to prison along with her sisters, brothers-in-law, brother, husband, and several of her father's vassals. They spent nine years, all of Enrique's reign, imprisoned; of all the prisoners, only Leonor and her husband survived.

From prison she went to the house of her maternal aunt, while her husband went off to try to recover the estate he had lost during the years of his imprisonment. Seven years later, Leonor was reunited with her husband, whose lack of success was all too evident to the ambitious Leonor. She had done well in her aunt's home, and by the end of the fourteenth century Leonor López de Córdoba had houses of her own. But she also earned the rancor of her cousins. She had not only displaced them in their mother's affections; she had received financial help from their mother as well.

Leonor López never distinguishes between her own personal suffering and the disgrace her family suffered. Her need to restore her family's good name after the debacle of having been allied with the losing side in a civil war gives her occasion to write — or dictate — a sympathetic version of her own life, for she considers it her duty to leave her children an illustrious past and lineage. As proof of her merit,

Leonor López offers a minute account of her prayers and pious works, but it is clear that she derives more comfort from her aunt's largesse, her father's noble name, and his former servants' continued service and reverence to her. The most deeply felt passages in the text are also focal points that constitute the internal structure of the autobiography. They concern the deaths of her father (decapitated by Enrique II), her brother (who died in prison of plague at thirteen years of age), and her twelve-year-old son (also a victim of the plague). These passages in the autobiography bring sadness, pain, and tenderness together with heroism and piety.

The autobiography ends in about 1401, with the pitiful image of Leonor López as mourning mother, cast away from her beloved aunt, but who, nevertheless, has managed to recover some of her lost position and fortune. Doña Leonor's extraordinary strength of spirit and will to survive and triumph bring her, in 1406, to the post of chief lady-in-waiting to Queen Catherine of Lancaster, one of King Pedro's daughters, whom Leonor's father had rescued in the war against Enrique de Trastámara. Later, Doña Leonor suffers another change of fortune. Once Catherine's favorite, she is banished from court under pain of death: the queen threatens to burn her alive if she so much as shows her face near the palace. So Leonor López returns once again to Córdoba, probably some time around 1412, where she prepares this memoir.

Autobiografía

En el nombre de Dios Padre, y del hijo, y del Espíritu Santo tres Personas, y un solo Dios verdadero en trinidad, al cual sea dada gloria al Padre, y al hijo, y al Espíritu Santo, así como era en el comienzo, así es ahora, y por el Siglo de los Siglos amén. En el nombre del cual Sobredicho Señor y de la Virgen Santa María su Madre, y Señora y Abogada de los Pecadores, y a honra, y ensalsamiento de todos los Ángeles, e Santos y Santas de la Corte del Cielo amén.

Por ende, sepan cuantos esta escritura vieren, como yo doña Leonor López de Córdoba, hija de mi señor el Maestre don Martín López de Córdoba, e doña Sancha Carrillo, a quien dé Dios gloria y Paraíso. Juro por esta significancia de † en que yo adoro, como todo esto que aquí es escrito, es verdad que lo vi, y pasó por mí, y escríbolo a honra y alabanza de mi Señor Jesu Cristo, e de la Virgen Santa María su Madre que lo parió, por que todas las criaturas que estuvieren en tribulación sean ciertos, que yo espero en su misericordia, que si se encomiendan de corazón a la Virgen Santa María, que Ella las consolará, y acorrerá, como consoló a mí; y por quien lo oyere sepan que la relación de todos mis hechos e milagros que la Virgen Santa María me mostró, y es mi intención que quede por memoria, mandélo escribir así como vedes; y así que yo soy hija del dicho Maestre, que fue de Calatrava, en el tiempo del Señor Rey Don Pedro, y el dicho Señor Rey le hizo merced de darle la Encomienda de Alcántara, que es en la ciudad de Sevilla; y luego le hizo Maestre de Alcántara, y a la postre de Calatrava, y el dicho Maestre mi padre era descendiente de la Casa de Aguilar y sobrino de don Juan Manuel, hijo de

Autobiography

In the name of God the Father and of the Son and of the Holy Ghost, three persons, and one single true God in trinity, glory be to the Father, the Son, and the Holy Ghost, as it was in the beginning, so it is now, and forever and ever, amen. In the name of that Lord and of the Holy Virgin Mary his Mother, Lady and Advocate of Sinners, and to the honor and exaltation of all the Angels and Saints in the Court of Heaven, amen.

Therefore, may all who see this testament know how I, Doña Leonor López de Córdoba, daughter of my lord, Grand Master Don Martín López de Córdoba and Doña Sancha Carrillo, may God grant them eternal glory, swear by this sign † that I worship, that all that is written here is true, for I saw it, and it happened to me, and I write it down for the honor and glory of my Lord Jesus Christ and his Mother, the Holy Virgin Mary, who bore him, so that all creatures in tribulation might be assured that I believe in her mercy and that if they commend themselves wholeheartedly to the Holy Virgin Mary she will console them and succor them as she consoled me. And so that whoever might hear it may know the story of my deeds and the miracles that the Holy Virgin Mary showed me, it is my intention that it be left as a record: I ordered it written as you see before you. And so, I am the daughter of the aforementioned Grand Master of Calatrava, in the time of King Pedro, who granted him the honor of bestowing upon him the Commandery of Alcántara in the city of Seville. And then he made him Grand Master of Alcántara, and finally of Calatrava. The Grand

una sobrina suya, hija de dos hermanos, y subió a tan grande estado, como se hallará en las Crónicas de España. E como dicho tengo soy hija de doña Sancha Carrillo, sobrina e criada del Señor Rey Don Alfonso, de muy esclarecida memoria (que Dios dé Santo Paraíso), padre del dicho Señor Rey Don Pedro, y mi madre falleció muy temprano, y así me casó mi padre de siete años con Ruy Gutiérrez de Henestrosa, hijo de Juan Ferrández de Henestrosa, camarero mayor del Señor Rey Don Pedro y su canciller mayor del sello de la puridad, y mayordomo mayor de la Reina Doña Blanca su mujer, el cual casó con doña María de Haro y los Cameros; y a mi marido quedáronle muchos bienes de su padre y muchos lugares, y alcanzaba trescientos de a caballo suyos, e cuarenta madejas de aljófar, tan grueso como garbanzos, e quinientos moros, e moras, y dos mil marcos de plata en vajilla, y las joyas, y preseas de su casa, no las pudieran escribir en dos pliegos de papel, y esto le cupo del dicho su padre y madre porque otro hijo y heredero no tenían. A mí me dio mi padre veinte mil doblas en casamiento y residíamos en Carmona con las hijas del Señor Rey Don Pedro, mi marido, y yo, e mis cuñados, maridos de mis hermanas; y un hermano mío que se llamaba don Lope López de Córdoba Carrillo. Llamábanse mis cuñados Fernán Rodríguez de Aza, señor de Aza, e Villalobos, e el otro Ruy García de Aza, el otro Lope Rodríguez de Aza, que eran hijos de Álvaro Rodríguez de Aza, e de doña Constanza de Villalobos. Y fue así, que cuando el Señor Rey Don Pedro quedó cercado en el Castillo de Montiel de su hermano el Señor Rey Don Enrique, mi padre bajó al Andalucía a llevar gente para socorrerlo. Y llevándola, halló que era muerto a manos de su hermano; y vista esta desgracia tomó el camino para Carmona donde estaban las

Master, my father, was a descendant of the House of Aguilar and nephew of Don Juan Manuel, son of a niece of his, a daughter with a brother. And he rose very high in rank, as can be found in the *Chronicles of Spain.*[1]

As I have said, I am the daughter of Doña Sancha Carrillo, niece and maid of honor of the most illustriously remembered King Alfonso (may God grant him Holy Paradise), father of the aforementioned King Pedro. My mother died very young, and so my father married me at the age of seven years to Ruy Gutiérrez de Henestrosa, son of Juan Ferrández de Henestrosa, High Chamberlain of King Pedro and his High Chancellor of the Secret Seal, and High Steward of his wife, Queen Blanca, and he married Doña María de Haro y los Cameros.

My husband inherited great wealth and many offices from his father. His men on horseback numbered three hundred, and he had forty skeins of pearls fat as chickpeas, and five hundred Moorish slaves, men and women, and two thousand marks of silver in tableware, and the jewels and gems of his household you could not write down on two sheets of paper. And his father and mother left all this to him for they had no other son or heir. As for me, my father gave me twenty thousand gold coins upon my marriage. And my husband and I resided in Carmona with the daughters of King Pedro, and my brothers-in-law, my sisters' husbands, and a brother of mine

1. The Orders of Alcántara and Calatrava were two of the principal military/religious orders of Catholic Spain. As head of both orders, Don Martín López de Córdoba was one of the most powerful men in the kingdom. He was the son of an important aristocratic family, but descended from the maternal line. As such, he had to earn his position, albeit with a considerable head start.

Señoras Infantas, hijas del Señor Rey Don Pedro, y parientas tan cercanas de mi marido, y mías por mi madre; y el Señor Rey Don Enrique viéndose Rey de Castilla se vino a Sevilla y puso cerco a Carmona y como es villa tan fuerte, estuvo muchos meses cercada, y acaso habiendo salido mi padre fuera de ella, y sabiéndolo los del Real Del Rey, como era salido de la dicha villa, y que no quedaría tan buen cobro en ella, ofreciéronse doce caballeros a escalar la villa, y subidos a ella a la muralla, fueron presos, y luego fue avisado mi padre de tal hecho, y vino luego y por el atrevimiento les mandó cortar las cabezas. Y el Señor Rey Don Enrique visto este hecho, y que no podía por fuerzas de armas entrarle a satisfacerse de este hecho, mandó al Condestable de Castilla tratase de medios con mi padre, y los medios que mi padre trató fueron dos, el uno que las Señoras Infantas las habían de poner libres a ellas y a sus tesoros en Inglaterra, antes que él entregase la villa dicha al Rey, y así fue hecho por qué mandó a unos escuderos, deudos suyos, naturales de Córdoba, y de su apellido que fuesen con ellas, y las demás gentes que le pareció. El otro capítulo fue que él, y sus hijos, y valedores, y los que habían asistido por su orden en aquella villa fuesen perdonados del Rey, y dados por leales a ellos, y a sus haciendas, y así se le dio firmado del dicho Condestable en nombre del Rey, y de allí fueron él, y sus hijos, y la demás gente a besar la mano del Rey; y el señor Rey Don Enrique mandólos prender, y poner en las Atarazanas de Sevilla, y el dicho Condestable visto que el Señor Rey Don Enrique, no le había cumplido la palabra que él había dado, en su nombre, al dicho Maestre, se salió de su corte, y nunca más volvió a ella, y el Señor Rey mandó que le cortasen la cabeza a mi padre en la Plaza de San Francisco de Sevilla, y que le fuesen confiscados

named Don Lope López de Córdoba Carrillo. My brothers-in-law were called Fernán Rodríguez de Aza, Lord of Aza and Villalobos, another was Ruy García de Aza, and another was Lope Rodríguez de Aza, sons of Alvaro Rodríguez de Aza and of Doña Constanza de Villalobos.

And so it was that when King Pedro was surrounded in the Castle of Montiel by his brother King Enrique, my father went down to Andalusia to fetch people to help him; and on the road back he discovered that Don Pedro was dead at the hands of his brother. Encountering this misfortune he took the road to Carmona where the princesses, King Pedro's daughters (who were related to me on my mother's side and were also my husband's close kin), were lodged. And Don Enrique, now king of Castile, took himself to Seville and put a blockade around Carmona, and as it was such a strong town, it was blockaded for many months.

My father chanced to leave the town, and the king's men of Real Del Rey learned of my father's absence and therefore that the town would no longer be so well protected. So twelve knights volunteered to scale the city walls, and when they reached the top they were captured. My father was advised of the deed, and he returned, and for their effrontery he ordered them beheaded. King Enrique, learning of this occurrence, and knowing that he could not take the town by force of arms to avenge it, sent the High Constable of Castile to negotiate with my father. And the conditions my father set were two: that the princesses were to be given their freedom to go to England together with their treasury before he surrendered the town to the king. This was done, and so he sent some gentlemen, kinsmen of his, born in Córdoba, to accompany them and the other people he

sus bienes, y los de su yerno, valedores, y criados; y yéndole a cortar la cabeza encontró con Mosén Beltrán de Clequín, caballero francés, que fue el caballero que el Rey Don Pedro se había fiado dél, que lo ponía en salvo estando cercado en el Castillo de Montiel, y no cumpliendo lo que le prometió, antes le entregó al Rey Don Enrique para que lo matase, y como encontró al Maestre díjole: —Señor Maestre, ¿no os decía yo que vuestras andanzas habían de parar en esto? Y él le respondió: —*Más vale morir como leal, como yo lo he hecho, que no vivir como vos vivís, habiendo sido traidor.* Y estuvimos los demás que quedamos presos nueve años hasta que el Señor Rey Don Enrique falleció; y nuestros maridos tenían sesenta libras de hierro cada uno en los pies, y mi hermano don Lope López tenía una cadena encima de los hierros en que había setenta eslabones. Él era niño de trece años, la más hermosa criatura que había en el mundo, e a mi marido en especial poníanlo en el aljibe de la hambre, e teníanlo seis, o siete días que nunca comía, ni bebía porque era primo de las Señoras Infantas, hijas del Señor Rey Don Pedro. En esto vino una pestilencia, e murieron todos mis dos hermanos e mis cuñados, e trece caballeros de la casa de mi padre; e Sancho Míñez de Villendra, su camarero mayor, decía a mí, y a mis hermanos: —Hijos de mi señor: Rogad a Dios que os viva yo, que si yo os vivo, nunca moriréis pobres—; e plugo a Dios que murió el tercero día sin hablar; e a todos los sacaban a desherrar al desherradero como moros, después de muertos e el triste de mi hermano don Lope López pidió al Alcaide que no nos tenían, que dijesen a Gonzalo Ruiz Bolante que nos hacía mucha caridad, e mucha honra por amor de Dios: —Señor Alcaide sea ahora vuestra merced que me tirase estos hierros en antes que salga mi ánima, a que no me sacasen al

deemed necessary. The other condition was that he and his children and his defenders, and those who had been present in the town by his order, be pardoned by the king, and that they and their estates be considered loyal. This too was granted, and signed by the High Constable in the name of the king. And by this agreement he gave the town over to the constable in the king's name. And from there, he, his family, and the rest of his people went to kiss the hand of the king.

But King Enrique ordered them taken prisoner and put in the arsenal of Seville. And the constable, when he learned that King Enrique had not kept his word, which he had given in his name to the Grand Master, left his court and never again returned. The king ordered that they cut off my father's head in the Plaza of San Francisco in Seville, and that all his belongings, and those of his sons-in-law, vassals, and servants, be confiscated.

As they were taking him to be beheaded, my father met Mosén Beltrán de Clequin, the French knight trusted by King Pedro, whom the king set free during the siege of the Castle of Montiel, and who had broken the oath he had sworn to the king, betraying him to King Enrique so he could kill him. And when Clequin encountered the Grand Master he said to him, "Lord Grand Master, did I not tell you that your exploits would end this way?" And my father answered him, "*It is better to die loyal, as I have done, than to live as you live, having been a traitor.*"

The rest of us were kept prisoner for nine years, until King Enrique died. Our husbands each had sixty pounds of iron on their feet, and my brother, Don Lope López, had a chain of seventy links on top of his irons. He was a child of thirteen, the most beautiful creature there was in the

desherradero—; a él díjole como a moro: —Si en mí fuese yo lo haría—; y en esto salió su ánima en mis manos; que había él un año más que yo, e sacáronlo en una tabla al desherradero como a moro, e enterráronlo con mis hermanos, e con mis hermanas, e con mis cuñados en San Francisco de Sevilla, e mis cuñados traían sendos collares de oro a la garganta, que eran cinco hermanos, e se pusieron aquellos collares en Santa María de Guadalupe, e prometieron de no quitárselos, hasta que todos cinco se los tirasen a Santa María, que por sus pecados el uno murió en Sevilla, y el otro en Lisboa, y el otro en Inglaterra, e así murieron derramados, e se mandaron enterrar con sus collares de oro, e los frailes con la codicia después de enterrados les quitaron el collar. Y no quedaron en la Atarazana de la casa de mi señor el Maestre, sino mi marido y yo. Y en esto murió el muy alto, y muy esclarecido Señor Rey Don Enrique de muy santa e esclarecida memoria, y mandó en su testamento que nos sacasen de la prisión, e nos tornasen todo lo nuestro e yo quedé en casa de mi señora tía doña María García Carrillo, e mi marido fue a demandar sus bienes, y los que los tenían preciáronle poco, porque no tenía estado, ni manera para los poder demandar, e los derechos ya sabéis cómo dependen a los lugares que han con qué se demandar, e así perdióse mi marido, e anduvo siete años por el mundo, como desventurado, y nunca halló pariente, ni amigo que bien le hiciese, ni hubiese piedad de él, e a cabo de siete años, estando yo en casa de mi señora tía doña María García Carrillo, dijeron a mi marido, que estaba en Badajoz con su tío Lope Fernández e Padilla en la Guerra de Portugal, que yo estaba muy bien andante, que me habían hecho mucho bien mis parientes.

Cabalgó encima de su mula, que valía

world. And they singled out my husband to be put in the hunger tank, where they held him six or seven days and never gave him food or drink because he was a cousin of the princesses, daughters of King Pedro.

Then a pestilence came, and my two brothers and my brothers-in-law and thirteen knights of my father's house all died. And Sancho Míñez de Villendra, my father's high chamberlain, said to me and to my brothers and sisters: "Children of my lord, pray God that I live for your sake, for if I do, you will never die poor." But it pleased God that he should die three days later, without uttering another word. After they died they took all of them out to the blacksmith's like slaves, to remove their irons. And my poor brother Don Lope López asked the jailor who held us to tell Gonzalo Ruiz Bolante to do us a great kindness and a great honor, for the love of God: "Sir jailer, be so kind as to strike these irons from me before my soul departs, so I may not be taken to the blacksmith." And he answered, as if to a slave, "If it were up to me I would do what you ask," and with that his soul departed as I held him. He was only one year older than I, and they took him out to the blacksmith's on a plank, like a slave, and they buried him with my brothers and my sisters and my brothers-in-law in the church of San Francisco in Seville.

Each of my brothers-in-law wore a gold chain at his throat, which they had put on in the church of Santa María de Guadalupe, for they were brothers; and they vowed not to remove those chains until all five met again to take them off in the church of Santa María. But for their sins, one perished in Seville and another in Lisbon, and another in England, and so they died scattered, and it was ordered that they be buried with their gold necklaces.

muy pocos dineros, e lo que traía vestido no valía treinta maravedís; y entróse por la puerta de mi señora mi tía. Yo como había sabido que mi marido andaba perdido por el mundo, traté con mi señora mi tía hermana de mi señora mi madre, que le decían doña Teresa Fernández Carrillo (estaba en la Orden de Guadalajara, que la hicieron mis bisabuelos, e dotaron precio para cuarenta ricas hembras de su linaje que viniesen en aquella orden) enviéle a demandar le pluguiese que yo fuese acogida en aquella orden, pues por mis pecados mi marido e yo éramos perdidos, y ella, y toda la orden alcanzáronlo en dicha, porque mi señora madre se había criado en aquellos monasterios, y de allí la sacó el Rey Don Pedro, e la dio a mi padre que casase con ella, porque ella era hermana de Gonzalo Díaz Carrillo e de Diego Carrillo, hijos de don Juan Fernández Carrillo, e de doña Sancha de Rojas, e porque estos mis tíos habían temor del dicho Señor Don Pedro que había muerto e desterrado muchos de este linaje, y a mi abuelo le había derribado las casas, e dado cuánto tenía a otro; estos mis tíos fuéronse dende a servir al Rey Don Enrique (cuando era conde) por este enojo. Y nací en Calatayud en casa del Señor Rey, que fueron las Señoras Infantas sus hijas mis madrinas, y trujéronme con ellas al Alcázar de Segovia con mi señora madre que ahí murió, y quedé yo de edad que nunca la conocí. Y después que mi marido vino, como dicho es, fuese a casa de mi señora tía, que era en Córdoba junto a San Hipólito, y a mí, y a mi marido me acogió allí en unas casas, junto a las suyas, y viéndonos con poco descanso, hice una oración a la Virgen Santa María de Belén treinta días, cada noche rezaba trescientas Aves Marías de rodillas, para que pusiese en corazón a mi señora, que consintiese abrir un postigo a sus casas, y dos días

But the friars in their greed removed their necklaces after they were buried. And no one from my lord the Grand Master's house remained in the arsenal but my husband and myself.

And then the most exalted and noble King Enrique, of most holy and illustrious memory, died: and he ordered in his will that they free us from prison and return all our belongings. I stayed in the house of my aunt, Doña María García Carrillo, and my husband went out to claim his property. And those who now held it esteemed him little, because he had no rank, nor means to claim what was his; and you well know how rights depend on the station one has on which to base a claim. And thus was my husband lost, and he wandered the world seven years, a wretched man, and never did he find kin or friend who did him a good turn or had pity on him. And at the end of seven years, while I was in the home of my aunt Doña María García Carrillo, they told my husband (who was in Badajoz with his uncle Lope Fernández e Padilla in the War of Portugal) that I was doing very well, and that my relatives had done me much benefit.

He rode on his mule, which was worth very little money, and what he wore on his back was not worth thirty copper coins, and he entered through my aunt's doorway. Since I had learned that my husband was faring so ill I spoke with my aunt, sister to my mother, whose name was Teresa Fernández Carrillo. (She was in the Order of Guadalajara, founded by my great-grandparents and endowed with the dowry of forty rich females of their line, so they could become nuns of the order.) I wrote to ask her to request that I might be taken in by the order, since for my sins my husband and I were bereft. And she and the entire order were happy to do it, be-

antes que acabase la oración, demandé a la señora mi tía que me dejase abrir aquel postigo, por que no viniésemos por la calle a comer a su mesa, entre tantos caballeros que había en Córdoba; e la su merced me respondió le placía, e yo fui muy consolada, e cuando otro día quise abrir el postigo, criadas suyas le habían vuelto su corazón, que no lo hiciese, y fui tan desconsolada, que perdí la paciencia, e la que me hizo más contradicción con la señora mi tía se murió en mis manos, comiéndose la lengua, e otro día, que no quedaba más que un día de acabar mi oración, sábado, soñaba pasando por San Hipólito, tocando el alba, vi en la pared de los corrales un arco muy grande, y muy alto, e que entraba yo por allí, y cogía flores de la sierra, y veía muy gran cielo, y en esto desperté, e hube esperanza en la Virgen Santa María que me daría casa. En esto vino un robo de la Judería, y tomé un niño huérfano, que tenía, para que fuese instruido en la fe, hícelo bautizar por que fuese instruido en la fe. Y un día viniendo con mi señora tía de misa de San Hipólito, vi repartir a los clérigos de San Hipólito, aquellos corrales, donde soñé yo que había el arco grande, y le supliqué a mi señora tía doña Mencía Carrillo, que fuese servida de comprar aquel sitio para mí, pues había diez y siete años que estaba en su compañía, y me las compró; diolas con la condición, que señalaba, que se hiciese una capellanía impuesta sobre las dichas casas por el alma del Señor Rey Don Alfonso que hizo aquella iglesia al nombre de San Hipólito, porque nació él, a tal día, e tienen estos capellanes otras seis o siete capellanías de don Alfonso Fernández, marido de la dicha señora mi tía, e don Alfonso Fernández Señor de Aguilar, e del Mariscal sus hijos, entonces hecha esta merced alcé los ojos a Dios, y a la Virgen María, dándole gracias por ello; y ende

cause my lady and mother had been raised in those monasteries, and King Pedro had taken her from there for my father to marry, because she was the sister of Gonzalo Díaz Carrillo, and of Diego Carrillo, sons of Don Juan Fernández Carrillo and of Doña Sancha de Rojas. And because these uncles of mine were afraid of Don Pedro, who had killed and exiled many of their family, and who had destroyed my grandfather's house and given what he owned to another, these uncles of mine went to serve King Enrique (when he was a count), for this affront. And I was born in Calatayud in the house of the king, and the princesses were my godmothers, and they took me with them to the castle in Segovia with my mother, who died there when I was so young that I never knew her.

After my husband arrived, as I have said, he went to the home of my aunt, which was in Córdoba, next to the church of San Hipólito, and she took me in with my husband, lodging us in some houses that were next door to hers. And seeing that we had so little peace, I prayed for thirty days to the Holy Virgin Mary of Bethlehem. Every night I prayed three hundred Hail Marys on my knees, so that she would put it in my aunt's heart to agree to open a passageway into her dwellings. And two days before my prayers ended, I asked my aunt to allow me to open that passage, so that we would not have to walk through the street, past all the nobility of Córdoba, to get to her table. And her grace responded that she would be happy to do so, and I was greatly consoled. When on the following day I tried to open the passageway, some of her maids had changed her mind, convincing her not to do it; and I was so disconsolate that I lost my patience, and the one who did most to set my aunt against me died in my hands, swallowing

llegó a mí un criado del Maestre mi señor e padre, que vive con Martín Fernández Alcaide de los Donceles, que allí estaba oyendo misa, y enviéle a pedir con aquel criado suyo, para que como pariente le diese las gracias a la señora mi tía de la merced que me había hecho, y a él plúgole mucho y así lo hizo con buena mesura diciéndole que esta merced recibía él por suya. E dádome la posesión abrí una puerta en el sitio y lugar que había visto el arco que la Virgen María me mostró, e a los abades les pesó que me entregasen el dicho solar, porque yo era de grande linaje, y que mis hijos serían grandes, y ellos eran abades, y que no habían menester grandes caballeros cabe sí, y yo túvelo por buen proverbio, y díjeles esperaba en Dios que así sería, y concertéme con ellos, de tal manera, que abrí la puerta en aquel lugar donde yo quería, e tengo que por aquella caridad que hice en criar aquel huérfano en la fe de Jesu Cristo, Dios me ayudó a darme aquel comienzo de casa, e de antes de esto, yo había ido treinta días a maitines ante Santa María el Amortecida, que es en la Orden de San Pablo de Córdoba con aguas y con vientos descalza, e rezábale 63 veces esta oración que se sigue con 66 Aves Marías, en reverencia de los 66 años que ella vivió con amargura en este mundo, por que ella me diese casa, e ella me dio casa, y casas, por su misericordia, mejores que yo las merecía, y comienza la oración, Madre Santa María—de vos gran dolor había vuestro hijo bien criado—vístelo atormentado con su gran tribulación, amortecióse vos el corazón, después de su tribulación, puso vos consolación, ponedlo vos a mí Señora, que sabéis mi dolor. En este tiempo plugo a Dios que con la ayuda de mi señora mi tía, y de la labor de mis manos, hiciese en aquel corral dos palacios, y una huerta, e otras dos o tres casas para

her tongue. And the next day, Saturday, with only one day remaining of my thirty days of prayer, I dreamed that when passing by San Hipólito with the morning bells ringing, I saw on the courtyard walls a very big, high arch, and that I entered there and picked flowers from the mountainside, and I saw the vast heavens. At this point I woke up and placed my hope in the Holy Virgin Mary that she would give me a house.

Then there was a plundering of the Jewish quarter, and I took from there an orphan child to instruct him in the faith, and I had him baptized so he might be instructed in the faith. And one day, returning with my aunt from mass at the church of San Hipólito, I saw the clerics of San Hipólito dividing up those courtyards where I dreamed the great arch was, and I begged my aunt Doña Mencía Carrillo to be so kind as to buy that place for me, as I had been in her company for seventeen years. She bought and gave them to me with the condition that a chaplaincy be laid upon those houses for the soul of King Alfonso, who built that church in the name of Saint Hippolotus, because he was born on his day. These chaplains have another six or seven chaplaincies belonging to Don Gonzalo Fernández, husband of this same aunt, and to their sons, the Marshall and Don Alfonso Fernández, Lord of Aguilar. This favor done, I raised my eyes to God and to the Virgin Mary, giving her thanks. And then there came a servant of the Grand Master, my lord and father, who lives with Martín Fernández, Castellan of Los Donceles, who was there hearing mass; and I sent that servant to him with the request that as a kinsman he give thanks to my aunt for the favor she had done me. And he was most happy to do so, and did it graciously, saying to her that he received this favor as if it had been done for him personally.

servicio. En este tiempo vino una pestilencia muy cruel, y mi señora no quería salir de la ciudad, e yo demandéle merced huir con mis hijuelos, que no se muriesen, y a ella no le plugo, mas diome licencia, y yo partíme de Córdoba, y fuime a Santa Ella con mis hijos; y el huérfano que yo crié vivía en Santa Ella, y aposentóme en su casa, y todos los vecinos de la villa se holgaron mucho de mi ida, y recibiéronme con mucho agasajo, porque habían sido criados del señor mi padre, y así me dieron la mejor casa que había en el lugar, que era la de Fernando Alonso Mediabarba, y estando sin sospecha entró mi señora tía con sus hijas, e yo apartéme a una cuadra pequeña, y sus hijas, mis primas nunca estaban bien conmigo, por el bien que me hacía su madre, y dende allí pasé tantas amarguras, que no se podían escribir, y vino allí pestilencia, y así se partió mi señora con su gente para Aguilar, y llevóme consigo aunque asaz, para sus hijas, porque su madre me quería mucho, y hacía grande cuenta de mí, e yo había enviado aquel huérfano que crié a Ezija. La noche que llegamos a Aguilar entró de Ezija el mozo con dos landres en la garganta, y tres carbunclos en el rostro, con muy grande calentura, y que estaba allí don Alfonso Fernández mi primo, y su mujer, y toda su casa, y aunque todas ellas eran mis sobrinas, y mis amigas, vinieron a mí en sabiendo que mi criado venía así, dijéronme: —Vuestro criado Alonso viene con pestilencia, y si don Alonso Fernández lo ve, hará maravillas estando con tal enfermedad—, y el dolor que a mi corazón llegó, bien lo podéis entender quien esta historia oyere, que yo venía corrida, y amarga; y en pensar que por mí había entrado tan grande dolencia en aquella casa, hice llamar un criado del señor mi padre el Maestre, que se llamaba Miguel de Santa Ella, e roguéle que llevase

The title now in my possession, I had a door cut open on the very site where I had seen the arch the Virgin showed me. And it disturbed the abbots that they should hand that piece of land over to me because I was of great lineage and my sons would be great, and they were abbots and had no need of great knights near them. But I took it for a good sign, and told them I hoped in God it would be thus, and I came to an agreement with them so that I placed the door where I wanted it. I believe for the charitable act I performed in raising that orphan in the faith of Jesus Christ, God helped me in giving me the beginnings of a house. Before this time I had gone barefoot in the wind and rain for thirty days to morning prayer to the shrine of María el Amortecida, which is in the monastery of the order of San Pablo de Córdoba, and I prayed this prayer to her sixty-three times, followed by sixty-six Hail Marys, in homage to the sixty-six years she lived with bitterness in this world, that she might give me a house; and because of her mercy she gave me a house, houses better than I deserved. And the prayer begins, "Holy Mother Mary, great pain did you feel for your son's sake—you saw him tormented with his great suffering, and your heart came close to death. After his agony he gave you comfort, so intercede with my aunt, for you know my pain." At this time it pleased God that with the help of my aunt and of the labor of my hands I built in that courtyard two palaces and a garden and another two or three houses for the servants.

Then there came a most cruel pestilence, and my lady did not want to leave the city. I begged her for mercy to flee with my little children so that they would not die, and this did not please her, but she gave me leave, and I departed from Córdoba, and I went to Santa Ella with my

aquel mozo a su casa, y el cuitado hubo miedo, y dijo: —Señora ¿cómo lo llevaré con pestilencia, que me mate?— y díjele: —Hijo no querrá Dios.— Y él con ver-güenza de mí llevólo; e por mis pecados trece personas, que de noche lo velaban, todos murieron y yo hacía una oración, que había oído, que hacía una monja ante un crucifijo parece que ella era muy devota de Jesu Cristo, y diz que después que había oído maitines, veníase ante un crucifijo, y rezaba de rodillas siete mil veces: —Piado-so hijo de la Virgen, vénzate piedad.—Y que una noche estando la monja cerca, donde ella estaba que oyó que le respondió el crucifijo e dijo: —Piadoso me llamaste *piadoso te seré.* —E yo había grande devo-ción en estas palabras, rezaba cada noche esta oración, rogando a Dios me quisiese librar a mí, y a mis hijos; si alguno hubiese de llevar, llevase el mayor porque era muy doliente; e plugo a Dios que una noche no hallaba quien velase aquel mozo doliente, porque habían muerto todos los que hasta entonces le habían velado, e vino a mí aquel mi hijo, que le decían Juan Fernán-dez de Henestrosa, como su abuelo, que era de edad de doce años y cuatro meses, e díjome: —Señora ¿no hay quien vele a Alonso esta noche?— e díjele: —Veladlo vos por amor de Dios—, y respondióme: —Señora ahora que han muerto otros ¿queréis que me mate?— E yo díjele: —Por la caridad que yo hago, Dios habrá piedad de mí—, e mi hijo por no salir de mi mandamiento lo fue a velar, e por mis pecados aquella noche le dio la pestilencia e otro día le enterré, y el enfermo vivió después habiendo muerto todos los di-chos; e doña Teresa, mujer de don Alfonso Fernández mi primo hubo muy gran eno-jo, porque moría mi hijo por tal ocasión en su casa, y la muerte en la boca lo mandaba sacar de ella, y yo estaba tan traspasada de

children. The orphan I brought up lived in Santa Ella, and he gave me lodging in his house, and all the residents of the town were very happy with my going there, and received me very warmly because they had been servants of my lord and father. And thus they gave me the best house that there was in the place, which belonged to Fer-nando Alonso Mediabarba. My aunt ar-rived unexpectedly with her daughters, and I removed myself to a small apart-ment. And her daughters, my cousins, were never favorably disposed toward me because of the kindness their mother showed me, and from then on I suffered so much bitterness that it cannot all be writ-ten down. And a pestilence came, and my lady departed with her people for Aguilar, and she took me with her, although her daughters thought that was doing too much, because she loved me greatly and thought highly of me. And I sent the or-phan whom I had raised to Ecija.

The night we arrived in Aguilar the young man came in from Ecija with two tumors on his throat and three dark blotches on his face and a very high fever. Don Alfonso Fernández, my cousin, was there, and his wife, with all his household; and although all of them were my nieces and my friends, they came to me when they discovered that my servant had come in such a state. They said to me: "Your servant Alonso has come here with the pestilence, and if Don Alfonso Fernández sees him, he will wreak havoc at being in the presence of such an illness." You who hear this story can well understand the pain that came to my heart, for I was angered and bitter. Thinking that such great suffering had en-tered the house on my account, I had a ser-vant of my lord and father, the Grand Mas-ter, summoned, whose name was Miguel de Santa Ella, and I begged him to take the

pesar, que no podía hablar del corrimiento que aquellos señores me hacían; y el triste de mi hijo decía: —Decid a mi señora doña Teresa que no me haga echar que ahora saldrá mi ánima para el cielo.— Y aquella noche falleció, y se enterró en Santa María la Coronada, que es en la villa, porque doña Teresa me tenía mala intención, y no sabía por qué, y mandó que no lo soterrasen dentro de la villa, y así cuando lo llevaban a enterrar fui yo con él, y cuando iba por la calle con mi hijo, las gentes salían dando alaridos, amancillados de mí, y decían: —Salid, señores, y veréis la más desventurada, desamparada, e más maldita mujer del mundo—, con los gritos que los cielos traspasaban, e como los de aquel lugar todos eran crianza, y hechura del señor mi padre, y aunque sabían que les pesaba a sus señores, hicieron grande llanto conmigo como si fuera su señora. Esta noche, como vine a soterrar a mi hijo, luego me dijeron que me viniese a Córdoba, e yo llegué a mi señora tía por ver si me lo mandaba ella. Ella me dijo: —Sobrina señora no puedo dejar de hacerlo, que a mi nuera y a mis hijas he prometido porque son hechas en uno, y en tanto me han aflijido que os parta de mí, que se lo hube otorgado, e esto no sé qué enojo hacéis a mi nuera doña Teresa que tan mala intención os tiene—, y yo le dije con muchas lágrimas: —Señora, Dios no me salve si merecí por qué—, y así víneme a mis casas a Córdoba.

young man to his house; and the poor man grew fearful and said: "My lady, how can I take him, sick with the pestilence, for it may kill me?" And I said to him: "Son, God shall not will it so." And he took him out of shame. And for my sins, thirteen people, who kept vigil over him during the night, all died. And I offered a prayer that I had heard a nun say before a crucifix. It seems she was very devoted to Jesus Christ, and it is said that after she heard morning prayers, she came before the crucifix and prayed on her knees seven thousand times: "Merciful Son of the Virgin, have pity." And one night the nun heard the crucifix answer her, saying: "Merciful you have called me, and *merciful I shall be.*" I placed great faith in these words and prayed this prayer every night, entreating God so he might wish to free me and my children, and if any of them had to be taken away, it should be the eldest one, for he was in great pain. And it was God's will that one night I could not find anyone to keep vigil over that suffering young man, because all those who had watched over him till then had died. And that son of mine whose name was Juan Fernández de Henestrosa, after his grandfather, and who was twelve years and four months of age, came to me and said: "My lady, is there no one who will watch over Alonso tonight?" And I said to him: "You watch over him, for the love of God." And he answered me: "My lady, now that the others have died, do you want me to die as well?" And I said to him: "For the act of charity I now do, God will have mercy on me." And my son, so as not to disobey me, went to watch over him, and for my sins, that night he came down with the plague and I buried him the next day. And the sick man survived, but all those I have mentioned died. And Doña Teresa, wife of Don Alfonso Fernández, my cousin, grew very

angry that for such a reason my son was dying in her house, and with death in his mouth she ordered him to be taken out.

And I was so wrought with anguish that I could not speak for the shame those noble people made me bear. And my sad little son said: "Tell Doña Teresa not to have me cast out, for my soul will soon depart for Heaven." And that night he died, and he was buried in the Church of Santa María la Coronada, which is in the town. But Doña Teresa had designs against me, and I did not know why; and she had ordered that he not be buried within the town. And so, when they took him to be buried I went with him, and when I was going down the street with my son, the people, offended for me, came out shouting: "Come out good people and you will see the most unfortunate, forsaken, and condemned woman in the world," with cries that rent the heavens. As the residents of that place were all liege and subject to my lord father, and although they knew it troubled their masters, they made great display of the grief they shared with me, as if I were their lady.

That night, after I returned from burying my son, they told me to go back to Córdoba, and I approached my aunt to see if she would order me to do so. She said to me: "My niece, I cannot fail to do this, for I have promised my daughter-in-law and my daughters, who are of one mind. As they have pressed me to remove you from my presence, I have granted their request. I do not know what vexation you have caused my daughter-in-law, Doña Teresa, that she feels such ill will toward you." And I said to her with many tears: "My lady, may God not grant me salvation if I have done anything to deserve this." And so I came back to my houses in Córdoba.

(Translated by Amy Kaminsky and Elaine Dorough Johnson)

Florencia Pinar

Among the fewer than half-dozen women whose names appear in the compilations of songs and poems of the fifteenth century is Florencia Pinar. The three poems reprinted here from the *Cancionero general* (General songbook, 1511) are the only ones that can be definitively attributed to her, but their quality and craft suggest that Pinar wrote others, about which we can now only speculate. Indeed, the history of women's poetry in Spain before the sixteenth century is, in great part, speculative. Medieval anonymity, together with the popular character of much early lyric, has made the attribution of specific poems impossible. The *cancioneros*, collections of poems and songs written largely by courtiers, contain few women's names among the poets they include, but the folk songs and popular love lyrics preserved in these compendia are testimony to a very old women's poetry tradition.

Early lyric poetry, *cantigas de amigo, villancicos,* and *jarchas,* are rooted in a prehistoric European lyric of women's poetry associated with religious rites and the work of planting and harvest. The *jarchas,* which are condensed poems about women's experience of love, are the oldest known written poems in any Romance language. Simple verses, with minimal vocabulary and written in everyday language, they owe their survival to the professional male poets of Al-Andalus (now Andalusia) who took them directly from the popular tradition, or who imitated them, appending them to the ends of poems they had written in classical Arabic or Hebrew.

In Muslim Spain women poets were associated with the court of the caliph of Córdoba. Aixa ben Ahmed and Ualada, the latter a daughter of Caliph Almostafi, are two who, in the eleventh century, were known for both their satiric and their erotic poetry. Nevertheless, it is necessary to wait until the fifteenth century before a woman puts her name to a poem written in Spanish. The first is a religious text, signed by María Sarmiento, that appeared in the *Cancionero de Martín Burgos* (Martin Burgos's song book), compiled in the 1460s.

The compilers of the *cancioneros* were Spain's first anthologists. They gathered and organized — after a fashion — examples of courtly poetry of their age. Among the poets they included are fewer than a half-dozen women. Of these, Florencia Pinar, with three poems that can be attributed to her with certainty, is the most fully represented. Other material in the *cancionero* texts, such as poems attributed to Marina Manuel, Catalina Manrique, María Sarmiento, and Juana de Portugal, in addition to

anonymous ones signed "a lady" or "a female dwarf," and semianonymous ones like the one signed "Vayona," suggesting that the writer is from Bayonne, together with poems that refer to women jongleurs or who name women poets directly, indicates that women took an active part in writing poetry during the fifteenth century.

The women poets of the songbooks did not set themselves apart, creating a separate women's poetry. The poetry of the *cancionero* is consciously intertextual, with an abundance of poetic conversations and glosses; and the women poets participated fully in this social poetic world. Vayona, for example, responds to the lines of a nobleman with a poem that defends the lady she serves. Women also initiate these poetic conversations. "Question of a Lady to Diego Núñez" presupposes that the lady expects an answer. The gloss that Florencia Pinar's brother writes, based on a poem by his sister, like other glosses written by other male poets on *motes* (aphorisms) by Marina Manuel, Catalina Manrique, and an anonymous lady, also indicates that men read and responded to the work of women writers, particularly, one supposes, when the lady was of a higher rank than the gentleman.

The *motes* were included in the *Cancionero general* because they justify the glosses that followed them. Like the *jarchas* that adorned and characterized the classical Arabic *moaxaja* and the folk songs (*villancicos* and *cantigas de amigo*) copied into the *cancioneros* because they served as inspiration for the courtly poets, these *motes* represent the assimilation of the feminine into the masculine and the subordination of women's texts as a condition of their survival.

It is possible that the compiler of the *Cancionero general* included the names of Marina Manuel and Catalina Manrique because they were from politically as well as poetically illustrious families. The *motes* that represent them in the songbook cannot have been their only literary foray, but rather the traces of a more extensive literary production. These published *motes* also suggest that other noblewomen participated in the literary games of the court, and that the lack of surviving texts signed by women is not due to their historical inexistence, but rather to their probably irrecoverable loss. It is interesting to note that another lady associated with the name Manrique, Doña Juana de Mendoza, wife of the poet Gómez Manrique, patronized Teresa de Cartagena's defense of women's writing.

Florencia Pinar did not come from an illustrious family, and Pinar herself is a shadowy figure. Her name appears in three songbooks from the fifteenth and sixteenth centuries, which contributes to the confusion about the attribution of her works. One text that appears attached to her name in one songbook has no such attribution in another. Scholars have generally believed that the poems signed simply "Pinar" were written by her brother. Thanks to the somewhat random organization of the songbooks, it is impossible to know for certain which poems were written by which Pinar. To add to the confusion, the *Cancionero general* contains one poem attributed to "Florencia," who might also be this poet. The conflicting evidence of the *cancioneros* is an annoyance, but the appearance of the name Florencia Pinar in three different compilations also indicates that she was widely known during her time.

Canción

¡Ay! que hay quien más no vive
porque no hay quien de ¡ay! se duele,
y si hay ¡ay! que recele,
hay un ¡ay! con que se esquive
quien sin ¡ay! vivir no suele.

Hay placeres, hay pesares,
hay glorias, hay mil dolores,
hay donde hay penas de amores
muy gran bien si de él gozares;
aunque vida se cautive,
si hay quien tal ¡ay! consuele,
no hay razón porque se cele,
aunque hay con que se esquive
quien sin ¡ay! vivir no suele.

Song

Alas! a lass there lives that does not live
because, alack, she lacks the lad she loves
and if the lassie sighs the cautious
sigh that says she's soft,
he sighs the sigh of scorn as hard as stone.

Joys there be and there be sorrows,
glories and a thousand woes.
Where love's pain lives abides delight
if you but take your pleasure so.
Though your life may be held captive,
captivated, be consoled;
if there's a sigh of consolation
there's no cause to hide from love,
even if you cautious sigh
the sigh that says you're soft
and his scornful sigh's
the sigh as hard as stone.

*(Translated by Amy Kaminsky
and Donna Lazarus)*

Canción
A unas perdices que la
enviaron vivas

De estas aves su nación
es cantar con alegría,
y de verlas en prisión
siento yo grave pasión,
sin sentir nadie la mía.

Ellas lloran que se vieron
sin temor de ser cautivas,
y a quien eran más esquivas
esos mismos las prendieron:
sus nombres mi vida son
que va perdiendo alegría,
y de verlas en prisión,
siento grave pasión,
sin sentir nadie la mía.

Song
To the Live Pheasants
Someone Sent Her

These birds are wont
to sing with joy,
and to see them caged
I feel a deep compassion
that no one feels for me.

They weep to think
they did not fear their captor,
and those they most disdained
were the first to seize them:
their names bespeak my life,
whose happiness is waning,
and to see them caged,
I feel a deep compassion,
that no one feels for me.

(Translated by Lou Charnon Deutsch)

Canción

El amor ha tales mañas
que quien no se guarda de ellas,
si se le entra en las entrañas,
no puede salir sin ellas.
   El amor es un gusano,
bien mirada su figura;
es un cáncer de natura
que come todo lo sano:
por sus burlas, por sus sañas,
de él se dan tales querellas,
que si entra en las entrañas,
no puede salir sin ellas.

Song

Love has such snares
that lest you guard against them,
it creeps into your heart,
it entangles you forever.
   Love is a worm,
though lovely to look at;
a cancer of nature
that devours the healthy:
with its deceit, with its passion,
it causes such upheaval
that once it creeps into your heart
it entangles you forever.

(Translated by Lou Charnon Deutsch)

Teresa de Cartagena

In the second half of the fifteenth century, Teresa de Cartagena, a nun, became the first Spanish woman to write a defense of women's writing. She was the only woman to participate in the so-called feminist debate that took place throughout the 1400s, and she embroiled herself in it to defend her own right to authorship.

Born to a powerful *converso* family, Teresa de Cartagena lived during an era of transition marked by profound spiritual and intellectual confusion.[1] The new humanism's notion of the preeminence of the mind confronted the religious consolidation of the peninsula under the banner of Catholicism, and neither dispelled a widely held belief in witchcraft. The mass uprisings against Jews, one of which Leonor López de Córdoba mentions, continued, while the popular mind credited magic for the political success and failure of some of the most powerful men of the era.

The century also saw an increase in the number of *conversos*. Their situation was tenuous: old Christians were suspicious of them for having been Jews and because the most visible of them now occupied positions of great influence. Jews, for their part, regarded *conversos* as traitors. The Inquisition would be particularly concerned with them, and as a community they were victims of Christian riots. They had alienated themselves from the consolation of their old religion and from the support of their former coreligionists.

The paradoxes of the era — political modernization faced with medieval religious preoccupation, the situation of the *conversos*, the glorification of the intellect accompanied by a belief in magic and witchcraft, the death knell of the most brutal aspects of feudalism as well as that of the autonomy of towns established by the charter laws — extended to the question of women.

Like the *converso*, "woman" did not get to define herself; the feminist debate took place throughout the century almost entirely without her participation. The best-known text of the debate, *El corbacho* (The whip), by the Archpriest of Talavera, is also one of the most misogynist; but other treatises, such as Don Alvaro de Luna's *Libro de las claras y virtuosas mujeres* (Book of pure and virtuous women), were written in defense of women.

Teresa de Cartagena's family played an important role in the religious, political, and literary upheavals of the era. Her maternal family had enough influence to oppose successfully the powerful Luna family. Teresa's grandfather had been Selomo

Ha-Levi, poet and chief rabbi of Burgos, before his conversion. Taking the name Pablo de Santa María, he traded his former title for that of bishop of the same city. Ha-Levi's conversion may have had more to do with his desire to extend his power than with religious zeal, but two generations later, Teresa was an orthodox Catholic, though with full awareness of the precarious situation of the *conversos*. Although the exact date of her birth is not known, she was old enough in 1449 — somewhere between fourteen and twenty-nine — to be fully aware of the massacre of the *conversos* that took place in Toledo that year.

Teresa also shared a family tradition of intellectual activity and literary expression. In addition to her poet grandfather, Teresa's father was a poet, and her uncle, Alfonso de Cartagena, who also became Bishop of Burgos, translated Seneca and Cicero and wrote didactic prose. She herself studied in Salamanca.

Teresa's two extant prose works are rooted in her own experience. *Arboleda de los enfermos* (Grove of the infirm), probably written a little after 1450, is a treatise based on her own infirmity. Teresa was deaf, and the *Arboleda* puts her deafness in a religious context, conceptualizing it as a gift from God. Referring to ecclesiastical authorities and generalizing from her own case (she almost always writes in the first person, either as "I" or "we"), Teresa reconciles her suffering with her religion, without losing sight of her infirmity. The experience of physical pain is never far from these pages. "And whoever says that the infirm person is lazy does not know what pain is," she writes.

Aside from some commonplaces in deference to notions of female modesty, Teresa writes the *Arboleda* without paying attention to her gender. The treatise, as a meditation on illness as a God-given path to spiritual health, tends to minimize the body and its limitations in favor of the soul. In fact, the physical limitations to which Teresa refers are those that men and women share. The issue of gender does not arise, and Teresa simply assumes that women and men alike have the ability to meditate and write on the spiritual and physical realities that she deals with in her treatise. Teresa includes women in humanity by the simple gesture of generalizing to all people from her own experience. She writes unpreoccupied, in sure and direct prose, as someone with the right to do so.

Being, as far as we know, the first Spanish woman to write a treatise destined for general circulation, Teresa de Cartagena could not have anticipated the reaction that the *Arboleda* would provoke. Her critics accused her of plagiarism, intimating that no woman could withstand the intellectual rigor required to produce such a work. Her following book, *Admiración operum Dey* (Wonder at the work of God), is a defense of her first treatise and of her right and her ability to take up the pen. She wrote it at the behest of another woman, Doña Juana de Mendoza, wife of the poet Gómez Manrique. Taking advantage of the rhetorical device offered by Doña Juana, Teresa addresses herself to the other woman and avoids a direct confrontation with those who attacked the *Arboleda*. Doña Juana's petition opened a space for a dialogue between

women, not isolated from the dialogue of masculine culture, but rather intertwined with questions of particular interest to women, created by that culture. Teresa de Cartagena defends women's participation in intellectual work by appealing to the surest authority of her age. Teresa's key argument, supported by considerable erudition, is that an omnipotent God can place talent, knowledge, and competence in a woman, if that is what God wishes to do.

1. *Converso* is the term used by Christians to refer to Jews who converted to Christianity.

Admiración operum Dey
(fragmentos)

Acuérdome, virtuosa señora, que me ofre-cí a escribir a vuestra discreción.[1] Si he tanto tardado de lo encomendar a la obra, no os debéis maravillar, ca mucho es enco-gida la voluntad cuando la disposición de la persona no concierta con ella, antes aun la impide e contrasta. Si considerardes, virtuosa señora, las enfermedades e corpo-rales pasiones que de continuo he por fa-miliares, bien conocerá vuestra discreción que mucho son estorbadoras de los movi-mientos de la voluntad e no menos turba-doras del entendimiento, el cual fatigado e turbado con aquello que la memoria e na-tural sentimiento del presente le ofrecen, así como constreñido de propia necesidad, recoge en sí mismo la deliberación de la voluntad con todos interiores movimien-tos. E tanto la detiene e detarda en la eje-cución de la obra cuanto ve que las sus fuerzas intelectuales son enflaquecidas por causa de los ya dichos exteriores trabajos. E aun con todo esto ya sería pagada este deuda que por mi palabra soy deudora si la soledad mía se contentase con solos mis corporales afanes y no me causase compa-ñía secreta e dañosa llena de interiores combates y espirituales peligros con mu-chedumbre de vanos e variables pensa-mientos, los cuales así como una hueste de gente armada cercan de cada parte la an-gustiada ánima mía. Pues ¿qué hará el en-tendimiento flaco y mujeril desque se ve puesto entre tantos e tan peligrosos lazos? Ca en defenderse de aquello que clara-mente es malo tiene asaz trabajo, e en co-nocer aquello que so color de bueno el nuestro adversario le ofrece son tanto

1. Se dirige a doña Juana de Mendoza, mujer de Gómez Manrique.

Wonder at the Work of God
(excerpts)

I recall, good lady, that I offered to write at your behest.[1] If it has taken me so long from your request to my writing this work, do not wonder, because one's will is much limited when one's disposition does not agree with it, or even contradicts and dis-agrees with it. If you consider, good lady, the illnesses and bodily afflictions that I continuously suffer, you will know well that they hinder my will's actions and dis-turb my mind, which, exhausted and agi-tated by those things that memory and any natural feelings of the moment put before it, as well as bound by its own limits, draws into itself the will's deliberations with all its inner movements. And it stops and de-lays so much in the execution of its work when it sees that its intellectual strength is weakened because of those external labors. And even with all this my debt would be already paid, for by my word I am in debt, if my solitude were to be content with only my bodily afflictions and did not impose on me its secret and destructive company filled with inner struggles and spiritual dangers, with many vain and contrary thoughts, which like an army of soldiers lay siege to each part of my anguished soul. Then, what will my weak and wom-anly understanding do, placed as it is among so many dangerous traps? Because it is very difficult to defend oneself from those things that are clearly evil, and to recognize those things whose appear-ance of good our adversary offers us; its strength is so weakened that if virtue does not help it or enlighten it, we cannot find in it any virtue or health. Therefore, most

1. She writes to Doña Juana de Mendoza, wife of the poet Gómez Manrique.

enflaquecidas sus fuerzas que si la Virtud soberana no le esfuerza e alumbra, no es en él virtud ni sanidad alguna. Así que, muy discreta señora, sienta vuestro discreto sentido la diversidad e calidad destos espirituales e ocultos escándalos con otros de no menor calidad e cantidad que vuestra prudencia puede bien entender, los cuales con la su gran fuerza así como avenidas de muchas aguas corrompieron el muro de mi flaca discreción e llevaron de raíz todo lo que hallaron que mi entendimiento tenía aparejado para encomendar la péñola. E sola la causa sobre que delibré escribir me representa la memoria; y pues el fundamento quedó sin hacer, sea el edificio, no tal ni tan bueno como a vuestra gran discreción presentar se debía, mas así pequeño e flaco como de mi pobre facultad se espera. Ca pues el árbol malo según sentencia de la soberana Verdad, no puede hacer buenos frutos, ¿qué palabra buena ni obra devota debéis esperar de mujer tan enferma en la persona e tan vulnerada en el ánima? Mas llevaré mis ojos a los montes donde viene a mí el auxilio, porque Aquél que da esfuerzo a los flacos e entendimiento a los pequeños quiera abrir el arca de su divinal largueza, dejando derramar de la fuente de su abundosa gracia sobre esta tierra estéril e seca, porque la mujer pecadora e apartada de virtud sepa formar palabra en loor y alabanza del Santo de los santos e Señor de las virtudes. E por no me alejar mucho del propósito e fundamento de mi escribir, es la causa ésta que se sigue.

wise lady, let your keen intelligence comprehend the diversity and magnitude of these spiritual and hidden scandals, together with others of no less magnitude or quantity that your wisdom can well understand, which, with their great, floodlike strength corroded the wall of my weak wit and took away completely all they found which my understanding had prepared to direct my quill. And only the cause about which I decided to write comes to my mind now; and since the foundation has been left undone, the resulting edifice is not nearly as good a presentation as your great wisdom merits. Rather it is small and paltry as is to be expected from my poor faculty. Because, according to the proverb that speaks God's truth, the bad tree cannot yield good fruit, what good words or devout work should you expect from such a woman so physically misfit and with such a damaged soul? But I will raise my eyes to the mountains whence help comes to me, so that He who gives strength to the weak and understanding to the small will deign to open the ark of His divine greatness, letting His abundant grace spill from its fountain upon this sterile and dry land, so that a woman, though sinful and separated from virtue, will know how to create words in praise and eulogy of the Saint of Saints and the Lord of virtue. And so as not to separate myself too much from the purpose and reason for my writing, I offer you the following words.

Introducción

Muchas veces me es hecho entender, virtuosa señora, que algunos de los prudentes varones e así mismo hembras discretas se maravillan o han maravillado de un

Introduction

I have been repeatedly informed, good lady, that some judicious men, as well as wise women, marvel or have marveled at a treatise that, divine grace directing my

tratado que, la gracia divina administrando mi flaco mujeril entendimiento, mi mano escribió. E como sea una obra pequeña, de poca sustancia, estoy maravillada. E no se crea que los prudentes varones se inclinasen a quererse maravillar de tan poca cosa, pero si su maravillar es cierto, bien parece que mi denuesto no es dudoso, ca manifiesto no se hace esta admiración por meritoria de la escritura, mas por defecto de la autora o componedora della, como vemos por experiencia cuando alguna persona de simple e rudo entendimiento dice alguna palabra que nos parezca algún tanto sentida: maravillámonos dello, no porque su dicho sea digno de admiración mas porque el mismo ser de aquella persona es así reprobado e bajo e tenido en tal estima que no esperamos della cosa que buena sea. E por esto cuando acaece por la misericordia de Dios que tales personas simples y rudas dicen o hacen algunas cosas, aunque no sea del todo buena, si no comunal, maravillámonos mucho por el respeto ya dicho. E por el mismo respeto creo ciertamente que se hayan maravillado los prudentes varones del tratado que yo hice, y no porque en él se contenga cosa muy buena ni digna de admiración, mas porque mi propio ser e justo merecimiento con la adversa fortuna e acrecentadas pasiones dan voces contra mí e llaman a todos que se maravillen diciendo: "¿Cómo en persona que tantos males asientan puede haber algún bien?" E de aquí se ha seguido que la obra mujeril e de poca sustancia que digna es de reprensión entre los hombres comunes, e con mucha razón sería hecha digna de admiración en el acatamiento de los singulares e grandes hombres, ca no sin causa se maravilla el prudente cuando ve que el necio sabe hablar. E diga quien quisiere que esta ya dicha admiración es loor, que

womanly understanding, my hand wrote. And since it is a small work, of little substance, I am myself amazed. And do not believe that wise men want to admire such an insignificant deed, for if they are indeed amazed, it seems to me that the insult cannot be doubted, because this admiration does not proceed from the merit of the writing, but is due rather to the author's or composer's imperfection; as experience shows us when a person of simple and unrefined understanding says something that seems remarkable to us we marvel at it, not because what was said is remarkable but because the person himself is despised as loathsome and considered in such a way that we do not expect from him anything noteworthy. And that which was a sign of God's mercy: that such simple and unrefined people say or do some things, although less than perfectly, because it is so unusual, surprises us greatly. And for the same reason I certainly believe that wise men have wondered at this treatise I wrote, not because it contains anything excellent or worthy of admiration, but because my own being and richly deserved adverse fortune, and my growing passions, accuse me and enjoin all who see me to ask in amazement: "How can a person with so many illnesses have any good qualities?" And from this it can be inferred that work that is of woman and of such minor content deserves reproach among common men, and it rightfully would have been considered deserving of wonder in the eyes of singular and great men, because not without reason does the wise man marvel when he sees that the fool can speak. And let anyone who wants to do so say that this afore-mentioned wonderment is praise; my will tells me that it is, rather, an insult. I think I prefer vile insults to vain praises, because neither can insults

a mi denuesto me parece e por la mi voluntad, antes se me ofrezcan injuriosos denuestos me parece que no vanos loores, ca ni me puede dañar la injuria ni aprovechar el vano loor. Así que yo no quiero usurpar la gloria ajena ni deseo huir del propio denuesto. Pero hay otra cosa que no debo consentir, pues la verdad no la consiente, ca parece ser no solamente se maravillan los prudentes del tratado ya dicho, mas aun algunos no pueden creer que yo hiciese tanto bien ser verdad: que en mí menos es de lo que se presume, pero en la misericordia de Dios mayores bienes se hallan. E porque me dicen, virtuosa señora, que el ya dicho volumen de papeles borrados haya venido a la noticia del señor Gómez Manrique e vuestra, no sé si la duda, a vueltas del tratado se presentó a vuestra discreción. E como quier que la buena obra que ante el sujeto de la soberana Verdad es verdadera e cierta, no empecé mucho si en el acatamiento e juicio de los hombres humanos es habida por dudosa, como ésta, puede estragar e estraga la sustancia de la escritura, e aun parece evacuar muy mucho el beneficio e gracia que Dios me hizo. Por ende a honor y gloria deste soberano e liberal Señor de cuya misericordia es llena la tierra, e yo, que soy un pequeño pedazo de tierra, atrévome a presentar a vuestra gran discreción esto que a la mía pequeña e flaca por ahora se ofrece.

Verdad es, muy discreta e amada señora, que todas las cosas que la omnipotencia de Dios ha hecho e hace en el mundo son de grande admiración a nuestro humano seso, así que la menor cosa que este soberano y potentísimo Hacedor ha hecho y hace, no es de menor admiración que la mayor. Esto es porque la más chica cosa en el mundo es, tampoco se pudiera arar como

harm me nor can I benefit from vain praise. Therefore, I do not wish to steal anyone's glory nor do I wish to avoid any insult. But there is another thing I should not allow, because truth does not allow it, and it is that not only do the wise marvel at this treatise, but there are even those who cannot believe that I have written such a good work: that there is less in me than there seems to be, but in God's mercy greater blessings can be found. And because they tell me that the aforementioned collection of roughly drafted papers has come to the attention of Gómez Manrique and to yours, I do not know if the doubt concerning the treatise was also presented for your consideration. And to ensure that the good work that comes before the subject of the sovereign truth is indeed truthful and certain, I would not have made a very good start if in the judgment of human men it were considered doubtful, as in this case, for it can spoil it and take away the substance of the writing, denying me much of the benefit and grace that God gave me. Therefore, to the honor and glory of the sovereign and liberal Lord of whose mercy the Earth is full, I, though but a small piece of the world, dare to present to you these products that my humble and weak understanding are presently able to offer.

It is true, most wise and beloved lady, that everything that God's omnipotence has done in this world is worthy of great wonder to our human mind; therefore the smallest thing that this sovereign and powerful Creator has done and does is no less worthy of admiration than the greatest. This is because neither the smallest nor the grandest thing in the world could ever have been imagined if God's omnipotence did not make it so ... Therefore, and

la mayor si la omnipotencia de Dios no la hiciera . . . Así que, tornando al propósito, creo yo, muy virtuosa señora, que la causa porque los varones se maravillan que mujer haya hecho tratado es por no ser acostumbrado en el estado fimineo, mas solamente en el varonil. Ca los varones hacer libros y aprender ciencias y usar dellas, tiénenlo así en uso de antiguo tiempo que parece ser habido por natural curso y por esto ninguno se maravilla. Y las hembras que no lo han habido en uso, ni aprenden ciencias, ni tienen el entendimiento tan perfecto como los varones, es habido por maravilla. Pero no es mayor maravilla ni a la omnipotencia de Dios menos fácil e ligero de hacer lo uno que lo otro, ca Él que pudo e puede engerir las ciencias en el entendimiento de los hombres, puede si quiere engerirlas en el entendimiento de las mujeres aunque sea imperfecto o no tan hábil ni suficiente para las recibir ni retener como el entendimiento de los varones. Ca esta imperfección y pequeña insuficiencia puédela muy bien reparar la grandeza divina e aun quitarla del todo e dar perfección e habilidad en el entendimiento fimineo así como en el varonil, ca la suficiencia que han los varones no la han del suyo, que Dios se la dio o da . . . Quiero preguntar cuál es la mayor y más principal preeminencia que Dios dio al varón más que a la hembra, y mi simpleza me responde que entre otras preeminencias de que Dios quiso dotar al sexo varonil más que al fimineo es ésta una e a mi ver principal: ca el hombre es fuerte e valiente e de grande ánimo e osado e de más perfecto e sano entendimiento, e la mujer, por el contrario, ca es flaca e pusilánime, de pequeño corazón e temerosa. Ca vemos con mayor osadía e esfuerzo esperará el varón un bravo toro que no la mujer esperaría un ratón que le pasase por las faldas.

returning to my purpose, I think, most virtuous lady, that the reason why men marvel that a woman has written this treatise is because such a skill is not common among women, only among men. Because for men to write books, learn sciences, and use them are activities that they have engaged in for a long time and it seems the natural course, and that is why no one marvels at it. And since women have not been accustomed to it, nor do they learn sciences or possess an understanding as perfected as that of men, it is considered extraordinary. But it is not a greater wonder nor is it easier for God's omnipotence to do either one or the other, because He who could or can engender men's understanding of the sciences could just as easily engender women's understanding of them, even if women's reason is imperfect or not as able or sufficient to receive or remember as men's reason. This imperfection and small insufficiency can be so easily repaired by God's greatness and even erased totally, and perfection and ability granted to female understanding as well as to male understanding, because the sufficiency that the male has is not inherent in him but was given or is given to him by God. I want to ask what is the greatest advantage that God gave men compared to women, and in my simplicity I answer that among other advantages that God provided the male sex compared to the female sex is this, to me, very important one: men are strong and brave and bold and daring and possess a more perfect and healthy understanding, and women, on the contrary, are weak and pusillanimous, with a small and fearful heart. For we see with what greater courage and strength the male will confront a wild bull than a woman suffer a mouse to jump on her skirts. And in the same way if we women see a bared sword,

E así mismo las mujeres si vemos una espada desnuda, aunque sabemos que con ella no nos hará daño alguno, pero naturalmente somos así temerosas que solamente de la ver habemos gran miedo. E los varones no han temor de usar della e aun de recibir en sus personas los crueles e fuertes golpes del hierro. E hizo Dios estas diferencias e contrariedades en una misma natura, e conviene saber, humana, por aquel solo fin e maravilloso secreto que Él mismo sabe. Yo, con mi simpleza, atrévome a decir que lo hizo el celestial Padre porque fuese conservación e adjutorio el uno de lo ál. Ca todo lo que el Señor crió e hizo sobre la faz de la tierra, todo lo proveyó e guarneció de maravillas provisiones e guarniciones. E si queredes bien mirar las plantas e árboles, veréis como las cortezas de fuera son muy recias e fuertes e sufridoras de las tempestades que los tiempos hacen, aguas e hielos e calores e fríos. Están así engeridas e hechas por tal son que no parecen sino un gastón firme e recio para conservar e ayudar el meollo que está encercado de dentro. E así por tal orden e manera anda lo uno con lo ál, que la fortaleza e recidumbre de las cortezas guardan e conservan el meollo, sufriendo exteriormente las tempestades ya dichas. El meollo así como es flaco e delicado, estando incluso, obra interiormente, da virtud e vigor a las cortezas e así lo uno con lo ál se conserva e ayuda e nos da cada año la diversidad o composidad de las frutas que vedes. E por este mismo respeto creo yo que el soberano e poderoso Señor quiso e quiere en la natura humana obrar estas dos contrariedades, conviene a saber: el estado varonil, fuerte e valiente, e el fimineo, flaco e delicado. Ca los varones con su fuerza e ánimo e suficiencia de entendimiento conservan e guardan las cosas de fuera, así en procurar e tratar e saber ganar los bienes

although we know that it will do us no harm, we are naturally so fearful that merely by seeing it we tremble with fear. And men are not afraid either of using it or of receiving the iron's cruel blows. And since God made these differences and oppositions in the same human nature, it is therefore important to realize that it was because of that one special and secret purpose that only He knows. My simple understanding tells me that this was done by the Heavenly Father in order that the sexes should preserve and complement one another. Because everything that the Lord created and made on the face of the Earth was provided for and given wonderful dispositions and faculties. And if you care to examine plants and trees, you will see that all the outside cortexes are very hard and strong and can endure the storms that the weather causes: water and ice, and heat and cold. They are created and made in such a way that they do not appear to be more than a strong and coarse cover to preserve and sustain the pith that is within. And thus in this order and manner, one thing is related to another, that the strength and coarseness of the bark keeps and preserves the pith, weathering the afore-mentioned storms. The pith, although weak and delicate, acts internally and gives virtue and strength to the bark and thus, one with the other, the tree preserves itself and helps us and gives us each year the diversity and quantity of fruits that you see. And because of this I think that the sovereign and powerful Lord wanted and wants to sustain these two contradictions in human nature, that is: the male state, strong and brave, and the feminine one, weak and delicate. Because men, with their strength, daring, and superior understanding, preserve and guard in the exterior realm, thereby providing,

de fortuna, como el regir e gobernar e defender sus patrias e tierras de los enemigos, e todas las otras cosas que a la conservación e provecho de la república se requiere, e por consiguiente a sus particulares haciendas e personas; para lo cual, mucho conviene y es menester que sean robustos e valientes, de grande ánimo e aun de grandes e de muy elevados entendimientos. E las hembras, así como flacas e pusilánimes e no sufridoras de los grandes trabajos e peligros que la procuración e gobernación e defensión de las sobredichas cosas se requieren, solamente estando inclusas o encercadas dentro en su casa, con su industria e trabajo e obras domésticas e delicadas dan fuerza e vigor, e sin duda no pequeño subsidio a los varones. E así se conserva e sostiene la natura humana, la cual es hecha de tan flaco almacén que sin estos ejercicios e trabajos no podría vivir. Así que estas preeminencias ya dichas de los varones, ser valientes e de gran ánimo e suficiente entendimiento, ni otra alguna que Dios les haya dado, no es en perjuicio de las hembras, ni la flaqueza e pusilinamidad del estado fimineo le otorga por eso, mayor excelencia al varón...

De ser la hembra ayudadora del varón, leémoslo en el Génesis, que después que Dios hubo formado el hombre del limo de la tierra e hubo inspirado en él el espíritu de vida, dijo: "No es bueno que sea el hombre solo; hagámosle adjutorio semejante a él." E bien se podría aquí arguir cuál es de mayor vigor, el ayudado o el ayudador: ya vedes lo que a esto responde la razón. Mas porque estos argumentos e cuestiones hacen a la arrogancia mundana e vana e no aprovechan cosa a la devoción e huyen mucho del propósito e final intención mía, la cual no es, ni plega a Dios que sea, de ofender al estado superior e honrable de los prudentes varones, ni tampoco favorecer al

dealing, and procuring the goods of fortune; ruling, governing, and defending our countries and lands from our enemies; and all other necessary things for the preservation of the republic and their own lands and people. For this reason it is very convenient and necessary that they be strong and brave, daring and of great and very high intelligence. And woman, since she is weak and pusillanimous and not able to endure the onerous tasks and perils that the providing and governing and defending of the aforementioned things require, but instead is protected and cloistered inside her home, with her industry and labor and her domestic and delicate works, provides strength and vigor, and undoubtedly no little help to the male. And human nature preserves and sustains itself in this fashion, which is made of such weak stuff that without these exercises or works it could not survive. Therefore, those afore-mentioned advantages that men possess, their daring, strength, and great understanding, and anything else that God has given them, are not in prejudice to the female, neither does the weakness nor the pusillanimity of woman's condition accord excellence to the male ...

On woman's being the helpmate of man, we read in Genesis that after God had formed man from the muck of the Earth and breathed into him the spirit of life, he said, "It is not good that man be alone, let us make him a helper like unto to him." And well could one question here which is of greater vigor, the one helped or the helper: see now what reason answers to this. But because these arguments and questions lead to mundane and vain arrogance and add nothing to devotion and stray much from my purpose and final intention, which is not, and pray God that it not be, offensive to the superior and

fimineo, mas solamente loar la omnipotencia e sabiduría e magnificencia de Dios, que así en las hembras como en los varones puede inspirar e hacer obras de grande admiración e magnificencia a loor y gloria del santo Nombre; aun si quisiere que los animales brutos le loen con lengua hablante, bien lo puede hacer. Pues, ¿qué deuda tan excusada es dudar que la mujer entienda algún bien e sepa hacer tratados o alguna otra obra loable e buena, aunque no sea acostumbrado en el estado fimineo? . . .

Decidme, virtuosa señora, ¿cuál varón de tan fuerte e valiente persona ni tan esforzado de corazón se pudiera hallar en el tiempo pasado, ni creo en este que nuestro llamamos, que osará llevar armas contra tan grande príncipe como fue Olinfernes, cuyo ejército cubría toda la faz y término de la tierra, e no hubo pavor de lo hacer una mujer? E bien sé que a esto dirán los varones que fue por especial gracia e industria que Dios quiso dar a la prudente Judit.[2] Y yo así lo digo, pero según esto, bien parece que la industria y gracia soberana exceden a las fuerzas naturales e varoniles, pues aquello que gran ejército de hombres armados no pudieron hacer, e hízolo la industria e gracia de una sola mujer. E la industria e gracia, ¿quién las ha por pequeñas preeminencias sino quien no sabe qué cosas son? Ciertamente son dos cosas así singulares que a quien Dios darlas quiere, ahora sea varón o sea hembra, maravillosas cosas entenderá e obrará con ellas si quisiese ejercitarse y no las encomendar a ociocidad e negligencia. Pues si Dios negó al estado fimineo gracia e industria para hacer cosas dificultosas que sobran a la fuerza de su natural condición,

honorable condition of wise gentlemen, nor otherwise to favor the feminine, but only to laud the omnipotence and the wisdom and the magnificence of God, who thus in women as in men can inspire and do works of great wonder and magnificence in praise and glory of His Holy Name; even if He desired that the dumb animals praise Him with speaking tongues, easily could He do it. Therefore, what offense is it to doubt that women understand some good work and know how to make treaties or some other praiseworthy and virtuous work, although it is not usual in the female condition? . . .

Tell me, good lady, what man of such strong and valiant nature or so forceful of heart could be found in times past, nor do I believe in that which we call our own, that would dare to bear arms against such a great prince as was Holofernes, whose army covered the length and breadth of the Earth, when a woman did not fear to do so? And well do I know that men will say that it was by special grace and abilities that God granted the prudent Judith.[2] And so say I, but accordingly it would appear that divine ability and grace exceed natural and manly forces, for that which a great legion of armed men could not do, the resourcefulness and grace of one woman achieved. And as for capability and grace, who takes them for small virtues but he who does not know what they are? Certainly they are two such important gifts that, be they male or female, those to whom they are granted by God will understand and work marvelous things with them if they wish to exercise them and not dedicate themselves to sloth and

---

2. Se refiere a la historia bíblica de Judit, quien emborrachó y decapitó a Holofernes, enemigo de los israelitas.

2. She refers to the biblical story of Judith, who feigned sexual interest in Holofernes, got him drunk, and decapitated him, thereby saving the Jewish people.

¿cómo los negará la gracia suya para que con ella y mediante ella sepan e puedan hacer alguna cosa que sea más fácil o ligera de hacer al sexo fimineo? Que manifiesto es que más a mano viene a la hembra ser elocuente que no ser fuerte, e más honesto la es ser entendida que no osada, e más ligera cosa le será usar de la péñola que de la espada. Así que deben notar los prudentes varones que Aquél que dio industria e gracia a Judit para hacer un tan maravilloso y famoso acto, bien puede dar industria o entendimiento e gracia a otra cualquier hembra para hacer lo que a otras mujeres, o por ventura algunos del estado varonil, no sabrían ...

Creo ciertamente que los bienes de gracia son mayores e más singulares que no los de natura e fortuna. Y el varón o hembra que de aquestos bienes o de alguno de ellos se siente proveído ¡en cuánta estima o precio los debe tener! ¡E cómo debe ser solícito e diligente en los guardar e dirigir al servicio e honor de Aquél de quien estos dichos y bienes emanan! No solamente quien lo recibe e tiene, más aun nosotros cuando viéremos relucir en alguna persona algunos de aquestos bienes de gracia, debemos nos maravillar devotamente, dirigiendo e enderezando nuestra admiración, no a respeto de la persona que los tiene, que sea varón o hembra, entendido o simple, mas solamente a respeto del misericordioso Padre que los da. E si a la alteza e unidad inestimable de aqueste soberano Señor dirigimos o elevamos nuestra admiración, no nos maravillaremos dudando aquello que vemos, mas aun maravillarnos hemos, creyendo que no solamente los bienes que vemos, mas aun los que no vemos ni podemos pensar, Dios pudo e puede inspirar e obrar en sus criaturas ...

Maravíllanse las gentes de lo que en el tratado escribí e yo me maravillo de lo que

negligence. Then if God denied to the female state the grace and resourcefulness to do difficult things that go beyond the power of women's natural condition, how will He deny them His grace so that with it and through it they will know how and be able to do anything that is easier or simpler for the female sex to do? It is well known that it comes more easily to woman to be eloquent than to be strong, and more natural for her to be understanding than daring, and easier for her to use the pen than the sword. So it is that wise men should note that He who gave resourcefulness and grace to Judith to achieve such a marvelous and famous feat alone can easily endow ability, understanding, and grace to any other female to do what other women, or perhaps some men, would not know how to do ...

I certainly believe that the benefits of grace are greater and more rare than those of nature and fortune. And the men or women who judge themselves bestowed with these blessings or any one of them, how greatly should they prize and esteem them! And how diligent and solicitous should they be in preserving them and using them in the service of Him from whom these virtues and blessings proceed! Not only he who receives and possesses them, but even we who see shining in someone any one of these gifts of grace, should devoutly marvel, sending and directing our admiration not in respect of the person who possesses them, whether man or woman, wise or simple, but only to honor the merciful Father who bestows them. And if to the majesty and incomprehensible oneness of the Sovereign Lord we direct and raise our admiration, let us not marvel, doubting that which we see, but marvel, believing not only those miracles we witness, but even those we do not

en la verdad callé; mas no me maravillo dudando ni hago mucho en me maravillar creyendo. Pues la experiencia me hace cierta, e Dios de la verdad sabe que yo no tuve otro Maestro ni me consejé con otro algún letrado, ni lo trasladé de libros, como algunas personas con maliciosa admiración suelen decir. Mas sólo ésta es la verdad: que Dios de las ciencias, Señor de las virtudes, Padre de las misericordias, Dios de toda consolación, Él que nos consuela en toda tribulación nuestra, Él solo me consoló, e Él solo me enseñó, e Él solo me leyó . . .

Por ende los que se maravillan dudando del tratado que yo hice, dejen la duda e maravíllense creyendo que hecho es el Señor Refugio del pobre, Ayudador en las oportunidades y en la tribulación . . .

Por ventura alguno querrá saber la exposición de aquesta palabra, conviene a saber: cómo mi entendimiento vio e siguió al Salvador magnificando a Dios. E para esto mejor entender e de decir primeramente la calidad de la dolencia, qué cosa es ceguedad de entendimiento e de qué humores procede esta intelectual tiniebla; para lo cual conviene considerar las potencias del ánima, las cuales son entendimiento, memoria, voluntad . . .

E porque así varones como hembras, todos generalmente somos llamados criaturas razonables, bien parece que este renombre e la verdad con él, nos compele e inclina a que naturalmente amemos e nos plega con nuestro propio bien, e aborrezcamos e nos pese del mal cuando nos acaece. Y pues esta natural inclinación es tanto aneja e familiar de todo animal razonable, mucho conviene y es menester que el entendimiento sea sano e tenga la vista bien sana e clara para que pueda entender e conocer e discernir cuál es lo bueno e cuál es lo malo, ca manifiesto es,

see nor are even able to imagine. God has and is able to inspire these deeds in his creatures . . .

People marvel at what I wrote in my treatise, and I am astonished at that which in truth I have not said, but I do not marvel doubting, nor do I do much to marvel believing. Because experience makes me certain and God truly knows that I have had no other Teacher nor have I consulted with any other scholar, nor did I take it from books, as some people claim with malicious envy. But only this is the truth: that the God of sciences, Lord of all virtues, Father of mercy, God of all consolation, He who consoles us in all our tribulations, He alone comforted me, and He alone taught me, and He alone tutored me . . .

Therefore, those of you who marvel doubting the treatise that I wrote, cease doubting and marvel believing as fact that the Lord has become the Refuge of the poor and an Aid in opportunity and in tribulation . . .

Perhaps someone would like to know of the exposition of that word, that is: how my mind saw and followed the Savior glorifying God. And for this it is best to understand and to speak first of the quality of illness, what a thing is blindness of the mind and from what humors this intellectual darkness proceeds; for which is worth considering the powers of the soul, which are intelligence, memory, and will. . . .

And because men as well as women are all generally called rational beings, well it seems that this renown, and the truth with it, compel us and incline us naturally to love and ply us with our own good and to abhor and repent our evils when we commit them. And therefore, this natural inclination is so close and familiar to all rational animals, it is very convenient and

cual él lo presentare a la memoria, tal lo reciba en su gracia la voluntad. E acuérdome que oí decir a los doctores de medicina que el cuerpo humano es regido por cuatro humores, e cuando alguno de aquéstos se altera e mueve demasiadamente, luego el cuerpo adolece gravemente. E así parece acaecer al entendimiento e los humores por que es regido e aun gobernado el nuestro entendimiento. E los humores creo ciertamente que son los cinco sentidos, e si éstos son bien ordenados e regidos, estará el entendimiento de aquél que bien los rigiere en buena sanidad. Pero si acaece que los cinco sesos corporales salen de regla e se ejercen demasiadamente en las cosas del siglo, adolece el entendimiento, e de que es hecho doliente no puede entender en su oficio, que es ser primera e principal potencia del ánima. E aun tanto puede ser excesiva la disolución de estos ya dichos intelectuales humores que podrán causar que el entendimiento pierda la vista. E ciertamente adolece el entendimiento por causa de los sentidos, ca ¿quién podrá vedar a su entendimiento que no entienda aquello que el ojo vio e la oreja oyó? Pues si aquello que ve e oye es dañoso e disolutamente tomado la salud del entendimiento se daña e la su interiora vista se oscurece. E desque el entendimiento está enfermo, creo en verdad, que la memoria e voluntad no están sanas. Pues si las potencias del ánima enflaquecen, ¿quién fortificará el espíritu? ¿Quién conocerá a Dios? Ca el entendimiento que nos es dado para le conocer ha perdido la vista. ¿Quién se membrará de Aquél que tantos beneficios nos hace, pues la memoria está enferma e absorta en membranzas mundanas? ¿Quién amará Aquél que soberanamente debe ser amado, pues la voluntad nuestra está dañada e ocupada en afecciones con los ojos

necessary that the mind be healthy and have clear and healthy vision so that it may understand and know and discern that which is good and that which is evil, since it is clear that, as the understanding presents it [the good or the evil] to the memory, so the will receives it into its favor. And I remember hearing physicians say that the human body is governed by four humors, and when one of these is excited or moves excessively, the body then suffers seriously. And thus it seems to occur as well with the mind and the humors by which our mind is guided and even governed. And the humors, I believe with certainty, are the five senses, and if these are in good order and well governed, then the mind of the one who governs them well will be in good health. But if it so happens that the five corporal senses falter and exercise themselves too much in worldly concerns, the mind suffers, and that which is suffering cannot execute well its office, which is to be the first and foremost power of the soul. And the dissolution of the afore-mentioned intellectual humors can even be so excessive as to cause understanding to be blinded. And the mind certainly suffers because of the senses, but who would be able to forbid his mind to understand that which he sees with his eyes and hears with his ears? And if that which is seen and heard is dangerous and taken dissolutely, the health of man's reason is damaged and his interior sight is darkened. And when the reason is ill I truly believe that memory and will also must be infirm. And if the powers of the soul weaken, who will fortify the spirit? Who will know God? Because the intelligence that is given us so that we may know Him has lost its vision. Who will remember Him who has bestowed so many blessings upon us when memory is ill and absorbed

del entendimiento contrarias del amor de Dios? E de esta manera e por causa de los sentidos se ciegan los ojos del entendimiento, ca ciego se puede decir el entendimiento de aquél que ve la luz accidental del curso del día e no ve ni considera las tinieblas de la noche de su oscuro vivir, las cuales le apartan de la Luz verdadera e le llevan por pasos contados a la eternal tiniebla. Pues aquél tiene la vista bien clara que ve las tinieblas e astordimientos de sus pecados e conoce la miseria en que vive e conoce la bondad de Dios que le espera a penitencia. E por cierto gran luz luce en el entendimiento de aquél que conoce a sí mismo e conoce a Dios ... Pues el verdadero Médico conociendo la calidad de mi dolencia espiritual, para me guarecer de aquélla ¿qué hizo? Cerró las puertas de mis orejas por donde la muerte entraba al ánima mía e abrió los ojos de mi entendimiento, e vi e seguí al Salvador ...

E de esta manera el mi ciego entendimiento vio, e siguió e sigue al Salvador, magnificando a Dios. E magnificar a Dios e acatar con diligencia debo la grandeza de sus beneficios e misericordias e gracias, e manifestarlas a las gentes recontándolo a gloria e a magnificencia del su santo Nombre, lo cual yo, aunque con poca devoción e menos prudencia, pero según la mi mujeril e pequeña suficiencia, hice. E ... escribí aquel tratado que trata de aquesta intelectual Luz e sobredicha ciencia, la cual es alabanza e conocer a Dios e a mí misma e negar mi voluntad e conformarme con la voluntad suya, e tomar la cruz de la pasión que padezco en las manos del entendimiento interior, e ir en pos del Salvador por pasos de aflicción espiritual ...

Así que estas tres potencias del ánima [entendimiento, memoria y voluntad], las cuales por la disolución excesiva de los sentidos corporales se turban e hacen

in worldly thoughts? Who will love Him who, as Sovereign, should be loved, if our will is injured and the eyes of our mind are occupied with affections contrary to the love of God? And in this manner and because of the senses the mind's eyes are blinded, since one may call blind the reasoning of one who sees only with the accidental light of day and does not see or consider the nightly shadows of his dark existence, which lead him away from the true Light and draw him with counted steps down the path of eternal darkness. But he sees clearly who sees the shadows and darkness of his sins and knows the misery in which he lives and knows the goodness of God that awaits him in penance. And it is true that a great light shines in the understanding of one who knows himself and knows God ... And the true Physician, knowing the nature of my spiritual illness, to save me from that, what did He do? He closed the doors of my ears through which death was entering into my soul and opened the eyes of my mind, and I saw and followed the Savior. ...

And in this manner my unseeing mind saw, and followed and follows the Savior, glorifying God. And I bear witness to this glorification of God and to the fulfillment of His commandment and the greatness of His blessings and mercy and grace, which I, although possessing little devotion and less wisdom, but according to my minimal, feminine capacity, manifested to everyone and recounted to the greater glory and magnificence of His holy name. And ... I wrote that treatise concerning intellectual Light and the above-mentioned science, which is the praise and knowledge of God and of myself and the denial of my will and the conforming of my will to His, and the taking up of the cross of passion in the hands of my internal understanding to

ociosas por la estrecha abstinencia de aquéllos, se pueden hacer e hacen curiosas e diligentes en sus propios oficios. E parece acaecer al entendimiento, memoria e voluntad, lo que acaece a algunas mujeres comunes que salen de su casa a menudo e andan vagando por casas ajenas, las cuales, por esta mala costumbre, se hacen así negligentes e perezosas en el ejercicio fimineo e obras domésticas e caseril, que ellas por esto no valen más e su hacienda e casa valen menos. Por consiguiente parece acaecer al entendimiento cuando desampara e deja mucho a menudo su propia casa, que es el estudio interior de la secreta cogitación dentro de las paredes del corazón; ca así como las hembras estando inclusas dentro de las puertas de su casa se ejercen en sus propios e honestos oficios, así el entendimiento, retraído de las cosas de fuera y encerrado dentro de las puertas de la secreta cogitación, se ejerce con más vigor en su propio oficio. Mas aquel entendimiento que anda vagando fuera de la posada o estudio interior e se envuelve mucho a menudo en las negociaciones mundanas, él por esta causa no vale más, e su hacienda, que es el ánima, vale menos. E así como la mujer andariega es constreñida de tornar a su casa por el acercamiento de la noche, mas viene tan escandalizada e mal vezada a trabajar, que ese poco de tiempo que le queda, no se puede ejercitar en cosa que convenga al bien suyo ni al provecho de su casa, e bien así acaece al entendimiento, ca la hora que los sentidos se recogen e apartan de sus trabajos por el acostamiento de la noche, en la cual es hecho silencio a todo negocio e trato foráneo, el entendimiento así como constreñido de necesidad, es compelido de acoger a su propia casa, que es la cogitación secreta e soliloquio de su interior pensamiento. Pero viene así alterado, escandalizado de la

follow my Savior in the path of spiritual affliction . . .

Thus these three powers of the soul [intelligence, memory, and will], which through the excessive dissolution of the bodily senses are perturbed and grow lazy through constant neglect, can be and are perfected in their own functions. And it seems to happen with intelligence, memory, and will, as with some common women who leave their house frequently and wander about to others' houses and who, because of this bad habit, become lazy and negligent in the exercise of domestic and feminine responsibilities of the hearth, and because of this are worth little, and their home and belongings worth less. So it seems to happen to the mind when it frequently leaves its own home unprotected, that is, the internal study of the secret cogitation that occurs inside the walls of the heart; so as women secluded inside the walls of the home apply themselves in their proper and honest duties, so the mind, withdrawn from external things and sealed within the doors of the mind's secret workings, applies itself more vigorously to its own responsibilities. But that mind which wanders far from its dwelling or inner reflection and involves itself frequently with worldly concerns, for this very reason is worth little, and its home, which is the soul, is worth even less. And just as the wandering woman is made to return to her home by nightfall, but approaches her work so scandalized and corrupted that the short amount of time that is left to her cannot be used for anything to her advantage or to the advantage of her household, thus it happens to our mind that each hour that the senses are lost to and taken away from their work by sleep, the mind is silenced for all effort and other business, and constrained by necessity to remain in its own

ociosidad del día, que el sosiego de la noche no le puede aprovechar, ni puede entender en cosa que convenga al bien suyo e provecho de su mal regida casa e hacienda, que es la salud espiritual. Pues para que el entendimiento entienda de reposo e asiento en lo que conviene al bien suyo e al provecho de su hacienda, que es la salud del ánima, necesario es que asosiegue y esté quedo en la ya dicha su posada. E cuando se devolviere dentro en sí mismo, tanto más curiosamente entenderá e aprovechará en su propio oficio, el cual es conocer a Dios e conocer los beneficios de Dios . . .

shelter, which is the secret cogitation and soliloquy of its internal thoughts. But it comes to this point so upset, so shocked by the idleness of the day, that it cannot take advantage of night's rest, nor can it meditate on anything worthwhile or of advantage to its ill-governed home and household, which is its spiritual health. For in order for the mind to make use of its repose and meditate upon that which is for its own benefit and to the advantage of its household, which is the health of the soul, it is necessary that it rest and remain in the afore-mentioned abode. And when it turns inward upon itself, with what greater curiosity will it ponder and delight in its own true office, which is to know God and know the goodness of God . . .

(Translated by Ana Menéndez Collera)

The Sixteenth Century

Saint Teresa of Ávila

Saint Teresa was the mother of the nuns of her reformed order whose work in the kitchen taught her that God was to be found among the pots and pans. She was also the itinerant founder of convents who, over a period of twenty years, spent long months traveling through Spain negotiating the creation of her nunneries. She wrote simple, unpretentious prose for the edification of a few spiritual daughters. She was named a Doctor of the Church, whose books have been translated and read worldwide.[1] A friendly woman desirous of pleasing others, she nevertheless challenged the authorities of her order and earned the enmity of other nuns by proposing strict reform. She was energetic and sickly, simple and cunning, defiant and obedient, a woman in whom mysticism and common sense coexisted.

George Eliot's redoubtable Dorothea Brooke was inspired by Teresa of Ávila's life, as have been many real-life women. Some of those whose lives were directly affected by Teresa's reforms expressed their devotion to her through poetry. But Teresa also threatened the relatively comfortable lives of many others who had entered the convent not because of fervent vocation but because the cloister was the only legitimate alternative to marriage for those who could not or would not marry.

This energetic figure — convent founder, mystic, and writer — flowered late. By the time she went out into the world to reform her order (and, by implication, the church as a whole, which needed to take stock of itself in the face of that other Reformation), she had already experienced and scrutinized her visions, knew she could distinguish authentic divine experiences from those inspired by the devil, and had progressed from visions to mystical ecstasy. She was sure of her spiritual life after having submitted her experiences to the most rigorous meditation and skepticism; she was ready, at the age of forty-six, to confront the church authorities with her plans for reform.

Saint Teresa attributed her late-blooming activity to a second birth that began with divine visions, but in a certain sense this was a third incarnation, which, like the one it followed, initiated a new stage in her life. Both new stages were preceded by a long and arduous transition period, and Teresa emerged from them transformed.

Teresa de Cepeda y Ahumada was born in Ávila on March 28, 1515. She spent her childhood in her father's spacious home, surrounded by siblings and relatives. It was

her father, Don Alonso Sánchez de Cepeda, who taught her to read; but Teresa preferred the novels her mother loved to the dry, serious tomes he pressed on her. Doña Beatriz de Ahumada, mother of nine and stepmother of two, told her children stories and allowed them to read the novels she enjoyed. Teresa had two sisters, one rather older than she and the other much younger. Her childhood companions were her brothers, in particular her brother Rodrigo. He was eleven years old and she seven when they undertook their famous aborted adventure of running off to be martyred in the land of the Moors. Returned home well before they could achieve their goal of being beheaded and going straight to heaven, they settled for playing hermit in the family garden. Some years later they abandoned their attempt to live lives of adventure and began writing. Sadly, the chivalresque novel written by the Cepeda children has disappeared.

Teresa also played with her female cousins, one of whom her mother considered a bad influence on the child. After Doña Beatriz's death at thirty-three (Teresa was almost twelve at the time), this cousin's influence increased. Teresa refers vaguely to this adolescent episode, but the result was that her father sent her off to the Convent of Santa María de Gracia to separate her from her vivacious, worldly cousin. Teresa spent more than a year there, until she became seriously ill. After returning home to recover, she decided, after a great deal of soul-searching, to take the habit, though not in Santa María de Gracia but in the Carmelite Convent of the Incarnation, where she had a friend.

The years of transition between Teresa's lively adolescence and her incorporation into convent life were difficult. Her father opposed her decision to become a nun, and when she entered the convent the change in diet and the privations of monastic life made Teresa ill. Two years after professing, she suffered such a terrible illness that she was given the last rites and her tomb was prepared. Returned to life, she was partially paralyzed for three years. The second stage of Teresa's life, thus begun, is marked by a series of symptoms — chest pain, fainting spells, headaches, fever — that were somewhat alleviated only when the third stage began; but they never left her completely.

The transition to the third stage of Teresa's life began in 1555, with her first vision. She records achieving the ecstasy of mystic union three years later, and in 1560 she made a vow to reform the Carmelites. She achieved her first success in 1562 with the founding of the Convent of Saint Joseph in Ávila. Teresa spent five years there — the best of her life, she writes — before leaving to organize the foundation of her other reformed convents. At the request of her confessor she also began to write, first the book of her life (*Vida*, 1562-65), then *Camino de perfección* (Way of perfection, 1565-70); *Las moradas* (The walls), written in four weeks in 1577; and *Libro de las fundaciones* (Book of the foundations), begun in 1573 and finished shortly before her death in 1582.

The selections included here come from Saint Teresa's *Vida.* Chapters 1 and 2, couched in didactic terms, recount her childhood and early adolescence, including memories of her parents and siblings and the friendship with her cousin. Chapter 32 begins with Teresa's vivid description of her preview of hell and ends with her recollection of the obstacles she encountered and overcame when she decided to found her first convent.

1. One of the delights of Teresa's prose is her idiosyncratic spelling, which I have not tried to "correct."

Vida
(fragmentos)

Capítulo 1

*En que trata cómo comenzó el Señor a
despertar a esta alma en su niñez a cosas
virtuosas, y la ayuda que para esto es serlo
los padres.*

El tener padres virtuosos y temerosos de
Dios me bastara, si yo no fuera tan ruin,
con lo que el Señor me favorecía para ser
buena. Era mi padre aficionado a leer buenos libros, y ansí los tenía de romance para
que leyesen sus hijos. Estos, con el cuidado
que mi madre tenía de hacernos rezar, y
ponernos en ser devotos de Nuestra Señora y de algunos Santos, comenzó a desper-
tarme de edad, a mi parecer, de seis u siete
años. Ayudábame no ver en mis padres favor sino para la virtud. Tenían muchas.
Era mi padre hombre de mucha caridad
con los pobres y piadad con los enfermos y
aún con los criados; tanta, que jamás se
pudo acabar con él tuviese esclavos, porque los había gran piadad; y estando una
vez en casa de un su hermano, la regalaba
como a sus hijos. Decía, que de que no era
libre, no lo podía sufrir de piadad. Era de
gran verdad; jamás nadie le vio jurar ni
mormurar. Muy honesto en gran manera.

Mi madre también tenía muchas virtudes, y pasó la vida con grandes enfermedades; grandísima honestidad. Con ser de
harta hermosura, jamás se entendió que
diese ocasión a que ella hacía caso de ella;
porque con morir de treinta y tres años, ya
su traje era como de persona de mucha
edad, muy apacible y de harto entendimiento. Fueron grandes los trabajos que
pasaron el tiempo que vivió. Murió muy
cristianamente.

Éramos tres hermanas y nueve hermanos; todos parecieron a sus padres, por la

Life
(excerpts)

Chapter 1

*In which it is seen how the Lord began
to awaken her young soul
to virtue, and what a help it is
to have good parents.*

Having been provided with virtuous and
God-fearing parents would have sufficed
to make me good, had I not been so
wicked. My father was fond of reading
books, and he even collected ones in Spanish for his children to read. Thanks to
these books, and to the care with which
my mother taught us to pray and to be de-
votees of Our Lady and the other saints, I
began at the early age of six or seven to
awaken to virtue. It helped me to see in my
parents no other care than for virtue. They
possessed many. My father was exceedingly charitable to the poor, generous to
the sick and even his servants; so much so,
that he refused to keep slaves, because
he felt such pity for them. Once when he
was staying in the home of his brother, he
treated the slave as he would his own children. He said he could not bear to see her
in slavery. He was an honest man; and no
one ever heard him swear or complain. He
was an exceedingly upright man.

My mother had many virtues as well,
and she suffered from numerous infirmities; she was exceedingly chaste. Although
she was very beautiful, she never let it be
seen that she gave the slightest care for her
beauty; even though she was only thirty-
three when she died, she already wore the
garb of an older woman. She suffered
many trials during her life, and died a
Christian death.

We were three sisters and nine brothers;
all of them, thanks be to God, resembled

bondad de Dios; en ser virtuosos, si no fui yo, aunque era la más querida de mi padre. Y antes que comenzase a ofender a Dios, parece tenía alguna razón, porque yo he lástima cuando me acuerdo las buenas inclinaciones que el Señor me había dado y cuán mal me supe aprovechar de ellas. Pues mis hermanos ninguna cosa me desayudaban a servir a Dios.

Tenía uno casi de mi edad. Juntábamonos entramos a leer vidas de Santos, que era el que yo más quería, aunque a todos tenía gran amor y ellos a mí. Como vía los martirios que por Dios las Santas pasaban, parecíame compraban muy barato el ir a gozar de Dios, y deseaba yo mucho morir ansí; no por amor que yo entendiese tenerle, sino por gozar en tan breve de los grandes bienes que leía haber en el cielo, y juntábame con este mi hermano a tratar qué medio habría para esto. Concertábamos irnos a tierra de moros, pidiendo por amor de Dios, para que allá nos descabezasen; y paréceme que nos daba el Señor ánimo en tan tierna edad, si viéramos algún medio, sino que el tener padres nos parecía el mayor embarazo. Espantábanos mucho el decir que pena y gloria era para siempre, en lo que leíamos. Acaecíanos estar muchos ratos tratando de esto y gustábamos de decir muchas veces: ¡para siempre, siempre, siempre! En pronunciar esto mucho rato era el Señor servido me quedase en esta niñez imprimido el camino de la verdad.

De que vi que era imposible ir adonde me matasen por Dios, ordenábamos ser ermitaños, y en una huerta que había en casa procurábamos, como podíamos, hacer ermitas, puniendo unas pedrecillas, que luego se nos caían, y ansí no hallábamos remedio en nada para nuestro deseo; que ahora me pone devoción ver cómo me daba Dios tan presto lo que yo perdí por mi culpa.

their parents in goodness and virtue, except myself, although I was the most loved by my father. And before I began to offend God, it seems that I did possess certain virtues, because now I am ashamed when I remember the good inclinations the Lord had given me and how poorly I availed myself of them. My brothers and sisters did nothing to dissuade me from serving God.

One of my brothers was nearly my same age. We often sat together to read the lives of saints, and I loved him more than all the rest, although I loved all of them as they also loved me. When I read of the martyrdom the saints suffered for the sake of God, it seemed that they had paid a small price indeed for the great pleasure they took in God, and I wanted to die like these women; not for the love that I felt for Him, but to be able to feel instantly the heavenly pleasures I had read about. My brother and I thought about ways to fulfill this desire. We conspired to go to the land of the Moors, to beg in the name of God so that the infidels would behead us; and it seemed that despite our tender age, God had inspired us so that if there had been a way we would have gone, except that having parents seemed like a serious impediment. We shivered to think of the pain and also the eternal glory we read about in books. We spent hours talking of these things, and we loved to repeat: "Forever, for eternity, forever!" We repeated this so often that God was pleased to impress on me the path to truth.

When I realized that it was impossible to go where I would be killed for God's sake, we decided to become hermits, and in the garden behind our house we managed as best we could to build hermit cells from piles of stones that were forever falling down. Thus we found no remedy for our desire. And now I am filled with devotion just to think how readily God show-

Hacía limosna como podía, y podía poco. Procuraba soledad para rezar mis devociones, que eran hartas, en especial el Rosario, de que mi madre era muy devota, y ansí nos hacía serlo. Gustaba mucho, cuando jugaba con otras niñas, hacer monasterios, como que éramos monjas; y yo me parece deseaba serlo, aunque no tanto como las cosas que he dicho.

Acuérdome que cuando murió mi madre, quedé yo de edad de doce años, poco menos. Como yo comencé a entender lo que había perdido, afligida fuíme a una imagen de Nuestra Señora y supliquéla fuese mi madre, con muchas lágrimas. Paréceme, que aunque se hizo con simpleza, que me ha valido; porque conocidamente he hallado a esta Virgen soberana en cuanto me he encomendado a Ella, y en fin, me ha tornado a sí. Fatígame ahora ver y pensar en qué estuvo el no haber yo estado entera en los buenos deseos que comencé.

¡Oh Señor mío!, pues parece tenéis determinado que me salve, plega a Vuestra Magestad sea ansí, y de hacerme tantas mercedes como me habéis hecho, ¿no tuviérades por bien, no por mi ganancia, sino por vuestro acatamiento, que no se ensuciara tanto posada adonde tan contino habíades de morar? Fatígame, Señor, aun decir esto, porque sé que fue mía toda la culpa; porque no me parece os quedó a Vos nada por hacer, para que desde esta edad no fuera toda vuestra. Cuando voy a quejarme de mis padres, tampoco puedo; porque no vía en ellos sino todo bien y cuidado de mi bien. Pues pasando de esta edad comenzé a entender las gracias de naturaleza que el Señor me había dado, que sigún decían eran muchas, cuando por ellas le había de dar gracias, de todas me comencé a ayudar para ofenderle, como ahora diré.

ered his gifts on me and how quickly I lost them.

I gave alms to the poor when I could, which was not often. I sought solitude in order to say my devotions, which were numerous, especially the Rosary, which my mother especially loved and urged us to pray. When playing with my friends, I loved most to play at building convents, as if we were nuns; and it seems I did want to become one, although not as much as the other things I have mentioned.

I recall that at the time my mother died, I was nearly twelve years old. As I began to fathom what I had lost, I went in my distress to an image of Our Lady and, weeping, begged her to be a mother to me. I believe that even though my prayer was naive, it served me well, because whenever afterward I have approached her, the Virgin Queen of heaven has interceded for me, and brought me back to her. I am saddened now to see how I turned away from the path that at one time I had begun to follow with such good intentions.

Oh my Lord, since You seem determined to save me, may it please your Majesty to do so. And since You have showered me with your mercy, would You not deem it well, not for my sake but for your own, not to allow the dwelling you so often inhabit to become defiled? It grieves me, Lord, to say these things because I know that the fault was mine alone, and there remained nothing for you to do to make me entirely yours from that time on. Nor can I possibly complain of my parents, seeing nothing but good in them, with no other care than for my welfare. As I grew older, I came to understand the natural graces that the Lord had given me, which some say were many, and while I should have given thanks for them, instead I began to offend Him, as I will now explain.

Capítulo 2

Trata cómo fue perdiendo estas virtudes, y lo que importa en la niñez tratar con personas virtuosas.

Paréceme que comenzó a hacerme mucho daño lo que ahora diré. Considero algunas veces cuán mal lo hacen los padres que no procuran que vean sus hijos siempre cosas de virtud de todas maneras; porque con serlo tanto mi madre, como he dicho, de lo bueno no tomé tanto en llegando a uso de razón, ni casi nada, y lo malo me dañó mucho. Era aficionada a los libros de caballerías, y no tan mal tomaba este pasatiempo como yo le tomé para mí, porque no perdía su labor; sino desenvolvíamonos para leer en ellos, y por ventura lo hacía para no pensar en grandes trabajos que tenía, y ocupar sus hijos que no anduviesen en otras cosas perdidos. De esto le pesaba tanto a mi padre, que se tenía que haber aviso a que no lo viese. Yo comencé a quedarme en costumbre de leerlos, y aquella pequeña falta que en ella vi, me comenzó a enfriar los deseos y comenzar a faltar en lo demás; y parecíame no era malo, con gastar muchas horas de el día y de la noche en tan vano ejercicio, aunque ascondida de mi padre. Era tan en extremo lo que en esto me embebía, que si no tenía libro nuevo, no me parece tenía contento.

Comencé a traer galas, y a desear contentar en parecer bien, con mucho cuidado de manos y cabello, y olores, y todas las vanidades que en esto podía tener, que eran hartas, por ser muy curiosa. No tenía mala intención, porque no quisiera yo que nadie ofendiera a Dios por mí. Duróme mucha curiosidad de limpieza demasiada, y cosas que me parecía a mí no eran ningún pecado, muchos años; ahora veo cuán malo debía ser. Tenía primos hermanos algunos, que en casa de mi padre no

Chapter 2

Tells how she lost her virtues, and how important it is for children to associate with virtuous persons.

I believe that what I am about to tell you caused me great harm. I think at times how mistaken parents are who do not provide their children only those things in every respect virtuous. My mother, as I have said, was virtuous herself, but I barely derived anything from her goodness as I grew older. On the contrary, I was very much harmed by whatever bad came my way. She was fond of books of chivalry, and, unlike me, she was not harmed at all by this pastime, for she never ceased her work because of it. We arranged to read these books together, she perhaps to distract herself from her many cares or to keep her children from more pernicious activities. Since my father did not approve of our pastime, we saw to it that he did not witness it. I grew accustomed to reading them, and this little fault I saw in her caused me to lose my good resolve and to begin to be lax in my duty. Even though I hid it from my father, it did not seem improper that I should waste many hours of the day and night in such a worthless exercise. I was so immersed in this reading that I would only be content when I had a new book to read.

Eventually I began to take care of my attire, contriving to become pleasing to the eyes of others. I took great trouble with my hands and hair and perfume, any vain pursuit I could conceive of, which were many because I was so eager to indulge in them. My intentions were not dishonest; I wanted no one to offend God on account of me, but for several years I took exaggerated interest in my personal appearance and other seemingly innocent activi-

tenían otros cabida para entrar, que era muy recatado, y pluguiera a Dios que lo fuera de éstos también; porque ahora veo el peligro que es tratar en la edad que se han de comenzar a criar virtudes con personas que no conocen la vanidad del mundo, sino que antes despiertan para meterse en él. Eran casi de mi edad, poco mayores que yo. Andábamos siempre juntos; teníanme gran amor; y en todas las cosas que les daba contento, los sustentaba plática, y oía sucesos de sus aficiones y niñerías, nonada buenas; y lo que peor fue, mostrarse el alma a lo que fue causa de todo su mal.

Si yo hubiera de aconsejar, dijera a los padres que en esta edad tuviesen gran cuenta con las personas que tratan sus hijos; porque aquí está mucho mal, que se va nuestro natural antes a lo peor que a lo mijor. Ansí me acaeció a mí, que tenía una hermana de mucha más edad que yo, de cuya honestidad y bondad, que tenía mucha, de ésta no tomaba nada y tomé todo el daño de una parienta que trataba mucho en casa. Era de tan livianos tratos, que mi madre la había mucho procurado desviar que tratase en casa (parece adevinaba el mal que por ella me había de venir), y era tanta la ocasión que había para entrar, que no había podido. A ésta que digo, me aficioné a tratar. Con ella era mi conversación y pláticas; porque me ayudaba a todas las cosas de pasatiempo que yo quería, y aun me ponía en ellas y daba parte de sus conversaciones y vanidades. Hasta que traté con ella, que fue de edad de catorce años, y creo que más (para tener amistad conmigo, digo, y darme parte de sus cosas), no me parece había dejado a Dios por culpa mortal, ni perdido el temor de Dios, aunque le tenía mayor de la honra. Éste tuvo fuerza para no la perder del todo, ni me parece por ninguna cosa del mundo en esto me podía mudar, ni había amor de persona de

ties. Now I see how wrong it must have been. During that period I saw several of my cousins, the only people my father, who was very strict, allowed to enter the house. I wish to God he had not even allowed them to enter, for I see now the danger, during the period when one should be awakening to virtue, of keeping company with persons who, although ignorant of worldliness, arouse a desire for the world in others. My cousins were about the same age as I, perhaps a bit older. We went everywhere together; they loved me dearly and we spoke of anything that amused them. I heard tales of all their less-than-innocent exploits and desires, and what was worse, I exposed my soul to the source of all its evil.

If I were to advise parents, I would tell them to be very vigilant of the company their children keep, because children are at great risk of choosing evil over good. This is what befell me: I had a sister much older than I from whose goodness and modesty I learned nothing, whereas I learned every form of evil from another relative who frequented our home. She was so frivolous that my mother, perhaps sensing the harmful effect she was to have on me, had tried to keep her from entering our house. But there were so many reasons for her to visit, that visit she did; and I took a great liking to her company. It was with her I conversed and gossiped the most, because she accompanied me in whatever pastime I devised and she likewise devised vain pastimes and conversations for me. Until I began to keep company with her, at about age fourteen, or perhaps later when we became constant companions and confidants, I do not believe that I had ever committed a mortal sin against God, or lost my fear of God, although more than anything I was concerned about my

él que a esto me hiciese rendir. Ansí tuviera fortaleza en no ir contra la honra de Dios, como me la daba mi natural para no perder en lo que me parecía a mí está la honra del mundo, y no miraba que la perdía por otras muchas vías.

En querer ésta vanamente tenía extremo. Los medios que eran menester para guardarla, no ponía ninguno; sólo para no perderme del todo tenía gran miramiento. Mi padre y hermana sentían mucho esta amistad; reprendíanmela muchas veces. Como no podían quitar la ocasión de entrar ella en casa, no les aprovechaban sus diligencias; porque mi sagacidad para cualquier cosa mala era mucha. Espántame algunas veces el daño que hace una mala compañía, y si no hubiera pasado por ello, no lo pudiera creer; en especial en tiempo de mocedad, debe ser mayor el mal que hace: querría escarmentasen en mí los padres para mirar mucho en esto. Y es ansí, que de tal manera me mudó esta conversación, que de natural y alma virtuoso, no me dejó casi ninguna, y me parece me imprimía sus condiciones ella y otra que tenía la mesma manera de pasatiempos.

Por aquí entiendo el gran provecho que hace la buena compañía, y tengo por cierto, que si tratara en aquella edad con personas virtuosas, que estuviera entera en la virtud; porque si en esta edad tuviera quien me enseñara a temer a Dios, fuera tomando fuerzas el alma para no caer. Después, quitado este temor del todo, quedóme sólo el de la honra, que en todo lo que hacía me traía atormentada. Con pensar que no se había de saber, me atrevía a muchas cosas bien contra ella y contra Dios.

Al principio dañáronme las cosas dichas, a lo que me parece, y no debía ser suya la culpa, sino mía; porque después mi malicia para el mal bastaba, junto con tener criadas, que para todo mal hallaba en ellas

honor. This I managed not to lose altogether, and nothing in the world would have induced me to relinquish it, nor was there anyone I loved so well, for whose sake I would forfeit my honor. Thus did I have the strength not to sin against godly honor because I was by nature loath to lose it in the eyes of the world, and I did not even see that I lost it in many other ways.

My vain care was to save my reputation at all cost, though I thought not at all about leading a truly virtuous life. I took care only not to lose my honor completely. My father and sister suffered because of this friendship and often chided me for it. But since they were unable to prevent my friend from coming to the house, their diligence was useless, because I was very clever at seeking out evil. Sometimes I am astonished at the ill that can result from bad company. I can only appreciate its gravity because I myself suffered its influence, greater the ill effects during adolescence than at any other time. I would ask parents to take a lesson from me and heed my warning. So great was the effect of this friendship on me that I lost nearly all virtue by nature endowed me, and I believe I was greatly influenced by her and another companion who partook in our same pastimes.

Now I understand what advantage comes from good company, and I am certain that had I conversed only with good people when I was young, my virtue would have remained intact; if I had had someone to teach me to be God-fearing, my soul would have fortified itself against a fall. After I lost this fear completely, my only concern was for my reputation, which tormented me with my every deed. Believing that what I did would never be revealed, I ventured many things against both my honor and my God.

buen aparejo. Que si alguna fuera en aconsejarme bien, por ventura me aprovechara; mas el interés las cegaba, como a mí la afeción. Y pues nunca era inclinada a mucho mal, porque cosas deshonestas naturalmente las aborrecía, sino a pasatiempos de buena conversación; mas puesta en la ocasión, estaba en la mano el peligro, y ponía en él a mi padre y hermanos. De los cuales me libró Dios, de manera que se parece bien procuraba contra mi voluntad que del todo no me perdiese, aunque no pudo ser tan secreto que no hubiese harta quiebra de mi honra y sospecha en mi padre; porque no me parece había tres meses que andaba en estas vanidades, cuando me llevaron a un monesterio que había en este lugar, adonde se criaban personas semejantes, aunque no tan ruines en costumbres como yo; y esto con tan gran disimulación, que sola yo y algún deudo lo supo; porque aguardaron a coyuntura que no pareciese novedad; porque haberse mi hermana casado y quedar sola sin madre, no era bien.

Era tan demasiado el amor que mi padre me tenía y la mucha disimulación mía, que no había de creer tanto mal de mí, y ansí no quedó en desgracia conmigo. Como fue breve el tiempo, aunque se entendiese algo, no debía ser dicho con certinidad; porque como yo temía tanto la honra, todas mis diligencias eran en que fuese secreto, y no miraba que no podía serlo a quien todo lo ve. ¡Oh, Dios mío, qué daño hace en el mundo tener esto en poco y pensar que ha de haber cosa secreta que sea contra Vos! Tengo por cierto que se excusarían grandes males si entendiésemos que no está el negocio en guardarnos de los hombres, sino en no nos guardar de descontentaros a Vos.

Los primeros ocho días sentí mucho, y más la sospecha que tuve se había entendido la vanidad mía, que no de estar allí;

Soon these things did me great harm, but I believe that it was not her fault, for my own malice sufficed to lead me to evil together with the fact that I had maidservants to help me on my way. If one of them had taken upon herself to reform me, perhaps I would have profited from it, but they were as blinded by possible gain as I was by my desire. I was never inclined to great evil, because immodest deeds naturally repelled me, and I enjoyed engaging in good conversation; but when the occasion arose, I exposed myself and my family to grave danger. God saw fit to remove me from all this, perhaps thereby preventing me from being lost altogether, although not before my honor was blemished and my father's suspicions aroused. After less than three months of my vain pastimes, I was taken to a nearby convent where children like myself, though perhaps not as wicked as I, were raised. The reason for this remained so well hidden that no one, except for a few family members, knew of it. To avoid suspicion, they waited until my sister had married and my mother had died and it was no longer fitting for me to remain at home.

My father's blinding love for me, to-gether with my own dissimulation, prevented him from seeing any of my wrongdoing, and thus did I avoid being disgraced in his eyes. Even though my deeds gave rise to some suspicion, since the period that I engaged in them was brief nothing was known for certain. Because I regarded my reputation so highly, I did everything in my power to keep what I did secret, without realizing it could never be so for the One who sees all things. Oh my God, what harm comes to those who forget this and believe anything could be kept secret from You! I believe much evil would be avoided if we understood that

porque ya yo andaba cansada, y no dejaba de tener gran temor de Dios cuando le ofendía, y procuraba confesarme con brevedad. Traía un desasosiego, que en ocho días, y aun creo menos, estaba muy más contenta que en casa de mi padre. Todas lo estaban conmigo, porque en esto me daba el Señor gracia, en dar contento adonde quiera que estuviese, y ansí era muy querida. Y puesto que yo estaba entonces ya enemiguísima de ser monja, holgábame de ver tan buenas monjas, que lo eran mucho las de aquella casa, y de gran honestidad y religión y recatamiento.

Aun con todo esto no me dejaba el demonio de tentar, y buscar los de fuera cómo me desasosegar con recaudos. Como no había lugar, presto se acabó, y comenzó mi alma a tornarse a acostumbrar en el bien de mi primera edad, y vi la gran merced que hace Dios a quien pone en compañía de buenos. Paréceme andaba Su Majestad mirando y remirando por dónde me podía tornar a sí. Bendito seáis Vos, Senor, que tanto me habéis sufrido. Amén.

Una cosa tenía que parece me podía ser alguna disculpa, si no tuviera tantas culpas; y es, que era el trato con quien por vía de casamiento me parecía podía acabar en bien, y informada de con quien me confesaba y de otras personas, en muchas cosas me decían no iba contra Dios. Dormía una monja con las que estábamos seglares, que por miedo suyo parece quiso el Señor comenzar a darme luz, como ahora diré.

we must be on guard not against men, but rather against offending You.

The first week I was very sad, more so because I worried lest others know of my secret vanity. But because I was already weary of my previous life, and still feared for having offended God, I confessed as quickly as possible. I was very restless at first, but after a week, or even less, I was happier in the convent than I had been in my father's house. Everyone was pleased with me, for in this regard the Lord had blessed me, that I always was able to please people, and everyone was fond of me. Although I was very much opposed to becoming a nun at that time, I took pleasure in seeing the nuns, who were all so good there, and of such great chastity, modesty, and religious devotion.

Despite this, the devil continued tempting me and disturbing my peace, devising ways to have messages from the outside brought to me. But since it was difficult, this soon ceased, and my soul began to revert to its former virtue and I realized the great favor God bestowed on me by granting me such good company. He must have searched again and again for ways to bring me back to Him. Blessed be the Lord who suffered me for so long. Amen.

One thing that I believe may have served to justify my behavior, had I not so many other faults, was that I believed that the person with whom I was intimate would soon be married and all would end well. And my confessor as well as others all told me that in many respects I was not sinning against God. A nun slept with those of us who were not novices, and I think that out of respect for her, God allowed me to begin to see the light, as I will now explain.

Capítulo 32

En que trata cómo quiso el Señor ponerla en espíritu en un lugar de el infierno, que tenía por sus pecados merecido. Cuenta una cifra de lo que allí se le representó, para lo que fue. Comienza a tratar la manera y modo cómo se fundó el monesterio, adonde ahora está, de San Josef.

Después de mucho tiempo que el Señor me había hecho ya muchas de las mercedes que he dicho, y otras muy grandes, estando un día en oración, me hallé en un punto toda, sin saber cómo, que me parecía estar metida en el infierno. Entendí que quería el Señor que viese el lugar que los demonios allá me tenían aparejado, y yo merecido por mis pecados. Ello fue en brevísimo espacio, mas, aunque yo viviese muchos años, me parece imposible olvidárseme. Parecíame la entrada a manera de un callejón muy largo y estrecho, a manera de horno muy bajo, y escuro y angosto; el suelo me pareció de un agua como lodo muy sucio y de pestilencial olor, y muchas sabandijas malas en él; a el cabo estaba una concavidad metida en una pared, a manera de una alacena, adonde me vi meter en mucho estrecho. Todo esto era deleitoso a la vista en comparación de lo que allí sentí. Esto que he dicho va mal encarecido.

Estotro me parece que a un principio de encarecerse cómo es, no puede haber, ni se puede entender; mas sentí un fuego en el alma, que yo no puedo entender cómo poder decir de la manera que es. Los dolores corporales tan incomportables, que, con haberlos pasado en esta vida gravísimos, y, sigún dicen los médicos, los mayores que se pueden acá pasar, porque fue encogérseme todos los nervios cuando me tullí, sin otros muchos de muchas maneras que he tenido, y aun algunos, como he dicho, causados de

Chapter 32

Tells how God removed her spirit to the place in hell she had earned for herself, and what was shown to her there. It also tells of how the Convent of Saint Joseph was founded in the place it now stands.

Long after God had granted the favors I have described, and others even greater, I was one day at prayer when suddenly I felt as if I had been transported to hell. I understood that the Lord wished me to see the place that the devils had prepared for me there, and which I had earned through my sins. It was over in an instant, but I will never be able to forget it no matter how long I live. The entrance seemed like a long and narrow alleyway, like a furnace, dark and confining; the ground was wet with mud and smelled of pestilence, with evil reptiles all about. At the end there was a wall with a niche hollowed out, where I found myself tightly fitted in. But what I saw there was delightful compared with what I felt.

What I saw can barely be exaggerated, but what I felt is beyond description or even comprehension. I felt a burning in my soul that I am at a total loss to describe. All forms of unbearable physical pain, which I have indeed felt most acutely according to my doctors, the worst pain one can feel on earth, such as when my nerves retracted during my paralysis, and many other forms of pain, some of them, as I have said, caused by the devil, are nothing when compared with what I felt then. And to think they were to be eternal, that they would never end! This pain is nothing compared with the agony my soul experienced: a feeling of oppression and suffocation, a feeling of such anguish and desperate, unrelenting discontent that I cannot begin to describe it. To say that it

el demonio, no es todo nada en comparación de lo que allí sentí, y ver que habían de ser sin fin y sin jamás cesar. Esto no es, pues, nada en comparación de el agonizar de el alma, un apretamiento, un ahogamiento, una aflición tan sentible y con tan desesperado y afligido descontento, que yo no sé cómo lo encarecer. Porque decir que es un estarse siempre arrancando el alma, es poco; porque aun parece que otro os acaba la vida; mas aquí el alma mesma es la que se despedaza. El caso es que yo no sé cómo encarezca aquel fuego interior, y aquel desesperamiento sobre tan gravísimos tormentos y dolores. No vía yo quién me los daba, mas sentíame quemar y desmenuzar a lo que me parece; y digo que aquel fuego y desesperación interior es lo peor.

Estando en tan pestilencial lugar, tan sin poder esperar consuelo, no hay sentarse, ni echarse, ni hay lugar, aunque me pusieron en éste como agujero hecho en la pared; porque estas paredes, que son espantosas a la vista, aprietan ellas mesmas, y todo ahoga; no hay luz, sino todo tinieblas escurísimas. Yo no entiendo cómo puede ser esto, que, con no haber luz, lo que a la vista ha de ser pena, todo se ve. No quiso el Señor entonces viese más de todo el infierno; después he visto otra visión de cosas espantosas, de algunos vicios el castigo. Cuanto a la vista, muy más espantosos me parecieron; mas como no sentía la pena, no me hicieron tanto temor; que en esta visión quiso el Señor que verdaderamente yo sintiese aquellos tormentos y aflición en el espíritu, como si el cuerpo lo estuviera padeciendo. Yo no sé cómo ello fue, mas bien entendí ser gran merced, y que quiso el Señor yo viese por vista de ojos de dónde me había librado su misericordia. Porque no es nada oírlo decir, ni haber yo otras veces pensado en diferentes

was as if my soul were being wrenched from my body is to say very little, for it would be like saying that someone else were striking me down when it is my own soul that was breaking itself apart. The truth is that I am unable to find the words to describe that inner fire and the despair I felt at such excruciating torment and pain. I could not see who was inflicting them on me, but I felt as if I were burning and being torn apart; and I repeat that there is nothing worse than that inner fire and despair.

When one is in such a pestilential place, with no hope of consolation, it is impossible to sit or lie; there was no place to do so for I was pressed tightly into that niche in the wall. The surrounding walls, with their terrifying aspect, pressed in on me and completely stifled me; there was no light, only the blackest shadows. I do not understand how it can be that, though everything was in darkness, yet it was possible to see clearly all the things that produced pain. It was not the Lord's will at that time to show me more of that hell, but I have since seen another appalling vision that represents the punishment for certain sins. This seemed to my eyes even more dreadful; but since I felt no pain, I was not as frightened. In the first vision the Lord deemed that I should really feel those torments and spiritual pain as if my body were truly suffering them. I cannot say how it was, but I understood what a great mercy the Lord showed by allowing me to witness the place from which His great mercy had delivered me. It means nothing to read a description of or to think of these tortures, as I have done before, although not often, for my soul out of fear could not bear it; of how the devils tear your flesh apart, or other tortures I have heard of— none of these can compare with this pain,

tormentos, aunque pocas, que por temor no se llevaba bien mi alma, ni que los demonios atenazan, ni otros diferentes tormentos que he leído, no es nada con esta pena, porque es otra cosa. En fin, como de debujo a la verdad, y el quemarse acá es muy poco en comparación de este fuego de allá.

Yo quedé tan espantada, y aun lo estoy ahora escribiéndolo, con que ha casi seis años, y es ansí, que me parece el calor natural me falta de temor aquí donde estoy. Y ansí, no me acuerdo vez, que tenga trabajo ni dolores, que no me parezca nonada todo de lo que acá se puede pasar; y ansí me parece, en parte, que nos quejamos sin propósito. Y ansí, torno a decir, que fue una de las mayores mercedes que el Señor me ha hecho, porque me ha aprovechado muy mucho, ansí para perder el miedo a las tribulaciones y contradiciones de esta vida, como para esforzarme a padecerlas y dar gracias a el Señor, que me libró, a lo que ahora me parece, de males tan perpetuos y terribles.

Después acá, como digo, todo me parece fácil en comparación de un memento que se haya de sufrir lo que yo en él allí padecí. Espántame cómo habiendo leído muchas veces libros adonde se da algo a entender las penas de el infierno, cómo no las temía, ni tenía en lo que son. ¿Adónde estaba? ¿Cómo me podía dar cosa descanso de lo que me acarreaba ir a tan mal lugar? Seáis bendito, Dios mío, por siempre, y como siempre, y como se ha parecido que me queríades Vos mucho más a mí que yo me quiero. ¡Qué de veces, Señor, me librastes de cárcel tan tenebrosa, y cómo me tornaba yo a meter en ella contra vuestra voluntad!

De aquí también gané la grandísima pena que me da las muchas almas que se condenan, de estos luteranos en especial,

because it is something other. In fact, like a picture beside a real scene, any burning on earth is but a very small matter compared with that fire.

I was so terrified by this, as I am even now just to speak of it though it happened six years ago; it is as if my fear were draining away my natural warmth. I do not recall any early trials or pains, as grave as they might be, that can compare with this; and yet we complain here without reason. And so, I repeat, this was one of the greatest mercies that the Lord has shown me, because I derived such a great benefit from it, losing any fear of life's tribulations and contrariness, gaining the strength to suffer them and give thanks to the Lord who has freed me, it seems, from terrible and perpetual torments.

Everything here, as I have stated, seems insignificant in comparison with a single moment of what I suffered there. I am amazed that having read so many times about the pains of hell, I was neither afraid of them nor did I even recognize their gravity. What could I have been thinking? How could I ever enjoy what was driving me to such a terrible place? My God, may You be blessed forever. How clear it is to me that You must have loved me far dearer than I have loved myself. How many times, oh Lord, have You freed me from that dark prison, and how many have I returned against your will!

This vision has also caused me to suffer terribly at the sight of those many souls who bring damnation upon themselves, especially the Lutherans, since they were, by virtue of being baptized, already members of the church. And so great was my urge to save even one of these condemned souls from such indescribable tortures that I would have been more than willing to die many times over to do so. Just as here when

porque eran ya por el bautismo miembros de la Iglesia, y los ímpetus grandes de aprovechar almas, que me parece, cierto, a mí que por librar a una sola de tan gravísimos tormentos, pasaría yo muchas muertes muy de buena gana. Miro que si vemos acá una persona que bien queremos, en especial, con un gran trabajo u dolor, parece que nuestro mesmo natural nos convida a compasión, y si es grande nos aprieta a nosotros. Pues ver a un alma para sin fin en el sumo trabajo de los trabajos, ¿quién lo ha de poder sufrir? No hay corazón que lo lleve sin gran pena; pues acá con saber que, en fin, se acabará con la vida y que ya tiene término, aun nos mueve a tanta compasión; estotro que no le tiene, no sé cómo podemos sosegar viendo tantas almas como lleva cada día el demonio consigo.

Esto también me hace desear que en cosa que tanto importa no nos contentemos con menos de hacer todo lo que pudiéramos de nuestra parte; no dejemos nada, y plega a el Señor sea servido de darnos gracia para ello. Cuando yo considero que, aunque era tan malísima, traía algún cuidado de servir a Dios y no hacía algunas cosas que veo que, como quien no hace nada, se las tragan en el mundo, y en fin, pasaba grandes enfermedades y con mucha paciencia, que me la daba el Señor; no era inclinada a mormurar, ni a decir mal a nadie, ni era codiciosa, ni envidia jamás me acuerdo tener, de manera que fuese ofensa grave del Señor, y otras algunas cosas, que, aunque era tan ruin, traía temor de Dios lo más contino, y veo adónde me tenían ya los demonios aposentada; y es verdad que, sigún mis culpas, aun me parece merecía más castigo; mas con todo, digo que era terrible tormento, y que es peligrosa cosa contentarnos, ni traer sosiego ni contento el alma que anda cayendo a cada paso en pecado mortal; sino que, por

we see a person we love dearly suffering a great sorrow or pain, we are naturally moved to compassion; and if the pain is very great, it oppresses us as well. Just so, who can bear to see a soul condemned to eternal suffering? No heart can bear it without great affliction. Even with the knowledge that here all suffering will end with death, it still moves us to compassion. That other pain is endless. I do not understand how we can remain calm while the devil carries off so many souls every day.

This makes me wish that in such important matters we were not satisfied until we had done all in our power to do; let us leave nothing undone; and may the Lord be pleased to grant us the grace to do so. I recall that, as wicked as I was, I took care to serve God in some things, and I refrained from doing certain things that are tolerated in the world; that I suffered terrible infirmities with great patience, which the Lord bestowed upon me; that I was not inclined to complain nor to speak ill of anyone, nor was I covetous, nor do I recall ever being envious to the point of mortally offending the Lord; and that I refrained from doing other things, and despicable as I was, always feared the Lord. Yet I see the place the devils had prepared for me; and it is true that with all my faults I deserved an even worse punishment. Still, I say that it was a terrible pain, and that it is a very dangerous thing to be content or to allow our soul to be content or satisfied when we can fall into mortal sin at every step; rather we should, for the love of God, avoid temptation for the Lord will help us as he has me. May it please Your Majesty not to let me fall from your grace into sin again, for I know the place that awaits me. Do not permit this, Lord, for Your Majesty's sake. Amen.

After having seen this vision, and other

amor de Dios, nos quitemos de las ocasiones, que el Señor nos ayudará como ha hecho a mí. Plega a Su Majestad que no me deje de su mano para que yo torne a caer, que ya tengo visto adónde he de ir a parar. No lo primita el Señor, por quien Su Majestad es. Amén.

Andando yo después de haber visto esto y otras grandes cosas y secretos, que el Señor por quien es me quiso mostrar, de la gloria que se dará a los buenos y pena a los malos, deseando modo y manera en que pudiese hacer penitencia de tanto mal, y merecer algo para ganar tanto bien, deseaba huir de gentes, y acabar ya de en todo en todo apartarme del mundo. No sosegaba mi espíritu, mas no desasosiego inquieto, sino sabroso; bien se vía que era de Dios, y que le había dado Su Majestad a el alma calor para disistir otros manjares más gruesos de los que comía.

Pensaba qué podría hacer por Dios, y pensé que lo primero era seguir el llamamiento que Su Majestad me había hecho a relisión, guardando mi Regla con la mayor prefeción que pudiese. Y aunque en la casa adonde estaba había muchas siervas de Dios y era harto servido en ella, a causa de tener gran necesidad, salían las monjas muchas veces a partes adonde con toda honestidad y relisión podíamos estar. Y también no estaba fundada en su primer rigor la Regla, sino guardábase conforme a lo que en toda la Orden, que es con Bula de relajación; y también otros muchos inconvenientes, que me parecía a mí tenía mucho regalo, por ser la casa grande y deleitosa. Mas este inconveniente de salir, aunque yo era la que mucho lo usaba, era grande para mí, ya porque algunas personas, a quienes los perlados no podían decir de no, gustaban estuviese yo en su compañía, y importunados, mandábanmelo, y ansí, sigún se iba ordenando, pudiera poco estar

great and secret things that the Lord, being who He is, deigned to show me, of the glory to be had by the righteous and the suffering of the wicked, I was moved to do penance for such evil as I had done. As my desire was to become worthy of such a great blessing, I wanted to flee from others and to withdraw from the world once and for all. My spirit was restless, yet my disquiet was not disturbing but pleasant, for I understood that it had come from God and that His Majesty had given my soul the ardor to digest much stronger food than what I usually consumed.

I pondered what I could do for God, and I thought that the first thing was to heed His Majesty's call to enter a religious order, conforming to the rule as best I could. And even though in the house where I was living there were many servants of God, and He was very well served there, many of the sisters were forced out of necessity to leave the house and go wherever we could live honestly and our vows would permit us. Also, our house did not follow strictly its original rule; rather, we observed the general rule of the order, according to the Bull of Mitigation. And there were many other disadvantages; life there seemed unduly pleasant because the house was such a large and agreeable place to be. The fact that I often left the house was also a great disadvantage for me, because certain persons, to whom the superiors could refuse nothing, enjoyed my company, and when they were thus importuned, my superiors would send me to keep them company. And, as I was ordered to leave, I was able to spend very little time in the convent, and the devil in part must have helped to bring this about. Yet because I repeated to the nuns some of the things that others had taught me, great profit was derived from this as well.

en el monesterio, porque el demonio en parte debía ayudar para que no estuviese en casa, que todavía, como comunicaba con algunas lo que los que me trataban me enseñaban, hacíase gran provecho.

Ofrecióse una vez estando una persona,[1] decirme a mí y a otras, que si no seríamos para ser monjas de la manera de las Descalzas, que aun posible era poder hacer un monesterio. Yo, como andaba en estos deseos, comencélo a tratar con aquella señora mi compañera viuda,[2] que ya he dicho que tenía el mesmo deseo. Ella comenzó a dar trazas para darle renta, que ahora veo yo que no llevaban mucho camino, y el deseo que de ello teníamos nos hacía parecer que sí. Mas yo, por otra parte, como tenía tan grandísimo contento en la casa que estaba, porque era muy a mi gusto y la celda en que estaba, todavía me detenía. Con todo concertamos de encomendarlo mucho a Dios.

Habiendo un día comulgado, mandóme mucho Su Majestad lo procurase con todas mis fuerzas, haciéndome grandes promesas de que no se dejaría de hacer el monesterio, y que se serviría mucho en él, y que se llamase San Josef, y que a la una puerta nos guardaría Él y Nuestra Señora la otra, y que Cristo andaría con nosotras, y que sería una estrella que diese de sí gran resplandor; y que, aunque las relisiones estaban relajadas, que no pensase se servía poco en ellas; que qué sería de el mundo si no fuese por los relisiosos; que dijese a mi confesor esto, que me mandaba, y que le rogaba Él que no fuese contra ello ni me lo estorbase.

Era esta visión con tan grandes efetos, y de tal manera es esta habla que me hacía el Señor, que yo no podía dudar que era Él. Yo

On a certain occasion a woman to whom I was talking[1] asked why I and the other nuns did not join the Discalced order so that we could establish our own convent. Since I had always been eager to do just that, I began to speak of it with a companion of mine, a widow who, as I have mentioned, shared my desire.[2] And she began to take steps to finance this project, and I see now how this would not have taken us very far, although in our desire we thought we had taken a great step. On the other hand, I was very content in the house where I was living, because it and the cell where I slept were much to my liking, and this made me hold back. Still we determined to commend this matter to God.

One day, after Communion, His Majesty ordered me to dedicate all my energies to this project, making me great promises that the convent would be built and that He would be greatly served in it, and that it should be called Saint Joseph's, and that He at one door and Our Lady at the other would watch over us, and that Christ would walk with us, and that the convent would be a star of great splendor and that even though religious orders had become relaxed, He was still served by them, for what would the world be without religious orders, and that I should tell all this to my confessor, that I was ordered by God to do this, and that God wished him not to oppose or hinder our plan.

This vision had such a great effect on me, and as it was so clearly the Lord whose speech I had heard, I could not doubt that it was He. I was greatly distressed because I imagined the great inconveniences and trials that this project would cost me. I had talked about doing it before, but never

---

1. María de Ocampo, prima de Teresa.
2. Doña Guiomar de Ulloa.

1. Teresa's cousin, María de Ocampo.
2. Doña Guiomar de Ulloa.

sentí grandísima pena, porque en parte se me representaron los grandes desasosiegos y trabajos que me había de costar, y como estaba tan contentísima en aquella casa, que, aunque antes lo trataba, no era con tanta determinación ni certidumbre que sería. Aquí parecía se me ponía premio, y como vía comenzaba cosa de gran desasosiego, estaba en duda de lo que haría. Mas fueron muchas veces las que el Señor me tornó a hablar en ello, puniéndome delante tantas causas y razones, que yo vía ser claras y que era su voluntad, que ya no osé hacer otra cosa sino decirlo a mi confesor, y dile por escrito todo lo que pasaba.

Él no osó determinadamente decirme que lo dejase, mas vía que no llevaba camino conforme a razón natural, por haber poquísima y casi ninguna posibilidad en mi compañera, que era la que lo había de hacer. Díjome que lo tratase con mi perlado, y que lo que él hiciese, eso hiciese yo. Yo no trataba estas visiones con el perlado, sino aquella señora trató con él, que quería hacer este monesterio; y el Provincial vino muy bien en ello, que es amigo de toda relisión, y diole todo el favor que fue menester, y díjole que él admitiría la casa. Trataron de la renta que había de tener, y nunca queríamos fuesen más de trece, por muchas causas. Antes que lo comenzásemos a tratar, escribimos al santo Fray Pedro de Alcántara todo lo que pasaba, y aconsejónos que no lo dejásemos de hacer, y dionos su parecer en todo.

No se hubo comenzado a saber por el lugar, cuando no se podía escribir en breve la gran persecución que vino sobre nosotras; los dichos, las risas, el decir que era disbarate. A mí, que bien me estaba en mi monesterio, a la mi compañera tanta persecución que la traían fatigada. Yo no sabía qué me hacer; en parte me parecía que tenían razón. Estando ansí muy fatigada

with great determination or certitude, for I was quite content in the house where I was. And I felt a great burden was being placed on me and I saw that a troubling period was beginning for me and I was not sure what I should do. But the Lord spoke repeatedly to me about it, placing before me so many reasons and arguments that I saw everything clearly and understood His will, and I dared not do other than to speak of it to my confessor and write to him about all that was happening.

My confessor did not dare to tell me expressly to abandon our plan, but he believed that there was very little chance for success, since my companion, who was to fund the project, had insufficient resources. He instructed me to speak of it to my superior, and to do whatever he advised. I did not mention my visions to the superior; rather, my friend, who so wanted to establish the convent, spoke with him. The provincial, who is a great friend of religious orders, was at first very receptive to our project, giving us all of his help and promising to sanction the house. They spoke of the revenue that would be required and it was decided that, for many reasons, the number of nuns should never exceed thirteen. Before we took this step, we wrote to the saintly Father Pedro de Alcántara about all that had transpired, and he advised us not to desist in our plan and he gave us his opinion about the whole matter.

Barely had our plan begun to be known here when an indescribable persecution descended upon us; the criticism, the derision, everyone thought it was ridiculous. For my part, they said I was fine in the monastery, while my companion wearied of so much criticism. I did not know what to do; in part it seemed to me that they were correct. Just when I was weary, com-

encomendándome a Dios, comenzó Su Majestad a consolarme y a animarme. Díjome que aquí vería lo que habían pasado los santos que habían fundado las relisiones; que mucha más persecución tenía por pasar de las que yo podía pensar, que no se nos diese nada. Decíame algunas cosas que dijese a mi compañera, y lo que más me espantaba yo, es que luego quedábamos consoladas de lo pasado y con ánimo para resistir a todos. Y es ansí, que de gente de oración y todo, en fin, el lugar no había casi persona que entonces no fuese contra nosotras y le pareciese grandísimo disbarate.

Fueron tantos los dichos y el alboroto de mi mesmo monesterio, que a el Provincial le pareció recio ponerse contra todos, y ansí mudó el parecer y no la quiso admitir. Dijo que la renta no era sigura, y que era poca, y que era mucha la contradicción; y en todo parece tenía razón, y, en fin, lo dejó y no lo quiso admitir. Nosotras, que ya parecía teníamos recibidos los primeros golpes, dionos muy gran pena; en especial me la dio a mí de ver a el Provincial contrario, que con quererlo él, tenía yo disculpa con todos. A la mi compañera ya no la querían asolver si no lo dejaba porque decían era obligada a quitar un escándalo.

Ella fue a un gran letrado, muy gran siervo de Dios, de la Orden de Santo Domingo, a decírselo y darle cuenta de todo. Esto fue aún antes que el Provincial los tuviese dejado, porque en todo el lugar no teníamos quien nos quisiese dar parecer, y ansí decían que sólo era por nuestras cabezas. Dio esta señora relación de todo y cuenta de la renta que tenía de su mayorazgo a este santo varón, con harto deseo nos ayudase, porque era el mayor letrado que entonces había en el lugar y pocos más en su Orden. Yo le dije todo lo que pensábamos hacer, y algunas causas. No le dije cosa de revelación ninguna, sino las razones

mending myself to God, His Majesty began to console and encourage me. He told me that I could now understand what saints who had founded religious orders had to endure, they had had to suffer greater persecution than I could possibly imagine, but that we should not be troubled by it. He told me some things to tell my companion, and what amazed me most is that with these words we were consoled and encouraged to resist everyone. And the fact is that both among men of prayer and everyone else, there was hardly anyone who was not against us and who did not judge our plan to be the greatest folly.

There was so much discussion and commotion in my own convent that the provincial decided not to oppose everyone, and thus he changed his mind and refused to sanction our plan. He said that the revenue was not assured, and that it was insufficient, and that there was much opposition; and he seemed to be right about everything and, finally, he dropped the matter and refused to sanction it. Having now received the first blows, we were brokenhearted. I was especially sad to see the provincial turn against us since had he approved the plan, everyone would have accepted it. My friend could not be absolved unless she desisted in her plan because, they said, she was obliged to end the scandal.

She approached a renowned man of letters, a Dominican priest who was a devout servant of God, to speak to him of it and to give him a full account of everything. This was even before the provincial had withdrawn his support, because no one in the entire place wished to advise us about it, and that is why they said that the whole plan was just our own silly notion. My companion gave a full account of everything to him, about the revenue she

naturales que me movían; porque no quería yo nos diese parecer sino conforme a ellas. Él nos dijo que le diésemos de término ocho días para responder, y que si estábamos determinadas a hacer lo que él dijese. Yo le dije que sí, mas aunque yo esto decía, y me parece lo hiciera, porque, nunca jamás se me quitaba una siguridad de que se había de hacer. Mi compañera tenía más fe; nunca ella por cosa que la dijesen se determinaba a dejarlo.

Yo, aunque como digo, me parecía imposible dejarse de hacer, de tal manera creo ser verdadera la revelación, como no vaya contra lo que está en la Sagrada Escritura u contra las leyes de la Iglesia que somos obligados a hacer; porque, aunque a mí verdaderamente me parecía era de Dios, si aquel letrado me dijera que no lo podíamos hacer sin ofenderle, y que íbamos contra conciencia, paréceme luego me apartara de ello y buscara otro medio; mas a mí no me daba el Señor sino éste. Decíame después este siervo de Dios, que lo había tomado a cargo con toda determinación de poner mucho en que nos apartásemos de hacerlo, porque ya había venido a su noticia el clamor de el pueblo, y también le parecía desatino como a todos, y en sabiendo habíamos ido a él, le envió a avisar un caballero, que mirase lo que hacía, que no nos ayudase, y que, en comenzando a mirar en lo que nos había de responder, y a pensar en el negocio y el intento que llevábamos y manera de concierto y relisión, se le asentó ser muy en servicio de Dios, y que no había de dejar de hacerse. Y ansí nos respondió nos diésemos priesa a concluirlo, y dijo la manera y traza que se había de tener; y aunque la hacienda era poca, que algo se había de fiar de Dios; que quien lo contradijese fuese a él, que él respondería; y ansí siempre nos ayudó, como después diré.

possessed from her estate, expressing her fervent hope that he would assist us, since he was at that time the most learned man of that place or even of the entire order. I told him everything we were thinking of doing, and some of our reasons. I did not mention any of my visions, but rather the earthly motives that had inspired me, because I wanted him to base his opinion only on these motives. He told us to allow him a week to respond, and asked if we were resigned to do whatever he decreed. I agreed to this, but although I said this, and I believe I would have done so, I never lost the confidence that we would succeed. My friend had more faith; she would not have given up for anything anyone could have possibly said to her.

Although, as I said, I thought it was impossible not to continue, I was convinced that the revelation was true only provided that it did not go against the Holy Scriptures or the laws of the church to which we are bound; because although I sincerely believed that it had come from God, if that learned man told me that we could not continue without offending Him and that we were going against our conscience, I believe that I would have abandoned that route and sought another; but the Lord was giving me only this one route. Later this servant of God told me that he had at first determined to dissuade us from our plan at any cost, because the clamor of the townspeople had already reached his ears, and he was also inclined to think it was folly like everyone else. And when a certain gentleman saw we were going to ask this man for his help, he asked him to think the matter over carefully, but as he began to think about what he would respond to us, and to consider our motives and the great effort we had invested in our project, and our concern for religion, he was convinced

Con esto fuimos muy consoladas, y con que algunas personas santas, que nos solían ser contrarias, estaban ya más aplacadas, y algunas nos ayudaban. Entre ellas era el caballero santo, de quien ya he hecho mención, que, como lo es, y le parecía llevaba camino de tanta perfeción, por ser todo nuestro fundamento en oración, aunque los medios le parecían muy dificultosos y sin camino, rendía su parecer a que podía ser cosa de Dios, que el mesmo Señor le debía mover. Y ansí hizo a el Maestro, que es el clérigo siervo de Dios que dije que había hablado primero, que es espejo de todo el lugar, como persona que le tiene Dios en él para remedio y aprovechamiento de muchas almas, y ya venía en ayudarme en el negocio. Y estando en estos términos, y siempre con ayuda de muchas oraciones, y tiniendo comprada ya la casa en buena parte, aunque pequeña; mas de esto a mí no se me daba nada, que me había dicho que el Señor que entrase como pudiese, que después yo vería lo que Su Majestad hacía: ¡y cuán bien que lo he visto! Y ansí, aunque vía ser poca la renta, tenía creído el Señor lo había por otros medios de ordenar y favorecernos.

that God would be greatly served by it, and that we should continue at all cost. And thus he responded that we should hasten to complete our plan and he told us the manner and the ways that we should proceed, that although our revenues were small, we should trust in God; that whoever was still against the plan should seek him out and he would respond for us, and he has always helped us in this way, as I will describe later.

With that we were much consoled, and certain saintly persons who once were against us were now more disposed to us, and some even helped us. Among them was the holy gentleman whom I have already mentioned. When he saw that our project was founded on prayer he judged that it would lead to perfection, even though the means seemed very difficult and unpromising. He ventured to say that the plan could be from God; it must have been the Lord who had moved him. And he also inspired that Master, that devoted cleric of God who, as I said, had spoken first, who is the mirror of the entire place, whom God holds there as a remedy and a profit of many souls, and he began to help me with our plan. And in these terms, being helped by many prayers, we nearly had completed our purchase of the house. Although it was small, I did not mind, for the Lord had told me that we should be there however we could, so that afterward I could see what His Majesty would do for us: and how well I had seen this! And thus, though I saw that our revenues were small, I trusted that the Lord would provide us with other means to arrange everything and to favor us.

(Translated by Lou Charnon Deutsch)

Luisa Sigea

Among the educated gentlewomen and women artists who served the Portuguese Princess María was the Renaissance humanist Luisa Sigea. Together with Paula Vicente (daughter of writer Gil Vicente), the poet Juana Vaz, and her own sister, Angela, Luisa Sigea participated in the intellectual life of the court for thirteen years, from 1542 to 1555. Fruit of the humanist flowering that allowed a small group of women a classical education, Luisa Sigea wrote almost exclusively in Latin. This gave her stature in her time but almost guaranteed her anonymity for the future. Latin texts by women were not deemed important enough to warrant translation into Spanish.

Luisa Sigea was born between 1526 and 1530, probably in Tarrancón, where her mother, Doña Francisca de Velasco, grew up. The aristocratic Doña Francisca married into the new nobility of learning, wedding the humanist scholar Diego Sigeo. Of their four children, two were girls. Luisa very early showed a talent for the study of the classics, and her sister Angela's musical ability was admired by her contemporaries.

Diego Sigeo moved his family to the Portuguese court in 1542, to make his fortune. As he rose to the position of preceptor to the prince, Don Juan, his daughters entered the service of Princess María. Luisa's dialogue in Latin, *Duarium Virginum Colloquium* (1552), written ten years into her life at court, portrays her experience in the exclusive women's academy surrounding the princess. It is the writer's testament to the disillusionment brought on by the intrigues of the princess's humanist circle and by the lack of remuneration for her services. When the family left Lisbon in 1555, they settled in Torres Novas. There Luisa married Francisco Cuevas, a nobleman from Burgos; and she went to that city to live with him that same year.

In 1556 Queen María of Hungary, sister of the Spanish monarch Charles V, retired to Spain to spend her last years in her native country. In 1558, Luisa Sigea obtained positions in Doña María's entourage for herself and her husband. Unfortunately, the queen died shortly thereafter, and at the end of 1558 Sigea was once again without patronage and with no more economic resources than a small income left to her by Doña María. Sigea's letter to King Philip II, requesting a post and reminding him of her merits and her former service to the royal family, went unanswered, and her petition to Queen Isabel of Valois was rejected. Disillusioned, she died — of grief, according to her contemporaries — on October 13, 1560. She left a daughter.

The melancholy of those final years is expressed in the texts that follow, but what

is most notable in these poems is the intellectual insight into an experience so rooted in emotion. Sigea was able to express her deepest feelings while distancing herself sufficiently to examine and analyze them. In her poems she maintains the measure and control so highly valued in the Renaissance, at the same time that she reveals the depth of her disillusionment and pain.

In addition to her scant literary production in Spanish (three poems and a handful of letters), Sigea wrote a long poem in Latin entitled "Cintra," inspired by the Portuguese river of that name, several short poems, many letters, and the aforementioned dialogue. The latter was translated into French, and in France her renown lasted longer than it did in Spain. Taking advantage of Luisa Sigea's fame, the French writer Nicholas Chorier wrote a pornographic work, affixed her name to it, and published it in Grenoble in 1680. This act condemned Sigea to general opprobrium and may be one of the causes of her disappearance from Spanish cultural history. In the nineteenth century Carolina Coronado wrote a novel very loosely based on Sigea's life, but it was not enough to rescue its subject from the near oblivion that has lasted until this day.

Canción

Habui menses vacuos et noctes laboriosas,
et numeravi mihi. (Job 7:3)

Pasados tengo hasta ahora
muchos meses y largos
tras un deseo en vano sostenido,
que tanto hoy día mejora
cuanto los más amargos
y más desesperados he tenido;
lo que en ellos sentido
no puedo yo contarlo;
el alma allá lo cuente;
mas ella no lo siente
tan poco que no calle como callo;
¡Oh grande sentimiento!
que a veces quita el alma al pensamiento,
y cuando esto acaece,
según veo las señales,
ya creo que el remedio está cercano;
la vida se amortece,
no se sienten los males
tanto como si esté el cuerpo más sano;
pero todo es en vano,
que al fin queda la vida
y torna el alma luego
en el costumbrado fuego
a ser muy más que antes encendida;
así que en fantasías
se me pasan los meses y los días;
en fantasías y cuentos
la vida se me pasa;
los días se me van con lo primero,
las noches en tormentos,
que el alma se traspasa
echando cuenta a un cuento verdadero
cual es dende que espero
el fin de mi deseo;
¡cuántas habré pasadas
de noche trabajadas
sufriéndolas por ver lo que aún no veo!
Éstas muy bien se cuentan,

Song

Habui menses vacuos et noctes laboriosas,
et numeravi mihi.

I have had empty months, and have
numbered to myself wearisome days.

(Job 7:3, from Douay Bible)

I leave behind the long, dull months
that I have passed till now
pursuing hope, one hope sustained in
   vain,
which even today can render
sweeter those that have been
most bitter to me, filled with most
   despair;
what I have known of pain
is past my powers of telling—
my soul on high may tell my grief
but she does not feel it
so sharply as to be silenced as I am silent.
Alas, such grief is mine,
at times my soul is severed from my mind;
when I am in this state
and I perceive its signs,
I trust the only cure is near at hand
then life itself grows faint,
while every ill withdraws
just as though the body were hale and
   strong;
but such hope is in vain—
at length I am left with life,
and my soul again returns
to daily flames that burn
with ever hotter and rekindled light.
Thus in idle dreams
my months and days recede;
in idle dreams and tales
my very life is spent,
in dreams my days go by
and my nights upon the rack,
for my soul is rent
rendering accounts to a true account
   untold
in which lies all my hope
of the goal that I desire.

mas ¡ay, que las que quedan más me
     afrentan!
En esto un pensamiento
me acude a consolarme
de cuantos males solo dél recibo
pensando en mi tormento;
no oso de alegrarme
según que se me muestra tan esquivo;
con todo, allí recibo
con tan nuevo consuelo,
y aunque parece sano
no oso echarle mano,
que a quien vive el dolor todo es recelo,
y al fin helo por bueno
y huelgo que acogerle acá en el seno.
Ésta es una esperanza
que viene acompañada
de razón, que en mi parte no ha faltado,
que habrá de hacer mudanza
en la fortuna airada
que ha tantos años contra mí durado,
y aunque fuera hado
o destino invencible
de cruda avara estrella,
muriera el poder de ella
con el de la razón que es más terrible,
y con su ser perfecto
traerán de mi deseo buen efecto;
mas ¡¡ay!! no sean aquesto
consolaciones vanas,
que ansí como se sienten no esperadas
ansí se van tan presto
que dejan menos sanas
las almas donde fueren gasajadas;
las noches trabajadas
ajenas de alegría,
los días, meses y años
llenos de graves daños
habré de pensar siempre noche y día;
si en esto el remedio halle
no sentiré el trabajo de esperarle.
Porque no seas de las gentes creída,
canción, conmigo queda,
que yo te encubriré mientras que pueda.

What might their number be,
those broken nights of worry,
borne through to see what still lies out of
     sight?
I can count easily,
but oh, how those remaining frighten me!
With this, a single thought
arises and brings comfort:
amongst so many ills, this thought alone
relieves my thoughts of torment;
I dare not take real pleasure
because the thought's elusive and aloof;
and yet I find I'm given
a newer consolation,
yet though it may seem strong,
I dare not grasp it fully,
for all things, to one in pain, provoke
     mistrust;
in the end I think it best
and am well pleased to hide it at my
     breast.
The hope I have described
is followed close behind
by reasoning—a trait not rare in me—
that Fortune's lofty ire
must undergo some change
having persisted all these years against me;
and even destiny
or yet unconquered fate
under harsh and greedy stars,
must sometime meet its end
through reason's power, more terrible and
     great;
in reason's perfect being
a happy end shall come to all my longing—
but oh! may these not be
empty consolations,
for the very moment they think them
     selves unhoped for,
that instant will they flee,
leaving in worse decline
the souls that extended every welcome to
     them.
My nights of broken worry

are strangers to all joy;
my days and months and years,
filled with threatening fears:
for I must think through every night and
    day.
If in this plight I find some remedy
I shall not mind the weary wait and
    worry.
As other folk may doubt all that you say,
my song, stay here with me,
and I shall harbor you while yet I may.

(Translated by Amanda Powell)

Octavas

Un fin, una esperanza, un como, un
    cuando
tras sí traen mi derecho verdadero;
los meses y los años voy pasando
en vano, y paso yo tras lo que espero;
estoy fuera de mí, y estoy mirando
si excede la natura lo que quiero;
y así las tristes noches velo y cuento,
mas no puedo contar lo que más siento.

En vano se me pasa cualquier punto,
mas no pierdo yo punto en el sentirlo;
con mi sentido hablo y le pregunto
si puede haber razón para sufrirlo;
respóndeme: sí puede, aunque difunto;
lo que entiendo de aquél no sé decirlo,
pues no falta razón y buena suerte,
pero falta en el mundo conocerte.

En esto no hay respuesta, ni se alcanza
razón para dejar de fatigarme,
y pues tan mal responde mi esperanza
justo es que yo responda con callarme;
fortuna contra mí enristró la lanza
y el medio me fuyó para estorbarme
el poder llegar yo al fin que espero,
y así me hace seguir lo que no quiero.

Por sola esta ocasión atrás me quedo,

Octaves

One goal, one hope, a way and a why, a
    when
bear after them what should be mine to
    claim;
in vain I make my way through months
    and years
and am waylaid by all that I await;
I am beside myself, and I must wonder
if what I want exceeds some natural law;
thus I keep watch and count the nights of
    grief,
but I cannot recount what I most feel.

In vain, each chance that I might seize
    goes by
but I lose not a chance to mourn my loss;
I speak to my good sense, of it inquire
whether in suffering so I have good
    cause—
Sense answers, *yes indeed*, though it be
    dead;
what I hear spoken I cannot express
for reason and fortune still abound,
save that you, Sense, are nowhere to be
    found.

To this there is no answer, nor can
    there be

y estando tan propincuo el descontento,
las tristes noches cuento, y nunca puedo
hallar cuento en el mal que en ella cuento;
ya de mí propia en esto tengo miedo
por lo que me amenaza el pensamiento;
mas pase así la vida, y pase presto,
pues no puede haber fin mi presupuesto.

reason for me to leave off being weary;
and, as my hope makes such a stingy
    answer,
I answer fairly when I keep my peace.
Against me, destiny has couched its lance;
means fled me, so impossibility
would bar me from the goal to which I
    aspire,
which makes me follow what I do not
    desire.
    For this one motive I remain behind,
and as unhappiness is very near,
I count the long, sad nights and cannot
    find
a way to count the ills encountered there;
and in this state I come to fear my mind
because my thinking threatens me with
    fear;
thus may my life go on, go on with speed,
since I cannot reach the end of what I
    need.

(Translated by Amanda Powell)

Beatriz Bernal

Beatriz Bernal was one of a handful of women to write a novel of chivalry, a genre almost exclusively cultivated by men and considered unsuitable for women even to read. These immensely popular tales of knights and monsters, damsels in distress and wicked sorcerers, were severely criticized for their immorality. Juan Luis Vives, author of a treatise on women's education, *De institutione feminae christianae*, was one of many experts who believed that such stories of love and adventure were particularly dangerous to women's sensitive nature. Saint Teresa survived their ill effects, but she was a woman of uncommon spiritual fortitude, and she too criticized them in a more sober period of her life. Imagine, then, women who not only abandoned themselves to the pleasure of reading what Vives called these "pestiferous books," but who actually went to the extreme of writing them. Yet not only one, but three, women did this: the anonymous Burgos author of *Palmerín de Oliva* and *Primaleón* (whose gender, though not her name, was revealed by a poet praising her work); Leonor Coutinho, the Portuguese author of *Don Belindo*; and Beatriz Bernal, who wrote *Don Cristalián de España*.[1]

Beatriz Bernal came from a noble family of Valladolid with roots in France. Her ancestor, Bernard de Foix, was given the villa and county of Medinaceli for his loyal service to Enrique de Trastámara (the same one who imprisoned the child Leonor López de Córdoba). De Foix had a bastard son named Mondisón Bernal who established himself in Valladolid, where his descendants maintained the aristocratic custom of perpetuating certain given names in the family. Beatriz Bernal was one of at least four Valladolid women of her era to bear that name. This Doña Beatriz married the university-educated Torres de Gatos, also of noble descent. They had at least one child, a daughter, Juana Bernal de Gatos, who played an important role in rescuing her mother from anonymity as a writer.

Beatriz Bernal published *Don Cristalián de España* at the high point of the popularity of the chivalresque narrative, which had begun in the first years of the sixteenth century and would see its demise toward the beginning of the seventeenth. In 1545, the year *Don Cristalián* came out, several new editions of well-known works such as *Amadís of Gaul* were issued, and three new novels of chivalry were published. In no other year, before or after, did so many new titles appear. It is impossible to know whether Beatriz Bernal was impelled by economic reasons or by aesthetic ones to

write her novel, by the desire to express herself or simply to amuse herself writing the sort of book she liked to read. It is possible that she was inspired by *Floriseo, el caballero del desierto* (Floriseo, the knight of the desert, 1516), written by Fernando Bernal, who was almost certainly a relative of hers. We do know that she had the precedent of another woman writer of novels of chivalry to ease her entry into the field, namely, the anonymous author of the first two books in the popular series about the knight Palmerin, *Palmerín de Oliva* and *Primaleón.*

Before 1590, *Palmerín de Oliva* (1511) and *Primaleón* (1512) went through at least ten Spanish editions each, several of which appeared before the publication of *Don Cristalián* in 1545. Bernal could see for herself the immense popularity of these novels, written by a woman who, despite her decision not to divulge her name, did allow her gender to be known. The model was useful to Bernal, for she too declined to sign the book she wrote. Her identity was still unknown in the Italian translation of the book, which came out in Venice in 1557-58. Only in the posthumous Spanish edition of 1587 was the author's name revealed.

After Bernal died, her daughter requested official permission to reissue *Don Cristalián de España*, requiring that she state her mother's name and thereby breaking Beatriz Bernal's anonymity. Juana Bernal de Gatos needed the money: the permission conceding to her the rights to the profits from sales of the novel says that she "was poor and in need" ("era pobre y padecía necesidades"). Thus, even after she died the mother could provide for her daughter. And Juana Bernal de Gatos, widowed and impoverished, the sole heir of Beatriz Bernal, revealed her mother's name to prove her right to the earnings of the book.

Don Cristalián de España, which goes on for more than three hundred double-columned pages, has an appropriately contorted plot, filled with monsters, enchanted castles, beautiful princesses, powerful queens, magic mountains, giants, and dragons. Of particular interest is the figure of the unprotected damsel, who achieves almost mythic stature, whether through the magic that is used to imprison her (and that she tries to use to free herself) or the atmosphere of ritual sacrifice that envelops her. In her treatment of this figure, Beatriz Bernal might be considered a precursor of María de Zayas, who a century later would compose scenes of horror similar to those of *Don Cristalián* to denounce the victimization of women.

In the novel's short prologue, reprinted and translated here, Bernal adopts an authorial persona to bring her own voice close to the surface of the text, using the common device of the found manuscript in a way that radically alters conventions concerning gender. The speaker who finds the manuscript is a woman in the company of women who has the gumption to stick her hand into a coffin containing an embalmed corpse in order to retrieve the large book that is at its feet. Not only does she display considerable cool when she pilfers the manuscript, but she is impatient to immerse herself in the pleasures of reading and "translating" the text. This macabre beginning barely hints at the high adventure Bernal is capable of inventing.

1. The first English translation of a Spanish novel of chivalry, printed late in the sixteenth century, was also prepared by a woman, Margaret Tyler. In the prologue to her translation of *Espejo de príncipes y caballeros* (*Mirror of Princes and Knights*), by Diego Ortúñez de Calahorra, Tyler anticipates the objections to a woman's meddling in affairs of chivalry.

Don Cristalián de España

Proemio a Felipe Segundo (fragmento)

Yendo un viernes de la Cruz con otras dueñas a andar las estaciones (ya que la aurora traía el mensaje del venidero día) llegamos a una iglesia adonde estaba un muy antiguo sepulcro, en el cual vimos estar un defunto embalsamado; y yo siendo más curiosa que las que conmigo iban de ver y saber aquella antigüedad, lleguéme más cerca, y mirando todo lo que en el sepulcro había, vi que a los pies del sepultado estaba un libro de crecido volumen, el cual (aunque fuese sacrilegio) para mí apliqué; y acuciosa de saber sus secretos, dejada la compañía me vine a mi casa, y abriéndole hallé que estaba escrito en nuestro común lenguaje, de letra tan antigua que ni parecía española, ni arábiga ni griega. Pero todavía creciendo mi deseo y abrazándome con un poco de trabajo, vi en él muy diversas cosas escritas, de las cuales, como pude, traduje y saqué esta historia, pareciéndome de más sutil estilo que ninguna otra cosa, donde se cuentan las hazañas y grandes hechos en armas que este valoroso príncipe don Cristalián de España y el infante Luzescanio, su hermano, hicieron.

Segunda Parte
Trata cómo el infante Luzescanio
fue armado caballero, y de las grandes
cosas en armas que el príncipe
don Cristalián y él hicieron
andando por el mundo buscando
aventuras.

Capítulo xliij
*De cómo el infante Luzescanio fue armado
caballero y también por este capítulo
sabrán quien en su poder le tenía.*

Escribe el sabio Doroteo que en Cantaria reinaba un rey, asaz noble y de buenas

Don Cristalián of Spain

Proem to Philip II (excerpt)

On my way one Good Friday with other gentlewomen to walk the Stations of the Cross (with the dawn now announcing the coming day) we came to a church with a very old tomb in which we saw the embalmed remains of the deceased; and I, being more curious to see and know that relic than were those who came with me, went up to it, and gazing at all that the tomb held, saw that at the feet of the deceased was a voluminous book and (though it were a sacrilege) I took it; and keen to know its secrets, I left those I was with and went to my house, and opening it, I discovered that it was written in our vernacular, in a letter so old-fashioned that it seemed not to be Spanish, nor Arabic, nor Greek. But as my desire grew greater yet and making a bit of an effort, I saw in it a great variety of things written, from which, as well as I was able, I translated and took this story, it seeming to me, more than any other, to be of the subtlest style, in which are told the adventures of great deeds in arms performed by this courageous prince Don Cristalián of Spain and Prince Luzescanio, his brother.

Part Two
Wherein we hear of how
Prince Luzescanio was knighted,
and of the great deeds in arms performed
by him and the prince Don Cristalián
as they wandered the world
in search of adventures.

Chapter xliij
*Of how Prince Luzescanio was knighted
and in this chapter we will also learn of her
whose command he was under.*

The wise Doroteo writes that in Cantaria there ruled a king, most noble and well-

costumbres, cuyo nombre era Barciano; y a la sazón estaba viudo, y no tenía sino una sola hija llamada Ceilna. Esta princesa fue muy aficionada a aprender las artes; y como el rey Barciano su padre la amase tanto, hizo venir a su reino grandes maestros, para que su hija fuese enseñada. Esta hermosa princesa aprendió tanto, que pasó en su saber a todos los maestros que la mostraron.

Poco tiempo después que aquellos sabios salieron del reino de Cantaria, fue el rey su padre muerto. Y como pasó desta presente vida, la princesa fue alzada por reina. Los altos hombres le pidieron en las primeras que hizo que tomase marido, porque el reino no estuviese sin señor. Ella respondió diciéndoles que la diesen tiempo para tomar su acuerdo sobre tan gran hecho como le pedían. Ellos respondieron que su alteza tomase el tiempo que quisiese.

La reina estuvo quince días que jamás hizo sino mirar y revolver sus libros, y a la fin ella supo por sus artes que en la Devisa del Valle Hermoso estaba encantado un caballero llamado Sonabal de Fenusa, rey de la Diserta, a maravilla muy preciado caballero. Ella tuvo mucha voluntad de lo haber por marido, pero no sabía cómo lo librar de aquel encantamiento. Y tornando a revolver sus libros halló que no podía ser libre sino fuese por la mano del segundo hijo del valiente y muy esforzado emperador Lindelel de Trapisonda.

Como ella esto supo, hizo llamar a los altos hombres de su reino, y hablóles en esta manera, —Tengo en la memoria lo que en las cortes pasadas me pedisteis, y es que tomase marido, para que este reino no estuviese sin señor. Yo conozco que vosotros tenéis mucha razón, y yo así lo quiero, y tengo voluntad de lo hacer. Pero mucho quería rogaros que me lo dejásedes

bred, whose name was Barciano; and, at that time he was a widower and had only one daughter named Ceilna. This princess was very eager to learn the arts of magic; and as King Barciano her father loved her so well, he brought to his kingdom the great masters to teach his daughter. This beautiful princess learned so much that she surpassed in her learning all that the masters taught her.

Not long after those wise men left the kingdom of Cantaria, her father the king died. And as he had passed away, the princess became queen. The distinguished nobles asked that among the first things she did she take a husband so that the realm would not be without a lord. She responded by telling them that they must give her time to make a decision on so important a request. They responded that her highness might take all the time she wished.

The queen spent two weeks doing nothing more than looking through and pondering her books, and at the end she knew, by means of her arts, that in the Shrine of the Beautiful Valley there was a knight named Sonabal of Fenusa, the king of Diserta, a wondrous knight held in very high esteem, upon whom a spell had been cast. She was most determined to have him for her husband, but she knew not how to free him from that spell. And consulting her books once again, she learned that he could not be freed except by the hand of the second son of the valiant and very courageous emperor, Lindelel of Trapisonda.

When she discovered this, she sent for the distinguished lords of her realm and spoke to them thus, "I have not forgotten what you in past councils asked of me, and that is that I take a husband, so that this kingdom be not without a lord. I know that

tomar tal, conque vosotros estuviésedes por honrados, y yo volviese contenta el tiempo que Dios en esta vida me dejase.— El duque de Orbala (caballero antiguo y sabio) en nombre de todos le respondió que estaban aparejados para tener por bueno lo que su alteza mandase. La reina se lo agradeció mucho y les dijo, —Sabed que yo he mirado mucho con quién me podría casar, y en todos estos reinos comarcanos ya sabéis que no hay con quién. Yo tengo en voluntad (si a vosotros parece) de tomar por marido a Sonabal de Fenusa, que es rey de la Diserta. Está encantado en la Devisa del Valle Hermoso. Yo he hallado por mis artes que cuantos hoy en el mundo son no le podrían librar de aquel encantamento en que está si no fuere el segundo hijo del emperador Lindelel de Trapisonda. Yo os ruego y mando que por la fidelidad que como buenos y leales vasallos me debéis, por mi amor tengáis por bien que yo esté sin marido hasta que el rey sea libre, que será lo más presto que yo pudiere.— Todos aquellos caballeros holgaron de servir a la reina en lo que les mandaba; y le dijeron que aguardarían todo lo que su alteza mandase. Ella les dio muchas gracias por ello. Y luego envió a Constantinopla a la doncella y caballeros que oísteis por el infante Luzescanio. Esta reina Ceilna lo tuvo consigo a muy gran vicio.

En este tiempo le hizo aparejar muy ricas armas. Ellas eran verdes, y todas labradas de unas llamas doradas. El escudo era de un hueso verde, que no parecía sino una fina esmeralda. Por devisa tenía un corazón, y la orla del escudo era los mismos fuegos dorados que en las armas estaban sembrados, puestos por tal concierto que todos parecían quemar el corazón. El caballo era el mejor que en aquellas partes había. Esto aparejado, la reina le dijo al

you are most correct, and this is also what I wish, and have determined to bring about. But I would like to beg you that you allow me to choose such, and that you honor my wish, so that I may be content for the time God sees fit that I live." The Duke of Orbala (an old and wise knight) responded in the name of all that they were prepared to follow her majesty's orders. The queen gave many thanks and said, "Know you that I have considered at length whom I might marry, and in all of the neighboring realms you know that there is no one suitable. I have thus decided (if it seem right to you) to take for my husband Sonabal of Fenusa, the king of Diserta. He is under a spell in the Shrine of the Beautiful Valley. I have found him through my arts but though these are vast they are not sufficient to free him from the spell cast on him except through the second son of Emperor Lindelel of Trapisonda. I beg and order you that through the loyalty you, as good and faithful vassals, owe me, that because of my love you accept that I remain without a husband until the king be free, which will be as soon as I am able to bring that about." All of those knights were glad to serve the queen as she ordered; and they told her that they would wait as long as her highness mandated. She thanked them profusely for that. And then she sent the maiden and knights you have already heard of to Constantinople for Prince Luzescanio. Queen Ceilna was most pleased.

At this time she ordered rich arms made ready for him. These were green and worked with gold flames. The shield was of green bone, that seemed nothing less than fine emerald. In the center was a heart, and the border of the shield contained the same golden flames that appeared on the armor, placed in such profusion that they all seemed to consume the heart. The

infante Luzescanio: —Ya es tiempo que re-
cibáis orden de caballería. —Ese es el mayor deseo que yo tengo, —dijo el infante.
—Pues que así es, vuestro deseo será cumplido, y a mí me haréis la más bien andante de cuantas nacieron. Y no quiero que
más nos detengamos, sino que luego nos
partamos para el reino de Romania, que
allí seréis caballero por la mano del príncipe Bores de Mar.

Mucho holgó el infante Luzescanio en
ver que tan breve era la partida. La reina tenía hechas ricas y muy preciadas vestiduras
para sí, y luego las mandó traer; y vistióse
una ropa de una seda verde, cubierta de
una red de oro, y en el campo que de lo verde quedaba, estaban puestas perlas de mucho valor. Vestida que fue, pusiéronle una
rica corona encima de sus hermosos cabellos. La corona era tal, que no tenía precio,
tantas y tan ricas piedras tenía. Acabada
que fue de vestir, la reina mandó a veinte y
cuatro doncellas que de ricas vestiduras
verdes se vistiesen. Ellas hicieron su mandado. La reina mandó traer las armas que
para el infante había mandado hacer. Y
como él las miró, fue muy ledo en las ver
tan lucientes. La reina le dijo, —Mi señor,
estas armas verdes y doradas traeréis vos en
señal que yo tengo esperanza de cobrar lo
que tanto tiempo ha que por mí es desea-
do. Los fuegos que por ellas están sembrados, y el corazón que en este escudo veis,
traeréis vos en señal que por una hermosa
doncella vuestro corazón ha de arder en vivas llamas de fuego de amor. Y no pasará
mucho tiempo que la vista de aquella doncella os haga triste, tantas cuitas y mortales
deseos pasaréis el tiempo que la sirviére-
des.— El infante pidió muy ahincadamen-
te a la reina que le dijese quién era aquella
doncella por quien tanto afán había de pasar. La reina no se lo quiso decir más de
cuanto le dijo, que le hacía cierto que en

horse was the finest to be found in those
parts. When it was provisioned, the queen
said to Prince Luzescanio, "Now it is time
for you to receive the order of knighthood." "I desire nothing more," said the
prince. "Then so be it, your desire will be
granted, and you will make me the happi-
est woman that ever was born. I do not
wish to waste any more time, but to depart
at once for the kingdom of Romania, and
there you will be knighted by the hand of
Prince Bores de Mar."

Prince Luzescanio was very glad to see
that they would be taking their leave so
soon. The queen had made for herself rich
and expensive garments, and she ordered
them brought; and she dressed in a garment of green silk covered with gold net,
and to the green background pearls of
great value had been attached. When she
was dressed, they placed a very rich crown
on her lovely locks. The crown was such
that it was priceless, so many and so rich
were the stones it held. When she had finished dressing, the queen ordered twenty-
four maidens to dress in rich garments of
green. They did as ordered. The queen ordered that the arms she had made for the
prince be brought. And as he gazed at
them, he felt gladdened on seeing them
shine so. The queen said, "My lord, these
green and golden arms you will bear as a
sign of the hope I have in acquiring that
which I have for so long desired. The
flames with which they are adorned, and
the heart you see on this shield, you will
bear as a sign that, for a beautiful maiden,
your heart burns with the live fire of love.
And before long the sight of that beautiful
maiden will have saddened you, so many
afflictions and mortal desires you will suffer throughout the time you serve her."
The prince asked the queen with great eagerness to tell him who this beautiful

aquel camino que iban ella se la mostraría. Como esto oyó el infante, no la quiso más importunar.

Él fue luego armado de aquellas armas verdes que ya oístes, y trajéronle el caballo con guarniciones todas verdes. El infante subió en él y parecía tan apuesto armado, que a quien lo miraba le semejaba no haber visto otro caballero que mejor que él pareciese. La reina subió en su palafrén ricamente guarnido, y las veinte y cuatro doncellas subieron en sus palafrenes. Con la reina iban grandes compañas de caballeros.

Y así como oído habéis salieron del reino de Cantaria, y tomaron el camino del reino de Romania. Y en todo él no les avino cosa que enojo les hiciese. Un día a hora de nona llegaron a tres millas de la ciudad de Laudana. La reina llamó a una doncella de las suyas y díjole, —Amiga véte a la ciudad, que allí nos han dicho que está el rey y su hijo el príncipe Bores de Mar; y di al rey, como yo voy a su corte, a le pedir merced, que un doncel me arme caballero el príncipe Bores de Mar.

La doncella se despidió de la reina y se fue para la ciudad, y entró en el palacio acabando el rey de comer. Todos pararon mientes en la doncella, que muy apuesta era. Ella se fue a donde el rey estaba, y humillándose ante él le quiso besar las manos. Él no se las quiso dar; antes le dijo, —Amiga, ¿de quién traéis nuevas?— La doncella le respondió, —Tráigolas de la reina de Cantaria. —Vos vengáis mucho en buen hora. Decidme, ¿qué tal queda la reina? —Ella está muy buena, —dijo la doncella, —y queda tres millas de aquí. Manda por mí besar vuestras reales manos, y haceos saber que la su venida a vuestra tierra es, a pedir a la vuestra merced que el príncipe vuestro hijo tenga por bien de le armar un doncel caballero.

maiden was for whom so many anxieties he would suffer. The queen refused to tell him anything more than she had already said, but assured him that on the road they were taking she would point her out. When the prince heard this, he had no wish to importune her further.

Then he was armed with those green arms of which you have heard, and they brought to him a horse fitted out in green. The prince mounted and so handsome was he in armor that to those who looked upon him he seemed the finest knight they had ever seen. The queen mounted her own richly adorned horse, and the twenty-four maidens mounted theirs. With the queen went a great retinue of knights.

And as you have heard, they left the kingdom of Cantaria and took the road to the kingdom of Romania. And nothing occurred to trouble them the entire way. One day, at the hour of nones, they came within three miles of the city of Laudana. The queen called to one of her maidens and said to her, "Friend, go to the city, for they have informed us that the king and his son, Prince Bores de Mar, are there. And say to the king that I go to his court to ask that his highness, Prince Bores de Mar, knight one of my pages."

The maiden took leave of the queen and went to the city and entered the palace just as the king was finishing his meal. All turned their eyes to the maiden, who was most lovely. She went up to the king and, kneeling before him, attempted to kiss his hand. He refused to allow her to do so and said instead, "Friend, from whom do you bring news?" The maiden replied, "I bring news from the queen of Cantaria." "You have come at a good time. Tell me, how is the queen?" "She is very well," said the maiden, "and she awaits three miles from here. She sent me to kiss your royal hands,

Como el rey oyó decir que la reina estaba tan cerca de la su ciudad, fue muy espantado y dijo, —Por cierto el doncel debe de ser de alta guisa, pues la reina de Cantaria salió de su tierra por le acompañar. Amiga, diréis a la reina que la su merced sea muy bien venida a esta tierra, y que yo y el príncipe mi hijo estamos aparejados para la servir en todo lo que mandar nos quisiere.

La doncella besó las manos al rey, y tomada su licencia se volvió a donde su señora estaba. Y besándole las manos, le dijo la buena voluntad que en el rey de Romania había hallado. Así mismo le dijo todo lo que el rey le enviaba a decir, de lo cual la reina y el infante fueron muy alegres.

Así como la doncella salió del palacio del rey de Romania, luego él hizo saber al príncipe Bores de Mar la venida de la reina, enviándole a decir como estaba tan cerca de la ciudad que muy presto se aparejase para salirla a recibir. Como Bores de Mar dejó el mandado del rey, luego lo hizo saber a la princesa Archesidela, diciéndole que se aparejase para cuando la reina viniese al palacio del rey. La princesa holgó mucho con la su venida, y el príncipe hizo llamar a los altos hombres que en la corte estaban, y todos se fueron al aposento del rey. Y como el rey los vio, dijo al príncipe que él también quería salir a recibir a la reina.

Y así salieron dos millas de la ciudad, que ya allí llegaron. El rey de Romania y Bores de Mar se apearon por más honrar a la reina. Y como ella los vio, luego se apeó así mismo el infante Luzescanio. La reina se humilló al rey, y él a ella, y habláronse con mucho acatamiento. Y así mismo Bores de Mar se humilló ante la reina y ella le habló muy mesuradamente. El infante Luzescanio se humilló ante el rey y ante Bores de Mar. Ellos le hablaron con mucha alegría

and to inform you that she comes to your land to ask of your majesty that the prince, your son, be so kind as to knight one of her pages."

When the king heard that the queen was so close to his city he was amazed and said, "The man must certainly be of high rank, since the queen of Cantaria left her land to accompany him. Friend, tell the queen that her majesty is welcome to this land, and that I and the prince, my son, are prepared to serve her in any way that she may wish."

The maiden kissed the king's hands, and taking her leave returned to where her lady waited. And kissing her hands, she told her that she had found the king of Romania favorably disposed. She also told her all the king had ordered that she report, and with this news the queen and the prince were most glad.

And when the maiden had left the palace of the king of Romania, he informed Prince Bores de Mar of the queen's arrival, sending a messenger to tell him that as she was so close to the city he must make haste to prepare himself to meet her. When Bores de Mar left the king's messenger, he went to inform the princess Archesidela, telling her to prepare herself for the arrival of the queen at the king's palace. The princess was most glad over her coming, and the prince summoned the most distinguished nobles of the court, and all went to the king's chamber. And when the king saw them, he told the prince that he too would go to receive the queen.

And thus they traveled two miles from the city, for that was where they met. The king of Romania and Bores de Mar dismounted in order to show greater reverence to the queen. And when he saw them, Prince Luzescanio also dismounted. The queen knelt before the king, and he before

aunque no le conocían. Y así tornaron todos a cabalgar, y se entraron en la ciudad. Todas las gentes salieron por las rúas a mirar a la reina y al doncel que consigo traía, que maravillosamente parecía armado.

Como en el palacio fueron, el rey rogó a la reina que mandase al doncel que se quitase las armas. Ella lo hizo por el ruego del rey. Y luego las doncellas de la reina ayudaron a desarmar al doncel. Como el yelmo le quitaron, todos cuantos en el palacio estaban fueron muy espantados de la su gran hermosura. El rey le mandó dar un rico manto. Y como todos fueron sentados, la reina dijo al rey, —Ya mi señor sabe la vuestra merced la causa de mi venida a esta tierra. Al príncipe Bores de Mar ruego yo que luego por la mañana dé orden de caballería a este doncel, que cuando él sepa quién es, se tendrá por bienandante en se la haber dado.— El príncipe le respondió que haría en todo su mandado. A esta hora ya salía de su aposento la princesa Archesidela, acompañada de muchas dueñas y doncellas de alta guisa. La reina de Cantaria y ella se hablaron muy cortésmente, humillándose la una a la otra. Y así se vinieron a asentar, maravillándose cada una de la extraña hermosura de la otra.

Aquella noche hizo el rey muy gran fiesta a la reina, así de la cena (que fue la más preciada que nunca jamás se dio a mesa de rey), como de muchos juegos y danzas que en el palacio se hicieron. Cuando fue la hora de dormir el príncipe Bores de Mar tomó al infante, y llevólo a la capilla del rey, dejando en su compañía a las doncellas de la reina, que con él velaron aquella noche. Bores de Mar dijo al infante, —Aquí mi señor velaréis esta noche las armas, y por la mañana seréis caballero.— Y despidiéndose de él se volvió al palacio y halló que ya el rey era ido a su aposento. Y

her, and they spoke with much respect. Bores de Mar likewise knelt before the queen, and she spoke to him with great courtesy. Prince Luzescanio knelt before the king and before Bores de Mar. They spoke to him with much cheer, though they did not know him. And then they all mounted their horses and rode to the city. All the people gathered in the village streets to see the queen and the page she had with her, who was so wonderfully armed.

When they arrived at the palace, the king entreated the queen to order her page to remove his armor. She did as the king requested. And the queen's maidens helped the page to remove his armor. When they took off his helmet, all who were in the palace were struck by his great beauty. The king ordered that he be given a rich robe. And when they all were seated, the queen said to the king, "My lord already knows the favor that has brought me to this land. I beg of Prince Bores de Mar that tomorrow morning he confer on this page the order of knighthood, and when he knows who this is, he will think himself fortunate for having done so." The prince replied that he would do all that was asked. At that moment Princess Archesidela was just emerging from her chamber, accompanied by many ladies and maidens of high rank. The queen of Cantaria and she spoke most respectfully to one another, each of them kneeling before the other. And then they sat down, marveling each of them at the rare beauty of the other.

That night the king gave a great feast in honor of the queen, including a dinner (which was the most highly prized ever given at a king's table), and many games and dances were held in the palace. When it came time to sleep, Prince Bores de Mar took the prince and led him to the king's

la reina de Cantaria así mismo era ida a dormir. Él se fue a su aposento.

Y otro día por la mañana todos se levantaron, y se fueron a la capilla donde el infante Luzescanio había velado las armas, y halláronle que se estaba confesando, y aguardaron hasta que acabase, que la misa se comenzó. Y cuando fue acabada, el infante tomó el cuerpo de Nuestro Redentor Jesucristo con mucha devoción, y le rogó que siempre le tuviese de su mano, para que no hiciese nada en su deservicio. Luego Bores de Mar se levantó, y calzándole la espuela derecha le dio paz en el rostro, diciéndole, —Caballero sois, la espada podéis tomar de quien os plugiere pero por daros aquella honra que vuestra hermosa apostura merece, yo quiero que la toméis de la más hermosa doncella que hoy es en el mundo nacida, después de la princesa Penamundi.— Y diciendo esto dijo al duque Camposileno que fuese por la hermosa Bellaestela.

El duque hizo su mandado. Y a poco rato vino con ella, trayéndola del brazo, acompañada de siete doncellas. Era de edad de trece años, y traía ricas y muy preciadas ropas vestidas, guarnidas de muy ricas perlas y piedras de gran valor. Traía un collar de hombros, que no había persona que apreciarlo pudiese. Traía un rico tocado, hecho por tal arte que los sus hermosos cabellos todos se mostraban. La falda le traía un enano ricamente guarnido. Así como en la capilla entró, fueron todos espantados de ver su gran hermosura.

La reina de Cantaria dijo al rey de Romania, —La vuestra merced sea de me decir quién es esta hermosa doncella.— El rey le respondió, —El doncel sea caballero, que después sabréis la su hacienda.— La reina le dijo, —Hermosa doncella aquí sois venida para acrecentar más en la honra deste caballero. —El príncipe Bores de Mar dijo

chapel, leaving him in the company of the queen's maidens, who would keep vigil with him that night. Bores de Mar said to the prince, "Here, my lord, will you keep vigil over your arms, and tomorrow morning you will be knighted." And taking his leave he returned to the palace and found that the king had already retired to his chamber. And the queen of Cantaria had also gone to sleep. He went to his chamber.

And the morning of the following day all rose and went to the chapel where Prince Luzescanio had kept vigil over his arms, and they found him confessing, and they waited until he had finished and the mass had begun. And when it was over, the prince took the body of Our Redeemer Jesus Christ with much devotion, and he prayed to Him to be always at his side, so that he would never be of disservice to Him. Bores de Mar rose, and, placing his right spur on his leg, he made the sign of peace on his forehead, saying to him, "Thou art a knight; thy sword mayest thou take from whomever may please thee, but to give us the honor that thy graceful bearing merits, I beg thee take it from the loveliest maiden ever to be born into this world, after the princess Penamundi." And saying this he told the Duke of Camposileno to summon the lovely Bellaestela.

The duke did as he was ordered. And not long thereafter he returned with her, leading her by the arm, accompanied by seven maidens. She was thirteen years old and was dressed in rich and precious raiment, adorned with costly pearls and gemstones of great value. On her shoulders she wore a necklace, and there was not one who could place a price on it. She wore a rich headdress arranged with such art that her lovely hair could be seen. Her train was carried by a dwarf dressed in

a Bellaestela, que así había nombre aquella doncella, —Mi señora dad vos la espada a este caballero, porque tomándola él de vuestra mano no podrá sino ser alta la su caballería.— Aquella hermosa doncella tomó la espada (que en las manos de la reina estaba), y dándola al infante dijo, —Pues que vos caballero de mí esta merced recibís, yo quiero ser luego pagada, y pediros que me otorguéis un don. —El don, mi señora, yo le otorgo, —dijo el infante. —Por eso ved lo que mandáis, que por bien andante me tendría en gastar mi tiempo en servicio de tan hermosa doncella como vos lo sois.— Bellaestela le dio muchas gracias por el don que le había otorgado, y díjole, —Sabed que el don que me habéis otorgado es éste, que yo no conozco a mi padre ni a mi madre, ni sé cuya hija soy, y quería señor caballero que vos entrásedes en esta demanda de los buscar. Porque hasta que yo lo sepa, jamás en mi corazón entrará entera alegría.— El infante le dijo, —Mi señora, en mandarme cosa en que yo os sirva, me tengo por el más bien andante de cuantos hoy son en el mundo, y de aquí prometo (si la reina de Cantaria no me manda algo en que detenerme pueda) de luego entrar en esa demanda.— Bellaestela le dio infinitas gracias.

La reina de Cantaria le dijo, —Hermosa doncella, y más que cuantas nacieron, este caballero primero que entre en la vuestra demanda, le es forzado sacar de encantamiento al rey de la Diserta, que encantado está en la Devisa del Valle Hermoso. Esto hecho, yo os prometo que él no se entremeta en otra cosa, sino en vuestro servicio. Y de ello sé yo que será él bien contento, según lo mucho que serviros desea.— Bellaestela le dijo que hiciese como ella lo mandaba. Del infante Luzescanio os digo, que estaba tan pagado de aquella hermosa doncella, que súbitamente fue

rich garments. And as she came into the chapel, all were amazed to see her great beauty.

The queen of Cantaria said to the king of Romania, "Would your majesty be so kind as to tell me who this beautiful maiden is." The king replied, "Let the page first be knighted, then you will know of her situation." The queen said to her, "Fair maiden, you have become fairer still in honor of this knight." Prince Bores de Mar said to Bellaestela, for such was the name of that maiden, "My lady, give your sword to this knight, so that in taking it from your hand, he may do nothing other than honor his knighthood." That beautiful maiden took the sword (which was in the hands of the queen), and giving it to the prince said, "Then do you, knight, from me receive this favor, I wish later to be repaid, and ask that you grant me a boon." "The boon, my lady, I will grant you," said the prince. "Thus ask what you will, and I will consider myself fortunate if I spend my time in the service of a maiden as lovely as you." Bellaestela gave him many thanks for the boon and said to him, "Know that the boon you have given me is this, that I know not my father nor my mother nor whose daughter I am, and I wish, sir knight, that you undertake the task of finding them. For until I know this, never will complete happiness enter my heart." The prince said to her, "My lady, in ordering me to do something to serve you, I hold myself the luckiest knight errant in the world, and from this moment, I promise (if the queen of Cantaria does not order that I do something that would cause delay) immediately to undertake this task." Bellaestela gave him infinite thanks.

The queen of Cantaria said, "Fair maiden, more beautiful by far than so

herido su corazón, y por ella pasó grandes afanes, andando por el mundo en la demanda que oído habéis, acabando muchas y muy extrañas aventuras, como esta historia os lo contará.

Pues como el infante Luzescanio fue armado caballero, el rey de Romania y el príncipe Bores de Mar lo tomaron consigo, y la reina de Cantaria y la princesa Archesidela tomaron a Bellaestela. Y así salieron al gran palacio, y todos se asentaron con mucho placer. El infante Luzescanio fue desarmado, y cubierto de un rico manto. Y luego se asentó junto al príncipe Bores de Mar. El rey dijo a la reina de Cantaria y al infante Luzescanio, —Yo quiero deciros lo que deseáis saber, porque el novel caballero tenga más voluntad del servicio de la doncella. Sabed la más extraña cosa que jamás oístes.

—Yo salí de esta mi ciudad habrá cinco meses, acompañado de mis altos hombres, y así mismo de todos mis cazadores, con intención de me estar en una casa de placer (que en un monte tengo) algunos días, porque allí hay mucha caza de todas maneras. Yendo mi camino acompañado de la manera que oído habéis, en un llano a hora de sexta, súbitamente volvió el día claro en una obscura noche. No dejé de recibir alguna congoja, con pensar que Dios cuando por bien lo tiene consume las vidas de los hombres. Como yo esta maravilla vi, dije a los que conmigo iban, —Vosotros atinaréis a algún lugar si hay por aquí cerca.— Ellos me respondieron que no, por cuanto no veían cielo ni tierra. Finalmente acordamos de nos estar quedos, hasta saber lo que Dios de nos tenía ordenado de hacer. En la obscuridad que habéis oído estuvimos, hasta que faz hora de nona, que vimos venir de lejos por el aire a esta hermosa doncella, guarnida de muy ricas y preciadas vestiduras. Ella venía asentada en una silla,

many who have been born, before seeing to your demand this prized knight must rescue the king of Diserta from the spell he is under in the Shrine of the Beautiful Valley, where he was bewitched. When this is done, I promise you that he will not be engaged in anything other than your service. And in that I know he will be well pleased, as he dearly wishes to serve you." Bellaestela said that she would do as commanded. Of Prince Luzescanio I tell you that he was so taken with that lovely maiden, that suddenly his heart ached, and he took great risks for her, wandering the world over in the quest you have heard, accomplishing many and most strange exploits, as this story will tell you.

Once Prince Luzescanio was knighted, the king of Romania and Prince Bores de Mar took him with them, and the queen of Cantaria and Princess Archesidela accompanied Bellaestela. And thus they went to the great palace, and all sat down with great pleasure. Prince Luzescanio was relieved of his armor and cloaked in a sumptuous robe. And then he sat next to Prince Bores de Mar. The king said to the queen of Cantaria and Prince Luzescanio, "I wish to tell you what you would like to know, so that the new knight will be more willing to serve the maiden. You are about to learn the strangest thing you have ever heard.

"I left this, my city, five months ago, accompanied by my distinguished lords and likewise by all my hunters, with the intention of spending a few days in a country house that I have in the mountains, because the hunting there is good. On the way, accompanied as I have told you, on a plain at the hour of sext, the clear day suddenly turned dark as night. I could not help but feel some anxiety, with thoughts of how God, when He so desires, consumes the lives of men. When I had seen

tan ricamente guarnida, que era cosa extraña de ver. De la silla venían asidos cuatro
jayanes. Delante venía otro mucho más
desemejado. En las sus manos traía una
rica corona. Era tal que de las muchas y ricas piedras que de la corona traía, parecía
salir rayos de sol. Era tan grande el resplandor que daban, que parecía venir delante
una antorcha encendida. Todos fuimos
maravillados de ver tal aventura; y estuvimos aguardando, para ver qué cosa podría
ser. No tardó mucho tiempo, cuando todos
fueron ante mí. Como yo de cerca vi lo que
en la silla venía, fui extrañamente espantado. Y antes que yo hablase, el jayán que la
corona en sus manos traía me dijo, —Mucho estarás maravillado, rey de Romania,
de esta aventura que hoy te ha acaecido.
Pues no menos lo será, cuando supieres la
causa de nuestra venida a tu corte. El sabio
Diante te manda por mí saludar, por cuanto tú eres el más preciado rey que hay en estas comarcas. Él te hace saber cómo los dioses han tenido por bien que los sus días
feneciesen. Y antes que el alma del cuerpo
le saliese te envía esta hermosa doncella,
que él en el su poder tenía desde el día de su
nacimiento. Mucho te ruega que la tengas
en el tu palacio, y le hagas aquella honra
que la su gran hermosura merece, porque
él te hace cierto que es la más alta doncella,
así en señorío, como en el linaje que en
gran parte del mundo se puede hallar. Mas
te hace saber, que ella ni tú no sabréis quién
es, hasta que el doncel de las armas verdes
venga a tu corte a recibir orden de caballería, por ruego de la reina de Cantaria. Este
doncel tomará la demanda de saber cuya
hija es esta doncella, y será llamado por
mucho tiempo el Caballero de la Esperanza. Éste acabará todo lo que la doncella desea saber, y tú te llamarás bien andante en
haber tenido en tu poder tan alta señora
como ella es. Yo he dicho el mandado de mi

this marvel I said to those who were with
me, 'Go look for some place safe nearby.'
They refused, for they could see neither
sky nor land. Finally, we agreed to remain
where we were until we could determine
what God had in mind for us to do. We remained in this darkness until there came
the hour of nones, when we saw in the distance, coming through the air, this lovely
maiden, adorned with most sumptuous
and precious garments. She came seated
on a chair, just as richly decorated, and this
was a strange sight to see. Four giants bore
the chair. And another came at the fore,
one much larger still. In his hands he carried a rich crown. It was such that, from
the many and rich gemstones, rays of sun-
light seemed to blaze from the crown. So
great was the splendor from these that it
seemed that a burning torch came before.
We all marveled at seeing such a sight; and
we waited, to see what this thing might be.
Not long thereafter, they were all before
me. When from up close I saw what had
arrived in the chair, I was strangely
amazed. And before I could speak, the giant bearing the crown in his hands said to
me, 'You will be most astounded, King of
Romania, at this sight that today befalls
you. But your amazement will be no less
when you hear the reason we have come to
your court. The wise Diante sends me to
greet you, as you are the king most esteemed in these parts. He advises you that
the gods have decided that his days are
coming to an end, and that before his soul
leaves his body, he sends you this lovely
maiden, whom he has had in his charge
from the day she was born. He begs that
you take her into your palace, and that you
provide her with the honor that her great
beauty merits, because he assures you that
she is the most noble of maidens, both in
his domain and in the lineage that in most

señor el sabio Diante; aquí no tenemos más que hacer sino saber la tu voluntad.

—Por cierto, amigo, —dije yo, —que huelgo en hacer lo que el sabio Diante me envía a rogar. Yo tendré y serviré a esta doncella, de tal manera que ella sea bien contenta de estar en el mi palacio, porque de aquí prometo de la tener en más que a la infanta Archesidela, mi hija.— Y como esto dije, los cinco jayanes me besaron las manos, y se despidieron de mí, dejando en mi poder esta hermosa doncella. Y como de mí partieron, luego tornó el día claro.

Cuando el rey acabó de decir lo que oído habéis, la reina y el infante quedaron muy espantados de oír tal aventura. El infante Luzescanio tenía mucha congoja en su corazón, que le parecía que se detenía mucho, que él luego quisiera partirse para la Devisa del Valle Hermoso y librar al rey de la Diserta, para luego entrar en la demanda de su señora Bellaestela. La reina de Cantaria dijo al rey, —Mucha razón es que esta hermosa doncella sea tenida en mucho, pues por tan extraña aventura es venida al vuestro poder.

A esta hora fueron puestas las mesas, y allí fueron muy bien servidos, como a mesa de tan alto rey convenía. Acabada que fue la comida, el infante Luzescanio dijo a la reina que si a la su merced le parecía que sería bien partirse luego. —Hágase lo que mandáis, —dijo ella, —si el rey para ello da licencia.— El rey de Romania dijo a la reina, —Mucho más contento fuera yo con tener aquí algunos días a la vuestra merced y a este caballero. Pero pues más no puede ser, hágase lo que mandáis. Antes que os partiésedes, querría que se me otorgase un don.

—Vuestra alteza mande y pida lo que quisiere, que muy aparejada soy para os servir en todo lo que yo pudiere.

El rey se le humilló y le dijo, —Sabed

of the world one will find. But he advises you that neither she nor you will know who she is until the page with the green arms comes to your court to be knighted at the request of the queen of Cantaria. This knight will take it upon himself to discover whose daughter this maiden is, and he will be called for many years the Knight of Hope. He will find out all the maid wishes to know, and you will be called most fortunate for having in your charge a lady as wellborn as she. I have given you the order of my lord the wise Diante; here we have no more to do other than to know your will.'

"'Of course, my friend,' said I, 'I am glad to do as the wise Diante has sent you to request. I will keep and serve this maiden in such a fashion that she will be well content to be in my palace, because from this moment on I promise to hold her in even higher esteem than the princess Archesidela, my daughter.' And when I had thus spoken, the five giants kissed my hands and said farewell, leaving in my charge this fair maiden. And when they had left, the day brightened once more."

When the king had finished telling what you have just heard, the queen and the prince were much amazed to hear of such an event. Prince Luzescanio felt much anxiety in his heart, as it seemed to him that they were wasting time, and he wanted to leave for the Shrine of the Beautiful Valley and free the king of Diserta, so he might then put himself at the command of the lady Bellaestela. The queen of Cantaria said to the king, "There is good reason for the lovely maiden to be held in such esteem, as by such strange means has she come under your protection."

At that hour the tables were prepared, and there they were well served, as befitting a king of such high estate. When the

mi señora que el don que me habéis otorgado es que la vuestra merced sea servida de nos decir quién es este caballero que en la vuestra compañía traéis.

La reina miró al infante y díjole, —Mi señor, dad licencia para decir lo que el rey me manda.

El infante se le humilló y le dijo que para aquello y para lo demás la su merced lo tenía. La reina dijo al rey, —La vuestra merced sabrá que este caballero es hijo del Emperador Lindelel de Trapisonda, y hermano del príncipe don Cristalián.

Cuando el rey de Romania esto le oyó, luego se levantó de la silla, y ansí mismo el príncipe Bores de Mar. Y abrazándole dijo el rey, —Ay, buen caballero, por Dios perdonad, que si aquí no se os ha hecho aquel servicio que a vuestra real persona convenía, la culpa sea de la reina, que no nos dijo quién érades.

Bores de Mar así mismo le abrazó, diciéndole, —Yo soy el que orden de caballería di a vuestro hermano el príncipe don Cristalián, y Dios por la su merced me ha hecho tan bien andante que así mismo a vos mi señor hiciese caballero. Grande es el alegría que en mi corazón está, y no menos haría yo vuestro mandado que lo haría por el príncipe don Cristalián.— El infante se le humilló. Y despidiéndose del rey y de Bores de Mar y así mismo de la princesa Archesidela, él se puso de hinojos ante su señora, pidiéndole las manos para se las besar.

La hermosa Bellaestela le dijo, —Daros las hía yo, pero no quiero comenzar a pagar antes que se me hagan los servicios.

—Mi señora, —dijo el infante, —pues que yo esta merced no merezco, a lo menos reciba otra de la vuestra merced, antes que de su presencia me aparte, si no sois servida que los mis tristes días fenezcan con deseo de la vuestra vista. Y la merced

meal was over, Prince Luzescanio said to the queen that, if her majesty agreed, it would be well to depart. "Do as you wish," she said, "if the king give you his leave." The king of Romania said to the queen, "I would be much more pleased if I had your majesty and this knight with me for a few days. But as that cannot be, do as you wish. Before you depart, I ask that you grant me a favor."

"May your highness order and ask what he wishes, as I am most ready to serve in any way I can."

The king fell to his knees and said, "May my lady know that the favor you have granted me is that your majesty be so kind as to reveal to us who this knight is that you bring in your company."

The queen looked at the prince and said to him, "My lord, grant me leave to tell the king what he wishes to know."

The prince knelt and said that it was his duty to serve her highness in that and in anything else she wished. The queen said to the king, "Your majesty will know that this knight is the son of Emperor Lindelel of Trapisonda, and brother of Prince Don Cristalián."

When the king of Romania heard this, he rose from his chair, and so did Prince Bores de Mar. And embracing him, the king said, "Ah, good knight, for the love of God forgive me, and if here you have not received the service a royal personage of your rank merits, the queen is to blame for not telling us who you were."

Bores de Mar likewise embraced him, saying, "I am he who knighted your brother, Prince Don Cristalián, and God in His mercy has made me so fortunate in allowing me to knight you as well, my lord. Great is the joy that is in my heart, and no less could I do for you than I would for Prince Don Cristalián." The prince fell to

que se me ha de hacer es recibirme por vuestro caballero. Bien conozco que es grande la merced que pido, pero mayor es el deseo que de serviros tengo.

La hermosa Bellaestela estuvo muy atenta oyendo al infante. Y como él acabó de hablar, a ella le vino una viva color al rostro, y tendiendo sus hermosas manos se las dio, para que se las besase, y lo recibió por su caballero. Bien se puede creer que ésta fue mayor merced para el infante Luzescanio que si del mundo le hiciera señor. Haciéndole gran acatamiento se despidió della. Y la reina de Cantaria se había despedido del rey y de los príncipes. Y luego el infante Luzescanio fue armado, y poniendo a la reina en su palafrén, subió en su caballo, y acompañados de sus caballeros y doncellas se salieron del palacio del rey de Romania, y tomaron el camino a Cantaria.

La reina iba con mucha alegría porque se le acercaba la vista del rey de la Diserta. Y el infante Luzescanio iba demasiado de triste por se apartar de su señora Bellaestela. Y en todo el camino no les avino cosa alguna. Y así llegaron al reino de Cantaria, a una ciudad que Olimpa había nombre, donde sabida su venida, la salieron a recibir. Y todos besaron las manos a la reina, y ella los recibió con mucho placer. Y así entraron en la ciudad. Y como en el palacio fueron, el infante Luzescanio fue desarmado y cubierto con un rico manto. Y luego se sentaron y estuvieron hablando en lo que más les agradaba.

his knees. And taking his leave of the king and of Bores de Mar, and also of Princess Archesidela, he knelt before his lady, asking for her hands to kiss.

The fair Bellaestela said, "Give them to you I would, but I do not wish to begin payment before you have served me."

"My lady," said the prince, "as I do not merit this favor, may your majesty at least concede another before I leave your sight, and if you are not served may my sad days come to an end with the desire for a glimpse of you. And the favor I would have you grant me is to receive me as your knight. I well know that the favor I ask is great, but greater is the desire I have to serve you."

The fair Bellaestela listened most carefully to the prince. And when he had finished speaking, a bright color came to her face, and, extending her lovely hands, she gave them to him so that he might kiss them and received him as her knight. Well it might be imagined that this was a greater honor for Prince Luzescanio than if she had made him lord of the world. And with a low bow he took his leave of her. And the queen of Cantaria had taken her leave of the king and the prince. And then Prince Luzescanio was armed, and lifting the queen to her saddle, he mounted his horse; and accompanied by her knights and ladies they left the palace of the king of Romania and started off on the road to Cantaria.

The queen was most glad because the sight of the king of Diserta was drawing near. And Prince Luzescanio was most sad at having to leave his lady Bellaestela. And nothing untoward occurred along the way. And thus they came to the kingdom of Cantaria, to a city called Olimpa, where, when their arrival had been announced, the people gathered to receive them. And

all kissed the hands of the queen, and she received them with much pleasure. And in this manner they entered the city. And when they had gone to the palace, Prince Luzescanio's armor was removed and he was covered with a sumptuous robe. And then they sat and spoke of those things that most pleased them.

Capítulo xliiij

En que se cuenta cómo el infante Luzescanio fue a la Devisa del Valle Hermoso, y de lo que allí le acaeció.

Venida que fue la mañana, el infante dijo a Bridamor (que así había nombre su escudero) que le diese de vestir. Él hizo su mandado, y luego se fue al aposento de la reina y díjole, —Mi señora, si la vuestra merced me da licencia, yo me querría partir para la Devisa del Valle Hermoso.

La reina le respondió, diciéndole, —Mi señor, ser la vuestra partida tan presta me da tanta alegría que no lo sé decir.

—Pues que de vuestra alteza licencia tengo, denme mis armas.— Bridamor se las trujo, y luego fue armado con ayuda de la reina, y besándole las manos, se despidió de ella y de los altos hombres que en el palacio estaban. Todos lo encomendaron a Dios. Y él subió en su caballo solo con Bridamor que la lanza le llevaba; tomó el camino de la Devisa del Valle Hermoso. Y en todo él no le avino cosa que de contar sea.

Anduvieron quince días. En este tiempo un día a hora de prima llegó a vista del valle; y conoció ser él, por la devisa que de lejos le parecía, y diose mucha priesa a andar. Y como en él fue, espantóse mucho en ver la hermosura dél, y dijo en su corazón, —Mucha razón es que este valle se llame hermoso, que cosa deleitosa es de mirar.

Ca sabed que el valle era un llano, y todo el llano de muchos y muy deleitosos

Chapter xliiij

Wherein the story of Prince Luzescanio's journey to the Shrine of the Beautiful Valley is told, and what happened to him there.

When morning arrived the prince told Bridamor (for that was his squire's name) to help him dress. When that was done he went to the queen's chamber and said to her, "My lady, if your majesty will give me leave, I would like to depart for the Shrine of the Beautiful Valley."

The queen replied by saying to him, "My lord, that you have chosen to leave so soon gives me such joy that I do not have words to express it."

"Very well, as I have your majesty's permission, bring me my arms." Bridamor brought them and he was armed with the help of the queen, and kissing her hands, he said farewell to her and to the great lords who were in her palace. All commended him to God. And he mounted his horse, taking with him only Bridamor, who carried his lance. He took the road to the Shrine of the Beautiful Valley. And throughout his journey there befell him nothing that bears telling.

They journeyed for fifteen days. During that time, one day at the hour of prime, they came within sight of the valley. And he recognized it because from the distance it looked to him like a shrine, and he made haste to resume his march. And when he reached it, he was amazed to see

árboles, y en los árboles había yerbas de maravilloso olor. Tenía cuatro fuentes, a cada una esquina la suya. En medio deste valle estaba un pilar maravillosamente labrado, encima del cual estaba un arca de cristal, y por algunas partes dorada. Era tan luciente que de gran parte relumbraba, y por causa della había nombre la Devisa del Valle Hermoso. Dentro de aquella arca estaba encantado el rey de la Diserta. Era tan claro el cristal que muy bien se veía el rey tendido en ella, que al parecer de quien lo miraba se semejaba que estaba muerto. En torno del pilar estaban cinco sepulcros, en medio de los cuales había un padrón de cobre, y en él una imagen de doncella, que en las sus manos tenía un letrero, que decía así: "Cualquier caballero que en la aventura del rey de la Diserta se quisiere probar, ha de haber batalla con cinco caballeros que dentro de los sepulcros están. Y si los venciere, luego el rey de la Diserta será libre de su encantamiento. Y si con los cinco caballeros quisiere haber batalla, ha de tocar en cualquiera de los sepulcros, y luego el caballero que dentro está será con él en batalla."

Como el infante acabó de leer las letras que la imagen tenía en sus manos, luego se fue para el primer sepulcro; y tomando la lanza a su escudero, hirió con ella en él. Así como el golpe sonó, luego el sepulcro fue abierto, y dél salió un caballero armado de todas armas. Luego ante él se apareció un escudero con un caballo, y el caballero del sepulcro subió muy presto en él, y tomó una gruesa lanza (que aquel escudero le traía) y dijo con voz airada, —Vos, don caballero, que en el Valle Hermoso osastes entrar, y atrevimiento tuvistes de tocar en mi sepulcro, ¿qué es lo que aquí demandáis?

—Caballero, —dijo el infante, —lo que yo en este valle vengo a buscar es al rey de

the beauty of it and said in his heart, "It is with good reason that this valley is called beautiful, as it is a delight to behold."

Let it be said that the valley was a plain, and the plain was covered with many and very delightful trees, and on the trees there were herbs with marvelous scent. It had four fountains, one in each of its corners. In the middle of the valley was a pillar wondrously carved, on top of which was a crystal coffin adorned with gold. It was so bright that it shone all over, and because of it the place was known as the Shrine of the Beautiful Valley. Inside the coffin was the bewitched king of Diserta. The crystal was so clear that the king lying inside could be seen, and to those who gazed upon him, he appeared to be dead. About the pillar were five tombs, and in the middle of them a column of copper and on it the image of a maiden who held in her hands a sign that said: "Any knight wishing to prove himself by coming to the aid of the king of Diserta will first have to do battle with the five knights lying inside these tombs. And if he defeats them, then will the king of Diserta be freed from his spell. And if he wishes to do battle with the five knights, he must knock on any of the tombs, and the knight who is within will be he who does battle."

When the prince finished reading the words held in the hands of the image, he went to the first tomb, and, taking the lance from his squire, he knocked on the tomb with it. And when the blow sounded the tomb opened, and from it emerged a knight, fully armed. Then before him a squire appeared with a horse, and the knight of the tomb quickly mounted, and he took a heavy lance (which the squire brought to him) and said in an angry voice, "You, Sir Knight, who have dared

la Diserta; porque os hago saber que a mí me ha de costar la vida, o lo tengo de poner en su libertad.

—Bien creo yo, —dijo el caballero, —que antes que de aquí os partáis, compraréis caramente la vuestra grande y crecida locura, como lo han hecho otros muchos que esta aventura del rey han querido acabar. Y porque me parecéis buen caballero, os aconsejo que os volváis por donde venistes, si aquí no queréis acabar vuestra vida.

El infante le dijo, —Caballero, si conmigo no habéis gana de hacer batalla, mandadme dar al rey libre, como de antes solía estar. Y si dármelo no quiéredes, en la batalla sois conmigo, y sea luego, porque aquí me detengo mucho.

Como el caballero del sepulcro así oyó hablar al infante, fue muy airado, y díjole, —Vos, don caballero, no conocéis los caballeros deste valle.

—No, —dijo el infante, —que los nunca vi. Pero yo os prometo que yo sepa presto quién son y lo que valen; y apartaos de mí, sino heriros he como a mi mortal enemigo.

El caballero se apartó, y el infante así mismo, y encontráronse de las lanzas y de los escudos de tan poderosos encuentros que las lanzas volaron en piezas. El caballero de la devisa quebró su lanza en el escudo del infante, pero no se lo falsó que muy bueno era, aunque la lanza fue hecha en dos partes. El infante le encontró de tal manera, que dio con él por las ancas del caballo en tierra, tal caída que el caballero se sintió mal della. Pero como era valiente y muy ligero, fue muy presto en pie, y tomando su espada se vino para el infante, diciéndole, —No penséis que porque de las lanzas me habéis derribado, por eso me tenéis ventaja alguna.

El infante le respondió, —La ventaja

enter the Beautiful Valley, and who are so bold as to knock at my tomb, what is it that you want here?"

"Knight," said the prince, "I have come to this valley in search of the king of Diserta; and thus I inform you that it will either cost me my life or I will free the king."

"I do believe," said the knight, "that before you leave here, you will have paid dearly for your great and swelling madness, as have so many others who have wished to put an end to the king's adventure. And because you seem to me a noble knight, I advise you to return whence you came, if here you do not wish to end your life."

The prince said to him, "Knight, if with me you have no desire to do battle, order that the king be free, as once he was. And if you do not wish to give him to me, in battle you will have me, and let it be at once, because I am overly detained here."

When the knight of the tomb heard the prince speak so, he was most angered and said to him, "You, Sir Knight, do not know the knights of this valley."

"No," said the prince, "I have never seen them. But I assure you that soon I shall know who they are and what they are worth; so make way, or I will be forced to wound you as I would a mortal enemy."

The knight moved back, and the prince did as well, and their lances met with their shields with such force that the lances flew to pieces. The knight of the shrine broke his lance on the prince's shield, but it withstood the blow because it was very good, though the lance was broken in two. The prince came upon him in such a way that his horse went to the ground on its haunches, and his fall was such that the knight was weakened as a result. But as he was valiant and swift, he was immediately on his feet, and taking his sword, he came

que os tengo es estar a caballo, y vos a pie; yo no la quiero.— Y diciendo esto, descendió del caballo y embrazó su escudo, y tomando su espada en la mano se fue para el caballero, y comenzáronse a herir de muy pesados golpes. Duró la batalla cerca de media hora. En este tiempo ya el caballero de la devisa andaba muy laso, que tenía muchas heridas, y salíale mucha sangre. Como el infante tal le viese comenzóle a dar priesa, por manera que el caballero de la devisa fue herido en el brazo derecho de tal golpe que se lo cortó. Y con gran dolor que sintió, y como la sangre se le había salido, enflaquecióle el corazón y dio consigo en el suelo.

El infante, que así lo vio, fue muy presto sobre él, y cortándole las enlazaderas del yelmo, violo que estaba tal como muerto; y comenzóle a hablar pensando que le respondiera, pero no tuvo fuerzas para ello, que mientras el infante le hablaba se le salió el ánima. Como muerto lo vio, subió en su caballo. Bridamor le dijo si tenía alguna herida. —No, —dijo él.

Y diciendo esto, movió para el segundo sepulcro, y con el espada que en la mano llevaba tocó en él lo más recio que pudo. Luego fue el sepulcro abierto, y dél salió un gran caballero armado de unas ricas y fuertes armas. Y como en el suelo fue, dijo contra el infante Luzescanio, —Caballero, ¿vos pensáis hacer de mí lo que del otro caballero habéis hecho? No lo penséis. Y salid luego del caballo, sino muerto sois.

Como el infante así le oyó hablar, díjole, —Caballero, ¿habéis de hacer la batalla a pie o a caballo?

—A pie, —dijo él, —por eso descended del vuestro sino matároslo he.

El infante le respondió, —Si vos el caballo me matáis, costar os ha la vida.— Y diciendo esto, descendió dél, y embrazó su escudo, y tomando su espada, se fue para

at the prince, saying, "Do not assume that because of the lances you have defeated me, or that for that reason you have any advantage whatever."

The prince replied, "The advantage I have is that I am mounted and you are on foot. It is not an advantage I seek." And so saying, he got down off his horse and took up his shield, and taking his sword in hand he advanced on the knight, and he began to thrust at him with most forceful blows. The battle lasted for almost half an hour. During that time the knight of the shrine became increasingly weary, as he had many wounds and was losing a great deal of blood. When the prince saw him thus, he rushed to the attack, so that the knight of the shrine was wounded in the right arm by a blow so strong that it cut his arm off. And with the great pain he felt, and with the blood he had lost, his heart gave way and he fell to the ground.

When the prince saw him in that state, he was immediately upon him, and cutting the bindings of his helmet, he saw that he was as if dead; and he began to speak to him, thinking that he would respond, but he did not have the strength for that, for as the prince spoke to him, his soul left his body. As he saw that he was dead, he mounted his horse. Bridamor asked if he was hurt. "No," he replied.

And so saying, he went to the second tomb, and with his sword in hand he knocked as hard as he could. The tomb then opened, and a great knight armed with rich and powerful weapons emerged. And when he was on the ground, he said to Prince Luzescanio, "Knight, do you propose to do to me as you have done to the other knight? Don't even think of it. And come down off your horse, or you are dead."

When the prince heard him speak thus,

el caballero, y comenzáronse a herir, como aquellos que cada uno quería para sí lo mejor. El caballero de la devisa era gran heridor de espada, pero contra la bondad del infante poco le aprovechaba su herir, que era a maravilla ligero, y hería tan amenudo al caballero de la devisa que muchas veces lo hacía desatinar. Pero como era valiente y de gran fuerza, luego tornaba en sí, y pugnaba por dar muerte al infante. Pero no le avino como él lo pensó, que el infante le dio tal golpe encima de la cabeza que se la hendió hasta los dientes. Luego el caballero cayó muerto.

Como el infante tal le vio, fuese sin más al tercero sepulcro, y dando en él un golpe, muy presto salió un caballero, asaz grande, y bien hecho, armado como convenía para entrar en la batalla. Y como al infante vio, le dijo, —Yo te perdono el daño que en este valle has hecho, y porque sé que eres buen caballero, te dejaré ir libre, sin hacer batalla contigo. Y mira si quieres recebir esto que por ti quiero hacer.

El infante le respondió, —Enemigo soy de gastar el tiempo en palabras. Guardaos de mí, que no tengo pensamiento de hacer lo que me dices aunque del mundo me hiciésedes señor.— Y diciendo esto se fue para el caballero, y comenzáronse a herir muy de corazón. Y duró la batalla cerca de una hora. En este tiempo el caballero de la devisa andaba muy cansado, y dijo al infante, —Señor caballero, si os plugiere descansemos un poco, que según veo bien lo habemos menester.

—Ese descanso no pienso tomar, —dijo el infante, —hasta ver al rey de la Diserta libre.— Y diciendo esto, comenzó a herir al caballero de tal priesa, que a poco rato le hizo desatinar. Y como así le vio diole de toda su fuerza un golpe con el escudo en los pechos, que dio con él en el suelo. Y el infante fue muy presto sobre él, y quitándole

he said, "Knight, would you do battle on foot or on horseback?"

"On foot," he said, "so get down from yours or I will kill him."

The prince replied, "If you kill my horse, it will cost you your life." And saying that, he dismounted and picked up his shield, and taking his sword, he went for the knight, and they began to strike at one another, like those determined to get the better, each of the other. The knight of the shrine was good at thrusting with his sword, but his thrusts produced little advantage against the skill of the prince, who was marvelously quick and thrust so often at the knight of the shrine that over and over he made him reel. But as he was courageous and most strong, he regained his balance and struggled to kill the prince. But things did not turn out as he thought, because the prince struck him such a blow to the head that he split it down to his teeth. Then the knight fell dead.

When the prince saw him in that state, he went without pause to the third tomb, and at the sound of his blow there immediately appeared a knight, extremely large and well formed, armed as if he were about to enter battle. And when he saw the prince he said, "I forgive you for the damage you have done in this valley, and because I know that you are a noble knight, I will let you go free without doing battle with you. And see if you would receive this that I wish to do for you."

The prince answered, "I hate wasting time in words. Take care with me as I have not the slightest intention of doing what you suggest, though you make me lord of the world." And so saying, he went for the knight; and they began to thrust eagerly at one another. And the battle lasted for nearly an hour. During this time the knight of the shrine became very tired and

las enlazaduras del yelmo, le cortó la cabeza. Esto hecho, limpió su espada.

Bridamor le dijo, —Señor, paréceme que estáis herido, que la falda de la loriga tenéis tinta de sangre.— El infante miró la herida que tenía, y vio que no era nada, aunque sangre le salía, y sin más se detener se fue para el otro sepulcro, y diole un golpe con el espada, así como a los otros había hecho. Y luego el sepulcro fue abierto, y dél salió un caballero de unas armas negras, y por ellas una banda colorada, y su paso a paso se vino para el infante, y le dijo, — ¿Qué es lo que quieres, que con tanta osadía tocaste a mi sepulcro?

—Quiero, —dijo el infante, —la libertad del rey de la Diserta, que es lo que a este valle hermoso me ha traído.

—Caballero, —dijo el de la devisa, — por lo que debéis a la orden de caballería y a la cosa del mundo que más amáis, que vos me digáis por cuyo mandado sois aquí venido.

Como el infante así se vio conjurar, díjole, —Caballero, yo soy aquí venido por mandado de la reina de Cantaria.

Como el caballero esto le oyó decir, sospiró muy fieramente, y dijo, —A mí me conviene morir.— Y apartándose del infante, embrazó su escudo, y tomando su espada en la mano, vínose para él, que ya aguardando le estaba, y acometiéronse con demasiado saña, como aquellos que cada uno deseaba dar fin a su batalla, y heríanse de muchos y muy pesados golpes, de manera que en muy poco rato viérades el campo cubierto de sangre, y de rajas de los escudos. El caballero de la devisa era de grande esfuerzo, y hería con mucho corazón, pero aprovechábale poco, que el infante no quería lo peor de la batalla para sí, que andaba tan ligero que no parecía sino una ave, hería tan amenudo al caballero, que espanto ponía a quien lo miraba. Y

said to the prince, "Sir Knight, I beg you let us rest a bit for, as I see it, it would do us both good."

"I do not intend to rest," said the prince, "until I see the king of Diserta free." And saying this, he began thrusting at the knight with such speed that soon he had him staggering. And when he saw him in that state, he came at him with all his might, giving him a blow to the chest with his shield. And the prince was immediately upon him, and cutting the bindings of his helmet, he cut off his head. That done, he cleaned his sword.

Bridamor said to him, "My lord, it seems to me that you are wounded; there are blood stains on the side of your cuirass." The prince looked at his wound, and seeing that though he was bleeding it was not serious, he went to the other tomb and brought his sword down on it, as he had done with the others. And then the tomb opened and from it stepped a knight with black weapons and around them a red band, and step by step he came toward the prince and said to him, "What is it you want that you knock so boldly at my tomb?"

"I want," said the prince, "the freedom of the king of Diserta, and that is what has brought me to this beautiful valley."

"Knight," said he of the shrine, "upon your knighthood and the thing you love more than any other, tell me by whose order you have come."

As the prince saw himself thus entreated, he said, "Knight, I am here on the order of the queen of Cantaria."

When the knight heard this, he took a deep, angry breath and said, "For this would I die." And backing away from the prince, he took up his shield, and taking his sword in hand, he came at him, and he was already waiting, and they came at one

tanta priesa le dio, como en él sintió flaqueza, que a poco rato lo traía a su voluntad.

Ya el caballero no entendía en otra cosa sino en se amparar de los grandes y pesados golpes que el infante le daba. Y como tan aquejado se vio, arrojó lo que del escudo le quedaba, y tomó la espada a dos manos, y vínose para el infante, pensándole herir en la cabeza. Pero como el infante era muy ligero, dio un salto al través, por manera que el caballero erró el golpe, y el infante le hirió en la pierna derecha, que se la cortó. Y luego el caballero de la devisa cayó muerto.

El infante fue sobre él pensando que vivo era, para le cortar la cabeza, y como el yelmo le quitó y lo vio muerto, limpió su espada y miró si tenía alguna herida de que daño recibiese, y vio que aunque algunas tenía, no era de peligro. Y así dio gracias a Dios y fuese para el quinto sepulcro, y tocándole con su espada muy presto así como de las otras salió un caballero tan desemejado que extraña cosa era de lo ver; de grandeza de un jayán, armado de todas armas. Como al infante vio a pie, con voz muy airada le dijo, —Caballero, subid en vuestro caballo, que no quiero haber batalla con vos a pie, que por mal andante me tendría si vos vivo de las mis manos saliésedes. Venido sois a tiempo que pagaréis el daño que en este valle habéis hecho.

El infante pidió su caballo a Bridamor, y dijo al caballero, —No me conocéis bien, aun obras no temo, cuanto más palabras.

—Agora lo veréis, —dijo el caballero, —que mal haya yo si te he merced.

Y como esto dijo, detrás de una mata salió un escudero con un hermoso caballo de diestro, y dos gruesas lanzas que en las manos traía. El gran caballero subió en su caballo, y tomó una de las lanzas que su escudero traía, y dijo contra el infante, —

another with such fury, as those intent upon bringing the battle to an end, and they lunged at one another with many ferocious blows, so that before long the field was covered with blood, and with splinters from the shields. The knight of the shrine was most strong and thrust with energy, but he gained little by this, as the prince was determined not to come out badly from this battle, and he moved so swiftly that he seemed like nothing so much as a bird; he thrust so quickly at the knight that whoever watched was amazed. And such was his speed that the other felt weak, and before long he had him where he wanted him.

Now the knight gave thought to nothing else than shielding himself from the great and heavy blows the prince meted out to him. And as he was suffering so, he cast away what remained of the shield and rushed at the prince, intending to wound him in the head. But as the prince was most agile, he jumped aside, so that the knight erred with the blow, and the prince wounded him in the right leg, which he cut off. And then the knight of the shrine fell dead.

The prince stood over him, thinking that he was still alive, ready to cut off his head, and when he cut off the helmet and saw him dead, he cleaned his sword and looked to see if he had any wounds from the blows he had received, and he saw that although there were some, they were not serious. And he gave thanks to God and went to the fifth tomb, and knocking with his sword, there emerged as quickly as from the others a knight of such extraordinary size that he was a strange sight to behold: as large as a giant, armed with all manner of weapons. When he saw the prince on foot, in an angry voice he said, "Knight, mount your horse, as I do not

Caballero, tomad esotra, que yo no tengo de haber batalla con vos sino a guisa de buen caballero.

El infante la tomó, y muy presto se apartaron el uno del otro, y viniéronse a encontrar de los escudos y caballos tan poderosamente que las lanzas volaron en piezas, y el infante perdió la una estribera, tan desatinado fue el encuentro que recibió. Pero como era buen caballero, presto la tornó a cobrar. El caballero de la devisa fue a tierra, él y su caballo, y de la gran caída que dio, sintióse algo quebrantado. Pero como era de gran fuerza, muy presto se levantó. Su caballo hubo la pierna derecha quebrada, por manera que el caballero a pie embrazó su escudo, y con su espada en la mano se vino para el infante esgrimiéndola, que parecía quererla quebrar, y díjole, —Caballero, guardaos de mí.— Y arremetió al infante, y diole tal golpe en la cabeza de su caballo que se la hendió, y luego cayó muerto. El infante salió muy presto dél, y fue tan airado contra el caballero por le haber muerto el caballo, que si como era uno sólo fueran diez, todos no se le hicieran nada. Y embrazando su escudo y con su espada alta en la mano, fue a herir de toda su fuerza al caballero. Y fue la ventura tan contraria que el golpe acertó en el brazo del escudo del caballero. Y así por ser el golpe tal, como porque el escudo del caballero era uno de los mejores que había en el mundo, la espada del infante fue quebrada en dos partes. Como el caballero le vio sin espada, a grandes voces comenzó a decir, —Caballero, date a mi prisión, que porque he conocido de ti que eres buen caballero, te habré merced de la vida. Y esto ha de ser para quedar en este valle para siempre jamás.

—Mucho pesar habría la reina de Cantaria, —dijo el infante, —si yo con vos hiciese tal conveniencia.

wish to do battle with you on foot, as I would have me for a base knight if you slipped through my hands alive. In good time you will pay for the damage you have done in this valley."

The prince asked Bridamor to bring his horse and said to the knight, "You do not know me well; actions I do not fear, words even less."

"We will soon see," said the knight, "may I be damned if I let you come out of this favored."

And when he said that, from behind a bush a squire came, leading a beautiful horse by the halter and carrying two heavy lances in his hands. The great knight mounted the steed, took one of the lances from his squire, and said to the prince, "Knight, take this other, as I do not wish to do battle with you except as a noble knight would."

The prince took it, and they immediately separated, and they came at one another so forcefully with shields and horses that the lances flew to pieces, and the prince lost one of his stirrups, so forceful was the blow he received. But as he was a good horseman, he soon recovered it. The knight of the shrine went to the ground, he and his horse, and from the hard fall he took he felt something break. But as he was so strong, he very quickly got to his feet. His horse's right leg was broken, so that the knight took his shield on foot, and with his sword in hand came at the prince, brandishing it, as though he wished to break it, and he said, "Knight, take care." And he rushed at the prince, and he gave his horse a blow to the head that split it, and it fell dead. The prince jumped quickly from the horse, and he was enraged with the knight for having killed his steed, so that even had the one been ten, together they would not have

—Pues ¿qué piensas hacer de ti, que ya eres puesto en mi poder?

—Yo te lo diré, —dijo el infante. Y en diciendo esto, tomó lo que del espada le quedaba, y arrojólo con tanta fuerza al caballero, que acertándole en la cabeza le torció el yelmo, y antes que el caballero tuviese lugar para herir al infante, como era uno de los más ligeros que en el mundo había nacido, arremetió con él, y sacóle el espada de la mano. Y como en su poder la vio, comenzóle a herir muy amenudo; el cual como le vio haber perdido su espada, echó mano a una masa que del lado con una cadena traía colgada, y con ella comenzó a herir al infante. Pero no le aprovechaba nada su afán, que todos los golpes daba en vacío, que la ligereza del infante era tanta que jamás le acertó golpe a derecho. Y heríale de tales golpes que le rompía las armas, y la carne de tal manera que el caballero andaba ya muy laso, y muy quebrantado, y había perdido mucha sangre. Agora sabed que el caballero de la devisa era tal que en ninguna parte no se hallaría mejor. A esta hora dio el infante tal golpe al caballero por encima de un hombro, que el brazo con parte del costado le echó en el suelo. Luego el caballero de la devisa cayó muerto.

El infante hincó los hinojos en el suelo y dio muchas gracias a Dios por la victoria que le había dado. Bridamor llegó a su señor, y miróle algunas heridas que tenía, y vio que no eran de peligro, y se las apretó lo mejor que pudo. Esto hecho, el infante miró a donde el rey de la Diserta estaba; y el pilar que sostenía el arca de cristal en que estaba encantado, vio que era muy alto, y no sabía qué manera tener para lo alcanzar. Estando de la manera que habéis oído, mirando cómo al rey podría de allí alcanzar, vio venir cuatro grifos a gran priesa volando, y todos cuatro tomaron el

harmed him. And taking his shield and with his sword held high, he went to lunge at the knight with all his strength. And his luck was so bad that the blow fell on the arm bearing the knight's shield. And because the blow was such, and also because the knight's shield was one of the best in the world, the prince's sword broke in two. As the knight saw him without a sword, he said in a loud voice, "Knight, you will be my prisoner and since I have seen you are a noble knight, I will spare your life. And this I do so that you will remain in this valley forever."

"It would pain the queen of Cantaria greatly," said the prince, "if I were to make such an agreement with you."

"Well, then, what do you plan to do with yourself, as you are now in my power?"

"I will tell you," said the prince. And so saying, he picked up what was left of his sword and threw it at the knight with such force that when it hit him in the head it twisted his helmet, and before the knight had a chance to wound the prince, who was one of the nimblest men the world had ever seen, he rushed at him and grabbed the sword from his hand. And as it was in his power, he began to lunge at him again and again; and he, having seen that he had lost his sword, put his hand to a mace that he had hanging by a chain at his side, and with it he began to swing at the prince. But his efforts did him no good, as all his blows fell on thin air, because the agility of the prince was such that a blow never met its target. And he struck at him with such blows that he broke his armor and his flesh, such that the knight was by now most weak, and nearly broken, and had lost much blood. Now you must know that the knight of the shrine was such that nowhere was a finer one to be found. At this moment the prince

arca con sus picos, y la pusieron en el valle, y luego se fueron volando por el mismo camino que habían venido.

Como el infante Luzescanio esto vio, fue extrañamente ledo. Luego abrió el arca, y vio al rey que estaba sin ningún sentido, que más parecía muerto que vivo. El infante fue muy triste de tal lo ver, y comenzólo a mover a una y otra parte, pero no le aprovechó nada. En ver esto fue la su tristeza doblada. Y no sabiendo qué hacer de sí, vio venir un ave blanca volando, y en el pico traía una redoma; y anduvo una pieza revolando encima del rey, y a la fin soltó la redoma. Y como de lo alto cayó fue quebrada encima del rey; así como el agua que en la redoma traía al rey tocó, luego fue libre de todos los encantamentos, y muy presto se levantó. Y como al infante viese armado, y por algunas partes las armas tintas de sangre, fue muy espantado, y díjole, —Señor caballero, muy gran merced recibiría si me dijésedes cuál ventura os trujo a este valle.

—Trújome el deseo de veros libre, — dijo el infante, —de los encantamentos en que estábades.

—Según me semeja, —dijo el rey, — ¿vos sois el que me habéis sacado de este captiverio en que estaba?

—Ha sido Dios, —dijo el infante, — que es el que hace mercedes a todo el mundo. Y tal es la que a mí me ha hecho, pues me hizo tan bien andante que mis fuerzas bastasen a haceros este pequeño servicio.

Como el rey esto oyó, fuese a humillar ante el infante, diciéndole, —Señor caballero, dadme vuestras manos, pues sois el que después de Dios me sacó del poder de Darsia la encantadora, que siete años ha que en este valle me tiene de la manera que visto habéis.

El infante se humilló ante el rey, y tomándole por las manos entrambos se

gave the knight such a blow to the shoulder that his arm and part of his side fell to the ground. Then the knight of the shrine fell dead.

The prince fell to his knees and gave many thanks to God for the victory He had given him. Bridamor came to his lord and looked at the wounds that he had and saw they were not grave, and he bound them the best he could. That done, the prince looked to where the king of Diserta was, and he saw that the pillar that held the coffin of crystal wherein he lay bewitched was most high, and he knew not how to go about reaching it. And in that state which you have just heard described, wondering how he would be able to reach the king so high up, he saw four griffins approach, flying at great speed, and all four picked up the coffin with their beaks and set it down in the valley, and then they flew back the way they had come.

When Prince Luzescanio saw this, he was amazed and cheered. Then he opened the coffin and gazed upon the king, who, giving no signs of life, seemed more dead than alive. The prince was most sad to see him thus, and he began to move this part and that, but it was for naught. Seeing this his sadness doubled. And not knowing what to do by himself, he saw a white bird come flying, and in its beak it carried a vial. And as it fell from a height, it broke on the king; and as the water in the vial touched the king he was freed from all spells, and very soon he got to his feet. And when he saw the armed prince with bloodstained armor, he was much amazed and said, "Sir Knight, I would be most grateful if you were to tell me what fortune has brought you to this valley."

"The wish to see you free from the spells cast on you," said the prince, "brought me here."

levantaron, y haciéndose gran acatamiento, se fueron a una hermosa fuente, y allí se
asentaron, y el infante se desarmó las manos y la cabeza. El rey fue muy maravillado
de ver la su gran hermosura, y díjole, —Mi
buen señor, mucho sería alegre si me dijésedes quién sois.

—Quien quier que yo sea, —dijo el infante, —deseo más vuestro servicio que
cuántos nacieron. Y lo demás que mi señor
queréis saber, yo soy un caballero andante,
que poco tiempo ha que recibí orden de caballería, y por no haber hecho cosa alguna
en que honra ganase, no digo quién soy;
por tanto la vuestra merced me perdone.

Como el rey vio que se quería encubrir,
no le preguntó más. El infante se lavó las
manos y el rostro del sudor y del polvo que
había cogido. Allí les dio Bridamor de comer de lo que llevaba para su señor. Acabada que fue la comida, el rey dijo al infante,
—Yo os quiero dar cuenta de mi vida, que
me semeja que es mucha razón, pues que la
libertad me distes. —El infante se lo agradeció mucho. El rey le dijo, —Vos, mi señor, sabréis que estando yo en una mi villa
que en el reino de la Diserta está, a mí me
vinieron embajadores del rey Abimar, y la
embajada que me traían era que el rey me
rogaba que yo tuviese por bien de tomar a
una sola hija que tenía por mujer, que me
daría grandes haberes con ella, y después
de sus días que el reino de Abimar sería
mío. Oída la embajada del rey, yo fui algo
triste, por no le dar mala respuesta, que yo
no tenía voluntad de me casar con su hija,
por cuanto ella tiene más parte de virtudes
que de hermosura. Yo mandé honrar mucho los embajadores, y al tercero día les
dije, —Caballeros, vosotros os podéis volver, y diréis al rey vuestro señor que yo me
tuviera por contento en tomar a la princesa
su hija por mujer, mas que por agora yo
no tengo voluntad de me casar, que la su

"It would appear to me," said the king,
"that you are he who has freed me from
my captivity?"

"It was God," said the prince, "as it is He
who provides His favors for all. And thus it
is that He has done for me, as He made me
so fortunate that my strength was sufficient
to do for you this small service."

When the king heard this, he fell to his
knees before the prince, saying to him, "Sir
Knight, give me your hands, as it is you
who, after God, freed me from the power
of the witch Darsia, who for seven years
has held me in this valley as you have
seen."

The prince got to his knees before the
king, and taking one another's hands they
rose, and with great reverence they went to
a lovely fountain, and there they sat, and
the prince removed the armor from his
hands and head. And the king was most
amazed to see his great beauty, and said to
him, "My good sir, I would be most pleased
if you were to tell me who you are."

"It matters little who I am," said the
prince. "I wish more than any man born to
be of service to you. And as for the rest that
my lord wishes to know, I am a knight errant who not long ago received the order
of knighthood, and as I have done nothing
whatsoever to deserve that honor, I will
not say who I am; for that I ask your grace
to forgive me."

As the king saw that he wished to reveal
no more, he refrained from asking. The
prince washed from his hands and his face
the sweat and the dust that had collected
there. Then Bridamor gave them what he
had brought his lord to eat. When the meal
was over, the king said to the prince, "I
wish to tell you about my life, and that
seems right to me, as you have given me
freedom." The prince thanked him profusely. The king said to him, "You, my lord,

merced me perdone.— Cuando los embajadores oyeron la mi respuesta, fueron muy
tristes, y luego se partieron para el reino de
Abimar. Y como al rey su señor dieron la
mi respuesta, él fue muy airado contra mí,
y túvose por escarnido, y juró de jamás ser
alegre, hasta tomar de mí la enmienda. Y
no lo olvidando, en el su reino había una
dueña encantadora, que había nombre
Darsia; a esta envió a llamar la princesa, y
con muchas lágrimas le rogó que con el su
gran saber la diese enmienda de mí, que
tan malamente la había escarnido en no
me querer casar con ella. La encantadora le
prometió de le dar tal venganza, que ella y
el rey fuesen bien contentos. La princesa se
lo agradeció mucho.

—Sabed mi señor, que estando yo un
día en mi lecho en el mi palacio demandé
de vestir a mis caballeros: y así como fui
vestido, estando hablando con ellos súbitamente el mi palacio comenzó a temblar,
de tal manera que todos cuantos en el estábamos pensamos ser muertos, y ninguno
tuvo poder para salir dél, sino todos caí-
mos en el suelo sin sentido. Y entre todos
me tomaron a mí, y me pusieron a donde
vistes, sin que sintiese cosa alguna, hasta la
hora en que estoy.

Mucho fue el infante espantado de oír
tal aventura, y dijo, —Malditos sean los
encantamentos que tanto mal hacen en el
mundo. Ya mi señor sois vos libre del poder de esa encantadora.

—Muchas gracias doy yo a Dios, y a
vos mi buen señor, que de las sus manos
me librastes.

Estando hablando en esto y en otras cosas que placer les daba, vieron entrar en el
valle gran compaña de caballeros. El rey y
el infante estuvieron aguardando por ver
qué cosa era. Y cuando más cerca fueron, el
infante los conoció, que eran de la reina de
Cantaria. Como los caballeros vieron al rey

will know that when I was in my castle in
the kingdom of Diserta, ambassadors
from King Abimar came to me, and the
message they brought me was that the
king begged me to agree to take his only
daughter for a wife, that he would give me
a great fortune with her, and that after his
days were spent the kingdom of Abimar
would be mine. Having heard the king's
message I was somewhat sad, because I did
not want to give a negative reply, that I did
not wish to marry his daughter, as she had
more virtue than beauty. I ordered that the
ambassadors be given every comfort, and
on the third day I said to them, 'Gentlemen, you may return and say to the king
your lord that I would be very happy to
take the princess his daughter as my wife,
but at the moment I have no wish to marry, and I beg his highness forgive me.'
When the ambassadors heard my response
they were most sad, and then they left for
the kingdom of Abimar. And when they
gave the king their lord my reply, he was
most displeased with me, and he took it
for an insult, and he swore he would not
be content until he forced me to make
amends. And not forgetting this, in his
kingdom there was an enchantress, who
was called Darsia; the princess summoned
her, and with many tears begged her to use
her great learning to take revenge on me,
who had so badly insulted her in not wishing to marry her. The enchantress promised she would have her revenge, that she
and the king would be well pleased. The
princess thanked her profusely.

"Know, good sir, that one day lying in
bed in my palace I ordered my knights to
help me dress. And when I was dressed
and talking with them, suddenly my palace
began to tremble so that all of us who were
inside thought we were about to die, and
no one had the strength to leave. Instead

y al infante demasiadamente fueron ledos. Y luego se apearon, y besaron las manos al rey y al infante. Un caballero le dijo, —La reina de Cantaria mi señora os manda saludar muchas veces, y que ella ha sabido como el rey de la Diserta es ya libre. Pide os por merced y al rey así mismo, pues que el su reino de Cantaria estaba más cerca del valle que otro, que tuviesen por bien de recebir en su tierra el servicio que ella les deseaba hacer. Aquí señor traemos caballos bien guarnidos para el rey y para la vuestra merced, si menester los hubiese.

El infante se volvió al rey, y le dijo, —¿Qué es lo que vuestra alteza responde a la reina?

—Vos mi buen señor, pues yo estoy en el vuestro poder, haced lo que por bien tuviésedes.

El infante dijo, —Caballeros, diréis a la reina vuestra señora que el rey de la Diserta y yo queremos recebir en su tierra aquellas mercedes que sin haberle hecho ningún servicio nos quiere hacer. Dejadnos los caballos que la reina nos envía, por que dellos tenemos necesidad, que el rey está sin caballo, y a mí me mataron el mío. Hacerse ha lo que la vuestra merced manda.

Luego se partieron dos caballeros a gran priesa para que la reina supiese cómo el rey y el infante iban. Los otros se quedaron para los acompañar. Aquella noche todos albergaron en el Valle Hermoso, porque ya era tarde. Venida que fue la mañana, el infante se armó las manos y la cabeza, que desarmado tenía, y subiendo en sus caballos, con mucho placer salieron del Valle Hermoso. Y tomaron su camino para el reino de Cantaria, y en todo él no les avino cosa en que se detuviesen.

we all fell to the ground unconscious. And they took me alone, and placed me where you found me, though I felt nothing until now."

The prince was amazed to hear of the adventure and said, "Damned be the sorcery that has brought so much evil to the world. But now, my lord, you are free of the power of that enchantress."

"I give great thanks to God, and to you, my good sir, who freed me from her hands."

As they were enjoying their conversation on this and other matters, they saw a large company of knights enter the valley. The king and the prince waited to see what this was all about. And as they drew nearer, the prince recognized them as coming from the queen of Cantaria. When the knights saw the king and the prince they were overwhelmed with joy. Then they dismounted and kissed the hands of the king and the prince. One knight said to him, "My lady, the queen of Cantaria, sends warm greetings and that she has received word that the king of Diserta is now free. She asks your leave and that of the king that since her kingdom of Cantaria is closer than any other to the valley, that you accept in her land the service she wishes to provide. We have brought, sir, horses well-equipped for the king and for your grace, if you have need of them."

The prince turned to the king and said, "How would your highness respond to the queen?"

"It is your decision, my good sir, as I am in your debt. Do as you wish."

The prince said, "Gentlemen, tell our lady the queen that the king of Diserta and I wish to receive in her land those favors that, though we have done her no service, she wishes to grant us. Leave with us the horses the queen has sent, as we have need

of them, since the king is without a mount and mine was killed. Do what your highness orders."

The two knights left with great haste to tell the queen that the king and the prince were on their way. The rest remained to accompany them. That night they all took shelter in the Beautiful Valley, as it was already late. When morning came, the prince put on his gauntlets and his helmet, which he had removed; and, mounting their horses, they left the Beautiful Valley in high spirits. And they took the road to the kingdom of Cantaria, and along the way nothing occurred to detain them.

Capítulo xlv

De cómo el infante y el rey de la Diserta llegaron a la ciudad de Olimpa, a donde la reina a la sazón estaba, y de lo que después que a Olimpa llegaron les sucedió.

Un día a hora de vísperas llegaron una milla de la ciudad de Olimpa a donde la reina estaba, y vieron salir della los caballeros y altos hombres que a la sazón en la corte estaban. Y como al rey y al infante llegaron, todos se apearon por besar las manos al rey y al infante. El rey los habló muy cortésmente, como aquél que muy mesurado era. El infante así mismo holgó mucho con la su vista. Y así se fueron todos a la ciudad, los caballeros muy contentos de ver la buena apostura del rey.

Como en el palacio fueron, la reina salió a recebillos hasta la puerta de la sala. Ella venía ricamente guarnida, y eran tan ricas las vestiduras que traía que acrecentaban mucho en la su hermosura. Sus hermosos cabellos traía cogidos en una red de oro sembrada de piedras de gran valor. Traía encima de la red una rica corona. Como a la puerta de la sala llegó, el rey de la Diserta fue muy espantado de la su gran

Chapter xlv

Of how the prince and the king of Diserta came to the city of Olimpa, where the queen then was, and of what happened to them after arriving at Olimpa.

One day at vespers they were within a mile from where the queen was in the city of Olimpa, and they watched the approach of the knights and noble lords who were already at court. And when they neared the king and the prince they all dismounted to kiss the hands of the king and the prince. The king spoke most courteously to them, as he was a man of measured words. The prince, for his part, was greatly pleased with this sight. And then they all went into the city, the knights well pleased to see the fine bearing of the king.

When they were within the palace, the queen came to the door leading to the hall in order to receive them. She was richly clothed, and the garments she wore were so sumptuous that they increased her beauty greatly. Her lovely hair was arranged in a gold net adorned with priceless gems. When he reached the door of the hall, the king of Diserta was most

hermosura, y parecíale no haber visto en su vida otra que más hermosa que la reina fuese. Él se humilló ante ella, y por fuerza le tomó las manos, y se las besó.

La reina le hizo grande acatamiento, y hablóle como aquella que era la más entendida que en aquellas partes había. Acabado que hubo de hablar al rey, llegó el infante, y humillándose ante ella, le quiso besar las manos. La reina las tiró afuera, y le dijo paso, que nadie lo oyó, —Mi señor, no tenía yo menos esperanza de la vuestra gran bondad, sino que habíades de hacer mi corazón alegre.

El infante le tornó a humillar; y así se fueron a asentar. La reina rogó mucho al infante que le dijese cómo había librado al rey, que holgaría de lo oír. El infante hizo su mandado, y se lo contó todo como lo habéis oído. Y así mismo le contó cómo y por qué el rey había sido encantado. Mucho fue la reina espantada de lo oír. En esto y en otras cosas estuvieron hablando, hasta que fue hora de cenar, que los aparadores y mesas fueron puestas. Fueron muy bien servidos de muchos y muy preciados manjares.

Acabada que fue la cena, y alzadas las tablas, la fiesta se comenzó de muchas doncellas y caballeros. En todo este tiempo nunca el rey de la Diserta quitó los ojos de la reina, que muy pagada estaba de ver la su hermosura. La fiesta duró muy poco por amor del infante. La reina dijo al rey que se fuese a dormir, que ya era hora, porque ella quería estar a ver curar el infante. El rey se levantó, y haciéndole aquel acatamiento que a su real persona le convenía, obedeció su mandado, y fue llevado a un aposento que la reina había mandado aparejar, y con él fueron siete caballeros para le servir.

La reina se fue al aposento del infante. Ya los maestros eran venidos (que aunque había muchos días que habían partido de

amazed by her great beauty, and it seemed to him that never in his life had he seen another more beautiful than the queen. He knelt before her and insisted upon taking her hands and kissing them.

The queen bowed to him deeply and spoke to him like the wisest woman in the kingdom. When she finished speaking to the king, the prince went to her, and, kneeling before her, he attempted to kiss her hands. The queen pulled them away and said softly to him, so that no one might hear, "My lord, I had no little hope of your great goodness that you would make my heart happy."

The prince knelt again and then went to sit down. The queen begged the prince to recount how he had freed the king, for it would please her to hear. The prince did as he was ordered, telling all that you have heard. And at the same time, he recounted how and why a spell had been cast upon the king. The queen was truly amazed to hear it. On this and other matters they conversed until it was time for supper and the sideboards and tables were set. They were well served with many rare delicacies.

When the supper was over and the tables cleared, the celebration began, with many maidens and knights. During the entire time the king of Diserta never once took his eyes from the queen, so well pleased was he in gazing on her beauty. Out of devotion for the prince, the celebration lasted only a short time. The queen told the king to go to bed, that it was now time, because she wanted to see to the prince's wounds. The king rose, and making that reverence due her royal personage, obeyed her command and was taken to a chamber that the queen had ordered made ready, and with him seven knights went to wait upon him.

la Devisa del Valle, aun no estaba bien gua-
rido de las llagas que tenía) y luego fue cu-
rado. Los maestros le dijeron que bien podía caminar si dello tuviese necesidad.
Como el infante oyó estas nuevas, fue muy
ledo, por se detener poco tiempo en Cantaria, que no era otro pensamiento el suyo
sino en servir a su señora Bellaestela, y luego entrar en la demanda de sus padres, y
jamás della salir, hasta cumplir lo que prometido había. La reina se despidió del infante, y se fue a su aposento.

Venido que fue otro día, todos se levantaron. La reina se vistió muy más ricamente que el día pasado; y así se estuvo en su
cámara hasta que fue hora de oír misa. El
rey de la Diserta se levantó luego que fue el
día venido, que en toda la noche no pudo
reposar, pensando en la gran hermosura
de la reina; y llamábase bien andante si la
reina con él quisiese casar. Y con estos pensamientos se fue a la cámara del infante
para le rogar que de su parte hablase a la
reina. Cuando el infante lo vio, fue muy espantado de lo ver tan de mañana, y díjole,
—Mi señor, ¿qué venida es ésta? ¿Cómo
vuestra alteza madrugó tanto?

—Mi buen señor, yo soy venido ante
vos para quejarme de la vuestra merced, y
juntamente pediros misericordia, pues
creo yo que en la vuestra mano está dar el
remedio para mi vida, que tan cercana está
a la muerte. Y pues vos mi señor me sacas-
tes del poder de Darsia, que allí me tenía
sin que yo sintiese mal ni bien, habéisme
puesto en poder de la reina de Cantaria a
donde siento tales cuitas y mortales deseos
que mis días fueran muy pocas si vos mi
señor no os doléis de mí.

Como el infante oyó así hablar al rey,
holgóse mucho, porque ya él sabía la voluntad de la reina. Con alegre semblante
respondió al rey diciéndole, —Mi señor,
pues que yo he sido la causa de vuestro

The queen went to the prince's chamber. The physicians had arrived (though it
was many days since they had left the
shrine of the valley, his wounds had yet to
be properly treated), and then he was
cured. The physicians said that he might
go if it were necessary. When the prince
heard this news, he was most pleased at
having to spend little time in Cantaria, for
his wish was none other than to serve his
lady Bellaestela, and to enter in the demand regarding her parents, and never desist until he had fulfilled that promise. The
queen took her leave of the prince and
went to her chamber.

They all rose at dawn the following day.
The queen dressed in robes more sumptuous than the day before, and she remained
thus in her chamber until it was time to
hear mass. The king of Diserta arose before dawn, as he could not rest the entire
night thinking of the queen's great beauty;
and he would have called himself fortunate were the queen to agree to marry
him. And with these thoughts he went to
the prince's chamber to beg that he speak
to the queen on his behalf. When the
prince saw him, he was much surprised at
seeing him so early in the morning and
said to him, "My lord, why have you come?
Why has your highness arisen so early?"

"My good sir, I have come before you
to plead for your help and also to beg your
mercy, as I believe that in your hands is the
solution for my life, so near as it is to
death. And you, my lord, who freed me
from the power of Darsia, who had me
there feeling neither good nor ill, have
now put me in the power of the queen of
Cantaria, where I feel such anxiety and
mortal desires that my days will be numbered if you, my good sir, do not take pity
on me."

When the prince heard the king speak

mal, de aquí me ofrezco a daros la medicina que vuestro corazón desea. Pero con tal condición, que la reina sea vuestra mujer.

—En eso me hará Dios a mí el más bienandante de cuantos nacieron en el mundo.

—Pues que así es, —dijo el infante, —la vuestra merced se vaya a su aposento, que yo voy luego a hablar a la reina.

El rey dio muchas gracias al infante por la buena voluntad que en él halló. Y así se despidió dél, y se fue a su cámara. El infante se vistió luego en yéndose el rey, y fuese al aposento de la reina, y hallóla tan hermosa y ricamente guarnida, como ya oísteis. Cuando la reina lo vio, díjole, —Señor Luzescanio, ¿qué venida es la vuestra a tal hora?

—Mi señora, —dijo el infante, —el que ha de pedir mercedes es razón que madrugue.

—Ya pluguiese a Dios, —dijo la reina, —que vos tuviésedes de mí necesidad, y fuese tal que yo os pudiese pagar algo de lo mucho que debo.

—Pues que en la vuestra merced hallo tan buena voluntad para me hacer mercedes, luego las quiero pedir. —Y diciendo esto, se asentó junto a la reina, y díjole todo cuanto con el rey había pasado. Como ella lo oyó fue extraño el placer que sintió. Y sin responder al infante, hincó los hinojos en el suelo, y alzando las manos al cielo, dio muchas gracias a Dios por las mercedes que le hacía de traerle tan buen fin los sus deseos.

Esto hecho, dijo al infante, —Mi señor, ya vos sabéis la mi voluntad, que ha mucho tiempo que no he otro deseo sino haber por marido al rey de la Diserta. Yo señor os ruego mucho que vos le habléis como cosa vuestra propia, y en lo demás lo hagáis todo como mandásedes.

El infante besó las manos a la reina, y se

thus he was most pleased, for he already knew the will of the queen. With a joyful countenance he responded to the king, saying, "My lord, as I have been the cause of your ills, in this instant I offer to provide the medicine your heart desires. But only on the condition that the queen become your wife."

"In so doing will God make of me the most fortunate man ever born into this world."

"Then so be it," said the prince, "now return, your majesty, to your chamber; and I will speak to the queen."

The king gave the prince many thanks for the goodwill he had shown. The prince dressed after the king had gone and went to the queen's chamber and found her as beautiful and richly dressed as you have already heard. When the queen saw him she said, "Sir Luzescanio, for what purpose have you come to see me at this hour?"

"My lady," said the prince, "when one needs to ask a favor, there is reason to rise early."

"And please God," said the queen, "that you had need of me, and that matters were such that I could repay you some of all I owe you."

"Given that I find such goodwill in your majesty to do me favors, then I will ask." And thus saying, he sat down next to the queen and told her all that had happened with the king. When she heard this she felt a strange pleasure. And without replying to the prince, she got to her knees, and raising her hands to the heavens gave many thanks to God for the favors he had brought to her by bringing a fine end to her wishes.

That done, she said to the prince, "My lord, you know my will already, that since long past I have desired nothing other than that the king of Diserta be my

fue al aposento del rey; y hallólo, que solo se andaba paseando. Como el rey lo vio venir, luego lo salió a recebir, diciéndole, — Mi señor, ¿qué nuevas me traéis de la reina mi señora?

El infante le abrazó, y le dijo, — Mi señor, siendo vos quien sois no os las puedo traer sino como las deseáis. Yo he trabajado tanto con la reina hasta que me prometió de hacer lo que todos deseamos. Y a mí me parece que sería bien que luego se hagan los desposorios.

El rey le dijo, —Si vos, mi señor, eso hacéis, de aquí me ofrezco de ser vuestro vasallo.

—Pues yo me vuelvo a la reina para lo concertar.— Y así se despidió del rey, y se fue al aposento de la reina, y díjole lo que con el rey dejaba concertado. La reina envió luego a llamar a todos los altos hombres de su corte. Y venidos que fueron, les contó todo lo que estaba concertado. Y demás desto les dijo que ella no quería tomar marido sino con voluntad de los de su reino. Todos respondieron que eran muy contentos de tomar al rey por señor, que su persona y gran señorío merecía mucho. La reina les respondió, —Pues que así es, hágase, y todo sea para servicio de Dios.

El infante dijo a la reina que se saliese la su merced a la sala, que ya el rey estaba aguardando. La reina se levantó, tomándola de brazo el infante Luzescanio, y un arzobispo que su tío era. Y así se salieron de la sala.

Y como el rey la vio, hincó los hinojos ante ella. La reina le hizo grande acatamiento. Y luego fueron desposados por mano de aquel arzobispo. Hechos que fueron los desposorios, en el palacio y en la ciudad se hicieron grandes alegrías y fiestas. La reina estaba muy contenta, y el rey así mismo.

Pasados que fueron ocho días después

husband. I, sir, beg that you speak to him of this as though it were your own idea, and as for the rest, that you do as he commands."

The prince kissed the queen's hands and went to the king's chamber, and he found him there alone walking to and fro. When the king saw him coming he went to greet him, saying, "My lord, what news do you bring me of my lady the queen?"

And the prince embraced him and said, "My lord, because you are who you are I can do none else than bring you the news you desire. I have entreated the queen so heartily on your behalf that she has promised to do that which we all desire. And it seems to me that it would be well that the betrothal be announced."

The king said to him, "If you, my lord, do this, from this moment I offer myself as your vassal."

"Then I will return to the queen to arrange it." And so he took his leave of the king and went to the queen's chamber and told her what he had just arranged with the king. The queen then summoned all the noble lords of her court. And when they had come, she told them what had been arranged. And in addition to this she told them that she had no wish to take a husband unless it were the will of her kingdom. They all replied that they were most pleased to have the king as their lord, for his person and his great majesty were much valued. The queen replied, "Then so be it, let it be done, and may all we do be in the service of God."

The prince said to the queen that her highness should go to the hall, for the king was already there awaiting her. The queen rose, taking Prince Luzescanio's arm and that of an archbishop who was her uncle. And thus they repaired to the hall.

And when the king saw her he fell to his

de los desposorios, el infante pidió licencia al rey y a la reina para se ir a la corte del rey de Romania. A ellos les pesó mucho por la su partida, pero hubiéronse de sufrir, pues que aquélla era su voluntad. El infante les dijo que luego otro día quería partir, y así lo hizo. Venida que fue la mañana, luego se armó de todas sus armas, y así se fue a la cámara del rey y de la reina, y despidióse dellos, y tomó su camino para el reino de Romania a donde le dejaremos hasta su tiempo.

knees before her. The queen bowed deeply before him. Then they were betrothed by the hand of the archbishop. When the betrothal had been made, there was much merrymaking and feasting in the palace and in the city. The queen was most pleased, and the king as well.

Eight days after the betrothal the prince asked leave to go to the court of the king of Romania. They were most saddened at his departure, but they could do no other than suffer this, for such was his will. The prince told them he wished to leave the following day, and so he did. When morning came he dressed in full armor, and thus he went to the chamber of the king and queen and bade them farewell and set out on the road to the kingdom of Romania, where we will leave him for the time being.

(Translated by Mary Ellen Fieweger)

Sor María de la Antigua

It is hard to imagine a life more innocent of the world than Sor María de la Antigua's. Cloistered before she was a year old, she dedicated her entire life to the demands of her religious community, first as a lay sister serving the nuns, and then as a nun herself, serving God. The child of servants, taken in by the sisters, Sor María de la Antigua must have learned humility and obedience early. Waiting on the nuns as a lay sister meant rising above her parents' station, and being able to profess as a nun was a crowning achievement.

Ana Rodríguez, born in Cádiz, and Baltazar Rodríguez, from the Portuguese town of Elvas, were living in Cazalla de la Sierra, near Seville, when their daughter María was born. She was baptized there on November 25, 1566, but a few months later the family moved to Utrera. The Rodríguez couple needed work, and in Utrera they found servant positions in the convent of Nuestra Señora de la Antigua, where the prioress took over the task of raising María. Once in the nun's care, the little girl would have learned her catechism and how to read and write.

At the age of thirteen, after living for six years in the care of the prioress's nephew and niece in Seville, María entered the convent of the Clarisas de Marchena, as a lay sister in the Franciscan order of St. Clair. Her parents certainly would have lacked the dowry necessary for profession. She kept the white veil of a lay sister until she was thirty-seven years old, when she moved to the convent of Discalced Sisters of Mercy of Lora, where she was able to profess. She remained there until her death in 1617, at the age of fifty-one.

In the many years she was in the convent, Sor María de la Antigua documented her religious experiences and her moral meditations in verse and prose. According to her contemporary, Father Pedro de San Cecilio, Sor María filled "more than thirteen hundred notebooks of high and substantial doctrine, dictated by God."[1] Seventy-one years after her death, Sor María's devotional writings were edited and published in Seville under the title *Desengaño de religiosos, y de almas que tratan de virtud* (Admonition of religious, and of souls that treat of virtue). The book, in prose, relates her visions of Jesus, the Virgin, and various saints, and contains forty-one poems interspersed throughout the text. This volume, of more than eight hundred pages, was published for the first time in 1678, and was reissued several times, including twice in Barcelona in 1697 and 1720. A fragment of the manuscript, copied in the second half

of the seventeenth century, contains fifty-two poems, twenty-four of which are different from those appearing in the 1678 edition.

Sor María de la Antigua lived isolated from the artificial cultural world of her era, with its system of patronage and its courtly games, but she did not lack for poetic models. She knew the metrical forms and the commonplace phrases of devotional poetry. Her rhyme and meter are traditional, and her language is similar to that of the mystics. God is lover, husband, sovereign goodness; the body is a dark prison; divine love is a fire of burning flames. She describes God's absence as the cruel toying of a lover, and mystic union in sexual terms. The strength of her poems lies in their passion. The crucifixion becomes present and personal in her poetry, and her pain when she cannot achieve union with God is intimate and striking.

Fray Andrés de San Agustín, Chronicler General of the Discalced Order of Our Lady of Mercy of the Redeemed Captives, the order in which Sor María spent the last fourteen years of her life, wrote the nun's spiritual biography. This *Vida ejemplar* (Exemplary life) was probably published at approximately the same time as *Desengaño de religiosos*, because it was approved by the censor in Cádiz just a year before Sor María's writings received their approval in Seville. The labor invested by the order in gathering and publishing Sor María's writing and in composing her hagiography, and the almost simultaneous publication of these two books in two different cities, suggest that the Mercedarians were trying to get Sor María beatified.

Sor María's upbringing in the restricted atmosphere of the convent channeled her considerable emotional and spiritual energy into orthodox religion, where it found its outlet in the search for an intimate relationship with God that is expressed in her poetry. The church created not only the conditions that animated mystic experience but also the technology that assured the preservation of the poetry that gave voice to it. Sor María infused the received pattern of mysticism with her own spiritual experience and combined the available forms in her own manner. She succeeds in evoking in her readers what she herself experienced in her spiritual struggles and ecstasies.

1. "más de 1300 cuadernos de alta y sustancial doctrina, dictados por Dios," cited in Manuel Serrano y Sanz, *Apuntes para una biblioteca de escritoras españolas* (Madrid: Real Academia Española, 1903-5, repr. 1975), 1:42.

| *Poesías sacras* | *Sacred Poems* |

1
Canción

1
Song

Alma, que estando muerta
y en horrores de vicios sepultada,
Dios te llama y despierta
con una voz tan dulce y regalada;
¿Qué haces, que no escuchas
sus amorosos ecos? ¿Con quién luchas?
  ¿Qué miedos te combaten?
¿Qué temores te impiden? ¿Qué recelos
hay en ti que dilaten
el logro de tus ansias y desvelos?
Responde a quien te llama,
y no te hieles cuando Dios te inflama.
  Concede al ocio justo
la piadosa atención que está pidiendo,
y con intenso gusto
escucharás a un cisne que muriendo
entre las ansias suyas
se acuerda así de las miserias tuyas.
  —¡Pobre ovejuela! —dice—:
¿qué quieres, ignorante de tu daño
malograrte, infelice?
¿No ves que vas huyendo del rebaño
de mis mansos corderos,
a ser manjar de lobos carniceros?
  De ti te compadece;
ten lástima de ti, que vas perdida,
y si no te parece
que es muy grande tu culpa y tu caída,
mira, fiel, con cuidado,
verás lo que me cuesta tu pecado.
  Mira estas nobles sienes
coronadas de espinas rigurosas,
y si en tu pecho tienes
piedad, mira estas puntas dolorosas
que el cerebro me pasan
y el corazón y el alma me traspasan.
  Mira estos ojos bellos,
por tu culpa sangrientos y eclipsados,
y estos rubios cabellos,

Poor soul, while you are lying dead
there in your dreadful vices deep
    entombed,
God calls and bids you waken,
His honeyed voice so sweetly wooing
    you—
What are you doing, not to listen
to those loving tones? With whom are you
    fighting?
  What terrors battle with you;
what fears stand in your way? And what
    suspicions
within you can delay
fulfillment of your sleepless nights and
    longings?
Respond to Him who calls you—
do not grow icy when your God inflames
    you.
  Give to our righteous quiet
the worshipful attention He requires,
and then with deep delight
you'll listen to a swan whose dying song,
in all His fears and longings,
even so remembers your own sufferings.
  "Poor little lamb!" says He.
"Can you be wanting, heedless of your
    harms,
to come to ruin and misery?
Don't you see how you flee from the flock
of my obedient sheep
only to be a morsel for wolves' teeth?"
  He speaks compassionately,
"Have pity on yourself, for you are lost,
and if it does not seem
that yours is a very grievous fault and fall,
then look, believer, closely,
and see what your great sin is costing me.
  "See this noble brow
crowned severely with a ring of thorns,

en mi sangre teñidos y bañados;
verás al sol ponerse
y al oro entre la púrpura esconderse.

    Mira aquestas mejillas
que a esmaltes de carmín fondo de nieve
daban, ya amarillas,
sin su beldad hermosa cuanto breve;
mira, y verás mis labios
cárdenos lirios de sufrirte agravios.

    Mira estas manos santas
que ocupadas en tales ejercicios,
misericordias tantas
obraron, por hacerte beneficios,
y para tu remedio
las verás taladradas por el medio.

    Mira ésta de rubíes
puerta, que en mi costado generoso
con pompas carmesíes
abrió un golpe de lanza impetuoso,
verás con este hierro
pagar mi amor lo que debió tu yerro.

    Mira estos pies divinos
que, descalzos, por una y otra parte
tan diversos caminos
anduvieron gustosos a buscarte,
y en ellos castigada
verás tu liviandad desenfrenada.

    Mira, si acaso puedes
mirar sin compasión, todo llagado
mi cuerpo, y si no excedes
en fiereza al león y al tigre airado,
viendo no lo merezco,
te dolerá lo que por ti padezco.

    Mira que si en el verde
leño se hace tan cruel castigo,
es para que se acuerde
cuál será aquel que se hará contigo,
que, dada a tus placeres,
seca de gracia y de virtudes eres.[1]

1. San Lucas 23:31, "Porque si en el árbol verde
hacen estas cosas, ¿qué no se hará en el seco?"
Aquí Jesús, en el camino del Calvario, les habla
a las mujeres ("hijas de Jerusalén") de su pró-
xima crucifixión.

and if your breast can know
pity at all, then see these piercing wounds
fixed into my skull
and transfixing both my heart and soul.

    "See these lovely eyes
that through your fault are bloodied and
    obscured,
and golden locks of hair
all stained and wetted with my very blood;
you'll see the sun sunk low,
and see gold hidden in that purple flow.

    "See how these cheeks once formed
a snowy background to enamels bright
as crimson, now turned wan,
and quit of beauty great as it was brief;
look, and you'll see my lips—
lilies battered for you, bruised and livid.

    "See these blessed hands,
which, busy with such daily tasks and
    deeds
as miracles and signs
did labor for your good untiringly;
and for your soul's relief,
you'll see these same hands cruelly gouged
    and pierced.

    "See this door of rubies,
which was struck open in my generous
    side
with crimson ceremony
by a blow a reckless lance applied,
and you shall see how my love pays
the debt of all your errors, by that blade.

    "See these holy feet
that went about unshod both high and low
and were well pleased to seek
where you might be, on every sort of road;
in my feet you'll see punished
your errant and unruly wantonness.

    "Look, if you can indeed
behold my wounded body without pity—
if you do not exceed
the tiger in fury and the lion in frenzy,
seeing this all undeserved—
you'll ache with what I, for your sake,
    endured.

Pero si estás tan dura
que no te mortifican mis dolores,
y tu vana locura
los oídos le niega a mis clamores,
alma, repara y mira
que cuanta es mi piedad, tanta es mi ira.

"See how this punishment
falls upon wood that is both fresh and
    green,
and know that this is meant
to call to mind what your deserts must be;
for, to your pleasures given,
you're dry of grace and from all virtue
    riven.[1]
"But if you've grown so hard
my pains can cause you no mortification,
and so vainly mad
your ears are deafened to my lamentations,
then, soul, pause and consider
that as my mercy flows, so grows my ire."

(Translated by Amanda Powell)

2
Invocación al favor divino que puso la venerable madre Sor María de la Antigua a esta obra[2]

Socorredme, Señor mío,
si no queréis que perezca
entre dos mares metida
de quien soy y tus grandezas
hechas en la criatura
peor que el Cielo sustenta,
que cuanto mayores fueron,
tanto lo son las ofensas.
Mandáisme, mi Dios, que escriba
las soberanas larguezas
que habéis hecho con mi alma,
y cómo respondo a ellas.
Sépase mi ingratitud;
no tengas, alma, vergüenza;
pues sin vergüenza pecasteis,
decid que sois sinvergüenza.
Yo soy la ingrata que di
a mi Señor con las puertas
tantas veces en la cara,

2
Invocation to Divine Favor, Which the Venerable Mother Sor María de la Antigua Added to This Work[2]

Uphold and save me, oh my Lord,
if I am not to perish
between the devil and the blue sea
of my nature and your blessings
bestowed upon the lowliest
of creatures nursed by Heaven;
for as mighty as your blessings are,
so great are my offenses.
Please send me, God, the power to write
of royal, rich largesses
you have extended to my soul,
and then of my responses.
Let my ingratitude be known;
soul, there is no shame in it—

1. Luke 23:31, from Douay Bible: "For if in the green wood they do these things, what shall they do in the dry?" Here Jesus, on the road to Calvary, speaks of his approaching crucifixion to the women ("daughters of Jerusalem") following him.
2. The work referred to is *Desengaño de religiosos*.

2. Se refiere al *Desengaño de religiosos*.

como si Él algo perdiera.
Y habiéndole menester,
yo le traté de manera
que en no echarme en el Infierno
mostró su amor y grandeza.
Ojalá estuviera en él
primero que le ofendiera,
que no siento mis tormentos,
sino sólo sus ofensas.

since you commit sins shamelessly—
shamelessly to tell it.
I am the selfsame wretch who closed
so many doors, so often,
in the face of my dear Lord,
as if *He* were thus the loser.
And in my need of Him alone,
I treated Him so poorly
that His not casting me into Hell
shows His love and bounty to me.
Fain would I rather be in Hell
than in any way offend Him,
for I feel no torments done to me,
but only offenses done Him.

(Translated by Amanda Powell)

3
Romance

Después de una larga ausencia
que hizo el amante Dios,
dejando a su pastorcilla
sola y quemada del sol,
 después de haber padecido
de su ausencia el gran rigor
que es el martirio más fuerte,
con que lastima su amor,
 cuando tan sola ha quedado,
que no la calienta el sol,
aunque la abrasa y quema
de su ausencia el gran rigor,
 cuando mandó a los demonios,
pues licencia que les dio,
que la cerquen y la aprieten
poniéndola en tentación,
 cuando viéndose cercada,
no halla consolación,
porque la noche y el día
lo pasa en tribulación;
 en la oración está triste,
fuera della muy peor,
disimulando y sufriendo

3
Poem in Ballad Meter

After a weary absence, while
the lover, God, was gone,
leaving his faithful shepherdess
sunburned and alone;
 when the harshness of His absence
she had long undergone,
which is the cruelest martyrdom
by which He wounds her love;
 when she has been so much alone
the sun no longer warms her
(though the great harshness of His loss
sets fire to her and burns her);
 when the wicked demons had been
  sent—
for He gave them permission
to trap her and press close around
and set her sore temptations;
 when she finds herself besieged about
with comfort nowhere near,
because she passes day and night
in trial and in fear;
 when, at her prayers, her grief is great
and worse she's not praying,

por no mostrar su pasión,
   y suspirando no puede,
que parece que secó
la tristeza las corrientes
de su castísimo amor,
   y dando suelta al contrario,
solas pasiones dejó
de las culpas, que otro tiempo
la cuitada cometió.

   Y porque en todo merezca
la pena en que la dejó,
la fatigan y la aprietan
otras que no cometió:
   culpas de que estuvo libre
por sola su inclinación
como soberbio y envidia
y la pasión del rencor.

   Y si en aquesta tormenta
saliera un rayo de sol
de decir, no me han vencido,
no fuera tal confusión,
   todas juntas acometen,
sin saber el cómo o no,
revolviendo torbellinos
y aprietos de confusión;
   mas es tan grande el nublado
que oscurece el corazón,
que no parece una estrella
después de escondido el sol.

   Aunque viéndola con pena,
le da un rayo de su amor,
mas no por eso se quitan
las tinieblas del rigor.

   Entre sueños la fatiga,
despierta pasa dolor,
en la cama no hay reposo,
en la comida peor;
   de sus padres la desvía,
porque sabe su Señor
que ellos en cierta manera
son para el alma su Dios,
   porque ella reconoce
en ellos más que a su Dios,

as she goes to lengths to hide her woe
and not to show her suffering;
   she sighs that she can do no more,
for it seems that sorrow's blast
has dried the flowing currents
of her love most pure and chaste;
   and giving reign to all the rest,
more passions now beset her,
those of sins that in years past
the wretched girl committed.

   That she may thoroughly deserve
the woe in which He left her,
still more sins that were never hers
come to harass and vex her;
   sins of which she once was free
by her holy inclination,
like haughty pride and jealousy
and anger's fiery passion.

   And if, amidst this frightful storm,
a ray of light should shine
to say, "They have not vanquished me"—
would that be rash confusion?
   All passions now join the attack
with neither rhyme nor reason,
to gather in great whirlwind clouds
and press her with confusion;
   so mighty is the cloud that forms
her very heart is darkened,
and not one little star appears
after the sun has hidden.

   And though He sees how she is grieved
and sends a ray of love,
that brightest beam cannot relieve
the shadows of her hurt.

   Her sleep brings only weariness,
and waking is a curse;
she finds no rest upon her bed;
to eat is even worse.
   He severs her from kith and kin;
this is because her Lord
knows that in some way they can
be to her soul a God,
   and that she might see more in them

y con sus padres recibe
los efectos de su amor.

Estando en estas fatigas
el demonio me apretó;
era tiempo de tinieblas,
no me daba luz el sol.

Quedé deste golpe tal,
que me dolió, y con razón;
que tanto en paz como en guerra
es un mar el corazón.

Como si fuera pecado
la llaga deste dolor,
a su hermano de mi padre
me ha quitado mi Señor.

No fue suyo aqueste golpe,
mas pues Él lo permitió,
quéjome deste tormento
a mi amante y mi Señor.

Conozco que es traza suya,
que en castigo me envió
de la culpa del desvío
con que yo olvidé su amor.

Hágase tu voluntad:
no pido nada, Señor,
que no es justo que te pida
quien tantos tiempos huyó.

Trátame como a tu esclava,
que ser hija de tu amor
no merece la basura
que tanto tiempo ofendió.

Mas cuando más afligida
ya nace el sol del amor,
que es la misa la corriente
donde hallo mi Señor.

Ya pasaron los nublados,
ya me alegra el corazón,
ya me dices: "¿De qué temes?
¿no ves que tu Padre soy?"

¿El vestido que me diste,
si lo he manchado, Señor,
si ha habido defecto o culpa
sin que lo supiera yo?

than in her very God,
and from her kin think to receive
the effects of His dear love.

In just these wearisome travails,
the devil pressed me sorely;
it was a time of shadows,
the sun shed no light for me.

The blow that fell hurt me full sore,
for many a day, with reason:
because the heart, in peace or war,
is vast as any ocean.

And as if there were some sin
to be wounded by such pain,
my father's own dear brother
by my Lord was taken.

This blow did not fall from His hand,
and yet He gave His leave,
so I complain to my Lord and love
of my anguish and my grief.

I know this is Your own design
and sent to chastise me
for the sin of turning from His love
toward my family.

So may His holy will be done—
I ask for nothing, Lord,
for it is not right that she who fled
so often, should now plead.

Treat me as you would your slave;
mere rubbish can't deserve
after long offending you
to be daughter of your love.

But when I most must suffer,
love's sun begins to shine,
and the Mass is the flowing river
wherein my Lord I find.

And now the clouds are passed way,
and now my heart takes flight
to hear, "Am I not your Father?
Then how can you take fright?"

Have I stained the spotless garment
my Lord, that you once gave,
or committed sin or error

¿o si hice algún disgusto
en el vestido de amor,
o si en tela tan subida
alguna culpa cayó?

　　Viendo mi Bien su querida
dentro desta confusión,
dícele: "Querida mía,
abracémonos los dos."

　　No huyas, ni estés extraña,
que trazas son de mi amor
el huir, por acercarme
con más miel que no rigor.

　　Acabemos, regalada,
que esto lo permito Yo,
para ver cómo mi oveja
dé balidos al pastor.

　　No penséis que son olvidos,
mirad que os quiero bien Yo,
y que entre vuestros amantes
he sido el primero Yo.

　　Yo te acojo, hija, en ellos,
que estoy en tu corazón;
y así rogando a María,
salgo a recibirla Yo.

　　No te apartes, pastorcilla,
que tu compañero soy,
y para ver si eres buena,
un rato te dejo Yo.

　　¿Es posible que te extrañas,
hija de mi corazón,
acosada y perseguida
con la fuerza del azor?

　　Mira que en solos mis brazos
tu regalo se libró,
por lo cual tu Catalina
te lastima el corazón.

　　No busques otro consuelo,
que buen amigo te soy;
yo porque no te me vayas,
descubro a todos tu amor.

　　Con tantas cadenas presa
aseguro tu temor,
temiendo no te me vayas,
porque te tengo afición.

when I was unaware?
　　Have I made some transgression
against the garment of your love,
or let some error fall upon
such a priceless cloth?

　　Then my Beloved sees His bride
troubled by confusion,
and comforts her, "Now, dearest mine,
let us embrace in union.

　　"Flee not from me nor stand aloof,
for my flight was love's design
by which I could in time approach
like honey, all harshness aside.

　　"Let's hear no more, my treasured love;
for I let all this happen
that I might see my little sheep
come bleating to her Shepherd.

　　"Don't think that I forget you
for you see I love you true,
and that among all your lovers
I am the first to woo.

　　"I shelter you, daughter, among them,
and I live in your very heart;
and so, with a prayer to Mary,
I go out to take her arm.

　　"Don't leave me, little shepherdess,
for I am your betrothed,
and just to prove that you are good
I'll leave you some time alone.

　　"But could you possibly wander off,
oh daughter of my heart,
to be harried and beset
with the force of a mighty hawk?

　　"See how only in my arms
your treasure could be found,
which is why your Catherine
on your heart inflicts a wound.

　　"You must seek no other comfort,
for I am your true friend;
and that you may not leave me,
your love I shall reveal.

　　"By holding you in many chains
I make sure of your fear
in fear that you might leave me—

Pues si Yo soy tu regalo,
sepamos: ¿Por qué razón
así te extrañas y encoges
en faltándote mi amor?

for truly I hold you dear.
　"If I am your Lord and treasure,
now say, how can it be
that when you fail to feel my love,
then you withdraw from me?"

(Translated by Amanda Powell)

The Seventeenth Century

Leonor de la Cueva y Silva

Leonor de la Cueva y Silva wrote poems about nature and about love, about jealousy and about people she knew. Her voice is sometimes personal and sometimes well masked by a poetic persona. Born at the beginning of the seventeenth century in Medina del Campo to Doña Leonor de Silva and Don Agustín de Rúa, she was one of several children of this aristocratic family. Serrano y Sanz notes that one of her brothers was a cleric, Jerónimo de la Rúa, and two were military men: Antonio de la Cueva y Silva, lieutenant general of the Flemish cavalry, and Juan de la Rúa, who was posted in Seville. She also had a sister, whose name was María Jacinta de la Cueva. Leonor's uncle was the poet-dramatist Francisco de la Cueva, whose daughter Magdalena also wrote poetry. Leonor and her uncle were on close terms, dedicating poems to each other. When Francisco de la Cueva died in 1621, his niece wrote a sonnet in his memory.

The manuscript that contains Leonor de la Cueva's poetry was begun in 1592 (i.e., probably before Leonor de la Cueva was born, and certainly before she began to write). It contains a number of anonymous poems as well as a series of *romances*, some of which were written by the most famous poets of the era, among them Luis de Góngora, Lope de Vega, and Juan de Salinas. These are followed by a cluster of poems by Leonor's uncle, Francisco de la Cueva, and then by some ninety pages of poetry written by Leonor de la Cueva y Silva herself. This manuscript, produced over a long period of time, is written in various hands. Leonor de la Cueva's poems show that she utilized the wide variety of poetic forms popular in her day: *romances*, octaves, sonnets, *liras*, *endechas*, *sextinas*, *décimas*, *quintillas*, and *redondillas*.

Leonor de la Cueva composed poems to celebrate her brother's promotion and to lament the deaths of members of her own and the royal family. She wrote as well about love and nature, about such historical figures as Don Álvaro de Luna, and about her native city. Her love poetry is filled with the constancy of pastoral love and the deceptions of the love of courtiers. Leonor de la Cueva also wrote a play, *La firmeza en el ausencia* (Constancy in absence, n.d.).

The theme of this play is similar to that of María de Zayas's tale, *La perseguida, triunfante* (The persecuted, triumphant), in which a woman struggles to maintain her honor against a man who, despite his high rank, behaves like a scoundrel in his efforts

to take advantage of her sexually. In the works of both writers the woman is finally rewarded, but not before she undergoes considerable suffering.

Little is known of Leonor de la Cueva y Silva's life. No documents referring to her birth, marriage (if any), or death have come to light, but she probably died sometime after 1650.

<table>
<tr><td>

Poesías líricas

1
Soneto

Ni sé si muero ni si tengo vida,
ni estoy en mí, ni fuera puedo hallarme,
ni en tanto olvido cuido de buscarme,
que estoy de pena y de dolor vestida.

Dame pesar el verme aborrecida
y si me quieren, doy en disgustarme;
ninguna cosa puede contentarme,
todo me enfada y deja desabrida;

ni aborrezco, ni quiero, ni desamo;
ni desamo, ni quiero, ni aborrezco,
ni vivo confiada ni celosa;

lo que desprecio a un tiempo adoro
    y amo;
vario portento en condición parezco,
pues me cansa toda humana cosa.

</td><td>

Lyric Poems

1
Sonnet

I know not if I die or if I live,
I find myself not in myself, nor yet
    elsewhere,
nor myself in such oblivion do I trouble
    yet to seek,
for I wear the garb of pain, the dress of
    sorrow.
    It grieves me deep to see I am
        abhorred,
and vexed am I as well if truly loved,
with not a single thing am I content;
annoyed am I by all, and I am bored.
    I do not hate, nor love, nor cease to
        love,
nor cease to love, nor love, nor do I hate.
Jealousy I do not feel, nor do I, foolish,
    trust;
I despise at one same time the thing I love.
    In this state an aimless marvel do I
        seem
for I am sore weary of every human thing.

(Translated by Amy Kaminsky)

</td></tr>
<tr><td>

2
*Introduce un pretendiente, desesperado
de salir con su pretensión, que con
el favor de un poderoso la consiguió
muy presto*

Sin esperanza en su tormenta esquiva
un navegante, por el mar perdido,
de mil olas furiosas combatido,
rota la nave, al agua se derriba;

y aunque su furia del sentir le priva,
se anima contra el mar embravecido
y sale al puerto de una tabla asido,
muerta su pena ya, su gloria viva.

</td><td>

2
*In which a suitor is introduced who was
impatient to press his intentions and
did so very quickly, having gained the
favor of a powerful ally*

Bereft of hope, a sailor, in his tempest
rides against the current, lost at sea,
battled by a thousand furious waves
his broken ship demolished on the water;

    and though its fury stuns him,
he rallies 'gainst the raging sea,
and grasping at his plank is washed ashore,
his grief now dead, his glory now alive.

</td></tr>
</table>

¡Ay, débil pretensión, que ansina eres
navegante en un mar de mil temores!
Rota la nave, muerta la esperanza,
    al agua del olvido echarte quieres,
donde, asiendo la tabla de favores,
sales triunfante al puerto de bonanza.

Oh, paltry suitor, you are as
the wretched, sea-torn sailor
Ship broken, hope dead, you would fling
    yourself into oblivion's waters,
where, seizing fortune's wheel,
you moor triumphant at victory's port.

(Translated by Amy Kaminsky)

3
¿De qué sirve querer
un imposible?

Basta, amor, el rigor con que me has
    muerto;
cese un poco, rapaz, tu ardiente fuego,
pues ya del alma el señorío entrego
por los ojos no más a dueño cierto;
    y aunque es el bien que adoro tan
        incierto,
que no pasa de vista, a sentir llego
tu fuerza de manera, que me anego
en mil mares de amar sin hallar puerto.
    Riño unas veces a mis libres ojos,
mas por respeto de lo que han mirado,
detengo el castigarlos lo posible,
    y viendo que padezco estos enojos,
digo entre mí a mi pecho enamorado:
¿de qué sirve querer un imposible?

3
What good is it to want
what can't be had?

Cease, love, your murderous harshness;
damp your burning fire, thieving lad.
For now do I submit my soul's dominion,
through my eyes to its true lord alone.
    Though the object of my love is so
        uncertain,
that it is naught but vision, still do I come
to feel your power with such force
that in love's thousand seas I drown and
    find no port.
    I scold sometimes my own free eyes,
but with respect for what they've seen
I mete not out full punishment
    And seeing that I suffer from these
        tempers
I address my self to my enamored breast:
what good is it to want what can't be had?

(Translated by Amy Kaminsky)

4

Introduce una dama que se aficionó
a un galán que estaba prendado
a otra, y dándole a entender su amor,
le correspondió hasta que vino a
saber que quería a otra, y enojada
le hace este soneto dando de mano
a su amor

Puse los ojos, ¡ay! que no debiera,
en quien ya de las flechas de Cupido
mostraba el tierno corazón herido,
para que yo sin esperanza muera.

Huir fácil me fue de la primera
ocasión que a tal daño me ha traído
con resistir mirar tan atrevido,
mas fui mujer, y al fin mujer ligera.

Grillos amor me puso a los sentidos,
y la causa cruel de tantos daños
con sus regalos aumentó mis glorias,

pero sabiendo, ¡ay Dios! que eran fingidos,
he sepultado en caros desengaños
mi firmeza, mi amor y sus memorias.

4

Introducing a lady who became fond of
a youth who was attached to another,
and making her love known to him, he
reciprocated until she found out that he
loved another, and angrily the lady
writes him this sonnet to strike a blow
at her love

I placed my eyes, oh! would that I had
  not,
on one whose tender breast
already bore the wounds of Cupid's darts,
so now bereft of hope, I hopeless die.

How easily I could have fled,
merely by resisting daring glances,
the first of the encounters that brought
  me to such harm,
but I was a woman, and frivolous at that.

Love draped chains about my senses,
and my grievous harm's cruel author
with his gifts increased my glory;

but once I learned that they were
  feigned,
dear God, I buried, in costly disillusion,
my constancy, my love, and its reminders.

(Translated by Amy Kaminsky)

5
Endechas

Arroyos cristalinos
que murmuráis soberbios,
sobre azules pizarras
mi pena y mi tormento;

altas desiertas cumbres
a quien esmalta Febo
con los dorados rayos
de sus claros reflejos;

veisme aquí sola y triste,
que en busca de Liseno
paso riscos de nieve
y montañas de hielo;

5
Dirges

Crystalline streams,
smug and whispering,
run my pain and torment
over slates of blue,

high, deserted peaks
that Phoebus enamels
with the golden rays
of his bright reflections.

You see me here, alone and sad
searching for Liseno.
I tread the snowy crags
and icy peaks.

si viéredes acaso
aquel mi ingrato dueño,
contadle mis pesares,
decidle cómo quedo;
    mas ¡ay! que sois peñascos
y no escucháis mi acento,
mas con mi llanto triste
enterneceros puedo,
    y vive presa el alma
entre el amor y celos;
ausente de la causa
padezco en dos extremos:
    sigo a quien me desprecia
y a quien me estima dejo;
adoro deslealtades,
firmezas aborrezco,
    y entre el temor y la pena,
lo amargo del recelo
en dudas por el alma
esparce su veneno;
    ingratitudes coge
por penas y desvelos,
que en campos agostados
mis esperanzas siembro.
    Mas cesen ya mis quejas,
yo sólo poner quiero
en este verde sauce
que es Floris de Liseno.

If you should see
my ungrateful lord,
recount to him my sorrows,
tell him of my state;
    but oh! you are but rugged stone
and do not hear my plea,
yet with my sad weeping
might I melt you,
    and my soul lives imprisoned
between jealousy and love;
absent from their author
I suffer two extremes:
    I follow who disdains me,
who admires me I leave;
I adore disloyalty,
steadfastness I abhor,
    and between fear and grief
suspicion's bitterness
spreads, in doubt,
its poison through my soul.
    It reaps ingratitude
for pain and worry;
for in withered fields
do I sow my hopes.
    But my complaints, be quiet now,
for now I would but inscribe
on this green willow
that Floris is Liseno's.

(Translated by Amy Kaminsky)

6

Liras a los tiempos del año

Arroja escarcha helada
el anciano Noviembre,
y el caduco Diciembre
muestra su faz nevada,
tirando por los chopos
el agua congelada en blancos copos.
    Viste el prado de nieve,
que lo estuvo de flores,
y entre tales rigores

6

Poem on the Seasons of the Year

Hoary November
flings his icy frost
and withered December
shows his snowy face,
scattering o'er the poplars
water frozen in whitened flakes.
    The meadow dressed in snow
that once wore flowers,
now enduring hardship

los carámbanos bebe,
en vez de aguas gustosas,
con que la fuente sustentó sus rosas.
　　Los árboles desnuda
que el Mayo vistió ufano,
y con su airada mano
todo lo trueca y muda
y todo lo despoja,
a la tierra de flor y al árbol de hoja.
　　El viejo Jano sigue
hecho estatua de hielo,
y arrojando del cielo
montes de agua, persigue
con sus lluvias la tierra,
siempre acosada de su eterna guerra.
　　Entra Februo tras Jano,
y menos riguroso,
aunque si bien nubloso,
nos anuncia el verano,
dando el Marzo embajada
que presto acabará su furia helada.
　　Pasa, en fin, su carrera,
y en el Abril vistoso,
con paso presuroso
hace la primavera,
de lo verde su ensayo
para mostrarse más bizarra en Mayo.
　　Con olorosas flores
a la vista deleita,
y su hermosura afeita
de mil varias colores
con que el alma enamora
en los jardines que compone Flora.
　　Festéjanla las aves
cuando despierta el alba,
haciendo dulce salva
con canciones süaves,
y el ruiseñor parlero
es quien la canta el parabién primero.
　　Todo alegre y vistoso
se manifiesta ufano,
y en brazos del verano
se pinta victorioso;

no longer slakes its thirst
with the water of the fount that fed its
　　roses;
it now drinks icicles.
　　December strips the trees
that May had proudly dressed;
with a pitiless hand
he changes and unsettles
and denudes the land,
the earth of its flower and the tree of its
　　leaf.
　　Old January, sculpted ice,
is next and,
hurling watery mountains
from the sky,
hounds the ever vexèd earth
with his eternal war of rain.
　　Februs follows Janus,
and less severe,
although still gloomy,
foretells summer,
March giving his solemn pledge
his icy fury soon will end.
　　His race now run,
spring's swift step
makes of gaudy April
the green rehearsal
of May's most brilliant show.
　　With scented flowers
she delights the eye
and her beauty gains
the soul's true love
with a thousand different hues
she paints in Flora's garden.
　　The birds regale her
when the dawn awakes
and make of gentle song
the sweetest balm,
and the nightingale, sweet singer,
sings to her the morning's first gay call.
　　All bright and full of joy
his pride and cheer displayed,
in summer's arms

mas cuanto él resucita
seca Agosto y con su ardor marchita.

he paints himself victorious.
But all that he brings back to life
August sears and with his ardor withers.

*(Translated by Donna Lazarus
and Amy Kaminsky)*

<table>
<tr><td>

7
Glosa

¡Ah, larga esperanza vana!
¡Cuántos días ha que voy
engañando el día de hoy,
esperando el de mañana!—

    Pásase el tiempo ligero,
no por mi amor, por mis años,
que éste está como primero,
y sin darme desengaños;
esperando desespero
en mi desdicha inhumana
adorando un imposible,
deidad más que soberana.
¡Pensar que ha de ser posible!
¡Ah, larga esperanza vana!
    Quiero con tal perfección,
que aunque pierdo en ello el gusto
y se abrasa el corazón,
contra amor y a mi disgusto,
me sujeto a la razón;
a mi pena treguas doy,
sirviéndome de consuelo
en el encanto en que estoy,
que tome en cuenta tu cielo
cuantos días ha que voy.
    Sólo mirando tus ojos,
Norte de mi pensamiento,
se deshacen mis enojos,
y se acaba mi tormento
en viendo sus rayos rojos;
y cuando no, en calma estoy
en un mar de mil amores,
donde firme roca soy,

</td><td>

7
Gloss

Oh vain, unending dream.
However long I dally
today deceiving,
as I await tomorrow.

    Time goes quickly
not for my love, but for my years.
as this one is just like the first
and still I see not clear.
In hope do I despair,
in my inhuman misery
worshiping an impossibility,
a more than sovereign god.
To think it might be possible!
Oh vain, unending dream.
    I love with such perfection
that though I lose all pleasure
and my heart is charred,
against love's logic, and to my disgust,
I am subject to reason;
I give my pain some respite,
consoling myself thus
in my bewitchèd state
that I keep in mind your heaven
however long I dally.
    Merely looking in your eyes,
the lodestone of my thoughts,
my anger fades;
when I see their rosy lights,
my torment dies—
and when I do not, I am becalmed
on a sea of countless loves
where I am a rock, and firm

</td></tr>
</table>

y vivo con tus favores
engañando el día de hoy.

    Susténtame la esperanza
con verdes de tu hermosura,
aunque mi desconfianza
me dice que es mal segura
de mujer la confianza;
mas todo mi alma se allana,
que si falta mi alegría
porque hoy no hablé a mi Diana,
llevo en paciencia este día
esperando el de mañana.

and with your favor live,
today deceiving.

    Hope alone sustains me
with the promise of your beauty,
though my mistrust reminds me
that trusting in a woman's hardly sure;
but my soul all falls to ruins—
if my joy flags
because I did not speak today to my
    Diana,
I bear this day in patience,
as I await tomorrow.

(*Translated by Amy Kaminsky*)

8
Liras en la muerte
de mi querido padre y señor

8
Verses on the Death
of My Beloved Father and Lord

    Dejad, cansados ojos,
el justo llanto que os convierte en fuentes,
detened los enojos
y enjugad vuestras líquidas corrientes,
que al mal que oprime el pecho
el alma y corazón le viene estrecho.
    En tan terrible pena,
ni hallo descanso, gusto ni alegría;
de todo estoy ajena,
y sólo tengo la desdicha mía
por alivio y consuelo
que de todo lo más me priva el cielo.
    Quitóme en breves días,
airado y riguroso, un bien amado,
a las fortunas mías
añadiendo este golpe desdichado.
¡Oh suerte fiera y dura!
¡Llorad, ojos, llorad mi desventura!
    Contenta el alma estaba
en sus trabajos, penas y dolores
con el bien que gozaba;
mas la Parca cruel, con mil rigores,
fiera y embravecida,
cortó el hilo al estambre de su vida.

    Cease, weary eyes,
the rightful weeping that makes of you
    fountains.
End your suffering
and dry your watery currents,
for to hold the pain that presses on my
    breast,
soul and heart are chambers far too
    narrow.
    In pain so terrible
I find not rest, nor joy, nor pleasure;
I am apart from every thing,
I have nothing but my sorrow
for respite and for comfort;
Heaven has taken all else from me.
    In these few days, wrathful and severe,
it stole from me a dear beloved,
adding to my fortunes this unhappy blow.
Oh, cruel, hard fate!
Weep, eyes, weep for my misfortune!

    Content had been my soul
in its sorrows, pains, and tasks,
with the good that it enjoyed.

Musa, detente un poco,
que si de tantos males hago suma
y en el presente toco,
no es suficiente mi grosera pluma,
que pues estoy penando,
cuanto puedo decir callando.

But that cruel Sister, harsh a thousandfold,
furious and fierce,
cut the thread and loosed
the spindle of his life.
    Muse, stay a while,
for if I sum so many woes
and in this song recount them,
my coarse pen is inadequate—
for I am suffering—
what I might say in silence.

*(Translated by Donna Lazarus
and Amy Kaminsky)*

María de Zayas y Sotomayor

Baptized in Madrid on December 12, 1590, María de Zayas y Sotomayor was the daughter of Don Fernando de Zayas y Sotomayor, Knight of the Order of Santiago, and Doña María de Barasa. It is likely that she was in Naples in 1616, where her father served under the Duke of Lemos, and that she lived for some time in Zaragoza, where she published her first volume of tales; but she lived the greater portion of her life in Madrid. It was probably there, during her residency at court, that Zayas became friends with the poet and dramatist, Ana Caro Mallén de Soto. It is not known if Zayas married, nor has her date of death been established. There are documents that refer to the death of two widows named María de Zayas in Madrid, one dated 1661, the other 1669, but her name was a common one, and it is unlikely that either of these two women was this author.

María de Zayas was active in Madrid literary circles in the 1620s and 1630s. She contributed satirical and love poems to poetic competitions, and she wrote occasional poetry, including a panegyric to Lope de Vega (1636) and verse congratulating other poets on the publication of their books. Together with the poems she intersperses throughout her prose works, these scattered verses are what survive of Zayas's poetic output, since no volume of her poetry was ever published. After a 1639 poem in commemoration of the death of her friend, the writer Pérez de Montalbán, no more of Zayas's poems appear, and her name disappears from the list of poets participating in Madrid's literary contests. On the other hand, her fame as a prose writer grows during these years. Her two prose collections, *Novelas amorosas y ejemplares* (1637, translated as *The Enchantments of Love*) and *Parte segunda del sarao y entretenimiento honesto* (1647, Part two of the chaste entertainment and soiree), better known as the *Desengaños amorosos* (Disenchantments [or Disabusals] of love), were published in Zaragoza, suggesting that she might have moved to that city. After the publication of the *Desengaños*, Zayas disappears from the literary scene, though there is an unflattering reference to her in a later Catalán poem that may place her in Barcelona after 1647.

Zayas's only dramatic work, *Traición en la amistad* (Betrayal in friendship), is undated. This play deals with friendship among women, and it criticizes the flirtatious woman who steals her friends' suitors. Zayas's interest in questions concerning women is also discernible in the *Novelas amorosas y ejemplares*, and to an even greater extent in the *Desengaños amorosos*, where it becomes central. The *Desengaños* are narrated

exclusively by women characters; and they have as their avowed purpose warning women of the dangers of love, convincing men to change their ways, and, most pointedly, recovering women's good reputation ("volver por la fama de las mujeres"). The point of view of the narrators in this volume is, almost without exception, consciously feminist, if by that we mean that they are aware of, and working to remedy, the systematic subordination of women to men. The tales of the *Desengaños* denounce a system that defames women, believing its own misogynist propaganda, and that violently punishes women who are its victims. Zayas does not transcend the limits of her class and era in her treatment of servants and slaves in these tales, but the limitations of her own class do not escape her scrutiny either; Emilia Pardo Bazán characterized her writing as a picaresque of the aristocracy.

The tale chosen for inclusion here, "La esclava de su amante" (Her lover's slave), is the first of the *Desengaños amorosos*, and the only one narrated by its protagonist, a woman who combines the strength and will of the protagonists of the *Novelas amorosas* with the role of victim of those of the *Desengaños*. "La esclava de su amante" is a rousing story of a woman's adventure as well as a sophisticated character study. It deals with a woman's sexual vulnerability, but also with her integrity; with her reckless behavior for love of a man, but also with the power of her love for other women.

During the seventeenth century, Zayas's books went through several Spanish editions, and a number of tales from them were translated into French and English, indicating that she was widely read in her own time. But Zayas was criticized for her outspokenness as well. The prologue to the *Desengaños amorosos* contains a response to the critics of the first volume, and the characters she creates to narrate often preface their tales with a defense of their right to tell the stories of women's lives. Zayas's popularity continued after her death, and her work has been continuously in print, in either full or partial editions, to this day. Still, Zayas fared badly with critics and literary historians, who, well into the twentieth century, charged that her tales were lascivious and even pornographic.

La esclava de su amante

—Mi nombre es doña Isabel Faxardo, no Zelima, ni mora, como pensáis, sino cristiana, e hija de padres católicos, y de los más principales de la ciudad de Murcia; que estos hierros que veis en mi rostro no son sino sombras de los que ha puesto en mi calidad y fama la ingratitud de un hombre; y para que me deis más crédito, veislos aquí quitados; así pudiera quitar los que han puesto en mi alma mis desventuras y poca cordura.— Y diciendo esto, se los quitó y arrojó lejos de sí, quedando el claro cristal de su divino rostro sin mancha, sombra ni oscuridad, descubriendo aquel sol los esplendores de su hermosura sin nube. Y todos los que colgados de lo que intimaba su hermosa boca, casi sin sentido, que apenas osaban apartar la vista para no perderla, pareciéndoles que como ángel se les podía esconder. Y por fin, los galanes más enamorados, y las damas más envidiosas, y todos compitiendo en la imaginación sobre si estaba mejor con hierros o sin hierros, y casi se determinaban a sentir viéndola sin ellos, por parecerles más fácil la empresa; y más Lisis, que como la quería con tanta ternura, dejó caer por sus ojos unos desperdicios; mas, por no estorbarla, los recogió con sus hermosas manos. Con esto, la hermosa doña Isabel prosiguió su discurso, viendo que todos callaban, notando la suspensión de cada uno, y no de todos juntos.

—Nací en la casa de mis padres sola, para que fuese sola la perdición de ella; hermosa, ya lo veis; noble, ya lo he dicho; rica, lo que bastara, a ser yo cuerda, o a no ser desgraciada, a darme un noble marido. Criéme hasta llegar a los doce años entre las caricias y regalos de mis padres; que claro es que no habiendo tenido otro de su

Her Lover's Slave

"My name is Doña Isabel Faxardo, not Zelima, nor am I a Moor, as you believed, but a Christian, and the daughter of Catholic parents, and of one of the finest families of the city of Murcia; and these brands that you see on my face are no more than a reflection of those a thankless man has caused to mar my worth and good name; and so that you are more inclined to believe me, you see them here removed; oh that I could remove those misfortune and imprudence have fixed on my soul." And thus saying, she removed them and hurled them far from her, leaving the crystal clarity of her divine face, without mark, shadow or stain, that sun revealing the splendors of her cloudless beauty. And all those present hanging on to every word uttered by that lovely mouth, as though entranced, hardly dared to take their eyes from her for fear of losing sight of her, seeming to them as she did an angel who might hide from them. And at last, the most enamored of the swains, and the most envious of the ladies, and all debating in their minds over whether she was lovelier with or without the brands, were inclined to think that she was so without them, as that seemed to them to require less effort; and especially Lisis who, as she loved her with such tenderness, let fall from her eyes some useless tears; but, so that they not disturb her, she brushed them away with her beautiful hands. With that, the beautiful Doña Isabel continued her discourse, seeing that all fell silent, noting the suspense of each individual, rather than all together.

"I alone was born in the house of my parents, so that I alone would be the cause of its perdition; beautiful, as you see; noble, as I have already said; rich, or at least sufficiently so, if I had been prudent (or

matrimonio, serían muchos, enseñándome entre ellos las cosas más importantes a mi calidad. Ya se entenderá, tras las virtudes que forman una persona virtuosamente cristiana, los ejercicios honestos de leer, escribir, tañer y danzar, con todo lo demás competente a una persona de mis prendas, y de todas aquellas que los padres desean ver enriquecidas a sus hijas; y más los míos, que, como no tenían otra, se afinaban en estos extremos; salí única en todo, y perdonadme que me alabe, que, como no tengo otro testigo, en tal ocasión no es justo pasen por desvanecimiento mis alabanzas; bien se lo pagué, pero más bien lo he pagado. Yo fui en todo extremada, y más en hacer versos, que era el espanto del reino, y la envidia de muchos no tan peritos en esta facultad; que hay algunos ignorantes que, como si las mujeres les quitaran el entendimiento por tenerle, se consumen de los aciertos ajenos. ¡Bárbaro, ignorante! si lo sabes hacer, hazlos, que no te roba nadie tu caudal; si son buenos los que no son tuyos, y más si son de dama, adóralos y alábalos; y si malos, discúlpala, considerando que no tiene más caudal, y que es digna de más aplauso en una mujer que en un hombre, por adornarlos con menos arte.

Cuando llegué a los catorce años, ya tenía mi padre tantos pretensores para mis bodas, que ya, enfadado, respondía que me dejasen ser mujer; mas como, según decían ellos, idolatraban en mi belleza, no se podían excusar de importunarle. Entre los más rendidos se mostró apasionadísimo un caballero, cuyo nombre es don Felipe, de pocos más años que yo, tan dotado de partes, de gentileza y de nobleza, cuanto desposeído de los de fortuna, que parecía que, envidiosa de las gracias que le había dado el cielo, le había quitado los suyos. Era, en fin, pobre; y tanto, que en la ciudad era desconocido, desdicha que padecen muchos.

had not been so unfortunate) to find myself a noble husband. I was raised up to the age of twelve amidst caresses and gifts from my parents, which, of course, were many, as they had no other child from their marriage; and they taught me, between the two of them, the things most important to my station. You understand, in addition to the virtues that form a virtuous Christian, the honest exercises of reading, writing, playing a musical instrument, and dancing, and all other matters appropriate to a person of my natural gifts, and all those by which parents wish to see their daughters enriched; and mine, who had no other, were especially attentive in this respect. I was first in all, and forgive me for singing my own praises, but, as I have no other witness, on such an occasion as this it is not just that my praise be taken as presumption; well did I repay, and even more have I paid. And I excelled in everything, especially in composing verses, which was the wonder of that kingdom, and the envy of many not as skilled in this gift; and there are some ignorant individuals who are pained by the achievements of women as though, by virtue of possessing intelligence, they deprived others of it. Barbarous, ignorant! If you know how to compose, compose them, since your plenty takes nothing from anyone; if another displays well gifts you do not possess, and especially if the individual in question is a lady, adore them and praise them; and if they are poorly displayed, forgive her, keeping in mind that this is all she has, and that from a woman it merits more applause than from a man, for being graced with less artifice.

When I turned fourteen, so many already sought to have me in marriage that my father, by now angry, responded that they should let me grow to be a woman;

Éste era el que más a fuerza de suspiros y lágrimas procuraba granjear mi voluntad; mas yo seguía la opinión de todos; y como los criados de mi casa me veían a él poco afecta, jamás le oyó ninguno, ni fue mirado de mí, pues bastó esto para ser poco conocido en otra ocasión; pluguiera al cielo le mirara yo bien, o fuera parte para que no me hubieran sucedido las desdichas que lloro; hubiera sabido excusar algunas; mas, siendo pobre, ¿cómo le había de mirar mi desvanecimiento?, pues tenía yo hacienda para él y para mí; mas mirábale de modo que jamás pude dar señas de su rostro, hasta que me vi engolfada en mis desventuras.

Sucedió en este tiempo el levantamiento de Cataluña, para castigo de nuestros pecados, o sólo de los míos, que aunque han sido las pérdidas grandes, la mía es mayor: que los muertos en esta ocasión ganaron eterna fama, y yo, que quedé viva, ignominiosa infamia.[1] Súpose en Murcia cómo Su Majestad (Dios le guarde) iba al ilustre y leal reino de Aragón, para hallarse presente en estas civiles guerras; y mi padre, como quien había gastado lo mejor de su mocedad en servicio de su rey, conoció lo que le importaban a Su Majestad los hombres de su valor, se determinó a irle a servir, para que en tal ocasión le premiase los servicios pasados y presentes, como católico y agradecido del rey; y con esto trató de su jornada, que sentimos mi madre y yo ternísimamente, y mi padre de la misma suerte; tanto, que a importunidades de mi madre y mías trató llevarnos en su compañía, con que volvió nuestra pena en gozo, y más a mí, que como niña, deseosa de ver tierras, o por mejor sentir mi desdichada suerte, que me guiaba a mi perdición, me llevaba contenta. Prevínose la partida, y

but as they worshiped my beauty, or so they said, they could not leave off importuning him. Among the most devoted, a knight by the name of Don Felipe showed himself consumed by passion; he was only a few years older than I, so well endowed with gifts, with gentility and nobility, though so lacking in those of fortune that it seemed that, envious of the gifts the heavens had given him, she had withheld her own. He was, in short, poor; and to such an extent that he was unknown in the city, a misfortune suffered by many. It was he above all who with sighs and tears tried to win my approval; but I followed the opinion of others; and as the servants in my house saw in me little affection for him, none of them ever interceded for him, nor did I take any notice of him, and that assured that he would continue to be little known on future occasions. I wish to the heavens that I had looked with favor on him, or that I had taken his side so that the misfortunes I lament would not have befallen me; he would have known how to prevent some; but, being poor, how was he to deal with my indifference, though I had enough wealth for him and for me? But because of the way I beheld him I never even recognized his face, until I saw myself engulfed in my misfortunes.

The uprising in Catalonia took place at this time, to punish us for our sins, or just me for mine, for although the losses have been great, mine are greater: those who died on this occasion earned eternal glory, and I, who remained alive, ignominious infamy.[1] I learned in Murcia how His Majesty (may God keep him safe) went to the illustrious and loyal kingdom of Aragon, in order to participate in these

---

1. El levantamiento de Cataluña ocurrió en junio de 1640.

1. The uprising in Catalonia took place in June of 1640.

aderezado lo que se había de llevar, que fuese lo más importante, para, aunque a la ligera, mostrar mi padre quién era, y que era descendiente de los antiguos Faxardos de aquel reino. Partimos de Murcia, dejando con mi ausencia común y particular tristeza en aquel reino, solemnizando en versos y prosas los más divinos entendimientos la falta que hacía a aquel reino.

Llegamos a la nobilísima y suntuosa ciudad de Zaragoza, y aposentados en una de sus principales casas, ya descansada del camino, salí a ver, y vi y fui vista. Mas no estuvo en esto mi pérdida, que dentro en mi casa estaba el incendio, pues sin salir me había ya visto mi desventura; y como si careciera esta noble ciudad de hermosuras, pues hay tantas, que apenas hay plumas ni elocuencias que basten a alabarlas, pues son tantas que dan envidia a otros reinos, se empezó a exagerar la mía, como si no hubieran visto otra. No sé si es tanta como decían; sólo sé que fue la que bastó a perderme; mas, como dice el vulgar, lo nuevo aplace. ¡Oh, quien no la hubiera tenido para excusar tantas fortunas! Habló mi padre a Su Majestad, que, informado de que había sido en la guerra tan gran soldado, y que aún no estaban amortiguados sus bríos y valor, y la buena cuenta que siempre había dado de lo que tenía a su cargo, le mandó asistiese al gobierno de un tercio de caballos, con título de Maese del Campo, honrando primero sus pechos con un hábito de Calatrava;[2] y así fue fuerza, viendo serlo, el asistir allí, en enviar a Murcia por toda la hacienda que se podía traer, dejando la demás a cuenta de deudos nobles que tenía allá.

Era dueña de la casa en que vivíamos una señora viuda, muy principal y

2. Orden de caballería.

civil wars; and my father, as one who had spent the best years of his youth in service to the king, knew how important men of his caliber were to His Majesty, and decided to go to serve him, so that on that occasion he would be rewarded for services, past and present, by a Catholic and grateful king; and with that he prepared his journey, which deeply pained my mother and me, and my father as well, to such a degree that, at my mother's importunings and my own, he agreed to take us with him, so that our suffering turned to joy, and especially mine, who, as a girl eager to see new lands, or better to experience the ill luck that guided me to my perdition, was happy that he took me along. Our departure had been readied, and the supplies prepared, and though these were only no more than what was essential, they demonstrated, in a superficial way, who my father was, that he was a descendant of the ancient Faxardos of that kingdom. We departed from Murcia, my absence leaving a general and special sadness in that realm, and the most divine interpretations of the void felt in that realm were rendered in verse and prose.

We came to the most noble and sumptuous city of Zaragoza, and lodged in one of the principal houses, and once rested from the journey, I went out to see, and I saw and was seen. But my downfall was not in that, since the fire was within my house, because before I walked out the door my misfortune had already seen me; and though this noble city did not lack beauties, my own began to be exaggerated, as if they had never seen another, when in fact there are so many that there are barely enough pens or eloquent words to praise them sufficiently, so many are there who spark the envy of other realms. I know not if mine is as great as they said; I only know

medianamente rica, que tenía un hijo y una hija; él, mozo y galán y de buen discurso, así no fuera falso traidor, llamado don Manuel; no quiero decir su apellido, que mejor es callarle, pues no supo darle lo que merecía. ¡Ay qué a costa mía he hecho experiencia de todo! ¡Ay, mujeres fáciles, y si supiésedes una por una, y todas juntas, a lo que os ponéis el día que os dejáis rendir a las falsas caricias de los hombres, y cómo quisiérades más haber nacido sin oídos y sin ojos; o si os desengañásedes en mí, de que más vais a perder, que a ganar! Era la hija moza, y medianamente hermosa, y concertada de casar con un primo, que estaba en las Indias y le aguardaban para celebrar sus bodas en la primera flota, cuyo nombre era doña Eufrasia. Ésta y yo nos tomamos tanto amor, como su madre y la mía, que de día ni de noche nos dividíamos, que, si no era para ir a dar el común reposo a los ojos, jamás nos apartábamos, o yo en su cuarto, o ella en el mío. No hay más que encarecerlo, sino que ya la ciudad nos celebraba con el nombre de *las dos amigas*; y de la misma suerte don Manuel dio en quererme, o engañarme, que todo viene a ser uno. A los principios empecé a extrañar y resistir sus pretensiones y porfías, teniéndolas por atrevimientos contra mi autoridad y honestidad; tanto, que por atajarlos me excusaba y negaba a la amistad de su hermana, dejando de asistirla en su cuarto todas las veces que sin nota podía hacerlo, de que don Manuel hacía tantos sentimientos, mostrando andar muy melancólico y desesperado, que tal vez me obligaba a lástima, por ver que ya mis rigores se atrevían a su salud. No miraba yo mal las veces que podía, sin dárselo a entender, a don Manuel, y bien gustara, pues era fuerza tener dueño, fuera él a quien tocara la suerte; mas, ¡ay!, que él iba con otro intento, pues con haber tantos que

that it was that which sufficed to seal my fate; but, as the saying goes, novelty gives pleasure. Oh, who would not have renounced it to avoid so many misfortunes! My father spoke to His Majesty, who, informed that he had been such a great soldier in the war, and that his vigor and valor had not yet dimmed, and the good account those under his command had always given, awarded him the title of field marshall and sent him to assist in leading a cavalry regiment, after first rewarding his courage with the habit of Calatrava;[2] and having received this assignment, it was necessary to send to Murcia for all the wealth that could be brought, leaving the rest in the care of noble kin he had there.

The owner of the house in which we lived was a widow, very important and relatively rich, who had one son and one daughter; he, handsome and gallant and well-spoken, had he not been so perfidious, was called Don Manuel; I would rather not mention his surname, as it is better to remain silent on that, since he did not know how to honor it. Oh, at my own expense I have experienced it all! Oh, easy women, if only you knew, each and every one of you, what you give away the day you surrender yourselves to the false caresses of men, and how you would prefer to have been born without ears and without eyes; or if only you saw the truth in me, of how much more you stand to lose than to win! The daughter was a girl, more or less pretty, and promised in marriage to a cousin, who was in the Indies, and they were waiting for him to return on the first ship to celebrate the wedding; and her name was Doña Eufrasia. She and I came to love one another so, as did her mother and mine, that neither by day nor by night

2. Quasi-religious order of knights.

pretendían este lugar, jamás se opuso a tal pretensión; y estaba mi padre tan desvanecido en mi amor, que aunque lo intentara, no fuera admitido, por haber otros de más partes que él, aunque don Manuel tenía muchas, ni yo me apartara del gusto de mi padre por cuanto vale el mundo. No había hasta entonces llegado amor a hacer suerte en mi libertad; antes imagino que, ofendido de ella, hizo el estrago que tantas penas me cuesta. No había tenido don Manuel lugar de decirme más de con los ojos y descansos de su corazón su voluntad, porque yo no se le daba; hasta que una tarde, estando yo con su hermana en su cuarto, salió de su aposento, que estaba a la entrada de él, con un instrumento, y sentándose en el mismo estrado con nosotras, le rogó doña Eufrasia cantase alguna cosa, y él extrañándolo, se lo supliqué también por no parecer grosera; y él, que no deseaba otra cosa, cantó un soneto, que si no os cansa mi larga historia, diré con los demás que se ofrecieren en el curso della.

Lisis, por todos, le rogó lo hiciese así, que les daría notable gusto, diciendo:

—¿Qué podréis decir, señora doña Isabel, que no sea de mucho agrado a los que escuchamos? Y así, en nombre de estas damas y caballeros, os suplico no excuséis nada de lo que os sucedió en vuestro prodigioso suceso, porque, de lo contrario, recibiremos gran pena.

—Pues con esa licencia, —replicó doña Isabel—, digo que don Manuel cantó este soneto; advirtiendo que él a mí y yo a él nos nombrábamos por Belisa y Salicio.

A un diluvio la tierra condenada,
    que toda se anegaba en sus enojos,
    ríos fuera de madre eran sus ojos,
    porque ya son las nubes mar airada.
La dulce Filomena retirada,
    como no ve del sol los rayos rojos,

were we separated, and, had it not been necessary to rest our eyes, we would never have separated; either I was in her room or she in mine. So evident was our friendship that throughout the city they referred to us *as the two girlfriends;* and in that same way, Don Manuel came to love me, or to deceive me, as it is all the same. At first I was puzzled and resisted his pretensions and persistence, taking them for impertinences against my dignity and good name; to put a stop to his advances I even made excuses to his sister and denied myself her company, avoiding visits to her room as often as I could without raising suspicion, and this caused Don Manuel to grieve so, making a show of walking about with an air so melancholy and desperate that perhaps I felt obliged to pity him, seeing how my severity threatened his health. Although I was not open about it, I did not look upon Don Manuel so unfavorably as I might have, and in fact I would have been pleased had he been the one chosen for my husband as one must, of necessity, have one; but, oh! he had other intentions and thus never objected to the many others who sought that role; and my father was so unimpressed by this my love that even had Don Manuel announced such an intention he would not have been approved, since, although he had much to recommend him, there were others with more gifts than he; nor would I have opposed my father's wishes for all the riches in the world. Up until then love had not come to affect my freedom; but I suspect that, offended by that liberty, it wreaked the havoc that has caused me so much suffering. Don Manuel had no opportunity to speak to me of his desires, other than with his eyes and with his heartfelt sighs, because I did not allow him that; until one afternoon, when I was with his sister in her room, he

no le rinde canciones en despojos,
　por verse sin su luz desconsolada.
Progne lamenta, el ruiseñor no canta;
　sin belleza y olor están las flores,
　y estando todo triste de este modo,
con tanta luz, que al mismo sol espanta,
　toda donaire, discreción y amores,
　salió Belisa, y serenóse todo.

Arrojó, acabando de cantar, el instrumento en el estrado, diciendo:

—¿Qué me importa a mí que salga el sol de Belisa en el oriente a dar alegría a cuantos la ven, si para mí está siempre convertida en triste ocaso?

Diole, diciendo esto, un modo de desmayo, con que, alborotadas su madre, hermana y criadas, fue fuerza llevarle a su cama, y yo retraerme a mi cuarto, no sé si triste o alegre; sólo sabré asegurar que me conocí confusa, y determiné no ponerme más en ocasión de sus atrevimientos. Si me durara este propósito, acertara; mas ya empezaba en mi corazón a hacer suertes amor, alentando yo misma mi ingratitud, y más cuando supe de allí a dos días que don Manuel estaba con un accidente, que a los médicos había puesto en cuidado. Con todo esto, estuve sin ver a doña Eufrasia hasta otro día, no dándome por entendida, y fingiendo precisa ocupación con la estafeta de mi tierra; hasta que doña Eufrasia, que hasta entonces no había tenido lugar asistiendo a su hermano, le dejó reposando y pasó a mi aposento, dándome muchas quejas de mi descuido y sospechosa amistad, de que me disculpé, haciéndome de nuevas y muy pesarosa de su disgusto. Al fin, acompañando a mi madre, hube de pasar aquella tarde a verle; y como estaba cierta que su mal procedía de mis desdenes, procuré, más cariñosa y agradable, darle la salud que le había quitado con ellos, hablando donaires y burlas, que en

emerged from his chamber, which was near the entrance to hers, with a musical instrument, and after he sat down on the divan with us, Doña Eufrasia begged him to sing something, and to his amazement, I also begged in order not to appear rude; and he, who had hoped for that very thing, sang a sonnet, and if this long account of mine is not tiring you, I will recite it with others offered in the course of this tale."

Lisis, on behalf of everyone, urged her to do so, saying that it would give them great pleasure:

"What could you say, Lady Doña Isabel, that would not be most pleasing to those of us who are listening? And so, in the name of these ladies and gentlemen, I entreat you not to leave out a thing that has befallen you in your prodigious experience, for if you do, we will be greatly pained."

"Very well, with your permission," replied Doña Isabel, "as I have said, Don Manuel sang this sonnet. And you should know first that he and I called one another Belisa and Salicio.

The earth condemned to a deluge,
　that swept away all in its wrath,
　its eyes were rivers overflowing their
　　banks,
　for the clouds had become an angry
　　sea.
The sweet Philomena withdrawn,
　as she now sees not the sun's red rays,
　offers no songs to the ruins,
　so heartsick is she without its light.
The swallow laments, the nightingale does
　not sing,
　the flowers are lacking in beauty and
　　scent,
　and when all has been saddened in this
　　way,
with so much light, the very sun is
　amazed,

don Manuel causaban varios efectos, ya de alegría, y ya de tristeza, que yo notaba con más cuidado que antes, si bien lo encubría con cauta disimulación. Llegó la hora de despedirnos, y llegando con mi madre a hacer la debida cortesía, y esforzarle con las esperanzas de la salud, que siempre se dan a los enfermos, me puso tan impensadamente en la mano un papel, que, o fuese la turbación del atrevimiento, o recato de mi madre y de la suya, que estaban cerca, que no pude hacer otra cosa más de encubrirle. Y como llegué a mi cuarto, me entré en mi aposento, y sentándome sobre mi cama, saqué el engañoso papel para hacerle pedazos sin leerle, y al punto que lo iba a conseguir, me llamaron, porque había venido mi padre, y hube de suspender por entonces su castigo, y no hubo lugar de dársele hasta que me fui a acostar, que habiéndome desnudado una doncella que me vestía y desnudaba, a quien yo quería mucho por habernos criado desde niñas, me acordé del papel y se le pedí, y que me llegase de camino la luz para abrasarle en ella.

Me dijo la cautelosa Claudia, que éste era su nombre, y bien le puedo dar también el de cautelosa, pues también estaba prevenida contra mí, y en favor del ingrato y desconocido don Manuel:

—¿Y acaso, señora mía, ha cometido este desdichado algún delito contra la fe, que le quieres dar tan riguroso castigo? Porque si es así, no será por malicia, sino con inocencia; porque antes entiendo que le sobra fe y que no le falta.

—Con todo mi honor le está cometiendo —dije yo—, y porque no haya más cómplices, será bien que éste muera.

—¿Pues a quién se condena sin oírle? —replicó Caludia—. Porque, a lo que miro, entero está como el día que nació. Óyele, por tu vida, y luego, si mereciere

all charm, discretion, and love,
Belisa emerged, and all was calmed.

After ending his song, he threw the instrument to the divan saying:

"Why should it matter to me that the sun of Belisa emerges in the east to give cheer to all who see it, if for me the sun will be forever sadly setting?"

After saying this, he fell into a kind of faint that caused his mother, sister, and the maids to become agitated, and it was necessary to take him to his bed, and then I retired to my room, whether sad or happy I know not; I can only say for certain that I felt confused, and determined never again to create, by my presence, occasion for further impertinences. That resolve, had it lasted, would have been correct; but now love began to draw lots in my heart, and I myself fanned the flames of my feelings of ingratitude, and especially when I learned two days later that Don Manuel had fallen ill, that he was under the care of physicians. Nevertheless, I did not go to see Doña Eufrasia until the following day, pretending to know nothing and feigning some business with the courier from my land; until Doña Eufrasia, who up to then had not had time, having been caring for her brother, left him resting and came to my chamber, scolding me for my careless and suspicious friendship, for which I apologized, pretending not to have known and feeling regret at her displeasure. In the end, accompanying my mother, I was to go that afternoon to see him; and as it was certain that his illness was caused by my slights, I attempted to be more affectionate and agreeable and to return to him the health that I had taken, uttering charming phrases and telling jokes that brought about varied effects in Don Manuel, first of joy, and then of sad-

pena, se la darás, y más si es tan poco venturoso como su dueño.

—¿Sabes tú cúyo es? —le torné a replicar.

—¿De quién puede ser, si no es admitido, sino del mal correspondido don Manuel, que por causa tuya está como está, sin gusto y salud, dos males que, a no ser desdichado, ya le hubieran muerto? Mas hasta la muerte huye de los que lo son.

—Sobornada parece que estás, pues abogas con tanta piedad por él.

—No estoy, por cierto —respondió Claudia—, sino enternecida, y aun, si dijera lastimada, acertara mejor.

—¿Pues de qué sabes tú que todas esas penas de que te lastimas tanto son por mí?

—Yo te lo diré —dijo la astuta Claudia—. Esta mañana me envió tu madre a saber cómo estaba, y el triste caballero vio los cielos abiertos en verme; contóme sus penas, dando de todas la culpa a tus desdenes, y esto con tantas lágrimas y suspiros, que me obligó a sentirlas como propias, solemnizando con suspiros los suyos y acompañando con lágrimas las suyas.

—Muy tierna eres, Claudia —repliqué yo—; presto crees a los hombres. Si fueras tú la querida, presto le consolaras.

—Y tan presto —dijo Claudia—, que ya estuviera sano y contento. Díjome más, que en estando para poderse levantar, se ha de ir donde a tus crueles ojos e ingratos oídos no lleguen nuevas de él.

—Ya quisiera que estuviera bueno, para que lo cumpliera —dije yo.

—¡Ay, señora mía! —respondió Claudia—, ¿es posible que en cuerpo tan lindo como el tuyo se aposente alma tan cruel? No seas así, por Dios, que ya se pasó el tiempo de las damas andariegas que con corazones de diamantes dejaban morir los caballeros, sin tener piedad de ellos. Casada has de ser, que tus padres para este estado

ness, and this I noted with more care than before, though I concealed this interest with careful dissimulation. It came time to take our leave, and approaching with my mother to bestow the courtesy expected, and to encourage him with wishes for his health, such as are always offered to the sick, I was taken completely aback when he placed a note in my hand; and, due either to confusion caused by his impudence, or discretion caused by the presence of my mother and his own, I could do nothing other than hide it. And when I came to my quarters, I entered my chamber and, seated on my bed, I took out the treacherous note in order to rip it to pieces without reading it, and just as I was about to do so, they called me because my father had arrived, and I had to suspend for the moment its destruction, and there was no time to carry it out until I went to bed; and after being undressed by a handmaiden who dressed and undressed me, whom I loved a great deal as we had been raised together since we were children, I remembered the note and asked her for it, and that she bring the light along in order to burn it in the flame.

The clever Claudia, for that was her name, and well might I call her clever too, for she was also disposed against me, and in favor of the ungrateful stranger Don Manuel, said to me:

"And has, my lady, this unfortunate note committed some crime against the faith, perhaps, that brings you to mete out such harsh punishment? Because if it has, it will not be due to malice, but to innocence; because it is my understanding that it has faith to spare, in that it is not wanting."

"It commits one against my very honor," I said, "and so that there be no further accomplices, it is best that it die."

"But who is condemned without first

te guardan; pues si es así, ¿qué desmerece don Manuel para que no gustes que sea tu esposo?

—Claudia —dije yo—, si don Manuel estuviera tan enamorado como dices, y tuviera tan castos pensamientos, ya me hubiera pedido a mi padre. Y pues no trata de eso, sino de que le corresponda, o por burlarme, o ver mi flaqueza, no me hables de él, que me das notable enojo.

Lo mismo que tú dices —volvió a replicar Claudia —le dije yo, y me respondió que cómo se había de atrever a pedirte por esposa incierto de tu voluntad; pues podrá ser que aunque tu padre lo acepte, no gustes tú de ello.

—El gusto de mi padre se hará el mío —dije yo.

—Ahora, señora —tornó a decir Claudia—, veamos ahora el papel, pues ni hace ni deshace el leerle, que pues lo demás corre por cuenta del cielo.

Estaba ya mi corazón más blando que cera, pues mientras Claudia me decía lo referido, había entre mí hecho varios discursos, y todos en abono de lo que me decía mi doncella, y en favor de don Manuel; mas, por no darla más atrevimientos, pues ya la juzgaba más de la parte contraria que de la mía, después de haberla mandado no hablase más en ello, ni fuese adonde don Manuel estaba, porfié a quemar el papel y ella a defenderle, hasta que, deseando yo lo mismo que ella quería, le abrí, amonestándola primero que no supiese don Manuel sino que le había rompido sin leerle, y ella prometídolo, vi que decía así:

"No sé, ingrata señora mía, de qué tienes hecho el corazón, pues a ser de diamante, ya le hubieran enternecido mis lágrimas; antes, sin mirar los riesgos que me vienen, le tienes cada día más endurecido; si yo te quisiera menos que para dueño de mí y de cuanto poseo, ya parece que se

being heard?" Claudia replied. "Because, as I see it, it is as unblemished as the day it was born. Hear it out, for your own sake, and then, if it deserves a sentence, impose it, above all if it be as unfortunate as its owner."

"Do you know who that is?" I said in reply.

"Who can it be, if this not be accepted, but the ill-requited Don Manuel, who because of you is in the state he is in, without joy and health, two ills that, were he not so unfortunate, would have killed him by now. But death itself flees from such as him."

"You have been bribed, it seems, because you plead for him with such compassion."

"I have not, I assure you," responded Claudia. "It is, rather, tenderness I feel, and were I to say pain, that would be truer still."

"But how do you know that I am to blame for all of these pains you feel so deeply?"

"I will tell you," said the cunning Claudia. "This morning your mother sent me to find out how he was, and the sad gentleman saw the skies clear on seeing me; he recounted all his sorrows, blaming all of them on your disdain, and all of that with a wealth of tears and sighs, that he obliged me to feel them as my own, adding my sighs to his and accompanying his tears with my own."

"You are very tender, Claudia," I replied, "and quick to believe men. Were you the beloved, you would be quick to console him."

"And so quick," said Claudia, "that by now he would be well and content. He told me more, that when he is able to get up he will go off to some place where your cruel eyes and ungrateful ears will have no news of him."

hallara disculpa a tu crueldad; mas, pues gustas que muera sin remedio, yo te prometo darte gusto, ausentándome del mundo y de tus ingratos ojos, como lo verás en levantándome de esta cama, y quizá entonces te pesará de no haber admitido mi voluntad."

No decía más que esto el papel. Mas, ¿qué más había de decir? Dios nos libre de un papel escrito a tiempo; saca fruto de donde no hay, y engendra voluntad aun sin ser visto. Mirad qué sería de mí, que ya no sólo había mirado, mas miraba los méritos de don Manuel todos juntos y cada uno por sí. ¡Ay, engañoso amante, ay, falso caballero, ay, verdugo de mi inocencia! ¡Y, ay, mujeres fáciles y mal aconsejadas, y cómo os dejáis vencer de mentiras bien afeitadas, y que no les dura el oro con que van cubiertas más de mientras dura el apetito! ¡Ay, desengaño, que visto, no se podrá engañar ninguna! ¡Ay, hombres!, y ¿por qué siendo hechos de la misma masa y trabazón que nosotras, no teniendo más nuestra alma que vuestra alma, nos tentáis, como si fuéramos hechas de otra pasta, sin que os obliguen los beneficios que desde el nacer al morir os hacemos? Pues si agradecierais los que recibís de vuestras madres, por ellas estimarais y reverenciarais a las demás; ya, ya lo tengo conocido a costa mía, que no lleváis otro designio sino perseguir nuestra inocencia, aviltar nuestro entendimiento, derribar nuestra fortaleza, y haciéndonos viles y comunes, alzaros con el imperio de la inmortal fama. Abran las demás los ojos del entendimiento, y no se dejen vencer de quien pueden temer el mal pago que a mí se me dio, para que dijesen en esta ocasión y tiempo estos desengaños, para ver si por mi causa cobrasen las mujeres la opinión perdida y no diesen lugar a los hombres para alabarse, ni hacer burla de ellas, ni sentir mal de sus flaquezas y malditos intereses, por los cuales

"I wish he were well, that he might do so," said I.

"Ah, my dear lady!" Claudia responded. "Is it possible that in a body as lovely as yours there resides a soul so cruel? Do not be like that, for the love of God; the time has passed when flighty ladies with hearts hard as diamonds allowed gentlemen to die, without taking pity on them. You ought to marry; your parents have saved you for that. And as that is the case, what is there so unworthy in Don Manuel that you would not have him for a husband?"

"Claudia," I said, "were Don Manuel as enamored as you claim, and were his thoughts as chaste, he would already have spoken for me with my father. But this is not the case, and since his concern is either to mock me, or to test my weakness, do not speak of him to me, as it makes me very angry."

"I said to him," Claudia responded yet again, "exactly what you have just finished saying, and he replied that how could he dare ask for your hand being uncertain of your wishes; for it might turn out that though your father accepted him, you would not."

"That which my father accepts, so will I," said I.

"Now then, my lady," Claudia spoke again, "let us see the note, since the reading neither makes nor breaks anything; all of that is up to the heavens."

My heart was by now softer than wax, because while Claudia said what I have recounted, there were within me a number of arguments and all lent weight to what my servant said, and were in Don Manuel's favor. But, in order not to give her an opportunity for further liberties, since I now judged her more on the opposing side than mine, after ordering her to speak no more of the matter, nor to go

hacen tantas, que, en lugar de ser amadas, son aborrecidas, aviltadas y vituperadas.

Volví de nuevo a mandar a Claudia y de camino rogarle no supiese don Manuel que había leído el papel, ni lo que había pasado entre las dos, y ella a prometerlo, y con esto se fue, dejándome divertida en tantos y tan confusos pensamientos, que yo misma me aborrecía de tenerlos; ya amaba, ya me arrepentía; ya me repetía piadosa, ya me hallaba mejor. Airada y final, me determiné a no favorecer a don Manuel, de suerte que le diese lugar a atrevimientos; mas tampoco desdeñarle, de suerte que le obligase a algún desesperado suceso. Volví con esta determinación a continuar la amistad de doña Eufrasia, y a comunicarnos con la frecuencia que antes hacía gala: si ella me llamaba cuñada, si bien no me pesaba de oírlo, escuchaba a don Manuel más apacible, y si no le respondía a su gusto, a lo menos no le afeaba el decirme su amor sin rebozo; y con lo que más le favorecía era decirle que me pidiese a mi padre por esposa, que le aseguraba de mi voluntad; mas como el traidor llevaba otros intentos, jamás lo puso en ejecución.

Llegóse en este tiempo el alegre de las carnestolendas, tan solemnizado en todas partes, y más en aquella ciudad, que se dice, por ponderarlo más, carnestolendas de Zaragoza. Andábamos todos de fiesta y regocijo, sin reparar los unos en los desaciertos de los otros. Pues fue así, que pasando sobre tarde al cuarto de doña Eufrasia a vestirme con ella de disfraz para una máscara que teníamos prevenida, y ella y sus criadas y otras amigas ocupadas adentro en prevenir lo necesario, su traidor hermano, que debía de estar aguardando esta ocasión, me detuvo a la puerta de su aposento, que, como he dicho, era a la entrada de los de su madre, dándome la

to Don Manuel, I persisted in my wish to burn the note, and she to defend it, until, desiring exactly what she did, I opened it, admonishing her first that Don Manuel was not to find out, but was to be told that I had ripped it up without reading it, and she promised, and I read the following:

"I know not, my ungrateful lady, what your heart is made of, as were it of diamond, my tears would by now have softened it; but, taking no heed of the dangers that befall me, it has become harder each day. If I loved you less than as the mistress of my being and all that I possess, then it seems that your cruelty might be excused; but, since it pleases you that I die without remedy, I promise to give you that pleasure, taking my leave from this world and from your ungrateful eyes, as you will see when I rise from this bed; and perhaps then the fact that you have not entertained my desire will weigh on you."

The note said no more than this. But what more was there to say? May the Lord free us from a note opportunely written; it bears fruit where there is none, and engenders desire even without being read. See what happened to me after I had looked not only at it, but at all the merits together of Don Manuel, and each one in and of itself. Oh, treacherous lover, oh, false gentleman, oh, executioner of my innocence! And, oh, easy women badly counseled; how you let yourselves be won over by honeyed lies, and the gold with which they are covered, that last not a moment longer than does the appetite! Oh, disabusal, that once revealed, no woman will any more be deceived! Oh, men! And why, being made of the same matter and consistency as we, our souls being no different than yours, do you tempt us, as though we were made of other stuff, feeling not the least obliged by the benefits that from birth to death we

bienvenida, como hacía en toda cortesía otras veces; yo, descuidada, o, por mejor, incierta de que pasaría a más atrevimientos, si bien ya habían llegado a tenerme asida por una mano, y viéndome divertida, tiró de mí, y sin poder ser parte a hacerme fuerte, me entró dentro, cerrando la puerta con llave; yo no sé lo que me sucedió, porque del susto me privó el sentido un mortal desmayo.

¡Ah, flaqueza femenil de las mujeres, acobardadas desde la infancia y aviltadas las fuerzas con enseñarlas primero a hacer vainicas que a jugar las armas! ¡Oh, si no volviera jamás en mí, sino que de los brazos del mal caballero me traspasaran a la sepultura! Mas guardábame mi mala suerte para más desdichas, si puede haberlas mayores. Pues pasada poco más de media hora, volví en mí, y me hallé, mal digo, no me hallé, pues me hallé perdida, y tan perdida, que no me supe ni pude volver ni podré ganarme jamás, y infundiendo en mí mi agravio una mortífera rabia, lo que en otra mujer pudiera causar lágrimas y desesperaciones, en mí fue un furor diabólico, con el cual, desasiéndome de sus infames lazos, arremetí a la espada que tenía a la cabecera de la cama, y sacándola de la vaina, se la fui a envainar en el cuerpo; hurtóle al golpe, y no fue milagro, que estaba diestro en hurtar, y abrazándose conmigo, me quitó la espada, que me la iba a entrar por el cuerpo por haber errado el del infame, diciendo de esta suerte: "Traidor, me vengo en mí, pues no he podido en ti, que las mujeres como yo así vengan sus agravios." Procuró el cauteloso amante amansarme y satisfacerme, temeroso de que no diera fin a mi vida, disculpó su atrevimiento con decir que lo había hecho por tenerme segura; y ya con caricias, ya con enojos mezclados con halagos, me dio palabra de ser mi esposo. En fin, a su parecer

provide to you? Because if you were grateful for what you receive from your mothers, in their name you would esteem and revere other women; but now, now I have learned, at my own cost, that you have no design other than to pursue our innocence, weaken our understanding, destroy our strength, and, through reducing us to vile and common beings, raise yourselves up with the imperiousness of immortal fame. Open, all of you, your eyes of understanding and do not allow yourselves to be conquered by those from whom you may fear to be as badly paid as I have been, and thus here and now these disabusals are revealed so that, after learning from me, women may recover their good name and not give way to men who flatter and mock them, nor suffer from their weaknesses and damned interests; as do so many who are then abhorred, debased, and reviled instead of loved.

I again sent Claudia away and in passing begged her not to let Don Manuel know I had read the note, nor what had passed between us, and she promised and, with that, she left, leaving me distracted by so many and such confusing thoughts that I was annoyed with myself for having them. First I loved, then I repented; then I felt piteously moved again, then I felt calmer. Irritated and determined, I decided not to favor Don Manuel, as that would only give him reason to feel emboldened; but also not to disdain him, in order not to force him to take some desperate measure. That decided, I resumed my friendship with Doña Eufrasia, and we spoke with the frequency that before had delighted us so: if she called me sister-in-law, and if hearing that did not trouble me, I listened to Don Manuel in a calmer fashion, and though I did not respond to him as he would have liked, at least I did

más quieta, aunque no al mío, que estaba hecha una pisada serpiente, me dejó volver a mi aposento tan ahogada en lágrimas, que apenas tenía aliento para vivir. Este suceso dio conmigo en la cama, de una peligrosa enfermedad, que fomentada de mis ahogos y tristezas, me vino a poner a punto de muerte; estando de verme así tan penados mis padres, que lastimaban a quien los veía.

Lo que granjeó don Manuel con este atrevimiento fue que si antes me causaba algún agrado, ya aborrecía hasta su sombra. Y aunque Claudia hacía instancia por saber de mí la causa de este pesar que había en mí, no lo consiguió, ni jamás la quise escuchar palabra que de don Manuel procurase decirme, y las veces que su hermana me veía era para mí la misma muerte; en fin, yo estaba tan aborrecida, que si no me la di yo misma, fue por no perder el alma. Bien conocía Claudia mi mal en mis sentimientos, y por asegurarse más, habló a don Manuel, de quien supo todo lo sucedido; pidióle me aquietase y procurase desenojar, prometiéndole a ella lo que a mí, que no sería otra su esposa. Permitió el cielo que me mejorase de mi mal, porque aún me faltaban por pasar otros mayores. Y un día que estaba Claudia sola conmigo, que mi madre ni las demás criadas estaban en casa, me dijo estas razones:

—No me espanto, señora mía, que tu sentimiento sea de la calidad que has mostrado y muestras; mas a los casos que la fortuna encamina y el Cielo permite para secretos suyos, que a nosotros no nos toca el saberlo, no se han de tomar tan a pechos, y por el cabo que se aventure a perder la vida y con ella el alma. Confieso que el atrevimiento del señor don Manuel fue el mayor que se puede imaginar; mas tu temeridad es más terrible, y supuesto que en este suceso, aunque has aventurado

not reproach him for declaring his love openly; and the most I conceded was to tell him that if he asked my father for my hand, I would most assuredly consent; but as the traitor had other plans, he never put that one into practice.

Carnival came around that time, a festivity so popular in these parts, and especially in that city, where it was called the Carnival of Zaragoza to distinguish it further. We were all in a gay, festive mood, and no one was paying any notice to the affairs of others. Matters were such that, on my way one afternoon to Doña Eufrasia's room where I was going to put on my costume for the masked ball we planned to attend, and where she and her maids and other friends were already busy getting ready, her traitorous brother, who must have been waiting for just such an occasion, stopped me at the door to his chamber, which as I have said, was near the entryway to those of his mother, and greeted me, as courteously as he had on other occasions. I was careless, or rather, I doubted that he would become bolder, since he had already grasped my hand, and seeing I was distracted, he pulled at me, and as I did not have the strength to resist, he had me inside the room, and locked the door with a key. I do not know what happened, because due to fright a dead faint deprived me of my senses.

Oh, the feminine weaknesses of women, turned into cowards from infancy and their strengths weakened because rather than playing at war they are taught how to make a hemstitch! Oh, if only I had never come to my senses, but had gone from the arms of the evil gentleman to the grave! But my bad luck was saving me for greater misfortunes, if anything worse were possible. Because, after a little more than a half hour had passed, I came to, and I found

mucho, no has perdido nada, pues en siendo tu esposo queda puesto el reparo, si tu pérdida se pudiera remediar con esos sentimientos y desesperaciones, fuera razón tenerlas. Ya no sirven desvíos para quien posee y es dueño de tu honor, pues con ellos das motivo para que, arrepentido y enfadado de tus sequedades, te deje burlada; pues no son las partes de tu ofensor de tan pocos méritos que no podrá conquistar con ellas cualquiera hermosura de su patria. Puesto más acertado es que se acuda al remedio, y no que cuando le busques no le halles, hoy me ha pedido que te amanse y te diga cuán mal lo haces con él y contigo misma, y que está con mucha pena de tu mal; que te alientes y procures cobrar salud, que tu voluntad es la suya, y no saldrá en esto y en todo lo que ordenares de tu gusto. Mira, señora, que esto es lo que te está bien, y que se pongan medios con tus padres para que sea tu esposo, con que la quiebra de tu honor quedará soldada y satisfecha, y todo lo demás es locura y acabar de perderte.

Bien conocí que Claudia me aconsejaba lo cierto, supuesto que ya no se podía hallar otro remedio; mas estaba tan aborrecida de mí misma, que en muchos días no llevó de mí buena respuesta. Y aunque ya me empezaba a levantar, en más de dos meses no me dejé ver de mi atrevido amante, ni recado que me enviaba quería recibir, ni papel que llegaba a mis manos llevaba otra respuesta que hacerle pedazos. Tanto, que don Manuel, o fuese que en aquella ocasión me tenía alguna voluntad, o porque picado de mis desdenes quería llevar adelante sus traiciones, se descubrió a su hermana, y le contó lo que conmigo le había pasado y pasaba, de que doña Eufrasia, admirada y pesarosa, después de haberle afeado facción tan grosera y mal hecha, tomó por su cuenta quitarme el

myself—no that is not true, I did not find myself as I found that I was lost, and so very lost; and I did not recognize myself nor did I know how to return nor will I be able to return to myself ever again, and my affront filled me with a deadly rage, and what in another woman might cause tears and desperation, in me became diabolical fury, with which, tearing myself from his infamous embrace, I rushed for the sword he had at the head of the bed, and removing it from its scabbard, I went to plunge it into his body. He dodged the blow, and this was no miracle; he was good at dodging, and embracing me, he took away the sword that, having missed the body of the scoundrel, I was about to thrust into my own, saying to him something like, "Traitor, I will take my revenge on myself as I have not been able to on you, since it is thus that women like myself avenge their wrongs." My wary lover, fearful that I would take my own life, tried to calm and reassure me, apologizing for his boldness, saying that he had done it to assure that I would be his; and first with caresses, then with anger mixed with flattery, he promised that he would be my husband. In the end, as I seemed calmer to him, though not to me, for I was turned into a trampled serpent, he allowed me to return to my chamber choking so with tears that I barely had breath to go on living. This event sent me to bed with a dangerous illness that, complicated by my anguish and pain, brought me near death; and my parents suffered so on seeing me in that state that those who saw them were sorely moved.

If before Don Manuel pleased me to a degree, now, with this affront, he caused me to detest even his shadow. And though Claudia made an effort to know the cause of this sorrow that was in me, she did not

enojo. Finalmente ella y Claudia trabajaron tanto conmigo, que me rindieron. Y como sobre las pesadumbres entre amantes las paces aumentan el gusto, todo el aborrecimiento que tenía a don Manuel se volvió en amor, y en él el amor aborrecimiento: que los hombres, en estando en posesión, la voluntad se desvanece como humo. Un año pasé en estos desvanecimientos, sin poder acabar con don Manuel pusiese terceros con mi padre para que se efectuasen nuestras bodas; y otras muchas que a mi padre le trataban no llegaban a efecto, por conocer la poca voluntad que tenía de casarme. Mi amante me entretenía diciendo que en haciéndole Su Majestad merced de un hábito de Santiago que le había pedido, para que más justamente mi padre le admitiese por hijo, se cumplirían mis deseos y los suyos. Si bien yo sentía mucho estas dilaciones, y casi temía mal de ellas, por no disgustarle, no apretaba más la dificultad.

En este tiempo, en lugar de un criado que mi padre había despedido, entró a servir en casa un mancebo, que, como después supe, era aquel caballero pobre que jamás había sido bien visto de mis ojos. Mas ¿quién mira bien a un pobre? El cual, no pudiendo vivir sin mi presencia, mudado hábito y nombre, hizo esta transformación. Parecióme cuando le vi la primera vez que era el mismo que era; mas no hice reparo en ello, por parecerme imposible. Bien conoció Luis, que así dijo llamarse, a los primeros lances, la voluntad que yo y don Manuel nos teníamos, no creyendo de la entereza de mi condición que pasase a más de honestos y recatados deseos, dirigidos al conyugal lazo. Y él estaba cierto que en esto no había de alcanzar, aunque fuera conocido por don Felipe, mas que los despegos que siempre callaba, por que no le privase de verme, sufriendo como amante

find out, nor did I ever again want to hear from her a word that Don Manuel tried to tell me, and the times his sister came to see me were like death itself. In short, I so detested myself that if I did not take my own life, it was so as not to lose my soul. Claudia knew well that my illness was due to my feelings, and to assure herself further, she spoke to Don Manuel, from whom she learned all that had happened. He begged that I be calm and try to rid myself of anger, promising her what he had promised me, that no one else would be his wife. The heavens allowed me to recover from my misfortune, since there were others, more serious, yet to come upon me. And one day when Claudia was alone with me, and neither my mother nor the other servants were in the house, she told me the following:

"It does not surprise me, my lady, that your feelings be of the sort you have displayed and still display; but that which fortune brings and the heavens permit for their own secret reasons not revealed to us ought not be taken so seriously that in the end one risks losing one's life, and with it one's soul. I confess that the boldness of Lord Don Manuel was the most serious that can be imagined; but your temerity is even worse, and though as a result you have ventured much, you have lost nothing, as in being your husband the damage will have been repaired; if your loss could be remedied with these feelings and this desperation, you would have reason to feel them. But cutting off one who possesses and is owner of your honor serves no purpose, as with that you give him reason to become regretful and angered with your curtness, and to leave you deceived, since your offender is not so little endowed that he could not win with his gifts some other beauty of his land. A more certain course

aborrecido y desestimado, dándose por premiado en su amor con poderme hablar y ver a todas horas. De esta manera pasé algunos meses, que aunque don Manuel, según conocí después, no era era su amor verdadero, sabía tan bien las artes de fingir, que yo me daba por contenta y pagada de mi voluntad. Así me duraron estos engaños, mas ¿cómo puede la mentira pasar por verdad sin que al cabo se descubra? Acuérdome que una tarde que estábamos en el estrado de su hermana, burlando y diciendo burlas y entretenidos acentos como otras veces, le llamaron, y él, al levantarse del asiento, me dejó caer la daga en las faldas, que se la había quitado por el estorbo que le hacía para estar sentado en bajo. A cuyo asunto hice este soneto:

Toma tu acero cortador, no seas
   causa de un exceso inadvertido,
   que puede ser, Salicio, que sea Dido
   si por mi mal quisieses ser Eneas.
Cualquiera atrevimiento es bien que creas
   de un pecho amante a tu valor rendido,
   muy cerca está de ingrato el que es
      querido;
   llévale, ingrato, si mi bien deseas.
Si a cualquiera rigor de aquesos ojos
   te lloro Eneas y me temo Elisa,
   quítame la ocasión de darme muerte,
Que quieres la vida por despojos,
   que me mates de amor, mi amor te
      avisa;
   tú ganarás honor, yo dulce suerte.[3]

Alabaron doña Eufrasia y su hermano más la presteza de hacerle que el soneto; si bien don Manuel, tibiamente, ya parecía que andaba su voluntad achacosa, y la mía

3. Dido (también llamada Elisa), fundadora y reina de Cartago, se suicidó, según el poeta Virgilio, al ser abandonada por su amante, Eneas.

is to take immediate advantage of the remedy, because if you wait until later to seek him out, you may not find him. Today he has asked me to calm you and to tell you how badly you do him and yourself, and that your illness gives him much grief; that you take heart and try to recover your health, that your will is his, and that he will not go back on that and on all that you see fit to ordain. Mark, my lady, how this is for your own good, and see to it that measures are taken with your parents to make him your husband, with which the damage to your honor will be repaired and satisfied, and everything else is madness and will end up being your loss."

I full knew that Claudia advised me well, given that now there was no other remedy to be found; but I so detested my very self, that for many days she did not have from me a suitable response. And though I now began to get out of bed, for more than two months I did not allow my bold lover to see me, nor did I receive any message he sent, nor did any note that came to my hands receive a response other than being torn to pieces. Matters were such that Don Manuel, either because at that time he had some desire to have me, or because piqued by my disdain he wanted to carry on with his treachery, went to his sister and told her what had happened with me and was happening, so that Doña Eufrasia, surprised and grieved, after having condemned an act so rude and badly done, took it upon herself to relieve me of my anger. Finally she and Claudia together worked on me to bring me to surrender. And because the suffering of lovers increases the joy of making amends, all the loathing I felt for Don Manuel turned to love, and in him love to loathing; because desire in men fades like smoke the moment they have what they want. I spent a

temerosa de algún mal suceso en los míos, y a mis solas daban mis ojos muestra de mis temores, quejábame de mi mal pagado amor, dando al cielo quejas de mi desdicha. Y cuando don Manuel, viéndome triste y los ojos con las señales de haberles dado el castigo que no merecían, pues no tuvieron culpa en mi tragedia, me preguntaba la causa, por no perder el decoro de mi gravedad, desmentía con él los sentimientos de ellos, que eran tantos, que apenas los podía disimular. Enamoréme, rogué, rendíme; vayan, vengan penas, alcáncense unas a otras. Mas por una violencia estar sujeta a tantas desventuras, ¿a quién ha sucedido sino a mí? ¡Ay, damas hermosas y avisadas, y qué desengaño éste, si le contempláis! Y ¡ay, hombres, y qué afrenta para vuestros engaños! ¡Quién pensara que don Manuel hiciera burla de una mujer como yo, supuesto que, aunque era noble y rico, aun para escudero de mi casa no le admitieran mis padres!, que éste es el mayor sentimiento que tengo, pues estaba segura de que no me merecía y conocía que me desestimaba.

Fue el caso que había más de diez años que don Manuel hablaba una dama de la ciudad, ni la más hermosa, ni la más honesta, y aunque casada, no hacía ascos de ningún galanteo, porque su marido tenía buena condición: comía sin traerlo, y por no estorbar, se iba fuera cuando era menester; que aun aquí había reprehensión para los hombres; mas los comunes y bajos que viven de esto no son hombres, sino bestias. Cuando más engolfada estaba Alejandra, que así tenía nombre esta dama, en la amistad de don Manuel, quiso el cielo, para castigarla, o para destruirme, darle una peligrosa enfermedad, de quien, viéndose en peligro de muerte, prometió a Dios apartarse de tan ilícito trato, haciendo voto de cumplirlo. Sustentó esta devota

year in this unsteady state, without succeeding in bringing Don Manuel to speak to my father so that the wedding could take place; and many others who went to my father were unable to win his consent, knowing, as he did, how weak was my desire to marry. My lover distracted me by saying that when His Majesty gave him the habit of Santiago as he had requested, precisely so that my father would feel more justified in accepting him as a son, he would fulfill my desires and his own. Though I felt these delays deeply, and almost feared that no good would come of them, I did not press the issue so as not to annoy him.

At that time, a young man was added to the household staff to replace a servant my father had dismissed; I later learned that he was the same poor gentleman who had never found favor in my eyes. But who looks favorably upon a poor person? It was he who, unable to live without my presence, changed his habit and his name, thus transforming himself. I seemed to recognize him the first time I saw him; but I did not give it a second thought, as it seemed to me impossible. Luis, for that was what he called himself, was immediately aware of the plans that Don Manuel and I had, and not fully understanding my situation, did not know that it went beyond an honest and chaste wish to marry. And he was certain that this he himself would not achieve, even were he known as Don Felipe, but he never said a word about my indifference so that he would not lose sight of me altogether, suffering like a despised lover held in low esteem, considering his love rewarded in being able to talk to me and see me at all hours. Matters went on like this for several months, and though I later found out that Don Manuel's love was not true, so skillful was he in the arts

promesa, viéndose con la deseada salud, año y medio, que fue el tiempo en que don Manuel buscó mi perdición, viéndose despedido de Alejandra; bien que, como después supe, la visitaba en toda cortesía, y la regalaba por la obligación pasada. ¡Ah, mal hayan estas correspondencias corteses, que tan caras cuestan a muchas! Y entretenido en mi galanteo, faltó a la asistencia de Alejandra, conociendo el poco fruto que sacaba de ella; pues esta mujer, en faltar de su casa, como solía mi ingrato dueño, conoció que era la ocasión otro empleo, y buscando la causa, o que de criadas pagadas de la casa de don Manuel, o mi desventura que se lo debió de decir, supo cómo don Manuel trataba su casamiento conmigo. Entró aquí alabarme mi hermosura y su rendimiento, y como jamás se apartaba de idolatrar en mi imagen, que cuando se cuentan los sucesos, y más si han de dañar, con menos ponderación son suficientes. En fin, Alejandra, celosa y envidiosa de mis dichas, faltó a Dios lo que había prometido, para sobrarme a mí en penas; que si faltó a Dios, ¿cómo no me había de sobrar a mí? Era atrevida y resuelta, y lo primero a que se atrevió fue a verme. Pasemos adelante, que fuera hacer este desengaño eterno, y no es tan corto el tormento que padezco en referirle que me saboree tan despacio en él. Acarició a don Manuel, solicitó que volviese a su amistad, consiguió lo que deseó, y volvió de nuevo a reiterar la ofensa, faltando en lo que a Dios había prometido de poner enmienda. Parecerá, señores, que me deleito en nombrar a menudo el nombre de este ingrato, pues no es sino que como para mí es veneno, quisiera que trayéndole en mis labios, me acabara de quitar la vida. Volvióse, en fin, a adormecer y transportar en los engañosos encantos de esta Circe, y como una división causa mayores deseos entre los

of deception I believed myself content and my desires fulfilled. And in this way his deceit continued. But how can a lie pass for truth without at last being uncovered? I remember that one afternoon when we were in his sister's chamber, teasing and telling jokes and playing word games as on other occasions, they called him, and he, on rising from his chair, let fall into my lap the dagger he had removed as it bothered him because he was on a low seat. The incident inspired me to compose this sonnet:

Take your cutting steel, do not let it be
   the cause of some unwanted excess,
   for it might be, Salicio, that I be Dido,
   if to hurt me you wish to become
     Aeneas.
No doubt you believe a lover's every
   boldness
   a sign of surrender to your qualities,
   very near to being an ingrate is he who
   is loved;
   take it away, ingrate, if my well-being
   you desire.
If at every sign of disdain in those eyes
   I cry to you Aeneas and I fear I am
   Elisa,
   take from me the occasion to bring
   death to myself.
If to you life is worth so little,
   then kill me with love, my love advises
   you;
   you will win honor, I sweet fortune.[3]

Doña Eufrasia and her brother praised more my quickness in making up the sonnet than the song itself; and in fact Don Manuel was cool, as it now seemed that his desire had waned, and I became fearful of something bad to come; and when I was

3. Dido, also called Elisa, legendary founder and queen of Carthage, killed herself, according to Virgil, when her lover Aeneas abandoned her.

que se aman, fue con tanta puntualidad el asistencia en su casa, que fue fuerza hiciese falta en la mía. Tanto, que ni en los perezosos días del verano, ni en las cansadas noches del invierno no había una hora para mí. Y con esto empecé a sentir las penas que una desvalida y mal pagada mujer puede sentir, porque si a fuerza de quejas y sentimientos había un instante para estar conmigo, era con tanta frialdad y tibieza, que se apagan en ella los encendidos fuegos de mi voluntad, no para apartarme de tenerla, sino para darle las sazones que merecía. Y últimamente empecé a temer; del temer nace el celar, y del celar buscar las desdichas y hallarlas. No le quiero prometer a un corazón amante más perdición que venir a tropezar en celos, que es cierto que la caída será para no levantarse más; porque si calla los agravios, juzgando que los ignora, no se recatan de hacerlos; y si habla más descubiertamente, pierden el respeto, como me sucedió a mí, que no pudiendo ya disimular las sinrazones de don Manuel, empecé a desenfadarme y reprehenderlas, y de esto pasar a reñirle, con que me califiqué por enfadosa y de mala condición, y a pocos pasos que di, me hallé en los lances de aborrecida. Ofréceseme a la memoria un soneto que hice, hallándome un día muy apasionada, que, aunque os canse, le he de decir:

No vivas, no, dichosa, muy segura
    de que has de ser toda la vida amada;
    llegará el tiempo que la nieve helada
    agote de tu dicha la hermosura.
Yo, como tú, gocé también ventura,
    ya soy, como me ves, bien desdichada;
    querida fui, rogada y estimada
    del que tu gusto y mi dolor procura.
Consuela mi pasión, que el dueño mío,
    que ahora es tuyo, fue conmigo
      ingrato,

alone my eyes revealed my fears, I complained of my love poorly paid, sending to the heavens complaints of my misfortune. And when Don Manuel, seeing me sad and my eyes with signs of having suffered punishment they did not merit, since they were not to blame for my tragedy, asked me why, so as not to forgo the respect seriousness commands, I denied to him the sentiments they held, though they were so many that I could barely hide them. I fell in love, I entreated, I surrendered; let sufferings come and go, let them catch up with one another. But to be subject to such misfortunes as a result of violence, to whom has this happened but me? Oh, beautiful ladies forewarned, and what a disabusal this is when you think of it! And, ah, men, what an unmasking of your vile deceits! Who would have thought Don Manuel capable of mocking a woman such as I, given that, though he was noble and rich, my parents would not have admitted him into my house even as a squire. And this is the greatest wound I feel, that I was certain that my worth was greater than his, and knew that he disdained me.

It happens that for more than ten years Don Manuel had been seeing a lady in the city, not even one of the most beautiful, nor the most honorable, and though married, she did not turn up her nose at any flattery, because her husband had a fine situation; he ate without earning a thing, and so as not to be in the way, he left the house when it was necessary; and even here men are to be reprehended; but the common and low who live like this are not men, but beasts. When Alexandra, for that was this lady's name, was most swept up in her friendship with Don Manuel, the heavens decided to bring upon her, either to punish her or to destroy me, a dangerous ailment, and she, seeing herself in

también contigo lo será, dichosa.
Pagarásme el agravio en su desvío;
  no pienses que has feriado muy barato,
  que te has de ver como yo estoy celosa.

Admitía estas finezas don Manuel, como quien ya no las estimaba; antes con enojos quería desvanecer mis sospechas, afirmándolas por falsas. Y dándose más cada día a sus desaciertos, venimos él y yo a tener tantos disgustos y desasosiegos, que más era muerte que amor el que había entre los dos; y con esto me dispuse a averiguar la verdad de todo, porque no me desmintiese, y de camino, por si podía hallar remedio a tan manifiesto daño, mandé a Claudia seguirle, con que se acabó de perder todo. Porque una tarde que le vi algo inquieto, y que ni por ruegos ni lágrimas mías, ni pedírselo a su hermana, no se pudo estorbar que no saliese de casa, mandé a Claudia viese dónde iba, la cual le siguió hasta verle entrar en casa de Alejandra. Y aguardando a ver en lo que resultaba, vio que ella con otras amigas y don Manuel se entraron en un coche y se fueron a un jardín. Y no pudiendo ya la fiel Claudia sufrir tantas libertades cometidas en ofensa mía, se fue tras ellos, y al entrar en el vergel, dejándose ver, le dijo lo que fue justo, si, como fue bien dicho, fuera bien admitido. Porque don Manuel, si bien corrido de ser descubierto, afeó y trató mal a Claudia, riñéndola más como dueño que como amante mío; con lo cual la atrevida Alejandra, tomándose la licencia de valida, se atrevió a Claudia con palabras y obras, dándose por sabidora de quién era yo, cómo me llamaba y, en fin, cuanto por mí había pasado, mezclando entre estas libertades las amenazas de que daría cuenta a mi padre de todo. Y aunque no cumplió esto, hizo otros atrevimientos tan grandes o mayores, como era venir a la posada de

danger of dying, promised God to end this illicit pact, making a vow to do just that. This devout promise lasted for one and a half years after she regained the health she desired, which was the time during which Don Manuel sought my perdition, seeing himself dismissed by Alexandra; so that, as I later found out, he visited her with all due courtesy, and gave her presents for past obligations. Ah, evil are these courtly connections, that cost so many women so dear! And enjoying his flirtation with me, he missed a visit with Alexandra, knowing the little fruit she provided; so this woman, when he missed their meeting, as my ungrateful husband was wont to do, realized that it was because he was busy elsewhere, and in her search for information, either from maidservants from Don Manuel's house who had been paid or from what must have been common knowledge about my misfortune, she found out that Don Manuel planned to marry me. He then began to praise my beauty and his submission, and as he never once left off praising my good looks, when what happened next is revealed, especially that destined to cause trouble, the reason will be clear. In short, Alexandra, jealous and envious of my good fortune, broke her promise with God, so that I might have suffering to spare; for if she broke her promise to God, what might she care for my suffering? She was daring and determined, and the first thing she dared was to see me. Let us move on, so that this disabusal not go on forever, as the torment I suffer on telling it is not so short-lived that I need to savor it slowly. She caressed Don Manuel, asked that their friendship be renewed, succeeded in her designs, and thus returned to her offense, breaking her promise to God to make amends. It would seem, gentlemen, that I delight in repeat-

don Manuel a todas horas. Entraba atro-
pellándolo todo, y diciendo mil libertades;
tanto, que en diversas ocasiones se puso
Claudia con ella a mil riesgos. En fin, para
no cansaros, lo diré de una vez. Ella era
mujer que no temía a Dios; ni a su marido,
pues llegó su atrevimiento a tratar quitarme la vida con sus propias manos. De todos estos atrevimientos no daba don Manuel la culpa a Alejandra, sino a mí, y tenía
razón, pues yo, por mis peligros, debía sufrir más; estaba ya tan precipitada, que
ninguno se me hacía áspero, ni peligroso,
pues me entraba por todos sin temor de
ningún riesgo. Todo era afligirme, todo
llorar y todo dar a don Manuel quejas;
unas veces, con caricias, y otras con despegos, determinándome tal vez a dejarle y no
tratar más de esto, aunque me quedase
perdida, y otras pidiéndole hablase a mis
padres, para que siendo su mujer cesasen
estas revoluciones. Mas como ya no quería, todas estas desdichas sentía y temía
doña Eufrasia, porque había de venir a parar en peligro de su hermano; mas no hallaba remedio, aunque le buscaba. A todas
estas desventuras hice unas décimas, que
os quiero referir, porque en ellas veréis mis
sentimientos mejor pintados, y con más fi-
nos colores, que dicen así:

Ya de mi dolor rendida,
    con los sentidos en calma,
    estoy deteniendo el alma,
    que anda buscando salida;
    ya parece que la vida,
    como la candela que arde
    y en verse morir cobarde
    vuelve otra vez a vivir,
    porque aunque desea morir,
    procura que sea más tarde.
Llorando noches y días,
    doy a mis ojos enojos,

ing so often that ingrate's name, but it is
simply that because it is like poison to me,
I wish that in bringing it to my lips, I were
able to end this life. He returned, in short,
to be soothed and transported by the
treacherous charms of this Circe, and as a
separation creates greater desire between
those who love, his attendance in her
house was so constant that it was necessary that he be absent from mine. Matters
were such that neither in the lazy days of
summer nor the long nights of winter was
there an hour for me. And with that I began to feel the suffering that a helpless and
ill-rewarded woman might feel, because if
as a result of complaints and sentiments
he spent a moment with me, it was with
such coldness and distance that the burning fires of my desire were thus put out,
not that desire ended, but it was without
the spice it merited. And lately I began to
fear; from fear jealousy is born, and from
jealousy the search for and the finding of
unhappiness. I would not wish on a loving
heart greater perdition than that which
comes from an encounter with jealousy,
for it is true that so heavy will be the fall
that getting up again will forever be impossible; because if the heart is silent
about the offenses, believing itself ignorant of them, they have no shame about
repeating them; and if it speaks more
openly, they lose respect, as happened to
me who, no longer able to hide the
wrongs of Don Manuel, began to get angry and to reproach him on that account,
and from that I went on to nag him, and
with that I judged myself a harpy and of
little worth, and before long, I was engulfed in self-loathing. There comes to
mind a sonnet I composed one day in the
grips of passion, and though it tire you, I
must recite it:

como si fueran mis ojos
causa de las ansias mías.
¿Adónde estáis, alegrías?
Decidme, ¿dónde os perdí?
Responded, ¿qué causa os di?
Mas ¿qué causa puede haber
mayor que no merecer
el bien que se fue de mí?
Sol fui de algún cielo ingrato,
si acaso hay ingrato cielo;
fuego fue, volvióse hielo;
sol fui, luna me retrato,
mi menguante fue su trato;
mas si la deidad mayor
está en mí, que es el amor,
y éste no puede menguar,
difícil será alcanzar
lo que intenta su rigor.
Celos tuve, mas, querida,
de los celos me burlaba:
antes en ellos hallaba
sainetes para la vida;
ya, sola y aborrecida,
Tántalo en sus glorias soy;
rabiando de sed estoy,
¡ay, qué penas! ¡ay, qué agravios!,
pues con el agua en los labios,
mayor tormenta me doy.
¿Qué mujer habrá tan loca,
que viéndose aborrecer,
no le canse el padecer
y esté como firme roca?
Yo sola, porque no toca
a mí la ley de olvidar,
venga pesar a pesar,
a un rigor otro rigor,
que ha de conocer amor
que sé cómo se ha de amar.
Ingrato, que al hielo excedes;
nieve, que a la nieve hielas,
si mi muerte no recelas,
desde hoy más temerla puedes,
regatea las mercedes,
aprieta más el cordel,

Do not live, no, fortunate woman,
    so certain
        that yours will be an entire life filled
        with love;
        the time will come when the frozen
        snow
    wears away the beauty that is your joy.
I, like you, enjoyed much fortune,
    now I am, as you see me, most
    unfortunate;
        I was loved, entreated, and esteemed
        by that whence comes your pleasure
        and my pain.
My passion finds consolation that my
    master,
    who now is yours, was with me an
    ingrate,
        and with you, fortunate one, will be as
        well.
In your error, you will pay me for the
    offense;
    do not think that you have bartered
    well,
        as you will come to be as I am, jealous.

Don Manuel received these manifesta-
tions as one for whom they meant nothing;
he first, in anger, tried to dismiss my suspicions, insisting they were unfounded. And
as he daily gave himself over more to his
erring ways, he and I came to have so many
quarrels and tensions that what was between us was more like death than love;
and with that I decided to find out the
whole truth, so that he could not deny it,
and at the same time to see if I could find a
remedy for so evident an injury; I ordered
Claudia to follow him, and with that all
was lost for good. Because one afternoon
when I saw him restless, and when neither
my pleas nor my tears, nor the requests of
his sister, would bring him to change his
plans to leave the house, I sent Claudia to
find out where he went, and she followed

mata esta vida con él,
sigue tu ingrata porfía;
que te pesará algún día
de haber sido tan cruel.
Sigue, cruel, el encanto
de esa engañosa sirena,
que por llevarte a su pena,
te adormece con su canto;
huye mi amoroso llanto,
no te obligues de mi fe,
porque así yo esperaré
que has de ser como deseo
de aquella arpía Fineo,
para que vengada esté.
Préciate de tu tibieza,
no te obliguen mis enojos,
pon más capote a los ojos,
cánsate de mi firmeza;
ultraja más mi nobleza,
ni sigas a la razón;
que yo, que en mi corazón
amor carácter ha sido,
pelearé con tu olvido,
muriendo por tu ocasión.
Bien sé que tu confianza
es de mi desdicha parte,
y fuera mejor matarte
a pura desconfianza;
todo crüel se me alcanza,
que como te ves querido,
tratas mi amor con olvido,
porque una noble mujer,
o no llegar a querer,
o ser lo que siempre ha sido.
Ojos, llorad, pues no tiene
ya remedio vuestro mal;
ya vuelve el dolor fatal,
ya el alma a la boca viene.
Ya sólo morir conviene,
porque triunfe el que me mata;
ya la vida se desata
del lazo que al alma dio,
y con ver que me mató,
no olvido al que me maltrata.

him until she saw him go into Alexandra's house. And, waiting to see what would happen next, she saw her with other friends and Don Manuel getting into a coach and going to a park. And as the faithful Claudia was unable to bear the offense against me in the many liberties taken, she followed them, and on entering the park, allowing herself to be seen, she told him what justice demanded be said, and since her words were well chosen, it would have been well for them to have been received. Because Don Manuel, though abashed at having been discovered, turned ugly and treated Claudia badly, assuming the mien of master rather than that of my lover; and with that the bold Alexandra, taking upon herself the liberties of the favored party, dared to respond to Claudia with words and deeds, announcing that she knew who I was, what my name was, and, in short, all that had happened on my account, mixing with these liberties threats to reveal all to my father. And though she did not carry this out, she did things equally bold or bolder, such as coming to Don Manuel's room at all hours. She entered trampling everything underfoot, and saying a thousand outrageous things, to such an extent that, on a number of occasions, Claudia confronted her at great risk to herself. In short, in order not to tire you, I will say it once and for all. She was a woman who feared neither God nor her husband, as her daring reached such heights as to attempt to take my life with her own hands. And for all this insolence Don Manuel did not blame Alexandra but me, and he was right, since I, for the risks I exposed myself to, deserved to suffer more. I was now so desperate that none of these dangers seemed harsh, or dangerous, since I embarked upon all of them without fear of any risk. Everything afflicted me, everything made

Alma, buscad dónde estar,
 que mi palabra os empeño,
 que en vuestra posada hay dueño
 que quiere en todo mandar.
 Ya, ¿qué tenéis que aguardar,
 si vuestro dueño os despide,
 y en vuestro lugar recibe
 otra alma que más estima?
 ¿No veis que en ella se anima
 y con más contento vive?
¡Oh cuántas glorias perdidas
 en esa casa dejáis!
 ¿Cómo ninguna sacáis?
 Pues no por mal adquiridas,
 mal premiadas, bien servidas,
 que en eso ninguno os gana;
 pero si es tan inhumana
 la impiedad del que os arroja,
 pues veis que en veros se enoja,
 idos vos de buena gana.
Sin las potencias salís,
 ¿cómo esos bienes dejáis?,
 que a cualquier parte que vais
 no os querrán, si lo advertís.
 Mas oigo que me decís
 que sois como el que se abrasa,
 que viendo que el fuego pasa
 a ejecutarle en la vida,
 deja la hacienda perdida,
 que se abrase con la casa.
Pensando en mi desventura,
 casi a la muerte he llegado,
 ya mi hacienda se ha abrasado,
 que eran bienes sin ventura.
 ¡Oh, tú, que vives segura
 y contenta en casa ajena!:
 de mi fuego queda llena,
 y algún día vivirá,
 y la tuya abrasará;
 toma escarmiento en mi pena.
Mira, y siente cuál estoy,
 tu caída piensa en mí,
 que ayer maravilla fuí,
 y hoy sombra mía no soy:

me cry, and everything made me complain to Don Manuel; sometimes I treated him with affection and at others with indifference, determined perhaps to leave him and to have nothing more to do with this, though that would have meant I was lost; at other times I asked that he speak to my parents, so that by being his wife these scenes would cease. But as he no longer wanted to, all of these miseries were felt and feared by Doña Eufrasia, because they would eventually put her brother in danger; but there was no remedy, though I searched for it. From all of these misfortunes I invented some verses, which I would like to recite to you, because in them you will see my sentiments better painted and with finer colors; they go like this:

Now having bowed to my pain,
 with my senses calm,
 I am soothing the soul,
 that looks for a way out;
 now it seems that life,
 like the candle that burns
 and on seeing itself die a coward
 comes to life again,
 because though it wishes to die,
 it attempts to delay that moment.
Crying nights and days,
 I vex my eyes,
 as though my eyes were
 the cause of these my anxieties.
 Where are you, joy?
 Tell me, where did I lose you?
 Answer, what cause did I give?
 But what cause can there be
 greater than not meriting
 the good that slipped away from me?
The sun I was of some ungrateful sky,
 if, that is, there be ungrateful skies;
 fire was he, turned to ice;
 sun I was, moon I picture myself,
 his conduct caused my waning;

lo que va de ayer a hoy
podrá ser de hoy a mañana.
Estás contenta y lozana;
pues de un mudable señor
el fiarse es grande error:
no estés tan alegre, Juana.
Gloria mis ojos llamó;
mis palabras, gusto y cielo.
Diome celos, y tomélos
al punto que me los dio.
¡Ah, mal haya quien amó
celosa, firme y rendida,
que cautelosa y fingida
es bien ser una mujer,
para no llegarse a ver,
como estoy, aborrecida!
¡Oh amor, por lo que he servido
a tu suprema deidad,
ten de mi vida piedad!
Esto por premio te pido:
no se alegre este atrevido
en verme por él morir;
pero muriendo vivir,
muerte será, que no vida;
ejecuta amor la herida,
pues yo no acierto a pedir.

Sucedió en este tiempo nombrar Su
Majestad por Virrey de Sicilia al señor Almirante de Castilla, y viéndose don Manuel engolfado en estas competencias que
entre mí y Alejandra traíamos, y lo más
cierto, con poco gusto de casarse conmigo,
considerando su peligro en todo, sin dar
cuenta a su madre y hermana, diligenció
por medio del mayordomo, que era muy
íntimo amigo suyo, y le recibió el señor Almirante por gentilhombre de su cámara, y
teniéndolo secreto, sin decirlo a nadie, sólo
a un criado que le servía, y había de ir con
él hasta la partida del señor Almirante, dos
o tres días antes mandó prevenir su ropa,
dándonos a entender a todos quería ir por

but if the greatest deity
is in me, that is love,
and this cannot wane,
his disdain hard-pressed will be
to attain that which it seeks.
Jealous I was but, loved,
I mocked jealousy:
rather, in jealousy I found
reason to go on living;
now, alone and detested,
Tantalus in his glories am I;
furious with thirst am I,
ah, what sorrows! ah, what offense!
because, with water on my lips,
I only torture myself that much more.
Is there a woman so mad,
who seeing herself despised,
does not tire of suffering
and become hard as stone?
To me alone, whom the law
of forgetting does not touch,
comes sorrow after sorrow,
one slight begets another,
so that love ought to know
that I know how one should love.
Ingrate, you are worse than ice;
and snow, the snow you freeze,
if my death you do not fear,
from now on you will fear more,
leave off with your favors,
pull tighter the cord,
kill this life with it,
go on in your ungrateful offense;
that will weigh on you one day
for having been so cruel.
Follow, cruel one, the charm
of that treacherous siren,
who, for taking you at her expense,
lulls you with her song;
flee from my loving cries,
let not my trust oblige you,
because I will wait
until you become what I wish,

seis u ocho días a un lugar donde tenía no
sé qué hacienda; que esta jornada la había
hecho otras veces en el tiempo que yo le conocía. Llegó el día de la partida, y despedido de todos los de su casa, al despedirse de
mí, que de propósito había pasado a ella
para despedirme, que, como inocente de su
engaño, aunque me pesaba, no era con el
extremo que si supiera la verdad de él, vi
más terneza en sus ojos que otras veces,
porque al tiempo de abrazarme no me
pudo hablar palabra, porque se le arrasa-
ron los ojos de agua, dejándome confusa,
tierna y sospechosa; si bien no juzgué sino
que hacía amor algún milagro en él y conmigo. Y de esta suerte pasé aquel día, ya
creyendo que me amaba, vertiendo lágrimas de alegría, ya de tristeza de verle ausente. Y estando ya cerrada la noche, sentada en una silla, la mano en la mejilla, bien
suspensa y triste, aguardando a mi madre,
que estaba en una visita, entró Luis, el criado de mi casa, o por mejor acertar, don Felipe, aquel caballero pobre, que por serlo
había sido tan mal mirado de mis ojos, que
no había sido ni antes ni en esta ocasión
conocido de ellos, y que servía por sólo ser-
virme. Y viéndome, como he dicho, me
dijo:

—¡Ay, señora mía!, y cómo si supieses
tu desdicha, como yo la sé, esa tristeza y
confusión se volviera en pena de muerte.

Asustéme al oír esto; mas, por no im-
pedir saber el cabo de su confusa razón,
callé; y él prosiguió, diciéndome:

—Ya no hay que disimular, señora,
conmigo, que aunque ha muchos días que
yo imaginaba estos sucesos, ahora es diferente, que ya sé toda la verdad.

—¿Vienes loco, Luis? —le repliqué.

—No vengo loco —volvió a decir—;
aunque pudiera, pues no es tan pequeño el
amor que como a señora mía te tengo, que
no me pudiera haber quitado el juicio, y

by that harpy Phineus,
  I will be avenged.
Take pride in your coldness,
  let not my anger oblige you,
  close your eyes,
  tire of my resolve;
  offend yet again my dignity,
  and do not what is just;
  for I, who in my heart
  a loving character have been,
  will fight your forgetting,
  and die on your account.
Well I know that your confidence
  is the cause of my misfortune,
  and better would it have been to kill
    you
  out of pure distrust;
  you are all cruel, I see it clearly,
  who, on seeing yourself loved,
  treat my love with forgetting,
  because a noble woman
  either finds not love or,
  on finding it, loves forever.
Eyes, weep, as your ill
  has now no remedy;
  the fatal pain has now returned,
  now my heart is in my mouth.
  Now only death will do,
  so that he who kills me triumph;
  now life is unleashed
  from the ties that bound it to the soul,
  and on seeing that he killed me,
  I do not forget him who treated me so.
Soul, seek another home,
  with my word I compel you,
  as in our chamber there is a master
  who wants to command in all.
  Now, what have you to await,
  if your master dismisses you,
  and in your place receives
  another soul he esteems more?
  Do you not see that in her he comes
    alive
  and more content he lives?

aun la vida, lo que hoy he sabido. Y porque no es justo encubrírtelo más, el traidor don Manuel se va a Sicilia con el Almirante, con quien va acomodado por gentilhombre suyo. Y demás de haber sabido de su criado mismo, que por no satisfacerte a la obligación que te tiene ha hecho esta maldad, yo le he visto por mis ojos partir esta tarde. Mira qué quieres que se haga en esto, que a fe de quien soy, y que soy más de lo que tú te imaginas, como sepa que tú gustes de ello, que aunque piense perder la vida, te ha de cumplir lo prometido, o que hemos de morir él y yo por ello.

Disimulando mi pena, le respondí:

—¿Y quién eres tú, que cuando aqueso fuese verdad, tendrías valor para hacer eso que dices?

—Dame licencia —respondió Luis—, que después de hecho, lo sabrás.

Acabé de enterarme de la sospecha que al principio dije había tenido de ser don Felipe, como me había dado el aire, y queriéndole responder, entró mi madre, con que cesó la plática. Y después de haberla recibido, porque me estaba ahogando en mis propios suspiros y lágrimas, entré en mi aposento, y arrojándome sobre la cama, no es necesario contaros las lástimas que dije, las lágrimas que lloré y las determinaciones que tuve, ya de quitarme la vida, ya de quitársela a quien me la quitaba. Y al fin admití la peor y la que ahora oiréis, que éstas eran honrosas, y la que elegí, con la que me acabé de perder; porque al punto me levanté con más ánimo que mi pena prometía, y tomando mis joyas y las de mi madre, y muchos dineros en plata y oro, porque todo estaba a mi poder, aguardé a que mi padre viniese a cenar, que habiendo venido, me llamaron; mas yo respondí que no me sentía buena, que después tomaría una conserva. Se sentaron a cenar, y como vi acomodado

Oh, how many glories were lost
   in that house you left behind!
Why did you not take them with
   you?
For though not ill-acquired,
ill-rewarded, still they serve,
and in that no one bests you;
but if so inhumane is the irreverence
   of him, who casts you off,
then you will see that in seeing you,
he is angered, thus leave him of your
   will.
Without these virtues you left,
   how could you leave those goods?
so that no matter where you go
they will not love you, you will see.
But I hear that you say to me
that you are like one who burns,
and who seeing the fire pass
to take one's life away,
leaves all wealth behind,
so that with the house it burn.
Thinking on my misfortune,
   near to the point of death have I come;
now my fortune has burned,
goods, these were, without future.
Oh you, you live secure
and content in another's house:
of my fire remain full,
and one day it will come to life,
and what is yours it will burn;
take heed from my sorrow.
Look, and feel what I am,
   your fall is much like mine,
who yesterday a marvel was,
and today not even a shadow of myself
   am I:
that which has been from yesterday to
   today
may well be from today to tomorrow.
You are content and vigorous;
but a changeable lord
to trust is a great error:
do not be so joyful, Juana.

lugar para mi loca determinación, por estar los criados y criadas divertidos en servir la mesa, y si aguardara a más, fuera imposible surtir efecto mi deseo, porque Luis cerraba las puertas de la calles y se llevaba la llave, sin dar parte a nadie, ni a Claudia, con ser la secretaria de todo, por una que salía de mi aposento a un corredor, me salí y puse en la calle.

A pocas de mi casa estaba la del criado que he dicho había despedido mi padre cuando recibió a Luis, que yo sabía medianamente, porque lastimada de su necesidad, por ser anciano, le socorría y aun visitaba las veces que sin mi madre salía fuera. Fuime a ella. El buen hombre me recibió con harto dolor de mi desdicha, que ya sabía él por mayor, habiéndole dado palabra que, en haciéndose mis bodas, le traería a mi casa.

Reprendió Octavio, que éste era su nombre, mi determinación; mas visto ya no había remedio, hubo de obedecer y callar, y más viendo que traía dineros, y que le di a él parte de ellos. Allí pasé aquella noche, cercada de penas y temores, y a otro día le mandé fuese a mi casa, y sin darse por entendido, hablase a Claudia y le dijese que me buscaba a mí, como hacía otras veces, y viese qué había y si me buscaban.

Fue Octavio, y halló el remate de mi desventura. Cuando llego a acordarme de esto, no sé cómo no se me hace pedazos el corazón. Llegó Octavio a mi desdichada casa, y vio entrar y salir toda la gente de la ciudad, y admirado entró él también con los demás, y buscando a Claudia, y hallándola triste y llorosa, le contó cómo acabando de cenar entró mi madre donde yo estaba, para saber qué mal me afligía, y como no me halló, preguntó por mí, a lo que todos respondieron que sobre la cama me habían dejado cuando salieron a servirla, y que habiéndome buscado por toda la casa

Glory called out to my eyes;
    my words, delight and heaven.
    He made me jealous,
    and I felt it at once.
    Ah, ill come to her who loved
    jealous, resolved, and devoted,
    when caution and pretense
    better serve a woman,
    in order that she come not to be,
    as I am, despised.
Oh, love, for that which I have served
    your supreme deity,
    take pity on my life!
    This for a reward I beg:
    that he so bold not take joy
    in seeing me die for him;
    but to live dying,
    is not life, but death.
    Let love avenge the offense,
    as I am no longer able to ask.

It happened at this time that His Majesty appointed the Lord Admiral of Castile to be Viceroy of Sicily, and Don Manuel, seeing himself deeply involved in the competition between Alexandra and myself, and clearly with little desire to marry me, considering the dangers on all sides, without thinking of his mother and sister, made the necessary inquiries through the majordomo, who was a very intimate friend of his, and was accepted by the admiral to work as a gentleman in waiting; and keeping this a secret, he said not a word to anyone, except to one of his servants, who was to accompany him until the Lord Admiral's departure, and two or three days prior to this he ordered his clothing prepared, giving all to understand that he wanted to go for six or eight days to a place where he had some sort of business to deal with; and he had made this journey on other occasions during the time I knew him. The day of his de-

y fuera, como hallasen las llaves de los escritorios sobre la cama, y la puerta que salía al corredor, que siempre estaba cerrada, abierta, y mirados los escritorios, y vista la falta de ellos, luego vieron que no faltaba en vano. A cuyo suceso empezó mi madre a dar gritos; acudió mi padre a ellos, y sabiendo la causa, como era hombre mayor, con la pena y susto que recibió, dio una caída de espaldas, privado de todo sentido, y que ni se sabe si de ella, o si del dolor, había sido el desmayo, tan profundo, que no volvió más de él.

De todo esto fue causa mi facilidad. Díjole cómo aunque los médicos mandaban se tuviese las horas que manda y pide la ley, que era excusado, y que ya se trataba de enterrarle; que mi madre estaba poco menos, y que con estas desdichas no se hacía caso de la mía si no era para afear mi mal acuerdo; que ya mi madre había sabido lo que pasaba con don Manuel, que en volviendo yo las espaldas, todos habían dicho lo que sabían, y que no había consentido buscarme, diciendo que pues yo había elegido el marido a mi gusto, que Dios me diese más dicha con él que había dado a su casa.

Volvió Octavio con estas nuevas, bien tristes y amargas para mí, y más cuando me dijo que no se platicaba por la ciudad sino mi suceso. Dobláronse mis pasiones, y casi estuve en términos de perder la vida; mas como aún no me había bien castigado el cielo ser motivo de tantos males, me la quiso guardar para que pase los que faltaban. Animéme algo con saber que no me buscaban, y después de coser todas mis joyas y algunos doblones en parte donde los trujese conmigo sin ser vistos, y dispuesto lo necesario para nuestra jornada, pasados cuatro o seis días, una noche nos metimos Octavio y yo de camino, y partimos la vía de Alicante, donde iba a embarcarse mi ingrato amante. Llegamos a ella, y viendo

parture arrived, and after saying farewell to all in his house, on saying farewell to me, for he had deliberately come to the house to say good-bye to me, and I, innocent of his ruse, was pained, though not as greatly as I would have been had I known the truth, and I saw more tenderness in his eyes than I had at other times, because as he embraced me he could not say a word, because his eyes filled with tears, leaving me confused, tender, and suspicious; but I did not judge, except to assume that love had worked some miracle in him and toward me. And in this way I spent that day, believing now that he loved me, crying tears of joy, then of sadness on finding him absent. And when night had fallen, seated in a chair, my hand on my cheek, very tense and sad, waiting for my mother, who was with visitors, Luis, the servant from my house— or, to be more exact, Don Felipe—arrived, that same poor gentleman, who for being such had been regarded by me with such disfavor, who on past occasions and on this one had gone unrecognized, and who served only to serve me. And on seeing me, as I have described, he said:

"Oh, my lady! And if only you knew your misfortune as well as I do, that sadness and confusion would become a death sentence."

I was startled by these words, but in order to hear out his confusing tale, I remained silent; and he continued, saying to me:

"There is no longer reason to pretend, my lady, not with me, because for days now I have imagined what was about to happen, but now it is different, because now I know for certain."

"Have you gone mad, Luis?" I replied.

"No, I have not gone mad," he said, "though I might have, because the love I

que no habían llegado las galeras, tomamos posada hasta ver el modo que tendría en dejarme ver de don Manuel.

Iba Octavio todos los días adonde el señor Almirante posaba; veía a mi traidor esposo (si le puedo dar este nombre), y veníame a contar lo que pasaba. Y entre otras cosas, me contó un día cómo el mayordomo buscaba una esclava, y que aunque le habían traído algunas, no le habían contentado. En oyendo esto, me determiné a otra mayor fincza, o a otra locura mayor que las demás, y como lo pensé lo puse por obra. Y fue que, fingiendo clavo y S para el rostro, me puse en hábito conveniente para fingirme esclava y mora, poniéndome por nombre Zelima, diciendo a Octavio me llevase y dijera era suya, y que si agradaba, no reparase en el precio.[4] Mucho sintió Octavio mi determinación, vertiendo lágrimas en abundancia por mí; mas yo le consolé con advertirle este disfraz no era más de para proseguir mi intento y traer a don Manuel a mi voluntad, y ausentarme de España, y que teniendo a los ojos a mi ingrato, sin conocerme, descubriría su intento. Con esto se consoló Octavio, y más con decirle que el precio que le diesen por mí se aprovechase de él, y me avisase a Sicilia de lo que mi madre disponía de sí.

En fin, todo se dispuso tan a gusto mío, que antes que pasaron ocho días ya estuve vendida en cien ducados, y esclava, no de los dueños que me habían comprado y dado por mí la cantidad que digo, sino de mi ingrato y alevoso amante, por quien yo me quise entregar a tan vil fortuna. En fin, satisfaciendo a Octavio con el dinero que dieron por mí, y más de los que yo tenía, se despidió para volverse a su casa con tan tierno sentimiento, que por no verle verter tiernas lágrimas, me aparté de él sin

4. "S" + "clavo" = esclavo, marca tiznada en la cara de los esclavos.

have for you as my lady is so great that well might I have taken leave of my senses, and even my life, because of what I have learned today. And because it is not right to hide it from you any longer, that traitor Don Manuel is on his way to Sicily with the admiral, with whom he travels as a gentleman-in-waiting. And the rest I have learned from his own servant, that in order to escape the obligation he has to you, he has committed this evil act. I saw him leave this afternoon with my own eyes. Decide what you wish to do in this respect, and on the strength of who I am, and I am more than you imagine, as soon as I know your wishes in this regard, though I lose my life, he will comply with what he has promised, or the two of us will die, he and I, as a result."

Hiding my sorrow, I responded:

"And who are you that, even if that be the truth, you have the courage to do what you say you will?"

"By your leave," Luis responded, "after the deed is done, you will know."

I then remembered the suspicion I mentioned earlier, that he was Don Felipe, and when I had taken a deep breath and was about to respond, my mother entered, and with that the exchange ended. After having greeted her, because I was choking on my own sighs and tears, I went to my chamber and, throwing myself on the bed, I do not need to tell you the laments I expressed, the tears I cried, and the decisions I made, first to take my own life, and then to take the life of him who had taken mine. And in the end I chose a worse course, which you will now hear about, for those were the honorable choices, but the one I elected led to my final perdition; because at that point I got up with more spirit than my sorrow warranted, and taking my jewels and those of my mother, and many

hablarle, quedando con mis nuevos amos, no sé si triste o alegre, aunque en encontrarlos buenos fui más dichosa que en lo demás que hasta aquí he referido; demás que yo les supe agradar y granjear, de modo que antes de muchos días me hice dueño de su voluntad y casa.

Era mi señora moza y de afable condición, y con ella y otras dos doncellas que había en la casa me llevaba tan bien, que todas me querían como si fuera hija de cada una y hermana de todas, particularmente con una de las doncellas, cuyo nombre era Leonisa, que me quería con tanto extremo, que comía y dormía con ella en su misma cama. Esta me persuadía que me volviese cristiana, y yo la agradaba con decir lo haría cuando llegase la ocasión, que yo lo deseaba más que ella. La primera vez que me vio don Manuel fue un día que comía con mis dueños. Y aunque lo hacía muchas veces por ser amigo, no había tenido yo ocasión de verle, porque no salía de la cocina, hasta este día que digo, que vine a traer un plato a la mesa; que como puso en mí los aleves ojos y me reconoció, aunque le debió de desvanecer su vista la S y clavo de mi rostro, tan perfectamente imitado el natural, que a nadie diera sospecha de ser fingidos. Y elevado entre el sí y el no, se olvidó de llevar el bocado a la boca, pensando qué sería lo que miraba, porque por una parte creyó ser la misma que era, y por otra no se podía persuadir que yo hubiese cometido tal delirio, como ignorante de las desdichas por su causa sucedidas en mi triste casa; pues a mí no me causó menos admiración otra novedad que vi, y fue que como le vi que me miraba tan suspenso, por no desengañarle tan presto, aparté de él los ojos y púselos en los criados que estaban sirviendo. En compañía de dos que había en casa, vi a Luis, el que servía en la mía. Admiréme, y

coins in silver and gold, because everything was entrusted to me, I waited until my father came to supper, and when he had, they called me; but I responded that I did not feel well, that I would have some conserves later. They sat down to dinner, and I saw the opportunity to act on my mad decision, because the servants and maids were busy serving at the table, and if I were to wait any longer, it would be impossible to put my plan into effect, because Luis closed the gates to the street and took the key with him; and without saying a word to anyone, not even to Claudia, who knew all my secrets, I left by a door that connected my room to the corridor, and left the house.

A short distance from my house was that of the servant whom, as I mentioned, my father dismissed when he hired Luis, and whom I knew somewhat, because taking pity on him, as he was old, I aided him and even visited him when I went out without my mother. I went there. The good man greeted me expressing great pain for my misfortune, about which he already knew in detail, as I had given word that, when I married, I would bring him into my house.

Octavio, for that was his name, scolded me for my plan; but seeing that I was not to be dissuaded, he saw fit to be silent and to obey, and especially when he saw that I brought coins and gave him some of them. There I spent the night, engulfed in sorrow and fear, and the following day I told him to go to my house and, pretending not to know what was happening, to talk to Claudia and to tell her that he was looking for me, as he had done in the past, and to find out what was happening and if they were looking for me.

Octavio went, and found my misfortune consummated. When I come to

vi que Luis estaba tan admirado de verme en tal hábito como don Manuel. Y como me tenía más fija en su memoria que don Manuel, a pesar de los fingidos hierros, me conoció. Al tiempo del volverme adentro, oí que don Manuel había preguntado a mis dueños si era la esclava que habían comprado.

—Sí —dijo mi señora—. Y es tan bonita y agradable, que me da el mayor desconsuelo el ver que es mora; que diera doblado de lo que costó porque se hiciese cristiana, y casi me hace verter lágrimas ver en tan linda cara aquellos hierros, y doy mil maldiciones a quien tal puso.

A esto respondió Leonisa, que estaba presente:

—Ella misma dice se los puso por un pesar que tuvo de que por su hermosura le hubiesen hecho un engaño. Y ya me ha prometido a mí que será cristiana.

—Bien ha sido menester que los tenga —respondió don Manuel—, para no creer que es una hermosura que yo conozco en mi patria; mas puede ser que Naturaleza hiciese esta mora en la misma estampa.

Como os he contado, entré cuidadosa de haber visto a Luis, y llamando un criado de los de la casa, le pregunté qué mancebo era aquel que servía a la mesa con los demás.

—Es —me respondió— un criado que este mismo día recibió el señor don Manuel, porque el suyo mató un hombre, y está ausente.

—Yo le conozco —repliqué— de una casa donde yo estuve un tiempo, y cierto que me holgara hablarle, que me alegra ver acá gente de donde me he criado.

—Luego —dijo— entrará a comer con nosotros y podrás hablarle.

Acabóse la comida, y entraron todos los criados dentro, y Luis con ellos. Sentáronse a la mesa, y cierto que yo no podía

remember this, I do not know why my heart does not shatter. Octavio arrived at my unfortunate house and saw that everyone in the city was entering and leaving. Amazed, he too entered with the rest, looking for Claudia, and finding her saddened and teary-eyed, she told him how, after finishing supper my mother went to my room to learn by what ailment I was afflicted, and as she did not find me, she asked for me, and everyone responded that they had left me on my bed when they went to serve her, and having looked through the entire house and outside as well, they found the keys to the drawers on the bed, and the door that connected to the corridor and was always shut, open, and looking into the drawers, and seeing them empty, they then realized the reason they were empty. And at that discovery, my mother began to cry out; my father joined them, and when he was told the cause, as he was an older man, he fell senseless to the floor with sorrow and fright from the news, and either because of the fall or the pain, it is not known which, he fell into a faint so profound that he never came to.

And for all of that my thoughtlessness was to blame. They said that even though the physicians ordered that the waiting period provided for and required by the law be observed, the order was suspended, and that now it was a matter of burying him; that my mother's state was only slightly better, and that with these misfortunes no attention was paid to mine except to besmirch my evil memory; that now my mother had been told what had happened with Don Manuel, that the moment my back was turned, everyone had recounted what they knew, and that she had not agreed to look for me, saying that since I had elected a husband to my tastes, may God bring me more happiness

contener la risa, a pesar de mis penas, de ver a Luis, que mientras más me miraba, más se admiraba, y más oyéndome llamar Zelima, no porque no me había conocido, sino de ver al extremo de bajeza que me había puesto por tener amor. Pues como se acabó de comer, aparté a Luis, y díjele:

—¿Qué fortuna te ha traído, Luis, adonde yo estoy?

—La misma que a ti, señora mía; querer bien y ser mal correspondido, y deseos de hallarte y vengarte en teniendo lugar y ocasión.

—Disimula, y no me llames sino Zelima, que esto importa a mis cosas, que ahora no es tiempo de más venganzas que las que amor toma de mí; que yo he dicho que has servido en una casa donde me crié, y que te conozco de esta parte, y a tu amo no le digas que me has conocido ni hablado, que más me fío de ti que de él.

—Con seguridad lo puedes hacer —dijo Luis—, que si él te quisiera y estimara como yo, no estuvieras en el estado que estás, ni hubieras causado las desdichas sucedidas.

—Así lo creo —respondí—; mas dime, ¿cómo has venido aquí?

—Buscándote, y con determinación de quitar la vida a quien ha sido parte para que tú hagas esto, y con esta intención entré a servirle.

—No trates de eso, que es perderme para siempre; que aunque don Manuel es falso y traidor, está mi vida en la suya; fuera de que yo trato de cobrar mi perdida opinión, y con su muerte no se granjea sino la mía, que apenas harías tú tal cuando yo misma me matase. —Esto le dije por que no pusiese su intento en ejecución—. ¿Qué hay de mi madre, Luis?

—Qué quieres que haya —respondió—, sino que pienso que es de diamante, pues no la han acabado las penas que tiene.

with him than He had brought to that house.

Octavio returned with this news, so sad and bitter for me, especially when he told me that they talked of nothing in the city other than my affairs. My suffering doubled, and I was very near to losing my life; but heaven had not yet punished me enough for being the cause of so many ills; it wanted to save me to go through those yet to come. My spirits were somewhat lifted on learning that they were not looking for me, and after sewing all my jewels and some doubloons in places where they would be with me without being noticed, and having prepared what was necessary for our journey, after four or six days had passed, one night Octavio and I set out on our way, and we left for Alicante, from where my ungrateful lover was going to set sail. We arrived there, and seeing that the galleys had not yet come in, we took lodgings until we could find a way that would allow me to be seen by Don Manuel.

Octavio went every day to the Lord Admiral's lodgings; he saw my traitorous husband (if I can call him that) and he returned to tell me what had occurred. And among other things, he told me one day that the majordomo was looking for a slave, and though they had brought several women to him, these had not satisfied him. On hearing this, I decided on another, grander plan, or another madness grander than the others; and as I thought about it, I set to work on it. And it was this: fashioning an imitation of a nail and an S for my face, I put on a robe like those worn by slaves and Moors, and I chose for myself the name Zelima, telling Octavio to take me and to say that I was his, and that if he was pleased, to not worry about the

Cuando yo partí de Zaragoza, quedaba disponiendo su partida para Murcia; lleva consigo el cuerpo de tu padre y mi señor, por llevar más presentes sus dolores.

—Y por allá ¿qué se platica de mi desacierto? —dije yo.

—Que te llevó don Manuel —respondió Luis—; porque Claudia dijo lo que pasaba. Con que tu madre se consoló algo en tu pérdida, pues le parece que con tu marido vas, que no hay que tenerte lástima; no como ella, que le lleva sin alma. Yo, como más interesado en haberte perdido, y como quien sabía más bien que no te llevaba don Manuel, antes iba huyendo de ti, no la quise acompañar, y así, he venido donde me ves, y con el intento que te he manifestado, el cual suspenderé hasta ver si hace lo que como caballero debe. Y de no hacerlo, me puedes perdonar: que aunque sepa perderme y perderte, vengaré tu agravio y el mío. Y cree que me tengo por bien afortunado en haberte hallado y en merecer que te fíes de mí y me hayas manifestado tu secreto antes que a él.

—Yo te lo agradezco —respondí—. Y por que no sientan mal de conversación tan larga, vete con Dios, que lugar habrá de vernos; y si hubieras menester algo, pídemelo, que aún no me lo ha quitado la fortuna todo, que ya tengo qué darte, aunque sea poco para lo que mereces y yo te debo.

Y con esto y darle un doblón de a cuatro, le despedí. Y cierto que nunca más bien me pareció Luis que en esta ocasión; lo uno, por tener de mi parte algún arrimo, y lo otro por verle con tan honrados y alentados intentos.

Algunos días tardaron las galeras en llegar al puerto, uno de los cuales, estando mi señora fuera con las doncellas, y sola yo en casa, acaso don Manuel, deseoso de satisfacerse de su sospecha, vino a mi casa a buscar a mi señor, o a mí, que es lo más

price.[4] Octavio was very upset by my plan, shedding abundant tears for me; but I consoled him by telling him that this disguise was for no other purpose than to proceed with my plan and to force Don Manuel to do as I wished, and to leave Spain, and that by having the ingrate in my sight, without recognizing me, I would uncover his intentions. Octavio was consoled by this, and more when I told him that the price that they gave for me would be his, and that he should send word to me in Sicily of what my mother had done with herself.

In short, all went as I had hoped, and before eight days had passed I was sold for one hundred ducats, and was a slave, not of the masters who had bought me and given for me the amount mentioned, but of my ungrateful and perfidious lover, for whom I chose to deliver myself up to such a base destiny. In short, Octavio being satisfied with the money they gave for me, and even more with what I had given, he said farewell before returning to his house with such tender feeling that, in order not to see him shed tender tears, I walked away from him without speaking, remaining with my new masters, whether sad or happy I do not know, though on finding them kind I was happier than in anything that up to now I have recounted; and I knew how to please them and to win their sympathy so that before many days had passed I was the mistress of their will and their household.

My lady was lovely and affable, and with her and the other maids who were in the house I got on so well that all loved me as though I were the daughter of each and the sister of all, especially one of the

---

4. The S plus the image of a nail is a rebus that reads "esclavo," "slave," the sign branded on the face of slaves.

cierto. Y como entró y me vio, con una se-
quedad notable, me dijo:

—¿Qué disfraz es éste, doña Isabel? ¿O
cómo las mujeres de tus obligaciones, y
que han tenido deseos y pensamientos de
ser mía, se ponen en semejantes bajezas?
Siéndolo tanto, que si alguna intención tenía de que fueses mi esposa, ya la he perdido, por el mal nombre que has granjeado
conmigo y con cuantos lo supieron.

—¡Ah traidor engañador y perdición
mía! ¿Cómo tienes vergüenza de tomar mi
nombre entre tus labios, siendo la causa de
esa bajeza con que me baldonas, cuando
por tus traiciones y maldades estoy puesta
en ella? Y no sólo eres causador de esto,
mas de la muerte de mi honrado padre,
que porque pagues a manos del cielo tus
traiciones, y no a las suyas, le quitó la vida
con el dolor de mi pérdida. Zelima soy, no
doña Isabel; esclava soy, que no señora;
mora soy, pues tengo dentro de mí misma
aposentado un moro renegado como tú,
pues quien faltó a Dios la palabra que le
dio de ser mío, ni es cristiano ni noble,
sino un infame caballero. Estos hierros y
los de mi afrenta me los has puesto, no
sólo en el rostro, sino en la fama. Haz lo
que te diere gusto, que si se ha quitado la
voluntad de hacerme tuya, Dios hay en el
cielo y rey en la tierra, y si éstos no lo hicieran, hay puñales, y tengo manos y hay valor para quitarte esa infame vida, para que
deprendan en mí las mujeres nobles a cas-
tigar hombres falsos y desagradecidos. Y
quítateme de delante, si no quieres que
haga lo que digo.

Víome tan colérica y apasionada, que, o
porque no hiciese algún desacierto, o porque no estaba contento de los agravios y
engaños que me había hecho, y le faltaban
más que hacer, empezó a reportarme con
caricias y halagos, que yo no quise por
gran espacio admitir, prometiéndome

maids, whose name was Leonisa, who
loved me so much that I ate and slept with
her in the same bed. She persuaded me to
become a Christian, and I pleased her by
saying that I would do so when the occasion arrived, that I wanted this more than
she. The first time that Don Manuel saw
me was one day when he dined with my
masters. And though he did so on many
occasions as he was a friend, I had not had
an opportunity to see him because I did
not leave the kitchen, until the day of
which I speak, when I brought a dish to
the table; and he laid his treacherous eyes
on me and recognized me, though the
sight of the S and the nail on my face must
have disconcerted him, so perfectly did
they resemble authentic ones that no one
would have suspected that they were false.
And debating between yes and no, he forgot to bring his food to his mouth, trying
to decide what it was he was looking at, because on the one hand he believed that I
was who I was, and on the other he could
not believe that I would have gone to such
mad lengths, as he was ignorant of the
misfortunes that on his account had happened in my sad house; and as for me, I
was just as amazed by a different novelty
that I saw, and as I saw that he looked at
me so expectantly, in order not to unde-
ceive him too quickly, I took my eyes from
him and looked at the servants who were
serving. I saw Luis, who had served in my
own house, in the company of two household servants. I was amazed, and saw that
Luis was just as amazed as Don Manuel on
seeing me so dressed. And as he had me
more fixed in his memory than Don
Manuel, in spite of the false brands he recognized me. Just as I was leaving the room,
I heard Don Manuel ask my masters if I
was the slave they had bought.

"Yes," the lady said. "And she is so lovely

remedio a todo. Queríale bien, y creíle. (Perdonadme estas licencias que tomo en decir esto, y creedme que más llevaba el pensamiento de restaurar mi honor que no el achaque de la liviandad.) En fin, después de haber hecho las amistades, y dádole cuenta de lo que me había sucedido hasta aquel punto, me dijo que pues ya estas cosas estaban en este estado, pasasen así hasta que llegásemos a Sicilia, que allá se tendría modo como mis deseos y los suyos tuviesen dichoso fin. Con esto nos apartamos, quedando yo contenta, mas no segura, de sus engaños; mas para la primera vez no había negociado muy mal. Vinieron las galeras y embarcamos en ellas con mucho gusto mío, por ir don Manuel en compañía de mis dueños y en la misma galera que yo iba, donde le hablaba y veía a todas horas, con gran pena de Luis, que como no se le negaban mis dichas, andaba muy triste, con lo que confirmaba el pensamiento que tenía de que era don Felipe, mas no se lo daba a sentir, por no darle mayores atrevimientos.

Llegamos a Sicilia, y aposentámonos todos dentro de Palacio. En reconocer la tierra y tomarla cariño se pasaron algunos meses. Y cuando entendí que don Manuel diera orden de sacarme de esclava y cumplir lo prometido, volvió de nuevo a matarme con tibiezas y desaires; tanto, que aun para mirarme le faltaba voluntad. Y era que había dado en andar distraído con mujeres y juegos, y lo cierto de todo, que no tenía amor; con que llegaron a ser mis ahogos y tormentos de tanto peso, que de día ni de noche se enjugaban mis tristes ojos, de manera que no fue posible encubrírselo a Leonisa, aquella doncella con quien profesaba tanta amistad, que sabidas debajo de secreto mis tragedias, y quién era, quedó fuera de sí.

Queríame tanto mi señora, que por

and pleasant that it distresses me even more that she is a Moor; I would give double what she cost if she were to become a Christian, and it almost makes me shed tears to see those brands on such a lovely face, and I damn a thousand times him who put them there."

To which Leonisa, who was present, responded:

"She says she herself put them there for her sorrow, that because of her beauty people deceived her. And she has already promised me that she will be a Christian."

"Then it is fitting that she has them," Don Manuel responded, "so that she not be mistaken for a beauty that I know from my own land; but it would seem that nature has made a Moor from the same mold."

As I have told you, I left the room cautiously on having seen Luis, and calling one of the servants from the household, I asked him about the youth who served at table with the rest.

"He is," he told me, "a servant Don Manuel took on this very day, because his own killed a man and has fled."

"I know him," I replied, "from a house I served in for a time, and it would certainly please me to speak to him, as it makes me very glad to see people here from where I grew up."

"Later," he said, "he will be here to eat with us and you may talk to him then."

The meal ended, and all the servants came in, and Luis with them. They sat at the table, and the truth is that, in spite of my sorrow, I could not contain my laughter on seeing Luis, whose astonishment grew each time he looked at me, and especially when he heard me called Zelima, not because he had not recognized me, but because of the depths to which I had fallen as a result of love. Then, when dinner ended, I took Luis aside, and I said to him:

dificultosa que era la merced que le pedía, me la otorgaba. Y así, por poder hablar a don Manuel sin estorbos y decirle mi sentimiento, le pedí una tarde licencia para que con Leonisa fuera a merendar a la marina, y concedida, pedí a Luis dijera a su amo que unas damas le aguardaban a la marina; mas que no dijese que era yo, temiendo que no iría. Nos fuimos a ella, y tomamos un barco para que nos pasase a una isleta, que tres o cuatro millas dentro del mar se mostraba muy amena y deleitosa. En esto llegaron don Manuel y Luis, que, habiéndonos conocido, disimulando el enfado, solemnizó la burla. Entramos todos cuatro en el barco con dos marineros que le gobernaban, y llegando a la isleta, salimos a tierra, aguardando en el mismo barquillo los marineros para volvernos cuando fuese hora (que en esto fueron más dichosos que los demás).

Sentámonos debajo de unos árboles, y estando hablando en la causa que allí me había llevado, yo dando quejas y don Manuel disculpas falsas y engañosas, como siempre, de la otra parte de la isleta había dado fondo en una quiebra o cala de ella una galeota de moros corsarios de Argel, y como desde lejos nos viesen, salieron en tierra el arráez y otros moros, y viniendo encubiertos hasta donde estábamos, nos saltearon de modo que ni don Manuel ni Luis pudieron ponerse en defensa, ni nosotras huir; y así, nos llevaron cautivos a su galeota, haciéndose, luego que tuvieron presa, a la mar, que no se contentó la fortuna con haberme hecho esclava de mi amante, sino de moros, aunque en llevarle a él conmigo no me penaba tanto el cautiverio. Los marineros, viendo el suceso, remando a boga arrancada, como dicen, se escaparon, llevando la nueva de nuestro desdichado suceso.

Estos corsarios moros, como están

"What fortune has brought you here, Luis, to where I am?"

"The same as has brought you, my lady; for loving well and being badly repaid, and a wish to find you and to avenge you when the time and place are right."

"Pretend I am who I say, and call me nothing other than Zelima, because that is important to what I have planned. This is not the time for any revenge other than that which love demands of me; and I have said that you have served in a house where I grew up, and that I know you from there, and to your master do not say that you have met or spoken with me, for I trust you more than I do him."

"You may surely do so," said Luis, "because if he loved and esteemed you as I do, you would not be in your present state, nor would you have caused the misfortunes that have come to pass."

"So also do I believe," I responded, "but tell me, how is it you have come here?"

"Looking for you, and determined to take the life of him who has brought you to this, and with that intention I entered his service."

"Do not do it, for then I would be forever lost; because though Don Manuel is false and a traitor, my life is in his; apart from which I am trying to recover my good name, and with his death nothing more than my own is achieved, and were you to do such a thing I would kill myself." This I told him so that he would not carry out his plan. "How is my mother, Luis?"

"As you might imagine," he responded. "I think she must be made of diamond, because her sorrows have not put an end to her. When I left Zaragoza, she was preparing her journey for Murcia; she is taking the body of your father and my lord, in order to keep her sorrows nearby."

diestros en tratar y hablar con cristianos, hablan y entiende medianamente nuestra lengua. Y así, me preguntó el arráez, como me vio herrada, quién era yo. Le dije que era mora y me llamaba Zelima; que me habían cautivado seis años había; que era de Fez, y que aquel caballero era hijo de mi señor, y el otro su criado, y aquella doncella lo era también de mi casa. Que los tratase bien y pusiese precio en el rescate; que apenas lo sabrían sus padres, cuando enviarían la estimación. Y eso lo dije fijada en las joyas y dineros que traía conmigo. Todo lo dicho lo hablaba alto, porque los demás lo oyesen y no me sacasen mentirosa.

Contento quedó el arráez, tanto con la presa por su interés, como por parecerle había hecho un gran servicio a su Mahoma en sacarme, siendo mora, de entre cristianos, y así lo dio a entender, haciéndome muchas caricias, y a los demás buen tratamiento, y así, fuimos a Argel y nos entregó a una hija suya hermosa y nina, llamada Zaida, que se holgó tanto conmigo, porque era mora, como con don Manuel, porque se enamoró de él. Vistióme luego de estos vestidos que veis, y trató de que hombres diestros en quitar estos hierros me los quitasen; no porque ellas no usan tales señales, que antes lo tienen por gala, sino porque era S y clavo, que daba señal de lo que yo era; a lo que respondí que yo misma me los había puesto por mi gusto y que no los quería quitar.

Queríame Zaida ternísimamente, o por merecerlo yo con mi agrado, o por parecerle podría ser parte con mi dueño para que la quisiese. En fin, yo hacía y deshacía en su casa como propia mía, y por mi respeto trataban a don Manuel y a Luis y a Leonisa muy bien, dejándolos andar libres por la ciudad, habiéndolos dado permiso para tratar su rescate, habiendo avisado a don Manuel hiciese el precio de todos tres,

"And there, what do they say about my misfortune?" I asked.

"That Don Manuel took you with him," Luis responded, "because Claudia told them what had happened. So that your mother was somewhat consoled with your loss, because she thinks that you have gone with your husband, that there is no reason to feel sorry for you, unlike her; for sorrow has taken her soul. I, being more interested in having lost you, and as one who well knew that Don Manuel had not taken you, but had fled from you, refused to accompany her, and thus, I have come to where you see me, and with the intention I have revealed to you, which I will suspend until I see whether he does what as a gentleman he is honor bound to do. And if he does not, you will pardon me: that although I know myself lost and you lost, I will avenge your offense and my own. And believe me that I consider myself fortunate in having found you and in meriting your trust and that you have told me your secret instead of telling him."

"I am grateful to you," I responded. "And so that they do not think badly of this lengthy conversation, go with God. We will certainly meet again soon; and if you have need of something, ask it of me. Fortune has not yet taken everything from me; I still have something to give you, though it be little compared to what you are worth and what I owe you."

And with that and giving him a doubloon, I said good-bye to him. And it is certain that Luis had never looked better to me than on this occasion; first because in him I had someone to support me, and second for seeing him with such honorable and encouraging intentions.

The galleys were delayed for some days in coming to port, and on one of those, my lady being out with the maids, and I alone

que yo le daría joyas para ello, de lo cual mostró don Manuel quedar agradecido; sólo hallaba dificultad en sacarme a mí, porque, como aviara, cierto es que no se podía tratar de rescate; aguardamos a los redentores para que se dispusiese todo.

En este tiempo me descubrió Zaida su amoroso cuidado, pidiéndome hablase a don Manuel, y que le dijese que si quería volverse moro, se casaría con él y le haría señor de grandes riquezas que tenía su padre, poniéndome con esto en nuevos cuidados y mayores desesperaciones, que me vi en puntos de quitarme la vida. Dábame lugar para hablar despacio a don Manuel, y aunque en muchos días no le dije nada de la pasión de la mora, temiendo su mudable condición, dándole a ella algunas fingidas respuestas, unas de disgusto y otras al contrario, hasta que ya la fuerza de los celos, más por pedírselos a mi ingrato que por decirle la voluntad a Zaida; porque el traidor, habiéndole parecido bien, con los ojos deshacía cuanto hacía. Después de reñirme mis sospechosas quimeras, me dijo que más acertado le parecía engañarla; que le dijese que él no había de dejar su ley, aunque le costase, no una vida que tenía, sino mil; mas si ella quería venirse con él a tierra de cristianos y ser cristiana, que la prometía casarse con ella. A esto añadió que yo la sazonase, diciéndole cuán bien se hallaría, y lo que más me gustase para atraerla a nuestro intento, que en saliendo de allí, estuviese segura que cumpliría con su obligación. ¡Ah, falso, y cómo me engañó en esto como en lo demás!

En fin, para no cansaros, Zaida vino en todo muy contenta, y más cuando supo que yo también me iría con ella. Y se concertó para de allí a dos meses la partida, que su padre había de ir a un lugar donde tenía hacienda y casa; que los moros en todas las tierras donde tienen trato tienen

in the house, Don Manuel, perhaps anxious to satisfy himself regarding his suspicions, came to my house in search of my lord, or of me, which is more probable. And when he came in and saw me, with notable dryness, he said to me:

"What kind of a disguise is this, Doña Isabel? Or rather, how is it that a woman of your station and who has had desires and thoughts of being mine, stoops to such a level? It pains me so that if ever I had some intention of making you my wife, I have now lost it, for the bad repute you have earned with me and with all those who learn of this."

"Oh deceitful traitor and my perdition! How dare you utter my name, being the cause of that lowly state for which you insult me, since because of your deceptions and evil I find myself thus? And not only of this are you the cause, but of the death of my honorable father, so that you will answer to the heavens for your betrayal and not to him, as he lost his life with the pain of my loss. Zelima I am, not Doña Isabel; a slave I am, and not a lady; a Moor I am, because I have within me dwelling so detestable a Moor as you, since he who breaks the promise he made to God to be mine is neither Christian nor noble, but an infamous gentleman. These brands and those of my affront you have placed, not only on my face but also on my good name. Do what you wish, because if you no longer desire to make me yours, God is in heaven and the king on earth, and if these do not do it, there are poniards, and I have hands and the courage to take from you that shameful life, so that noble women learn from me how to punish false and disgraceful men. Now get out of my sight, if you do not want me to do as I have said."

Seeing me so filled with rage and passion that, either because he did not want to

mujeres e hijos. Ya la venganza mía contra don Manuel debía de disponer el cielo, y así facilitó los medios de ella; pues ido el moro, Zaida hizo una carta en que su padre la enviaba llamar, porque había caído de una peligrosa enfermedad, para que el rey le diese licencia para su jornada, por cuanto los moros no pueden ir de un lugar a otro sin ella. Y alcanzada, hizo aderezar una galeota bien armada, de remeros cristianos, a quien se avisó con todo el secreto el designio, y poniendo en ella todas las riquezas de plata, oro y vestidos que sin hacer rumor podía llevar, y con ella, yo y Leonisa, y otras dos cristianas que la servían, que mora no quiso llevar ninguna, don Manuel y Luis, caminamos por la mar la vía de Alicante, donde con menos riesgo se pudiese salir.

Aquí fueron mis tormentos mayores, aquí mis ansias sin comparación; porque como allí no había impedimento que lo estorbase, y Zaida iba segura que don Manuel había de ser su marido, no se negaba a ningún favor que pudiese hacerle. Ya contemplaban mis tristes ojos a don Manuel asido de las manos de Zaida, y miraban a Zaida colgada de su cuello, y aun beberse los alientos en vasos de coral; porque como el traidor mudable la amaba, él se buscaba las ocasiones. Y si no llegó a más, era por el cuidado con que yo andaba siendo estorbo de sus mayores placeres. Bien conocía yo que no gustaban de que yo fuese tan cuidadosa; mas disimulaban su enfado. Y si tal vez le decía al medio moro alguna palabra, me daba en los ojos con que qué podía hacer, que bastaban los riesgos que por mis temeridades y locuras había pasado, que no era razón por ellas mismas nos viésemos en otros mayores; que tuviese sufrimiento hasta llegar a Zaragoza, que todo tendría remedio.

Llegamos, en fin, en próspero viaje a

commit some error, or because he was not content with the insults and deceit he had already done to me, and he still had more to add, he began to comfort me with caresses and praise, that I was far from wishing to accept, promising me to remedy all. I loved him well, and I believed him. (Forgive me the liberties I take in saying this, and believe me that my thoughts were more concerned with restoring my honor and not with licentious temptations.) And thus, after having made up, and listening to what had happened to me to that point, he said to me that since matters were already in this state, they should go on as they were until we arrived in Sicily, that there we would find a way to bring my desires and his to a happy end. With that we parted, and I was content, but not entirely convinced by his deception; but for the moment I had not negotiated badly. The galleys came and we boarded them and I was very glad, for Don Manuel was going in the company of my masters and in the same galley in which I went, where I spoke to him and saw him at all hours, to the great sorrow of Luis, who since my happiness was not denied, was very sad, and thus the belief I had that he was Don Felipe was confirmed, but I did not let him know that, in order not to give him cause for taking liberties.

We came to Sicily, and all of us lodged at the palace. A number of months passed in getting to know that land and coming to feel affection for it. And when it seemed to me that it was time for Don Manuel to give the order to take me out of slavery and to fulfill the promise he had made, he began anew to kill me with coolness and affronts; and matters were such that he had no desire to look at me. And this was because he had given himself to distractions with women and gambling, and it was more

Cartagena; tomada tierra, dada libertad a los cristianos, y con que pudiesen ir a su tierra, puesta la ropa a punto, tomamos el camino para Zaragoza, si bien Zaida descontenta, que quisiera en la primera tierra de cristianos bautizarse y casarse; tan enamorada estaba de su nuevo esposo. Y aun si no lo hizo, fue por mí, que porque no deseaba lo mismo. Llegamos a Zaragoza, siendo pasados seis años que partimos de ella, y a su casa de don Manuel. Halló a su madre muerta, y a doña Eufrasia viuda, que habiéndose casado con el primo que esperaba de las Indias, dejándola recién parida de un hijo, había muerto en la guerra de un carabinazo. Fuimos bien recibidos de doña Eufrasia, con la admiración y gusto que se puede imaginar. Tres días descansamos, contando los unos a los otros los sucesos pasados, maravillada doña Eufrasia de ver la S y clavo en mi rostro, que por Zaida no le había quitado, a quien consolé con decirle eran fingidos, que era la fuerza tenerlos hasta cierta ocasión.

Era tanta la priesa que Zaida daba que la bautizasen, que se quería casar, que me obligó una tarde, algo antes de anochecer, llamar a don Manuel, y en presencia de Zaida y de su hermana y la demás familia, sin que faltase Luis, que aquellos días andaba más cuidadoso, le dije estas razones:

—Ya señor don Manuel, que ha querido el cielo, obligado de mis continuos lamentos, que nuestros trabajos y desdichas hayan tenido fin con tan próspero suceso como habernos traído libre de todos a vuestra casa, y Dios ha permitido que yo os acompañase en lo uno y lo otro, quizá para que, viendo por vuestros ojos con cuanta perseverancia y paciencia os he seguido en ellos, paguéis deudas tan grandes. Cesen ya engaños y cautelas, y sepa Zaida y el mundo entero que lo que me debéis no se paga con menos cantidad que

certain than ever that he did not love me; and with that my depression and torment became so heavy, that during the day and at night my sad eyes filled with tears, so that it was not possible to hide this from Leonisa, the maid with whom I had become such good friends; and learning in secret my tragedies, and who I was, she was beside herself.

My lady loved me so well that no matter how much trouble a favor I asked of her might cause, she granted it. And thus, in order to speak with Don Manuel unhindered and tell him my feelings, I asked one afternoon for time off so that I could go with Leonisa to the seaside for lunch, and when permission was given, I asked Luis to tell his master that some ladies were waiting for him on the marina, but not to say that it was I, fearing that he would not be there. We went there, and we hired a boat to take us to an islet that was three or four miles out to sea and looked very inviting and delightful. Then Don Manuel and Luis arrived, who, recognizing us, hid his anger and went along with the game. The four of us got into the boat with two sailors who guided it, and coming to the islet, we landed, while the same sailors waited in the little boat to take us back when it was time (and in that they were more fortunate than the rest of us).

We sat under some trees, and as we were speaking of the reason that had taken me there, I complaining and Don Manuel pleading falsely and deceitfully as always for forgiveness, on another part of the islet, in an inlet or a cove, a galleon of Moorish corsairs from Algiers was anchored, and as they saw us from afar, the captain and other Moors came to shore, and coming stealthily to where we were, they were upon us so suddenly that neither Don Manuel nor Luis could come to

con vuestra persona, y que de estos hierros que están en mi rostro, cómo por vos sólo se los podéis quitar, y que llegue el día en que las desdichas y afrentas que he padecido tengan premio; fuerza es que ya mi ventura no se dilate, para que los que han sabido mis afrentas y desaciertos sepan mis logros y dichas. Muchas veces habéis prometido ser mío, pues no es razón que cuando otras os tienen por suyo, os tema yo ajeno y os llore extraño. Mi calidad ya sabéis que es mucha; mi hacienda no es corta; mi hermosura, la misma que vos buscaste y elegiste; mi amor no lo ignoráis; mis finezas pasan a temeridades. Por ninguna parte perdéis, antes ganáis; que si hasta aquí con hierros fingidos he sido vuestra esclava, desde hoy sin ellos seré verdadera. Decid, os suplico, lo que queréis que se disponga, para que lo que os pido tenga el dichoso lauro que deseo, y no me tengáis más temerosa, pues ya de justicia merezco el premio que de tantas desdichas como yo he pasado os estoy pidiendo.

No me dejó decir más el traidor, que, sonriéndose, a modo de burla, dijo:

—¿Y quién os ha dicho, señora doña Isabel, que todo eso que decís no lo tengo muy conocido? Y tanto, que con lo mismo que habéis pensado obligarme, me tenéis tan desobligado, que si alguna voluntad os tenía, ya ni aun pensamiento de haberla habido en mí tengo. Vuestra calidad no la niego, vuestras finezas no las desconozco; mas si no hay voluntad, no sirve todo eso nada. Conocido pudiérades tener en mí, desde el día que me partí de esta ciudad, que pues os volví las espaldas, no os quería para esposa. Y si entonces aún se me hiciera dificultoso, ¿cuánto más será ahora, que sólo por seguirme como pudiera una mujer baja, os habéis puesto en tan civiles empeños? Esta resolución con que ahora os hablo, días ha que la pudiérades tener

our defense, nor could we flee; and so they took us captives to their small galley, directing it, after taking prisoners, to sea; because fortune, not content that I was already my lover's slave, made me also a slave of the Moors, though in having him with me I was not so pained by captivity. The sailors, seeing what had occurred, rowing strong, as they say, escaped, taking the news of what had befallen us.

Those Moorish corsairs, as they are skilled in dealing and speaking with Christians, spoke and understood something of our tongue. And thus, the captain, upon seeing that I was branded, asked me who I was. I told him I was a Moor and I was called Zelima; that they had taken me six years before; that I was from Fez, and that the gentleman was my lord's son, and the other his servant, and that the maid was also from my household. I asked that they treat us well and fix a ransom; that the moment his parents found out, they would send the amount settled upon. And I told him that with the jewels and money I had brought with me in mind. I said all of this in a loud voice, so that the rest would hear and would not make of me a liar.

The captain was satisfied, both for having taken prisoners who would provide ransom and for apparently having done a great service to his Mohammed in freeing me, a Moor, from the Christians, and he let me know this, caressing me much, and treating the rest well, and thus, we went to Algiers and they handed us over to his daughter, a beautiful girl named Zaida, who was as glad with me, because I was a Moor, as with Don Manuel, because she fell in love with him. She dressed me then in these robes you see, and they wanted to have these brands removed by men skilled in such tasks; not because they did not use those signs—in fact, they were thought

conocida. Y en cuanto a la palabra que decís os he dado, como ésas damos los hombres para alcanzar lo que deseamos, y pudieran ya las mujeres tener conocida esta
treta, no dejarse engañar, pues las avisan
tantas escarmentadas. Y, en fin, por esa parte me hallo menos obligado que por las demás, pues si la di alguna vez, fue sin voluntad de cumplirla, y sólo por moderar
vuestra ira. Yo nunca os he engañado; que
bien podíais haber conocido que el dilatarlo nunca ha sido falta de lugar, sino que no
tengo ni he tenido tal pensamiento; que
vos sola sois la que os habéis querido engañar, por andaros tras mí sin dejarme. Y
para que ya salgáis de esa duda y no me andéis persiguiendo, sino que viéndome imposible os aquietéis y perdáis la esperanza
que en mí tenéis, y volviéndoos con vuestra
madre, allá entre vuestros naturales busquéis marido que sea menos escrupuloso
que yo, porque es imposible que yo me fiase de mujer que sabe hacer y buscar tantos
disfraces. Zaida es hermosa, y riquezas no
le faltan; amor tiene como vos, y yo se lo
tengo desde el punto que la vi. Y así, para
que en siendo cristiana, que será en previniéndose lo necesario para serlo, le doy la
mano de esposo, y con esto acabaremos,
vos de atormentarme y yo de padecerlo.

De la misma suerte que la víbora pisada me pusieron las infames palabras y aleves obras del ingrato don Manuel. Y queriendo responder a ellas, Luis, que desde el
punto que él había empezado su plática se
había mejorado de lugar y se puso al mismo lado de don Manuel, sacando la espada
y diciendo:

—¡Oh, falso y mal caballero!, ¿y de esta
suerte pagas las obligaciones y finezas que
debes a un ángel?

Y viendo que a estas voces le levantaba
don Manuel metiendo mano a la suya, le
tiró una estocada tal, que, o fuese cogerle

elegant—but because mine was an S and a
nail, and these were signs of what I was; to
them I responded that I myself had put
them there at my own behest and that I
did not want them taken off.

Zaida loved me so tenderly, either because I merited it for being agreeable or
because she thought I would take up her
case with my master and he would love
her. In short, I did what I liked in that
house as though it were my own, and out
of respect for me they treated Don Manuel
and Luis and Leonisa very well, allowing
them to wander about the city freely, having given them permission to see to their
ransom, and I advised Don Manuel to
work out a price for all three, and that I
would give my jewels for the cause, for
which Don Manuel showed his gratitude;
but there was difficulty in getting me out
because, as matters stood, there certainly
was no way to speak of ransom; we waited
for the redeemers to settle everything.

During that time Zaida revealed to me
her amorous designs, asking that I talk to
Don Manuel, and that I tell him that if he
were to become a Moor she would marry
him and make him lord of her father's
great riches, providing me, as a result, with
new worries and greater despair, so that I
was at the point of taking my life. She gave
me leave to take my time in speaking with
Don Manuel, although for many days I
said nothing to him of the Moor's passion,
fearing his unpredictable condition, making up stories for her, some of rejection
and others to the contrary, until jealousy
forced me to it, more to see my ingrate's
reaction than to tell him of Zaida's wish;
and having taking a liking for her, the traitor's eyes betrayed his words. After scolding me for my fanciful suspicions, he told
me that it seemed wisest to lead her on;
that I was to tell her that he could not leave

desapercibido, o que el cielo por su mano le envió su merecido castigo y a mí la deseada venganza, que le pasó de parte a parte, con tal presteza, que al primer ¡ay! se le salió el alma, dejándome a mí casi sin ella, y en dos saltos se puso a la puerta y diciendo:

—Ya, hermosa doña Isabel, te vengó don Felipe de los agravios que te hizo don Manuel. Quédate con Dios, que si escapo de este riesgo con la vida, yo te buscaré.

Y en un instante se puso en la calle. El alboroto, en un fracaso como éste, fue tal, que es imposible contarle; porque las criadas, unas acudieron a las ventanas dando voces y llamando gente, y otras a doña Eufrasia, que se había desmayado, de suerte que ninguna reparó en Zaida, que como siempre había tenido cautivas cristianas, no sabía ni hablaba mal nuestra lengua. Y habiendo entendido todo el caso, y viendo a don Manuel muerto, se arrojó sobre él llorando, y con el dolor de haberle perdido, le quitó la daga que tenía en la cinta, y antes que nadie pudiese, con la turbación que todos tenían, prevenir su riesgo, se la escondió en el corazón, cayendo muerta sobre el infeliz mozo.

Yo, que como más cursada en desdichas, era la que tenía más valor, por una parte lastimada del suceso, y por otra satisfecha con la venganza, viéndolos a todos revueltos y que ya empezaba a venir gente, me entré en mi aposento, y tomando todas las joyas de Zaida que de más valor y menos embarazo eran, que estaban en mi poder, me salí a la calle, lo uno porque la justicia no asiese de mí para que dijese quién era don Felipe, y lo otro por ver si le hallaba, para que entrambos nos pusiésemos en salvo; mas no lo hallé.

En fin, aunque había días que no pisaba las calles de Zaragoza, acerté la casa de Octavio, que me recibió con más admiración que cuando la primera vez fui a ella, y

his religion, though it cost him not the single life he had but a thousand; but if she wanted to accompany him to the land of the Christians and to become a Christian, he promised to marry her. To this he added that I should spice the tale, telling her how well-off she would be, and anything else I wished to bring her to agree, that once we had left there I was to be assured that he would fulfill his obligation. Oh, false one, and how you deluded me in this as in everything else!

In short, so as not to tire you, Zaida agreed to everything, very content, and even more so when she found out that I, too, would go with her. And the departure was planned for two months hence, when her father had to go to a place where he had some affairs and a house; and the Moors, wherever they have business, have wives and children. And my revenge against Don Manuel depended on the heavens, and they provided the means for this; for as soon as the Moor had gone, Zaida wrote a letter saying that her father had sent for her, because he had become dangerously ill, so that the king would give permission for her journey, since without that the Moors cannot go from one place to another. And once granted, she had a well-armed galleon made ready, with Christian rowers, who were advised with all the secrecy the plan required, and putting in the vessel all her riches in silver, gold, and clothing that she could take without arousing suspicion, and with her, I and Leonisa and two other Christians who served her, as she did not wish to take a single Moorish woman, and Don Manuel and Luis, we traveled by sea toward Alicante, where our journey was less likely to be beset by dangers.

Here my torments increased, here was my anxiety without compare; because

contándole mis sucesos, reposé allí aquella noche (si pudo tener reposo mujer por quien habían pasado y pasan tantas desventuras), y así, aseguro que no sé si estaba triste, si alegre; porque por una parte el lastimoso fin de don Manuel, como aún hasta entonces no había tenido tiempo de aborrecerle, me lastimaba el corazón; por otra, sus traiciones y malos tratos junto, considerándole ya no mío, sino de Zaida, encendía en mí tal ira, que tenía su muerte y mi venganza por consuelo; luego, considerar el peligro de don Felipe, a quien tan obligada estaba por haber hecho lo que a mí me era fuerza hacer para volver por mi opinión perdida. Todo esto me tenía en mortales ahogos y desasosiegos.

Otro día salió Octavio a ver por la ciudad lo que pasaba, y supo como habían enterrado a don Manuel y a Zaida, al uno como a cristiano, y a ella como a mora desesperada, y cómo a mí y a don Felipe nos llamaba la Justicia a pregones, poniendo grandes penas a quien nos encubriese y ocultase. Y así, fue fuerza estarme escondida quince días, hasta que se sosegase el alboroto de un caso tan prodigioso. Al cabo, persuadí a Octavio fuese conmigo a Valencia, que allá, más seguros, le diría mi determinación. No le iba a Octavio mal con mis sucesos, pues siempre granjeaba de ellos con que sustentarse, y, así, lo concedió. Y puesto por obra, tres o cuatro días estuve después de llegar a Valencia sin determinar lo que dispondría de mí. Unas veces me determinaba a entrarme en un convento hasta saber nuevas de don Felipe, a quien no podía negar la obligación que le tenía, y a costa de mis joyas sacarle libre del peligro que tenía por el delito cometido, y pagarle con mi persona y bienes, haciéndole mi esposo; mas de esto me apartaba el temer que quien una vez había sido desdichada, no sería jamás dichosa. Otras veces

there was nothing to stop it, and as Zaida was convinced that Don Manuel was to be her husband, she did not refuse any favor he asked. My sad eyes first contemplated Don Manuel holding Zaida's hands, then they watched Zaida with her arms around his neck, and even drinking in each other's brew from coral cups; because since the fickle traitor loved her, he looked for opportunities. And if it did not go beyond that, it was because of the care I took to block their greater pleasures. I knew well that they were not pleased with my close attentions; but they hid their anger. And if perhaps I said a word to the half-Moor, he looked at me and with eyes that said, What can I do? and that he had had enough of the risks that for my willfulness and madness he had endured, that there was no reason that we should find ourselves facing others more serious still; that if I suffered until we got to Zaragoza, that all would be resolved.

We arrived, in short, after a safe journey, in Cartagena; once landed, and the Christians freed, and with the means to return to their lands, the clothing readied, we took the road to Zaragoza, though Zaida was unhappy, having wanted to be baptized and get married the moment she set foot on Christian land—so in love was she with her new husband. And if this did not come to pass, it was my doing, not because he did not want the same. We came to Zaragoza, six years after we left that place, and to Don Manuel's house. He learned that his mother had died, and that Doña Eufrasia was a widow. Having married the cousin whose return from the Indies she awaited, leaving her soon after she gave birth to a child, he had died of carbine wounds in the war. We were well received by Doña Eufrasia, with the amazement and pleasure that might be imagined. We

me resolvía a irme a Murcia con mi madre, y de esto me quitaba con imaginar cómo parecería ante ella, habiendo sido causa de la muerte de mi padre y de todas sus penas y trabajos.

Finalmente, me resolví a la determinación con que empecé mis fortunas, que era ser siempre esclava herrada, pues lo era en el alma. Y así, metiendo las joyas de modo que las pudiese siempre traer conmigo, y este vestido en un lío, que no pudiese parecer más de ser algún pobre arreo de una esclava, dándole a Octavio con que satisfice el trabajo que por mí tomaba, le hice me sacase a la plaza, y a pública voz de pregonero me vendiese, sin reparar en que el precio que le diesen por mí fuese bajo o subido. Con grandes veras procuró Octavio apartarme de esta determinación, metiéndome por delante quién era, lo mal que me estaba y que si hasta entonces por reducir y seguir a don Manuel lo había hecho, ya para qué era seguir una vida tan vil. Mas viendo que no había reducirme, quizá por permisión del cielo, que me quería traer a esta ocasión, me sacó a la plaza, y de los primeros que llegaron a comprarme fue el tío de mi señora Lisis, que aficionado, o por mejor decir, enamorado como pareció después, me compró, pagando por mí cien ducados. Y haciendo a Octavio merced de ellos, me despedí de él, y él se apartó de mí llorando, viendo cuán sin remedio era ya el verme en descanso, pues yo misma me buscaba los trabajos.

Llevóme mi señor a su casa y entregóme a mi señora doña Leonor; la cual poco contenta, por ver a su marido travieso de mujeres, quizá temiendo de mí lo que le debía de haber sucedido con otras criadas, no me admitió con gusto. Mas después de algunos días que me trató, satisfecha de mi proceder honesto, admirando en mí la gravedad y estimación que mostraba, me

rested for three days, exchanging tales of past events, Doña Eufrasia marveling on seeing the S and nail on my face, which for Zaida had not been removed, and I consoled her, telling her they were false, that it was necessary that they remain until a certain moment.

So great was Zaida's hurry to get baptized so that she could marry that she obliged me one afternoon, a little before nightfall, to call Don Manuel, and, in the presence of Zaida and his sister and the rest of the family, along with Luis, who in those days was always alert, I told them the following:

"Very well, Lord Don Manuel, the heavens have wished, obliged by my continuous laments, that our tribulations and misfortunes come to so fortunate an end as this, to have been brought free to your house, and God has permitted that I accompany you time and again, perhaps so that, on seeing with your own eyes with what perseverance and patience I have followed you throughout, you will pay your great debts. Let delusions and excuses now cease, and let Zaida and everyone else know that what you owe me cannot be paid with less than your person, and that these brands that are on my face can only be removed by you, and that the day has come when the misfortunes and affronts that I have suffered will be rewarded. Essential is it that my good fortune be no longer delayed, so that those who have known of my affronts and errors may know my achievements and joys. Many times you have promised to be mine, so it is not right that because others consider you theirs, I fear your loss and weep over your absence. You already know that I have much to offer; my wealth is not inconsiderable, my beauty, the same you sought out and chose; my love you are not

cobró amor, y más cuando, viéndome perseguida de su marido, se lo avisé, pidiéndole pusiese remedio en ello, y el que más a propósito halló fue quitarme de sus ojos. Con esto ordenó enviarme a Madrid, y a poder de mi señora Lisis; quedándome allá nuevas de su afable condición, vine con grandísimo gusto en mejorar de dueño, que en esto bien le merezco ser creída, pues por el grande amor que la tengo, y haberme importunado algunas veces le dijese de qué nacían las lágrimas que en varias ocasiones me veía verter, y yo haberle prometido contarlo a su tiempo, como lo he hecho en esta ocasión; pues para contar un desengaño, ¿qué mayor que el que habéis oído en mi larga y lastimosa historia?

—Ya señores —prosiguió la hermosa doña Isabel—, pues he desengañado con mi engaño a muchas, no será razón que me dure toda la vida vivir engañada, fiándome en que tengo de vivir hasta que la fortuna vuelva su rueda en mi favor; pues ya no ha de resucitar don Manuel, ni cuando esto fuera posible, me fiara de él, ni de ningún hombre, pues a todos los contemplo en éste engañosos y taimados para con las mujeres. Y lo que más me admira es que ni el noble, ni el honrado, ni el de obligaciones, ni el que más se precia de cuerdo, hace más con ellas que los civiles y de humilde esfera; porque han tomado por oficio decir mal de ellas, desestimarlas y engañarlas, pareciéndoles que en esto no pierden nada. Y si lo miran bien, pierden mucho, porque mientras más flaco y débil es el sujeto de las mujeres, más apoyo y amparo habían de tener en el valor de los hombres. Mas en esto basta lo dicho, que yo, como ya no los he menester, porque no quiero haberlos menester, ni me importa que sean fingidos o verdaderos, porque tengo elegido Amante que no me olvidará, y Esposo que no me despreciará, pues le

ignorant of; I have been more than foolhardy in proving it to you. At no point do you lose, but rather you gain; so that while up to now with false brands I have been your slave, from now on without them I will be your true slave. Decide, I beg you, what you would have happen, so that what I ask you be granted as the joyous reward I desire, and do not keep me in fear any longer, for now in all justice I merit the prize I am asking of you for the many misfortunes I have suffered."

The traitor did not allow me to say more, but, smiling, in a mocking way, said:

"And who has told you, Lady Doña Isabel, that all you have said I am not well acquainted with? So thoroughly, that with all that you have thought to oblige me, you have so well disobliged me, and if I once felt some desire for you, now not even a memory of having felt so do I have. Your station I do not deny, I am not unacquainted with the expressions of your love; but if there is no desire, none of that serves any purpose. You should have known that about me from the day I left this city, that when I turned my back on you, I did not want you for a wife. And if it was already difficult for me to love you then, how much more so is it now, when, by following me as only a common woman could, you have put yourself in such vulgar straits? This resolve of which I now speak to you, days ago you might well have realized. And as for the word you claim I have given you, words like those we men give to get what we want, and women should by now be familiar with this ruse, and they should not allow themselves to be deluded since so many are there, who have learned from experience, to advise them. And, in short, for that reason I feel even less obliged than for the others; since if I gave it to you at one time, it was

contemplo yo los brazos abiertos para recibirme. Y así, divina Lisis —esto dijo poniéndose de rodillas—, te suplico como esclava tuya me concedas licencia para
entregarme a mi divino Esposo, entrándo-
me en religión con compañía de mi señora
doña Estefanía,[5] para que en estando allí,
avise a mi triste madre, que en compañía
de tal Esposo ya se holgará hallarme, y yo
no tendré vergüenza de parecer en su presencia, y ya que le he dado triste mocedad,
darle descansada vejez. En mis joyas me
parece tendré para cumplir el dote y los
demás gastos. Esto no es razón me lo ne-
guéis, pues por un ingrato y desconocido
amante he pasado tantas desdichas, y
siempre con los hierros y nombre de su esclava, ¿cuánto mejor es serlo de Dios, y a Él
ofrecerme con el mismo nombre de la Esclava de su Amante?

Aquí dio fin la hermosa doña Isabel
con un ternísimo llanto, dejando a todos
tiernos y lastimados; en particular Lisis,
que, como acabó y la vio de rodillas ante sí,
la echó los brazos al cuello, juntando su
hermosa boca con la mejilla de doña Isabel, le dijo con mil hermosas lágrimas y
tiernos sollozos:

—¡Ay, señora mía!, ¿y cómo habéis permitido tenerme tanto tiempo engañada,
teniendo por mi esclava a la que debía ser y
es señora mía? Esta queja jamás la perderé,
y os pido perdonéis los yerros que he cometido en mandaros como esclava contra
vuestro valor y calidad. La elección que
habéis hecho, en fin, es hija de vuestro entendimiento, y así yo la tengo por muy justa, y excusado es pedirme licencia, pues
vos la tenéis para mandarme como a vuestra. Y si las joyas que decís tenéis no basta-
ren, os podéis servir de las mías, y de cuanto yo valgo y tengo.

5. Doña Estefanía, prima de doña Lisis quien
cuenta un desengaño más adelante, es monja.

without the intention of keeping it, and
only to lessen your ire. I have never deluded you; well you might have known this, as
there has been no lack of occasions for
coming to this realization, but I have not
now, nor have I ever had such a thought;
and you alone are she who has wished to
be deluded, by following after me without
leaving me in peace. And thus leave off
with these doubts and stop pursuing me,
and seeing that I am out of reach, calm
yourself and forget the hope you had in
me, and return to your mother, and there
among your own people look for a husband who is less scrupulous than I, because it is impossible for me to trust a
woman who knows how to make and seek
out so many disguises. Zaida is beautiful,
and she does not lack riches; she feels love
as do you, and I have felt it for her from the
moment I saw her. And thus, in being a
Christian, which she will be when all that
is necessary has been prepared, I give her
my hand as her husband, and with that we
will put an end to this, the torments you
cause and the suffering I feel."

On hearing the vile and treacherous
words of the ungrateful Don Manuel, I felt
like a viper that has been trodden upon.
And Luis, who from the time he began his
speech had worked his way forward and
now stood at Don Manuel's side, took out
his sword by way of response, and said:

"Oh, false and evil sir! Is this the way
you pay the obligations and favors you
owe an angel?"

And seeing that with these words Don
Manuel rose and moved his hand to his
own, he thrust his sword in such a way
that, either because he caught him unaware or because by his hand the heavens
sent him the merited punishment and to
me the desired vengeance, he ran him
through, with such celerity that with his

Besaba doña Isabel las manos de Lisis, mientras le decía eso. Y dando lugar a las damas y caballeros que la llegaban a abrazar y a ofrecérsele, se levantó, y después de haber recibido a todos y satisfecho a sus ofrecimientos con increíbles donaire y despejo, pidió arpa, y sentándose junto a los músicos, sosegados todos, cantó este romance:

Dar celos quita el honor;
    la presunción, pedir celos;
    no tenerlos no es amor,
    y discreción es tenerlos.
Quien por picar a su amante
    pierde a su honor el respeto
    y finge lo que no hace,
    o se determina a hacerlo,
ocasionando el castigo,
    se pone a cualquiera riesgo;
    que también supone culpa
    la obra como el deseo.
Quien pide celos, no estima
    las partes que le dio el cielo,
    y ensalzando las ajenas,
    abate el merecimiento.
Está a peligro que elija
    su mismo dueño por dueño,
    lo que por reñir su agravio
    sube a la esfera del fuego.
Quien tiene amor y no cela,
    todos dicen, y lo entiendo,
    que no estima lo que ama
    y finge sus devaneos.
Celos y amor no son dos:
    uno es causa; el otro, efecto.
    Porque efecto y causa son
    dos, pero sólo un sujeto.
Nacen celos del amor,
    y el mismo amor son los celos,
    y si es, como dicen, dios,
    una en dos causas contemplo.
Quien vive tan descuidado
    que no teme, será necio;

first cry his soul left, nearly leaving me without mine, and in two strides he was at the door and saying:

"There, lovely Doña Isabel, Don Felipe has avenged the offenses done to you by Don Manuel. May God be with you. And if I escape this peril with my life, I will come looking for you."

And in a moment he was out the door. The confusion caused by a disaster such as this is impossible to describe; some of the servants ran to the windows shouting and calling out to people, and others to Doña Eufrasia, who had fainted, so that no one paid any attention to Zaida, who, because she had always had Christian slaves, knew and spoke our language quite well. And having understood all that went on, and seeing Don Manuel dead, she threw herself on him weeping, and with the pain of having lost him, she took the dagger she had at her waist, and with the uproar everyone was in, before anyone could stop her, she buried it in her heart, falling dead on her wretched young man.

I, mose versed in misfortune, was the one with the greatest courage; on the one hand pained by the event, and on the other satisfied with the vengeance, seeing everyone in a state of confusion and people beginning to come, I went to my chamber, and taking Zaida's smallest but most valuable jewels, which were in my possession, left, first so that justice would not come to me to find out who Don Felipe was, and second to see if I could find him, so that together we might escape. But I did not find him.

Finally, though I had not walked the streets of Zaragoza in many a day, I found Octavio's house, and he received me with more amazement than the first time I had gone there, and telling him what had happened to me, I rested there that night

pues quien más estado alcanza,
    más cerca está de perderlo.
Seguro salió Faetón
    rigiendo el carro febeo,
    confiado en su volar
    por las regiones del cielo.
Icaro, en alas de cera,
    por las esferas subiendo,
    y en su misma confianza,
    Icaro y Faetón murieron.
Celos y desconfianza,
    que son una cosa es cierto;
    porque el celar es temer;
    el desconfiar, lo mesmo.
Luego quien celos tuviere
    es fuerza que sea discreto,
    porque cualquier confiado
    está cerca de ser necio.
Con aquesto he desatado
    la duda que se ha propuesto,
    y responderé a cualquiera
    que deseare saberlo.
De que en razón de celos,
    es tan malo darlos
    como tenerlos.
Pedirlos, libertad;
    darlos, deprecios.
Y de los dos extremos,
    malo es tenerlos; pero aqueste quiero,
    porque mal puede amor serlo sin ellos.

(if rest is within reach of a woman who had experienced and continues to experience so many misfortunes), and thus I truly cannot say whether I was sad or happy; because, on the one hand, Don Manuel's pitiful end, as up to then there had not been time to despise him, pained my heart; on the other hand, his treachery and evil ways together, thinking of him now not as mine but as Zaida's, enraged me so that I took his death and my revenge as consolation; then, I thought of the danger faced by Don Felipe, to whom I owed so much for having done what had to be done for me to recover the good name I had lost. All of that had me in mortal distress and anxiety.

The next day Octavio went about the city to see what was happening and found out that they had buried Don Manuel and Zaida, the one as a Christian and the other as a desperate Moor, and as justice was calling publicly for my arrest and that of Don Felipe, anyone who sheltered or hid us faced serious risks. And thus I was obliged to remain hidden for fifteen days, until the uproar of such a prodigious case had calmed. At the end of that time, I persuaded Octavio to go with me to Valencia, where, safer, I would decide what to do. Octavio did not do badly with my adventures, as he always got out of them something with which to sustain himself, and thus he conceded. And we set out, and for three or four days after arriving in Valencia, I was unable to decide what to do with myself. At times I was determined to enter a convent until I had news of Don Felipe, to whom I could not deny the obligation I owed, and with my jewels, free him from the danger he was in for the crime committed, and pay him with my person and my goods, making him my husband. But from that I was dissuaded by the fear that a

woman who had once been unhappy would never know happiness. At other times I was resolved to go to Murcia to be with my mother, but from that I was dissuaded by images of how I would appear in her eyes, having been the cause of the death of my father and of all her sufferings and tribulations.

In the end, I made the decision with which my fortunes had begun, and that was to be always a branded slave, since thus was I in my heart. And so, arranging the jewels in such a way that I would always have them on my person, and this dress in a bundle that would seem nothing more than some poor appurtenances of a slave, paying Octavio for the trouble he had taken on my behalf, I told him to take me to the plaza, and in the loud voice of a crier to sell me, without paying any mind if the price they gave for me was high or low. Octavio took great pains to dissuade me from this decision, arguing about who I was, how wrong I was, and if up to then I had done it to convince and follow Don Manuel, now what reason was there to continue in such a wretched life. But seeing that there was no way to convince me, perhaps with the permission of the heavens, that wanted to bring me to this state, he took me to the plaza, and among the first who came to buy me was the uncle of my lady Lisis, who, because he liked me, or better said, was in love as it later seemed, bought me, paying for me one hundred ducats. And repaying Octavio's favors with those, I said farewell to him, and he left me crying, understanding, on seeing me now at peace, that there was no other remedy, since I myself looked for these tribulations.

My master took me to his house and handed me over to my lady, Doña Leonor. But she was little pleased, knowing her

husband to be a philanderer around women; perhaps fearing of me what must have happened with other servants, she did not receive me with pleasure. But after having dealt with me for some days, satisfied with my honest behavior, admiring the seriousness and esteem I displayed, she came to love me, and even more when, seeing myself pursued by her husband, I advised her, asking that she find a remedy for this situation, and the most convenient she found was to remove me from his sight. So she ordered me sent to Madrid, and in the care of my lady Lisis; and though this confirmed the excellent qualities of my former mistress, I came with great joy for having found a better master, and in this I well deserve to be believed, that for the great love I have for her, and she having importuned me now and again to tell her whence came the tears that on a number of occasions she saw me shed, and I having promised to tell her in good time, thus have I done on this occasion; and as misfortunes go, what greater than that which you have heard in my long and pitiful story?

"Now sirs," the beautiful Doña Isabel continued, "since with my illusions I have disillusioned so many, it is not right that I spend an entire life deluded, assuming that what I have will be sufficient to keep me alive until fortune's wheel turns in my favor; as now Don Manuel will certainly not return to life, nor if that were possible would I trust him, nor any other man, as in him I see them all, treacherous and cunning toward women. And what most amazes me is that neither the noble, nor the honest man, nor he with obligations, nor he who thinks himself most wise, treats women any differently than do those from the lower, humble spheres; because they have taken it as their duty to speak ill

of them, undervalue and deceive them, believing that in this they lose nothing. But if you consider it well, they lose much, as the weaker and more vulnerable a woman's character, the more support and protection she ought to receive from men. But of that enough said, as I no longer have need of them, because I do not wish to have need of them, nor does it matter to me that they be false or true, because I have chosen as Lover one who will not forget me, and as husband one who will not despise me, and as I gaze at Him His arms open to receive me. And thus, divine Lisis"—this she said falling to her knees—"I beg you as your slave that you give me permission to deliver myself to my divine Husband, entering into a religious order accompanied by my Lady Doña Estefanía,[5] so that once there, she may advise my sad mother, who will be delighted to find me in the company of such a Spouse; and I will not be ashamed to appear in her presence, and now that I have given her a sad youth will I give her a peaceful old age. I believe that my jewels will be sufficient to cover the dowry and other expenses. This is not a reason for you to deny me, since because of an ungrateful, thankless lover I have lived so many misfortunes, and always with these brands and known as his slave; how much better it is to be that of God, and to offer myself to Him with the same name, that of Her Lover's Slave."

Here the lovely Doña Isabel ended, weeping most tenderly, leaving everyone sad and moved, especially Lisis, who, as she had finished and was kneeling before her, threw her arms around her neck, and, pressing her lovely mouth against Doña

5. Estefanía, Lisis's cousin and narrator of a subsequent tale, is a nun.

Isabel's cheek, said to her with a thousand lovely tears and tender sobs:

"Ah, my lady! and why have you allowed me to go on for so long deluded, taking her, who should be and is my lady, for a slave? For this I will never forgive you; and I beg that you pardon the errors I have committed in ordering you about as a slave, contrary to your dignity and station. The choice you have made, in the end, is the result of your judgment, and thus I take it for most just, and there is no need to ask my permission, as it is your right to treat me as yours. And if the jewels you speak of are not sufficient, you may use mine and all that I am worth and possess."

Doña Isabel kissed the hands of Lisis as she said that. And making way for the ladies and gentlemen who had come forward to embrace her and offer themselves to her, she rose; and after having received all and accepted the words they offered with amazing grace and ease, she asked for a harp, and sitting next to the musicians, everyone at peace, she sang this song:

In giving cause for jealousy, honor is lost;
　　presumption it is to look for jealousy;
　　to be not jealous is to love not,
　　and prudence demands that one feel
　　　thus.
He who to make his lover jealous
　　loses respect for his good name
　　and pretends to do that which he does
　　　not,
　　or is determined to do thus,
occasioning punishment,
　　puts himself at great risk;
　　intention must be taken
　　to be as sinful as the act.
He who give cause for jealousy, does not
　　　esteem
　　the gifts the heavens have given,

and by magnifying those of another,
diminishes the merits of the first.
She is in danger who elects as master
the master of another,
who in avenging her affront,
finds herself engulfed in flames.
They say, and this I understand,
that he who loves and is not ever
vigilant,
does not esteem his love's object
and hides his indifference.
Jealousy and love are not two:
one is the cause; the other, effect.
Because effect and cause are
two, but the subject one.
From love jealousy is born,
and love itself is jealousy,
and if it is, as they say, a god,
one in two causes I contemplate.
He who lives so carelessly
that he does not fear, will be foolish;
since the greater the power achieved,
the nearer is its loss.
Phaeton went out certain,
guiding the Phoebean chariot,
trusting in his ability to fly
through the regions of the sky.
Icarus, with wings of wax,
to the heights rising,
and for their very confidence,
Icarus and Phaeton perished.
Jealousy and mistrust,
that they are one and the same is
certain;
because to be jealous is to fear;
to mistrust, to do so as well.
Then he who were jealous
must needs take care,
because he who is trusting
is very near to being a fool.
With this I have resolved
the problem posed,
And I will respond to any
who wishes to know.

As wrong is it
 to inspire as it is
 to feel jealousy.
To look for signs of this, freedom,
 to be its cause, disdain.
And of the two extremes,
 both are evil; but this I wish because
 without it love does not exist.

(Translated by Mary Ellen Fieweger)

Ana Caro Mallén de Soto

The only image history permits us to trace of Ana Caro Mallén de Soto is that of professional writer. Stripped of her personal life by time and oblivion, this dramatist and poet-chronicler does not exist outside the memory of her work, and her work was not autobiographical. As what tradition tells us is an anomalous case — a woman who entered the public world — Ana Caro Mallén de Soto left traces of her participation in public events without leaving any official record of her private existence. The only life we can reconstruct for Ana Caro is that which can be glimpsed in and around her work.

Aside from the year of death of her brother, who was old enough to have been a grandfather when he died in 1655, the only dates we have to situate Ana Caro historically are those that refer to her writing. The first is the poetic recounting of public festivities dated 1628, and the last a lost religious drama for which she was paid in 1645. (The publication of another play in 1653 may have occurred years after it was written.) It is unlikely that these dates mark the parameters of Caro's literary life, for the greater part of her work seems to have disappeared. In the last several years, Francisco López Estrada has disinterred and published four of Caro's poems, and it is possible that more may be discovered, extending the dates we now have. But it is doubtful that we will ever have access to Ana Caro's complete works. Her contemporary, and perhaps kin, Rodrigo Caro, writing about her in his book *Varones insignes en Letras Naturales de la Ilustrísima Ciudad de Sevilla* (Famous men of letters from the illustrious city of Seville), calls her "a famous poet, who has written many plays, presented in Seville, Madrid, and other places to great acclaim, and she has written many and diverse other works of poetry, entering in many literary tournaments, in which, almost always, she has won first prize."[1] Other contemporaries also write about her. In *La Garduña de Sevilla* (The marten of Seville), Alonso Castillo Solórzano situates her in Madrid, in the company of María de Zayas, and she shows up in Luis Vélez de Guevara's *El Diablo Cojuelo* (The gimpy devil), reading a poem in the Academy in Seville.

Ana Caro's surviving poetry is long, formal, and academic. The majority of the poems that have been preserved, or rediscovered, function to spread news, even propaganda. One of these, "Romance por la victoria de Tetuán" (Ballad for the victory at Tetuán, 1633), celebrates a minor battle won by an obscure hero in the seemingly endless story of Spanish imperialism. Others recount public celebrations, rich in

detailed and solemn description of ceremonies and rituals, and praise the key play-ers and their patrons of the feasts. These are chronicles of public events, in which the poet's role is to commemorate some ephemeral occurrence, to inflate the impor-tance of particular actors without making herself visible. Equally professional, though more intimate, given their recipient, is the poem that Caro composed in honor of the publication of the *Novelas ejemplares y amorosas* written by her friend, María de Zayas y Sotomayor.

One of the few historical references we have of Ana Caro concerns her religious plays, which have since been lost. These were to be performed during the Festival of Corpus Christi in 1641, 1642, and 1645. Although we do not know very much about the plays, we do know that she was paid for them; that is, the only evidence we have of Caro's participation in devotional theater is underlined by its pecuniary aspect.

Caro is not a particularly humble writer. She goes against the custom of offering anonymous tributes during religious festivals, by signing her multilingual dramatic panegyric for the Corpus Christi celebration of 1639. As far as her occasional poetry is concerned, after begging her reader's pardon for her lack of experience as a poet (this is in the earliest poem we have of hers, "Relación de las fiestas por los mártires del Japón" [Story of the feast for the martyrs of Japan, 1628]), the only inferiority Ana Caro admits to refers to class. She is deferential when she addresses the Countess of Salvatierra, to whom she dedicates her "Relación de la fiesta y octava celebradas con motivo de los sucesos de Flandes" (Story of the festival and octave celebrated for the events in Flanders, 1635).[2] Significantly, this dedicatory prologue seems to have a sec-ondary object: Caro asks the countess for permission to remain always in her service, and it is possible that Caro's move to Madrid was facilitated by being patronized by the countess. In the following lines, which introduce "Romance por la victoria de Tetuán," the poet rejects feminine modesty, manifesting instead a poetic attitude that today might be described as phallic:

> Take courage, cowardly pen,
> transcend celestial spheres,
> scale the clouds undaunted;
> pierce lightning with valor.
>
> Take courage, glorious fame,
> so your eyes and tongues
> may eternalize hyperbole
> to the question of my enterprise.[3]

Like her poems, her panegyric and surely her religious drama support the insti-tutions and the ideology of her day: expansionist monarchy and church. In her two extant plays, however, state and religion are relegated to the background, while the author calls into question the less obviously visible gender ideology and its institu-

tions: love, marriage, male dominance, female passivity. Ana Caro shows another face here, a subversive one. Both Queen Rosaura in *El conde de Partinuplés* (The count of Partinuplés), who, obliged to marry, uses her magic arts to maintain control over the dangerous process of choosing a husband, and Leonor, who intends to kill the man who deceived her in *Valor, agravio y mujer* (Valor, Outrage, and Woman), are strong and decisive women characters who call into question the apparatus of sexual hierarchy.

Valor, agravio y mujer takes on the theme of honor, common in the theater of the Spanish Golden Age, in which a woman's sexual transgression tarnishes the good name of the men in her family. Caro pokes fun at the honor code in a scene in which three men are so embroiled in each other's sexual and romantic lives that they can see no escape other than their mutual deaths. Unlike her male contemporaries, for whom honor is primarily a man's issue, Caro's heroine sets out to avenge her own lost honor by killing — or winning back — the man who seduced her with the promise of marriage. The complex chain of events orchestrated by the protagonist belies the play's pat ending, which bows to the conventions of the genre. In the course of the play, Caro questions norms of class as well as gender, creating a woman hero who is an able swordswoman and who knows how to court a lady, as well as a servant (the familiar *gracioso*) who is both wise and respected by his mistress.

1. "insigne poeta, que ha hecho muchas comedias, representadas en Sevilla, Madrid y otras partes con grandísimo aplauso, y ha hecho otras muchas y varias obras de poesía, entrando en muchas justas literarias, en las cuales, casi siempre, se le ha dado el primer premio" (Rodrigo Caro, n.d., 73).

2. An octave (*octava*) is the period of eight days that comprise a church festival.

3. ¡Aliento, cobarde pluma! / Pasa celestes esferas; / atrevida, escala nubes; / valiente, rayos penetra . . . / Ánimo, gloriosa fama, / porque tus ojos y lenguas / hipérboles eternicen / al asunto de mi empresa.

Valor, agravio y mujer

Hablan en ella las personas siguientes:

Don Fernando de Ribera
Doña Leonor, su hermana
Ribete, lacayo
Don Juan de Córdoba
Tomillo, criado
Estela, Condesa de Sora
Lisarda, su prima
Ludovico, Príncipe de Pinoy
Flora, criada
Fineo, criado
Tres bandoleros

Jornada Primera

Debe haber a los dos lados del tablado dos escalerillas, cubiertas de murta a manera de riscos, que llegan a lo alto del vestuario, y por ellas bajan Estela y Lisarda, de cazadoras, con venablos. Se fingen truenos y torbellino al bajar.

LISARDA　　　Por aquí, gallarda Estela
de este inaccesible monte,
de este gigante soberbio
que a las estrellas se opone
podrás bajar a este valle,
en tanto que los rigores
del cielo, menos severos
y más piadosos deponen
negro encapotado ceño:
sígueme, prima.

ESTELA　　　　　　　　　¿Por dónde?
Que soy de hielo. Mal hayan
mil veces mis ambiciones,

(Van bajando poco a poco, y hablando.)

y el corzo, que dio ligero
ocasión a que malogre
sus altiveces mi brío,
mi orgullo bizarro, el golpe
felizmente ejecutado,
pues sus pisadas veloces
persuadieron mis alientos,
y repiten mis temores.
¡Válgame el cielo! ¿No miras
cómo el cristalino móvil

Valor, Outrage, and Woman

Cast of characters

Don Fernando de Ribera
Doña Leonor, his sister
Ribete, lackey
Don Juan de Córdoba
Tomillo, servant
Estela, Countess of Sora
Lisarda, her cousin
Ludovico, Prince of Pinoy
Flora, servant
Fineo, servant
Three bandits

Act 1

At each side of the stage there are steps draped in myrtle, made to look like craggy cliffs, that reach to the top of the set. Estela and Lisarda, dressed for hunting and carrying spears, descend from one. Thunder and lightning.

LISARDA   This way, graceful Estela,
from this lofty mountain,
from this haughty giant,
that challenges the stars,
can you make your way to the valley,
while heaven's rigors,
less severe and more merciful,
prepare their black and gloomy frown.
Follow me, cousin.

ESTELA   Which way?
I am frozen. A thousand
curses on my ambition,

(They speak as they descend slowly.)

and on the roe deer that so lightly
caused my spirit and my gallant pride
to falter, as it escaped
my so expertly executed blow.
For its swift steps
persuaded my spirits
and repeated my fears.
Heaven protect me! See you not
how the crystalline movement of heaven's court

de su asiento desencaja
las columnas de sus orbes?
¿Y cómo, turbado, el cielo,
entre asombros y entre horrores,
segunda vez representa
principios de Faetonte?[1]
¿Cómo temblando sus ejes
se altera, y se descompone
la paz de los elementos,
que airados y desconformes
granizan ruidosos truenos,
fulminan prestos vapores,
congelados en la esfera
ya rayos, ya exhalaciones?
¿No ves cómo, airado Eolo,
la intrépida cárcel rompe
al Noto y Boreas,[2] porque
desatadas sus prisiones,
estremeciendo la tierra
en lo cóncavo rimbomben
de sus maternas entrañas
con prodigiosos temblores?
¿No ves vestidos de luto
los azules pabellones,
y que las preñadas nubes,
caliginosos ardores
que engendraron la violencia,
hace que rayos aborten?
Todo está brotando miedos,
todo penas y rigores,
todo pesar, todo asombro,
todo sustos y aflicciones,
no se termina un celaje
en el opuesto horizonte.
¿Qué hemos de hacer?

LISARDA   No te aflijas.

ESTELA   Estatua de piedra inmóvil
me ha hecho el temor, Lisarda.
¡Qué así me entrase en el bosque!

(Acaban de bajar.)

LISARDA   A la inclemencia del tiempo,
debajo de aquestos robles
nos negaremos, Estela,
en tanto que nos socorre

disjoins the columns of its celestial orbs,
and how the sky, troubled,
amidst dread and horror
a second time does stage
the precipices of Phaëton?[1]
How with its trembling shafts
it alters, and undoes
the peace of the elements
that, angered and irate,
hail down noisy thunder,
explodes in sudden mists
frozen in the spheres,
now lightning, now vapors?
See you not how angry Aeolus
sunders the intrepid prison of
Notus and Boreas,[2] so that
freed from their confinement,
shaking the earth
with prodigious tremors,
they might resound in the concavity
of their maternal entrails?
See you not the blue pavilions
hung with mourning vestment,
and how the pregnant clouds,
sultry ardors by violence engendered,
make the lightning bolts abort?
Everything erupts in fear;
all is trouble, all is harshness,
all is grief, all is dread,
all fear, and all affliction.
Nor do the clouds cease
on the far horizon.
What are we to do?

LISARDA   Be not afraid.

ESTELA   A statue of immobile stone
has fear made me, Lisarda.
Thus should I enter the forest!

(They have completed their descent.)

LISARDA   Beneath those oaks let us take shelter,
Estela, from this inclement weather,
till the heavens rescue us,

el cielo, que ya descubre
al Occidente arreboles.

(Desvíanse a un lado, y salen Tibaldo, Rufino y Astolfo, bandoleros.)

TIBALDO   Buenos bandidos, ¡por Dios!
de más tenemos el nombre,
pues el ocio o la desgracia
nos está dando lecciones
de doncellas de labor:
bien se ejerce de Mavorte[3]
la bélica disciplina
en nuestras ejecuciones:
¡bravo orgullo!

RUFINO   Sin razón
nos culpas. Las ocasiones
faltan; los ánimos, no.

TIBALDO   Buscarlas, porque se logren.

ASTOLFO   Por Dios, si no me engaño,
no es mala la que nos pone
en las manos la ventura.

TIBALDO   Quiera el cielo que goce.

ASTOLFO   Dos mujeres son; bizarras;
y hablando están. ¿No las oyes?

TIBALDO   Acerquémonos corteses.

ESTELA   Lisarda, ¿no ves tres hombres?

LISARDA   Sí, hacia nosotras vienen.

ESTELA   Gracias al cielo, señores;
¿está muy lejos de aquí
la quinta de Enrique, el Conde
de Velflor?

TIBALDO   Bien cerca está.

ESTELA   ¿Queréis decirnos por dónde?

TIBALDO   Vamos, venid con nosotros.

ESTELA   Vuestra cortesía es norte,
que nos guía.

RUFINO   Antes de mucho
con más miedos, más temores
zozobrará vuestra calma.

(Llévanlas, y baja don Juan de Córdoba, muy galán, de camino, por el risco opuesto al que bajaron ellas, y dice:)

DON JUAN   ¡Qué notables confusiones!
¡Qué impensado terremoto!
¡Qué tempestad tan disforme!
Perdí el camino, en efecto,
y será dicho que tope

for in the west the sky
is beginning to turn red.

(They go off to one side. Enter the bandits Tibaldo, Rufino, and Astolfo.)

TIBALDO	We are sorry bandits, by God!
	All we have's the name,
	for laziness or ill fortune
	gives us lessons
	fit for girls at needlework.
	So well is Mars's warlike discipline
	exercised in our exploits!³
	What fierce pride!
RUFINO	You have no cause to blame us.
	The opportunities are lacking,
	not our spirit!
TIBALDO	Seek them out, to make them happen!
ASTOLFO	By God, if I'm not mistaken,
	'tis no bad wind that's put us
	in the hands of fortune!
TIBALDO	May the heavens permit this pleasure!
ASTOLFO	'Tis two gentlewomen,
	and they are talking. Do you not hear them?
TIBALDO	Let us approach, like gentlemen.
ESTELA	Lisarda, see you not three men?
LISARDA	Aye, they are coming toward us.
ESTELA	Thank heavens! Sirs,
	is the estate of Enrique,
	Count of Velflor, very far from here?
TIBALDO	'Tis close by.
ESTELA	Be you so good as to tell us where?
TIBALDO	Let us take you; come with us.
ESTELA	Your courtesy is the compass
	that will guide us.
RUFINO	Before long, with greater fear,
	more terror, will your calm be afflicted.

(They take them away. Enter Don Juan de Córdoba, very gallant, descending the path opposite the cliff the cousins came down.)

DON JUAN	What notable confusion!
	What an unexpected earthquake!
	What a violent storm!
	I lost my way, in fact,
	and will be fortunate to meet

quien me le enseñe; tal es
la soledad destos montes.

(Va bajando.)

Ata estas mulas, Tomillo,
a un árbol, y mientras comen
baja a este llano.

(Tomillo, arriba, sin bajar)

TOMILLO   ¿Qué llano?
Un tigre, un rinoceronte,
un cocodrilo, un caimán,
un Polifemo cíclope,
un ánima condenada,
y un diablo, Dios me perdone
te ha de llevar.

DON JUAN   Majadero,
¿sobre qué das esas voces?

TOMILLO   Sobre que es fuerza que pagues
sacrilegio tan enorme,
como fue dejar a un ángel.

DON JUAN   ¿Hay disparates mayores?

TOMILLO   Pues, ¿qué puede sucedernos
bien cuando tú. . .

DON JUAN   No me enojes;
deja estas locuras.

TOMILLO   Bueno.
¿Locuras y sinrazones
son las verdades?

DON JUAN   Escucha:
mal articuladas voces
oigo.

TOMILLO   Algún sátiro o fauno.

(Salen los bandoleros con las damas, y para atarles las manos ponen en el suelo las pistolas y gabanes; y estáse don Juan retirado.)

TIBALDO   Perdonen, o no perdonen.

LISARDA   Pues, bárbaros, ¿qué intentáis?

ASTOLFO   No es nada, no se alboroten,
que será peor.

(Tomillo acaba de bajar.)

DON JUAN   Escucha, oye.

TOMILLO   ¿Qué he de oír? ¿Hay algún paso
de comedia, encanto, bosque,
o aventura en que seamos
yo Sancho, tú don Quijote,
porque busquemos la venta,

someone to set me on my course.
These mountains are so lonely.

(He continues down.)

Tie these mules, Tomillo,
to a tree, and while they eat
come down to this plain.

(Tomillo, above, does not go down.)

TOMILLO	What plain?
	A tiger, a rhinoceros,
	a crocodile, an alligator
	a Poliphemous cyclops,
	a damned soul,
	and a devil, God forgive me,
	will take you.
DON JUAN	Fool!
	What do you rail about?
TOMILLO	About how you must pay for the great sacrilege
	of abandoning an angel.
DON JUAN	What foolishness!
TOMILLO	Well, what good do you think
	will come to us, when you . . .
DON JUAN	Anger me not;
	stop your nonsense!
TOMILLO	Fine. Is truth
	nonsense and foolishness?
DON JUAN	Listen; I hear muffled voices.
TOMILLO	Some satyr or faun.

(The bandits enter with the ladies. To tie their hands the bandits place their cloaks and pistols on the ground. Don Juan is a little way off.)

TIBALDO	Pardon us or not.
LISARDA	Well, savages, what do you intend?
ASTOLFO	Nothing. Make no noise
	or it will go the worse for you.

(Tomillo reaches the stage.)

DON JUAN	Listen, do you hear?
TOMILLO	What am I to hear?
	Some scene of wit,
	enchantment, woods, or adventure
	in which I am Sancho and you Don Quixote,

los palos, y Maritornes?[4]

DON JUAN Paso es, y no poco estrecho,
a donde es fuerza que apoye
sus osadías mi orgullo.

TIBALDO Idles quitando las joyas.

ESTELA Tomad las joyas, traidores,
y dejadnos. ¡Ay, Lisarda!

DON JUAN ¿No ves, Tomillo, dos soles
padeciendo injusto eclipse?
¿No miras sus resplandores
turbados, y que a su lumbre
bárbaramente se opone?

TOMILLO Querrás decir que la tierra.
No son sino salteadores
que quizá si nos descubren,
nos cenarán esta noche,
sin dejarnos confesar,
en picadillo, o gigote.

DON JUAN Yo he de cumplir con quien soy.

LISARDA Matadnos, ingratos hombres.

RUFINO No aspiramos a eso, reina.

(*Póneseles delante don Juan con la espada desnuda; Tomillo coge en tanto los gabanes y pistolas, y se entra entre los ramos, y ellos se turban.*)

ESTELA ¿Cómo su piedad esconde
el cielo?

DON JUAN   Pues, ¿a qué aspiran,
a experimentar rigores
de mi brazo y de mi espada?

TIBALDO O, ¡qué irresistibles golpes!

DON JUAN ¡Villanos, viles, cobardes!

TOMILLO Aunque pese a mis temores,
les he de quitar las armas
para que el riesgo se estorbe,
que de ayuda servirá.

TIBALDO ¡Dispara, Rufino!

RUFINO   ¿Dónde
están las pistolas?

TOMILLO   Pistos
les será mejor que tomen.

ASTOLFO No hay que esperar.

TIBALDO   Huye, Astolfo,
¡que éste es demonio, no es hombre!

RUFINO ¡Huye, Tibaldo!

(*Vanse, y don Juan tras ellos.*)

as we look for the inn, whacks, and Maritornes?[4]

DON JUAN	A scene it is and not a little narrow
	where I have no choice but to challenge
	their brazenness with my pride.
TIBALDO	Remove their jewels.
ESTELA	Take the jewels, traitors,
	and leave us. Oh, Lisarda!
DON JUAN	See you not, Tomillo, two
	suns suffering an unjust eclipse?
	See you not their perturbed
	splendor, and their dazzle
	so barbarously set upon?
TOMILLO	You mean the earth.
	They are nothing but highway
	robbers who may, if they discover us,
	make chopped meat or stew
	from us for supper tonight
	before we can confess.
DON JUAN	I must act in accordance
	with who I am.
LISARDA	Kill us, ungrateful men.
RUFINO	To that we do not aspire, my queen.

(Don Juan steps in front of them with his sword unsheathed; Tomillo picks up the cloaks and pistols, and steps among the branches, and they are alarmed.)

ESTELA	How heaven does hide its mercy!
DON JUAN	Now, to what do you aspire,
	to test the strength of
	my arm and my sword?
TIBALDO	Oh, what powerful blows!
DON JUAN	Villains! vile cowards!
TOMILLO	Despite my fear
	must I take their weapons
	to hamper this attack on us
	and be of some help to my master.
TIBALDO	Shoot, Rufino!
RUFINO	Where are the guns?
TOMILLO	Gone, and you'd be better so.
ASTOLFO	There's no time to spare.
TIBALDO	Flee, Astolfo, this is a
	demon, not a man!
RUFINO	Flee, Tibaldo!

(Exit bandits, with Don Juan close behind.)

TOMILLO   ¡Pardiez,
              que los lleva a lindo trote
              el tal mi amo; y les da
              lindamente a trochemoche
              cintarazo como tierra,
              porque por fuerza la tomen!
              Eso sí, pléguete Cristo;
              ¡qué bien corrido galope!

ESTELA   ¡Ay, Lisarda!

LISARDA   Estela mía,
              ánimo, que bien disponen
              nuestro remedio los cielos.

(Sale don Fernando de Ribera, Capitán de la Guardia, y gente.)

DON FERNANDO ¡Que no parezcan, Godofre!
              ¿Qué selva encantada, o qué
              laberinto las esconde?
              Mas, ¿qué es esto?

ESTELA   ¡Ay, don Fernando!
              Rendidas a la desorden
              de la suerte.

DON FERNANDO   ¿Qué fue? ¿Cómo?

LISARDA   Unos bandidos enormes
              nos han puesto. . .

DON FERNANDO   ¿Hay tal desdicha?
(Desátalas.)

LISARDA   Mas un caballero noble
              nos libró.

(Sale don Juan.)

DON JUAN   Ahora verán
              los bárbaros que se oponen
              a la beldad de esos cielos,
              sin venerar los candores
              de vuestras manos, el justo
              castigo.

DON FERNANDO   ¡Muera!
(Empuña la espada.)

ESTELA   No borres
              con ingratitud, Fernando,
              mis justas obligaciones;
              vida y honor le debemos.

DON FERNANDO Dejad que a esos pies me postre,
              y perdonad mi ignorancia.

TOMILLO   Y ¿será razón que monde
              nísperos Tomillo, en tanto

TOMILLO	Good God, my lord is
	making them run a nice trot;
	and nicely sending them
	helter-skelter over the ground,
	he's really giving them what for!
	Sure enough, Christ, what a gallop they've run!
ESTELA	Oh, Lisarda!
LISARDA	My Estela, take heart.
	How well the heavens
	have arranged our rescue.

(Enter Don Fernando de Ribera, Captain of the Guard, with others.)

DON FERNANDO	They cannot be found, Godofre!
	What enchanted jungle or
	what labyrinth hides them?
	But what is this?
ESTELA	Oh, Don Fernando!
	We yield to the disorder of our fortune.
DON FERNANDO	What happened? How?
LISARDA	Some terrible bandits held us …
DON FERNANDO	What greater calamity?

(He unties them.)

LISARDA	But a noble gentleman saved us.

(Enter Don Juan.)

DON JUAN	Now the savages who
	oppose the beauty of these skies
	and refused to venerate the innocence of your hands
	will see just punishment.
DON FERNANDO	Die!

(He brandishes his sword.)

ESTELA	Do not erase my just obligations, Fernando,
	with ingratitude;
	we owe him life and honor.
DON FERNANDO	Allow me to prostrate myself at those feet
	and beg forgiveness for my ignorance.
TOMILLO	And is there some reason for Tomillo
	to let the grass grow under his feet

	que estos testigos, conformes
	o contestes, no declaran
	mis alentados valores?
DON FERNANDO	Yo te premiaré.
DON JUAN	Anda, necio.
	Guárdeos Dios, porque se abone
	en vuestro valor mi celo.
ESTELA	Decid vuestra patria y nombre,
	caballero, si no hay
	causa alguna que estorbe,
	sepa yo a quién le debo tanto,
	porque agradecida logre
	mi obligación en serviros,
	deseos por galardones.
DON FERNANDO	Lo mismo os pido, y si acaso
	de Bruselas en la Corte
	se ofrece en qué os sirva, si
	no porque se reconoce
	obligada la Condesa,
	sino por inclinaciones
	naturales de mi estrella.
	Venid, que cuanto os importe
	tendréis en mi voluntad.
TOMILLO	Más que doscientos Nestores
	vivas.[5] ¡Qué buen mocetón!
LISARDA	Tan justas obligaciones
	como os tenemos las dos,
	más dilatará el informe
	que juntos os suplicamos.
DON JUAN	Con el afecto responde
	mi obediencia agradecida.
DON FERNANDO	¡Qué galán! ¡Qué gentilhombre!
DON JUAN	Nací en la ciudad famosa
	que la antigüedad celebra
	por madre de los ingenios,
	por origen de las letras,
	esplendor de los estudios,
	claro archivo de las ciencias,
	epílogo del valor
	y centro de la nobleza:
	la que en dos felices partos
	dio al mundo Lucano y Séneca,
	éste filósofo estóico.
	aquél, insigne poeta;

	while these witnesses, agreeing or confirming,
	fail to declare my tireless bravery?
DON FERNANDO	I will reward you.
DON JUAN	Go on, dolt. God keep you,
	as my devotion vouches for your valor.
ESTELA	Tell us your name and country, sir,
	if there is no reason to
	conceal them, so that I may know
	to whom I owe so much, and so that
	gratefully my obligation to serve you
	may be fulfilled, as well as
	my desires to reward you.
DON FERNANDO	I ask the same of you, and,
	that the Court of Brussels may
	offer to serve you, not only because
	the Countess recognizes her obligation,
	but for the natural inclinations of my star.
	Come, it is my wish that you may have
	what you most desire.
TOMILLO	More than two hundred living
	Nestors![5] What a good fellow!
LISARDA	We are both of us so justly
	obliged to you that we beg you
	to say how we may serve you.
DON JUAN	My grateful obedience
	responds with emotion.
DON FERNANDO	How gallant! What a gentleman!
DON JUAN	I was born in that famous city
	that antiquity celebrated as the
	mother of geniuses,
	as the birthplace of literature,
	the splendor of study,
	lucid archive of science,
	epilogue of valor,
	and center of nobility:
	the city that saw two happy
	births and gave the world
	Lucan and Seneca,
	the latter, Stoic philosopher
	and the former, renowned poet;

Otro Séneca y Aneo
Galión; aquél enseña
moralidad virtuosa
en memorables tragedias,
y éste oraciones ilustres,
sin otros muchos que deja
mi justo afecto, y entre ellos
el famoso Juan de Mena,
en castellana poesía;
como en la difícil ciencia
de matemática, raro
escudriñador de estrellas,
aquél Marqués generoso,
don Enrique de Villena,
cuyos sucesos admiran,
si bien tanto se adulteran
en los vicios que hace el tiempo;
Rufo y Marcial, aunque queda
el último en opiniones.
Mas porque de una vez sepas
cuál es mi patria, nació
don Luis de Góngora en ella;
raro prodigio del orbe,
que la castellana lengua
enriqueció su ingenio,
frasis, dulzura, agudeza.[6]
En Córdoba nací, al fin,
cuyos muros hermosea
el Betis, y desatado,
tal vez en cristal, los besa,
por verle antiguo edificio
de la romana soberbia,
en quien ostentó Marcelo[7]
de su poder la grandeza.
Heredé la noble sangre
de los Córdobas en ella;
nombre famoso, que ilustra
de España alguna excelencia.
Gasté en Madrid de mis años
floreciente primavera
en las lisonjas que acaban
cuando el escarmiento empieza.
Dejéla porque es la envidia
hidra que no se sujeta

another Seneca and Aneas Galion,
the first taught virtuous morality
in memorable tragedies, and the
latter remembered for illustrious
orations, not to mention many
others for whom I fairly feel
affection, among them the
famous Castilian poet
Juan de Mena; and in the
difficult science of mathematics,
the outstanding observer of stars,
that generous Marquis,
Don Enrique de Villena,
whose achievements were admired,
though they may be diminished
by the passing of time;
Rufus and Martial as well,
though the latter's achievement
is a matter of opinion.
I'll mention another to make
sure you know my homeland:
Don Luis de Góngora was born there;
rare prodigy of our world,
his genius enriched the Spanish language,
in style, sweetness, sharp wit.[6]
In Córdoba I was born, then,
whose walls beautify Andalusia,
which kisses them unrestrained,
marveling at the ancient monument
to Roman pride in which
Marcellus displayed the grandeur
of his power.[7]
I inherited there the noble
blood of the Córdobas;
the famous name that
illustrates some excellency in Spain.
I spent my years of flowering
youth in Madrid, on those
sweet nothings that end
when the lesson begins.
I left it because envy is a hydra
impossible to kill

a muerte, pues de un principio
saca infinitas cabezas;
por sucesos amorosos
que no importan, me destierran,
y juntos, poder y amor
mis favores atropellan.
Volví, en efecto, a la patria,
adonde triste, y violenta
se hallaba la voluntad
hecha a mayores grandezas;
y por divertir el gusto,
si hay alivio que divierta
el forzoso sentimiento
de una fortuna deshecha,
a Sevilla vine, donde
de mis deudos la nobleza
desahogo solicita
en su agrado a mis tristezas.
Divertíme en su hermosura,
en su alcázar, en sus huertas,
en su grandeza, en su río,
en su lonja, en su alameda,
en su iglesia mayor, que es
la maravilla primera,
y la octava de las siete
por más insigne y más bella
en su riqueza; y al fin. . .

(Sale el Príncipe Ludovico y gente.)

LUDOVICO	¿Don Fernando de Ribera
	decís que está aquí? ¡O amigo!
DON FERNANDO	¿Qué hay, Príncipe?
LUDOVICO	Que Su Alteza,

a mí, Fisberto, a Lucindo,
y al Duque Liseno, ordena
por diferentes parajes,
que sin Lisarda y Estela
no volvamos; y pues ya
libres de las inclemencias
del tiempo con vos están,
vuelvan presto a su presencia,
que al repecho deste valle
con una carroza esperan
caballeros y criados.

ESTELA   Vamos, pues; haced que venga

as it sprouts its infinite heads;
they banished me for love
affairs of no importance,
and love and power together have
trampled my good turns.
I returned, then, to my homeland,
where sadly and with violence
my will was subject to mightier powers;
and thus to raise my low spirits,
if a relief is possible for the
heavy heart that follows ill fortune,
I went to Seville,
where the nobility of my line sought solace,
my sadnesses to find comfort in its charm.
I amused myself
in its beauty, in its castle,
in its orchards, in its grandeur,
in its river, in its market,
on its promenade, in its great church,
which is the first marvel
and the eighth
of the seven wonders,
so outstanding and so beautiful
is it in its richness, and finally . . .

(Enter Prince Ludovico and others.)

LUDOVICO   Said you that Don Fernando de
Ribera was here? Oh, friend!

DON FERNANDO   How is it with you, Majesty?

LUDOVICO   His Highness has ordered us,
Fisberto, Lucindo, Duke Liseno,
and myself, to different parts to find
Lisarda and Estela, without whom
we could not return; but now
that we are freed of inclement
weather and they are with you,
they must return quickly.
On the hill over this valley
a coach awaits,
with gentlemen and servants.

ESTELA   Let us be gone, then;

	ese hidalgo con nosotros.
DON FERNANDO	Bueno es que tú me lo adviertas.
ESTELA	*(Aparte)* ¡Que no acabase su historia!
DON FERNANDO	Con el Príncipe, Condesa,

os adelantad al coche,
que ya os seguimos.

ESTELA   Con pena
voy por no saber, Lisarda,
lo que del suceso queda.

LISARDA   Después lo sabrás.

(Vanse con el Príncipe y la gente.)

DON FERNANDO   Amigo,
alguna fuerza secreta
de inclinación natural,
de simpatía de estrellas
me obliga a quereros bien,
venid conmigo a Bruselas.

DON JUAN   Por vos he de ser dichoso.

DON FERNANDO   Mientras a la quinta llegan,
y los seguimos a espacio,
proseguid por vida vuestra:
¿qué es lo que os trae a Flandes?

DON JUAN   *(Aparte)* Dicha tuve en que viniese
el Príncipe por Estela,
porque a su belleza el alma
ha rendido las potencias,
y podrá ser que me importe
que mi suceso no sepa.
Digo, pues, que divertido
y admirado en las grandezas
de Sevilla estaba, cuando
un martes en una iglesia,
día de la Cruz de mayo,
que tanto en mis hombros pesa,
vi una mujer, don Fernando,
y en ella tanta belleza,
que usurpó su gallardía
los aplausos de la fiesta.
No os pinto su hermosura
por no eslabonar cadenas
a los yerros de mi amor;
pero con aborrecerla,
si dijere que es un ángel,
no hayáis miedo que encarezca

	conduct that gentleman along with us.
DON FERNANDO	How good that you alerted me!
ESTELA	*(Aside)* May his story not end!
DON FERNANDO	Go you on ahead with the Prince, Countess,
	together in his coach, and we will follow you.
ESTELA	It grieves me to go, Lisarda,
	without knowing the rest of what happened.
LISARDA	You will hear more anon.

(Exit Estela and Lisarda, with the Prince and others.)

DON FERNANDO	Friend, some secret force
	of a natural tendency,
	an astrological affinity,
	obliges me to care for you.
	Come with me to Brussels.
DON JUAN	I have been fortunate to meet you.
DON FERNANDO	While they are on their way to the estate,
	and we are behind them at a distance,
	continue to recount your life;
	what brings you to Flanders?
DON JUAN	*(Aside)* I was lucky that the Prince
	came for Estela, because her beauty
	renders the soul powerless,
	and it may serve me that she not know of my affairs.
	I say, then, that while amusing
	myself in Seville and admiring its
	wonders, one Tuesday in a church—
	it was the Day of the Cross in May
	and heavily did that cross weigh
	upon my shoulders—I saw a woman,
	Don Fernando, and in her so much
	beauty that her loveliness stole
	the applause from the festival.
	I will not paint her beauty for you,
	as that would be but to link chains
	to the irons of my love;
	if I were to say that she is an angel
	and though I detest her,
	fear not that I praise

lo más de su perfección:
vila, en efecto, y améla;
supe su casa, su estado,
partes, calidad, hacienda;
y satisfecho de todo,
persuadí sus enterezas,
solicité sus descuidos,
facilité mis promesas,
favoreció mis deseos,
de suerte, que una tercera
fue testigo de mis dichas,
si hay dichas en la violencia.
Dila palabra de esposo:
no es menester que os advierta
lo demás, discreto sois,
yo muy ciego, ella muy tierna:
y con ser bella en extremo,
y con extremo discreta,
afable para los gustos,
para los disgustos cuerda;
contra mi propio designio
cuanto los designios yerran
obligaciones tan justas,
tan bien conocidas deudas
o su estrella, o su desdicha
desconocen, o cancelan.
Cansado, y arrepentido
la dejé, y seguí la fuerza,
si de mi fortuna no,
de mis mudables estrellas;
sin despedirme, ni hablarla,
con resolución grosera,
pasé a Lisboa, corrido
de la mudable influencia,
que me obligó a despreciarla:
vi a Francia, y a Inglaterrra;
y al fin, llegué a estos países,
y su corte de Bruselas,
donde halla centro el alma,
porque otra vez considera
las grandezas de Madrid:
asiento tienen las treguas
de las guerras con Holanda,
causa de que yo no pueda

too excessively her perfection:
I saw her, in effect, and I fell in love;
I found out her home, her estate,
lands, quality, all she owned,
and satisfied with all,
I persuaded her virtue,
courted her carelessness,
made easy promises,
and she favored my wishes,
and, as luck would have it,
a go-between was witness to my pleasures,
if in such violence pleasures might be had.
I swore I would be her husband:
I need not tell you more;
you are discreet.
I was very blind, she very tender;
as she was beautiful in the extreme
and extremely wise,
affable in pleasure,
and in displeasure's face, sensible;
against my own designs,
how designs do err.
Fortune or unhappiness
willfully ignore, or do annul,
just obligations and acknowledged debts.
Tired and repentant,
I left her, and followed the pull,
if not of my fortune,
then of my ever-changing stars;
neither taking my leave of her
nor even speaking to her.
With brusque resolution
I went to Lisbon, driven by
that unstable influence that had
obliged me to value her so little;
I saw France and England,
and finally I arrived in these countries,
and at your court in Brussels,
where my soul found its center
because it contemplates again
the grandness of Madrid:
the arrangement of a truce
in the wars with Holland

ejercitarme en las armas;
mas pues vuestra nobleza
me ampara, en tanto que a Flandes
algún socorro me llega,
favoreced mis intentos,
pues podéis con Sus Altezas,
porque ocupado en Palacio
algún tiempo me entretenga.
Don Juan de Córdoba soy,
andaluz; vos sois, Ribera,
noble, y andaluz también;
en esta ocasión, en ésta
es bien que el ánimo luzca,
es bien que el valor se vea
de los andaluces pechos,
de la española nobleza.
Éste es mi suceso, ahora,
como de una patria mesma,
y como quien sois honradme,
pues ya es obligación vuestra.

DON FERNANDO   Huélgome de conoceros,
señor don Juan, y quisiera
que a mi afecto se igualara
el posible de mis fuerzas.
A vuestro heroico valor,
por alguna oculta fuerza,
estoy inclinado tanto,
que he de hacer Su Alteza
como suya satisfaga
la obligación en que Estela,
y todos por ella, estamos:
y en tanto de mi hacienda,
y de mi casa os servid;
vamos juntos, donde os vea
la Infanta, para que os premie
y desempeñe las deudas
de mi voluntad.

DON JUAN   No sé,
por Dios, como os agradezca
tantos favores.

DON FERNANDO   Venid.
(Sale Tomillo.)

TOMILLO   Señor, las mulas esperan.

DON FERNANDO   ¿Y la carroza?

prevents me from taking up arms;
but your nobility will shelter me
until some assistance reaches me in Flanders;
favor my intentions.
You have influence with His Majesty
that he might make me welcome in his palace,
to pass some time.
I am Don Juan de Córdoba,
Andalusian; you are Ribera,
noble, and also Andalusian;
on this occasion it would be
well to let our spirit shine
and well that the valor of our Andalusian breasts
and our Spanish nobility be seen.
This is my story, then, and
as we are from the same homeland,
honor me because you are who you are,
and this is your obligation.

DON FERNANDO   Permit me your acquaintance,
Señor Don Juan,
and I hope that my affection
equals the potential of my might.
Moved by some hidden force,
I am so partial to your heroic valor
that I will have His Highness fulfill,
as if it were his own, this obligation
we all have to you for rescuing Estela:
meanwhile, may my estate and my home serve you;
let us go together to see the Princess
so that she may reward you and
settle these debts as I wish.

DON JUAN   By God, I know not how
to thank you for so many favors.

DON FERNANDO   Come.

(Enter Tomillo.)

TOMILLO   Sir, the mules are waiting.

DON FERNANDO   And the coach?

TOMILLO   Ya está
pienso que en la cuarta esfera,
por emular la de Apolo,
compitiendo con las selvas.[8]

(Vanse. Salen doña Leonor vestida de hombre, bizarra, y Ribete, lacayo.)

DOÑA LEONOR   En este traje podré
cobrar mi perdido honor.

RIBETE   Pareces al dios del amor:
¡Qué talle! ¡Qué pierna, y pie!
Notable resolución
fue la tuya, mujer tierna,
y noble.

DOÑA LEONOR   Cuando gobierna
la fuerza de la pasión,
no hay discurso cuerdo o sabio
en quien ama; pero yo,
mi razón, que mi amor no,
consultada con mi agravio,
voy siguiendo en las violencias
de mi forzoso destino,
porque al primer desatino
se rindieron las potencias.
Supe que a Flandes venía
este ingrato, que ha ofendido
tanto amor con tanto olvido,
tal fe con tal tiranía.
Fingí en el más recoleto
monasterio mi retiro,
y sólo a ocultarme aspiro
de mis deudos; en efeto,
no tengo quien me visite,
si no es mi hermana, y está
del caso avisada ya,
para que me solicite,
y vaya a ver con engaño,
de suerte, que aunque terrible
mi locura, es imposible
que se averigüe su engaño.
Ya, pues me determiné,
y atrevida pasé el mar,
o he de morir, o acabar
la empresa que comencé;
o a todos los cielos juro
que, nueva Amazona, intente,

TOMILLO	It is ready, and in the fourth sphere, I believe,
	competing with the wilderness
	in imitation of Apollo.[8]

(Exeunt. Enter Doña Leonor, dressed as a man and looking gallant, accompanied by Ribete, a lackey.)

DOÑA LEONOR	In these clothes will I be able
	to recover my lost honor.
RIBETE	You look like the god of love:
	What a figure! What a leg and
	what a foot! Tender lady,
	yours was a noble and
	outstanding resolution.
DOÑA LEONOR	There is no learned or wise
	discourse in one who loves
	when governed by the force of passion;
	but it is my reason and not my love
	that will meet with the affront I have suffered,
	and I will continue on in the violence of my unavoidable destiny,
	because my faculties surrendered
	at the first foolishness.
	I have discovered that this ingrate
	who offended so much love with so much neglect,
	and such faith with such tyranny,
	has come to Flanders.
	I have let it be known
	that I am in retreat
	at a most secluded monastery,
	as I wish to hide myself from my kin.
	In truth, no one but my sister
	might visit me, and she
	knows of my disguise.
	So let others be fooled,
	for no matter how terrible my madness,
	it is impossible to discover the deception.
	Thus, determined and daring,
	I crossed the sea,
	either to die or to finish
	the enterprise I have begun;
	I will attempt, I swear to all the heavens,
	like a new Amazon

o Camila más valiente,[9]
vengarme de aquel perjuro
aleve.

RIBETE   Oyéndote estoy,
y ¡por Cristo! que he pensado
que el nuevo traje te ha dado
alientos.

DOÑA LEONOR   Yo soy quien soy.
Engáñaste, si imaginas,
Ribete, que soy mujer:
mi agravio mudó mi ser.

RIBETE   Impresiones peregrinas
suele hacer un agravio:
ten, que la verdad se prueba
de Ovidio,[10] pues Isis nueva
de oro guarneces el labio;[11]
mas, volviendo a nuestro intento,
¿matarásle?

DOÑA LEONOR   Mataré,
¡vive Dios!

RIBETE   ¿En buena fe?

DOÑA LEONOR   ¡Por Cristo!

RIBETE   Otro juramento,
lástima es.

DOÑA LEONOR   Flema gentil
gastas.

RIBETE   Señor Magallanes,
a él, y a cuantos don Juanes,
ciento a ciento, y mil a mil
salieren.

DOÑA LEONOR   Calla, inocente.

RIBETE   Escucha, así Dios te guarde;
¿por fuerza he de ser cobarde?
¿No habrá un lacayo valiente?

DOÑA LEONOR   ¿Por eso te amohinas?

RIBETE   Estoy mal con enfadosos,
que introducen los graciosos
muertos de hambre, y gallinas.
El que ha nacido alentado,
¿no lo ha de ser si no es noble?
¿que no podrá serlo al doble
del caballero el criado?

DOÑA LEONOR   Has dicho muy bien, no en vano
te he elegido por mi amigo,

	or the bravest Camilla,
	to avenge myself on that lying traitor.[9]
RIBETE	I have been listening to you, and,
	by Christ, I think these new clothes
	have given you spirit.
DOÑA LEONOR	I am who I am.
	You deceive yourself, Ribete,
	if you imagine I am a woman:
	this affront has changed my being.
RIBETE	An offense produces strange impressions:
	see, Ovid[10] proves this truth
	since as the new Isis[11] you embellish your speech with gold;
	but returning to our intentions,
	will you kill him?
DOÑA LEONOR	I shall kill, by God!
RIBETE	In truth?
DOÑA LEONOR	By Christ!
RIBETE	For shame, another curse.
DOÑA LEONOR	You are too soft!
RIBETE	Circle the world like Magellan and you will find
	Don Juans by the hundreds
	and the thousands.
DOÑA LEONOR	Silence, fool!
RIBETE	Mark me, may God keep you;
	must I be a coward?
	Are there no brave lackeys?
DOÑA LEONOR	Is that what is annoying you?
RIBETE	I am sick of bothersome playwrights
	who put chickenhearted fools,
	dying of hunger, in their plays.
	He who was born inspired,
	is he only thus because he was born noble?
	Cannot the servant be the match of a gentleman?
DOÑA LEONOR	You have spoken very well, and
	not in vain have I chosen you,
	not for a servant, but as my friend.

no por criado.

RIBETE   Contigo
va Ribete el sevillano
bravo, que tuvo a laceria
reñir con tres algún día,
y pendón rojo añadía
a los verdes de la feria;
pero tratemos del modo
de vivir: ¿qué has de hacer
ahora?

DOÑA LEONOR   Hemos menester,
para no perderlo todo,
buscar a mi hermano.

RIBETE   ¿Y si te conoce?

DOÑA LEONOR   No
puede ser, que me dejó
de seis años, y está llano
que no se puede acordar
de mi rostro; y si privanza
tengo con él, mi venganza
mi valor ha de lograr.

RIBETE   ¿Don Leonardo, en fin, te llamas
Ponce de León?

DOÑA LEONOR   Sí, llamo.

RIBETE   ¿Cuántas veces, señor amo,
me han de importunar las damas
con el recado, o billete?
Ya me parece comedia,
donde todo lo remedia
un bufón medio alcahuete.
No hay fábula, no hay tramoya
a donde no venga al justo
un lacayo de buen gusto;
porque si no, aquí fue Troya.
¿Hay mayor impropriedad
en graciosidades tales,
que haga un lacayo iguales
la almohaza, y majestad?
Que siendo rayo temido
un rey, haciendo mil gestos,
le obligue un lacayo destos
a que ría divertido.

DOÑA LEONOR   Gente viene; hacia esta parte.
Desvía.

RIBETE	With you will go Ribete, the brave Sevillian
	who was injured in a fight with three one day,
	and added a reddened banner
	to the green ones of the fair;
	but let us speak of the present:
	what have you to do now?
DOÑA LEONOR	We must look for my brother
	so all may not be lost.
RIBETE	And if he recognizes you?
DOÑA LEONOR	It is not possible. He left me when
	I was six years old, and 'tis plain
	that he could not know my face;
	and if I find favor with him
	my bravery will achieve my revenge.
RIBETE	Don Leonardo, then, is your name
	Ponce de León?
DOÑA LEONOR	Yes, it is my name.
RIBETE	How many times, my master,
	will the ladies bother me
	with a message or love letter for you?
	Now it seems like a comedy to me
	in which a go-between buffoon cures all.
	There is no tale, no scheme,
	in which a lackey of good taste
	does not appear just in the nick of time.
	Because if he does not, alas,
	there would be nothing left but ruins.
	Is there greater impropriety
	than such gratuitousness
	in which a lackey treats equally
	a curry comb and majesty?
	A lackey making a thousand foolish
	gestures distracts a king
	frightened of lightning
	and makes him laugh.
DOÑA LEONOR	People are coming;
	let us conceal ourselves there.

(Sale don Fernando de Ribera, y el Príncipe.)

DON FERNANDO   Esto ha pasado.

LUDOVICO   Hame el suceso admirado.

DON FERNANDO   Más pudieras admirarte,
que de su dicha, aunque es tanta,
de su bizarro valor,
pues por él goza favor
en la gracia de la Infanta:
su mayordomo, en efeto,
don Juan de Córdoba es ya.

DOÑA LEONOR   ¡Ay, Ribete!

LUDOVICO   Bien está,
pues lo merece el sujeto;
y al fin, ¿Estela se inclina
a don Juan?

DON FERNANDO   Así lo siento,
por ser de agradecimiento
satisfacción peregrina.

(Hablan aparte los dos.)

DOÑA LEONOR   Don Juan de Córdoba ¡ay, Dios!
dijo. ¿Si es aquel ingrato?
Mal disimula el recato
tantos pesares.

DON FERNANDO   Por vos
la hablaré.

LUDOVICO   ¿Puede aspirar
Estela a mayor altura?
Su riqueza, su hermosura,
¿en quién la puede emplear,
como en mí?

DON FERNANDO   Decís muy bien.

LUDOVICO   ¿Hay en todo Flandes hombre
más galán, más gentilhombre?

RIBETE   Maldígate el cielo, amén.

DON FERNANDO   Fiad esto a mi cuidado.

LUDOVICO   Que me está bien sólo os digo:
haced, pues que sois mi amigo,
que tenga efecto.

(Vase Ludovico.)

DON FERNANDO   ¡Qué enfado!

DOÑA LEONOR   Ribete, llegarme quiero
a preguntar por mi hermano.

RIBETE   ¿Si le conocerá?

DOÑA LEONOR   Es llano.

(Enter Don Fernando de Ribera and the Prince.)

DON FERNANDO That is what happened.

LUDOVICO The event leaves me amazed.

DON FERNANDO You would have been more astonished
by his valiant courage than by his luck,
though it is notable, but for his
bravery he should enjoy favor
in the Princess's grace;
Don Juan de Córdoba is now,
in effect, her steward.

DOÑA LEONOR Oh, Ribete!

LUDOVICO That is as it should be.
He well deserves it.
Does Estela feel affection for Don Juan?

DON FERNANDO So it seems, although 'tis a
satisfaction born of gratitude.

(The two speak aside.)

DONA LEONOR Oh, God! He said Don Juan
de Córdoba. Is it that ingrate?
Discretion badly masks so many woes.

DON FERNANDO I will speak to her for you.

LUDOVICO Can Estela aspire to greater heights?
Her wealth, her beauty;
who is better fit to use them than I?

DON FERNANDO Well put.

LUDOVICO Is there a man in Flanders
more gallant, more a gentleman?

RIBETE Heaven curse you, amen.

DON FERNANDO Trust this to my care.

LUDOVICO All I can think to say to you is:
as you are my friend,
make sure that your care has its effect.

(Exit Ludovico.)

DON FERNANDO What bother!

DOÑA LEONOR Ribete, I want to ask him
about my brother.

RIBETE If he knows him?

DOÑA LEONOR Plainly.

DON FERNANDO   ¿Mandáis algo, caballero?

DOÑA LEONOR   No, señor; saber quisiera
de un capitán.

DON FERNANDO   ¿Capitán?
¿Qué nombre?

DOÑA LEONOR   Éstas lo dirán:
don Fernando de Ribera,
caballerizo mayor,
y Capitán de la Guardia
de Su Alteza.

DON FERNANDO   *(Aparte)*   ¡Qué gallarda
presencia! ¿Si es de Leonor?
Haced cuenta que le veis,
dadme el pliego.

DOÑA LEONOR   ¡O cuánto gana
hoy mi dicha!

DON FERNANDO   ¿Es de mi hermana?
(Dale el pliego.)

DOÑA LEONOR   En la letra lo veréis.
Ribete, turbada estoy.

RIBETE   ¿De qué?
(Lee don Fernando.)

DOÑA LEONOR   De ver a mi hermano.

RIBETE   ¿Ese es valor sevillano?

DOÑA LEONOR   Has dicho bien, mi honor hoy
me ha de dar valor gallardo
para lucir su decoro,
que, sin honra, es vil el oro.

DON FERNANDO   Yo he leído, don Leonardo,
esta carta, y sólo para
en que os ampare mi amor
cuando por mil de favor
vuestra presencia bastara.
Mi hermana lo pide así,
y yo a su gusto obligado
quedaré desempeñado
con vos, por ella y por mí:
¿cómo está?

DOÑA LEONOR   Siente tu ausencia,
como es justo.

DON FERNANDO   ¿Es muy hermosa?

DOÑA LEONOR   Es afable, y virtuosa.

DON FERNANDO   Esto le basta. ¿Y Laurencia,
la más pequeña?

DON FERNANDO	Is there something you require of me, sir?
DOÑA LEONOR	No, sir; I would simply like to know about a certain captain.
DON FERNANDO	Captain? What is his name?
DOÑA LEONOR	This letter will say: Don Fernando de Ribera, horse master and Captain of His Highness's Guard.
DON FERNANDO	*(Aside)* What charming presence! Could it be from Leonor? Know that you see him. Give me the letter.
DOÑA LEONOR	Oh, much has my good fortune won today!
DON FERNANDO	Is it from my sister?

(She gives him the letter.)

DOÑA LEONOR	You will see by the writing. Ribete, I am anxious.
RIBETE	Why?

(Don Fernando reads.)

DOÑA LEONOR	About seeing my brother.
RIBETE	Is that Sevillian bravery?
DOÑA LEONOR	You have spoken well, my honor must today give me gallant courage to allow its nobility to shine, for without honor even gold is vile.
DON FERNANDO	I have read this letter, Don Leonardo, but your presence is enough to assure you of my love and aid. My sister asks this and I am obliged and will fulfill her wish for you, for her, and for myself: how does she?
DOÑA LEONOR	As is just, she feels your absence.
DON FERNANDO	Is she very beautiful?
DOÑA LEONOR	She is affable and virtuous.
DON FERNANDO	That is enough. And Laurencia, the very youngest?

DOÑA LEONOR	Es un cielo,
	una azucena, un jazmín,
	un ángel, un serafín
	mentido al humano velo.
DON FERNANDO	Decidme, por vida mía,
	¿qué os trae a Flandes?
DOÑA LEONOR	Intento,
	con justo agradecimiento,
	pagar vuestra cortesía;
	y es imposible, pues vos,
	liberalmente discreto,
	acobardáis el conceto
	en los labios.
DON FERNANDO	Guárdeos Dios.
DOÑA LEONOR	Si es justa ley de obligación forzosa

¡O Ribera famoso! obedeceros,
escuchad mi fortuna rigurosa,
piadosa ya, pues me ha traído a veros;
el valor de mi sangre generosa
no será menester encareceros
pues por blasón de su nobleza muestro
el preciarme de ser muy deudo vuestro.

Serví una dama, donde los primores
de toda la hermosura cifró el cielo
gozó en secreto el alma sus favores,
vinculando la gloria en el desvelo;
compitióme el poder, y mis temores
apenas conocieron el recelo,
y no os admire, porque la firmeza
de Anarda sólo iguala a su belleza.

Atrevido mostró el Marqués Ricardo
querer servir en público a mi dama,
mas no por esto el ánimo acobardo,
antes le aliento a la celosa llama:
presumiendo de rico, y de gallardo,
perder quiso al decoro de su fama,
inútil presunción, respetos justos,
ocasionando celos, y disgustos.

Entre otras una noche, que a la puerta
de Anarda le hallé, sintiendo en vano
en flor marchita su esperanza muerta
al primero verdor de su verano,
hallando en su asistencia ocasión cierta,
rayos hizo vibrar mi espada, y mano

DOÑA LEONOR	She is heaven, a lily,
	jasmine, an angel,
	a cherub wrapped
	in a human veil.
DON FERNANDO	Tell me, for my life,
	what brings you to Flanders?
DOÑA LEONOR	I intend with just gratitude
	to repay your courtesy;
	it is not possible that you,
	generously discreet, would
	frighten me from speaking.
DON FERNANDO	Heaven forbid!
DOÑA LEONOR	If it is the just law of unavoidable
	obligation, oh famous Ribera,
	I will obey you.
	Hear how my fortune,
	once harsh, now merciful,
	has brought me to see you;
	the valor of my generous blood
	shall not be necessary to praise you excessively
	since it is by the coat of arms of your nobility
	that I show you, that you may
	esteem me, for I am your close kinsman.

I served a lady, where in secret
my soul reveled in the exquisiteness
of all the beauty that heaven could bestow,
and my glory was inseparable from my vigilance;
power competed with me, and my fears
scarcely admitted caution; be not amazed
by this because Anarda's constancy
was equal to her beauty.

The daring Marquis Ricardo let it
be known in public that he wished to
serve my lady, but this was not the
purpose of that cowardly spirit,
ignited by a jealous flame:
boasting of wealth, and of gallantry,
he lost the propriety of his reputation,
useless vanity and fair respect,
he occasioned jealousy and disagreements.

I found him one night at Anarda's door,
vainly mourning the withered flower
of his hope that had died in the first green
of summer, and finding his presence
reason to remove him, lightning
moved my sword and my hand

tanto, que pude solo retiralle
a él, y a otros dos valientes de la calle.

    Disimuló este agravio, mas, un día,
asistiendo los dos a la pelota
sobre jugar la suerte suya o mía,
se enfada, se enfurece, y alborota,
un "¡miente todo el mundo!" al aire envía,
con que vi mi cordura tan remota,
que una mano lugar buscó en su cara,
y otra de mi furor rayos dispara.

    Desbaratóse el juego, y los parciales
coléricos trabaron civil guerra,
en tanto que mis golpes desiguales
hacen que bese mi rival la tierra;
uno de meter paces da señales,
otro, animoso y despechado, cierra;
y al fin, entre vengados y ofendidos,
salieron uno muerto y tres heridos.

    Ricardo, tantas veces despreciado,
de mi dama, de mí, de su fortuna,
si no celoso, ya desesperado,
no perdona ocasión, ni traza alguna,
a la venganza aspira, y agraviado,
sus amigos y deudos importuna
haciendo de su ofensa vil alarde,
acción, si no de noble, de cobarde.

    Mas yo, por no cansarte, dando medio
de su forzoso enojo a la violencia,
quise elegir por último remedio
hacer de la querida patria ausencia;
en efecto, poniendo tierra en medio,
objeto no seré de su impaciencia,
pues pudiera vengarse como sabio,
que no cabe traición donde hay agravio.

    Previno nuestro tío mi jornada,
y antes de irme a embarcar, esta sortija
me dio por prenda rica, y estimada,
de Victoria, su hermosa, y noble hija;
del reino de Anfitrite la salada
región cerúlea vi,[12] sin la prolija
pensión de una tormenta, y con bonanza;
tomó a tus plantas puerto mi esperanza.

DON FERNANDO De gustoso, y satisfecho
suspenso me habéis dejado,

as well, sending him away, and
two others just as brazen.
    He did not reveal this offense,
but one day while we were playing ball,
a game that might decide his luck or mine,
he grew angry, and became furious, and rowdy,
and shouted "All the world is lying"
for everyone to hear, with which
my reason fled and one of my hands
hit his face, and the other pummeled with my fury.
    The game was ruined,
and the enraged onlookers joined in civil war;
my blows could not be matched
and made my rival kiss the ground;
one man made signs for peace,
another, heated and resentful, was closing in;
and finally, among offended and revenged,
were one dead and three wounded.
    Ricardo, so many times belittled,
by my lady, by me, by his fortune,
if not jealous, then desperate,
pardons no occasion but aspires
to vengeance; injured, he has
rallied his friends and his importunate
kin to make of his vile display
some art, if not noble, then cowardly.
    For myself, so as not to tire you,
I supposed that his unavoidable anger
would lead to violence and thus chose
as a last resort to leave my beloved
land, and in effect, at this distance
I will not be the object of his impatience,
so he may avenge himself wisely,
there being no space for betrayal
where there is injury.
    Our uncle prepared my flight,
and before I set out, gave me this
ring as a valuable and appreciated
jewel from Victoria, his beautiful
and noble daughter;
I saw Amphitrite's salty blue reign,[12]
without the wearisome aggravation of a storm,
and with good winds, my hope has found
its port at your feet.

DON FERNANDO   You have left me agreeably and
happily astonished, not on account

no es de la patria cuidado,
puesto que halláis en mi pecho
de pariente voluntad,
fineza de amigo, amor
de hermano, pues a Leonor
no amara con más verdad.
Esta sortija le di
a la hermosa Victoria
mi prima, que sea en gloria,
cuando de España partí.
Y aunque sirve de testigo
que os abona, y acredita
la verdad, no necesita
de prueba alguna conmigo.
Bien haya, amén, la ocasión
del disgusto sucedido,
pues ésta la causa ha sido
de veros.

DOÑA LEONOR   No sin razón
vuestro valor tiene fama
en el mundo.

DON FERNANDO   Don Leonardo,
mi hermano sois.

DOÑA LEONOR   ¡Qué gallardo!
Mas de tal ribera es rama.

DON FERNANDO   En el cuarto de don Juan
de Córdoba estaréis bien.

DOÑA LEONOR   ¿Quién es ese hidalgo?

DON FERNANDO   ¿Quién?
Un caballero galán
cordobés.

DOÑA LEONOR   No será justo,
ni cortés urbanidad,
que por mi comodidad
compre ese hidalgo un disgusto.

DON FERNANDO   Don Juan tiene cuarto aparte,
y le honra Su Alteza mucho
por su gran valor.

DOÑA LEONOR   (Aparte)   ¡Qué escucho!
¿Y es persona de buen arte?

DON FERNANDO   Es la primer maravilla
su talle, y de afable trato,
aunque fácil, pues ingrato
a una dama de Sevilla,

of my beloved country but because
you find in my kinsman's breast
the will and kindness of a friend,
a brother's love, as I could not
more truly love Leonor.
When I left Spain I gave
this ring to my cousin,
beautiful Victoria, may she be in heaven.
And though it serves as witness,
affirming the truth of your story,
you need offer me no proof.
Though unpleasant was the occasion that brings you here,
it was good in bringing us together.

DOÑA LEONOR Not without reason
is your courage renowned in the world.

DON FERNANDO Don Leonardo, you are my brother.

DOÑA LEONOR How magnanimous you are!
The branch could not be
of any other trunk.

DON FERNANDO You will be comfortable in the quarters
of Don Juan de Córdoba.

DOÑA LEONOR Who is that gentleman?

DON FERNANDO Who? An elegant fellow from
Córdoba.

DOÑA LEONOR It will not be just, nor civilized courtesy,
for that gentleman to be inconvenienced
on behalf of my comfort.

DON FERNANDO Don Juan has a room apart,
and Her Highness greatly honors
him for his enormous courage.

DOÑA LEONOR *(Aside)* What do I hear?
And is he a person of goodwill?

DON FERNANDO He is a wonder!
His figure is dashing and his manner is affable,
although fickle;
he broke faith with a lady of Seville
whom he enjoyed with guile;

THE SEVENTEENTH CENTURY

	a quien gozó con cautela,
	hoy la aborrece, y adora
	a la Condesa de Sora;
	que aunque es muy hermosa Estela,
	no hay en mi opinión disculpa
	para una injusta mudanza.
DOÑA LEONOR	(*Aparte*) Ánimo, altiva esperanza;
	los hombres no tienen culpa
	tal vez.
DON FERNANDO	Antes, de Leonor
	repite mil perfecciones.
DOÑA LEONOR	¿Y la aborrece?
DON FERNANDO	Opiniones
	son del ciego lince amor;
	por la Condesa el sentido
	está perdiendo.
DOÑA LEONOR	(*Aparte*) ¡Ah, cruel!
	¿Y ella le corresponde fiel?
DON FERNANDO	Con semblante agradecido
	se muestra afable, y cortés;
	forzosa satisfacción
	de la generosa acción
	de la facción, que después
	sabréis. ¿Fineo?

(*Sale Fineo.*)

FINEO	Señor.
DON FERNANDO	Aderezad aposento
	a don Leonardo al momento.
DOÑA LEONOR	(*Aparte*) ¡Muerta estoy!
RIBETE	Calla, Leonor.
DON FERNANDO	En el cuarto de don Juan.
FINEO	Voy al punto.
DON FERNANDO	Entrad, Leonardo.
DOÑA LEONOR	Ya os sigo.
DON FERNANDO	En el cuarto aguardo
	de Su Alteza.
RIBETE	Malos van
	los títeres: ¿a quién digo?
	¡Hola, hao! de allende el mar,
	volvámonos a embarcar,
	pues ya lo está aquel amigo;
	centellas, furias, enojos,
	viboreznos, basiliscos,
	iras, promontorios, riscos,

	today he abhors her
	and adores the Countess of Sora;
	although Estela is very beautiful,
	in my opinion there is no excuse
	for an unjust change of heart.
DOÑA LEONOR	*(Aside)* Courage, proud hope!
	Men, perhaps, do not bear guilt.
DON FERNANDO	He used to repeat Leonor's
	thousand perfections.
DOÑA LEONOR	And now he abhors her?
DON FERNANDO	Such are the ways
	of that sharp-eyed, blind boy, Love.
	He is losing his senses over the Countess.
DOÑA LEONOR	*(Aside)* Oh, how cruel!
	And she responds in kind?
DON FERNANDO	With grateful countenance
	she appears affable and polite;
	an inevitable gratitude felt
	for the generous action of this person,
	about which you will soon know.
	Fineo?

(Enter Fineo.)

FINEO	Master.
DON FERNANDO	Have the bed ready immediately
	for Don Leonardo.
DOÑA LEONOR	*(Aside)* I am dead!
RIBETE	Be still, Leonor.
DON FERNANDO	In Don Juan's quarters.
FINEO	At once.
DON FERNANDO	Enter, Leonardo.
DOÑA LEONOR	After you.
DON FERNANDO	I shall wait for Her Highness to come.
RIBETE	This farce is going badly:
	to whom do I speak?
	Hello! hey! since that friend is now here,
	let's board the boat from this side of the sea
	and go on back; sparks, fury,
	anger, vipers, cannonballs,
	rage, obstacles, crags

está echando por los ojos.
Si en los primeros ensayos
hay arrobos, hay desvelos,
hay furores, rabias, celos,
relámpagos, truenos, rayos,
¿qué será después? Ahora
está pensando a mi ver,
los estragos que ha de hacer
sobre el reto de Zamora:[13]
ah, señora. ¿Con quién hablo?

DOÑA LEONOR   Déjame, villano, infame.
(Dale.)

RIBETE   Belcebú que más te llame,
demándetelo el diablo:
¿miraste el retrato en mí
de don Juan? ¡Tal antubión!
¡Qué bien das un pescozón!

DOÑA LEONOR   ¡Déjame, vete de aquí!
(Vase Ribete.)

¿Adónde, cielos, adónde
vuestros rigores se encubren?
¿Para cuándo es el castigo?
La justicia, ¿dónde huye?
¿Dónde está? ¿Cómo es posible
que esta maldad disimule
la piedad en un aleve?
Injusta pasión arguye.
¿Dónde están, Jove, los rayos?
Ya vive ocioso e inútil
tu brazo: ¿cómo traiciones
bárbaras y enormes sufre?
¿No te ministra Vulcano,[14]
de su fragua, y de su yunque,
armas de fuego, de quien
sólo el laurel se asegure?
Némesis —¿dónde se oculta?[15]
¿A qué dios le sustituye
su poder, para que grato
mi venganza no ejecute?
Las desdichas, los agravios
hace la suerte comunes;
no importa el mérito, no
tienen precio las virtudes.
¿Tan mal se premia el amor

stream from your eyes.
If at first there are ecstasies
and anxieties, furies, rages,
jealousies, lightning, thunder,
flashes, what will there be later?
You are thinking now, it seems to me,
of the havoc to be wreaked on
this challenge of Zamora?[13]
Oh, lady, with whom do I speak?

DOÑA LEONOR   Leave me alone, brute, lowlife.
(She strikes him.)

RIBETE   They should call you Beelzebub,
the devil causes you to act this way.
Do I look to you like Don Juan?
What an attack! You certainly deal a
good blow to the neck!

DOÑA LEONOR   Leave me alone! Get out of here!
(Exit Ribete.)

Where, heaven, where
does your harshness hide itself?
When will the punishment be exacted?
Where has justice fled?
Where is it? How is it possible
that this evil pretends piousness in a traitor?
It passionately calls out injustice.
Where, Jupiter, are your thunderbolts?
Your arm is useless and lazy now:
how do you suffer barbarous
and enormous betrayals?
Does not with his anvil Vulcan[14] craft for you
fiery weapons in his furnace,
for you who need only the laurel for protection?
Nemesis, where do you hide?[15]
What god's whim took your power
so that my revenge be not executed?
Luck makes misfortunes and offenses
one and the same; no matter what
their worth, virtues have no price.
So badly is love rewarded

que a número no reduce
un hombre tantas finezas,
cuando de noble presume?
¿Qué es esto, desdichas, cómo
tanta verdad se desluce?
¿Tanto afecto se malogra?
¿Tal calidad se destruye?
¿Tal sangre se deshonra?
¿Tal recato se reduce
a opiniones? ¿Tal honor,
cómo se apura, y consume?
¿Yo, aborrecida, y sin honra?
¿Tal maldad los cielos sufren?
¿Mi nobleza despreciada?
¿Mi casta opinión sin lustre?
¿Sin premio mi voluntad?
¿Mi fe, que las altas nubes
pasó, y llegó a las estrellas,
es posible que la injurie
don Juan? Venganza, venganza,
cielos; el mundo murmure,
que ha de ver mi valor,
a pesar de las comunes
opiniones, la más nueva
historia, la más ilustre
resolución que vio el orbe:
y juro por los azules
velos de cielo, y por cuantas
en ellos se miran luces,
que he de morir, o vencer,
sin que me den pesadumbre
iras, olvidos, desprecios,
desdenes, ingratitudes,
aborrecimientos, odios,
mi honor en la altiva cumbre
de los cielos he de ver,
o hacer que se disculpen
en mis locuras mis yerros,
o que ellas mismas apuren
con excesos cuanto pueden,
con errores cuanto lucen,
Valor, agravio y mujer,
si en un sujeto se incluyen.

(Vase.)

that when a man is thought noble,
he cannot even reduce to a number
the many kindnesses he receives.
What is this, misfortune? How can
so much truth be tarnished?
So much affection be so badly placed?
Such quality be destroyed?
Such blood be dishonored?
Such discretion reduced by opinion?
Such honor, how is it drained and consumed?
I, abhorred, and without respect?
The heavens suffer such evil?
My nobility belittled?
My chaste opinion without luster?
Is my will without reward?
My faith that surpassed
the highest clouds
and reached the stars, is it possible that Don Juan
could injure it? Vengeance, vengeance,
heaven; the world insinuates
and my valor must be seen,
despite common opinion,
the latest story, the most illustrious
resolution that has seen the light of day;
and I swear by the blue veils of heaven,
and by the many lights
reflected there, that I will die
or triumph. Nor may rage, oblivion,
contempt, disdain, ingratitude,
abhorrence, hatred cause me
sorrow. I will see my honor raised
to the heavens' haughty summit.
My madness will excuse my erring ways
or exhaust itself in crimes
for all the world to see,
if one being must contain
Valor, Outrage, and Woman.

(Exit.)

Jornada segunda

(Salen Estela y Lisarda.)

LISARDA	¿Qué te parece don Juan, Estela?
ESTELA	Bien me parece.
LISARDA	Cualquier agrado merece por gentilhombre, y galán: ¡qué gallardo! ¡qué brioso! ¡qué alentado! ¡qué valiente anduvo!
ESTELA	Forzosamente será bizarro, y airoso que en la elección de tu gusto, calificó su buen aire.
LISARDA	Bueno está, prima, el donaire. ¿Y el de Pinoy?
ESTELA	No hay disgusto para mí como su nombre: ¡Jesús! Líbrenme los cielos de su ambición.
LISARDA	*(Aparte)* Mis desvelos premie amor.
ESTELA	¡Qué bárbaro hombre!
LISARDA	¿Al fin, no le quieres?
ESTELA	No.
LISARDA	Por discreto, y por gallardo, bien merece don Leonardo amor.
ESTELA	Ya, prima, llegó a declararse el cuidado, pues en término tan breve, tantos desvelos me debe, tantas penas me ha costado: la obligación de don Juan bien solicita en mi intento forzoso agradecimiento; mas este Adonis galán, este Fénix español, este Ganimedes nuevo, este Dios de Amor mancebo, este Narciso, este Sol, de tal suerte en mi sentido mudanza su vista ha hecho,

Act 2

(Enter Estela and Lisarda.)

LISARDA   What think you of Don Juan,
            Estela?

ESTELA   He seems a fine man.

LISARDA   He is deserving of any compliment
            a gentleman might receive:
            how gallant! how vigorous!
            how brave! how courageous he was!

ESTELA   Noble and elegant must he be.
            That you take note of him
            attests to his charm.

LISARDA   Oh, yes. He is charming, cousin.
            And Pinoy?

ESTELA   There's nothing so disgusting
            to me as that man. Jesus! Heaven
            free me from his designs.

LISARDA   *(Aside)* May love reward my sleepless nights.

ESTELA   What a brutish man!

LISARDA   Then you love him not?

ESTELA   No.

LISARDA   Don Leonardo well deserves love
            for his discretion
            and his charm.

ESTELA   Now, cousin, my true
            sentiments must be declared,
            in brief. It is to him I owe
            many sleepless nights, and much
            grief has he cost me.
            My obligation to Don Juan of course
            demands my inevitable gratitude,
            but this gallant Adonis,
            this Spanish Phoenix,
            this new Ganymede,
            this youthful God of Love,
            this Narcissus, this Sun,
            why the sight of him has
            wrought such a change in my senses

que no ha dejado en el pecho
ni aun memorias de otro olvido.[16]

LISARDA   ¡Gran mudanza!

ESTELA   Yo confieso
que lo es; mas si mi elección
jamás tuvo inclinación
declarada, no fue exceso
rendirme.

LISARDA   A solicitar
sus dichas le trae amor.

ESTELA   Las mías, mejor dirás.

(Salen don Fernando, doña Leonor y Ribete.)

DON FERNANDO   Ludovico, hermosa Estela,
me pide que os venga a hablar;
don Juan es mi amigo, y sé
que os rinde el alma don Juan,
y yo, humilde, a vuestras plantas:
¿por dónde he de comenzar?
que por Dios, que no me atrevo
a pediros. . .

ESTELA   Que pidáis
poco importa, don Fernando,
cuando tan lejos está
mi voluntad de elegir.

DON FERNANDO   Basta.

ESTELA   No me digáis más
de don Juan, ni Ludovico.

DON FERNANDO   *(Aparte)* ¡Qué dichoso desdeñar,
pues me deja acción de amante!

DOÑA LEONOR   *(Aparte)* Pues aborrece a don Juan,
¡qué dichoso despedir!

ESTELA   Don Leonardo, ¿no me habláis?
¿Vos sin verme tantos días?
¡O qué mal cumplís, qué mal
la ley de la cortesía,
la obligación de galán!

DON FERNANDO   Pues no os resolvéis, adiós.

ESTELA   Adiós.

DON FERNANDO   Leonardo, ¿os quedáis?

DOÑA LEONOR   Sí, primo.

ESTELA   A los dos, por mí,
don Fernando, les dirás,
que ni estoy enamorada,
ni me pretendo casar.

	that it has left in my breast
	no memory of that other
	forgotten man.[16]
LISARDA	What a great change!
ESTELA	I confess it is; but if
	my choice was never
	a declared inclination,
	to surrender myself was
	not excessive.
LISARDA	Love brings him to you
	for his delight.
ESTELA	Mine, it would be better to say.

(Enter Don Fernando, Doña Leonor, and Ribete.)

DON FERNANDO	Fair Estela, Ludovico has asked
	that I come speak with you;
	Don Juan is my friend, and I know
	that to you he has given up his soul,
	and I, humbly, at your feet,
	oh, where can I begin? By God
	I dare not ask you . . .
ESTELA	What you ask matters little,
	Don Fernando, when my will
	to choose is so distant.
DON FERNANDO	Enough.
ESTELA	Say no more to me of
	Don Juan nor of Ludovico.
DON FERNANDO	*(Aside)* How fortunate for me
	that she disdains; it leaves me
	free to act the lover.
DOÑA LEONOR	*(Aside)* Then she abhors Don Juan,
	what a fortunate turn.
ESTELA	Don Leonardo, speak you not to me?
	And having seen me not in so many days?
	Oh, how badly you comply
	with the law of courtesy,
	the obligation of the gallant man!
DON FERNANDO	As you have not agreed to a decision,
	I take my leave.
ESTELA	Farewell.
DON FERNANDO	Stay you, Leonardo?
DOÑA LEONOR	Yes, cousin.
ESTELA	Tell them both for me,
	Don Fernando, that I am not in love,
	and I do not intend to marry.

(Vase don Fernando.)

DOÑA LEONOR   Mi silencio, hermosa Estela,
mucho os dice sin hablar,
que es lengua el afecto mudo
que está confesando ya
los efectos, que estos ojos
sólo pudieron causar.
Soles, que imperiosamente
de luz ostentando están
entre rayos, y entre flechas,
bonanza y serenidad:
en el engaño, dulzura,
extrañeza en la beldad,
valentía en el donaire,
y donaire en el mirar.
¿En quién, si no en vos, se ve
el rigor y la piedad,
con que dais pena, y dais gloria,
con que dais vida, y matáis?
Poder sobre el albedrío,
para inquietarle la paz,
jurisdicción en el gusto,
imperio en la voluntad,
¿quién como vos le ha tenido?
¿Quién como vos le tendrá?
¿Quién, si no vos, que sois sola,
o ya sol, o ya deidad,
es dueño de cuanto mira?
Pues cuando más libre estáis,
parece que lisonjera,
con rendir y con matar,
hacéis ociosa la pena,
hacéis apacible el mal,
apetecible el rigor,
inexcusable el penar,
pues si no es de esta belleza
la imperiosa majestad,
gustosos desasosiegos
en el valle, ¿quién os los da?
Cuando más rendida el alma
pide a estos ojos piedad,
más rigores examina,
desengaños siente más;
y si humilde a vuestras manos

(Exit Don Fernando.)

DOÑA LEONOR   My silence, fair Estela,
tells you much without words,
mute affection is a tongue
that now confesses the effects
those eyes alone could cause.
Imperious suns that proudly cast
their light amongst the thunderbolts
and lightning, and midst
slings and arrows are
serenity and good fortune:
in deception, sweetness,
strangeness in beauty,
valor in charm,
and charm in the gaze.
In whom, if not in you, do
severity and mercy mingle?
Sorrow you bestow, and
you give glory; you grant
life, and you slay.
Power over free will,
to disturb its peace,
jurisdiction in matters of taste,
rule of another's conscience,
who owns all this but you?
Who if not you, who alone,
as sun or deity,
possesses all she sees?
The freer you are, the more
it seems to please you
to conquer or to kill;
you put pain to rest,
you make evil pleasing,
harshness appetizing,
and grief inexcusable.
If imperial majesty,
deep and pleasant longings,
are not of your beauty,
then who gives them to you?
When the soul, exhausted,
asks pity of those eyes,
it meets with greater harshness
and feels more disillusioned;
and if humble, to your hands

sagrado viene a buscar,
atreviéndose al jazmín,
mirándose en el cristal,
desengañada, y corrida
su designio vuelve atrás,
pues gala haciendo el delito,
y lisonja la crueldad,
el homicidio cautela,
que son, publicando están,
quien voluntades cautiva,
quien roba la libertad.
Discreta como hermosa,
a un mismo tiempo ostentáis
en el agrado, aspereza,
halago en la gravedad,
en los desvíos, cordura,
entereza en la beldad,
en el ofender, disculpa,
pues tenéis para matar,
altiveces de hermosura,
con secretos de deidad.
Gala es en vos lo que pudo
ser defecto en la que más
se precia de airosa, y bella,
porque el herir, y el matar
a traición, jamás halló
sólo en vos disculpa igual.
Haced dichosa mi pena,
dad licencia a mi humildad
para que os sirva, si es justo
que a mi amor lo permitáis:
que estas venturas, aquestos
favores que el alma ya
solicita en vuestra vista,
o busca en vuestra piedad,
si vuestros ojos lo niegan,
¿dónde se podrán hallar?

RIBETE   Aquí gracia, y despúes gloria,
amén, por siempre jamás:
¡qué difícil asonante
buscó Leonor! No hizo mal,
dele versos en agudo,
pues que no le puede dar
otros agudos en prosa.

sacred came it seeking,
daring the jasmine,
gazing in the glass,
disappointed, chased away,
it withdraws its plan,
for elegance makes crime,
flattery is cruelty,
and caution, murder.
Thus do they proclaim:
the one who captures hearts
robs freedom also.
As wise as you are beautiful,
you display, at once,
severity in charm,
allure in circumspection,
in diversion, prudence,
in beauty, integrity,
in offending, forgiveness;
for the haughtiness of beauty
and the secrets of some deity
are your most deadly arms.
What would be a defect in one
who is most vain of her style
and beauty, is grace in you;
for to wound or kill
to avenge betrayal would
find in you only forgiveness.
Make fortunate my woe,
give license to my humility
that it may serve you,
if it is just that you permit
my love. These adventures,
these favors that my soul now seeks
in your sight, or looks for in your mercy,
if your eyes deny them,
where might they be found?

RIBETE Here grace, and later glory,
amen, forever and always,
what difficult harmony
Leonor sought! She did not do badly,
declaiming her verses in sharp notes
since she cannot be so pointed
in prose.

ESTELA   Don Leonardo, bastan ya
               las lisonjas, que imagino
               que el ruiseñor imitáis,
               que no canta enamorado
               de sus celos al compás,
               porque siente, o porque quiere,
               sino por querer cantar.
               Estimo las cortesías,
               y a tener seguridad
               las pagara con finezas.

DOÑA LEONOR   Mi amor se acreditará
               con experiencias; mas no
               habéis comparado mal
               al canto del ruiseñor
               de mi afecto la verdad:
               pues si dulcemente grave,
               sobre el jazmín, o rosal
               hace facistol, a donde
               suele contrapuntear
               bienvenidas a la Aurora;
               Aurora sois celestial,
               dos soles son vuestros ojos,
               un cielo es vuestra beldad.
               ¿Qué mucho que ruiseñor
               amante quiera engañar
               en la gloria de miraros
               de no veros el penar?

ESTELA   ¡Qué bien sabéis persuadir!
               Basta, Leonardo, no más;
               esta noche en el terrero
               a solas os quiero hablar
               por las rejas, que al jardín
               se corresponden.

DOÑA LEONOR   Irá
               a obedeceros el alma.

ESTELA   Pues adiós.

DOÑA LEONOR   Adiós; mandad,
               bella Lisarda, en qué os sirva.

LISARDA   Luego os veré.

DOÑA LEONOR   Bien está.
(Vanse las damas.)

               ¿Qué te parece de Estela?

RIBETE   Que se va cumpliendo ya
               mi vaticinio, pues ciega,

ESTELA   Don Leonardo, stop this
flattery now; I believe you
imitate the nightingale,
which does not sing love's
jealousy in time for sentiment
or love but just because it likes to sing.
I appreciate the courtesy
and you may be sure it will be paid
with kindness.

DOÑA LEONOR   My love will be credited with
experience; but you have not
compared badly the song of
the nightingale with my affection:
if so sweetly serious upon the jasmine or rosebush
he places his lectern and there welcomes,
in counterpoint, the dawn;
you are Aurora celestial,
two suns are your eyes,
a sky is your beauty.
Is it hard to understand
that the loving nightingale wishes
to be deceived by the glory of looking
at you rather than to see your grief?

ESTELA   You know so well how to persuade!
Enough, Leonardo, no more,
Let me speak to you alone
tonight on the terrace through
the grillwork in the garden.

DOÑA LEONOR   My soul will be there to obey you.

ESTELA   Farewell, then.

DOÑA LEONOR   Farewell; tell me, fair
Lisarda, how may I serve you?

LISARDA   I will see you anon.

DOÑA LEONOR   As you wish.

(Exit Estela and Lisarda.)

     What think you of Estela?

RIBETE   She is already fulfilling
my prophecy as blindly

fuego imagina sacar
de dos pedernales fríos;
¡Qué bien se entablará
el juego de amor, aunque ella
muestre que picada está,
si para que se despique,
no la puedes envidar,
si no es de falso, por ser
limitado tu caudal
para empeño tan forzoso!

DOÑA LEONOR   Amor de mi parte está.
El Príncipe de Pinoy
es éste, su vanidad
se está leyendo en su talle;
mas me importa su amistad.

RIBETE   Linda alhaja.
(Sale el Príncipe.)

LUDOVICO   ¿Don Leonardo?

DOÑA LEONOR   ¡O Príncipe! Un siglo ha
que no os veo.

LUDOVICO   Bien así
la amistad acreditáis.

DOÑA LEONOR   Yo os juro por vida vuestra. . .

LUDOVICO   Basta; ¿para qué juráis?

DOÑA LEONOR   ¿Qué hay de Estela?

LUDOVICO   ¿Qué hay de Estela?
Fernando la vino a hablar,
y respondió desdeñosa,
que la deje, que no está
del Príncipe enamorada,
ni se pretende casar;
desaire que me ha enfadado,
por ser tan pública ya
mi pretensión.

DOÑA LEONOR   ¿Sois mi amigo?

LUDOVICO   ¿Quién merece la verdad
de mi amor, sino vos sólo?

DOÑA LEONOR   Mucho tengo que hablar
con vos.

RIBETE   *(Aparte)* Mira lo que haces.

DOÑA LEONOR   Esto me importa, escuchad.
Estela se ha declarado
conmigo; no la he de amar
por vos, aunque me importara

	she imagines seizing from the
	fire two cold flints.
	How well she will play
	the game of love, although
	she shows that she is smitten,
	and if it be not false you cannot
	wager on her losing interest
	though your resources are limited
	for such an involvement!
DOÑA LEONOR	Love is on my side.
	Here comes the Prince of Pinoy.
	His vanity is evident from
	his figure, but his friendship
	is important to me.
RIBETE	Not bad.

(Enter the Prince.)

LUDOVICO	Don Leonardo?
DOÑA LEONOR	Oh, Majesty, it has been a century
	since last I saw you.
LUDOVICO	You are a credit to friendship.
DOÑA LEONOR	I swear to you by your life . . .
LUDOVICO	Enough; why do you swear?
DOÑA LEONOR	What news of Estela?
LUDOVICO	What news, you ask?
	Fernando tried to speak with her
	and she responded disdainfully,
	that he should leave her be,
	that she is not in love with the Prince,
	nor does she intend to marry;
	a rebuff that angers me,
	as my wooing is so public.
DOÑA LEONOR	Are you my friend?
LUDOVICO	Who but you deserves the
	truth of my love?
DOÑA LEONOR	I have much to say to you.
RIBETE	*(Aside)* Watch what you do.
DOÑA LEONOR	Mark, this is important.
	Estela has declared herself to me;
	because of you, I cannot love her,
	even if my life depended on it,

la vida, que la amistad
verdadera se conoce
en aquestos lances, mas
del favor que me hiciere,
dueño mi gusto os hará.
Y para que desde luego
la pretensión consigáis,
al terrero aquesta noche
quiero la vais a hablar
disfrazado con mi nombre.

LUDOVICO   ¿Qué decís?

DOÑA LEONOR   Que me debáis
estas finezas, venid,
que yo os diré lo demás.

(Vanse los dos.)

RIBETE   ¿Qué intenta Leonor? ¿Qué es esto?
Mas es mujer; ¿qué no hará?
que la más compuesta tiene
mil pelos de Satanás.

(Sale Tomillo.)

TOMILLO   Vive Dios, que no sé dónde
he de hallar a don Juan.

RIBETE   Éste es el bufón, que a Flora
imagina desflorar:
Pregonadle a uso de España.

TOMILLO   ¡O paisano! ¿Qué será,
que las mismas pajarillas
se me alegran en pensar
que veo españoles?

RIBETE   Esa
es fuerza del natural.

TOMILLO   Al cuarto de don Fernando
creo que asistís.

RIBETE   Es verdad.
Criado soy de su primo
don Leonardo; ¿queréis más?

TOMILLO   ¿Cómo va de paga?

RIBETE   Paga
adelantado.

TOMILLO   ¿Y os da
ración?

RIBETE   Como yo la quiero.

TOMILLO   No hay tanto bien por acá;
¿de dónde sois?

for true friendship is revealed
in these turns, but if you were
to do me this favor,
my pleasure would make you master.
And so that you may obtain your desire,
I want you to go to the terrace tonight
and, disguised, speak in my name.

LUDOVICO   What are you saying?

DOÑA LEONOR   Come, you owe me this kindness,
and I will tell you the rest.

(Exeunt.)

RIBETE   What does Leonor intend? What is this?
But she is a woman; what will she not do?
The noblest woman has
a thousand hairs of Satan.

(Enter Tomillo.)

TOMILLO   For the love of God, I know not
where to find Don Juan.

RIBETE   This is the buffoon who imagines
deflowering Flora:
speak to him as it's done in Spain.

TOMILLO   Oh, fellow countryman!
How is it that I find such
delight whenever I see a Spaniard?

RIBETE   'Tis only natural.

TOMILLO   I believe that you serve in the
quarters of Don Fernando.

RIBETE   That is true. I am the servant
of his cousin Don Leonardo.
Would you know more?

TOMILLO   How do they pay you?

RIBETE   In advance.

TOMILLO   They give you meals?

RIBETE   As I wish.

TOMILLO   I have nothing so favorable here.
Where are you from?

RIBETE	De Madrid.
TOMILLO	¿Cuándo vinistes de allá?
RIBETE	¡Bravo chasco! Habrá seis meses.
TOMILLO	¿Qué hay en el lugar de nuevo?
RIBETE	Ya es todo muy viejo allá;

sólo en esto de poetas
hay notable novedad,
por innumerables, tanto,
que aun quieren poetizar
las mujeres, y se atreven
a hacer comedias ya.

TOMILLO   ¡Válgame Dios! ¿Pues no fuera
mejor coser e hilar?
¿Mujeres poetas?

RIBETE   Sí;
mas no es nuevo, pues están
Argentaria, Safo, Areta,
Blesilla,[17] y más de un millar
de modernas, que hoy a Italia
lustre soberano dan,
disculpando la osadía
de su nueva vanidad.

TOMILLO   Y decidme. . .

RIBETE   Voto a Cristo,
que ése es mucho preguntar.

(Vanse, y sale don Juan.)

DON JUAN   Tanta inquietud en el pecho,
tanta pasión en el alma,
en el sosiego tal calma,
en el vivir tal despecho:
tal penar mal satisfecho,
tal temblar, y tal arder,
tal gusto en el padecer,
sobornando los desvelos;
sin duda, si no son celos,
que infiernos deben de ser.
¿De qué sirvió la ocasión
en que me puso la suerte,
si della misma se advierte
cuan pocas mi dichas son?
Mi amor, y su obligación,
reconoce Estela hermosa:
mas ¿qué importa, si dudosa,
o no quiere, o no se atreve,

RIBETE	From Madrid.
TOMILLO	When came you from there?
RIBETE	When, you ask! Almost six months ago.
TOMILLO	What news from there?
RIBETE	Nothing's new; everything's now old.
	Just the poets offer some
	notable novelty; they are
	innumerable, so many in fact
	that now even women want to
	write poetry, and they have gone so far
	as to write plays.
TOMILLO	God Almighty! Would it not be better
	if they sewed and spun?
	Women poets?
RIBETE	Yes, but it isn't new; you have
	Argentaria, Sappho, Arete,
	Blesilla,[17] and today more than a thousand
	modern ones who now give Italy
	unsurpassed luster, in compensation for
	the boldness of their new vanity.
TOMILLO	And tell me . . .
RIBETE	I swear to Christ you've got
	a lot of questions.

(Exeunt. Enter Don Juan.)

DON JUAN	Such restlessness in my breast,
	such passion in my soul,
	in tranquillity such calm,
	in living, so much spite,
	so much suffering without satisfaction,
	so much trembling, and such ardor
	such taste for endurance,
	bribing sleeplessness.
	No doubt, if it be not jealousy
	it must be hell.
	What fortune is this
	to have this chance
	when Fortune herself knows
	how unfortunate I am?
	Lovely Estela recognizes
	my love, and its obligation,
	but what does it matter if, unsure,
	she either loves not, or dares not,

siendo a mis encendios nieve,
y a otro calor mariposa?
Con justa causa acobardo,
o el amor, o la esperanza,
pues tan poca dicha alcanza,
cuando tanto premio aguardo:
este primo, este Leonardo,
de don Fernando, en rigor,
galán se ha opuesto a mi amor;
pero no es bien que me asombre,
si habla, rostro, talle, y nombre
vino a tener de Leonor.
¿Que quién, sino quien retrata
su aborrecido traslado,
pudiera haber malogrado
suerte tan dichosa y grata?
Ausente me ofende, y mata
con aparentes antojos,
de suerte que a mis enojos
dice el gusto, y no se engaña,
que Leonor vino de España
sólo a quebrarme los ojos.
El de Pinoy sirve a Estela,
y amigo del de Pinoy
es don Leonardo, a quien hoy
su mudable gusto apela:
yo, perdida centinela,
desde lejos miro el fuego,
y al temor concedo y niego
mis penas y mis favores,
el pecho un volcán de ardores,
el alma un Etna de fuego.
"Más merece quien más ama,"
dijo un ingenio divino;
yo he de amar, porque imagino
que algún mérito me llama:
goce del laurel la rama
el que Fortuna eligió,
pues si indigno la gozó,
es cierto, si bien se advierte
que le pudo dar la suerte,
dicha sí, mérito no.

(Sale Ribete.)

RIBETE   ¡Qué ciegos intentos dan

being snow on my burning ardor,
and drawn like a butterfly to another's heat?
Justly I abash either love or hope,
so little luck is to be had
when I await such great reward.
This Leonardo, this cousin
of Don Fernando, undeniably
this youth has opposed my love;
but it is not well that it astonishes me,
for his speech, face, figure, and
name all resemble Leonor.
Who but the one who is
the portrait of her abhorrent image
could have been the one to ruin
luck so fortunate and pleasing?
Absent she offends me, and kills
with apparent caprice,
fortunately desire tells my anger,
and is not deceived, that Leonor
has come from Spain just
to smash my eyes.
This Pinoy serves Estela,
and a friend of Pinoy is Don Leonardo,
who appeals today to her fickle taste:
I, lost cinder,
from afar gaze at the fire,
and concede to fear and deny
my sorrows and my blessings,
my breast a volcano of ardor,
my soul an Etna on fire.
"He who loves most,
most deserves," said the sage;
I must love for I imagine
that some merit calls me.
May the man whom Fortune chooses
enjoy his branch of laurel,
and if he be unworthy
he must well know
it was luck brought him
good fortune, not his merit.

(Enter Ribete.)

RIBETE   What blind purposes disquiet

a Leonor desasosiego!
Mas si van siguiendo a un ciego,
¿qué vista tener podrán?
Mándame que dé a don Juan
este papel por de Estela,
que como amor la desvela,
por desvanecer su daño
busca engaño contra engaño,
cautela contra cautela.
¡A qué buen tiempo le veo!
Quiero darle el alegrón.

DON JUAN   Yo he de amar sin galardón
y conquistar sin trofeo.

RIBETE   A cierto dichos empleo
os llama fortuna ahora
por este papel.

DON JUAN   Ignora
la novedad mi desgracia.

RIBETE   Y es de Estela, por la gracia
de Dios, Condesa de Sora.

DON JUAN   El papel beso mil veces
por suyo; dejadme leer.

RIBETE   (Aparte) Leed, que a fe que ha de ser
más el ruido que las nueces.

DON JUAN   Dichoso, fortuna, yo
pues ya llego a persuadirme
a que merezco por firme
si por venturoso no;
mi constancia al fin venció
de Estela hermosa el desdén,
pues me llama. A espacio ven,
dicha, porque en gloria tal,
ya que no me mató el mal,
me podrá matar el bien.

RIBETE   Bien lo entiende.

DON JUAN   Esta cadena
os doy, y os quisiera dar
un mundo. ¡Dulce papel!

RIBETE   (Aparte) Pues a fe que lleva en él
menos de lo que ha pensado.

DON JUAN   No sé si es verdad o sueño,
ni me atrevo a responder.
Amigo, el obedecer
será mi gustoso empeño;

Leonor! But if they follow the blind,
what sight will they be able to procure?
She sends me to give this paper
to Don Juan, as if from Estela,
for as love keeps her from sleep
she seeks to dispel its damage
by posing deception against deception,
cunning against cunning.
What fortune that I see him now!
I long to give him this great joy.

DON JUAN I must love without reward
and conquer without triumph.

RIBETE Indeed I bring you happiness,
your fortune presents itself
in this piece of paper.

DON JUAN The news knows not
of my disgrace.

RIBETE The letter is from Estela,
by the grace of God, Countess of Sora.

DON JUAN Since it is from her I kiss the
paper a thousand times;
let me read it.

RIBETE (Aside) Read, by my lights. It
has to be more bark than bite.

DON JUAN Fortunate I am and can now
persuade myself that for my
firmness I deserve what for
being lucky I do not;
my constancy at last has won
over the disdain of Estela,
who now calls me.
Come, fortune, because I am in
such glory that though bad luck
killed me not, good luck may.

RIBETE He understands it well.

DON JUAN I give you this chain and would
well give you the world.
Sweet paper!

RIBETE (Aside) He carries less with him
than he thinks.

DON JUAN I know not if it is truth or dream,
nor do I dare to answer. Friend,
obedience will be my fondest pledge;

decid a mi hermoso dueño
que soy suyo.

RIBETE   Pues adiós.

DON JUAN   El mismo vaya con vos.
Oíd, procuradme hablar,
porque habemos que quedar
grandes amigos los dos.

RIBETE   ¡Oh! Pues claro está.

(Vase.)

DON JUAN   Aprisa, luciente coche,
da lugar al de la noche
que obsucro te sigue ya.
Hoy mi esperanza hará
de su dicha ostentación,
pues Estela me da acción,
y aunque el premio halle tardanza,
más vale una alta esperanza
que una humilde posesión.

(Vase, y sale doña Leonor, de noche.)

DOÑA LEONOR   ¿Dónde, ¡ay! locos desatinos,
me lleva con paso errante
de amor la bárbara fuerza?
¿Cómo en tantas ceguedades,
atropellando imposibles,
a creer me persuade
que he de vencer? ¡Ay, honor,
qué me cuestas de pesares,
qué me debes de zozobras,
en qué me pones de ultrajes!
¡Oh, si Ribete acabase
de venir, para saber
si tuvo dicha de darle
el papel a aquel ingrato
que a tantos riesgos me trae!
Mas ya viene: ¿qué hay, Ribete?

(Sale Ribete.)

RIBETE   Que llegué; que di a aquel ángel
el papel; que me rindió
este despojo brillante,
pensando que era de Estela;
que me dijo que dictase
por ella a su dueño hermoso
que era suyo y vendrá a hablarle.

DOÑA LEONOR   Bien está.

	tell my fair lord that I am hers.
RIBETE	Good-bye, then.
DON JUAN	May God go with you.
	Listen, tell her I will come to
	speak with her, as we must
	remain great friends.
RIBETE	Of course!

(Exit Ribete.)

DON JUAN	Hurry, shining coach,
	give up your place to that of night
	who dark is close behind you now.
	Today my hope will make a show of its good fortune,
	for Estela has made a gesture to me,
	and though the reward has been delayed,
	a high hope is worth more
	than a humble possession.

(Exit. Enter Doña Leonor. It is night.)

DOÑA LEONOR	Oh, unleashed madness, where
	does this barbaric force carry
	me with the erring step of love?
	How in so much blindness
	colliding with impossibilities,
	can I persuade myself that
	I shall win? Oh, honor,
	what have you cost me in sorrow?
	What do you owe me for my woes?
	What outrages will I meet on your behalf?
	Oh, if only Ribete would come
	so I might know if he was able to give
	my letter to that ingrate who brings
	me to so many risks! But there,
	he comes. How went it, Ribete?

(Enter Ribete.)

RIBETE	I arrived; I gave that angel the paper,
	and thinking that it was from Estela
	he gave me this glimmering booty,
	and he told me to tell her, his fair lord,
	that he is hers and will come to speak to her.
DOÑA LEONOR	Well done!

RIBETE	Y ¿estás resuelta?
DOÑA LEONOR	Esta noche ha de entablarse
	o mi remedio, o mi muerte.
RIBETE	Mira, Leonor, lo que haces.
DOÑA LEONOR	Esto ha de ser.
RIBETE	¡Quiera Dios
	que no des con todo al traste!
DOÑA LEONOR	¡Qué mal conoces mi brío!
RIBETE	¿Quién dice que eres cobarde?
	Cátate aquí muy valiente,
	muy diestra, muy arrogante,
	muy alentada, y, al fin,
	un sepan cuantos de Marte,
	que hace a diestros y a siniestros
	estragos y mortandades
	con el ánimo. Y la fuerza:
	di, señora, ¿dónde yace?
DOÑA LEONOR	Semíramis, ¿no fue heroica?
	Cenobia, Drusila, Draznes,
	Camila,[18] y otras cien mil,
	¿no sirvieron de ejemplares
	a mil varones famosos?
	Demás de que el encontrarle
	es contingente, que yo
	sólo quise adelantarme
	tan temprano, por hacer
	que el Príncipe a Estela hable
	sin ver a don Juan, Ribete.
RIBETE	Pues ánimo y adelante,
	que ya estás en el terrero,
	y aquestas ventanas salen
	al cuarto de la Condesa,
	que aquí me habló la otra tarde.
DOÑA LEONOR	Pues, Ribete, donde dije
	ten prevenidas las llaves
	que te dio Fineo.
RIBETE	Bien.
	¿Son las que a este cuarto hacen
	junto al de Estela, que tiene
	balcones a esotra parte
	de Palacio, y ahora está
	vacío e inhabitable?
DOÑA LEONOR	Sí; y con un vestido mío
	me has de esperar donde sabes

RIBETE	And you are determined?
DOÑA LEONOR	Tonight will see either my redress or my death.
RIBETE	Take care in what you do, Leonor.
DOÑA LEONOR	This must be.
RIBETE	For the love of God, do not destroy your life!
DOÑA LEONOR	You do not know my spirit!
RIBETE	Who says you are a coward? Try to find one here who is more valiant, more skillful, more arrogant, more spirited, and, furthermore, of those followers of Mars who helter-skelter wreaked destruction and slaughter, one with so much vigor. And strength: say, madame, where does it lie?
DOÑA LEONOR	Semiramis, was she not heroic? Zenobia, Drusilla, Draznes, Camilla,[18] and another hundred thousand, were they not more exemplary than a thousand famous men? Besides, meeting him is fortuitous, for I only wish to hasten so the Prince might speak to Estela without seeing Don Juan, Ribete.
RIBETE	Courage and onward, you are already on the terrace and at those windows of the Countess's room, where she spoke to me the other afternoon.
DOÑA LEONOR	Then, Ribete, have the keys that Fineo gave you ready where I said.
RIBETE	As you will. Are they the ones to the empty darkened room next to Estela's, with balconies that lead to the palace's main wing?
DOÑA LEONOR	Yes, and there must you await me with a gown of mine,

	porque me importa el vivir.
RIBETE	¿No importa más el quedarme
	y defenderte, si acaso
	don Juan. . .
DOÑA LEONOR	¡Oh, qué necedades!
	Yo sé lo que puedo, amigo.
RIBETE	Pues si lo que puedes sabes,
	quédate, señora, adiós.

(Vase Ribete.)

DOÑA LEONOR	Temprano vine, por ver
	si a don Juan también le trae
	su desvelo; y quiera Dios
	que Ludovico se tarde
	por si viniere.

(Sale don Juan.)

DON JUAN	No en vano
	temí que el puesto ocupase
	gente: un hombre solo es; quiero
	reconocerle.
DOÑA LEONOR	Bien talle
	tiene aqueste. ¿Si es don Juan?
	Quiero más cerca llegarme
	y conocer, si es posible,
	quién es.
DON JUAN	Si aquéste hablase,
	sabré si es el de Pinoy.

(Van llegando uno a otro.)

DOÑA LEONOR	Yo me determino a hablarle
	para salir desta duda.
	¿Quién va, hidalgo?
DON JUAN	Quien sabe
	ir a donde le parece.
DOÑA LEONOR	*(Aparte)* Él es. ¡Respuesta galante!
	No irá sino quiero yo.
DON JUAN	¿Quién sois vos para estorbarme
	que me esté o vaya?
DOÑA LEONOR	El diablo.
DON JUAN	¿El diablo? ¡Lindo descarte!
	Es poco un diablo.
DOÑA LEONOR	Ciento,
	mil millares de millares
	soy si me enojo.
DON JUAN	¡Gran tropa!
DOÑA LEONOR	¿Burláisos?

	for my life depends upon it.
RIBETE	Is it not more important that I remain and defend you in case don Juan . . .
DOÑA LEONOR	Oh, what foolishness! I know what I can do, my friend.
RIBETE	If you can do what you know, then stay, madame; good-bye.

(Exit Ribete.)

DOÑA LEONOR	I have come early to see if wakefulness brings Don Juan; may God wish Ludovico be delayed if he is coming.

(Enter Don Juan.)

DON JUAN	It was not in vain I feared that someone would be here upon this place. There is a man, alone; let me see if I recognize him.
DOÑA LEONOR	That man has a dashing figure. Is it Don Juan? I will go closer and find out, if I might, who he is.
DON JUAN	If that man were to speak, I would know if it is Pinoy.

(They approach each other.)

DOÑA LEONOR	I am determined to speak to him so I will have no doubt. Who goes there, sir?
DON JUAN	He who can where he pleases.
DOÑA LEONOR	*(Aside)* It is. Gallant answer! He will not go if I do not wish it.
DON JUAN	Who are you to disturb me and say whether I may go or remain?
DOÑA LEONOR	The devil.
DON JUAN	The devil? Nice play! But a single devil is of little consequence.
DOÑA LEONOR	One hundred, a thousand, tens of thousands am I if I get angry.
DON JUAN	Legions of them!
DOÑA LEONOR	Do you mock me?

DON JUAN   No soy bastante
a defenderme de tantos;
y así os pido, si humildades
corteses valen con diablos,
que los llevéis a otra parte,
que aquí, ¿qué pueden querer?
(Aparte) Estime que aquí me halle
este alentado, y que temo
perder el dichoso lance
de hablar a Estela esta noche.

DOÑA LEONOR   Digo yo que querrán darles
a los como vos ingratos
dos docenas de pesares.

DON JUAN   ¿Y si no los quiero?

DOÑA LEONOR   ¿No?

DON JUAN   Demonios muy criminales
traéis; moderaos un poco.

DOÑA LEONOR   Vos muy civiles donaires.
O nos hemos de matar
o solo habéis de dejarme
en este puesto, que importa.

DON JUAN   ¿Hay tal locura? Bastante
prueba es ya de mi cordura
sufrir estos disparates;
pero me importa: el matarnos
fuera desdicha notable,
y el irme será mayor;
que los hombres de mis partes
jamás violentan su gusto
con tan precisos desaires;
demás de que tengo dada
palabra aquí, de guardarle
el puesto a un amigo.

DOÑA LEONOR   Bien;
si como es justo guardasen
los hombres de vuestras prendas
otros preceptos más graves
en la ley de la razón
y la justicia, ¡qué tarde
ocasionaran venganzas!
Mas ¿para qué quien no sabe
cumplir palabras las da?
¿Es gentileza, es donaire,
es gala o es bizarría?

DON JUAN	I am not enough to defend myself from so many; and so I ask of you, if humble courtesy is worth anything with devils, that you take them somewhere else, for what would they want here? *(Aside)* Realize that this spirited being finds me here, and I am fearful of losing the fortunate opportunity to speak to Estela tonight.
DOÑA LEONOR	I say that they want to give to those ingrates like you two dozen sorrows.
DON JUAN	And if I want them not?
DOÑA LEONOR	No?
DON JUAN	You bring very criminal demons; restrain them a bit.
DOÑA LEONOR	You possess very civil charms. Either we must kill each other or you must leave me here on this spot, as you will.
DON JUAN	What madness is this? Enduring this wild nonsense has been enough test of my senses; but, yes, it does matter to me: killing each other may be a notable misfortune and my leaving will be a greater one; men such as I never affront their good taste with such unattractive behavior; besides, I have given my word to wait here for a friend.
DOÑA LEONOR	Agreed. If it is just that men of your rank keep other, graver precepts grounded in the law of reason and justice; how late may vengeance still be exacted! But, why does he who knows not how to keep his word give it? Is it courtesy, is it grace, is it elegance, or is it gallantry?

DON JUAN   (*Aparte*) Éste me tiene por alguien
                    que le ha ofendido; bien puedo
                    dejarle por ignorante.
                    No os entiendo, ¡por Dios vivo!

DOÑA LEONOR   Pues yo sí me entiendo, y baste
                    saber que os conozco, pues
                    sabéis que hablo verdades.

DON JUAN   Vuestro arrojamiento indica
                    ánimo y valor tan grande
                    que os estoy aficionado.

DOÑA LEONOR   Aficionado es en balde.
                    No es ésta la vez primera
                    que de mí os aficionasteis;
                    mas fue ficción, porque sois
                    aleve, ingrato, mudable,
                    injusto, engañador, falso,
                    perjuro, bárbaro, fácil,
                    sin Dios, sin fe, sin palabra.

DON JUAN   Mirad que no he dado a nadie
                    ocasión para que así
                    en mi descrédito hable,
                    y por estar donde estáis
                    escucho de vos ultrajes
                    que no entiendo.

DOÑA LEONOR   ¿No entendéis?
                    ¿No sois vos el inconstante
                    que finge, promete, jura,
                    ruega, obliga, persuade,
                    empeña palabra y fe
                    de noble, y falta a su sangre,
                    a su honor y obligaciones,
                    fugitivo al primer lance,
                    que se va sin despedirse,
                    y que aborrece sin darle
                    ocasión?

DON JUAN   Os engañáis.

DOÑA LEONOR   Más valdrá que yo me engañe.
                    ¡Gran hombre sois de una fuga!

DON JUAN   Más cierto será que falte
                    luz a los rayos del sol,
                    que dejar yo de guardarle
                    mi palabra a quien la di.

DOÑA LEONOR   Pues mirad: yo sé quién sabe
                    que disteis una palabra,

DON JUAN	*(Aside)* This person takes me
	for someone who has offended him;
	out of ignorance, I would do well to leave him.
	As I live and breathe,
	I do not understand you!
DOÑA LEONOR	Well do I understand myself, and
	as it is enough to say that I know you,
	then you know that I speak the truth.
DON JUAN	Your challenge shows spirit
	and such great bravery that I am
	growing fond of you.
DOÑA LEONOR	Your fondness is in vain.
	It is not the first time you
	took a liking to me, and that
	was a fiction because you are
	treacherous, ungrateful, fickle,
	unjust, deceptive, false,
	a liar, a light-minded barbarian,
	godless, faithless,
	with no word of honor.
DON JUAN	In faith, I have given no one
	cause to speak thus to my
	discredit, and being
	where you are I hear
	insults from you I do not understand.
DOÑA LEONOR	You understand me not?
	Are you not the inconstant man who
	woos, promises, swears,
	begs, obliges, persuades,
	insists on the nobility of
	his word and faith, and fails
	his blood, his honor, and his duty,
	who flees at the first difficulty,
	leaves with no farewell,
	and abhors without cause?
DON JUAN	You deceive yourself.
DOÑA LEONOR	It would have been better
	had I deceived myself.
	You are a great man, for fleeing!
DON JUAN	More certain must it be
	that the rays of sun might lose their light
	than that I would break my word, once given.
DOÑA LEONOR	See here, I know one who knows
	that you gave your word,

que hicisteis pleito homenaje
de no quebrarla, y apenas
disteis al deseo alcance,
cuando se acabó.

DON JUAN   Engañáisos.

DOÑA LEONOR   Más valdrá que yo me engañe.

DON JUAN   No entiendo lo que decís.

DOÑA LEONOR   Yo sí lo entiendo.

DON JUAN   Escuchadme.

DOÑA LEONOR   No quiero de vuestros labios
escuchar más falsedades,
que dirán engaños nuevos.

DON JUAN   Reparad. . .

DOÑA LEONOR   No hay que repare,
pues no reparasteis vos;
sacad la espada.

DON JUAN   Excusarme
no puede ya mi cordura
ni mi valor, porque es lance
forzoso.

(Comienzan a reñir y sale el Príncipe.)

LUDOVICO   Aquí don Leonardo
me dijo que le esperase,
y sospecho que tarda.

DON JUAN   Ya procuró acreditarse
mi paciencia de cortés,
conociendo que me hablasteis
por otro; pero no habéis
querido excusar los lances.

LUDOVICO   ¡Espadas en el terrero!

DOÑA LEONOR   ¡Ejemplo de desleales,
bien os conozco!

DON JUAN   ¡Ea, pues,
riñamos!

(Riñen.)

LUDOVICO   Fortuna, ¡acabe
mi competencia! Don Juan
es éste, y podré matarle
ayudando a su enemigo.

(Pónese al lado de doña Leonor.)
Pues estoy de vuestra parte,
¡muera el villano!

DOÑA LEONOR   No hará,

(Pónese al lado de don Juan.)

	and you made a pledge not to break it,
	and scarcely had you given it
	and gotten what you desired,
	when it was over.
DON JUAN	You deceive yourself.
DOÑA LEONOR	It would have been better if I had.
DON JUAN	I understand not what you say.
DOÑA LEONOR	I do understand.
DON JUAN	Listen to me.
DOÑA LEONOR	I do not wish to hear more
	lies from your lips that
	will speak new deceptions.
DON JUAN	Repair . . .
DOÑA LEONOR	There's nothing to repair since
	you did not. Take out your sword.
DON JUAN	Neither my reason nor my valor
	can excuse me from this
	unavoidable conflict.

(*They begin to fight. Enter the Prince.*)

LUDOVICO	Don Leonardo told me that
	I should await him here and
	I suspect he has been delayed.
DON JUAN	You have already seen my
	courteous patience, knowing
	you mistook me for another;
	you did not wish to forgo conflict.
LUDOVICO	Sword fighting on the terrace!
DOÑA LEONOR	An example for disloyal men,
	well I know you!
DON JUAN	Then we shall fight!

(*They fight.*)

LUDOVICO	Fortune, finish off my competition!
	Don Juan is my rival and I can kill
	him by helping his enemy.

(*He places himself at Doña Leonor's side.*)

	I am on your side.
	Die, villain!
DOÑA LEONOR	He will not;

(*She places herself at Don Juan's side.*)

	que basta para librarle
	de mil muertes mi valor.
DON JUAN	¿Hay suceso más notable?
LUDOVICO	¿A quien procura ofenderos
	defendéis?
DOÑA LEONOR	Puede importarme
	su vida.
DON JUAN	¿Qué es esto, cielos?
	Tal mudanza en un instante?
LUDOVICO	¡Ah, quién matara a don Juan!
DOÑA LEONOR	No os habrá de ser muy fácil,
	que soy yo quien le defiende.
LUDOVICO	¡Terribles golpes!
DOÑA LEONOR	Más vale,
	pues aquesto no os importa,
	iros, caballero, antes
	que os cueste...
LUDOVICO	(Aparte) El primer consejo
	del contrario es favorable.
	A mí no me han conocido;
	mejor será retirarme,
	no espere Estela.

(Váse retirando, y doña Leonor tras él.)

DOÑA LEONOR	Eso sí.
DON JUAN	Vos sois bizarro y galante.
	¡Válgame el cielo! ¿Qué es esto?
	¡Que este hombre me ocasionase
	a reñir, y con la espada
	hiciese tan desiguales
	el enojo y la razón!
	¡Que tan resuelto jurase
	darme muerte, y que en un punto
	me defendiese! Este es lance
	que lo imagino imposible.
	Que puede, dijo, importarle
	mi vida; y cuando brioso
	a reñir me persuade,
	¡al que me ofende resiste!
	¡No entiendo estas novedades!

(Sale doña Leonor.)

DOÑA LEONOR	¡Ea, ya se fue, volvamos
	a reñir!
DON JUAN	El obligarme
	y el ofenderme, quisiera

	my courage will free him from a thousand deaths.
DON JUAN	What remarkable act is this?
LUDOVICO	Do you seek to defend him, who has offended you?
DOÑA LEONOR	His life may be important to me.
DON JUAN	What is this, heaven? Such a change in an instant?
LUDOVICO	Oh! If only someone would kill Don Juan!
DOÑA LEONOR	That will not be easy, as I am the one who defends him.
LUDOVICO	What terrible blows!
DOÑA LEONOR	Since this matter concerns you not, sir, you had better leave before it costs you …
LUDOVICO	*(Aside)* The first word of advice from the opposition is favorable. They have not recognized me, and it will be better for me to retire so that Estela need not wait.

(Exit the Prince with Doña Leonor behind him.)

DOÑA LEONOR	Indeed.
DON JUAN	You are courageous and gallant. Bless me, heaven! What is this? This man provoked me into fighting, and made anger and reason ever more disparate with his sword! Sworn and so determined to have me die, yet he ended up defending me! This is a conflict I would have imagined impossible. That my life, he said, may matter to him; first, with spirit, he persuades me to fight, and then he resists my enemy! I do not understand these events!

(Enter Doña Leonor.)

DOÑA LEONOR	He has left now; let us return to our duel!
DON JUAN	You oblige me and you insult me, and by God, I would

saber, ¡por Dios! de qué nace.
Yo no he de reñir con vos,
hidalgo; prueba bastante
de que soy agradecido.

DOÑA LEONOR   Tendréis a favor muy grande
el haberos defendido
y ayudado. ¡Qué mal sabe
conocer vuestro designio
la intención de mi dictamen!
Con justa causa ofendido
de vos, no quise que nadie
tuviese parte en la gloria
que ya espero con vengarme,
pues no era victoria mía
que otro valor me usurpase
el triunfo, ni fuera gusto
o lisonja el ayudarme,
pues con eso mi venganza
fuera menos memorable,
cuando está toda mi dicha
en mataros solo.

DON JUAN   Si alguien
os ha ofendido, y creéis
que soy yo, engañáisos.

DOÑA LEONOR   Antes
fui el engañado, ya no.

DON JUAN   Pues decid quién sois.

DOÑA LEONOR   *(Aparte)*   En balde
procura saber quién soy
quien tan mal pagarme sabe.
El Príncipe de Pinoy
era el que seguí; bastante
ocasión para que vuelva
le he dado; quiero excusarme
de verle. Quedaos, que a mí
no me importa aquesto, y si antes
os provoqué, no fue acaso.

DON JUAN   ¿Quién sois? Decid.

DOÑA LEONOR   No se hable
en eso; creed que mi agravio
os buscará en otra parte.

DON JUAN   Escuchad, oíd.

DOÑA LEONOR   No es posible;
yo os buscaré, aquesto baste.

	know why! I have no reason, sir,
	to fight you; it is proof
	enough that I am grateful.
DOÑA LEONOR	You hold it a great favor
	that I helped and defended you;
	yet, how badly does your mind
	know my intention!
	I wished none to have a part
	in the glorious vengeance
	that awaits me now.
	With just cause have I insulted you,
	nor would it be my victory
	had another's bravery usurped my triumph.
	His aid pleased me not, nor flattered me.
	It would have but made
	less memorable my vengeance,
	when all my joy lies
	in killing you myself.
DON JUAN	If someone has offended you,
	and you believe that it was I,
	you deceive yourself.
DOÑA LEONOR	I was deceived before, but no longer.
DON JUAN	Then reveal yourself.
DOÑA LEONOR	*(Aside)* In vain does he seek to know
	who I am, he who treated me so ill.
	It was Pinoy I followed; I have
	given him enough time to return.
	I do not wish to see him.
	Stay, for he matters not to me,
	and if before I provoked you,
	it was not for nothing.
DON JUAN	Who are you? Tell me.
DOÑA LEONOR	That is not to be told;
	believe me, my affront
	will find you elsewhere.
DON JUAN	Listen, hear me!
DOÑA LEONOR	Impossible! I will look for
	you, and that is enough.

(Váse.)

DON JUAN   ¡Vive Dios!, que he de seguirle
            sólo por saber si sabe
            que soy yo con quien habló;
            que recuerdos semejantes
            de mi suceso, no sé
            que pueda saberlos nadie.

(Váse, y sale Estela a la ventana.)

ESTELA   Mucho Leonardo tarda;
            que se sosieguen en Palacio aguarda,
            si no es que de otros brazos
            le entretienen gustosos embarazos.
            ¡Oh, qué mal en su ausencia me divierto!
            Haga el amor este temor incierto.
            Ya sospecho que viene.

(Sale el Príncipe de Pinoy.)

LUDOVICO   ¡Válgame el cielo! ¿Dónde se detiene
            Leonardo a aquesta hora?
            Hablar oí.

ESTELA   ¿Es Leonardo?

LUDOVICO   Soy, señora,
            (quiero fingirme él mismo) vuestro esclavo,
            que ya por serlo mi ventura alabo.

ESTELA   Confusa os aguardaba mi esperanza.

LUDOVICO   Toda mi dicha ha estado en mi tardanza.

ESTELA   ¿Cómo?

LUDOVICO   Porque os ha dado,
            hermosísima Estela, ese cuidado.

ESTELA   ¿En qué os habéis entretenido?

LUDOVICO   Un rato
            jugué.

ESTELA   ¿Ganasteis?

LUDOVICO   Sí.

ESTELA   Dadme barato.

LUDOVICO   ¿Qué me queda que daros, si soy todo
            vuestro?

ESTELA   Para excusaros buscáis modo;
            llegaos más cerca, oíd.

LUDOVICO   ¡Dichoso empleo!

(Sale doña Leonor.)

DOÑA LEONOR Si le hablo, consigue mi deseo
            el más feliz engaño,
            pues teniendo de Estela desengaño,
            podrá dejar la pretensión. . .

(Exit Doña Leonor.)

DON JUAN   Good God! I must follow
          him if only to know if he knows
          that it is I with whom he spoke;
          I know not how anyone might
          know of my past.

(Exit. Estela comes to the window.)

ESTELA   Leonardo is much delayed;
        perhaps he waits for the palace
        to go to its night's rest—
        unless other arms now hold him
        in delicious embraces.
        Oh, how badly I amuse myself in his
        absence! Love creates this uncertain
        fear. I suspect that he is coming now.

(Enter the Prince of Pinoy.)

LUDOVICO   Bless me, heaven! Where does
          Leonardo detain himself at this
          hour? I heard a voice . . .

ESTELA   Is it Leonardo?

LUDOVICO   I am, madame, (I want to pretend
          that I am he) your slave, and being
          that, I celebrate my luck.

ESTELA   In confusion did
        my hope await you.

LUDOVICO   All my happiness has been in my delay.

ESTELA   How?

LUDOVICO   Because you have,
          most fair Estela,
          been thus concerned.

ESTELA   How have you spent your time?

LUDOVICO   I gambled a while.

ESTELA   Did you win?

LUDOVICO   Yes.

ESTELA   You offer me your winnings?

LUDOVICO   What is left for me to give you,
          if I am all yours?

ESTELA   How you try to make me forgive you!
        Come closer, listen.

LUDOVICO   A happy task!

(Enter Doña Leonor.)

DOÑA LEONOR   If I speak to him, my happy wish
             to trick him will come true;
             for if he be disillusioned by Estela,
             he might cease to woo her . . .

(Sale don Juan en busca de Estela.)

DON JUAN   ¡Que fuese
            siguiéndole, y al cabo le perdiese
            al volver de Palacio!

DOÑA LEONOR   *(Aparte)* Éste es don Juan: ¡a espacio, amor, a espacio,
            que esta noche me pones
            de perderme y ganarme en ocasiones!

DON JUAN   Ésta es, sin duda, Estela.

DOÑA LEONOR   ¿Quién es?

DON JUAN   Una perdida centinela
            de la guerra del amor.

DOÑA LEONOR   ¡Bravo soldado!
            ¿Es don Juan?

DON JUAN   Es quien tiene a ese sol dado
            del alma el rendimiento,
            memoria, voluntad y entendimiento,
            con gustosa violencia;
            de suerte que no hay acto de potencia
            libre en mí, que ejercite
            razón que juzgue, fuerza que milite,
            que a vos no esté sujeta.

DOÑA LEONOR   ¿Qué, tanto me queréis?

DON JUAN   Vos sois discreta,
            y sabéis que adoraros
            es fuerza si al cristal queréis miraros.

DOÑA LEONOR   Desengaños me ofrece, si ambiciosa
            tal vez estuvo en la pasión dudosa,
            la vanidad.

DON JUAN   Será cristal obscuro. . .

DOÑA LEONOR   Ahora señor don Juan, yo no procuro
            lisonjas al pincel de mi retrato,
            sólo os quisiera ver menos ingrato.

DON JUAN   ¿Yo, ingrato? ¡Quiera el cielo,
            si no os adora mi amoroso celo,
            que sea aqueste mi último fracaso!

DOÑA LEONOR   Que ¿no me conocéis?, vamos al caso.
            ¿Cómo queréis que os crea,
            si no era necia, fea,
            pobre, humilde, villana,
            doña Leonor, la dama sevillana?
            Y ya sabéis, ingrato, habéis burlado
            con su honor la verdad de su cuidado.

DON JUAN   ¿Qué Leonor o qué dama?

DOÑA LEONOR   Llegaos más cerca, oíd: nunca la fama

(Enter Don Juan, looking for Estela.)

DON JUAN   He went after him, and in the end
    he lost him returning from the palace!

DOÑA LEONOR   *(Aside)* Here comes Don Juan;
    and now to play love, to play,
    for tonight you place me in danger
    of losing or winning my own self!

DON JUAN   That is, without a doubt, Estela.

DOÑA LEONOR   Who goes there?

DON JUAN   A lost sentinel from love's war.

DOÑA LEONOR   Brave soldier! Is it Don Juan?

DON JUAN   It is he whose soul has, with joyful violence,
    given to that sun surrender, memory,
    will, and understanding;
    and, fortunately, there is no act of potency loose in me
    to exert reason that might judge,
    force that might militate,
    that is not subject to you.

DOÑA LEONOR   What, you love me that much?

DON JUAN   You are wise, and if you wish
    to behold yourself in the glass
    you know that to love you is unavoidable.

DOÑA LEONOR   It offers me disillusionment,
    vanity. I was perhaps ambitious
    in dubious passion.

DON JUAN   It must have been a darkened glass . . .

DOÑA LEONOR   Now, señor Don Juan, I seek no
    flattery from the paintbrush of my
    portrait, I would just like you to
    be less ungrateful.

DON JUAN   I, an ingrate? What does heaven want
    if not for my loving devotion to adore
    you and that it be my last failure!

DOÑA LEONOR   What, do you not know me? Let us
    examine the case. How can you
    wish me to believe you if
    Doña Leonor, the Sevillian lady,
    was not foolish, ugly, poor,
    humble, rustic? And now, you
    know, ingrate, you mocked her
    honor with the truth of her feeling.

DON JUAN   What Leonor? What lady?

DOÑA LEONOR   Look more closely, listen:

	se engaña totalmente,
	y yo sé que no miente.
DON JUAN	*(Aparte)* ¡Que me haya don Fernando descubierto!
LUDOVICO	De que soy vuestro esclavo estoy bien cierto,
	mas no de que os desvela
	mi amor, hermosa Estela.
	(Quiero saber lo que a Leonardo quiere.)
	Yo sé que el de Pinoy por vos se muere.
	Es rico, es noble, es príncipe, en efecto,
	y aunque atropella amor todo respeto,
	no me juzgo dichoso.
ESTELA	Por cansado, soberbio y ambicioso,
	aun su nombre aborrezco.
LUDOVICO	¡Ah, ingrata, bien merezco
	que anticipéis mi amor a sus favores!
DOÑA LEONOR	¿De qué sirven retóricos colores?
	Ya confesáis su amor.
DON JUAN	Ya lo confieso.
DOÑA LEONOR	Pues lo demás será traición, exceso.
DON JUAN	Que la quise es muy cierto;
	mas no ofendí su honor, esto os advierto.
DOÑA LEONOR	Muy fácil sois, don Juan: pues ¿sin gozalla
	pudisteis olvidalla?
DON JUAN	Sola vuestra beldad tiene la culpa.
DOÑA LEONOR	¿Mi beldad? ¡No está mala la disculpa!
	Si os andáis a querer a las más bellas,
	iréis dejando aquéstas por aquellas.
DON JUAN	Oíd, ¡por vida vuestra!
ESTELA	*(Aparte)* Yo haré de mis finezas clara muestra.
LUDOVICO	¿Qué decís de don Juan?
ESTELA	Que no me agrada
	para quererle; sólo a vos os quiero.
LUDOVICO	De que así me queráis me desespero.
DON JUAN	*(Aparte)* ¡Que ya lo sepa Estela! ¡Yo estoy loco!
DOÑA LEONOR	Decid, don Juan, decid.
DON JUAN	Oíd un poco:
	como el que ve de la aurora
	la estrella o claro lucero,
	de su lumbre mensajero,
	cuando el horizonte dora,
	que se admira, y se enamora
	de su brillante arrebol,
	pero saliendo el farol
	del cielo, luciente y puro,

	reputation never totally deceives,
	and I know that I lie not.
DON JUAN	*(Aside)* Don Fernando has revealed my secret!
LUDOVICO	That I am your slave I am certain,
	but not so that my love shall deprive
	you of sleep, beautiful Estela.
	(I want to know how she loves Leonardo.)
	I know that Pinoy dies for you.
	He is rich, he is noble, a prince,
	in truth, and though love tramples
	all respect, I do not judge myself fortunate.
ESTELA	He is tiresome, arrogant, and ambitious;
	and I abhor even his name.
LUDOVICO	Oh, ingrate, do I so deserve that
	you abandon my love to his favors!
DOÑA LEONOR	What use is colorful rhetoric?
	You have already confessed your love.
DON JUAN	And I confess it now.
DOÑA LEONOR	The rest shall be betrayal, excess.
DON JUAN	That I loved her is certain;
	but I advise you that I did
	not offend her honor.
DOÑA LEONOR	You are most wanton, Don Juan.
	Well, then, were you able to forget her,
	not having possessed her?
DON JUAN	It is your beauty that is at fault.
DOÑA LEONOR	My beauty? Not a bad excuse!
	If you set yourself to loving the most beautiful,
	you will leave one for another.
DON JUAN	Listen, I beg you!
ESTELA	*(Aside)* I will make a clear show of my love.
LUDOVICO	What say you of Don Juan?
ESTELA	That it would not please me
	to love him; I love only you.
LUDOVICO	That you love me thus
	makes me desperate.
DON JUAN	*(Aside)* And Estela knows of it! I am mad!
DOÑA LEONOR	Speak, Don Juan, speak.
DON JUAN	Mark: 'tis as if one sees the dawn,
	the stars, or the bright planet Venus,
	sees the horizon become gold,
	and its shining messenger is admired,
	and its brilliant rosiness is loved,
	but its lantern leaves the sky,
	shimmering and pure,
	as the brightest planet calls to the darkness

    el lucero llama obscuro,
    viendo tan hermoso el sol.
    Así yo, que a Leonor vi,
    o de lucero o de estrella,
    adoré su lumbre bella
    y su mariposa fui;
    mas luego, mirando en ti
    del sol lucientes ensayos,
    hallé sombras y desmayos
    en la vista de mi amor,
    que es poca estrella Leonor,
    y eres sol con muchos rayos.

LUDOVICO Pues yo sé que a don Juan se vio obligado
    vuestro amante cuidado.

ESTELA Negarlo, engaño fuera;
    mas fue… escuchad.

LUDOVICO   Decid.

ESTELA   Desta manera:
    como el que en la selva umbrosa
    o jardín ve de colores
    una provincia de flores,
    pura, fragante y hermosa,
    que se aficiona a la rosa
    por su belleza, y al fin
    halla en la selva o jardín
    un jazmín; y porque sabe
    que es el jazmín más suave,
    la deja y coge el jazmín.
    Así yo, que vi a don Juan,
    rosa que a la vista agrada,
    de su valor obligada,
    pude admitirle galán;
    mas siendo tu vista imán
    de mi sentido, escogí
    lo que más hermoso vi,
    pues aunque la rosa admiro,
    eres el jazmín, y miro
    más fragante gala en ti.

DOÑA LEONOR De suerte, que la estrella
    precursora del sol, luciente y bella
    ¿fue Leonor?

DON JUAN   Sí.

DOÑA LEONOR   *(Aparte)* ¡Con cuántas penas lucho!
    Pues escuchad.

that the beautiful sun is coming.
Thus it was that I saw Leonor,
as either a bright planet or a star,
I loved her glowing beauty and
I was a moth to her flame; but after,
seeing in you rehearsals of the sun,
I found shadows and dismay
in the sight of my love;
Leonor is a mere star, and you
are the sun with many rays.

LUDOVICO   Well I know that your loving attention
was bestowed upon Don Juan.

ESTELA   To deny it would be false; but
it was . . . listen.

LUDOVICO   Speak.

ESTELA   In this way: as one in a shady jungle
or garden full of colors,
a province of flowers,
pure, fragrant, and beautiful,
one is attracted to the rose
for its beauty, and finally
finds in the jungle or garden
a jasmine; and knowing that
it is the softest jasmine,
one picks and takes this flower.
Thus I was when I saw Don Juan,
a rose that pleases the sight,
obligated to his bravery,
I admit it gracefully;
but the sight of you was a magnet
to my senses; I chose what I
saw that was most beautiful,
and although I admire the rose,
you are the jasmine, and I
find more fragrant charm in you.

DOÑA LEONOR   So the star that was the precursor
of the sun, shining and beautiful,
was Leonor?

DON JUAN   Yes.

DOÑA LEONOR   (*Aside*) I struggle with so much pain!
Well, mark.

DON JUAN   Decid, que ya os escucho.

DOÑA LEONOR   El que en la tiniebla obscura
de alguna noche camina,
adora por peregrina
del lucero la luz pura;
sólo en su lumbre asegura
de su guía la esperanza,
y aunque ya del sol le alcanza
el rayo, está agradecido
al lucero, porque ha sido
de su tormenta bonanza.
Tú, en el obscuro contraste
de la noche de tu amor,
el lucero de Leonor
norte a tus penas miraste:
guióte, mas olvidaste,
como ingrato, la centella
de su lumbre clara y bella
antes de amar mi arrebol.
¿Ves cómo sin ver el sol
aborreciste la estrella?

LUDOVICO   Metáfora curiosa
ha sido, Estela, comparar la rosa
a don Juan por su gala y bizarría.

ESTELA   Engañáisos.

LUDOVICO   Oíd, ¡por vida mía!
El que eligió en el jardín
el jazmín no fue discreto;
que no tiene olor perfeto,
si se marchita, el jazmín;
la rosa hasta su fin,
porque aun su amor le alabe,
tiene un olor muy dulce y grave,
fragancia más olorosa;
luego es mejor flor la rosa,
y el jazmín menos suave.
Tú, que rosa y jazmín ves,
admites la pompa breve
del jazmín, fragante nieve
que un soplo al céfiro es;
mas conociendo después
la altiva lisonja hermosa
de la rosa codiciosa,
la antepondrás a mi amor,

DON JUAN Speak, for I am listening.

DOÑA LEONOR He who in night's dark shadow walks,
adores the pure light of the planet Venus as it wanders;
only in its light is hope assured
of some guide, and although the
rays of the sun already reach him,
he is grateful to the planet Venus
for it has been the fair weather
in the midst of his storm.
You, in the dark comparison
of the night to your love,
the planet Venus of Leonor was north on your compass of pains;
she guided you but you, ingrate,
had forgotten the spark of her clear
and beautiful light before you loved my rosy skies.
Do you see how without seeing
the sun you abhorred the star?

LUDOVICO Curious metaphor it was,
Estela, to compare the rose to
Don Juan for his charm and valor.

ESTELA You deceive yourself.

LUDOVICO Listen, I implore you!
He who chose the jasmine
in the garden was not discreet;
it has no perfect odor if it withers;
the rose, so that its love may
continue its praise, has scent sweet and profound,
a fragrance so perfumed,
until its end;
so the better flower is the rose,
and the jasmine is less fine.
You, who see both rose and
jasmine, admit the brief splendor
of the jasmine, fragrant snow
that in an instant is nothing;
but later knowing the beautiful
haughty flattery of the greedy rose,
you will prefer it to my love,

	que es el jazmín poca flor,
	mucha fragancia la rosa.
DON JUAN	¡Sofístico argumento!
DOÑA LEONOR	Perdonad; yo os he dicho lo que siento.
	Volved, volved a España,
	que no es honrosa hazaña
	burlar una mujer ilustre y noble.
DON JUAN	Por sólo amaros, la aborrece al doble
	mi voluntad, y ved qué premio alcanza.
DOÑA LEONOR	Pues perded la esperanza;
	que sólo os he llamado
	por dejaros, don Juan, desengañado.
ESTELA	¡Fáciles paradojas
	íntimas, don Leonardo, a mis congojas!
	Yo he de quererte firme,
	sin poder persuadirme
	a que deje de amar, desdicha alguna.
LUDOVICO	Triunfo seré dichoso de fortuna,
	o ya jazmín o rosa.
ESTELA	Adiós, que sale ya la aurora hermosa
	entre luz y arreboles.
LUDOVICO	No os vais, para que envidie vuestros soles.
ESTELA	Lisonjas. Vedme luego,
	y adiós.

(Vase Estela.)

LUDOVICO	Sin vuestros rayos quedo ciego.
DON JUAN	¡Que así se fuese Estela! ¿Hay tal despecho?
	El corazón da golpes en el pecho
	por dejar la prisión en que se halla;
	la vida muere en la civil batalla
	de sus propios deseos.
	Al alma afligen locos devaneos,
	y un confuso caos está dudando;
	la culpa desto tiene don Fernando.
	¿Qué haré, Estela ingrata?
LUDOVICO	Aunque tan mal me trata
	tu amor, ingrata Estela,
	mi engaño o mi cautela,
	ya que no el adorarte,
	en mis dichas tendrá la mayor parte.

(Vase.)

DON JUAN	Mas, ¿cómo desconfío?
	¿Dónde está mi valor? ¿Dónde mi brío?
	Yo he de seguir esta amorosa empresa,

	the rose is most fragrant,
	the jasmine, of short duration.
DON JUAN	What sophistry!
DOÑA LEONOR	Forgive me, I have told you what I feel.
	Return, return to Spain, for it is no honorable deed
	to mock an illustrious and noble woman.
DON JUAN	My will abhors her doubly for love of you,
	and you shall see what the reward will be.
DOÑA LEONOR	Give up hope, for I have
	only called on you, Don Juan,
	to leave you disillusioned.
ESTELA	To my sorrow, Don Leonardo,
	you speak easy paradoxes!
	My misfortune is that I must love you steadily
	without being able to persuade myself to stop loving you.
LUDOVICO	Whether it be rose or jasmine,
	I will be triumphant in my good fortune.
ESTELA	Good-bye, the beautiful dawn is now
	appearing amidst bright and rosy clouds.
LUDOVICO	Stay awhile, let her envy your suns.
ESTELA	Flattery. Look for me later, and adieu.

(Exit Estela.)

LUDOVICO	I am blind without your rays.
DON JUAN	That Estela left thus! Is there
	greater dejection? My heart beats in my breast
	pleading to leave the prison where it finds itself;
	life dies in the civil war of its own desires.
	Mad delirium troubles my soul,
	and a confused chaos of doubt arises;
	all this is Don Fernando's doing.
	What shall I do, ungrateful Estela?
LUDOVICO	Although your love treats me badly,
	ungrateful Estela, I cannot stop adoring you,
	and whether it is my illusion or my good luck,
	one or the other
	will have the main part of my fortune.

(Exit Ludovico.)

DON JUAN	But, where is my confidence?
	Where is my courage? Where is my spirit?
	I must continue this romantic endeavor,

yo he de amar la Condesa,
yo he de oponerme firme a todo el mundo,
yo he de hacer que mi afecto sin segundo
conquiste sus desdenes;
yo he de adorar sus males por mis bienes.
Confiéranse en mi daño
ira, enojo, tibieza, desengaño,
odio, aborrecimiento;
apóquese la vida en el tormento
de mi pena importuna,
que si ayuda fortuna
al que osado se atreve,
sea la vida breve,
y el tormento crecido.
Osado y atrevido,
con firmeza resuelta,
de su inconstancia me opondré a la vuelta.

Jornada Tercera

(Salen don Fernando y don Juan.)

DON FERNANDO   Si para satisfaceros
a mi crédito importara
dar al peligro la vida,
arrojar al riesgo el alma,
no dudéis, don Juan, lo hiciera.
¿Yo a Estela? Mi propia espada
me mate si...

DON JUAN   Don Fernando,
paso: mil veces mal haya
quien malquistó tantas dichas,
dando a tantos males causa.
Yo os creo; mas ¡vive Dios,
que no sé que en Flandes haya
hombre que sepa mi historia!

DON FERNANDO   En mi valor fuera infamia,
cuanto más en mi afición
que se precia muy de hidalga
y amante vuestra.

DON JUAN   Es agravio,
después de desengañada
la mía, satisfacerme.
¡Por Dios, que me sangra a pausas
la pena de no saber
quién tan descompuesto habla

I must love the Countess,
I must firmly stand up to the whole world,
I must make my affection, which has no
equal, conquer her disdain; my good
qualities must adore her defects.
Rage, anger, indifference, disillusion,
hatred, abhorrence have been bestowed
on my injury;
my life's to be humbled in torment;
this vexes my grief,
for if fortune helps him, who boldly
dares, though his life be shorter
and torment greater.
Bold and daring, with determined
firmness, I will return to oppose
her inconstancy.

Act 3

(*Enter Don Fernando and Don Juan.*)

DON FERNANDO   If I had to risk my life and
soul to satisfy you as to my
reputation, have no doubt, Don Juan,
I would do it. I to Estela disclose
confidences? May my own sword
kill me if . . .

DON JUAN   Don Fernando, I shall go on: a thousand
times may someone have set himself
against so much happiness and caused
so many evils. I believe you, but for
the life of God I know of no man in
Flanders who knows my tale!

DON FERNANDO   It would have profaned my worth,
no less my affection,
which I hold noble
in my love for you.

DON JUAN   Satisfaction itself outrages me
after suffering such scorn.
By God, the misery of not knowing who was so wild
as to speak of my affairs makes me feel as though
I were slowly bleeding to death.

de mis cosas! ¡Yo estoy loco!
¡Qué de penas, miedos y ansias
me afligen.

DON FERNANDO   Estela viene.

(Salen Estela y Lisarda.)

DON JUAN   Inquieta la espera el alma;
no le digáis nada vos.

DON FERNANDO   Estela hermosa, Lisarda
bella, hoy amanece tarde,
pues juntas el sol y el alba
venís.

LISARDA   Hipérbole nueva.

DON JUAN   No es nueva, pues siempre abrasa
el sol de Estela, y da luz
vuestro rostro, aurora clara.

ESTELA   Señor don Juan, bueno está.
¿Tantas veces obligada
a valor y a cortesías
queréis que esté?

DON JUAN   Mi desgracia
jamás acierta a agradaros,
pues siempre esquiva e ingrata
me castigáis.

ESTELA   No, don Juan;
ingrata, no; descuidada
puedo haber sido en serviros.

DON JUAN   Vuestros descuidos me matan.

ESTELA   Siempre soy vuestra, don Juan;
y quiera Dios que yo valga
para serviros. Veréis
cuán agradecida paga
mi voluntad vuestro afecto.

DON JUAN   Don Fernando, ¡gran mudanza!

DON FERNANDO   ¿Ves cómo estás engañado?
(Aparte) Hoy mis intentos acaban.

DON JUAN   Decidme ¡por vida vuestra!
una verdad.

ESTELA   Preguntalda.

DON JUAN   ¿Diréisla?

ESTELA   Sí, ¡por mi vida!

DON JUAN   ¿Quién os dijo que en España
serví, enamoré y gocé
a Doña Leonor, la dama
de Sevilla?

I am mad! Grief, fear, and anxiety torment me!

DON FERNANDO Estela is coming.

(Enter Estela and Lisarda.)

DON JUAN My soul restlessly awaits her;
say nothing to her.

DON FERNANDO Beautiful Estela, fair Lisarda,
sunrise is late today, for the sun
and dawn have just arrived.

LISARDA A new hyperbole.

DON JUAN New 'tis not, as the sun of Estela
always glows, and your face
is a clear, light-giving dawn.

ESTELA Señor Don Juan, how fine you are.
How many times do you intend
to place me in your debt
for your valor and your courtesy?

DON JUAN My disgrace never manages to
be agreeable to you since you,
cold and ungrateful, always
punish me.

ESTELA Nay, Don Juan, ungrateful no;
I may have been careless in serving you.

DON JUAN Your carelessness kills me.

ESTELA I am yours always, Don Juan,
and God will that I may be worthy
to serve you. You will see how gratefully
my goodwill repays your affection.

DON JUAN What a great change, Don Fernando!

DON FERNANDO You see how deceived you are?
(Aside) Today my attempts are finished.

DON JUAN By your life, tell me the truth!

ESTELA Ask me.

DON JUAN Will you tell me?

ESTELA I swear by my life, yes!

DON JUAN Who told you that in Spain
I served, loved, and enjoyed
Doña Leonor, the lady of Seville?

ESTELA   ¿Quién? Vos mismo.

DON JUAN   ¿Yo? ¿Cuándo?

ESTELA   ¿Ahora no acaba
de despertar vuestra lengua
desengaño en mi ignorancia?

DON JUAN   Y antes, ¿quién?

ESTELA   Nadie, a fe mía.

DON JUAN   Pues, ¿cómo tan enojada
me hablasteis en el terrero
la otra noche?

ESTELA   ¿Oyes, Lisarda?
Don Juan dice que le hablé.

LISARDA   Bien claro está que se engaña.

DON JUAN   ¿Cómo engaño? ¿No dijisteis
que una dama sevillana
fue trofeo de mi amor?

ESTELA   Don Juan, para burla basta,
que no lo sé hasta ahora,
no, ¡por quien soy! ni palabra
os hablé desto en mi vida
en terrero ni en ventana.

DON JUAN   *(Aparte)* ¡Vive el cielo, que estoy loco!
Sin duda Estela me ama
y quiere disimular
por don Fernando y Lisarda;
porque negar que me dijo
verdades tan declaradas,
no carece de misterio.
Ea, amor, ¡al arma, al arma!
Pensamientos amorosos,
volvamos a la batalla,
pues está animando Estela
vuestras dulces esperanzas.
Yo quiero disimular.
Perdonad, que me burlaba
por entretener el tiempo.

DON FERNANDO La burla ha sido extremada,
mas pienso que contra vos.

LISARDA   ¿Era, don Juan, vuestra dama
muy hermosa? Porque tienen
las sevillanas gran fama.

DON JUAN   Todo fue burla, ¡por Dios!

ESTELA   Si acaso quedó burlada,
burla sería don Juan.

ESTELA	Who? You yourself.
DON JUAN	I? When?
ESTELA	Has not your tongue just now
	awakened me from the illusion
	of my ignorance?
DON JUAN	And before, who?
ESTELA	No one, by my faith.
DON JUAN	Then why spoke you to me
	with so much anger
	last night on the terrace?
ESTELA	Do you hear, Lisarda?
	Don Juan says that I spoke with him.
LISARDA	It is quite clear that he deceives himself.
DON JUAN	Deceived how? Did you not say that
	a Sevillian lady was a trophy of my love?
ESTELA	Don Juan, that is mockery enough.
	I knew nothing until now, no, by my being,
	not a word did you speak of this ever on the terrace
	or at my window.
DON JUAN	(*Aside*) For the love of heaven, I must be mad!
	Without doubt Estela loves me and
	wishes to pretend in front of Don Fernando
	and Lisarda that she never heard these
	truths declared; well, there is no mystery in that.
	Oh love, to arms, to arms!
	With loving thoughts, let us return
	to battle, since Estela is enlivening
	your sweet hopes. I wish to pretend.
	Forgive me, I was joking
	to amuse myself and pass the time.
DON FERNANDO	The joke went too far,
	but I think the joke's on you.
LISARDA	Was your lady, Don Juan, very beautiful?
	The women of Seville have great fame.
DON JUAN	It was all in jest, by God!
ESTELA	If she was seduced,
	what jest is that, Don Juan!

DON JUAN   No, a fe. ¡Quién imaginara
              este suceso? ¡Oh amor!
              ¿Qué es esto que por mí pasa?
              Ya me favorece Estela,
              ya me despide, y se agravia
              de que la pretenda ya.
              Me obliga y me desengaña,
              ya niega el favorecerme,
              ya se muestra afable y grata;
              y yo, incontrastable roca
              al furor se sus mudanzas,
              mar que siempre crece en olas,
              no me canso en adorarla.

DON FERNANDO Sabe el cielo cuánto estimo
              que favorezcáis mi causa
              por lo que quiero a don Juan.
              (Aparte) Este equívoco declara
              amor a la bella Estela.
              Y así os pido, a quien hablara
              por sí mismo, que le honréis.
              ¡Oh amistad, y cuánto allanas!

ESTELA   Yo hablaré con vos después.
              Don Juan, tened con las damas
              más firme correspondencia.

DON JUAN   Injustamente me agravia
              vuestro desdén, bella Estela.

ESTELA   Leonor fue la agraviada.

DON JUAN   (Aparte) No quiero dar a entender
              que la entiendo, pues se cansa
              de verme Estela. Fernando,
              vamos.

DON FERNANDO   Venid. ¡Qué enojada
              la tenéis! Adiós, señoras.

ESTELA   Adiós. ¿Hay más sazonada
              quimera?

LISARDA   ¿Qué es esto, prima?

ESTELA   No sé, ¡por tu vida! Aguarda;
              curiosidad de mujer
              es ésta. A Tomillo llama,
              que él nos dirá la verdad.

LISARDA   Dices bien. Tomillo. . .
(Sale Tomillo.)

TOMILLO   ¿Mandas
              en qué te pueda servir?

DON JUAN	No, by faith!
	Who could imagine
	such a thing? Oh love! What is
	happening to me? Estela favors first
	and then dismisses me,
	offended by my wooing.
	She obliges me and spurns me,
	now refuses me her favor,
	now seems affable and charming;
	and I, to the fury
	of her changing moods
	am an unshakable rock,
	a sea whose waves increase;
	my adoration of her tires not.
DON FERNANDO	Heaven knows how much I wish
	you to favor my cause,
	for all Don Juan is dear to me.
	(Aside) This blunderer declares his love
	to the beautiful Estela.
	And thus I ask of you,
	who would speak for himself,
	that you honor that cause.
	Oh, friendship, how you smooth the path!
ESTELA	I will speak with you anon.
	Don Juan, have with the ladies
	firmer correspondence.
DON JUAN	Unjustly does your disdain
	injure me, fair Estela.
ESTELA	Leonor was the injured party.
DON JUAN	*(Aside)* I want Estela not to know I understand,
	lest she weary of seeing me.
	Let us go, Fernando.
DON FERNANDO	Come. How angry you have made her.
	Good day, ladies.
ESTELA	Good day. How bizarre that was!
LISARDA	What was that all about, cousin?
ESTELA	For the life of me, I know not.
	Wait, this woman's curiosity
	wants satisfaction. Call Tomillo;
	he will tell us the truth.
LISARDA	You are right. Tomillo . . .
(Enter Tomillo.)	
TOMILLO	How may I serve you?

ESTELA

> Si una verdad me declaras,
> aqueste bolsillo es tuyo.

TOMILLO

> Ea, pregunta.

ESTELA

>   ¿Quién fue,
> dime, una Leonor que hablaba
> don Juan en Sevilla?

TOMILLO

>   ¿Quién?
> ¡Ah, sí! ¡Ah, sí! No me acordaba:
> Norilla la Cantonera,
> que vivía en Cantarranas
> de resellar cuartos falsos.
> ¿No dices, a cuya casa
> iba don Juan?

ESTELA

>   Sí, será.

TOMILLO

> (Aparte) ¡Qué dulcemente se engaña!

ESTELA

> ¿Qué mujer era?

TOMILLO

>   No era
> mujer, sino una fantasma:
> ancha de frente, y angosta
> de sienes, cejiencorvada.

ESTELA

> El parabién del empleo
> pienso darle.

LISARDA

>   Yo la vaya.
> Y ¿la quería?

TOMILLO

>   No sé;
> sólo sé que se alababa
> ella de ser su respecto.

ESTELA

> ¿Hay tal hombre?

TOMILLO

>   ¿Esto te espanta?
> ¿No sabes que le parece
> hermosa quien sea dama?

ESTELA

> Dices bien; éste es Leonardo.

TOMILLO

> Yo le he dado por su carta.

(Sale doña Leonor.)

DOÑA LEONOR

> Preguntéle a mi cuidado,
> Estela hermosa, por mí,
> y respondióme que en ti
> me pudiera haber hallado;
> dudó la dicha, el temor
> venció, al temor la humildad,
> alentóse la verdad,
> y aseguróme el amor.
> Busquéme en ti, y declaré
> en mi dicha el silogismo,

ESTELA	If you tell me one truth,
	this purse will be yours.
TOMILLO	Ask me, then.
ESTELA	Tell me, who was this Leonor
	Don Juan courted in Seville?
TOMILLO	Who? Oh, yes. I had forgotten.
	Nora the Hussy, who lived near the Bog,
	and made her living counterfeiting coins. Do you mean
	the one whose house Don Juan would visit?
ESTELA	Yes, that may be.
TOMILLO	*(Aside)* How sweetly she's deceived!
ESTELA	What sort of woman was she?
TOMILLO	She was no woman, but a ghoul:
	a wide forehead, and long face,
	with crooked eyebrows.
ESTELA	I think to congratulate him on this.
LISARDA	And he loved her?
TOMILLO	I know not. I only know
	she bragged of his respect.
ESTELA	Might there be such a man?
TOMILLO	Does this shock you?
	Do you not know he likes the shape
	of anything in skirts?
ESTELA	Well said.
	Here comes Leonardo.
TOMILLO	I have told you what I know.

(Enter Doña Leonor.)

DOÑA LEONOR	I asked my cares, Estela fair,
	where I might be, and they replied
	that I might find myself in you.
	They doubted happiness, and gave way
	to fear, then fear to humility.
	Truth took heart and love assured me.
	I sought myself
	and declared the syllogism

pues no hallándome en mí mismo,
en tus ojos me hallé.

ESTELA   Haberte, Leonardo, hallado
en mis ojos, imagino
que no acredita de fino
de tu desvelo el cuidado;
y no parezcan antojos,
pues viene a estar de mi parte,
por mi afecto, el retratarte
siempre mi amor en mis ojos;
que claro está que mayor
fineza viniera a ser
que en ti me pudieras ver
por transformación de amor;
que sin mí hallarte en mí,
pues con eso me apercibes
que sin mis memorias vives,
pues no me hallas en ti.
Que es consecuencia notoria,
que si me quisieras bien,
como estás en mí, también
estuviera en tu memoria.

DOÑA LEONOR   Aunque más tu lengua intime
esa engañosa opinión,
no tiene el amante acción
que en lo que ama no se anime;
si amor de veras inflama
un pecho, alienta y respira
transformado en lo que mira,
animado en lo que ama.
Yo, aunque sé que estás en mí,
en fe de mi amor, no creo,
si en tus ojos no me veo,
que merezco estar en ti.

ESTELA   En fin, no te hallas sin verme.

DOÑA LEONOR   Como no está el merecer
de mi parte, sé querer,
pero no satisfacerme.

ESTELA   Y ¿es amor desconfiar?

LISARDA   Es, al menos, discreción.

DOÑA LEONOR   No hay en mí satisfacción
de que me puedas amar
si mis partes considero.

ESTELA   ¡Injusta desconfianza!

in my joy, for not finding me
in my own self, I found myself in your eyes.

ESTELA   Having found yourself, Leonardo,
in my eyes does not, I imagine,
credit with refinement
your sleepless nights of care.
And may my eyes
seem not flights of fancy,
as, due to my affection,
it is on my account
that my love paints your portrait
ever in my eyes.
Truly it would be a greater kindness
that in yourself you might see me,
by love's transformation;
for without me to find you in me,
since thus would you advise me,
without my memory you live,
for you find me not in you.
Such is the notorious consequence,
that if you loved me well,
as you are in me, would I also be
in your memory.

DOÑA LEONOR   Although your tongue conveys
that false opinion,
the lover makes no move
not inspired by the one he loves.
If a breast be truly inflamed by love,
it breathes transformed into what it sees,
come to life in what it loves.
I, although I know you are in me,
on my love's faith would not believe,
if in your eyes I saw not myself,
that I am worthy to be in you.

ESTELA   And so, you do not find
yourself without seeing me?

DOÑA LEONOR   As worthiness is not
in me, I can love
but not be satisfied.

ESTELA   And is love distrust?

LISARDA   It is, at least, discretion.

DOÑA LEONOR   I cannot be satisfied
that you might love me
if my parts do I consider.

ESTELA   Unjust mistrust!

Alentad más la esperanza
en los méritos. Yo quiero
salir al campo esta tarde;
sigue la carroza.

DOÑA LEONOR   Ajusto
a tu obediencia mi gusto.

ESTELA   Pues queda adiós.

(Vanse.)

DOÑA LEONOR   Él te guarde.
En males tan declarados,
en daños tan descubiertos,
los peligros hallo ciertos,
los remedios ignorados.
No sé por dónde ¡ay de mí!
acabar: amor intenta
la tragedia de mi afrenta.

(Sale don Juan.)

DON JUAN   Sí, estaba Leonardo aquí;
parece que le halló
la fuerza de mi deseo.

DOÑA LEONOR   ¡Qué ha de tener otro empleo,
y yo burlada! ¡Eso no;
primero pienso morir!

DON JUAN   Señor don Leonardo. . .

DOÑA LEONOR   Amigo. . .
(Aparte) ¡Pluguiera a Dios que lo fueras!
Mas eres hombre. ¿En qué os sirvo?

DON JUAN   Favorecerme podréis;
mas escuchad: yo he venido,
como a noble, a suplicaros,
como a quien sois, a pediros. . .

DOÑA LEONOR   ¡Ah, falso! ¿Cómo a muy vuestro
no decís, siendo el camino
más cierto para mandarme?

DON JUAN   Conózcoos por señor mío,
y, concluyendo argumentos,
quiero de una vez decirlo,
pues Estela me animó:
la Condesa. . .

DOÑA LEONOR   ¡Buen principio!
Ea, pasad adelante.

DON JUAN   La condesa Estela, digo,
o ya por gusto, o ya
porque dio forzoso indicio

	Encourage hope in your merits.
	I plan to go to the country this
	afternoon; follow the coach.
DOÑA LEONOR	I conform my desire to your will.
ESTELA	Farewell, then.

(Exit Estela and Lisarda.)

DOÑA LEONOR	May God keep you. In such
	apparent evil, in harm
	so evident, I find danger certain
	and the cure unknown.
	Oh me! I know not where to finish;
	love guides the tragedy of my affront.

(Enter Don Juan.)

DON JUAN	Yes, Leonardo was here;
	it seems that the force of
	my desire found him.
DOÑA LEONOR	It should have some other use
	than mocking me! I'd rather die than that!
DON JUAN	Señor Don Leonardo . . .
DOÑA LEONOR	Friend . . .
	(Aside) If it only pleased God that you were!
	But you are a man.
	How may I serve you?
DON JUAN	Grant me a service, if you will;
	Mark: I have come to you
	as a nobleman, to beg of you,
	as what you are, to ask of you . . .
DOÑA LEONOR	Oh, traitor! Why say you not
	you ask me as your own,
	being, to command me,
	the surest way.
DON JUAN	I know you as my lord,
	and, coming to the point,
	I wish to say this, once and for all,
	for Estela has encouraged me:
	the Countess . . .
DOÑA LEONOR	A good beginning!
	Pray, continue.
DON JUAN	The Countess Estela, I say,
	either as a whim, or because my bravery,
	on that occasion that you know
	gave her strong indication of my vigor,

mi valor en la ocasión
que ya sabéis, de mis bríos,
puso los ojos en mí.
Es mujer, no fue delito;
viose obligada, bastó,
porque el común desvarío
de las mujeres, comienza
por afecto agradecido.
Dio ocasión a mis desvelos,
dio causa a mis desatinos,
aliento a mis esperanzas,
acogida a mis suspiros;
de suerte que me juzgué
dueño feliz ¡qué delirio!
de su belleza y su estado.
De España a este tiempo mismo
vinisteis, siendo a sus ojos
vuestra gallardía hechizo,
que suspendió de mis dichas
los amorosos principios.
A los semblantes de Estela
Argos velador he sido,[19]
sacando de cierta ciencia,
que sus mudables indicios
acreditan que me estima;
y así, Leonardo, os suplico,
si algo os obliga mi ruego,
por lo que debe a sí mismo
quien es noble como vos
que deis a mi pena alivio,
dejando su pretensión,
pues anterior habéis visto
la mía, y con tanta fuerza
de heroicos empeños míos.
Haced por mí esta fineza,
porque nos rotule el siglo,
si por generoso a vos,
a mí por agradecido.

DOÑA LEONOR   (Aparte) ¡Ah, ingrato, mal caballero!
¡Bien corresponde tu estilo
a quien eres! Vuestras penas,
señor don Juan, habéis dicho
con tal afecto, tal ansia,
que quisiera ¡por Dios vivo!

cast her eyes upon me.
She is a woman, it was no offense;
she saw herself obliged and that sufficed,
because the common foolishness of women
begins with grateful affection.
It deprived me of sleep, it caused my follies,
gave breath to my hopes,
and shelter to my sighs;
and chance had it that I judged
myself the happy owner—what delusion!—
of her beauty and her being.
You came from Spain at this time,
and being in her eyes of such bewitching charm
that the good fortune of my love's
beginnings was suspended.
Like Argus,[19] I have been watching Estela's mien,
finding with certain science
that her changeable signs indicate she esteems me;
and thus, Leonardo, I ask you if my plea may persuade you,
for that which you owe yourself,
for one who is as noble as you,
give relief to my pain, leaving your suit
because you have seen that mine preceded it
and mine insists with much heroic strength.
Do for me this kindness;
as the century goes round,
if you are generous, I will be grateful.

DOÑA LEONOR (*Aside*) Oh, vile, ungrateful gentleman!
Your manner corresponds
so well with what you are!
Your pain, señor Don Juan, have you voiced
with such feeling, such anxiousness,
as God lives, I would fain

> (*Aparte*) poder sacaros el alma
> dar a su cuidado alivio.
> Confieso que la Condesa
> una y mil veces me ha dicho
> que ha de ser mía, y que soy
> el dueño de su albedrío,
> a quien amorosa ofrece
> por víctima y sacrificio
> sus acciones, mas ¿qué importa,
> si diferentes motivos,
> si firmes obligaciones,
> si lazos de amor altivos,
> me tienen rendida el alma?
> Que otra vez quisiera, digo,
> por hacer algo por vos
> como quien soy, por serviros
> y daros gusto, querer
> a Estela, y haberle sido
> muy amante, y muy fiel;
> mas creed que en nada os sirvo,
> pues mis dulces pensamientos
> me tienen tan divertido,
> que en ellos está mi gloria;
> y así, don Juan, imagino
> que nada hago por vos.

DON JUAN
> ¿Es posible que ha podido
> tan poco con vos Estela?

DOÑA LEONOR
> Si no basta a persuadiros
> mi verdad, este retrato,
> diga si es objeto digno
> de mis finezas. (*Aparte*) Ahora,
> ingrato, llega el castigo
> de tanto aborrecimiento.

DON JUAN
> ¡Válgame el cielo! ¿Qué miro?

DOÑA LEONOR
> Mirad si esa perfección,
> aquese garbo, ese aliño,
> ese donaire, ese agrado. . .

DON JUAN
> ¡Perdiendo estoy el juicio!

DOÑA LEONOR
> . . .merecen que yo le olvide
> por Estela.

DON JUAN
>   Basilisco
> mortal ha sido a mis ojos:
> parece que en él he visto
> la cabeza de Medusa,

(*aside*) tear out your soul
give your cares relief.
I confess that the Countess
has told me a thousand and one times that she will be mine,
and that I am the master of her will,
of her, who lovingly offers by her action
to be victim or sacrifice,
but what matters that if different motives,
if firm obligations, if ties of the highest love
have my soul in their power?
Again, I say, that it would please me,
as a favor to you
because of who I am,
to serve and give you pleasure,
to love Estela and to have been
her fine and faithful lover.
But think you not that I might help you,
for my sweet thoughts have me so distracted,
and in them is my glory,
and thus, Don Juan, I imagine
that there is nothing I can do for you.

DON JUAN   Is it possible that Estela has
meant so little to you?

DOÑA LEONOR   If it is not enough to persuade
you of my truth, this portrait
will say what a worthy object
she is of my kindnesses.
(*Aside*) Now, ingrate, suffer
the punishment that so much
abhorrence has begotten.

DON JUAN   Heaven bless me! What do I see?

DOÑA LEONOR   See if that perfection, that
elegance, that attractiveness,
that grace, that charm . . .

DON JUAN   I am losing my sanity!

DOÑA LEONOR   . . . all truly deserve to be
forgotten for Estela.

DON JUAN   A deadly basilisk has looked into my eyes:
it seems that in it I have seen Medusa's head,

	que en piedra me ha convertido,[20]
	que me ha quitado la vida.
DOÑA LEONOR	*(Aparte)* De conveniencias y arbitrios
	debe de tratar. Parece
	que estáis suspenso.
DON JUAN	Imagino
	que vi otra vez esta dama,
	¡ah, cielos! y que fue mío
	este retrato. *(Aparte)* Rindióse
	esta vez a los peligros
	de la verdad la razón.
DOÑA LEONOR	Advertid que le he traído
	de España, y que es de una dama
	a quien deben mis sentidos
	la gloria de un dulce empeño,
	y a cuyas dichas, si vivo,
	sucederán de Himeneo
	los lazos alternativos,[21]
	para cuya ejecución
	a Bruselas he venido,
	pues no he de poder casarme
	si primero no castigo
	con un rigor un agravio,
	con una muerte un delito.
DON JUAN	*(Aparte)* ¿Qué es esto que por mí pasa?
	¿Es posible que he tenido
	valor para oír mi afrenta?
	¿Cómo de una vez no rindo
	a la infamia los discursos,
	la vida, a los desperdicios
	del honor? Leonor fue fácil;
	y a los números lascivos
	de infame, ¿tanta lealtad,
	fe tan pura, ha reducido?
	Mas fue con nombre de esposo.
	Aquí de vosotros mismos,
	celos, que ya la disculpo;
	yo sólo el culpado he sido.
	Yo la dejé, yo fui ingrato.
	¿Qué he de hacer en el abismo
	de tan grandes confusiones?
	Doña Leonor. . .
DOÑA LEONOR	*(Aparte)* A partido
	quiere darse ya este aleve.

	that I have turned to stone,
	that my life has been taken.[20]
DOÑA LEONOR	(*Aside*) These must be plots and schemes.
	It seems you are taken aback.
DON JUAN	I imagined that once before I saw this lady,
	oh heaven! and that this portrait was mine.
	(*Aside*) Now has reason
	surrendered to the dangers of truth.
DOÑA LEONOR	Take notice that I have brought this from Spain,
	and that it is a lady
	to whom my feelings owe the glory of a sweet endeavor,
	and to whose charms, if I live,
	I will be bound by Hymen;[21]
	I have come to Brussels to assure the execution of my task;
	I cannot marry if first I do not punish with severity
	an offense, with a death this injury.
DON JUAN	(*Aside*) What is this that is happening to me?
	Might I have been given strength
	but to hear my disgrace?
	Why do I not give protest to this infamy,
	give up life to the spoils of honor?
	Leonor was wanton;
	has so much loyalty and pure faith been reduced
	to the lewd litany of the vile?
	But it was done in the name of husband.
	Here before you, jealousy, I forgive her now;
	I have been the only guilty one.
	I left her, I was ungrateful.
	What shall I do in the abyss of
	such great confusion?
	Doña Leonor . . .
DOÑA LEONOR	(*Aside*) This traitor wants to play.

¿Qué decís?

DON JUAN   No sé qué digo:
que me abraso en rabia y celos,
que estoy en un laberinto
donde no es posible hallar,
si no es con mi muerte, el hilo,
pues Leonor no fue Ariadna.[22]
En este retrato he visto
mi muerte.

DOÑA LEONOR   *(Aparte)*   ¡Ah, bárbaro, ingrato,
tan ciego, tan divertido
estás que no me conoces!
¿Hay más loco desatino,
que el original no mira,
y el retrato ha conocido?
Tal le tienen sus engaños.

DON JUAN   Mal mis pesares resisto.
¿Qué empeños de amor debéis
a esta dama?

DOÑA LEONOR   He merecido
sus brazos y sus favores;
a vuestro entender remito
lo demás.

DON JUAN   Ahora es tiempo,
locuras y desvaríos;
ahora, penas, ahora
no quede lugar vacío
en el alma; apoderaos
de potencias y sentidos;
Leonor fue común, desdichas;
rompa mi silencio a gritos
el respeto. Esa mujer,
ese monstruo, ese prodigio
de facilidad, fue mía;
dejéla, y aborrecido,
pueden más celos que amor;
ya la adoro, ya me rindo
al rapaz arquero alado.[23]
Pero ni aun hallo camino
matándoos para vivir,
pues la ofensa que me hizo,
siempre vivirá en mis oídos;
¿Quién imaginara el limpio
honor de Leonor manchado?

	What say you?
DON JUAN	I know not what I am saying;
	I burn with rage and jealousy,
	I am in a labyrinth and only my death
	will lead me to the thread,
	as Leonor was no Ariadne.[22]
	I have seen my death in this portrait.
DOÑA LEONOR	*(Aside)* Oh, brute, ingrate, you are so blind,
	so distracted that you recognize me not!
	Is there madder folly than to recognize the portrait
	and not to see the original?
	Thus do his illusions blind him.
DON JUAN	Ill do I resist my woes.
	What obligations of love owe you to this lady?
DOÑA LEONOR	I have earned her embrace and
	won her favor; I leave the rest
	to your imagination.
DON JUAN	Now is the time of madness
	and distraction, sorrows now,
	and there remains no vacant
	spot in my soul free of them;
	take hold of strength and reason:
	break my silence with loud cries;
	Leonor was base, alas!
	That woman, that monster,
	that epitome of wantonness,
	was mine; I left her, now abhorred,
	jealousy does more than love;
	I now adore her, I now surrender
	to the winged, rapacious archer.[23]
	But I cannot find the way to kill you so I might live,
	for the offense that she did me
	will always speak itself to me.
	Who could imagine the clean
	honor of Leonor stained?

DOÑA LEONOR   *(Aparte)* Declaróse este testigo,
    aunque en mi contra, en mi abono.
    Todo lo que sabe ha dicho;
    mas apretemos la cuerda.
    ¿De suerte que mi enemigo
     sois vos, don Juan?

DON JUAN   Sí, Leonardo.

DOÑA LEONOR   ¡Que jamás Leonor me dijo
    vuestro nombre! Quizá fue
    porque el ilustre apellido
    de Córdoba no quedase
    en lo ingrato obscurecido.
    Sólo dijo que en Bruselas
    os hallaría, y que aviso
    tendría en sus mismas cartas
    del nombre, y es buena ocasión
    para mataros.

(Sale don Fernando.)

DON FERNANDO   Mi primo
    y don Juan, de pesadumbre. . .

DON JUAN   ¡Don Fernando!

DOÑA LEONOR   ¿Si habrá oído
    lo que hablábamos?

DON JUAN   No sé;
    sépalo el mundo.

DOÑA LEONOR   Yo digo
    que os podré matar, don Juan,
    si no hacéis punto fijo
    en guardar aqueste punto.

DON JUAN   Jamás a esos puntos sigo,
    cuando me enojo, Leonardo.

DOÑA LEONOR   Yo tampoco cuando riño,
    porque el valor me gobierna,
    no del arte los caprichos,
    ángulos rectos o curvos;
    mas a don Luis he visto,
    de Narváez, el famoso.

DON FERNANDO   Los ojos y los oídos
    se engañan. Don Juan, Leonardo,
    ¿de qué habláis?

DOÑA LEONOR   Del ejercicio
    de las armas.

DON FERNANDO   ¿Cómo estáis,
    don Juan, tan descolorido?

DOÑA LEONOR	*(Aside)* Though this witness declared
	himself against me, he has spoken on my behalf.
	He has said all that he knows,
	but let us tighten the rope.
	Are you by any chance, Don Juan, my enemy?
DON JUAN	Yes, Leonardo.
DOÑA LEONOR	Leonor never told me your name!
	Perhaps it was so that the illustrious
	name of Córdoba would not linger
	in forgotten darkness. She told me
	only that in Brussels I would find
	you, and by letter she would tell me
	your name, and now
	is the proper time to kill you.

(Enter Don Fernando.)

DON FERNANDO	My cousin and Don Juan,
	quarreling . . .
DON JUAN	Don Fernando!
DOÑA LEONOR	Did he hear what we were saying?
DON JUAN	I know not; may the whole world know.
DOÑA LEONOR	I say that I will kill you,
	Don Juan, if you do not
	watch out for my sword's tip.
DON JUAN	I never follow tips as those
	when I am angry, Leonardo.
DOÑA LEONOR	Nor do I when I quarrel, for
	valor rules me and not art's whim,
	angles curved or straight,
	though I have seen the famous
	Don Luis of Narváez.
DON FERNANDO	My eyes and ears deceive me.
	Don Juan, Leonardo, what is it
	that you speak of?
DOÑA LEONOR	Of the exercise of weaponry.
DON FERNANDO	Why, Don Juan, are you so pale?

DON JUAN	En tratando de reñir,
	no puedo más, a honor mío.
	Leonardo, vedme.

(Yéndose.)

DOÑA LEONOR	Sí, haré,
	que he de seguir los principios
	de vuestra doctrina. *(Aparte)* ¡Ah, cielos!
DON JUAN	*(Aparte)* ¡Qué luego Fernando vino
	en esta ocasión!
DOÑA LEONOR	*(Aparte)* ¡Que en esta
	ocasión haya venido
	mi hermano! ¡Infelice soy!
DON JUAN	A los jardines de Armindo
	me voy esta tarde un rato.
	Venid, si queréis, conmigo,
	llevarán espadas negras.
DOÑA LEONOR	Iré con gusto excesivo.
DON JUAN	¿Quedáisos, Fernando?
DON FERNANDO	Sí.
DON JUAN	Pues adiós. Lo dicho, dicho,
	don Leonardo.
DOÑA LEONOR	Claro está.
DON FERNANDO	¿Fuese?
DOÑA LEONOR	Sí.
DON FERNANDO	Estela me dijo,
	no obstante que la pretende
	el Príncipe Ludovico
	de Pinoy, y que a don Juan
	debe estar agradecido
	su pecho, que sólo a ti
	inclina el desdén esquivo
	de su condición, de suerte...
DOÑA LEONOR	No prosigas.
DON FERNANDO	No prosigo,
	pues ya lo entiendes, Leonardo.
	A favor tan conocido,
	¿qué le puedes responder,
	sino desdeñoso, tibio?
	(Aparte) Sabe el cielo cuánto siento
	cuando de adorarla vivo,
	que me haga su tercero.
DOÑA LEONOR	Pues, Fernando, si he tenido
	acción al amor de Estela
	desde luego me desisto

DON JUAN	I cannot, on my honor, quarrel more.
	Leonardo, see me.

(He goes to him.)

DOÑA LEONOR	Aye, that I will; I must keep the
	principles of your doctrine.
	(Aside) Oh, heavens!
DON JUAN	*(Aside)* How lucky that Fernando came
	at this moment!
DOÑA LEONOR	*(Aside)* Why did my brother have to come at just this moment?
	How unhappy I am!
DON JUAN	I go to the gardens of Armindo
	to pass some time this afternoon.
	Come with me, if you wish.
	They will bear black swords.
DOÑA LEONOR	I will go with utmost pleasure.
DON JUAN	Stay you here, Fernando?
DON FERNANDO	Yes.
DON JUAN	Good-bye, then. What's said is said,
	Don Leonardo.
DOÑA LEONOR	To be sure.
DON FERNANDO	Has he gone?
DOÑA LEONOR	Yes.
DON FERNANDO	Estela told me, though
	Prince Ludovico of Pinoy
	courts her, and her heart owes
	Don Juan a debt of gratitude,
	it is, by chance, to you alone
	that her station's aloof disdain
	deigns to bow . . .
DOÑA LEONOR	Proceed no further.
DON FERNANDO	I shall not go on, as now
	you understand me, Leonardo.
	To such open favor how can
	you respond, but cooly and with scorn?
	(Aside) Heaven knows how I,
	who live only to adore her,
	am pained that she would make of me her go-between.
DOÑA LEONOR	Although, Fernando, I may have awakened Estela's love,
	I must, of course, desist from its pursuit.

de su pretensión.

DON FERNANDO   ¿Estáis
loco?

DOÑA LEONOR   No tengo juicio.
(Aparte) Deseando estoy que llegue
la tarde.

DON FERNANDO   De tus designios
quiero que me hagas dueño.

DOÑA LEONOR   Aún no es tiempo; *(Aparte)* divertirlo
quiero con algún engaño.
Ven conmigo.

DON FERNANDO   Voy contigo.

(Vanse, y sale Tomillo.)

TOMILLO   Después que bebí de aquel
negro chocolate, o mixto
de varias cosas, que Flora
me brindó, estoy aturdido;
los ojos no puedo abrir.

(Sale Flora.)

FLORA   Siguiendo vengo a Tomillo
por si ha obrado el chocolate.

TOMILLO   Doy al diablo lo que miro
si lo veo; aquí me acuesto
un rato.

(Échase.)

¡Qué bien mullido
está el suelo! No parece
sino que aposta se hizo
para quebrarme los huesos.
Esto es hecho; no he pedido
sustentar la competencia;
sueño, a tus fuerzas me rindo.

(Duerme.)

FLORA   Como una piedra ha quedado.
Lindamente ha obrado el pisto;
pero vamos al expolio,
en nombre de San Cirilo.

(Vale sacando de las faltriqueras.)

Comienzo: ésta es bigotera,
tendrá cuatrocientos siglos;
según parece, éste es
lienzo. ¡Qué blanco, qué limpio,
ostenta sucias ruinas
de tabaco y romadizo!

DON FERNANDO	Are you mad?
DOÑA LEONOR	I am quite out of my mind.
	(*Aside*) I am wishing the evening would arrive.
DON FERNANDO	Allow me, then, to know your plans.
DOÑA LEONOR	'Tis not yet time,
	(*Aside*) I wish to divert him
	with some deception.
	Come with me.
DON FERNANDO	With you I go.

(*Exeunt. Enter Tomillo.*)

TOMILLO
After drinking that black
chocolate or whatever mixture of
ingredients that Flora gave me,
I am quite dazed;
I cannot keep my eyes open.

(*Enter Flora.*)

FLORA
I am after Tomillo to see
if the chocolate's done its work.

TOMILLO
I'd give the devil all I see, if I could see it;
I'll lie down here awhile.

(*He lies down.*)

How nice and soft the ground is!
It seems as if it had been made
to break my bones. This is done;
I did not ask to win this game;
sleep, I surrender to your power.

(*He sleeps.*)

FLORA
He is sleeping like a stone.
The broth has worked nicely,
but let's to the loot,
by Saint Cyril's holy name.

(*She empties his pockets.*)

I begin: a moustache cover,
about four hundred centuries old.
This would be his handkerchief.
How whitely, how cleanly does it
show its stains of tobacco, and of snot.

Ésta es taba. ¡Gran reliquia
de mártir trae consigo
este menguado! Ésta es
baraja; devoto libro
de Fray Luis de Granada,
de oraciones y ejercicios.
El bolsillo no parece,
y de hallarle desconfío,
que en tan ilustres despojos
ni le hallo ni le miro.
¿Qué es aquesto? Tabaquera
de cuerno. ¡Qué hermoso aliño,
parto, al fin, de su cosecha,
honor de su frontispicio!
Hombres, ¡que aquesto os dé gusto!
Yo conozco cierto amigo
que se sorbió entre el tabaco
el polvo de dos ladrillos.
Doyle vuelta a estotro lado,
haré segundo escrutinio.

(Vuélvele.)

¡Cómo pesa el picarón!
¡San Onofre, San Patricio,
que no despierte! Éstas son
marañas de seda e hilo,
y el cigarro del tabaco,
que no se le escapa vicio
a este sucio, éste, sin duda,
es el precioso bolsillo,
a quien mis miedos consagro
y mis cuidados dedico.
¡Jesús, cuántos trapos tiene!

(Va quitando capas.)

Uno, dos, tres, cuatro, cinco,
seis, siete, ocho; es imposible
contar; mas ¡oh dulce archivo
de escudos y de esperanzas,
con reverencia te miro!

(Sácale.)

Depositario dichoso
de aquel metal atractivo
que a tantos Midas y Cresos
puede ocasionar delitos,
al corazón te traslado,

A knucklebone: the great relic
of some martyr this fool carries about!
Here's a deck of cards; Fray Luis de Granada's
book of devotions, full of prayers and exercises.
I do not see the purse
and I fear I'll find it not,
for in all this fine booty
I neither find nor see it.
What is this? A tobacco horn.
A charming ornament is this I reap,
the glory of his visage! Men, to think
this gives you pleasure! I know a
friend who sucked the
dust of two bricks mixed in his
tobacco. I'll turn him to his
other side and give another look.

(She turns him over.)

How this rascal weighs!
Saint Olaf, Saint Patrick,
don't wake up! These are
tangles of silk and thread,
and here's a cigarette; this filthy fellow
does not miss a single vice;
this, without doubt, is the
precious purse, to which I
consecrate my fears and
dedicate my cares. Jesus,
in how many rags has he
wrapped it!

(She takes layers off.)

One, two, three, four, five,
six, seven, eight; it is impossible
to count; but, oh sweet archive
of coin and hopes, I look at you
with reverence!

(She holds it up.)

Fortunate depository of that
attractive metal that causes
many Midases and Croesuses
to commit offenses;
I take you to my heart,

metal generoso y rico,
y voyme antes que despierte,
y esas alhajas remito
a su cuidado el guardarlas
cuando olvide el parasismo.

(Vase, y sale Ribete.)

RIBETE   Leonor anda alborotada
sin decirme la ocasión;
ni escucha con atención
ni tiene sosiego en nada.
Hame ocultado que va
aquesta tarde a un jardín
con don Juan, no sé a qué fin.
¡Válgame Dios! ¿Qué será?
Sus pasos seguir pretendo,
que no puedo presumir
bien de aquesto.

TOMILLO   Tal dormir. . .
un año ha que estoy durmiendo,
y no puedo despertar;
Vuélvome de estotro lado.

RIBETE   Este pobrete ha tomado
algún lobo.

TOMILLO   No hay que hablar.

RIBETE   ¡Ah, Tomillo! ¿Duermes?

TOMILLO   No.

RIBETE   Pues, ¿qué? ¿Sueñas?

TOMILLO   No, tampoco;
si duermo pregunta el loco,
cuando ya me despertó.

RIBETE   ¿Son aquestas baratijas
tuyas?

(Levántese Tomillo.)

TOMILLO   No; sí; ¿qué es aquesto?
¡Mi bolso!

(Turbado, busca.)

RIBETE   ¿Dónde le has puesto?

TOMILLO   No sé.

RIBETE   Aguarda, no te aflijas;
busquémosle.

TOMILLO   ¿Qué es buscar?
Quitádome ha de cuidado
el que tan bien ha buscado,
pues no le supe guardar.

rich and generous metal,
and so I'll leave before he awakes;
I leave for him these other gems
for him to put away
when he recovers from his fit.

(Exit Flora. Enter Ribete.)

RIBETE Leonor is upset but has not
told me why; she neither listens
with attention nor finds calm in
anything. She has hidden from me
that she is going this afternoon
to a garden with Don Juan, I do not
know for what purpose.
Bless me, God! What will happen?
I intend to follow her steps as I
cannot presume any good will
come of this.

TOMILLO Such sleep . . . I've been sleeping
for a year, and I can't wake up;
I'll turn over to my other side.

RIBETE This poor fool has gotten himself drunk.

TOMILLO Don't even talk about it!

RIBETE Oh, Tomillo! Are you sleeping?

TOMILLO No.

RIBETE What, then? Are you dreaming?

TOMILLO No, that neither. This crazy man asks me if I'm sleeping
now that I'm awake.

RIBETE Is this deck of cards yours?

(Tomillo gets up.)

TOMILLO No; yes; what is this?
My purse!

(Agitated, he looks about for it.)

RIBETE Where did you put it?

TOMILLO I do not know.

RIBETE Wait, do not be upset;
we'll look for it.

TOMILLO What is there to look for?
My most valuable possession has
been taken from me, that which was
well sought after, but I knew not
how to care for it. Oh, purse

	¡Ay, bolso del alma mía!
RIBETE	Hazle una presopopeya.
TOMILLO	*Mira, Nero de Tarpeya,*
	a Roma como se ardía.
	¿Partamos, quieres, Ribete,
	hermanablemente?
RIBETE	¿Qué?
	¡Voto a Cristo, que le dé!
	Mas déjole por pobrete.
	¿No me conoces?
TOMILLO	Ya estoy
	al cabo: ¡ay, escudos míos!
RIBETE	Por no hacer dos desvaríos
	con este triste, me voy,
	y porque no le suceda
	a Leonor algún disgusto.

(Vase.)

| TOMILLO | Flora me ha dado este susto; |
| | esta vez, vengada queda. |

(Vase, y sale don Juan.)

DON JUAN	El tropel de mis desvelos
	me trae confuso y loco,
	que el discurso enfrena poco
	si pican mucho los celos.
	No es posible hallar medio
	mi desdicha en tanta pena;
	mi ingratitud me condena,
	y el morir sólo es remedio.
	Pues morir, honor, morir,
	que la ocasión os advierte
	que vale una honrada muerte
	más que un infame vivir.
	Bien se arguye mi cuidado,
	¡ay, honor! pues no reposo;
	desesperado y celoso.

(Sale doña Leonor.)

DOÑA LEONOR	Perdonadme si he tardado,
	que me ha detenido Estela,
	mandándome que la siga.
DON JUAN	No me da su amor fatiga
	cuando mi honor me desvela;
	yo os he llamado, Leonardo,
	para mataros muriendo.
DOÑA LEONOR	Don Juan, lo mismo pretendo.

	of my soul!
RIBETE	Make up a poem for it.
TOMILLO	*Look, Nero of Tarpeya,*
	at Rome as it burns.
	Shall we share,
	Ribete, like brothers?
RIBETE	What? I swear to Christ, that
	I should give him . . . But I shall
	leave him be, poor soul.
	Do you not know me?
TOMILLO	I'm done for. Oh, my gold coins!
RIBETE	I shall take my leave so as
	not to do more harm
	to this sad soul, and so
	no ill may befall Leonor.

(Exit Ribete.)

| TOMILLO | Flora has given me this scare; |
| | this time, she's gotten even. |

(Exit. Enter Don Juan.)

DON JUAN	All my sleepless nights have
	left me confused and mad; when
	jealousy stabs so, reason holds
	little sway. I cannot find a way,
	my misfortune in the midst of so much pain,
	my ingratitude condemns me,
	and death is the only remedy.
	Then die, honor, die; the occasion
	presents itself, and an
	honorable death is more worthy
	than a disreputable life. Oh, honor!
	Though this be well argued,
	desperate and jealous
	still I find no rest.

(Enter Doña Leonor.)

DOÑA LEONOR	Pardon me for being late but
	Estela detained me and asked
	that I accompany her.
DON JUAN	'Tis not her love that wearies me
	but my honor that keeps me from
	sleep; I have called you, Leonardo,
	so that I may die by killing you.
DOÑA LEONOR	Don Juan, that is also my intention.

(Ribete a la puerta.)

RIBETE   ¡Grandes requiebros! ¿Qué aguardo?
                     No he temido en vano; apriesa
                     a llamar su hermano voy,
                     que está con Estela. Hoy,

(Vase.)   Leonor, se acaba tu empresa.

DOÑA LEONOR   Hoy, don Juan, se ha de acabar
                     toda mi infamia ¡por Dios!
                     porque matándoos a vos,
                     libre me podré casar
                     con quien deseo.

DON JUAN   Esa dicha
                     bien os podrá suceder,
                     mas no a mí, que vengo a ser
                     el todo de la desdicha;
                     de suerte, que aunque mi espada
                     llegue primero, no importa,
                     pues aunque muráis, no acorta
                     en mí esta afrenta pesada,
                     este infame deshonor;
                     porque no es razón que pase
                     por tal infamia, y me case
                     habiendo sido Leonor
                     fácil después de ser mía,
                     con vos; y si me matáis,
                     con ella viuda os casáis.
                     Mirad si dicha sería
                     vuestra; mas no ha de quedar
                     esta vez que aquesa suerte.
                     Yo os tengo que dar la muerte;
                     procuradme vos matar,
                     porque muriendo los dos,
                     con ambas vidas se acabe
                     un tormento en mí tan grave,
                     un bien tan dichoso en vos.

DOÑA LEONOR   Don Juan, mataros deseo,
                     no morir, cuando imagino
                     de aquel objeto divino
                     ser el venturoso empleo.
                     Acortemos de razones,
                     que en afrentas declaradas
                     mejor hablan las espadas.

DON JUAN   ¡Qué terribles confusiones!
                     Matar y morir pretendo.

(Ribete appears at the door.)

RIBETE   What delightful endearments!
Why do I hesitate?
I have not feared in vain;
quickly I'll go and call her brother,
who is with Estela.
Today, Leonor, your endeavor will be done with.

(Exit Ribete.)

DOÑA LEONOR   Today, Don Juan, all my infamy
will be finished, by God! for
by killing you I shall be free to
marry whom I desire.

DON JUAN   That good fortune may indeed
happen to you, but not to me
who has become the embodiment
of misfortune; if, by chance, my
sword strikes first, it will not
matter, since though you may die,
this dire disgrace of mine, this
base dishonor, will not be cut;
there is no reason to supplant such
vileness, and I would marry
Leonor having been wanton after being mine,
and if you kill me you would marry her, a widow.
Mark well if you believe this would
be fortunate for you; I see
but one end to this. I must
kill you, and you kill me,
for if we both die, with our two lives
will end what for me
is a grave torment, and for you
a bounty of good fortune.

DOÑA LEONOR   Don Juan, I wish to kill you,
not to die, when I think of being
the happy lover
of that divine object.
Let us cut short
this discussion, since swords
speak more eloquently when it
comes to declared dishonors.

DON JUAN   What terrible confusion!
I intend to kill and die.

(Sacan las espadas, y salen don Fernando y Ludovico.)

DON FERNANDO   En este instante me avisa
                Ribete que a toda prisa
                venga, Príncipe, y riñendo
                están don Juan y Leonardo.
                ¿Qué es esto?

LUDOVICO   Pues, caballeros,
                ¿amigos, y los aceros
                desnudos?

DON FERNANDO   Si un punto tardo,
                sucede. . .

DON JUAN   *(Aparte)*   ¿Fuera posible?
                Nada me sucede bien.
                ¡Ah, ingrata fortuna! ¿A quién,
                sino a mí, lance terrible?

DON FERNANDO   ¿Fue aquesto probar las armas,
                venir a ejercer fue aquesto
                las espadas negras? ¿Son
                éstos los ángulos rectos
                de don Luis de Narváez
                y el entretener el tiempo
                en su loable ejercicio?
                Don Juan, ¿con mi primo mesmo
                reñís? ¿Ésta es la amistad?

DON JUAN   ¡En qué de afrentas me has puesto,
                Leonor!

DON FERNANDO   ¿No hay más atención
                a que es mi sangre, mi deudo,
                a que es de mi propia casta,
                y a que soy amigo vuestro?
                ¿Tan grande ha sido el agravio,
                que para satisfacello
                no basta el ser yo quien soy?
                Vos, primo, ¿cómo tan necio
                buscáis los peligros? ¿Cómo
                os mostráis tan poco cuerdo?

DOÑA LEONOR   Yo hago lo que me toca.
                Sin razón le estás diciendo
                oprobios a mi justicia.

DON FERNANDO   Decidme, pues, el suceso.

DOÑA LEONOR   Don Juan lo dirá mejor.

DON JUAN   ¿Cómo declararme puedo,
                agraviado en las afrentas,
                y convencido en los riesgos?

(They unsheath their swords. Enter Don Fernando and Ludovico.)

DON FERNANDO	Ribete, in great haste,
	has just advised me in this instant
	to come, Majesty, and, indeed,
	Don Juan and Leonardo are fighting.
	What is this about?
LUDOVICO	Gentlemen, you are friends;
	why are those blades unsheathed?
DON FERNANDO	If I delay a moment, something may happen. . .
DON JUAN	*(Aside)* Is it possible? Nothing goes well for me.
	Oh, ungrateful fortune!
	To whom, but to me, would such horrors befall?
DON FERNANDO	Was it to test the weapons that
	you have come to practice with
	black swords? Are these the
	straight angles of Don Luis
	de Narváez and the way to
	pass the time at that laudable
	exercise? Don Juan, is it with
	my cousin himself that you
	quarrel? Is this friendship?
DON JUAN	In what disgrace have you
	placed me, Leonor!
DON FERNANDO	Pay you so little heed that
	this is my blood, my kin,
	a man of my own breeding,
	and that I am your friend?
	Was the offense so great that
	in order to avenge it it is not
	enough that I am who I am?
	You, cousin, how can you be so
	foolish as to look for danger?
	How can you show that you possess
	so little in the way of brains?
DOÑA LEONOR	I do that which I must.
	Without reason do you cast
	a dark light on my just cause.
DON FERNANDO	Tell me, then, the reason.
DOÑA LEONOR	Don Juan would tell it better.
DON JUAN	How can I explain myself
	when I am beset by dishonor
	and convinced of the risks?

DON FERNANDO   ¿Qué es esto, no respondéis?
DON JUAN   ¡Que esto permiten los cielos!
                 Diga Leonardo la causa;
                 (*Aparte*) de pesar estoy muriendo.
DOÑA LEONOR   Pues gusta de que publique
                 de tus mudables excesos
                 el número, Ludovico,
                 y Fernando, estad atentos.
                 Pues ya te hizo don Juan,
                 ¡o primo!, de los secretos
                 de su amor, y su mudanza,
                 como me dijiste, dueño;
                 que se vino, y lo demás
                 sucedido; y en efecto,
                 que sirvió a Estela, que aleve
                 intentó su casamiento.
                 Óyeme, y sabrás lo más
                 importante a nuestro cuento.
                 Doña Leonor de Ribera,
                 tu hermana, hermoso objeto
                 del vulgo, y las pretensiones
                 de infinitos caballeros,
                 fue. . . no sé cómo lo diga.
DON FERNANDO   Acaba, Leonardo, presto.
DON JUAN   Espera, espera, Leonardo;
                 todo me ha cubierto un hielo.
                 (*Aparte*) Si es hermana de Fernando,
                 ¡ay, más confuso tormento!
DOÑA LEONOR   Digo, pues, que fue tu hermana
                 doña Leonor, de los yerros
                 de don Juan causa.
DON JUAN   (*Aparte*)   Acabó
                 de echar la fortuna el resto
                 a mis desdichas.
DON FERNANDO   Prosigue,
                 prosigue, que estoy temiendo
                 que para oírte me falte
                 el juicio, y el sufrimiento.
                 (*Aparte*) ¡Ah, mal caballero, ingrato,
                 bien pagabas mis deseos,
                 casándote con Estela!
DOÑA LEONOR   Palabra de casamiento
                 le dio don Juan, ya lo sabes;
                 disculpa, que culpa ha hecho

DON FERNANDO	What is this, do you not answer?
DON JUAN	May the heavens permit me!
	Tell, Leonardo, the reason.
	(Aside) I shall die of misery.
DOÑA LEONOR	Enjoy my making public
	the list of your fickle excesses;
	be attentive, Ludovico and Fernando.
	Don Juan has made you,
	oh, cousin! as you told me,
	owner of the secrets of his love
	and his inconstancy; of how he came,
	and what things passed; and he,
	in fact, served Estela, and treacherously
	sought to marry her.
	Listen to me and you will know
	the most important part of our story.
	Doña Leonor de Ribera, your sister,
	beautiful object of worship of ordinary men,
	and of the pretensions of numberless
	gentlemen, was . . . I know not how to say it.
DON FERNANDO	Finish, Leonardo, with haste.
DON JUAN	Wait, wait, Leonardo;
	I am covered all with ice.
	(Aside) If she is Fernando's sister,
	oh, what confused torment!
DOÑA LEONOR	I say, then, that it was your sister,
	Doña Leonor, who was the victim
	of Don Juan's errors.
DON JUAN	*(Aside)* Now has Fortune cast
	the rest of my disgrace.
DON FERNANDO	Go on, go on; I fear that listening to you
	I may lose my judgment and patience.
	(Aside) Oh, vile gentleman, ingrate,
	how well you would repay my kindness,
	marrying Estela!
DOÑA LEONOR	You know now that Don Juan gave her
	his word that he would marry her—
	forgive her, for of such innocence

la inocencia en las mujeres;
mas dejóla ingrato, a tiempo
que yo la amaba, Fernando,
con tan notables afectos,
que el alma dudó tal vez
respiraciones, y alientos
en el pecho, y animaba
la vida en el dulce incendio
de la beldad de Leonor:
corrida en los escarmientos
de la traición de don Juan,
y obligándome primero
con juramentos (que amando,
todos hacen juramentos)
me declaró de su historia
el lastimoso suceso,
con más perlas[24] que palabras.
Mas yo, amante verdadero,
la prometí de vengar
su agravio, y dando al silencio,
con la muerte de don Juan,
la ley forzosa del duelo,
ser su esposo, y lo he de ser,
don Fernando, si no muero
a manos de mi enemigo.
A Flandes vine, sabiendo
que estaba en Bruselas. Soy
noble, honor sólo profeso;
ved si es forzoso que vengue
este agravio, pues soy dueño
dél, y de Leonor también.

DON JUAN	No lo serás, vive el cielo.
DON FERNANDO	¿Hay mayores confusiones?
	Hoy la vida, y honor pierdo:
	¡Ah, hermana fácil! Don Juan,
	mal pagaste de mi pecho
	las finezas.
DON JUAN	(*Aparte*) De corrido,
	a mirarle no me atrevo.
	A saber que era tu hermana...
DON FERNANDO	¿Qué hicieras? No hallo medio
	en tanto mal, Ludovico.
DOÑA LEONOR	Yo la adoro.
DON JUAN	Yo la quiero.

has women's guilt been wrought—
but ungrateful, he abandoned her.
In time I fell in love with her, Fernando,
with such great passion that
my soul might doubt its breath,
and the impulses of my breast; and
my life quickened in the sweet fire
of the beauty of Leonor. Ashamed by
Don Juan's lessons in betrayal,
and obligating me first with promises
(in love, all promise freely) she told me,
more with pearls[24] than with words,
the sorrowful events of her past.
And I, true lover, swore to her I would
avenge her insult, putting it to rest by
the inescapable law of the duel;
with the death of Don Juan, I would be her husband,
and that must I be, Don Fernando, if I do not die
at the hand of my enemy.
I came to Flanders knowing that
he was in Brussels. I am noble, I profess
only honor, judge for yourself if it is not
inevitable that I avenge that offense, since
I am the owner of it, and of Leonor as well.

DON JUAN You cannot be, by heaven.

DON FERNANDO Could there be greater confusion?
Today I lose my life and honor:
oh, wanton sister! Don Juan, how badly
you have repaid me my kindness.

DON JUAN *(Aside)* I dare not look at him, even quickly.
Had I known she was your sister . . .

DON FERNANDO What would you have done?
I see no way out of all this evil, Ludovico.

DOÑA LEONOR I adore her.

DON JUAN I love her.

DOÑA LEONOR	*(Aparte)* ¡Qué gusto!
DON JUAN	¡Qué pesadumbre!
DOÑA LEONOR	*(Aparte)* ¡Qué satisfacción!
DON JUAN	¡Qué celos!

DON JUAN   Yo no me puedo casar
con doña Leonor, es cierto;
aunque muera Leonardo,
antes moriré primero.
¡Ah, si hubiera sido honrada!

DON FERNANDO   ¡Qué laberinto tan ciego!
Dice bien don Juan, bien dice;
pues si casarla pretendo
con Leonardo, ¿cómo puedo,
vivo don Juan? Esto es hecho:
todos hemos de matarnos,
yo no hallo otro remedio.

LUDOVICO   Ni yo le miro, por Dios,
y ése es bárbaro y sangriento.

DOÑA LEONOR   En efecto, ¿si Leonor
no rompiera el lazo estrecho
de tu amor, y si no hubiera
admitido mis empeños,
la quisieras?

DON JUAN   La adorara.

DOÑA LEONOR   Pues a Leonor verás presto;
y quizá de tus engaños
podrás quedar satisfecho.

DON JUAN   ¿Dónde está?

DOÑA LEONOR   En Bruselas.

DON JUAN   ¿Cómo?

DOÑA LEONOR   Esperad aquí un momento.

(Vase, y salen Estela, Lisarda, Flora, Ribete y Tomillo.)

ESTELA   ¿Don Leonardo con don Juan
de disgusto?

RIBETE   Así lo entiendo.

TOMILLO   ¡Ay, mi bolso y mis escudos!

LISARDA   No está Leonardo con ellos.

ESTELA   Señores, ¿qué ha sucedido?

DON FERNANDO   No sé qué os diga; no puedo
hablar.

LISARDA   Ludovico, escucha.

LUDOVICO   De ver a Estela me ofendo,
después que oí a mis oídos
tan desairados desprecios.

DOÑA LEONOR	*(Aside)* What fun!
DON JUAN	What grief!
DOÑA LEONOR	*(Aside)* What satisfaction!
DON JUAN	What jealousy! I cannot marry
	Doña Leonor, that is certain,
	even if Leonardo were to die;
	I would die first. Oh, would
	that she'd been chaste.
DON FERNANDO	What labyrinth so blind! Well does
	Don Juan speak, aye, speaks he well;
	Even if I wish to marry her to Leonardo,
	how can I with Don Juan alive?
	This is the solution: we must all kill each other;
	I can find no other remedy.
LUDOVICO	I cannot even look at this, by God;
	it is so barbarous and bloody.
DOÑA LEONOR	In truth, had Leonor not broken
	the tight bonds of your love,
	and had she not admitted my endeavors,
	you would now love her?
DON JUAN	I would adore her.
DOÑA LEONOR	Then you shall soon see Leonor;
	and perhaps you will be able
	to vindicate your error.
DON JUAN	Where is she?
DOÑA LEONOR	In Brussels.
DON JUAN	How?
DOÑA LEONOR	Wait here a moment.

(Exit Leonor. Enter Estela, Lisarda, Flora, Ribete, and Tomillo.)

ESTELA	Don Leonardo in a quarrel
	with Don Juan?
RIBETE	Thus do I understand it.
TOMILLO	Oh, my purse and my coins!
LISARDA	Leonardo is not with them.
ESTELA	Gentlemen, what has happened?
DON FERNANDO	I know not what to tell you;
	I am speechless.
LISARDA	Ludovico, listen.
LUDOVICO	It offends me to see Estela
	after my ears have heard
	such disdainful contempt.

	¿Qué decís, Lisarda hermosa?
LISARDA	¿Don Leonardo —qué se ha hecho?
	¿Dónde está?
LUDOVICO	Escuchad aparte.
DON FERNANDO	¡Qué mal prevenidos riesgos!

DON FERNANDO
Hoy he de quedar sin vida,
o ha de quedar satisfecho
mi deshonor. ¡Ay, hermana!
El juicio estoy perdiendo.

TOMILLO   Vamos a la parte.

FLORA   ¿A qué parte, majadero?

TOMILLO   Ribete.

RIBETE   ¿Qué es lo que dices?

TOMILLO   Digo que soy un jumento.

RIBETE   ¿Dónde está Leonor? ¡Que se haya
metido en estos empeños!

(Sale doña Leonor, dama bizarra.)

DOÑA LEONOR   Hermano, Príncipe, esposo,
yo os perdono el mal concepto
que habéis hecho de mi amor,
si basta a satisfaceros
haber venido constante,
y resuelta.

RIBETE   ¿Qué es aquesto?

DOÑA LEONOR   Desde España hasta Flandes,
y haberme arrojado al riesgo
de matarme tantas veces;
la primera en el terrero
retirando a Ludovico,
y a mi propio esposo hiriendo;
y hoy cuando guardó a Palacio
mi valor justo respeto,
y deslumbrando a mi hermano,
fingir pude engaños nuevos;
y ahora, arrojada y valiente,
por mi casto honor volviendo,

(Se dirige a don Juan.)

salí a quitarte la vida,
y lo hiciera, vive el cielo,
a no verte arrepentido,
que tanto puede en un pecho
Valor, Agravio y Mujer.
Leonardo fui, mas ya vuelvo
a ser Leonor: ¿me querrás?

	What said you, fair Lisarda?
LISARDA	Don Leonardo—what has he done?
	Where is he?
LUDOVICO	Come here and I will tell you.
DON FERNANDO	What ill-foreseen perils!
	Today I must lose my life or
	vindicate my honor.
	Oh, sister! I am losing my reason.
TOMILLO	Let's get down to it.
FLORA	Down to what, you fool?
TOMILLO	Ribete.
RIBETE	What say you?
TOMILLO	I say that I'm an ass.
RIBETE	Where is Leonor? How could she
	have undertaken these endeavors?

(Enter Doña Leonor, an elegantly dressed lady.)

DOÑA LEONOR	Brother, Majesty, husband,
	I forgive you the wrong impression
	that you have had of my love.
	I hope it is enough to satisfy you
	that I have come, constant and resolved.
RIBETE	What is this?
DOÑA LEONOR	From Spain to Flanders,
	having hurled myself at the risk of death so many times;
	first on the terrace, making Ludovico withdraw,
	and injuring my own husband;
	and today when, at the palace, my valor kept its due respect,
	bewildering my brother, I feigned new deceits;
	and now, daring and valiant, recovering my chaste honor,

(She addresses Don Juan.)

	I came to take your life,
	and would have done, by heaven,
	had I not seen you contrite;
	for much can be done when
	Valor, Outrage, and Woman
	in a single breast unite.
	I was Leonardo, but now return
	as Leonor. Will you love me?

DON JUAN	Te adoraré.
RIBETE	Los enredos de Leonor tuvieron fin.
DON FERNANDO	Confuso, hermana, y suspenso me ha tenido tanto bien.
LUDOVICO	¡Ay, más dichoso suceso!
ESTELA	Leonardo, ¿así me engañabas?
DOÑA LEONOR	Fue fuerza, Estela.
ESTELA	Quedemos hermanas, Leonor hermosa. Fernando, de esposo, y dueño me dad la mano.
DON FERNANDO	Estas dichas causó Leonor; yo soy vuestro.
LUDOVICO	Ganar quiero tu belleza, Lisarda hermosa, pues pierdo a Estela; dame tu mano.
LISARDA	La mano y el alma ofrezco.
RIBETE	Flora, de tres para tres han sido los casamientos. Tú quedas para los dos, y entrambos te dejaremos para que te coman lobos, borrico de muchos dueños. . .
ESTELA	Yo te la doy, y seis mil escudos.
RIBETE	Digo que acepto por los escudos, pues bien los ha menester el necio, que se casa de paciencia.
TOMILLO	Sólo yo todo lo pierdo: Flora, bolsillo y escudos.
DOÑA LEONOR	Aquí, Senado discreto, *Valor, agravio y mujer* acaban; pídeos su dueño, por mujer y por humilde, que perdonéis sus defectos.

FIN

DON JUAN	I will adore you.
RIBETE	The tangles of Leonor are at an end.
DON FERNANDO	This unexpected good has me quite confused, sister, and astonished.
LUDOVICO	What a happy event!
ESTELA	So you deceived me, Leonardo?
DOÑA LEONOR	I had no choice, Estela.
ESTELA	Let us remain as sisters, fair Leonor. Fernando, as husband and master, give me your hand.
DON FERNANDO	Leonor caused this good fortune; I am yours.
LUDOVICO	I crave to win your beauty, fair Lisarda, since I lose that of Estela. Give me your hand.
LISARDA	I offer you my hand and soul.
RIBETE	Flora, the marriages have been made three for three. You remain for two, and between us both we will leave you, so that the wolves may eat you, like a donkey with many masters . . .
ESTELA	I give her to you, and six thousand crowns.
RIBETE	I say that I accept for the crowns, as the fool who marries out of patience has need of them.
TOMILLO	I'm the only one who loses: Flora, purse, and coins.
DOÑA LEONOR	Here, discerning Audience, ends *Valor, Outrage, and Woman.* Its author begs of you, as a woman and a humble soul, that you pardon its faults.

End

(*Translated by Donna Lazarus and Amy Kaminsky*)

1. Faetonte: figura de la mitología griega quien por poco prende fuego al mundo en su tentado de guiar la carroza solar por el cielo.

2. Eolo: dios de los vientos; Noto: viento del sur; Boreas: viento del norte.

3. Mavorte: dios de la guerra.

4. Maritornes: en *Don Quijote,* sirvienta a quien don Quijote trata como si fuera una dama.

5. Néstor: rey de Pilos, representado en *La Ilíada* como valiente y sabio.

6. Esta lista de hijos ilustres de Córdoba termina con un nombre que el público de Ana Caro seguramente reconocería, el del poeta Luis de Góngora (1561-1627).

7. Marcelo: comandante romano distinguido durante la segunda Guerra Púnica.

8. Apolo: dios de la luz y de la música.

9. Camila: reina guerrera de la mitología griega.

10. Ovidio: poeta romano, autor de *Metamorfosis.*

11. Isis: poderosa diosa egipcíaca.

12. Anfitrite: esposa de Neptuno, dios del mar.

13. Reto de Zamora: reto entre castellanos y zamoranos para resolver la cuestión de honor después de la muerte del rey don Sancho, durante la época del Cid, en el cual murieron todos los combatientes.

14. Vulcano: dios del arte de la metalurgia.

15. Némesis: diosa de la venganza.

16. Lisarda nombra varias figuras mitológicas masculinas conocidas por su gran belleza.

17. Mujeres doctas de la época clásica romana y griega. Pola Argentaria ayudó a su marido Lucano a escribir sus poesías; Safo es la gran poeta lírica; Areta fue filósofa; y Blesilla, concocida por su sabiduría, fue canonizada por la iglesia.

18. Figuras femeninas heroicas del mundo clásico. Semíramis: reina de Asiria y fundadora de Babilonia; Cenobia: historiadora y reina guerrera de Palmira; Drusila: hermana y amante del tirano Calígula; Draznes: referencia desconocida; Camila: cazadora y guerrera.

19. Argos: figura mitológica de más de cien ojos.

20. Medusa: En la mitología griega, mujer bella covertida en monstruo. Ver su rostro, como ser mirado por el basilico, significaba convertirse en piedra.

21. Himeneo: dios del matrimonio.

22. En la historia del Minotauro, Ariadna le dio un hilo a Teseo para que pudiera salir del laberinto.

23. Cupido, dios del amor.

24. Lágrimas.

1. Phaëton: figure in Greek mythology who nearly sets the earth afire in his attempt to drive the solar chariot.

2. Aeolus: god of winds; Notus: south wind; Boreas: north wind.

3. Mars: god of war.

4. Maritornes: in Cervantes's *Don Quixote,* a servant whom Don Quixote treats as if she were a lady.

5. Nestor: King of Pylos, depicted in Homer's *Iliad* as brave and wise.

6. This list of famous sons of Córdoba ends with a name that would be instantly recognizable to Caro's audience: her contemporary, the poet Luis de Góngora.

7. Marcellus: distinguished Roman commander of the second Punic War.

8. Apollo: god of light and music.

9. Camilla: warrior queen of Greek mythology.

10. Ovid: author of *Metamorphoses.*

11. Isis: powerful Egyptian earth goddess.

12. Amphitrite: wife of Neptune, god of the sea.

13. Challenge of Zamora: in eleventh-century Spain, the challenge to mortal combat between the knights of Zamora and those of Castile to settle an affair of honor caused by the death of the Castilian King Sancho; all the combatants died.

14. Vulcan: god of the art of metallurgy.

15. Nemesis: goddess of vengeance.

16. Lisarda refers to a number of male mythological figures known for their great beauty.

17. Learned women of the classical period in Greece and Rome. Pola Argentaria helped her husband, the poet Lucan, to compose his poems; Saphho was a great lyric poet; Arete was a philosopher; and Blesilla, known for her wisdom, was canonized by the church.

18. Heroic female figures of the classical era. Semiramis: queen of Assyria and legendary founder of Babylon; Zenobia: historian and warrior queen of Palmyra; Drusila: sister and lover of the tyrant Caligula; Draznes: obscure reference; Camilla: hunter and warrior.

19. Argus: mythological figure who had more than one hundred eyes.

20. Medusa: In Greek mythology, a beautiful woman who was turned into a monster. To look at her face, as to be looked in the eye by a basilisk meant to be turned to stone.

21. Hymen: god of marriage.

22. In the story of the Minotaur, Ariadne gave Theseus a thread to unwind as he entered the labyrinth so he could later find his way out.

23. Cupid, god of love.

24. Tears.

Sor Marcela de San Félix

Sor Marcela de San Félix was born in Toledo on May 8, 1605, to the actress Micaela Luján. Her father was Micaela's lover, Lope de Vega, perhaps Spain's best-known playwright. What happened to Micaela Luján is not known, but from an early age Marcela and her brother, Lope Félix, were raised by a servant. Then, shortly after Lope de Vega's wife died in 1613, Marcela and Lope Félix went to live with him. One year later, the first reference to Marcela appears in Lope's letters. In a detail that reveals that he took his responsibilities as a father seriously, Lope wrote that he could not travel from Toledo because Marcela had fallen ill. In 1616 he wrote of accompanying his daughter to San Isidro to fulfill a vow made on account of Marcela's illness.[1]

Lope's letters testify to the affection Marcela received from the famous poet-dramatist and from his patron, the Duke of Sessa. Both men indulged her. On one occasion the duke gave the young Marcela a pair of diamond earrings, and on another she herself asked him for some costly cloth out of which to make a gown. It was to the duke that Lope went for the dowry when Marcela decided to enter the convent.

For her part, Marcela loved and admired her father. On occasion she helped him correct and copy his writing. She went to the bullfights with him. And for almost a whole year, at her father's behest, Marcela stole back, a few at a time, the love letters Lope had written to another of his lovers, Marta de Nevares. From January to October 1617, Lope had his daughter, who then was eleven or twelve years old, go to Marta's house and bring back his letters so he could give them to his patron who seems to have wanted to own whatever he could of Lope's writing. At first Lope worried about the ethics of the situation (he was afraid he might corrupt his daughter), but Marcela accepted the job. She stole letters regularly, according to Lope's correspondence with the duke. Her primary motive was undoubtedly loyalty to her father, but she also had other reasons. She knew that she was serving Sessa, and she wanted to be paid: a new dress, trimmed in green and black.[2] Nevertheless, during this time Marcela and her father's lover became good friends. Marta was distressed when she discovered the thievery, but it seems that she later gave Marcela the letters so that the child would not have to steal them from her. Two years later, when Marta suddenly went blind, Marcela was profoundly affected and prayed for the woman she now called mother.

The adolescent Marcela had her unruly suitors. In 1617 or 1618 one of them stormed her house, and in 1619, according to Lope, a nephew of Marta de Nevares "started bothering little Marcela."[3] Lope, who by this time had become a priest as the result of a brief interlude of repentance in his exuberantly sexual life, wrote that he defended her despite his "[priest's] habit and [advanced] years."[4] At the end of 1621 Marcela decided to enter the Trinitarian Order, the most exclusive convent of Madrid; Lope arranged for her to do so, and pressed Sessa for the required dowry. When Marcela took her vows on February 13, 1622, Lope himself organized the ceremony and composed an epistle in her honor. As a priest, Lope had the privilege of visiting his cloistered daughter, and he did so frequently, since the convent was only about three blocks from his home; and Sor Marcela listened to her father's masses.

Sor Marcela de San Félix was twice the superior of her convent. She held other offices as well: she was three times *provisora* (keeper of the convent's pantry). Sor Marcela writes about that job in a number of humorous poems concerning the very real problem of food shortages in the convent. According to the caption on her portrait, "she served indefatigably in the ministries of prelate, teacher, and the like,"[5] and she was "of sovereign discretion, severe affability."[6] Sor Marcela de San Félix died January 9, 1687.

Both Sor Marcela and another of Lope's daughters wrote poetry, though the latter's poems have disappeared. Sor Marcela's religious verse expresses a desire for peace and tranquillity that might be obtained through solitude and prayer. Solitude was not always easy to come by in the communal world of the convent. Her peace was interrupted most notably in 1628, when Pedro de Villegas attacked the brother of the dramatist Calderón de la Barca and sought refuge in Sor Marcela's convent, with the Calderón brothers hard on their heels. The tumult produced a scandal, breaking the cloister of Sor Marcela and the other nuns.

Sor Marcela left a large body of work, but she wrote more than she left. Of the five volumes she filled, she burned four, and her spiritual autobiography was also consigned to the flames at the direction of her confessor. Like her father, Sor Marcela wrote both poetry and drama. Her six extant dramatic works are religious plays written to be performed in the convent. Much of her poetry also responded to the occasional needs of her religious community. The rites of the cloister provided a legitimate context for literary creation, but they also restricted the poet, who complained, jocularly, of having to bend her art to the demands of her order.

The majority of Sor Marcela's surviving poems are written in popular forms. In 1988 Electa Arenal and Georgina Sabat-Rivers edited Sor Marcela's complete works: twenty-two *romances,* two *seguidillas,* a *villancico,* a *décima,* an *endecha,* eight *loas* (dramatic monologues), and a *lira,* as well as six allegorical dramas (*coloquios espirituales*). She also wrote a short biography of another nun. Sor Marcela often experimented formally in her poems. Almost a third of her romances break the eight-syllable rule in favor of a seven syllable line, and five of the rest are *esdrújula* rhyme, where the

rhyming syllable is the third to last in the line. The poems offer an insight into the daily life of the convent and of the spiritual life of one of its inhabitants.

Sor Marcela's poems express her satisfaction with the spiritual freedom the convent offers her, her well-developed sense of humor, and a deep spiritual sensibility. The poems included here show both her pious and her playful sides. Poetry was the coin of the household in which she was raised, anything but pompous. The poet in the first *loa* laments his audience's lack of respect for his poetry; the writer of the poem herself enjoys the fun. Here and in the other *loa*, Sor Marcela satirizes the poverty of the convent and pokes fun at the sisters, but she seems most to enjoy making fun of her own ferocity and mendacity. The *loas* demonstrate the easy coexistence between the ordinary communal life of the convent and its deeper spiritual joys and demands; without negating their playfulness, Sor Marcela ends on a joyful, but serious, note. Her ballad "El jardín del convento" is a poem about the life of the spirit, but it too connects her physical and material experience of the convent (its fountain, the plants it contains) with a dedication to God.

Always the poet, Sor Marcela is proud of her somewhat unconventional parentage: she invokes her father's name in more than a few of her poems, and the inscription on her portrait tells us that Sor Marcela was "desirous, in the end, that her true and glorious lineage not be forgotten."[7]

1. "a cumplir una promesa de la enfermedad de Marcela," Agustín G. de Amezúa, *Lope de Vega en sus cartas* (Madrid: Real Academia Española, 1935), 1:1267.

2. "que los pasamanos sean verdes y negros," Amezúa, *Lope de Vega en sus cartas* (Madrid: Real Academia Española, 1941), 3:282.

3. "dio a ynquietar a Marcelica," Amezúa, *Lope de Vega en sus cartas* (Madrid: Real Academia Españada, 1940), 2:489.

4. "hábito y años," Amezúa, 2:489.

5. "sirvió infatigable en los ministros de prelada, maestra y semejantes," Amezúa, 2:699.

6. "de discreción soberana, apacibilidad severa," Amezúa, 2:699.

7. "deseosa, a la cuenta, de que no se olvidara nunca su verdadero y glorioso linaje," Amezúa, 2:700.

1
Loa a una profesión

Discretísimo senado,
en que religión, prudencia
y entendimiento se igualan
por no entrar en competencia,
    suplico a caridades
también a sus reverencias
(perdonen que van despúes
aunque el verso da licencia):
Loquitur carmina
totius frasis sonat.[1]

    En fin, suplico a vustedes
me estén un ratico atentas,
y a un diluvio de trabajos,
a un estanque de miserias,
    a un océano de males
presten piadosas orejas.
Vengo, madres y señoras,
con una muy grande pena,
    con una angustia mortal
por una inaudita ofensa;
no habrán oído en su vida
desgracia que lo parezca,
    afflicción que así lo indique,
ni pudrición con más lenguas.
Abundantiam malorum,
tacitum nunquam[2]

    Bien se acordarán que soy
un licenciado poeta,
que por ser tan conocidas,
no referiré mis prendas.

    Ya conté de mi prosapia,
mi linaje y descendencia,
de mi padre y de mi madre
dije hazañas y nobleza,
    mas, olvidóseme entonces
de contar... y es cosa cierta
que la vi con estos ojos
que encubaron a mi agüela,

1
Dramatic Prologue,
for the Profession of a Nun

Solemn and most enlightened conclave,
in each of whom sense, devotion,
and wisdom dwell in equal measure
(oh, may I steer clear of contention)—
    for refreshments, dear nuns,* I beseech
        you,
and I beseech your Reverences
—forgive me that I put you second,
but I have poetic license):
Loquitur carmina
tatius frasis sonat.[1]

    —To sum up, I beseech you all
for a minute now to heed me,
and heed a flood of tribulations,
and a reservoir of miseries;
    indeed to an ocean of misfortunes
please lend compassionate ears.
I come, good mothers and fine ladies,
with a hurt that grieves me sore,
    I suffer a great and mortal anguish
by an uheard-of offense;
never in all your lives have you heard
of a similar disgrace,
    nor affliction thus shown abroad,
nor of rot on so many tongues.
Abundantiam malorum,
tacitum numquam.[2]

---

* In this poem, the author speaks in the comic persona of a student-poet; see lines 27-28. Lines 5 and 6 engage in punning wordplay on *caridad* (literally, "charity") and *reverencias* (your Reverences). *Caridades* (plural) is both a term of respect used generally for nuns (as opposed to *reverencias*, for the prioress and mother superior, who would normally be mentioned first) and a form of light refreshment enjoyed on saints' days in religious orders. The student-poet speaker has his mind well set on food.—Trans.

1. "The poems speak for themselves, sounding like everyday speech." With these Latin interjections, Marcela continues her comic send-up of academic verse.

2. "An abundance of evils shall never be silenced."

---

1. Poemas; suena el discurso de todos.
2. A abundancia de males, nunca callado.

mas, vuelvo a lo que decía
que las cosas de la tierra,
por más que ensalcen a un hombre,
de vanidad están llenas.
Vanitas humana,
pessima infirmitas.[3]

Digo, pues, que ya les dije
una noche en cierta fiesta,
cómo era un estudiante
que pasaba con pobreza.
Necesitas magna
caret lege.[4]

Pues ésta me dio ocasión
a que contase mis menguas
en un convento de monjas,
mejor dijera, de fieras
en lo crüel, en lo acervo
más que víboras se ostentan.
No digo que lo son todas;
con decoro y con decencia
hablaré de las demás,
que sólo tres me atormentan:
éstas son las provisoras,
las mujeres más sangrientas,
monjidemonios escuadra
y el colmo de la miseria.
No soy hombre arrojadizo,
que no pronuncia mi lengua
palabras, que la razón
las ministra con gran fuerza,
no deja contar el caso
y la acción crüel y fiera
de estas de hierro mujeres,
el enojo y la vergüenza.
Si tienen por allí un trago,
me lo den sus reverencias
porque tengo la garganta,
con la cólera, muy seca.
Animum debilem
vinem corroborat.[5]

You all recall that I am a poet
of the highest—indeed bachelor's—
degree;
well-known as they are, I'll not rehearse
my talents and qualities.

Elsewhere I've told of my lineage,
my descent and ancestry;
of my good father and of my mother's
great deeds and nobility,
but somehow I forgot to tell—
and it's certainly a fact
I saw with my own eyes—that they
drowned
my old granny in a cask;[†]
but let me get back to the topic at hand,
for such worldly things as these,
though they greatly glorify a man,
are full of vanity.
Vanitas humana,
pessima infirmitas.[3]

—Well, then, as I say, I told you all
on a certain festive evening,
of how I was a worthy student
suffering poverty.
Necesitas magna
caret lege.[4]

Well, then, my poverty inspired me
to relate all of my needs
in this convent of goodly nuns—
or more aptly put, of beasts
who prove themselves far worse than
vipers
in cruel severity.
I shan't say this is true of all;
with decorum and decency

[†] "they drowned/my old granny in a cask" ("encubaron a mi agüela"): *encubar* refers to a punishment described by the *Diccionario de la Academia Real*, "To place the person accused of certain crimes, such as parricide, in a barrel with a rooster, a monkey, a dog, and a viper; a punishment used in times gone by"; *agüela* is a colloquial form of *abuela*, grandmother. These are not illustrious precedents.—Trans.

3. "Human vanity is the worst of all ills."
4. "Great need knows no law."

---

3. La vanidad humana es la peor enfermedad.
4. La gran necesidad carece de ley.
5. El vino fortalece el ánimo débil.

Supe que, en aquel convento,
había una fiesta grande
a las bodas celestiales
de un ángel que a Dios se entrega.

Y como sabía yo
que en ocasiones como ésta
recitan las religiosas
a lo devoto, comedias,

digo, coloquios divinos
que últimamente las divierta,
parecióme que podría
con mi ingenio y con mis letras,

haciéndoles una loa
salir de tanta miseria,
y por lo menos comer
un par de días siquiera.

Y luego se me ofreció
que el secretario Carencia,
liberal en tal acción,
la casa tendría llena.

Parto al convento en dos saltos,
mas, ¡ay!, que topé a la puerta
un león, un tigre hircano,
en fin, con una Marcela.

Lleguéme por un ladito
y díjele con modestia:
—Madre mía, tengo a dicha
hablar con su reverencia,

porque la traigo una cosa
que habrá menester por fuerza.
Aunque me ve capirroto
tengo un girón de poeta,

y me precio de discípulo
de aquella fecunda Vega
de cuyo ingenio los partos
dieron a España nobleza.

Hele compuesto una loa
para acompañar a la fiesta
y quisiera fuera tal
que a todas gusto las diera.

—¿Adónde tiene la loa?—
me respondió boquisesga,
boquiseca, boquiabrojos,
boquiespinas y asperezas;

you'll hear me speak of all the rest—
just three tormented me:
these were the nuns in charge of stores,
women most bloodthirsty,

they are a squadron of nunnydevils,
the very height of meanness.
I'm not a rash or daring man
and my tongue shall not pronounce

a single word not ministered
by the force of reason;
I'm not permitted to tell this tale,
nor the beastly and cruel actions

these women, forged of iron, per-
    formed,
by the force of my ire and shame.
If you might have somewhere a drop
your Reverences could share,

then let's have a sip, for my poor throat
has gone quite dry with rage.
Animum debilem
vinum corroborat [5]

I knew that, in this very convent,
festivities would be held
for the heavenly wedding feast
of an angel pledged to God;

therefore, because I knew full well
that on occasions like these
the blessed nuns enjoy performing
holy comedies

(I mean, the dialogues divine
in which lately they find some fun),
it seemed to me that I could surely
(given my wit and learning)

by writing a dramatic prologue
escape from poverty,
and, at the very least, could eat
for a day or two or three.

And then I thought the good secretary,
Señor Deficiency,
would be generous in this case and have
the house quite full indeed.

5. "Wine fortifies the weak spirit." Needless
to say, the student speaks ironically; he is about
to tell the tale.—Trans.

—Madre, en el seno la traigo,
véala su reverencia.
—Mire, amigo, Dios le guarde,
que me voy a rezar tercia.

—Madre mía,— repliqué,
—hágame su reverencia
caridad de darme algo,
que es muy grande mi pobreza.

—¡Jesús, amigo, Jesús!
mucho mayor es la nuestra:
a cuarenta y dos personas
este convento sustenta,

con cien mil obligaciones
y con poquísima renta,
y no cobramos un real
y tenemos muchas deudas.

—Yo lo creo cierto así—,
le dije, —madre, mas vea
que mi pobreza y mi hambre
con muy poco se remedia:

con que me dé una escudilla
de berzas u de lantejas
habrá cumplido conmigo
y hecho una obra muy buena—.

—En verdad que está eso bueno,
un real cuesta cada berza,
cada escarola seis cuartos,
cada hanega de lantejas

puestas aquí, y de subirlas,
bien llegarán a cincuenta;
y luego los mozos piden
ya de beber, ya merienda.

¿No es esta verdad, Mariana?
Y como todo nos cuesta
más que vale, sabe Dios
que quisiera no comieran

las monjas—. Esto decía
una de las compañeras,
y parecían hermanas
en lo mísero y la flema.

Mas la otra monjirripio,
la segunda compañera,
más piadosa aunque muy poco,
aqueste caso modera:

I left for the convent in a trice,
but oh! at the door I met
a lion, a savage Hircanian tiger:
I encountered, in short, a Marcela.

Approaching her ever so carefully,
I said with deference,
"Good mother, it is a happy chance
to run into your Reverence,

"because I have right here for you
just what you need, I know it.
Although my scholar's hood is ragged,
I fancy myself a poet,

"and proud to be a disciple of
that fertile riverbank, Vega,[§]
the many offspring of whose wit
gave Spain such grand resplendence.

"For you, a prologue I've composed
to accompany your fiesta,
and it is my wish that every nun
derive from it great pleasure."

"Where have you put this prologue, then?"
she rejoined with a mouth of thistles,
all slantymouthed and droughtymouthed
and thornymouthed and splintered.

"Good Mother, I carry it at my breast;
here it is, your Reverence."
"Show me the Prologue, good fellow; God
keep you,
I'm off to chapel for terce."[||]

"Now, my good Mother," I made reply,
"I beg you the charity
of giving me something, your Reverence,
for great is my poverty."

"In Jesus' name, my friend, see here!
far greater is our own need:
for the persons number forty and two
that this convent must house and feed;

§ Here, as elsewhere in her poetry, Marcela quips directly about her father, the dramatist and poet Lope de Vega.—Trans.

|| "terce": the service of the third canonical hour.—Trans.

—Mariana, tráele a este pobre,
que dejé en la cobertera
dos puerros y un güebo casi,
que sólo falta la yema—.
    —Esto tengo para mí,
con que ahorraré la cena;
no lo dé su caridad,
voy a cerrar la despensa.

    Bien se ve cuán poco sabe
su caridad lo que cuestan
las cosas pues tan sin tiento,
manirrota, las franquea—.

    Esto dijo aquella sierpe,
aquella áspera Marcela.
yo, un poco más atrevido,
que la razón da licencia,
    le dije: —Pues, madre mía,
en una fiesta como ésta,
¿No ha sobrado alguna cosa?
¿Es posible que una pera,
    un poquito de pescado,
un poco de pan no tengan?
—Si me ha sobrado pescado,
si fruta o cosas como éstas,
    ¿no ve, hermano, que me falta
casi toda una Cuaresma?
En ella: la Encarnación,
san Josef, que es la primera,
    Jueves Santo, que es forzoso
dar una comida buena,
Resurrección, cien apóstoles
que entre Pascuas se celebran,
    la Cruz de Mayo, santa Ana,
primero la Magdalena...—
Y yo no la atajara,
el calendario leyera
    sin dejar santo ni santa
en el cielo ni en la tierra
a quien esta mujer dura
en sus fiestas no metiera.

    Digo en su ponderación,
que en refitorio no entran
si no es en el Flosantoram
o en otra sacra leyenda.

"with a hundred thousand expenses to
        meet
and the scarcest revenue;
not a single penny do we collect,
and our debts are coming due."
    "I'm sure, good Mother, that it is so,"
I said, "but please see here,
for my poverty and my hunger too
have the very simplest cure:
    "Give me no more than a nice broad
        bowl
of cabbage and lentils, stewed,
and you'll have fulfilled all I could ask
with a deed most kind and good."
    "It surely would be good, in truth!"
each cabbage costs one whole penny,
six farthings each endive costs at the least,
and every measure of lentils
    "—what with prices rising, and carried
        on up—
why it easily comes to fifty;
and then the grocer's lads will want
a drink and a bit of luncheon.
    "Mariana, is it not just as I say?
Since everything costs us more
than it's worth, the good Lord Himself
        only knows
whether in fact God desires
    "that nuns should be fed!" These
        words were said
by the first of her dear companions,
and sisters indeed they might have been,
both miserly and phlegmatic.

    But the next nunnyverbiage,
her second companion dear,
more merciful—though little enough—
would restrain this sad affair:
    "Mariana, please bring this poor lad a
        bite,
for upon the tablecloth
I left two leeks and most of an egg,
missing nought but its yolk."
    I have kept those for myself,
so I may save on my supper;

—¿Es posible—, repliqué,
que un poco de pan les falta?—
—y cómo si falta, amigo—,
respondió la muy pelada,

—ya ven cuán caro es el pan,
y siete hanegas no bastan
para el gasto del convento
para una sola semana,

y estamos, si no lo sabe,
muy por extremo alcalzadas—.
No alcancéis, plegue a san Bruno,
a tener un poco de agua,

mujeres las más crüeles,
las más míseras y malas
que han contado las historias
ni que han fingido las fábulas.

Dios os dé hambre canina
y no podáis apagarla,
y siempre el pan que comáis
no os pase de la garganta.

Toda la demás comida
se os vuelva amarga o salada,
en el caldo halléis mil moscas,
en los güevos, garrapatas,

los higos despidan tierra
y mil gusanos las pasas;
en la cabeza os dé tiña,
en las manos os dé sarna;

veáis en vuestras despensas
ratones en abundancia.
y en este discurso largo
que de vuestro oficio os falta,

no quede muela ni diente
que a las monjas no se caiga;
déles grandes desconciertos,
todas vomiten sin tasa,

males de madre sin cuenta,
lombrices, dolor de ijada...
Gastéis a arrobas el vino,
a todas ofenda el agua,

no pueda comer ninguna
aceitunas ni ensalada;
destiérrese todo aquello
con que sois más aliviadas,

your Charity# must not give it away—
I am going to close up the cupboard.

"Now I can see how little you know
of costs, your Charity:
with so little caution, oh spendthrift
    woman!
you give things aways for free."

This was said by the serpent herself,
that harsh and sour Marcela.
Then I found myself somewhat
    emboldened (for
to be right grants some permission),

and I said to her, "Then, Mother mine,
in a fiesta like yours here,
can there be nothing that is left over?
Not even a little pear,

"nor perhaps a morsel of boiled fish,
nor a crust of bread today?"
"If fish or fruit has been left over,
or such things as you say,

"don't you see, brother, I still must face
the greater part of Lent?**
And in it the Annunciation occurs;††
but first Saint Joseph's is spent;§§

"Holy Thursday, obligatory to serve
a good substantial meal;||||

Again, "your Charity," like "your Rever-
ence," is a conventional term of respect, with a
pointedly ironic play on "charity," given the
stinginess shown.—Trans.

** Lent: the Christian fast before Easter,
comprising forty fasting days of penance and
abstinence in which only one meal a day,
excluding fish and meat, were permitted. The
persona of "Marcela" launches into the calendar of holy days (and meals to be served).—
Trans.

†† the Annunciation: the angel Gabriel's
announcement to the Virgin Mary that she
will give birth to the son of God; celebrated
March 25.—Trans.

§§ Saint Joseph's [Day]: the feast day honor-
ing Mary's husband; celebrated March 19.—
Trans.

|||| Holy Thursday: the Thursday before
Easter; more dramatic irony, in that the days
immediately preceding the crucifixion are a
period of specially observed fast and mourning.—Trans.

sólo gastéis lectuario,
bizcochos, nueces moscadas,
y todas digan a voces
que habéis querido matarlas.

Y a no ser yo tan paciente,
más maldiciones echara,
que el justo enojo me obliga
a demostración tamaña.

the Resurrection; a hundred Apostles
from Easter to Christmastide;##
    the Cross of May and Saint Anne's
        Day,***
but first the Magdalene. . ."†††
and if I had not interrupted, she would
have recited the calendar then,§§§

    leaving aside neither female nor male,
on earth nor in highest heaven,
whom this stingy woman would fail
to include in her saints' day planning.

    She'd not fail to *mention* them, I mean;
the refectory they'd not enter,
save in the "Garland of Saints" read aloud,
or some other holy legend.

    "But can it be," was my retort,
"you've not even a bit of bread?"
Miss Empty-Pockets answered me,
"And how should we have it, friend?

    "You see how expensive bread has
        become,
and seven whole measures won't keep
the convent supplied with enough for its
        use
for even a single week;

    "and we are, if indeed you do not know,
plunged in the direst hardship."
Then may it not soften (good Saint Bruno
        give aid)||||||
by so much as a bit of water!

a hundred apostles: that is, saints' feasts are observed between the two major cycles of the Christian year.—Trans.

*** the Cross of May and Saint Anne's Day: the "Invention" or Finding of the True Cross, celebrated on May 3; Saint Anne is the mother of the Virgin Mary, celebrated on July 26.—Trans.

††† the Magdalene: Saint Mary Magdalene, the legendary repentant woman sinner.—Trans.

§§§ The calendar of saints' days throughout the liturgical year.—Trans.

|||||| Saint Bruno: founder of the Carthusian order, renowned for austere fasting and penance.—Trans.

You three most miserable and cruel
and evil-hearted of ladies
that were ever described in bygone tales
or invented in stories:
    may God give you a ravening appetite
and never let you fill it;
when you break bread, may every bite
stick fast in your gullet.
    And may all the rest of your food
turn either salty or bitter,
may you find a thousand flies in your broth
and in your eggs find chiggers;
    may bits of dirt fall from your figs
and a thousand worms from your raisins;
may you have ringworm upon your scalps
and on your hands have scabies;
    and in your larders may you find
little mice aplenty.
And lest you take too great a part
in a speech so lengthy,
    may not a molar or tooth remain
in the mouth of any nun;
may their bones stick out all over,
may they vomit and never be done,
    and have cramps beyond all counting,
and tapeworms, and stitch in the side;
may all of you sicken at water,
so you go through gallons of wine;###
    may not a one be able to eat
simple olives or greens;
may everything be banished away
that brings you the slightest relief,
    may you only digest medicinal jams
and nutmeg and dry biscuit;
and may all the nuns, at the top of their lungs,
shout that you've tried to kill them.
    And so, were I not such a patient lad,
I'd spout more imprecations,
for a righteous anger requires of me
this impressive demonstration.

(Translated by Amanda Powell)

At the time, wine was used for medicinal
purposes.—Trans.

2
Loa en la profesión de la hermana Isabel del Santísimo Sacramento

Discretísimo senado,
dóminas santas y bellas
monji-serafines todas
en ardores y en pureza.
Jardín de diversas flores,
de abundantes frutas huerta
y de perfumes divinos
pomo hermoso y cazoleta.
Yo soy un pobre estudiante
tentado por ser poeta,
cosa que por mis pecados
me ha venido por herencia,
porque: *Qualis pater talis
filius,*[1] etcétera.
Supe que en aquesta casa
hoy la fiesta se celebra
de las bodas siempre alegres,
siempre felices, y exentas
de las humanas desgracias
que ha vinculada la tierra
en todos sus regocijos
por más lícitos que sean;
en fin, supe se consagra,
se dedica y hace entrega
la hermana Isabel dichosa,
que hoy su himeneo celebra
con la sacra Trinidad,
que la persona tercera
enlaza dos corazones,
que en la voluntad dispuesta
de Isabel, hace que Cristo
tome posesión entera.
Tan a lo tierno la mira
tan fino la galantea,
tan liberal la enriquece
y tan Maestro la enseña,
que esperamos ha de ser,
si humana correspondencia,

1. "Cual padre, tal hijo."

2
In Celebration of the Profession of Vows of Sister Isabel of the Blessed Sacrament

Most discrete senate,
blessed and beautiful teachers,
sister-angels all
of zeal and purity;
garden of many flowers,
of bounteous fruits a grove
and of divine perfumes
a vial, a vessel.
I am a lowly student
tempted to be a poet,
something which, for my sins
I have inherited,
for *Qualis pater talis filius,*[1] etc.
I learned that today in this convent,
you are celebrating
the joyful nuptials,
always happy and exempt
from human misfortune
with which life tempers
all our joys,
however innocent they are.
As I was saying, I learned that today
the happy Sister Isabel
will be consecrated,
and will devote and surrender herself
upon the celebration of her union
with the holy Trinity,
and the Holy Spirit
will join two hearts;
Isabel being so disposed,
Christ will take full possession of her.
How tenderly He gazes upon her,
how galantly He woos her
and lavishes her with riches
and masterfuly teaches her,
and we hope that though
her love be a human love
yet her zeal will be more than human,

1. "Like father, like son."

más que humano, su fervor,	and we bid you rejoice
y que a comenzar dispuesta	that she is now disposed
se halla para una vida	to begin a life
que de virtudes compuesta,	to virtue consecrated;
dé a Dios infinita gloria;	give God praise
y todas sus reverencias	for all your Reverences;
de tenerla por hermana	for having her as a sister
sumamente estén contentas.	be you supremely content.
Ya Isabel, con nuevos bríos,	And now, Isabel, with renewed zeal,
se dispone, y considera	is ready and believes
que con lo activo de Marta	that active like Martha
tendrá a María contenta,	she will best please Mary,
porque no hará división	for there could be no division
de dos hermanas tan buenas.	between two such good sisters.
Con esto, el divino Esposo	With this the divine Spouse,
que ama tanto cuanto cela,	who so loves all He watches over,
gustoso en su corazón	will gladly take residence
hará asiento, de manera	in her heart, so that she,
que ella, unida y transformada,	at one with Him and transformed,
goce del cielo en la tierra.	will enjoy heaven while on earth.
Pero porque en tanto día	But since if every day
si todo fuese de veras,	were such a solemn occasion
sería cosa cansada,	it would be a tiresome affair,
melancólica y funesta,	melancholy and unlucky,
quisiera templar, si acierto,	I would like, if I might, to temper
a lo humano, mi vigüela,	my guitar to a human range,
y que en estilo gracioso	and bid, in lighthearted manner,
me ayudasen las doncellas	the young maidens of Parnassus
del sacro monte Parnaso,	to come assist me,
sin que a lo serio compuestas	only I bid they come forward
vengan en esta ocasión.	adorned as for a festive occasion.
Con cuidado las espera	My empty gourd anxiously awaits them
mi calabaza, que en ayunas	and they also must be fasting still
lo mismo están; poca cena	after the paltry meal
como ha dispuesto y trazado	laid before them and prepared
la más lucida miseria,	with the matchless stinginess,
la poquedad más bizarra	the most bizarre miserliness
que ha sacado en quinta esencia	that the exceedingly dull Marcela
con indecible trabajo	has managed to distill for them
la gran flema de Marcela.	with untold labor.
El otro día apostaron,	The other day she
la madre ministra y ella,	and the Mother Superior wagered
a cuál haría más actos	who would obtain the greatest heights
de escasez y de miseria.	of scarcity and stinginess.

Y sucedió un caso raro
que pide atención entera:
que entrambas a dos ganaron
y quedaron muy contentas.
Quisiera, por mi consuelo,
el que la misma Marcela
relatara de sí misma
lo que hay en esta materia.
Mas dejémoslo al silencio
que no es posible que pueda
explicarse con palabras
una cosa que es inmensa.
Pero la madre ministra
bien quisiera que comieran,
pero que no se gastara,
sí, de milagro fuera.
Ya presumo que dirán,
con causa, sus Reverencias,
a qué propósito fue
el decir que era poeta.
Yo daré razón de mí,
que me he olvidado no entiendan
de lo que dije al principio.
Ninguna se me divierta,
ni me escupa ni me tosa,
se me recoja o se duerma,
que es tan sutil y delgado
mi ingenio, que si bostezan
o hacen acción semejante,
se me perturba y enreda.
Es cosa para admirar
tan grande delicadeza;
si oyese yo que respiran,
hagan cuenta que no hay fiesta.
En fin, los días pasados
quise hacer cierta comedia,
digo, un coloquio que fuese
del gusto de la profesa.
Levantéme una mañana
cuando, con boca de perlas,
despertaba el alba al sol
y acostaba a las estrellas,
porque: *Aurora gratissima musis.*[2]

2. "El alba es grata a las musas."

And a strange thing occurred
most worthy of note:
the two of them both won the wager
and were thus content.
For my consolation, I would prefer
for Marcela to explain the matter
in her own words.
But let us leave off speaking of it,
for how could she ever
explain in words
something so immense?
And no doubt Mother Superior
would wish you could all eat
without incurring any expense;
that would be a miracle indeed!
I imagine now your Reverences
will with good reason ask
what in the world I was talking about
when I called myself a poet.
But I will yet justify myself,
do not think I have forgotten
what I was saying when I began.
And let no one mock me,
nor spit on me, nor cough,
nor leave the room, nor fall asleep,
for so subtle and refined
is my genius that if you should yawn
or make any other gesture
I would become perturbed and lose my place.
Such great delicacy is
something to marvel at;
heed that if I should even
hear you breathing, the feast will be over.
Well, then, these past days
I strove to write a certain comedy,
that is, a discourse, that would be
pleasing to the professing novice.
I awoke one morning
just as, with her mouth of pearls,
the dawn was awakening the sun
and putting to sleep the stars,
because *Aurora gratissima musis.*[2]

2. "Dawn is most welcome to the muses."

Mas, con grandes aparatos
salieron todas compuestas
las Musas, digo, que Apolo
me influía su elocuencia.
Vestidas gallardamente,
tocadas por excelencia,
traían joyas muy ricas,
velos, bandas, flores, trenzas,
aunque una vino muy tosca,
mala Musa, Musa adversa.
El desaliño y desaire
pienso que imitar pudiera
María de San Francisco
que tan gustosa le ostenta.
No traía, cual las otras,
arte, preceptos y ciencia;
ninguna las profesaba,
gran defecto en la pobreza,
porque: *Necesitas caret leges.*[3]
Madres mías, ¿eso hacen?,
pues ya mi ingenio me deja;
si quieren que fiesta haya,
han de quedar como muertas.
Ríanse, pero de suerte
que no se oiga y se vea.
Quiero volver a decir
las dichas de la profesa.
No hay que tratar, yo no acierto;
¿no quieren estarse quedas?
¿Concepción háse sentado?
Que perturbará si entra
a la mitad del coloquio,
que no será cosa nueva.
Gracias al Señor que ya
se va rompiendo la vena,
y si va tomando brío,
tendremos galante fiesta.
Un poquito ha estado floja,
quiera el cielo que no vuelva
a enflaquecer, hagan, madres,
oración con toda priesa.

And, with great ceremony,
all the Muses appeared before me
and Apollo inspired me with
his eloquence.
Most elegantly attired,
flawlessly coiffed, they were
adorned with rich jewels,
veils, sashes, flowers, and braids;
yet one came who was poorly attired,
a bad Muse, a contrary Muse,
whose slovenliness and lack of grace
I believe Maria of San Francisco
could well imitate,
who so readily displays them.
She did not wear, like the others,
the garb of art, precepts, or science;
she professed none of these,
a great defect in one so poor,
for *Necesitas caret leges.*[3]
My dear mothers, is this how you treat me?
Well, then, my wit abandons me;
if you wish me to celebrate this day,
you will have to remain as still as death.
Laugh, but take care
I do not hear or see you.
But let me return to the
good fortune of the professing novice.
There is nothing to say, I cannot continue;
can you not be still?
Has Concepción seated herself?
She will surely make a commotion if she
    enters
in the middle of my discourse,
which would not be unusual.
Thanks to the Lord my inspiration
has finally broken out of its pen,
and if it gets up enough resolve,
we will have a fine feast yet.
It has been a bit sickly of late,
heaven grant it not
falter again, dear sisters;
quickly, say a prayer!

---

3. "La pobreza carece de preceptos."

3. "Poverty lacks precepts."

Atención, que va una cosa
con erudición muy nueva.
Válame Dios, ¡qué trabajo!
No hay hipérbole que pueda
encarecer lo que pasa
de aflicciones un poeta
si sale; embota el ingenio,
si la vena se le cierra:
no me ocurre de importancia
cosa que deciros pueda.
Corrido estoy y confuso,
¡quién escaparse pudiera!
Ea, consonantes tardos,
ea, gordas agudezas,
¿por qué me desamparáis
en ocasión tan de veras?
Señoras monjas, yo voy
a hacer luego una receta
de anacardina, y un parche
de galvano o girapliega,
que dicen es milagroso
para hacer que los poetas
en un momento disparen
los versos como escopetas;
también dicen, que es famoso,
unas rosquillas muy buenas.
vaya la madre ministra,
y venciendo su miseria,
de bollicos y rosquillas
me traiga una grande espuerta.
Con esto confío en Dios
que en seis semanas enteras
habré compuesto una copla
con cuatro pies, muy derecha.
Iré remitiendo así
algunas otras que ostentan
lo grande de mi talento,
lo lucido de mis letras.
Si de ello fueren gustando
mis madres, sus reverencias,
envíen a mi posada
ricos dulces y conservas;
así, madres, he pensado
el dejar hecha una hacienda.

Now heed, for you are about to
hear a singularly erudite discourse.
God help me, what a task!
There is no hyperbole to
describe the embarrassment the
poet faces if it happens that
his wit deserts him,
if his insipiration flags.
I cannot think of anything to say
that could be of any consequence.
I am ashamed and confused.
How to escape this?
Harken, tardy consonants
and you, wise witticisms,
why do you abandon me now
on such a solemn occasion?
Medames sisters, I am
going to compose a recipe for you
for cashew nut paste, a galvanizing
medicine plaster and purgative
they say works miraculously
to help poets
instantly discharge
verses like bullets;
as well as, and this is quite remarkable,
some most delicious sweet rolls.
Have Mother Superior
conquer her miserliness
and bring me a basket
full of sweet buns and pastries.
With them I trust in God
I will be able to compose a fine
poem complete from head to tail
in just six weeks.
I will send along with it
some others that will demonstrate
the magnitude of my talent
and the brilliance of my erudition.
And if, dear sisters, your Reverences,
you should fancy any of them,
please dispatch to my lodgings
some tasty sweets and conserves;
this is how, dear mothers, I have devised
to earn my fortune.

Quiero darles hoy las pascuas
de la Navidad que llega,
que aunque faltan cinco meses,
la prevención siempre es buena.
"Quien da luego, da dos veces",
dice el adagio en mi tierra,
pues recíbanlas con gusto,
tengan las Pascuas cual sean
los años que yo deseo:
no se la demos a medias,
además qué podrá ser
que ocupaciones me tengan
entonces sin atención,
y caiga en falta tan fea
como dejar de cumplir
obligación como ésta.
Mas, porque ya se hace tarde
y mi compañía espera,
que a recitar el coloquio
con grande afecto se apresta,
será bien que se cesen ya
las burlas, porque de veras
digamos a nuestra novia
una palabra siquiera.
Y daréla un documento
que, si bien común, encierra
una grande perfección
a que el alma santa ancla:
que es que piense cada día
que aquél es el que comienza
a servir y amar su esposo
muy desvelada y atenta,
a no hacer imperfección
que alguna advertencia tenga,
que en lo frágil de esta vida
es imposible que pueda
pasar sin el tropezar.
Pero es menester que advierta
que ha de sacar más virtud
con el pesar y la enmienda,
y que a la oración continua
tan aficionada sea
que ore sin intermisión
como San Pablo lo enseña.

I wish you all today
happy tidings in advance
of the approaching Christmastide.
Although it is still five months off,
it is always best to be prepared:
"Who gives promptly gives twice,"
as they say in my country.
So, receive my best wishes with pleasure.
I wish you a merry Christmas
for as many years as I hope to have:
let us not be stingy with our wishes,
for it is possible that in the future
other duties will have me so preoccupied
that I will fail miserably
to comply with such social obligations as
    this.
But since it grows late
and this company still awaits
with great eagerness
the recital of my discourse,
it were better to cease
this banter in order
to offer our bride
if but a few sincere words.
And I will give her advice
that, though very humble,
contains a great perfection
for the holy soul to adhere to:
which is that she regard each day
as if the very first she began
to serve and to love her husband
with great vigilance and attention;
that she not be guilty of any
imperfection of consequence,
though it is not possible
to pass through this fragile life
without stumbling.
She must remember
that she will become more virtuous
through repentance and reform;
and may she continue to
be fond of praying,
and do it without ceasing,
as Saint Paul recommended.

Mas crea que la oración
no puede ser muy intensa
si dejan de acompañarla
el silencio y la modestia,
sus sólidos fundamentos,
la humildad y la obediencia.
Levantará un edificio
con hermosura y grandeza;
compañera inseparable
la rica pobreza sea:
gozará de la abundancia
aunque tenga grandes menguas.
A la santa mansedumbre
ni la olvide ni la ofenda,
que es de la humildad hermana
y de la paz muy parienta.
Con esto será, sin duda,
tan ajustada y perfecta,
que sea Dios alabado
y engrandecido por ella.

But may she be mindful that her prayer
will not be as intense
if not accompanied
by silence and modesty,
and its solid foundations,
humility and obedience.
Thus will she raise an edifice
of beauty and grandeur;
let rich poverty be
her steady companion:
she will enjoy great wealth
though she suffer great want.
May she neither neglect nor offend
holy meekness,
who is sister to humility
and close kin to peace.
If she heeds this advice, no doubt
she will be so accomplished and perfected
that God will be praised
and glorified in her.

(Translated by Amanda Powell)

3
El jardín del convento

En estas verdes hojas
que aquesta fuente riega
con agua de mis ojos,
que suya no la lleva,
    contemplo, amado mío
tu grande providencia,
tu beldad soberana,
y tu hermosura inmensa.
    También, por el contrario,
conozco mi vileza,
mi imperfección sin par,
mi descuido y tibieza,
    pues las hojas y flores
que crecen tan apriesa,
con sus calladas voces
significan mis menguas,

3
The Convent Garden

Upon these green leaves
moistened by yonder fountain
with tears from my eyes,
the source of its water,
    I contemplate, my love,
your great bounty,
your sovereign beauty,
and your immense love.
    And, in contrast,
I am mindful of my lowliness,
my matchless imperfection,
my neglectfulness and indifference,
    since the leaves and flowers
that sprout so quickly,
with their silent voices
signify my paltriness,

y siempre que las miro
parece que me enseñan
que yo sola en el mundo
soy la que nunca medra.

Miro del cinamomo
aquella copia inmensa
de su olorosa flor
que tanto nos deleita.

Parece que a porfía
la multitud afecta
llevarse de las flores
la palma de belleza.

En las guardadas rosas
a quien espinas cercan,
de tus hermosas llagas
la memoria refrescan.

Los vistosos jazmines
en su candor ostentan
lo lindo de tus manos
y liberal franqueza,

porque, sin aguardar
que los cojan por fuerza,
ellos se dan al suelo
sin hacer resistencia.

Acuérdame tu olor
la fragante mosqueta,
tan linda entre las flores
y tan noble en sí mesma.

El clavel estimado
tu sangre representa,
y por esto merece
le traten con decencia.

De tus hermosos labios,
del coral dulce afrenta,
su cárdeno color
me muestran las violetas.

Majestuosa siempre
la cándida azucena,
tu bellísimo cuello
venturoso semeja.

La fecunda retama,
tan rubia como bella,
de tus cabellos de oro
me da memorias tiernas.

and whenever I gaze upon them
they seem to teach me
that I alone of all
have not flourished in this garden.

I look at the China tree,
the immense abundance
of its sweet-smelling flowers
that so delight us;

and it seems that, by its
abundance and persistence,
it strives to wear the crown
of beauty above all other flowers.

The reticent roses,
surrounded by thorns,
bring to mind
your beautiful wounds.

The colorful jasmines
in their candor reveal
the beauty of your hands
and your generosity,

for, not waiting to
be picked by force,
they cast themselves upon the ground
without the least resistance.

The fragrant white rose
reminds me of your scent,
so noble among all the flowers
and so beautiful of itself.

The esteemed carnation
signifies your blood,
and for this it is
held in such regard.

Of your beautiful lips
that tenderly shame the coral,
the violets display
their deep purple.

Ever majestic,
the white and guileless lily
is the happy likeness
of your perfect neck.

The bounteous furze,
so fair and lovely,
sparks tender memories
of your golden hair.

Muestra por abrazar
la siempre verde yedra;
a que busque tu unión
provoca mi tibieza.

Procurando ascender,
si presumida trepa,
humilde se aprisiona,
que de amante se precia.

Misericordia y paz
este olivo me enseña
que siempre las procure
por costosas que sean.

Las rojas clavellinas
y manutisas bellas,
de imitar tu color
parece que se precian,

pero el bizarro lirio,
con gravedad modesta,
porque a él te comparas
más ufano campea.

Süave el albahaca,
símbolo de pureza,
su verdor apacible
nuestra esperanza alienta.

Clavelones, adorno
de las últimas fiestas,
enseñan que la muerte,
como terrible, es cierta.

Recuerdo de humildad
es la hierba doncella,
aunque vistosa y grave
no sale de la tierra.

Los amargos ajenjos
me enseñan a que tenga
mortificado el gusto
y al apetito venza.

El robusto alhelí
que el invierno no seca,
me fuerza que haga rostro
a toda aspereza.

El funesto ciprés,
aunque árbol de tristeza,
provoca a devoción
y soledad enseña;

The ever verdant ivy
shows its desire to
unite with you in its embrace,
while bearing witness to my tepidness;

for, if attempting to ascend
it be too eager,
presuming itself a lover,
it becomes instead a humble prisoner.

Mercy and peace are
what this olive tree teaches me,
striving ever for these virtues
regardless of the sacrifice.

The rosy pinks
and handsome morning glories
seem to want
to presume your colors,

and the admirable iris,
with its grave modesty,
to compete with you
stands out most proudly.

Sweet basil,
symbol of purity,
inspires our hope
with its placid greenery.

Marigolds, adornment
of season's end,
teach that death
is as terrible as certain.

I am reminded that the grass
is the maiden of humility,
though verdant and grave
is does not climb above the earth.

The bitter wormwood
teaches me to mortify my appetite
and to conquer my hunger.

Robust stock,
that even winter does not wither,
urges me to confront
every adversity.

The forlorn cypress,
though the tree of sadness,
inspires devotion
and teaches solitude;

and that sweetly named plant,

y la del nombre dulce,
felicísima hierba
que de Santa María
nos acuerda y recrea.

Las ásperas ortigas,
intratables y fieras,
en igualar mi agrado
presumen competencia.

Entre todas las flores,
puede la gigantea
pretender por amante
que alaben tus finezas.

Del sol enamorada
siempre mirarle intenta,
y por vueltas que da
de seguirle no cesa.

¡Oh, cómo reprehende
el descuido y tibieza
con que busco, Dios mío,
a tu amable presencia!

Los árboles copados
alegres manifiestan
los sazonados frutos
que el justo te presenta.

Las abundantes parras,
alegres manifiestan
que a tu sangre real
accidentes le prestan.

Mis años mal gastados
me acuerda aquesta higuera,
pues ha crecido tanto,
y yo estoy tan pequeña,

y habiéndonos plantado
en esta santa tierra,
casi en un mismo tiempo
mil ventajas me lleva.

El riguroso invierno
con su mucha aspereza,
os quita los vestidos
y deja en gran pobreza;
  tolerando rigores,
y sufriendo inclemencias,
me enseñáis, apacibles,

most fortunate of grasses,
reminds us and re-creates
for us our holy Mary.

The harsh nettles,
untouchable and wild,
presume to compete
with my own charms.

Of all the flowers,
perhaps the loving sunflower
strives to have us best
praise your goodness;
  enamored of the sun,
it strives ever to face it,
which, with its turning,
it never ceases to do.

Oh, how it reprimands
the indifference and feebleness
with which, my Lord,
I seek your beloved presence!

The arching trees,
happy, bring forth
their ripened fruit
so justly offered to you.

The abundant vines
gladly bear witness
that your sacred blood
has been spilt.

Of my wasted years
I am reminded by that fig tree,
for it has grown so tall
while I have remained so small;
  and though we were both planted
on this holy ground at nearly the same
    time,
it has so many advantages over me.

Rigorous winter
with its bitter winds
tears your clothing to shreds,
leaving you in stark poverty.

Yet bearing these rigors,
and suffering inclemencies
so peacefully, you teach me
to have patience.

a que tenga paciencia.
  Con suave agasajo
la hermosa primavera
siempre os sirve gustosa
de madre y camarera.
  De la Resurrección
parece nos da nuevas,
cuando, sin menoscabo,
nos tornen nuestra tierra.
  Los árboles y plantas,
las flores y las hierbas
publican tu hermosura
y dicen tu grandeza.
  Todos, Señor, me animan,
me enseñan y me fuerzan
a que te sirva y ame,
te alabe y te engrandezca.

With its soft breezes
happy springtime
always serves you willingly
as mother and servant.
  It seems to be the harbinger
of the Resurrection
when, without detriment,
our land is plowed.
  Trees and plants,
flowers and grasses,
all herald your beauty,
and preach your greatness.
  All, my Lord, inspire me
and teach me and fortify me
to love you and to serve you,
to glorify and praise you.

(Translated by Amanda Powell)

Sor María de Santa Isabel (Marcia Belisarda)

Sor María de Santa Isabel is, from a biographical perspective, a virtual enigma. From what we can deduce from her poems, she was a nun in the Royal Convent of the Conception in Toledo during the seventeenth century. In an encomium to her, Montoya calls her "Toledana," for which reason we may guess that she was born in Toledo. According to her own testimony, she wrote her first poems at age twenty-seven. The few dates connected to her poems cover the period from 1642 to 1646. After that date she collected her poems in a manuscript, hoping to see them published.

Sor María de Santa Isabel wanted to publish her poetry. The manuscript she prepared was ready to be submitted to the censor; several encomia had been collected to precede Sor María's own poems; she had chosen a pseudonym, Marcia Belisarda, under which to publish her work; and she had written a prologue in which she announced her desire to see published not only a few poems here and there, but an edition of her complete works. The preliminary poems include one Sor María dedicated to "Lady María de Ortega, because she shepherded this book for me,"[1] which suggests that María de Ortega circulated Sor María's manuscript, collecting dedicatory poems, and acted as her representative. Furthermore, Sor María reveals in her prologue a sophisticated understanding of the importance of collecting her works and publishing them together so they might be judged not individually, but rather each in relation to the others, and as the product of a single pen.

Approximately two-thirds of the 138 poems included in Sor María's manuscript are on religious themes. Of these, many are dedicated to the lives of religious figures, including Saint Teresa; Saint Catherine of Siena; Santiago, the patron saint of Spain; and Beatriz de Silva, the legendary founder of the Conceptionist Order. Other religious poems are on emblematic themes, among them the Nativity, the sacrament of the Eucharist, the assumption of Mary, and the crucifixion. Still others celebrate convent occasions, such as professions or the visit of some ecclesiastical dignitary. Only one of the religious poems deals directly with a personal religious experience.

The predominant, though not exclusive, theme in Sor María's secular poetry is the failure of love. Like her religious verse, the antilove poems cannot be categorized as autobiographical. They rely on such familiar set pieces as the disenchanted lover, and they are remarkable not for the way in which they reveal the deepest reaches of

the poet's soul, but for the fluidity of the poetic voice, sometimes masculine, sometimes feminine, and sometimes of indeterminate gender. The beloved, similarly of no fixed gender, is frequently present only as an absence. In these poems, the poetic complaint is directed not to the beloved, but to love itself. The melancholy of some of Sor María's poems, as well as the jokes and satire of others, frequently have to do with love.

The Royal Convent of the Conception in Toledo did not isolate Sor María de Santa Isabel from the world. Her poems reveal not only that she was familiar with the poetic conventions of the day, but also that she kept current with the political and cultural events of the period. She knew popular songs and the works of other poets, lay as well as religious, with whom she sought to enter into conversation. A number of her poems are glosses on or replies to poems written by her contemporaries. As with the larger part of her religious work, these profane poems have their source in preexisting texts, and their author writes as one fully conscious of participating in the collective literary enterprise of her day. Sor María was generous to the poets of her era. In addition to the eulogies she wrote, she praised other women writers and incorporated several of their poems into her manuscript. She included, for example, a "Gloss that a Carmelite nun of Ocaña wrote, copied here because it is worthy of praise,"[2] a "very famous and justly sung *romance*,"[3] and a "*décima* by Doña Juana de Bayllo, nun of Santa Isabel el Real, to another, who had fainted."[4]

Sor María herself was sufficiently well known as a writer so that her poems appeared as encomia for novels and other literary works. She also wrote poetry at the behest of a number of people, among them a nun who was in love, a musician, and several ladies. A "great lady whose husband abhorred her,"[5] and a nun who "cried and cried at the death of another who had raised her,"[6] were two recipients of her poems. Such poetry was written to be read outside the convent. Equally public were the poems she wrote to celebrate professions, especially those the poet dedicated to postulants of religious orders other than her own. It is likely that Sor María reached the height of her fame between 1643 and 1646, when three of her poems were sung in the churches of Seville and Toledo. It was an ephemeral moment of glory. Despite the trouble she went to gathering, ordering, and introducing each poem with a short descriptive heading, Sor María de Santa Isabel never saw her poetry published.

We can only guess why Sor María's book was never issued. The process was suspended before the manuscript was sent to the censor, a necessary stage for the publication of any book of the era. It is possible that her death, whose date is unknown, interrupted the process, or that her confessor or mother superior forbade her to continue with such a profane project. Unlike Sor María de la Antigua, whose work was collected and published by the functionaries of her order, Sor María de Santa Isabel did not hold out the possibility to her sister Conceptionists of reflected glory through the publication of holy writing. Sor María's poems respond not to a pro-

found spirituality but to an aesthetic impulse nourished by a vital interest in the world, and as such they were of little use to her order. Whether the authorities withheld the support needed to publish her manuscript, or actively prohibited publication, the result was the same: a silence not inherent in Sor María de Santa Isabel, but constructed around her.

1. "Señora Doña María de Ortega, porque me condujo este libro," cited in Manuel Serrano y Sanz, *Apuntes para una biblioteca de escritoras españolas desde el año 1401 al 1833* (Madrid: Real Academia Española, 1905; repr. 1975), 2:363.

2. "Glosa que escribió una religiosa carmelita de Ocaña, puse aquí por digna de ser celebrada," Serrano y Sanz, 2:377.

3. "romance muy celebrado y cantado, con razón," Serrano y Sanz, 2:375.

4. "décima de Doña Juana de Bayllo, monja de Santa Isabel el Real, a otra que le dio un desmayo," Serrano y Sanz, 2:304.

5. "una gran señora, casada, a quien aborrecía su marido," Serrano y Sanz, 2:368.

6. "Una religiosa que lloraba sin medida la muerte de otra que la había criado," Serrano y Sanz, 2:369.

A quien leyere estos versos

Siendo pasión natural amar los hijos (aun sin ser hermosos, mayormente los del entendimiento), no se extrañará que estos del corto mío recoja mi amor; porque desperdiciados cada uno por sí, se exponen a padecer injustos naufragios en el crédito de las gentes; y juntos, podrán más bien valerse unos con otros, por cuanto la cadencia y las voces de ellos darán señas suficientes de ser, no hijos de muchos padres, sí de uno solo, tan honrosamente altivo que antes morirá de necesidad que buscarla socorro, estimando en más parecer pobre que valerse de prestado caudal para ostentarse lúcidamente rico; ociosa satisfacción para los que con discreta y urbana atención o intención deben advertir que quien dio el alma a la mujer la dio al hombre, y que no es de otra calidad que ésta, aquélla, y que a muchas concedió lo que negó a muchos; y si dando a conocer estos versos su legítimo autor (por serles en todos sus defectos parecidos) no bastare para que no se dude, la gloria que en la duda le adquirieren se deberá a Dios; y cuando no la goce no le falta la de su cielo, que es la que desea y pretende

Marcia Belisarda.

To the Reader of These Poems

As it is a common tendency[*] to love one's children (even when they are not beautiful, especially true of those that are offspring of the mind), it will not be thought strange that my love should gather up these, which are cut from my narrow cloth. If they are squandered about here and there with each one all alone, they risk suffering undeserved calamities among public opinion; whereas they can much better fend for themselves together; for jointly, their cadence and voices will suffice to show that they are not the children of various fathers but of one alone, and that one so honorably proud that he would sooner perish of want than seek any remedy for it, thinking it better to appear poor than to avail himself of borrowed treasure with which to show himself sumptuously rich. Such is the idle satisfaction of those who, with witty and urbane attentions or intentions, ought rather take note that the One who gave a soul to woman gave the same to man, and that the former soul is of no different quality than the latter; indeed, that One granted to many women what was denied to many men. And if the way in which these verses reveal their legititmate author (by the author's resemblance to them in every one of their defects) does not suffice to remove all doubt, then any glory they might obtain for their author by such doubt shall be due to God; but when the author enjoys no such glory, may that of God's heaven not be stinted. That is what is desired and sought by

Marcia Belisarda.

(Translated by Amanda Powell)

  * In the pre-Romantic context, the Spanish phrase "pasión natural" implies not so much sanctioned maternal feeling (deemed "natural" in nineteenth- and twentieth-century terms), but a lower order of feeling pertaining to the fallen world of nature.—Trans.

1
Romance

Procurad, memorias tristes,
divertir mi sentimiento
con penas que siempre son,
y no con gustos que fueron.

Representadme pesares,
dejad pasados contentos,
que son figuras de humo
en el teatro del viento.

Muy bien entiendo las voces
de vuestro mudo silencio,
que mal concertadas suenan
que acordes fueron un tiempo.

De mis muertas esperanzas
clamor parecen sus ecos,
o que se cantan endechas
a mi perdido sosiego.

Si con inciertos favores
olvidáis agravios ciertos,
guerra armáis al corazón,
no menos que a sangre y fuego.

No me deis en vaso de oro
disimulado veneno,
creyendo así lo que dice
quien no cree lo que siento.

Memorias, dejadme ya,
o acabad mi vida luego,
que no hay fuerzas en el alma
para tan crueles tormentos.

1
Poem in Ballad Meter

Make your attempt, sad memories,
to entertain my feeling
with sorrows that last eternally,
rather than joys that were fleeting.

Paint for me those heavy cares
and set aside past pleasures,
for the latter are but shapes of smoke
in the theater of rough weather.

I clearly understand the tones
of your dumbstruck silence;
they are all now out of tune,
that sounded once in unison.

Their echoes seem to ring the knell
for longings that have died,
or to sing a mournful dirge
of my lost, lamented quiet.

Forgetting definite attacks
to receive indefinite favors
does wage a war upon the heart
with no less than sword and fire.

Then give to me no golden cup
that holds a hidden poison;
I'll not believe words said by one
who disbelieves my feeling.

Leave me, memories, in peace
or let my life be ended;
my soul can surely not endure
to be so sore tormented.

(Translated by Amanda Powell)

2
Otro,
dándome el asunto

Escapé de tus cadenas
entregándome al sosiego,
amor, porque siempre al rostro
salen tus pesados hierros.

Cuando juzgué que me hallaba
libre de tu cautiverio,

2
Another Ballad,
on a Topic That Was Given to Me

I gave myself to rest and peace
and slipped your heavy chains,
oh love, because those weighty irons
always brand the face.

And just when I had thought myself
set free of your enslavement,

con otros nuevos me oprimes
fatigándome de nuevo.

¿De qué sirve atormentarme,
amor loco, niño ciego,
si ya me doy por vencido
a tus harpones soberbios?

Montes de dificultades
se oponen a mis deseos;
mas como te ves gigante
me animas al vencimiento.

Nací con honra y sin dicha;
a mucho obliga un respeto
y mucho más el amor;
¿qué haré, piadosos cielos?

Mi infeliz suerte maldigo,
del hado injusto me quejo,
pues muero de lo que callo
y de lo que digo muero.

Ni mi voluntad se logra,
ni en lo que callo merezco,
ni se cree lo que digo
por no asistir lo que quiero.

in newer fetters I am bound,
provoking new vexation.

What use then to toment me, Love—
—not only blind but daft—
when I've already given in
to your disdainful shafts?

Great peaks and towering obstacles
oppose all my desires;
but you incite me on to conquer
as you grow to giant's size.

I was born to honor but not good luck:
reverence makes one a mighty debtor,
but gracious heaven, what shall I do
when love's debt is even greater?

I curse my poor, unhappy lot
and moan my unjust fate;
of what I keep unsaid, I die,
and I die of what I say.

Neither is my will achieved,
nor has my silence merit,
nor is a word I say believed,
while my desire is absent.

(Translated by Amanda Powell)

3
*A una gran señora, casada,
a quien aborrecía su marido*

Divino hechizo de amor
en quien se admiran a un tiempo
la discreción y hermosura
en iguales paralelos.

A todo sentir del alma,
todo penar del deseo,
justamente querellosa
vives de tu injusto dueño.

Que como siempre el amor
sólo del alma hace empleo,
no se opusieron al tuyo
imperfecciones del cuerpo.

Alma irracional, sin duda,
tiene, pues no aspira a un cielo,

3
*To a Noble Married Lady,
Whose Husband Shunned Her*

Sweet love's divinest witchery
in whom we most admire
both beauty and sagacity
in strictly equal measure:

With all the feeling a soul attains,
all the yearning of desire,
it is only just that you complain
of your most unjust master.

As it is always true that love
inhabits but the soul,
against your love there never arose
the slightest bodily flaw.

Doubtless he has an irrational soul,
for he does not reach for heaven:

que tantas lleva en sus ojos
cuantos hacen movimientos.

Tantos dotes nobles, ricos
engrandecen tu secreto,
que el más discreto, en amarle
logra felices aciertos.

Que te adoran, no lo dudas,
que a tu dueño envidian, menos,
los que no alcanzan su dicha
con mejor conocimiento.

Vive, pues, siempre gozosa
de que los cielos te hicieron
deidad que sólo merecen
gozarla los cielos mesmos.

as many women fill his eyes
as those eyes make movements.

A noble dowry of such great worth
exalts what you keep hidden,
that the wisest man, in loving that,
finds happy realization.

You do not doubt that you are loved—
still less that your lord is envied—
by those who can't reach his good fortune
by means of greater wisdom.

Then know the heavens created you—
and so may you live and rejoice—
as a deity whom the heavens themselves
alone deserve to enjoy.

(Translated by Amanda Powell)

4
Décimas para una novela

Fatigado corazón
¿qué os aqueja? ¿ver el oro
de vuestro amado tesoro
convertido ya en carbón?
Apelad a la razón
si descansar pretendéis,
y en ella conoceréis
que ese de mi vida engaño
os libra del desengaño
que en su muerte hallar podréis.

No me admira que sintáis
padecer sin culpa alguna
desaires de mi fortuna,
cuando la pena pagáis;
mas si olvidado no estáis
de vos en vuestro desvelo,
pues sabéis que os hizo el cielo
tan valiente en el sufrir
en parte os pueden servir
las desdichas de consuelo.

Esforzad el sufrimiento
consultando a la cordura,
que es suerte, si no ventura,

4
Verses for a Novel

My heart, so sadly vexed and weary,
what can grieve you? Seeing the gold
had turned already into coal
that once was your beloved treasure?
You must have recourse to reason
if you seek to rest awhile;
through reason, then, you may espy
how my life met with illusion
delivering you from disillusion
you should have met with when love died.

No wonder, then, that you be grieved:
through no fault of your own, enduring
rebuffs and slights of my ill fortune
for which you pay the penalty;
but if, in your anxiety
and care, you don't forget yourself—
indeed, you know that heaven made you
courageous when there's cause to suffer—
your sad misfortunes may then offer
some measure even of consolation.

Find strength and courage as you suffer
by consulting your good sense,
for it is luck, if not happiness

ver a tiempo un escarmiento;
sufrid, que según yo siento,
grande hazaña viene a ser,
corazón mío, vencer
con sufrimiento el rigor,
por cuanto es mayor valor
el sufrir que el padecer.

Pues olvidar es forzoso,
determinaos, corazón,
a salir con la razón
de un abismo proceloso;
el tiempo es dificultoso
y en vos poco el valor fuera
si fácil guerra emprendiera;
si ésta os promete más gloria,
¡ea!, al arma, mi memoria,
muera el enemigo, muera.

to see in time a hard-won lesson;
to me it seems best, then, to suffer,
for it is a most heroic feat
to vanquish that severity,
my weary heart, with suffering,
and therefore there's more bravery
in suffering than endurance.

Because all things will be forgotten,
my heart, you must indeed determine
to find your way, by way of reason,
from the tempestuous abyss;
the hour is laborious,
and it says little of your mettle
to undertake an easy battle;
but this fight promises you more glory:
come then, to arms! my memory—
and may death come to the enemy!

(Translated by Amanda Powell)

5
*Décimas escritas muy de prisa,
en respuesta de otras en que
ponderaban la mudanza de las mujeres*

5
*Verses Written in a Great Hurry,
in Reply to Others, Which Considered
the Inconstancy of Women*

Hombres, no deshonréis
con título de inconstantes
las mujeres, que diamantes
son, si obligarlas sabéis.
Si alguna mudable veis,
la mudanza es argumento
de que antes quiso de asiento;
mas en vuestra voluntad
antes ni después, verdad
no se halló con fundamento.

Si mujer dice mudanza
el hombre mentira dice,
y si en algo contradice
es que el juicio no lo alcanza;
si se ajusta a igual balanza
por la cuenta se hallaría
en él mentir cada día
y en mudarse cada mes,

You men must no dishonor do
placing the label of "inconstant"
on women, firm as diamonds when
you can oblige them to be true.
If one seems changeable to you,
her change should serve as argument
that earlier she lacked good sense;
but when you come to your decision,
early and late, it lacks foundation
that might prove it to be true.

If true that woman speaks of change,
man in turn speaks of deception;
if there is any contradiction
it is that judgment's not attained;
if an equal balance were arranged
by all accounts we would then find
that every day he tells a lie
and changes once a month or so;

que el mentir vileza es;
mudar de hombres, mejoría.

to lie is base and vile and low—
'tis *betterment* for man to change.

(Translated by Amanda Powell)

6
Décimas para cantadas, dándome el asunto

Juré, Filis, de no verte
porque de verte moría:
aquesto jurar podía
mas no dejar de quererte;
confieso que es pena fuerte
que dos distantes estén,
Filis, queriéndose bien;
pero es de gusto sin igual
salir tan bien dese mal
que se pueda dar por bien.

   Cuerda fue en mi la locura
de no cumplir lo jurado,
porque amor no está obligado
a cumplir lo que se jura,
y porque así mi ventura
logró la mayor victoria
hallándome en tu memoria
cuando te juzgaba ajena,
con que salí de la pena
para entrar luego en la gloria.

   De valiente haciendo alarde
vencer quise en mí al amor,
y postrado a su valor
nunca me vi más cobarde;
sus leyes quiere que guarde
con decoro de rendido,
pues llego otra vez herido
de sus flechas a tus plantas,
donde vencedor levantas
al que se da por vencido.

   Ya no tengo de librarme
de más peligro de muerte
que el que ocasiona no verte,
pues sólo basta a matarme,

6
Verses to Be Sung, on a Topic That Was Given to Me

I swore, my Phyllis, not to see you,
for seeing you was death to me;
I could swear thus so not to see,
but could not swear to cease to love you;
'tis grief and sorrow, I must tell you,
that souls so distant parted be,
Phyllis, who love each other dearly;
but 'tis a joy without compare
to find such end to this despair
that in the end we think it goodly.

   'Twas madness prudent, wise, and sound
to break the vow I thus had sworn,
for surely love cannot be forced
to hold to every little vow;
indeed, this is precisely how
my luck achieved great victory,
remaining in your memory
though I feared you were another's;
so that I left behind my sorrows
to find myself in sudden glory.

   I boasted of my bravery
and thought to quell the love within;
by brave love I was overthrown
and saw myself most cowardly;
now love holds me to its decree
just as befits my great defeat,
for once again I'm at your feet
wounded by love's piercing shafts,
where, like a conqueror you lift
one who admits complete defeat.

   And now I have no cause to flee
from any risk of death besides
being distant from your sight,
for that alone means death to me;

que aunque puedan obligarme
celos a huir tu favor,
no me quitará el rigor
que amarte, señora, puede;
que adonde ceniza queda,
si no llamas, hay calor.

I might be obliged, by jealousy,
to avoid your kindly aid;
this would not keep me from the pain
that loving you may still impose,
for surely where the ashes glow
there's warmth, if not a flame.

(Translated by Amanda Powell)

7
Romance para una novela

Pues gustas, mi dueño hermoso,
que pinte así el sentimiento
del alma, va de pintura
aunque peligre el acierto.

Bien sé que en obedecerte
créditos de amante pierdo,
porque cuanto más te pinte
mi amor quedará en bosquejo.

Dije mucho y poco dije,
porque de mi amor los afectos
sólo amor puede decirlos
y él solo puede entenderlos.

Tus ojos vi por mi dicha
dos soles, digo, en un cielo,
a cuyo imperio el amor
rindió del alma trofeos.

Blasonaba mi albedrío
de leyes de amor exento,
mas ya en cárcel de hermosura
voluntario es prisionero;

preciado de que me quieras
estoy, pero aun más aprecio
que el amor con que te adoro
deba a mí conocimiento.

No sé, pues, cómo pintarte
este amor, dígale el pecho
que anhelos habla en suspiros
y ansias imprime en incendios.

¿No te han dicho ya mis ojos
la pasión de que adolezco?
No, pues, la aumenten tus dudas,
sea el creerla remedio,

7
Poem in Ballad Meter: For a Novel

Since you are pleased, my lovely lord,
that I should here portray
my soul's deep feeling, depict it I shall,
though the risk to good sense be grave.

I know well that by obeying you
I lose my good name as a lover;
the more I try to paint you, my lord,
my sketch of love grows rougher.

I've said but little, saying much,
because my love's affections
can only be expressed by love,
and love must comprehend them.

It was my luck to see your eyes,
two suns in heaven's one sphere;
at that, love offered to that realm
the spoils of my soul's war.

Once my free will made boastful claims
of freedom from love's duty;
now 'tis a willing captive, held
in the prison house of beauty.

'Tis my conceit that you love me,
but I hold in more esteem
that the love with which I worship you
owes its consciousness to me.

And so I cannot paint this love
for you; then let desires
spoken by sighs from the heart do so,
and longings published in fires.

Surely by now my eyes have told you
the passion that I endure?
Don't let your doubts increase it, when
your belief must be its cure;

que puesto que en que me quieras
todo bien a adquirir llego
será mal si dificultas,
que amor con amor granjeo.

   ¿Es posible que no sientes
el riguroso tormento
en que amor mi vida pone
cuando en tus ojos le veo?

   No es posible que le ignores;
¿mas, qué pretendes?; advierto
en el potro de tus dudas
ver en mí el morir postrero,

   sino es que la pena mía
la mires de tí tan lejos
que no atiendas que en el alma
está, de quien eres dueño;

   bien, que si amas como dices
sentirás lo que padezco
y si de ti no te fías
pregúntalo a mis desvelos

   de quien sabrás que entre glorias
que ocasiona el pensamiento
como en él solo se logran
soy Tántalo de deseos,[1]

   y que son en mi memoria
razones tuyas que observo,
discreta vida del alma,
gustosa muerte del cuerpo.

   En fin, te quiero; mal dije,
te adoro, no lo encarezco;
lo demás mi amor te diga
que yo explicarle no puedo;

   y si no crees te adoro
si dudas que por ti muero,
quíteme un puñal la vida
será más dulce instrumento;

   que quien ya no ha de gozarte
en el tranquilo himeneo
tendrá el morir por lisonja
como el vivir por desprecio;

for the minute you love me I shall
obtain all that is good;
it is wrong for you to pose obstacles,
for I capture love with love.

   Can you look indifferently
on tortures most severe
in which love plunges my own life
when I see it in your eyes?

   It cannot be you do not know it;
what do you seek? I seem to see
upon the rack of all your doubts
my own death, finally,

   as if you could behold my pain
and think it far from you,
all unawares it lies within
the soul that you do rule.

   Well, then, if you love just as you say,
you shall see what I endure,
and if you cannot trust yourself,
then ask my anxious cares,

   from whom you'll learn that, awaiting
    bliss
(which thought at times stirs up,
and only attainable in thought),
I'm a very Tantalus,[1]

   and that in my memory I heed
your closely reasoned motives,
the circumspect life of the soul,
and pleasing death of the body.

   In sum, I love you—I misspoke,
I adore you, 'tis scant praise—
my love shall tell you all the rest
and explain what I can't say;

   if you doubt that I adore you
and do not believe I die,
let a dagger take my life away,
'twill be a sweet device;

   for whoever can never possess you
in the peaceful wedding song
thinks death but a bit of flattery

---

1. Tántalo: figura mitológica griega castigada por los dioses con sufrir hambre y sed eternamente sin poder saciarse con el agua y la fruta que ve pero que no logra alcanzar.

1. Tantalus: figure in Greek myth whose punishment by the gods consists of suffering eternal hunger and thirst while water and fruit are in his sight and just beyond his reach.

mas no, que tuya es la vida;
viva yo a pesar del tiempo,
porque pises más envidias
y goces más rendimientos.

and holds her life in scorn;
　　but no—for life itself is yours—
let me live, though time may pass,
that you may tread upon more envy
and enjoy more submissiveness.

(Translated by Amanda Powell)

8

*Soneto, dándome por asunto
cortarse un dedo llegando
a cortar un jazmín*

Filis, de amor hechizo soberano,
cortar quiso un jazmín desvanecido,
y de cinco mirándose excedido
quedó del vencimiento más ufano.
　　No bien corta el jazmín, cuando tirano
acero, en rojo humor otro ha tenido,
mintiendo ramillete entretejido
de jazmín y clavel la hermosa mano.
　　Átropos bella a la tijera cede
piadosa ejecución si, inadvertida,
a su mano dolor ocasionando.[1]
　　Que si alma con su sangre dar no
　　　puede,
en vez de muerte, dio al jazmín la vida,
de amor el dulce imperio dilatando.

8

*A Sonnet, Having Been Given the Topic
of Cutting One's Finger in Reaching to
Cut a Jasmine*

Phyllis, sublime enchantment of love's
　　powers,
thought she would cut a haughty jasmine
　　branch;
itself undone by five buds on one hand,
this defeat left a still more boastful flower.
　　Just as she cut the jasmine, the tyrant
　　　blade
did stain one finger with a crimson flow,
so that her lovely hand now seemed to
　　show
a mingled nosegay, jasmine, and carnation.
　　The pretty Atropos allowed her shears
this part to play, as merciful as careless
inflicting pain upon her own soft hand.[1]
　　For as no soul with its own blood can
　　　meet,
she gave that jasmine life instead of death,
and love's sweet empire she did thus
　　extend.

(Translated by Amanda Powell)

---

1. Átropos: una de las tres Parcas, quienes hilaban y cortaban el hilo del destino humano.

1. Atropos: one of the three Fates, who spun the thread of human destiny and cut it with their shears.

Catalina Clara Ramírez de Guzmán

Baptized on July 16, 1611, Catalina Clara Ramírez de Guzmán was the daughter of Doña Isabel Sebastiana de Guzman, direct descendant of The Grand Master of the knightly order of Santiago, and Don Francisco Ramírez Guerrero, an official of the Inquisition of Llerena whose duties as a military man and governor often took him from home. Doña Catalina Clara was a prolific writer whose family comes to life in her verse. She dedicated poems to her mother, her father, her brothers, Lorenzo and Pedro, and her three sisters, Ana, Antonia, and Beatriz. These domestic poems bear witness to the traditional gender roles of the Spanish aristocracy of the era. The mother and the four daughters composed a society of the home while the men went out into the world for political or military purposes. The poems Catalina Clara Ramírez de Guzmán dedicated to her brothers were almost always sent far away; her poem-portraits of her sisters, on the other hand, assumed the presence of their models. She wrote about her mother's household tasks and, more frequently, about her father's absence. The poems on this theme run the gamut from lament to opportunism: the daughter writes the father, asking him poetically to bring gifts home from his travels.

Catalina Clara Ramírez de Guzmán's domestic poems deal with themes rooted in daily life and reflect the aristocratic habits and attitudes of her time. The poet observes and comments, sometimes acerbicly, on particular situations, providing us with an intimate view onto her world, a world in which women are as visible as men. She writes of a lady who wears her mourning much too long, of one who enjoys hunting, and of a third, an "outsider who complained of being uncomfortable in the place she came to because people whispered about her."[1] She also writes of "a young gallant who denies having courted a pastry maker."[2] There is a poem about a lady who eats mud, and one about a woman married to a hypochondriac, one dedicated to a gentleman to whom she sends a confection made of eggs, as well as one to a pregnant woman, and another to a woman who becomes engaged. She deals critically with a gentleman who, in a too vulgar manner, asked two ladies to buy him a silver chain, and with a man who does nothing but smile in order to show off his beautiful white teeth. She chastises the lady who did not cry when her sister entered a convent. This poem, along with "*Décimas* for two elegant ladies who thoughtlessly became nuns, to their parents' displeasure, in a convent that, when founded, was for wayward women,"[3] and her ballad "To Doña María Gago, a nun who, having been sought by many in her devotion was

caught by a lame man,"[4] imply that religious profession was not universally considered either admirable or desirable. When commenting on the lack of decision of "a lady who tried many times to become a nun, and upon achieving it changed her mind and left the convent,"[5] the poet suggests that religious vocation is not necessarily a divine calling but rather one option for women among several. The lack of reverence for convent life that informs these poems is reiterated in the poem "To the daughter of a sergeant major who, when entering the convent, was told by her father that if she did not want to be a nun the king would give her the habit of [the military order of] Santiago as he did for two of her sisters and all were called sergeant; they invited a marquise and a man not of her station to dine, and brought soldiers to the party,"[6] a poem whose title alone could serve as a basis for an extensive sociohistorical study.

The vicissitudes of the human body, always represented with reference to a particular individual of her acquaintance, are also a frequent theme in Catalina Clara Ramírez de Guzmán's poetry. She writes warmly to "a man with gout, cured by a lady;"[7] and the poem to her mother, "whose eyes were bad and she continued to sew, making them worse,"[8] provides a window on the life of this home, not only at the level of daily activities and their mundanely dangerous consequences, but also at the level of family affection. On the other hand, the poet unfeelingly dedicates a sonnet to a small man, calling attention to his stature; is hardly sensitive when she addresses a cross-eyed girl; and she is, to a modern sensibility, shocking in her racism in the poem "To a black woman who spent too much time on her hair."[9]

Catalina Clara Ramírez de Guzmán wrote tenderly "To a friend's absence"[10] and cruelly "To a man who wrote badly."[11] When she painted her own verbal portrait, she turned her satire on herself. The poet also wrote philosophical poems and love poems, many of which were written on behalf of someone else. She wrote about nature and, rarely, about religious themes. Her poems reveal a complicated individual, a direct and opinionated woman of good humor, a woman who as a careful observer of society could be both contemplative and critical.

Catalina Clara Ramírez de Guzmán left close to 150 poems, but, for the most part, her poetry remains in manuscript form in the National Library in Madrid. A dedicatory poem of hers appeared in a book published in 1663, from which it may be assumed that she died some time after that date.

1. "forastera, que decía que se hallaba mal en el lugar donde asistía porque la murmuraban," cited in Manuel Serrano y Sanz, *Apuntes para una biblioteca de escritoras españolas desde el año 1401 al 1833,* (Madrid: *Real Academia Española,* 1903; repr. 1975), 1:490.

2. "un galán que negaba el galanteo que hizo a una pastelera," Serrano y Sanz, 1:487.

3. "Décimas a unas damas muy bizarras que se entraron monjas impensadamente, sin gusto de sus padres, en un convento que su fundación fue de recogidas," Serrano y Sanz, 1:487.

4. "A Doña María Gago, una monja que habiendo pretentido muchos su devoción, la consiguió un cojo," Serrano y Sanz, 1:487.

5. "una dama que intentó muchas veces ser religiosa, y en consiguiéndolo mudaba de propósito y dejaba el convento," Serrano y Sanz, 1:487.

6. "A una hija de un sargento mayor que entrándola monja la dijo su padre que sino gustaba de serlo que le Rey le daría un hábito de Santiago como a otras dos hermanas suyas, y a todas las llaman sargentas; convidaron a comer a una marquesa y a un hombre muy desigual, y a la fiesta llevó soldados," Serrano y Sanz, 1:485.

7. "a un gotoso que le curaba una dama," Serrano y Sanz, 1:482.

8. "que tenía los ojos malos y hacía labor, con que se le ponían peores," Serrano y Sanz, 1:486.

9. "A una negra que cuidaba mucho del pelo," Serrano y Sanz, 1:490.

10. "A la ausencia de una amiga," Serrano y Sanz, 1:490.

11. "A un hombre que escribía mal," Serrano y Sanz, 1:486.

1
Redondillas

Recatándote de mí
vas, tiempo, tan sin ruido
que hasta mirarte perdido
no siento que te perdí.

Tan sin gozar de la vida
me vas llevando a morir,
que me puedo persuadir
a que la paso dormida.

Nada ocupa mi memoria,
que tengo por preeminencia
un limbo en cada potencia,
donde no hay pena ni gloria.

Tal vez de razón ajena
digo en vida tan ociosa:
por tener alguna cosa
me holgara de tener pena.

Tan zonza conformidad
no quiere el alma sufrir,
porque vivir por vivir
es mucha simplicidad.

1
Poem

You withdraw from me,
time, with such silent steps
that till I see you gone
I do not feel your going.

You are leading me to death
with so little joy for life
that I can persuade myself
I pass through life asleep.

Nothing fills my memory;
I am overwhelmed
by sheer emptiness of will,
bereft of pain or glory.

I speak perhaps with reason altered,
my life so filled with tedium
just to have some thing
I'd hold happily to pain.

My soul will not tolerate
such insipid resignation,
for living just to stay alive
is stupid in extreme.

*(Translated by Amy Kaminsky
and Bill Egerington)*

2
Romance

Despertad, que viene el alba,
mi bien, y os verán salir;
cansado estáis, bien lo veo,
pues sin cuidado dormís.

Ya la vecindad despierta
y preguntarán por mí
envidiosas centinelas
que envidian si estáis aquí.

De mis estimadas prendas
la de más estima os di:
pues la gozáis con el tiempo,
al mismo tiempo seguid.

2
Poem in Ballad Meter

Awake, the dawn is coming, love;
I fear you will be seen.
How well I see your weariness,
as I watch your peaceful sleep.

The neighbors are awakening
and soon will call for me;
envious sentinels are they,
jealous if you are here.

Of all my precious treasures
the most precious I gave to you,
that you may enjoy it again and again,
and enjoy it when you will.

Y pues tenéis, vida mía,
seguro lo que yo os di,
no me atormentéis el alma
pues dentro della vivís.

    Entre mis brazos os tengo;
si siento el veros partir
preguntádselo a mis ojos,
que ven de su gloria el fin.

    Volved temprano otra noche,
mi bien, que no os podréis ir
si el sol a la puerta llama
por donde habéis de salir.

    Esto cantaba una niña
no dando a sus penas fin,
y al partirse su querido,
llorando le dice así:

    Quiero que te vayas y que te quedes;
no sé, vida mía, porque me ofendes.

And since, my love, you do possess
so surely what I've given you;
do not then, love, torment my soul,
for there within you live.

    Within my arms I hold you;
do you wonder if I grieve
to see you go? Just ask my eyes
that in your parting see their glory end.

    Tomorrow night come early,
for you'll have to stay the day
if the sun comes calling at this door
through which, my love, you leave.

    This song a girl was singing
allowing her sorrows no end,
and when she sees her lover part,
weeping, she says to him:

    I want you to stay and I want you to go;
why, my life's love, do you make me grieve
       so?

(Translated by Bill Egerington
and Amy Kaminsky)

3
Romance

Triste memoria enemiga,
que sólo en mi daño vives:
¿por qué con perdidos dones
te cansas y me persigues?

    Cruel pensamiento, baste
el daño que me trujiste;
acaba, pues, murió
la causa de que naciste.

    Fácil razón, no augmentes
la llama en que me encendiste,
pues ves convertida en humo
la fe de un amor tan firme.

    Tus palabras me engañaron,
con ellas asiento hice;
mas palabras de mujer
no son fundamento firme.

3
Poem in Ballad Meter

Memory, sad enemy,
your life is but my suffering;
why do you haunt me
and weary yourself with treasures lost?

    Cruel thoughts,
cease the harm you brought me.
Stop, for that which gave you
birth has died.

    Fickle reason, do not increase
the flame you kindled in me;
for here you see the faith of solid love
transformed to smoke.

    Your words deceived me;
I clung to them.
But a woman's words
are no firm foundation.

Viví engañado y contento,
tan alegre cuanto quise;
de bienes tan regalado,
cuantos males hoy me afligen.
   Si de mi bien os cansáis,
no os espantéis que publique
ofensas y agravios vuestros
que me cansan y persiguen.

I lived deceived and happy,
as joyful as I might;
regaled with as much fortune
as misfortune plagues me now.
   If you weary of my love
do not marvel that I publish
offenses and affronts of yours
that bother and beset me.

*(Translated by Bill Egerington
and Amy Kaminsky)*

4
Romance pintando el invierno

Qué amenazado está el campo
de las iras de el diciembre,
que le ha dado soplo al aire,
que ha de abrasarlo con nieve.
   Los árboles prevenidos
desnudas las hojas tienen,
que el estorbo de estar preso
no embaraza al que es valiente.
   Piezas las nubes disparan
desde sus muros celestes,
siendo campo de batalla
el que de flores fue albergue.
   Balas de cristal esparce
sobre el florido tapete,
blanco de su puntería,
a pesar de tanto verde.
   Banderas tremola el cierzo
y las plantas se estremecen
porque, aunque son cosas de aire,
la debilidad las teme.
   Su miedo helados confiesan
los arroyos y las fuentes,
si no es que, muertas las flores,
ya ser expertos no quieren.
   Treguas les propone el marzo,
y abril socorros le ofrece,
con ejércitos de rosas
y escuadrones de mosquetas.

4
Ballad Painting the Winter

How threatened is the countryside
by December's anger,
who, blowing gusts into the air
scorches it with snow.
   The trees, forewarned and ready,
are naked of their leaves,
for the obstacle of prison
hinders not the brave.
   The clouds are shooting fragments
from their celestial walls,
making now a battlefield
of what once was sheltered bower.
   Crystal bullets scatter
o'er the floral carpet,
target of their deadly aim
despite flutterings of green.
   The north wind waves its banners,
the plants all shake and shudder;
for though this is the way of winds,
weakness fears and dreads it.
   The streams and fountains, frozen,
would confess their terror,
if they did not wish to learn
what the flowers knew, and killed them.
   March a truce proposes,
and April offers succor,
with armies of red flowers
and squadrons of musk roses.

(Translated by Amy Kaminsky)

The Eighteenth Century

María Gertrudis Hore

The story of María Gertrudis Hore has not come down to us as biography, in which the individuality of the subject is established in the details that modify the paradigms of biographical narrative. We have come instead to know her story in the form of a moralizing legend in which the norms of gender and genre have devoured the historical reality. As a result, Hore's story allows us to see with great clarity one of the models of traditional women's biography: the penitent adultress.

The legend of the Daughter of the Sun (la Hija del Sol) has eclipsed the story of María Hore's life; but it was, for many years, the only story the world had of her. Nevertheless, there are documents that tell us about Hore's birth, marriage, profession as a nun, and her death: the canonical contours of a woman's life. María Gertrudis Hore was born in Cádiz, on December 5, 1742. Her parents, Don Miguel Hore and Doña María Ley, were of Irish descent. It is said that in Cádiz María was called the Daughter of the Sun for her beauty, grace, and wit. In any case, she signed her poems HDS (Hija del Sol), turning sobriquet into pseudonym.

At the age of nineteen, María married Esteban Fleming, who was from Puerto de Santa María. Although they seem to have maintained their primary residence in Cádiz, the couple made frequent extended visits to Madrid. María became part of the social life of that city and apparently met the queen, though the two women did not get along. In 1778, when Hore decided to enter the convent, Hore and Fleming were once again living in Cádiz. Armed with a letter from her husband giving her permission to become a nun, Hore went to the bishop of that city. In 1779, while Fleming was in America, Hore was admitted into the novitiate at the Convent of Santa María. One year later, on February 14, 1780, she took religious vows.

All of Hore's dated poems were published after her profession, though others, written earlier, survive. Although she wrote for several provincial journals, most of her work appeared in the popular magazine *Correo de Madrid*, in 1787, 1795, and 1796. When she died, she left the manuscript containing her poems to her confessor, who passed it on to Doña Teresa de Figueroa. The manuscript was never published, and Hore was forgotten as a poet. She was, however, remembered as the center of a legend.

We cannot know to what extent her Apollonian pseudonym inspired the story of adultery and repentance that was woven around the historical figure of María Hore. This legend, collected by Fernán Caballero in 1857 and reprinted in the present

volume, kept Hore alive in the popular imagination until 1875, when some of her poems were collected and published by Leopoldo Cueto, Marquis of Valmar, in the *Biblioteca de autores españoles* (Library of Spanish authors).

Because of their epistolary form and conversational tone, it is easy to read many of Hore's poems as if they were personal letters filled with autobiographical revelations. The scarcity of documents and of other accounts of her life add to this temptation. This procedure becomes even more dangerous when we consider that so few of her poems survive. In her poem "Amado primo mío" (Dear cousin) she writes how she consigned her papers to the fire — which may or may not be true, of course. Still, we can confirm the effective loss of the poems her confessor bade her write but never published. Moreover, when Cueto finally published some of Hore's poems a century after her death, he first edited them heavily.[1]

In her epistolary poetry, Hore describes a process of disenchantment with the frenetic social whirl of Madrid. She said good-bye to her friends in Cádiz with a degree of sadness when she left for the capital, but once there she describes, in "A Gerarda," how delighted she is with the diversions of the great city. Nevertheless, another poem addressed to Gerarda, apparently written after the poet entered the convent, is a round denunciation of the frivolous life she previously embraced. Besides providing a certain affective trajectory of the poet's life, the warmth and intimacy of these epistolary poems are signs of a profound friendship between the two poetic personages, Gerarda and Fenisa. María Hore's withdrawal into a women's community after seven years of marriage, and her poems addressed to Filena and Cloe, also suggest that Hore sought out the company of women.

What the legend of the Daughter of the Sun relates as a passionate, adulterous love affair just a few months after her marriage, renounced as a result of a sign from heaven and followed by reclusion and repentance, did not happen quite that way. Although Hore had lovers and was concerned about her sins, she was married for seven years, not a matter of months, before she petitioned for entry into the convent. Moreover, centering the story on an adultery plot is a nineteenth century attempt to neutralize and make comprehensible the behavior of the eighteenth. During the years that Hore spent as a married woman in the capital, she undoubtedly participated in the custom of the *cortejo,* whereby married women were courted by unmarried men. According to Carmen Martín Gaite, this practice was common in the eighteenth century among Hore's social class, but it was gone by the nineteenth. According to the customs of the *cortejo,* a married woman would receive a gallant, who would accompany her both at home and to the social events in the capital. Well-bred husbands were expected to approve of this arrangement. Esteban Fleming, who so easily accepted her decision to break up their marriage to become a nun, and who, as a busy international merchant, was simply absent during a significant period of time, would probably not have been opposed to his wife's participating in the *cortejo.* For María Hore, young, beautiful, clever, and lively, there would have been no lack of candidates.

These *cortejos,* which might or might not have included a sexual relationship, did not bear the social opprobrium that similar behavior would a century later.

During her years in the convent Hore wrote a series of religious poems, among which is a long *silva* dedicated to the Virgin. Her poems to young women warning of the perils of the world are also of interest. A healthy woman who boasted of her robustness in her application to join the convent, María Hore nevertheless died in an epidemic on August 9, 1801.

A note on the Spanish texts: Hore's poems were much edited by Cueto, and I have tried to go back as much as possible to the pre-Cueto versions, which Constance Sullivan generously shared with me. Where I have kept Cueto's revisions (to fill in the lines or words he obliterated), I have marked those revisions by placing them in brackets.　—Ed.

---

1. Constance Sullivan, who did the archival work on Hore that uncovered Cueto's revision of Hore, was kind enough to share that work in progress with me.

1
A Gerarda,
la vida de la corte

Ya, Gerarda mía,
tu amistad severa
culpará mi olvido
con injusta queja;
    mas cuando a tu vista
disculpas ofrezca,
calmará tu enojo
mi amistad sincera.
    En el gran tumulto
que aquí se presenta,
los días se huyen,
las noches se vuelan.
    Aun aquel descanso
que naturaleza
prescribe preciso
á la subsistencia,
    si todo no lo hurta,
algo le cercena
a las diversiones
de alegre tarea.
    Los sentidos solo
son los que aquí reinan;
pues sujetan ellos
hasta las potencias.
    La música dulce,
la danza ligera,
la cómica farsa,
la triste tragedia;
    el bárbaro circo
de gentes y fieras,
a quien la costumbre
permite o tolera;
    sensibles afectos
ya olvidan, ya acuerdan,
agitando activas
pasiones diversas.
    Mira qué sosiego
tomará entre ellas
vacilante pulso,
si a escribir empieza.

1
To Gerarda,
Life at Court

By now, my dear Gerarda,
your stern friendship
must be faulting my neglect
with unfair resentment.
    But when you see
the apologies I offer,
my sincere friendship
will calm your anger.
    In the great tumult
that here prevails
days flee,
nights fly.
    Even that rest
which nature
decrees if we
are to survive,
    is pared away,
if not stolen altogether
by the delights
of gay and joyful tasks.
    The senses alone
rule this realm;
even the powerful
are held in their thrall.
    Sweet music,
graceful dance,
comic farce,
sad tragedy;
    a crude circus
of folks and savage beasts
whom custom
permits or tolerates;
    sensitive feelings
first forget and then remember,
bestirring and awakening
sundry passions.
    See what serenity
the hesitant hand
will find
if it begins to write.

Apenas la pluma
al papel se entrega,
cuando la retiran
distracciones nuevas.

Esto ha motivado
mi tarda respuesta,
que con mi deseo
volado se hubiera.

Mas ahora, torciendo
la llave a la puerta,
por ti mi amistad
a todo se niega.

¡Cuánto deseaba
mi fe verdadera
celebrar, amiga,
tus dulces endechas!

¡Dichoso Liseno!
tu pensar consuela,
pues tales memorias
te ofrece la ausencia.

Mas si acaso injusto
a olvidarlas llegas,
Amor y su madre
castigos prevengan;

los celos te acosen,
desdenes te ofendan,
y si amares a otra,
á rigores mueras...

Gerarda, perdona,
porque mi fineza
exhala expresiones
que tal vez no aprueba;

no tardará mucho
el día que pueda
abrazarte fina,
hablarte contenta.

Pues ahora tan sólo
repetir me dejan
que Fenisa es siempre
tu amiga y tu afecta.

Scarcely does the pen
yield to the paper
when new distractions
force the writer to withdraw.

This has been the reason
for my late reply;
it would have flown to you
had it been in my power.

But now, turning
the key in friendship's door,
my friendship will refuse
all save you.

My constancy desired
so very much, my friend,
the true celebration of
your sweet loving poems.

Fortunate Liseno
your thought consoles
for absence offers up to you
a bounty of memories.

But if by chance
unjustly you forget them,
may Love and his mother
prepare their fierce chastisement.

May jealousy accost you,
may rebuff offend you,
and if you love another,
may you, scorned, die.

Gerarda, do forgive me;
perhaps my poem
breathes expressions
most unseemly.

The day will soon arrive,
it will not now be long before
I can embrace you politely,
and happily converse.

For now I am left
only to repeat
that Fenisa is always
your dear and loving friend.

(Translated by Lou Charnon Deutsch)

2

Al poner unas flores,
después de amortajado, a un hijo
que se le murió de viruelas

"Anacreóntica"

Estas hermosas flores,
que adorno fueron mío,
y hoy con trémula mano
entretejo y matizo,
    a esas tus yertas sienes,
conforme, las dedico;
último don funesto
del maternal cariño.
    Entre tus fríos dedos,
conforme, sólo aplico
esta flor, que retrata
la aflicción que reprimo.
    Por lo que me has costado,
por lo que te he querido,
[pide que me dé fuerzas]
el Hacedor divino.
    [Su purísima Madre
también tu madre ha sido;
pídele que me otorgue
resignación y auxilio...]
    Tomad, piadosa gente,
ya os entrego mi hijo,
ya ni tocar su rostro
a mis labios permito.
    Ya su espíritu habita
en más dichoso sitio;
y tras sí se ha llevado
sentimiento y sentidos.
    De la naturaleza
ceda el infinito alivio
al superior decreto
de quien así lo quiso.

2

On Laying Some Flowers,
after the Shrouding, for Her Son
Who Died of Smallpox

"Anacreontics"

These beautiful flowers,
once my adornment,
that today I weave and intertwine
with shaking hands,
    dedicating them, resigned,
to those, your lifeless temples,
last, mournful gift
of maternal feeling.
    Between your cold fingers,
I place, resigned, just this flower;
how it portrays the grief
I now keep inside.
    For all you have cost me,
for all I have loved you,
ask of the Divine Maker
[that he give me strength.]
    [His most pure Mother
has been your mother too;
ask that she grant
comfort and resignation ...]
    Take him, merciful people;
I deliver my son to you.
I will not again permit my lips
to touch his face.
    His spirit dwells already
in that realm of bliss;
and with him he has borne
all sense and sentiment.
    May the infinite respite
of nature be ceded
to the highest decree
of the one who thus would have it.

(Translated by Lou Charnon Deutsch)

3
Endecasílabos

Los dulcísimos metros que tu pluma
hoy me dirige, amada amiga mía,
fueran el refrigerio más gustoso,
si admitieran alguno mis fatigas;
la paz, con que el amor y la fortuna
la bella unión coronan a porfía
de tantas bellas almas, que su culto
engrandecen con ver que se dedican,
celebrara, si acaso ser pudiera,
que por bien estimara la alegría;
mas yo, que la conozco cierto anuncio
de tristezas, pesares y fatigas,
compadezco las almas que, engañadas,
en su inconstante duración se fían,
y huyendo del contagio que las cerca,
me acojo a mí feliz melancolía.

Si ésta cede al encanto que le ofrecen
de tu discurso las pinturas vivas,
mil funestos objetos me prevengo
porque conserven las tristezas mías.
¡Qué estado tan feliz! Quien le conoce
no apetece más gustos ni más dichas,
pues libre del temor y la esperanza,
era la nada, y nada le lastima.

El aire brama en fuertes huracanes,
la tierra toda tiembla estremecida,
una escuadra se sorbe el mar airado,
destruye un edificio llama activa;
perecerá, si perecer le toca,
pero no temblará con cobardía
el sabio corazón que reconoce
que nada pierde con perder la vida.

No reirá cual Heráclito del mundo
vanas perecederas alegrías,
ni cual Demócrito llorará las tristes
funestas consecuencias que las sigan.[1]
Mas como aquel filósofo del Támesis,
huyendo, sí, sus engañosas dichas

1. Heráclito y Demócrito: filósofos griegos.

3
Poem

The sweet, sweet verses that your pen
directs to me today, my beloved friend,
would have been the most delightful con-
    solation
had they admitted some my weariness.
Peace, with which love and fortune
crown the union fair, urged on
by countless lovely souls, that
her cult do they exalt in their devotion,
would celebrate, if indeed she might hold
    joy
high in her esteem;
but I, who know her as some herald
    of woe, lament, and pain,
take pity on the souls that, deceived,
trust in their inconstant duration,
and fleeing from the contagion that
    envelops them,
I take refuge in sweet melancholy.

If it yields to the enchantment offered
by the living paintings of your discourse,
I forsee a thousand mournful matters
for they are records of my sadness.
What a happy state! Whoever knows it
    loses all desire
for pleasure and good fortune,
is free of fear and hope:
nothingness; and nothing can bring pain.

The air bellows in harsh hurricanes,
the whole earth shakes and trembles,
mighty squadrons swallow the angry sea,
raging flame destroys fortresses;
it will perish if its time has come to perish
but the wise heart that recognizes
that nothing is lost with loss of life
will not tremble with cowardice.

He will not laugh, like Heraclitus, at
    the world,
vain, perishable joys,
nor will he, like Democritus, weep

y los vanos objetos que interpone
para que la verdad se nos resista,
se entra por los altísimos cipreses
y con el mayor gusto ve y visita
sepulcrales cavernas, a quien sólo
de la muerte blandones iluminan;
y leyendo piadosos epitafios
de los pasados, su memoria viva
se complace en tan lúgubre ejercicio
y con cuidado pisa sus cenizas.

    Yo exclamaré con él, que aquel imperio
en que la muerte en trono de ruïnas
soberana se ostenta a los humanos,
un asilo le ofrece a sus desdichas.
Aquí el alma ha de entrar, y aquí es preciso
que el pensamiento siempre se dirija,
y para su consuelo y su remedio
como recreo este paseo admita.
¡Cuán mortal es ¡Oh Dios! para el orgullo
y cuán suave a la verdad benigna
de estos cóncavos siempre tenebrosos
el aire que gustoso se respira!

    ¡Sí, sí, divino Young![2] contigo entro,
al ver tu ejemplo, mi valor se anima,
y de ti acompañada sin recelo,
compararé la muerte con la vida.
De aquélla el horroroso y triste aspecto
me atreveré a mirar con frente altiva,
y en los sepulcros de las almas grandes
las palmas cogeré en tu compañía.

    Mas ¿dónde voy?. . . Perdona mis
      discursos,
mi distracción perdona, amiga mía,
que del inglés filósofo la cuarta
Noche me arrebató mi fantasía.

    No, aunque me ves gustosa en mi tris-
      teza,

for the sad and mournful consequences
    that follow.[1]
But, like that philosopher of the Thames,
fleeing, yes, its deceptive bliss
and the vain objects that it interposes
so truth might be taken from us,
he enters by the highest cypresses
and with pure delight he sees and visits
sepulchral caves; his was lit
by naught but death's own candelabra;
and reading pious epitaphs
of those who've passed, his living memory
is pleased by so gloomy an exercise
and with care he treads on ashes.

    I will exclaim with him that the empire
in which death on a sovereign throne of
    ruins
displays itself for humankind offers asylum
for its misfortunes.
Here the soul must enter, and here it is
that thought must be directed
and for its comfort and its cure
as recreation this excursion be admitted.
How deadly, God, for pride
and how benign, before the gentle truth
of these forever shadowy concavities,
is the air we breathe with such delight!

    Yes, yes, divine Young![2] With you I
      enter.
Seeing your example gives life to my
    courage,
and accompanying you without misgiving,
I will compare death to life;
I will dare to look with my head held up
at death's sad and fearful countenance
and in the tombs of great souls
will I, in your company, take their hands.

---

2. Edward Young (1683-1765): poeta inglés, autor de *Night Thoughts* (Pensamientos nocturnos, 1742-44), conocido por su poesía religiosa y filosófica.

1. Heraclitus and Democritus: Greek philosophers.

2. Edward Young (1683-1765): British religious and philosophical poet, author of *Night Thoughts* (1742-44).

dejes de condenarla y combatirla;
yo no merezco tu piedad, pues necia
huyo el remedio al punto que le indica.

    ¿Qué tengo, desgraciada? ¿Qué me
        aflige?
[¿Vencen mi corazón las penas mías?]
No, pues ya la costumbre las ha hecho
indiferentes cuasi, por continuas.

    ¿Es más que, te pregunto, el corto alivio
que hallaban mis pesares en el día
para el instante que alternar lograba
contristada mi voz melancolías?

    [A veces los delirios de la mente
deslumbran mi insaciable fantasía,]
Y este corto consuelo, rigurosas
leyes de esta república me privan
por un espacio, que cual siglos cuento,
aunque los cuenten todos como días.

    ¡Feliz tú, que viviendo en otro mundo,
[disfrutas de] la amable compañía
de tus amigas, sin que estorbo alguno
incomode lo firme de tu dicha.

But, whither do I go? . . . forgive my
    speeches,
pardon my distraction, my dear friend;
my imagination was seized by the English
philosopher's fourth *Night*.

    Condemn and fight my sadness,
although you see it pleases me.
I do not deserve your pity, so foolishly
do I flee the remedies that cure my ill.

    Why am I so unfortunate? What
    troubles me?
[Does my pain overcome my heart?]
No, habit has made it almost dull,
so continuous is it.

    Is it, I ask you, more than the brief
    respite
that my sorrows found on the day,
for the instant, that my saddened voice
could alternate melancholies?

    [At times the mind's delirium
dazzles my insatiable fancy,]
and this nation's harsh laws deprive
me, for a space, of this small comfort,
that are centuries to me,
though for others they be days.

    Happy you, who, living in another
    world,
[enjoy] the pleasant company
of your women friends, with no
    importune
disturbance to embitter your good
    fortune.

(Translated by Lou Charnon Deutsch)

4
Soneto

Estaba Apolo en el Parnaso un día
repartiendo guirnaldas diferentes,
y de Helicona al son de las corrientes
Terpsícore festivas danzas guía.[3]
Fenisa, que del Betis ascendía[4]
osada llega entre otras concurrentes,
y al ver de todas adornar las frentes,
¿Dónde está, dice, la corona mía?
Febo, al verla de galas adornada,
Aparta, le responde; la riqueza
con mi numen feliz no tiene entrada.
A que ella le replica con presteza:
Si eso no más en mí te desagrada,
coróname, que admito la pobreza.

4
Sonnet

Apollo on Parnassus was one day,
bestowing different wreathes,
and from Helicon, to the rhythms of the air
Terpsichore leads the festive dance.[3]
Fenisa, who from Betis was
    descended,[4]
boldly among the competitors arrives,
and seeing all the others' heads adorned,
"Where is," she says, "the crown that bears
    my name?"
Phoebus, seeing her adorned in
    raiment fine,
"Stay aside," replies; "wealth does not
enter in my happy realm."
To which she answers swiftly,
"If it be only that you disapprove in me,
crown me, I embrace poverty."

(Translated by Lou Charnon Deutsch)

5
A sus amigas

Ya llegó, en fin, el venturoso día;
¡Oh queridas amigas! que mi afecto
con su indecisa suerte me lastime
la tierna compasión de vuestro pecho.
Ya la nave que anduvo por el golfo,
expuesta al choque de contrarios vientos,
sin temor de huracanes y borrascas,

5
To Her Friends

The happy day has, at last, arrived;
oh, dear friends, that my feelings
with their wavering fortunes wound in me
the soft compassion of your breasts.
Now the ship that sailed the gulf,
exposed to the clash of opposing winds,
with no fear of storms and hurricanes,

---

3. Referencias mitológicas. Febo: otro nombre del dios del sol, Apolo; Parnaso: monte consagrado a Apolo y a las musas; Helicona: monte consagrado a las musas; Terpsícore: musa de la danza y de la música coral.
4. "Fenisa" es un nombre poético que Hore emplea para referirse a sí misma. Betis: nombre romano del río Guadalquivir, por el cual se entiende toda Andalucía.

3. Apollo: god of the sun, also called Phoebus. Parnassus: mountain dedicated to Apollo and the Muses; Helicon: one of the mountains of the nine Muses. Terpsichore, muse of the dance.
4. Fenisa: poetic name Hore often gives to her poetic persona. Betis: Roman name for the Guadalquivir River, metonymn for Andalusia.

logró tener del mar seguro puerto.
Ya aquella peregrina caminante
que vuestro lado disfrutó algún tiempo,
fijó el dudoso pie, para su dicha,
del desengaño en el sagrado templo.
En la santa quietud y sus murallas,
lejos de hallar el arrepentimiento
que tantas veces, casi persuadida,
temer le hicieron los avisos vuestros,
halló la paz, el gusto, la alegría,
los placeres, el gozo y el sosiego
que en este caos de contrariedades
en vano procuró buscar su esmero.
Aquí amanece el día, y sin cuidados,
su belleza a gozar sólo despierto,
y después de rendir como es debido
al Santuario aquel primer momento,
a la labor dedico algunos ratos;
otros en la lectura me divierto,
y la pluma me ponen en la mano
gusto y obligación al mismo tiempo.
Ya de algunas amigas la memoria,
en la reja me busca con esmero,
y con gusto dejando ocupaciones,
corro a mostrarles mi agradecimiento.
Pero de cuantas dichas proporciona
este feliz retiro que poseo,
no hay alguna que tanto me complazca
como la amable sociedad de adentro.
En el trato agradable de sus gentes
más atención disfruto que merezco,
y en la voluntad de cada cual que hablo,
es el favorecerme nuevo empeño.
Las ya de edad me tratan como hija,
yo les pago con todo mi respeto;
y con la juventud alegre logro
la diversión, compañía y juego.
Ved, amigas, si en esta nueva existencia
queda que apetecer a mis deseos,
sino que no escasééis a mi cariño
vuestra noticia que constante espero.

has found the sea's safe port.
Now that pilgrim traveler
who once enjoyed your company
has happily set her doubtful foot
to find truth in the sacred temple.
In the holy silence of its walls,
far from the regret she feared,
almost persuaded by your many warnings,
she found peace, delight, happiness,
pleasures, joy, and calm,
that in the chaos of the contradictions of
    the world,
she so carefully sought, in vain.
Here day breaks, and I carefree
awake for nothing more than to savor its
    beauty,
and after rendering the Sanctuary's due
for that first moment,
I give some time to my labors,
amuse myself at other times by reading;
pleasure and duty both
place pen in my hand.
Then my friends' careful remembrances
call me to the grill,*
and leaving my tasks I run
to them and show my gratitude.
But of all the many pleasures
this felicitous retreat bestows on me,
there is none that pleases me more
than its own sweet society.
In the pleasant company of its folk
I enjoy much more attention than I
    deserve,
and in the will of each to whom I speak
resides a new firm eagerness to favor me.
The older ones treat me like a daughter;
I pay them back with all of my respect;
and with the joyous young ones I achieve
candor and vivacity, playfulness and
    cheer.

*Cloistered nuns could speak to visitors to the
convent from behind a grill or grate.—Trans.

See, my friends, if in this new existence
there remains something that I yearn for,
unless it is that you not be miserly
toward my love for you
in giving me the news of you I long for.

(Translated by Lou Charnon Deutsch)

6

¿Hasta cuándo, Gerarda,
tu peregrino ingenio
en frívolos asuntos
malgastará conceptos?

¿Hasta cuándo has de darles
infelice fomento
a tus locas pasiones
con amorosos versos?

Esas luces tan claras
que te concedió el cielo
no le causen enojos,
mas tribútenle inciensos.

Yo también algún tiempo
templaba el instrumento,
creyéndolo sonoro
cuando más descompuesto.

Yo también invocaba
al que llaman Dios ciego
é hice (rara Locura!)
que me prohijara Febo.

Yo lloré ingratitudes,
yo celebraba afectos,
empleando en delirios
la dulzura del metro.

Pero ya, arrepentida
de tan frívolo empleo,
sólo a dignos asuntos
dedicarlo pretendo.

Tú, amada compañera,
sigue también mi ejemplo;
no aguardes que algún día
lo exija el escarmiento.

6

How long, Gerarda,
will your restless wit
squander its ideas
on frivolous affairs?

How long will you
foment, unhappy,
your own mad passions
writing poems of love?

That clear intelligence
awarded you by heaven
ought provoke not heaven's anger,
but burn incense to it in tribute.

I also once played
on that instrument
and believed it surely resonant
when it was most out of tune.

I too invoked
the god that they call blind
and made myself
(strange madness!) Phoebus's daughter.

I wept over ingratitudes,
I celebrated signs of love,
delirious I applied to each
poetry's own sweetness.

But now, regretful
of this abuse of poetry,
I will apply it only
to more worthy matters.

Heed, beloved companion,
my own example.
Wait not for the day
when harsh experience demands it.

Emprenda, emprenda mucho,
elévese tu ingenio,
remóntese tu numen,
cruce el numen volando,
no aletée rastrero.

No tejas más laureles
a ese contrario sexo,
que sólo en nuestra ruina
fabrica sus trofeos.

Y si se resistiere
á tu loable afecto
tu corazón departe
de todos tus afectos.

Si la mente se escusa
á darte pensamientos,
y sólo te sugiere
los frívolos y tiernos,

nuestra común amiga,
sea tu nuevo Febo,
ella te preste especies
á tus primeros versos.

Y luego que tus voces
llenen de gozo el viento,
verás qué diferentes
guirnaldas te tejemos.

Verás caer marchitas
esas rosas de Venus,
y perder la fragancia
que te encantó algún tiempo.

Del más sacro Parnaso
subirás a lo excelso,
y al monte de Helicona
mirarás con desprecio.

Ea, Gerarda mía,
remóntese tu vuelo,
y perdona a *Fenisa*
tan osado consejo.

Try and try again
to reach heights far more lofty;
let your genius soar,
not flit low to the ground.

Weave no more laurels
for that contrary sex;
out of our ruin and nothing more
do they craft their trophies.

And if your heart resists
your praiseworthy desire,
it must be separate from
all of your desires.

If your mind refuses
to provide you with ideas
and only suggests to you
frivolity and love,

may the friend we have in common
your new Phoebus be,
may she bestow images
on your first true poems.

And when your voice
fills the wind with joy
you'll see what different garlands
we weave in your honor.

Those roses of Venus
will fall dead and withered,
and lose the sweet fragrance
that once held you enchanted.

From most sacred Parnassus
you'll rise to the most sublime
and look down with disdain
upon Helicon's hill.

So, my Gerarda,
may you take flight and soar,
and forgive your *Fenisa*
her counsel so bold.

(Translated by Lou Charnon Deutsch)

Margarita Hicky y Pellizoni

Margarita Hicky y Pellizoni was born in Palma de Mallorca, probably in the 1740s. A few years later, her parents, Ana Pellizoni and Domingo Hicky, moved the family to Madrid, where Margarita spent the greater part of her life. It is likely that Ana Pellizoni was a member of the well-known operatic family whose members brought Italian opera to Madrid. Domingo Hicky, of Irish descent, was a lieutenant colonel in the Dragoons, and his sons — Margarita's brothers — followed him into military careers.

In 1763 Margarita Hicky married Juan Antonio Aguirre, who was half a century her senior. The couple lived at court, where Juan Antonio, who was from an aristocratic family, held the post of Chief of the Prince's Wardrobe. The next written record we have of Margarita Hicky is dated 1779 when, already widowed, she applied for permission to publish her translations and her poems. Hicky remained in Madrid after her husband died, and when her works were published in 1789, a full ten years after she submitted them to the censor, they bore neither her own name nor the pseudonym Antonia Hernanda de Oliva, under which she had requested the necessary license to publish, but just the epithet "a lady of this Court."[1]

A number of the poems in her collection *Poesías varias sagradas, morales y profanas* (Diverse sacred, moral, and profane poems) deal with love, from first blush to disillusionment. Like María de Zayas and the Mexican Sor Juana Inés de la Cruz, Margarita Hicky chastises men for the tawdry way they treat women. For Hicky, women are

> robbed of their estate,
> victims of honor,
> censured with love,
> and without it shunned;
> without affection courted,
> for appetite's sake sought,
> once attained, abused;
> their virtue unpraised,
> their youth without laurels,
> and in old age scorned.[2]

Men, on the other hand,

> are fickle monsters
> arrogant and base;

> humble, if disdained;
> if loved, irreverent;
> when favored, insolent;
> they desire, but they do not love;
> tepidity inflames them;
> they serve so they may rule;
> they stoop to conquer,
> and slander her who honors them.[3]

Like Zayas and Sor Juana, Hicky defends the intellectual and aesthetic ability of her sex:

> For the true sage, wherever
> he finds truth and reason,
> can take it up and use it
> without worrying overmuch about
> who it is that offers it.
> Because he cannot ignore,
> if in fact he knows,
> that the soul, as a spirit, has
> no sex.
>
> . . . .
>
> Every day, instant, moment,
> we see women surpass men
> in the arts and sciences,
> if they undertake their study
> with diligence.[4]

Hicky's book also contains translations of three French tragedies, two epic poems eulogizing a Captain General Don Pedro de Cevallos, and religious poetry.

Daughter of the century of such advocates of women's education as Father Feijóo and Josefa Amar de Borbón, Margarita Hicky received enough formal education that she could become interested in studying geography and translating Racine and Voltaire. The censor was pleased with her translations and approved of the changes she made in Voltaire's texts. Nevertheless, Hicky deplored the fact that another translator took liberties with Racine's *Andromaque*; for although she was quite willing to rectify the irregularities that undermined Catholic doctrine in Voltaire, Hicky did not sanction the restitution of the myth of female inconstancy in Racine.

Margarita Hicky's last work, "Descripción geográfica e histórica de todo el orbe conocido hasta ahora" (Geographical and historical description of the whole planet known as of this moment), was never published. A five- or six-volume octosyllabic poem (she sent three of the volumes to the censor, planning to send the other two or three later on), it represented an enormous effort in research and writing. Nevertheless, what Hicky's representative called a work "taken from the best geographic authors

that are known and all put in Castilian octosyllabic verse, very clear and intelligible, a work that could be very useful in its conduciveness in facilitating the possession of this very important science for those who apply themselves to it,"[5] was rejected by the readers of the Royal Academy. Those gentlemen pronounced the poem "useless and uncorrectable," since, according to the Royal Academy's secretary, "in the entire work we have found nothing but continuous errors and very notable mistakes in the names and situations of towns and provinces, for not having referred to good books, or for having copied or understood badly, confusing descriptions and definitions through lack of exactitude that, on occasion, the exigencies of poetic form required; the poem being, moreover, terribly written, without any rule or metric measure."[6]

The disappearance of this poem, testament to Hicky's autodidacticism, is a great loss. However "incorrect" it may have been, a poem of such wide scope, doubtless idiosyncratic—that is to say, original—would have been an incomparable lens through which to study this eighteenth century woman's vision of the world. After so cruel a rejection, the work disappeared, and Margarita Hicky stopped writing, or at least she stopped requesting that her work be published. The rejection by the Royal Academy is the last document we have concerning Margarita Hicky y Pellizoni. The date and place of her death are unknown.

1. I am grateful to Constance Sullivan, who had access to the manuscript of Hicky's book, as well as to other documents concerning Hicky's life, for this information. Sullivan also informed me that Hicky signed her name as I write it here, and not "Hickey," as Serrano y Sanz and his followers have spelled it.

2. de bienes destituidas, / víctimas del pundonor, / censuradas con amor, / y sin él desatendidas; / sin cariño pretendidas, / por apetito buscadas / conseguidas, ultrajadas; / sin aplausos la virtud / sin lauros la juventud, / y en la vejez despreciadas (cited in Manuel Serrano y Sanz, *Apuntes para una biblioteca de escritoras españolas desde el año 1401 al 1833* [Madrid: Real Academia Española, 1903; repr. 1975], 1:514).

3. son monstruos inconsecuentes / altaneros y abatidos; / humildes, si aborrecidos; / si amados, irreverentes; / con el favor, insolentes; / desean, pero no aman; / en las tibiezas se inflaman, / sirven para dominar; / se rinden para triunfar, / y a la que los honra infaman (cited in Serrano y Sanz, 1:514).

4. Que el verdadero sabio, donde quiera / que la verdad y la razón encuentre, / allí sabe tomarla, y la aprovecha / sin nimio detenerse en quién la ofrece. / Porque ignorar no puede, si es que sabe, / que el alma, como espíritu carece / de sexo . . . / Pues cada día, instantes y momentos, / vemos aventajarse las mujeres / en las artes y ciencias a los hombres, / si con aplicación su estudio emprenden (cited in Serrano y Sanz, 1:512).

5. "sacada de los mejores autores geográficos que se conocen y puesta toda en verso castellano octosílabo, muy claro e inteligible, obra que puede ser muy útil por lo muy conducente que es a facilitar la posesión de esta ciencia tan importante a los que se apliquen a ella" (cited in Serrano y Sanz, 1: 510).

6. "inútil e incorregible, ya que en toda la obra no han hallado sino continuos yerros y muy notables equivocaciones en los nombres y situaciones de los pueblos y provincias, por no haberse valido de buenos libros, o por haberlos copiado u entendido mal, confundiendo las descripciones y definiciones por falta de exactitud a que en ocasiones la obligaba la sujeción del verso; siendo éste, por otra parte, una pésima prosa, sin regla alguna ni medida métrica," (cited in Serrano y Sanz, 1:511).

1

Endechas expresando las contradicciones,
dudas y confusiones de una inclinación
en sus principios, y el plausible deseo
de poder amar y ser amada sin delito

Escucha, Fabio mío,
los contrarios afectos
y las opuestas ansias
que cruelmente batallan en mi pecho.

Y pues eres la causa,
atiende mis lamentos,
que a aquel que da los golpes
no es justo que le ofenda oír los ecos.

Yo te vi, Fabio mío,
si mal no me acuerdo,
de tu noble persona
tranquila contemplé el merecimiento.

Tratéte muy despacio,
mas con tanto sosiego,
que no recelé nunca
ni aun la menor centella de este incendio.

Confírmenlo las veces
que, amando otros objetos,
me fiastes tus triunfos
y ayudó a celebrarlos mi festejo.

Después, o por influjos
de los astros severos,
o de mudar cansado
tu corazón de tanto amante empeño,

no sé por qué, atraído
de gracias que no tengo,
fijar en mí emprendiste
lo vago y variable de tu afecto.

Llegaste a declararme
tu amoroso deseo;
desestiméle cuerda,
y encendió el desengaño más tu fuego.

Repetistes instancias
y yo desabrimientos,
y obstinándome firme,
a ser porfía ya llegó tu anhelo.

Pasando algunos días,
te dio ocasión el tiempo

1

Verses Expressing the Contradictions,
Doubts, and Confusions of a Love
Just Beginning, and the Reasonable Desire
to Love and Be Loved Without Sin

Listen, my Fabio,
to the conflicting feelings
and the opposing longings
that battle cruelly in my breast.

Hear my lamentations,
you who are their author:
it is unfair that the one who strikes
feel offended by the echoes of his blows.

I saw you, my Fabio,
if I am not mistaken,
and calmly contemplated
your noble bearing's worth.

So gently did I treat you
and with such tranquillity
that never once suspected
this fire's smallest spark.

The times you, in love with others,
shared your triumphs with me
and I helped celebrate them,
confirm what I now say to you.

Then what harsh star
has cast this spell?
Or was your heart just weary
of love's insistent changes?

I know not why, attracted
to me by charms I don't possess,
your inconstant, fickle love
set out to woo me too.

You came and swore to me
your lover's fierce desire;
I, no fool, disdained it,
but scorn only inflamed you.

You repeated your entreaties
and I met them rudely;
I was stubborn and unswerving,
as your passion turned insistent.

The moment came
just a few days later,

que oyese de más cerca
de tus amantes ansias los extremos.

Me aventuré a escucharte,
y mi atrevido esfuerzo
se persuadió, inocente,
que podía sin peligro oírte tierno.

Mas ¡ay! ¡cuán a mi costa
el daño experimento
que hay en oír atenta
de aquel que no disgusta ardientes ruegos!

En fin, compadecióme
tu amoroso tormento,
lastimóme tu llanto,
y acabó de obligarme tu respeto.

Tu respeto, sí, Fabio,
aquel noble respeto
que de un amor que es fino
y fijo es el seguro compañero.

Y con él embargando
mis rigores (¡no aliento,
triste de mí, a decirlo!),
mis fieras esquiveces suspendiendo,

lograste ver trocadas
por mi mal, en momentos,
las iras en piedades,
y en agrados cambiados los despegos.

Desde ese instante, Fabio,
yo misma no me entiendo:
ni sé decir si te amo,
ni sabré decir si te aborrezco.

Sólo sé que combaten
tantas ansias en mi pecho,
que, fieras, me persuaden
que está en mi corazón el mismo infierno.

Toda soy repugnancias,
gustos y desconsuelos;
ni acierto a aborrecerte,
ni con amarte (¡ay de mí!, triste) acierto.

Con tu presencia calman
algo mis sentimientos;
mas luego que te apartas,
¡qué ansia!, a despedazarme vuelven fieros.

Negarme a tu caricia
mil veces me he propuesto,

when your intensely loving anguish
could be heard more closely by.

Innocent, I ventured out to hear you
and was persuaded by this daring act
that I could listen to you tenderly
and not put myself in danger.

But, alas! It's cost me dear,
to discover listening's harm,
when the one who offers such
very ardent pleas does so tirelessly.

At last I pitied you
your lover's torment
and, wounded by your pain,
your regard it was that won me in the end.

Your regard, yes, Fabio,
that noble regard that is
of any love that's fine and
true, the sure companion.

And with it restraining
my severity (I find no solace
in so saying), suspending
my fierce disdain,

you beheld, to my misfortune,
my anger turn to pity
in but moments,
my indifference turn to welcome.

Since that moment, Fabio,
I know myself no longer;
I cannot say if I love you
nor know I if I hate you.

I only know that diverse sentiments
battle in my breast so fiercely
that I am confident
that hell itself resides within my heart.

Repugnance, pleasure, grief
are all I am; I cannot succeed in
abhorring you, nor (woe is me),
in loving you can I succeed.

In your presence are my feelings
calmed somewhat, but later,
when you leave—what anguish!—
savage they return to tear my flesh.

A thousand times I've thought
to refuse your caress,

y sin saber yo cómo
tu dicha desvanece mis intentos.
　　Me aflijo cuando logras
el favor que concedo,
y luego, arrepentida,
quisiera concederte el que te niego.
　　De mi altivez llevada,
quisiera verte muerto
antes que feliz verte,
y por darte la vida luego muero.
　　Y pues oyes qué penas
triste por ti padezco,
de agradecido sólo
haz por mí una fineza que pretendo.
　　Ya dejar de estimarte
aunque quiera no puedo;
mas si fuese posible,
poner quisiera a mi locura freno.
　　Para lograrlo, Fabio,
te pido que, contento,
con lo que has merecido,
de tu ambición moderes los excesos.
　　No te ofenda bien mío,
lo extraño de este ruego,
que el corazón lo llora,
mas lo quieren ansiosos mis respetos.
　　No huyo, no, de amarte,
ni que me olvides quiero,
mas sólo sin bochorno
poderte amar eternamente anhelo.
　　Y para conseguirlo,
hoy de tu amor pretendo
que no exijas del mío
pruebas que por principio negar debo.
　　Ésta es, Fabio del alma,
la fineza que espero
merecer de tu noble,
constante y bien nacido rendimiento.
　　Serán, si así lo hicieres,
tan tuyos mis afectos,
que usurparte no puedan
su posesión la envidia ni los celos.
　　Y con esto, adiós, Fabio,
que molestarte temo;

and without knowing how,
your pleasure erases my intentions.
　　It troubles me that you obtain
the favor I concede,
and then, regretful, I wish again
to give you what I would deny.
　　Transported by my pride,
I would rather see you dead
than see you happy,
though I would die to give you life.
　　Hear my grief,
sad I am and for your sake I suffer,
be grateful and grant to me
the kindness that I ask you.
　　I would cast you from my thoughts
but I cannot;
and fervently I wish to halt
this madness that I feel.
　　To this end, Fabio,
I beg you be content
with what you have achieved,
and your ambition's excess you restrain.
　　Be not, my love, offended,
by this petition's strangeness;
my heart cries for it and
yet more anxiously my spirit.
　　No, I do not flee from loving you,
nor do I wish you to forget me,
but I long only forever to love you
without this heat that suffocates me.
　　In order to attain this state,
today I seek your love,
and ask that you not ask of mine
proof, I must just now deny.
　　This, Fabio of my soul, is
the kindness I now hope
to merit of your noble, faithful,
most well born compliance.
　　If you do as I wish,
my affections will be so deeply yours
that neither jealousy nor envy
can ever take them from you.
　　And with this, farewell, Fabio,
I fear I may annoy you;

consérvate felice,
y prospere tu vida eterna el Cielo.

may you be happy
and Heaven bless your life eternal.

(Translated by Lou Charnon Deutsch)

2

*Endechas aconsejando a una jóven
hermosura no entre en la carrera del amor*

Deténte, hermosa Tirsi,
¿dónde va tu albedrío?
Mira que vas perdida
siguiendo un precipicio.

No prosigas, aguarda,
detén el paso, el brío,
porque es despeñadero
el que juzgas camino.
No te engañe el terreno
porque le ves florido,
que en esas mismas flores
está el mayor peligro.
Vuelve, vuelve la espalda
al reclamo fingido,
no te suceda, incauta,
lo que al fiel pajarillo,
que engañado en los ecos
del gorgeo mentido,
pensando que al consorte,
se entrega al enemigo.

Deténte, hermosa Tirsi,
¿dónde va tu albedrío?
Mira que vas perdida
siguiendo un precipicio.

Huye el mar proceloso
donde todo es conflicto,
tormentas y borrascas,
naufragios, peñas, riscos,
en donde se navega
sin fe, sin norte fijo,
sin socorros humanos,
sin auxilios divinos,
y en donde siendo todo

2

*Verses Advising a Young Beauty
Not to Enter the Lists of Love*

Stop, beautiful Tirsi.
Where does your caprice lead you?
See how you are wandering lost
at the precipice's edge.

Go no further, wait,
detain your step, your spirit,
for what you've judged
a road is hazardous terrain.
Be not deceived by the land's appearance
because you see it in flower,
for in those very blossoms
the greatest danger lies.
Turn, turn your back
on false allure,
let not happen to you, faithless girl,
what happened to the faithful bird
who, fooled by the faithless
echoes of song, believing them
to be her mate's own warbles,
fell into her enemy's snare.

Stop, beautiful Tirsi.
Where does your caprice lead you?
See how you are wandering lost
at the precipice's edge.

Flee the storm-tossed sea
where all is conflict,
squall, and tempest,
shipwrecks, rocks, crags,
on which one sails,
without faith, with no fixed compass,
without human succor,
without divine avail,
and where all is danger,

<table>
<tr><td>

contingencia y peligro,
desconocidas playas,
escollos y bajíos,
en tan urgentes riesgos
es el piloto un niño,
el rumbo la inconstancia,
y el bajel es de vidrio.

   Deténte, hermosa Tirsi,
¿dónde va tu albedrío?
Mira que vas perdida
siguiendo un precipicio.

   No malogres las gracias
de tus años floridos,
dando a tus perfecciones
empleos poco dignos.
A empresas más heroicas
eleva tus sentidos
y no abatida anheles
gozos tan fugitivos,
que aquél que más te haya,
por ser tu afecto expresivo,
merecedor de tanta
ventura parecido,
será quizá de todos
los que a tus pies invictos
solicitan tu gracia
el menos de ella digno.

   Deténte, hermosa Tirsi,
¿dónde va tu albedrío?
Mira que vas perdida
siguiendo un precipio.

</td><td>

unknown beaches,
reefs, and shallows,
and the perils so urgent
that the pilot's but a child,
the course, inconstancy,
and the ship is made of glass.

   Stop, beautiful Tirsi.
Where does your caprice lead you?
See how you are wandering lost
at the precipice's edge.

   Waste not the charms
of your years in flower
by wasting your perfections
on unworthy occupations.
Raise your sensibilities
to endeavors more heroic,
and do not yearn dejected
for such fleeting pleasures,
for the one that seems to you,
thanks to your expressive soul,
worthy of such risk,
may be of all the ones who,
at your triumphant feet,
ask you for your favors
the one who least deserves them.

   Stop, beautiful Tirsi.
Where does your caprice lead you?
See how you are wandering lost
at the precipice's edge.

(*Translated by Lou Charnon Deutsch*)

</td></tr>
</table>

3
Soneto definiendo el amor
o sus contrariedades

3
Sonnet Defining Love
or Its Contradictions

<table>
<tr><td>

   Borrasca disfrazada en la bonanza,
engañoso deleite de un sentido,
dulzura amarga, daño apetecido,
alterada quietud, vana esperanza.
   Desapacible paz, desconfianza,
desazonado gozo mal sufrido,
esclava libertad, triunfo abatido,
simulada traición, fácil mudanza.

</td><td>

   Tempest in the guise of weather fair,
one sensation's fraudulent delight,
bitter sweetness, longed-for pain,
anxious quietude, and hope in vain.
   Unpeaceful, worried peace, as well
     suspicion.
uneasy pleasure, borne ill,
liberty in chains and abject triumph,

</td></tr>
</table>

Perenne manantial de sentimientos,
efímera aprehensión que experimenta
dolorosas delicias y escarmientos.

Azarosa fortuna, cruel, violenta,
zozobra, sinsabor, desabrimientos,
risa en la playa y en la mar tormenta.

sham betrayal, easy fickleness.

Emotions' everlasting spring,
ephemeral understanding that perceives
painful joys, chastisements.

Hazardous fortune, cruel and violent,
anguish, pain, dejection,
laughter on the beach and storm at sea.

(Translated by Lou Charnon Deutsch)

The Nineteenth Century

Fernán Caballero

✳

With the possible exception of Leonor López de Córdoba, Cecilia Böhl de Faber, who wrote under the pseudonym Fernán Caballero, is the writer in this anthology most conscious of setting out a national program in her work. Resolved not to create what she called "Romanesque" novels, but rather to transmit the reality she observed, convinced of the validity of her parents' conservatism, and cloaked in an ultramasculine pseudonym with aristocratic medieval overtones, she affirms the values rooted in Spanish absolutism, Catholicism, and traditionalism. At the same time, however, she is forced to break one of the fundamental rules of that tradition — the silence of women.

Cecilia Böhl's Spanish identity was problematic, and perhaps for that very reason she clung so tightly to it. Her parents were Juan Nicolás Böhl de Faber, a German, and Francisca Larrea, of Spanish-Irish descent. She was born in Switzerland on December 24, 1796, when her mother was on her way to visit Germany, and spent the first few years of her life moving between Andalusia and Hamburg with her parents, who could not agree on where to establish permanent residence. Then, in 1806, Doña Francisca returned to Spain with her two youngest daughters, leaving Cecilia and her brother in Germany with their father. A combination of war in Europe and the parents' stubbornness kept the family apart until 1811, and it was not until 1813 that the whole family moved to Spain. Cecilia, who was then seventeen, spoke French and German fluently, but not Spanish. Nor did she spend much time in Spain. In 1816 she moved to Puerto Rico with her new husband, Antonio Planells y Bardají, who died a few months later. Cecilia remained in Puerto Rico for three years, and when she returned to Europe in 1819, her destination was not Spain, but Germany, to visit her grandmother. In 1820 she went back to Spain to stay.

Cecilia's parents were highly influential in both her political education and her writing career. Romantic reactionaries, Juan Nicolás Böhl de Faber and Francisca Larrea agreed on matters of national politics, religion, and literature. The folkloric themes as well as the didacticism and moralizing of Cecilia's works have their source in her parents' attitudes and writing. Her ambivalence with respect to her own position as an author of literary texts can also be explained, at least to some extent, with reference to her parents.

Juan Nicolás Böhl fully enjoyed being his wife's teacher, but he was much less

happy with her refusal to remain in the role of adoring, obedient disciple. Francisca Larrea hosted groups of learned people for discussions on politics and culture, she contributed to local newspapers in Cádiz, and, much to her husband's dismay, she read Mary Wollstonecraft. Juan Nicolás all the while believed that women had no business meddling in intellectual questions, and he did not hide his hostility toward women who displayed their intelligence: "When Icarus flew too near the sun, he fell to the water, and the same thing happened to Madame Wollstonecraft. Why are all intelligent women unhappy? Why are they *detested*? Why are they ridiculed, at least? I have not yet encountered a woman in whom the smallest intellectual superiority did not produce some moral deficiency."[1]

The husband who wrote these lines to his wife was also the father who encouraged and kept all his eldest daughter's youthful literary efforts, but it is clear that he never wished her to publish them. Cecilia, who had spent her formative years at her father's side, adopted his attitudes concerning women. Doña Francisca corrected, copied, and in many cases translated her daughter's writing, for Cecilia almost always wrote in French or German. Unlike her husband, Francisca Larrea wanted Cecilia to publish; and in 1835, when she took the liberty of submitting one of her daughter's stories to the magazine *El Artista,* Cecilia protested.

It is not surprising that such parents produced a daughter who, on the one hand, became a serious writer and, on the other, did not want to publish what she wrote. Cecilia was also ambivalent about the "intellectual superiority" that her father disliked and that her mother displayed in the local newspapers. She modestly rejected both authority and originality in her writing: "I have no more merit than the person who washes and removes the dust from an old painting that has been stashed away for years; one admires it, yes, but one admires the painting, not the person who cleans it and brings it to light."[2]

Nevertheless, she displays a certain amount of pride in having initiated a new kind of writing in Spain: "The tendency of my little works is to combat the novelistic . . . This is to make an innovation, giving a new spin to the passionate novel, bringing it to the simple path of duty and artlessness."[3] Fernán Caballero's role as a precursor of Spanish literary realism has been firmly established by literary historians, but they also follow her lead in underestimating her skill as a creative writer. Traditional criticism does not argue when she compares herself to a photographer, whose transparent style ostensibly transmits observed reality without leaving any trace of authorial presence. Paradoxically, the very desire to erase her personality from her texts and to write only what she has observed or what has been told to her leads her to use details from her own life in her work. Fernán Caballero's biographers consistently go back to her novel *Clemencia* (1852) for information on the author's life.

Cecilia Böhl remarried in 1822. Her new husband, the Marquis of Arco Hermoso, gave her entry into Seville's aristocracy as well as access to the Andalusian rural life that would serve as background to much of her writing. During the years she spent

as Marquise, Cecilia wrote two novels: *La familia de Alvareda* (1849; *The Alvareda Family*, 1872) and *Elia, o España treinta años ha* (1849; *Elia, or Spain Fifty Years Ago*, 1868). In 1836, a year after her second husband died, Cecilia traveled through Europe with her sister. On the trip she met and fell in love with an Englishman named Frederic Cuthbert. When she discovered he was not interested in marriage, she returned to Spain. In 1887 she was once again married, to Antonio Arrom, and once again she was writing.

Antonio was younger than Cecilia, but not as strong, and his illness quickly used up her savings. In 1848, motivated in part by necessity, and no longer obliged to obey her father, who had died in 1836, or to defy her mother, who died in 1838, she began to publish her writing. Within a year, she had published four novels and four short stories. One of them, "La Hija del Sol" (The daughter of the sun), comes from a story that circulated in Cádiz, loosely based on the life of María Hore. The narrator claims the tale is true, and it would appear to represent truly the era's myths surrounding both race and women's sexuality. Fernán Caballero ostensibly tells it for its moral; but it is also a mysterious story of love and death. In recording this highly fictionalized account of the eighteenth-century poet, Fernán Caballero pays homage to another woman writer, even as she presents a version of Hore's life that is so distorted that it suppresses even the fact that the protagonist was a writer.

The success of her writing did little to alleviate Cecilia Böhl's economic distress. It did, however, make it possible to send her husband abroad, as she prevailed upon one of her literary admirers to have Antonio named consul to Australia. The couple lived apart for five years, trying to improve their economic status. When Antonio returned for a visit in 1858, he had established a business, and Cecilia had gotten a house in the Alcázar (fortress) of Seville as a gift from the queen. Unfortunately, Antonio's business partner defrauded him; ruined, he committed suicide. Widowed for the third time, Cecilia tried to live a quiet life. To a certain extent she achieved her goal, always separating her private identity from her public one as Fernán Caballero. But Fernán Caballero was already a part of the international literary world, and she kept up her friendships and correspondence with many writers. Among her friends was the Cuban poet, novelist, and playwright Gertrudis Gómez de Avellaneda, whose political radicalism, sexual emancipation, and literary adherence to a romanticism linked to the expression of personal emotion did not get in the way of Cecilia's affection for her.

Cecilia Böhl lived in the Seville Alcázar until 1868, when the queen lost her throne and the author, as a result, lost her home. She moved to a small house where she lived until her death on April 7, 1877.

1. Cuando Ícaro se acercó demasiado al sol, cayó al agua, y lo mismo sucedió a madame Wollstonecraft. ¿Por qué son desgraciadas todas las mujeres sabias? ¿Por qué se las *detesta*? ¿Por qué se las ridiculiza, por lo menos? No he encontrado todavía una mujer a quien la más pequeña superioridad intelectual no produzca alguna deficiencia moral"; cited in Javier Herrero, *Fernán Caballero: Un nuevo planteamiento* (Madrid: Gredos, 1963), 39.

2. "No tengo más mérito alguno que aquél que lava y quita el polvo a una pintura vieja y arrumbada; se admira, sí, se admira pero. . . a la pintura, no al que la limpia y saca a luz," (Fernán Caballero, *Obras Completas*, [Madrid: Sucesores de Rivadeneyra, 1893-1914], 41-42).

3. "la tendencia de mis obritas es combatir lo novelesco . . . Esto es hacer una innovación, dando un giro nuevo a la apasionada novela, trayéndola a la sencilla senda del deber y de la naturalidad;" cited in Susan Kirkpatrick, *Las Románticas: Women Writers and Subjectivity in Spain, 1835-1850* (Berkeley: University of California Press, 1989), 331 n. 8.

La Hija del Sol

Est-ce vrai? —Oui: mais qu'importe?
BALZAC

Tocaban a ánimas las campanas de la ciudad de Sevilla, y muchos corazones religiosos se alzaban al cielo en aquella hora dedicada por la Iglesia a recordar a los muertos. Todo yacía frío, silencioso y triste en la invadiente obscuridad de una noche de diciembre; una espesa cortina de nubes cubría las estrellas, que son, según dice un poeta, los ojos con que mira el cielo a la tierra.

En la sala de una de las hermosas casas de Sevilla, que los extranjeros llaman palacios, frente a una chimenea en que ardía y daba luz como una antorcha la alegre leña del olivo, estaba sentada una señora, sumida en los pensamientos graves y tristes que infundían la hora y lo lóbrego de la noche. No se oía sino el gemido del viento, que daba tormento a los naranjos del jardín, y que, penetrando por el cañón de la chimenea, caía sobre la llama, a la cual abatía temblorosa, esparciendo ráfagas de vacilante luz por la estancia. Parecía que la soledad la abrumase, y cual si un genio benéfico se ocupase en prevenir sus deseos, abrióse la puerta, apareciendo en el umbral una persona cuya vista debió serle grata, puesto que, al verla, hizo la señora un ademán y exclamación de alegría, y se levantó para ir a su encuentro.

La recién entrada era una señora de edad, bajita, trigueña, cuyos ademanes animados y cuyos ojos vivos y alegres denotaban que los años habían pasado por aquella naturaleza juvenil y activa sin doblegarla y sin que su dueña los notase.

—Vaya, marquesa —dijo la recién llegada, —que para venir desde donde yo vivo hasta tu casa se necesitan *amor y coche*.

The Daughter of the Sun

Est-ce vrai? —Oui: mais qu'importe?
BALZAC

The bells of the city of Seville rang for the souls in purgatory, and many religious hearts were lifted to heaven at that hour dedicated by the church to the memory of the dead. Everything lay cold, silent, and sad in the encroaching darkness of a December night; a thick curtain of clouds covered the stars that, according to one poet, are the eyes through which heaven gazes at the earth.

In the living room of one of Seville's beautiful houses, which foreigners regard as palaces, before a fireplace where cheerful olive logs blazed and threw light like a torch, a lady was seated, immersed in the grave and sad thoughts that permeated the hour and the gloom of the night. There was no sound other than the moaning of the wind that whipped the orange trees in the garden and, entering the fireplace chimney, fell on the flames, reducing them to a tremulous glow, scattering sparks of flickering light through the room. It seemed that loneliness would overwhelm her when, as though a kind genie had taken it upon himself to foresee her desires, the door opened; and there appeared on the threshold a person the sight of whom must have been pleasing to her, for, when she saw her, the lady made a gesture and uttered words of joy, and got up to greet her.

The recent arrival was an elderly woman, short, olive-skinned, whose animated gestures and lively, gay eyes indicated that the years had passed by that youthful and active nature without bending it and without its owner taking note.

"I declare, Marquise," said the woman who had just arrived, "in order to get from

—Te ha bastado el amor. ¡Y cuánto te lo agradezco! Ahora conozco la verdad que encierra este refrán: "Amor con amor se paga". ¡Salir en una noche como ésta!

—Hija mía, no había otra —repuso la amiga. —¿Sabes —añadió— que te he estado mirando por los cristales, y he visto que tienes un aire de languidez, según dicen los poetas del día, que maldito si te sienta bien? Si te hubiese visto tu amigo el barón de Saint-Preux, diría que, echada como estás en tu sillón ante la chimenea, parecías la estatua de la Lealtad llorando ante la hoguera de un trono.

—Por fortuna —repuso riendo la marquesa, —el trono que arde aquí lo fue siempre de un jilguero.

—Si te viese Joaquín Bécker, le servirías de modelo para algún cuadro de la Viuda de Padilla, —prosiguió la que había entrado.[1]

—Desahoga ese buen humor que rebosa en ti como la alegría en los niños —respondió con resignación la marquesa.

—Tu recomendado sir Robert Bruce diría al verte, que lo que verdaderamente progresa en el mundo es el *spleen*.

—Pero, amiga mía —replicó la marquesa, —cuando se tienen penas...

—Si me hablas de penas, tomo el portante —interrumpió la señora; —tengo una cáfila de ellas a tu disposición, que me dejo en casa cuando salgo. Vengo a que nos distraigamos un rato en sabrosa plática, como dicen los buenos hablistas, exóticos ya entre nosotros. Dejemos las lamentaciones para Semana Santa.

—De ningún modo me entretendrías mejor y más a mi gusto —repuso la

where I live to your house one needs love and a carriage."

"You've managed it with love alone. And how grateful I am to you! Now I understand the truth held in the saying 'Love is by love repaid.' To have come out on a night like this!"

"My dear, I had no choice," the friend replied. "You know," she added, "that I have been watching you through the window and I have noticed an air of lassitude about you, as the fashionable poets would say, that does not become you. If your friend the Baron of Saint-Preux had seen you, he would have said that, stretched out as you are in your easy chair before the fireplace, you look like the statue of Loyalty weeping before an empty throne."

"Fortunately," the marquise replied laughing, "the empty throne in question was always that of a goldfinch."

"If Joaquín Bécker had seen you, you would have served as a model for a canvas of the Widow of Padilla," said the visitor.[1]

"The good humor that abounds in you like the joy of a child is a comfort," the marquise responded with resignation.

"If he saw you your highly thought-of Sir Robert Bruce would say that it is spleen that is truly on the increase in the world."

"But, my friend," the marquise replied, "when one has sorrows..."

"If you speak to me of sorrows, I shall leave," the woman interrupted. "I have a caravan of those—you are welcome to them—which remain at home when I go out. I've come so that we might entertain ourselves for a bit in a delicious chat, as the silver-tongued—now so rare among us—

1. Bécker fue un pintor sevillano de la época. Juan de Padilla fue ejecutado por ser jefe del ejército comunero que se levantó en contra de Carlos V.

1. Bécker was a noted contemporary painter from Seville. Juan de Padilla was executed as the leader of the popular revolt against Charles V.

marquesa— que contándome la historia de aquella hermosa dama que debió a su extraordinaria belleza el nombre por el que fue conocida.

—¿*La Hija del Sol*?. . . Verdad es que prometí referírtela; y cierto es también que nadie te la podrá contar con mejores datos que yo, habiéndolos adquirido en la Isla de León, teatro del suceso, donde pasé mi primera juventud, siendo mi padre capitán general del Departamento.

Sentáronse ambas amigas frente a la chimenea, avivaron el fuego, y la marquesa se puso a escuchar con ansiosa curiosidad el siguiente relato:

Quedó viuda la señora de *** con sólo una hija, de tan maravillosa belleza, que mereció el dictado de "la Hija del Sol", por el cual era conocida. Crióla su madre lejos del mundo, en silencio y soledad, velando incesantemente sobre su tesoro, hasta ponerla en manos del hombre digno y honrado que, uniéndose a la hermosa joven, le dio su nombre y hacienda. Don A. F. era un hombre de mérito, y la Hija del Sol se unió a él sin desear y sin oponérsele la boda: siguió en esta ocasión el dictamen de su madre, que nunca había hallado oposición en la dócil niña.

Gozaban hacía algún tiempo los esposos de una felicidad sin nubes, cuando un acaecimiento inútil de referir obligó a don A. F. a hacer un viaje a la Habana. Entonces rogó a su suegra que se encargase de su hija y la llevase fuera de Cádiz durante su ausencia. Hacíalo porque en aquella época —por los años de 1764— era Cádiz rica y poderosa, y el oro arrastraba en pos de sí ese lujo, esos placeres, esas vanidades, esa embriaguez y esas pasiones que son su séquito ordinario. Para alejarse de este foco de seducciones y peligros, don A. F. les suplicó que se trasladasen a la Isla, ciudad de

would put it. Let us save the laments for Holy Week."

"If you would like to entertain me, there is nothing that would please me more," the marquise responded, "than hearing the story of that lovely lady whose extraordinary beauty gave rise to the name by which she was known."

"*The Daughter of the Sun?* . . . It is true that I promised to tell you that story; and it is also true that no one could tell it better than I, having heard it on the Island of León, the scene of the event, where I spent the early years of my youth, when my father was captain general of the Department."

The two friends seated themselves before the fireplace, built up the fire, and the marquise settled down to listen, with eager curiosity, to the following story:

"When the wife of *** was left a widow, she had just one daughter, of such marvelous beauty, that she merited the title 'the Daughter of the Sun,' and by that she was known. Her mother brought her up far from the world, in silence and solitude, incessantly watching over her treasure, until she placed her in the hands of a dignified and honorable man who, taking the beautiful young woman in marriage, gave her his name and his fortune. Don A. F. was a man of merit, and the Daughter of the Sun married him neither desirous of nor opposed to the wedding: she followed on that occasion the dictates of her mother, whom the docile child had never opposed.

"The couple had lived some time enjoying a cloudless happiness, when an event of no importance to this story obliged Don A. F. to travel to Havana. So he implored his mother-in-law to take charge of her daughter and to take her away from Cádiz during his absence. He asked this because during that time—around 1764—

arsenales y de marina, vasta y solitaria, porque Cádiz lo absorbía todo en sus cercanías.

Mientras un barco salía lentamente de la bahía de Cádiz, entonces animada como una feria, una berlina con cuatro caballos, cuyos cascabeles sonaban alegremente, corría por el arrecife que conduce de Cádiz a la Isla, y que se alza entre dos mares, que se unen tanto en las altas mareas, que entonces, más que camino, parece el arrecife puente.

En la berlina se hallaban dos señoras: la una anciana, cuyo semblante expresaba cuidados y zozobras; la otra joven y hermosa, cuyo rostro estaba bañado de lágrimas. Frente de ambas iba sentada una negra aún joven, doncella y compañera desde su infancia de la que lloraba; la que por sus visajes, gracias y niñerías logró que a una legua de Cádiz las lágrimas de su ama llegaron a secarse, y que una sonrisa reemplazase los suspiros que antes salían de sus labios.

La Isla de León es una ciudad larga y angosta, que se levanta blanca y brillante entre los montones de sal, como un cisne rodeado de sus polluelos. Tres cosas descuellan en ella: las palmeras de su arenisco suelo, el Observatorio de su sabia marina y la cúpula de sus católicos templos. La Isla es triste como una bella mujer arrinconada por una feliz competidora; o más bien la Isla, con sus arsenales, sus diques, sus cordelerías, sus astilleros y machinas, parece la mujer del marino en su soledad, sentada en la playa y mirando al mar.

La berlina se paró delante de una hermosa casa, que, como la mayor parte, era de piedra y estaba solada de mármol, y cuyas puertas eran de caoba. Frente de la puerta de la calle se abría la del jardín. Precedíale una galería que formaban columnas de mármol, entre las cuales

Cádiz was wealthy and powerful, and the gold brought with it that luxury, those pleasures, those vanities, that drunkenness, and those passions that ordinarily follow in its train. In order that they be far from that center of seductions and dangers, Don A. F. begged that they move to the Island, a city of shipyards and beaches, vast and solitary, because Cádiz absorbed everything within its reach.

"As a boat slowly left the Bay of Cádiz, as animated as a country fair, a berlin carriage with four horses, its jingle bells sounding gaily, ran along the reef that led from Cádiz to the Island, and that rose above the two seas, that were united at high tide as they were then, and more than a road, the reef seemed a bridge.

"Two ladies rode in the berlin: the one was old, her face filled with cares and anxieties; the other young and beautiful, her face bathed in tears. Facing the two was a Negress, still young, a maid and the companion from childhood of the weeping woman; and with her joking, clever expressions, and cajoling, she managed to stop the tears of her mistress when they were a league from Cádiz, and then a smile replaced the sighs that before escaped from her lips.

"The Island of León is a long, narrow city that rises white and brilliant amid mounds of salt, like a swan surrounded by its chicks. Three things stand out there: the palm trees from the sandy soil, the observatory from its vital beach, and the domes of its Catholic churches. The Island is sad, like a lovely woman pushed into a corner by a happy competitor; or, better yet, the Island, with its shipyards, its dikes, its rope-making shops, its lumber yards and machines, seems like the lonely wife of a sailor, seated on the beach and looking out to the sea.

habían confeccionado los jazmines, las madreselvas y los rosales guirnalderos, columpios para mecer sus flores. Caminitos de ladrillos dividían el jardín en cuatro partes. Las paredes desaparecían bajo un espeso velo de enredaderas. En el centro del jardín había un cenador o merendero tan espesamente cubierto por rosales de pasión, que en lo obscuro y fresco, más que cenador, parecía gruta. En medio, sobre un pedestal, se hallaba un amorcito de mármol, que con una mano escondía sus flechas, y con un dedo de la otra que llevaba a sus labios, imponía silencio.

En este merendero era en el que pasaba la Hija del Sol largas y solitarias horas. Algunas veces le decía Francisca, su negra, después de prolongados ratos de silencio:

—Ese niño, mi señora, nos hace señas que callemos. Más valiera que nos mandase hablar, pues lo vamos a olvidar. Mi amo tiene en el barco la mar, los vientos y los peligros; pero acá nosotras no tenemos nada sino flores.

La Hija del Sol bostezaba y respondía:
—Mi marido piensa
que entre dos que bien se quieren
con uno que goce basta.

¡Así pasaba su vida aquella mujer, que, por desgracia, no había sido enseñada a llenar su tiempo y a ocupar su mente, y a la que pesaba la ociosidad como al desvelado las tinieblas! Necesitaba la vida activa para revolotear ligeramente y sin objeto, de flor en flor, como la mariposa.

Un día estaba la hermosa solitaria sentada, abanicándose, en su ventana o cierro de cristales. Francisca, echada en el suelo, se entretenía en teñir de azul con agua de añil el blanco perrito habanero de su señora.

—¿Sabe usted, mi ama —dijo de repente, —que ese oficial, ese brigadier de guardias marinas que nos sigue cuando vamos a misa, se ha mudado aquí enfrente?

"The berlin stopped in front of a lovely house that, like most of the houses, was made of stone and tiled with marble, its doors made of mahogany. The door to the street was opposite the one opening on to the garden. This was followed by a corridor formed by marble pillars, and between these the jasmines, the honeysuckles, and the climbing roses had grown together to form swings in which to rock their flowers. Paths of brick divided the garden into four parts. The walls were hidden behind a thick veil of vines. In the center of the garden was a bower or arbor so heavily covered with passion roses that its darkness and coolness made it seem more like a grotto than a bower. In the middle, on a pedestal, stood a marble Cupid; in one hand he held his arrows hidden behind his back, and a finger of the other, held to his lips, demanded silence.

"It was in this bower that the Daughter of the Sun spent long, solitary hours. At times Francisca, her Negress, after prolonged periods of silence, said to her:

"'That child, my lady, is signaling to us to keep quiet. But it would be better if he ordered us to speak, because we are going to forget how. My master has, in his boat, the sea, the wind, and peril; but here we have nothing but flowers.'

"The Daughter of the Sun yawned and replied:

"'My husband believes
that between two who love so well,
sufficient it is that one enjoy.'

"And thus that woman spent her life because, unfortunately, she had not been taught to fill her time and occupy her mind, and idleness weighed on her like the gloom on one who cannot sleep! She needed an active life where she could whirl about lightly and for no purpose, from flower to flower, like a butterfly.

"One day the beautiful recluse was

La Hija del Sol, al oír a su negra, volvió la cabeza por un irreflexivo e involuntario impulso, y vio en el balcón de la casa a que Paca aludía a un joven, el cual, aprovechando el instante en que ella fijó su vista en él, la saludó con la finura y gracia que ha distinguido siempre a los oficiales de la Marina Real.

La reconvención que iba a hacer la Hija del Sol a su negra expiró en sus labios al ver al joven, en el que de sobra había reparado anteriormente. Así que Francisca prosiguió:

—Se llama don Carlos de las Navas, tiene veinticuatro años y es el mejor mozo de la brigada. Es tan bueno y tan llano, que todo el mundo le quiere. . .

—Parece que estás muy impuesta en todo lo concerniente a ese caballero —dijo su ama interrumpiendo a la negra. —Pero como todo eso ni me atañe ni me importa, guárdalo para ti y otros curiosos.

—Aquí tiene mi ama a su perrito, más azul que una pervinca —dijo la humilde muchacha para distraer a su ama.

Pero la Hija del Sol no pensaba ni en el perrito azul, ni en su doncella negra. Días había que un gallardo joven la seguía por todas partes: ¡le veía en todas partes: en la calle, en la iglesia, en sus pensamientos, en sus sueños! ¡Ahora se le encuentra alojado frente a su ventana; se le han nombrado; se halla casi en relaciones con él, por medio de un saludo que no ha podido excusar.

De más está el que se añada que las Navas, que fue uno de los más cumplidos caballeros de su época, al ver a la Hija del Sol, había concebido por ella una de aquellas pasiones que en tiempos en que no absorbía la política completamente a los hombres, henchían y exaltaban sus almas a punto de intentar lo posible, movidos por ellas.

Mucho tiempo fueron inútiles todas sus

seated, fanning herself in her bay window. Francisca, stretched out on the ground, amused herself with her mistress's little white Havana dog, dying it blue with indigo water.

"'Did you know, my mistress,' she said suddenly, 'that the officer, that brigadier from the marine guard who follows us when we go to mass, has moved in across the street?'

"The Daughter of the Sun, on hearing her Negress, turned her head in an unthinking and involuntary impulse, and saw on the balcony of the house to which Paca alluded a young man who, taking advantage of the moment during which she fixed her gaze on him, greeted her with the courtesy and grace that has always distinguished the officers of the Royal Navy.

"The rebuke the Daughter of the Sun was going to make to the Negress died on her lips when she saw the young man whom she had previously noticed more than once. And so Francisca continued:

"'His name is Don Carlos de las Navas, he is twenty-four years old and is the finest young man in the brigade. He is so good and so straightforward that everyone loves him . . .'

"'It appears that you are very well informed about everything concerning the gentleman,' her mistress said, interrupting the Negress. 'But as none of that concerns nor interests me, save it for yourself and others who are curious.'

"'Here my lady has her little dog, bluer than a periwinkle,' said the humble girl to distract her mistress.

"But the Daughter of the Sun was thinking neither of her little blue dog, nor of her Black maid. For days the charming young man had followed her everywhere: she saw him at every turn: in the street, in church, in her thoughts, in her dreams!

gestiones, porque a la Hija del Sol habían sido infundidos principios religiosos, que si no siempre alcanzan en vista de la fragilidad humana, a evitar una culpa, siempre llegan a enmendarla o corregirla. Las Navas estaba desesperado; la Hija del Sol, por su parte, había trocado su anterior tranquilo fastidio por un constante dolor que la consumía. Francisca, la negra, llena de compasión por los sufrimientos de ambos, y cediendo a sus instintos de raza incivilizada, sin reflexionar en la culpable causa de estos voluntarios sufrimientos, ni en las transcendentales consecuencias de su necia complacencia, cedió a los ruegos de las Navas, y una noche en que estaba su ama tristemente sentada en el cenador del jardín, le abrió una puertecita que éste tenía y que daba a la *Albina*, sitio solitario y pantanoso que se extiende entre la Isla y el mar.

Es una verdad muy conocida la de que el primer paso es el que cuesta. La puerta que tan imprudentemente abrió la negra, lo fue ya cada noche. En aquella galería, poco ha tan sola y vacía; entre aquellas flores, poco ha tan desdeñadas; a la claridad de aquella luna, poco ha tan desatendida, pasaban los amantes noches de encanto, y cuya felicidad adormecía hasta la conciencia. De esta suerte pasó un año.

Entonces acaeció que el capitán general del Departamento, que había ido a Jerez, murió allí repentinamente; toda la brigada de guardias marinas tuvo que trasladarse a aquel pueblo para acompañar el entierro. Esta ausencia, por corta que fuese, causó un vivo dolor en dos seres que había un año que no podían vivir sino en la misma atmósfera, y para los cuales era la ausencia un compuesto de dolor, de inquietud, de ansiedad, de temor y de celos.

En la noche del segundo día estaba sentada la Hija del Sol en la galería de su jardín: Francisca lo estaba a sus pies. La luna

Now she discovered him lodged opposite her window; his name had been brought up; she found herself almost involved with him as a result of a greeting that she had been unable to avoid.

"There is no need to add that when las Navas, who was one of the most outstanding gentlemen of his time, first saw the Daughter of the Sun, he had conceived for her one of those passions that, during periods when politics did not completely absorb men, filled and exalted their souls to such a degree that, for it, they were willing to attempt anything.

"For a long time all of his gestures were in vain, because the Daughter of the Sun had been steeped in religious principles, and though these do not always enable one to avoid sin, human frailty being what it is, they do provide for making amends or correcting errors. Las Navas was desperate; the Daughter of the Sun, for her part, had exchanged her former tedious interior peace for a constant pain that consumed her. Francisca, the Negress, filled with compassion for the sufferings of both, and yielding to the instincts of her uncivilized race, without reflecting on the sinful cause of these voluntary sufferings, nor on the transcendent consequences of their foolish satisfaction, yielded to the pleas of las Navas; and one night, when her mistress was sitting sadly in the garden bower, she opened for him a tiny door that led from the garden to the *Albina,* a solitary and marshy site that stretched between the Island and the sea.

"It is a widely known truth that the first step is the hardest. The door that the Negress so imprudently opened was now left so every night. In that gallery, a short while before so lonely and empty; among those flowers, a short while before so disdained; in the glow of that moon, a

se levantaba pura y tranquila, como un corazón exento de pasiones y de inquietudes.

—Mi ama —dijo Francisca poniéndose de un salto en pie, —ahí está el señorito de Navas. ¿No ha oído su mercé la señal?

—No es posible, Francisca —respondió azorada y con el corazón palpitante la Hija del Sol.

—Escuche, mi ama, escuche, —repuso la negra.

La Hija del Sol aplicó el oído, y oyó distintamente el silbido particular que usaba las Navas para darse a conocer.

Francisca corrió a buscar la llave del postigo, corrió hacia él, lo abrió, y las Navas, envuelto en su capa, entró con paso acelerado.

Pero Francisca no pudo volver a cerrar el postigo, porque le empujaron dos hombres que entraron y siguieron a las Navas.

Sobrecogida de un asombro que la paralizó, la negra no pudo ni moverse ni gritar. Los que habían entrado alcanzaron a las Navas, y antes que pudiese defenderse ni parar el golpe, le clavaron sus puñales en el pecho. Las Navas cayó sin dar un gemido; cuando le vieron tendido en el suelo, los asesinos huyeron.

Por algún tiempo el más profundo silencio siguió reinando en aquel lugar, mudo testigo de la catástrofe. Francisca permanecía paralizada bajo la doble impresión del espanto y del horror. La Hija del Sol yacía desmayada sobre las gradas de mármol de la galería; ¡las Navas no daba señal de vida! La luna plateaba tranquilamente este cuadro, y las flores lo embalsamaban.

Al cabo de un rato, vuelta Francisca en sí por la activa angustia que sucedió a su pánico espanto, vuela hacia su ama, a quien ya mira deshonrada y perdida; la coge en sus brazos, la despierta, la anima.

—¡Ama mía! ¡Ama mía! —exclama. —

short while before so unnoticed, the lovers spent their nights of enchantment; and their happiness put even their consciences to sleep. In this way a year passed.

"Then it happened that the captain general of the Department, who had gone to Jerez, died there suddenly: the entire brigade of marine guards had to go to that town to be present at the burial. This absence, though it was brief, caused a burning pain in two beings who for a year had been unable to live except by breathing the same air, and for whom the absence was a combination of pain, uneasiness, anxiety, fear, and jealousy.

"On the night of the second day, the Daughter of the Sun was seated in the gallery of her garden: Francisca was at her feet. The moon rose pure and peaceful, like a heart free of passions and worries.

"'My mistress,' Francisca said, jumping to her feet, 'Master de las Navas is here. Has not your grace heard the signal?'

"'That is not possible, Francisca,' The alarmed Daughter of the Sun responded, her heart racing.

"'Listen, my mistress, listen,' replied the Negress.

"The Daughter of the Sun strained to listen and distinctly heard the special whistle that las Navas used to announce his presence.

"Francisca ran to look for the key to the gate, then ran to it, opened it; and las Navas, wrapped in his cape, quickly entered.

"But Francisca was unable to close the gate, because two men pushed against it, then entered and followed las Navas.

"Overcome by a fright that paralyzed her, the Negress could not move or cry out. The men who had entered reached las Navas, and before he could defend himself or ward off the blow, they drove their dag-

¡Sois perdida si aquí hallan ese cadáver! Ama mía, vuestra honra y vuestra suerte dependen de lo que podamos hacer en estos momentos; ¡y son contados! Es preciso sacar de aquí ese cadáver, que os compromete. ¡Valor, mi señora, valor! ¡Si no lo hacéis por vos, hacerlo por el amo! Saquemos de aquí ese cadáver para evitar el escándalo y la afrenta. Ayudadme a arrastrarlo a la *Albina*, que yo no puedo hacerlo sola.

Y la valerosa negra arrastra a su infeliz ama, y la obliga a ayudarle a arrastrar el cadáver a la *Albina*.

—¡Basta! ¡Que no puedo más! —gemía su ama.

—¡Más todavía, mi señora! —replicaba con angustia la negra. —¿Queréis aparecer ante los tribunales?

Y las dos, dominando su dolor, su asombro y su flaqueza, volvían a coger el yerto cadáver para alejarlo más de allí.

Después, Francisca, sosteniendo a su señora, la acuesta, vuelve al jardín, echa agua sobre las manchas de sangre y hace desaparecer todo rastro, todo vestigio de aquel lúgubre crimen, con esa energía, hija del cariño, que es la más perseverante. Regresa al lado de su señora, y al verla tendida, tan blanca y tan inmóvil como si fuese aquel lecho su féretro, cae de rodillas, y elevando hacia su señora sus temblorosas manos, prorrumpe en sollozos, exclamando:

—¡Ama mía, yo os perdí!

—No, Francisca, no —murmuró su señora; —¡me has salvado!

Y echando uno de sus brazos de marfil al cuello de ébano de la esclava, la atrajo a sí, prorrumpiendo en sollozos.

—Ya viene el alba —dijo poco después Francisca, que fue a abrir las ventanas como para poner cuanto antes fin a aquella espantosa noche.

Por más que digan los poetas, que, por

gers into his chest. Las Navas fell without so much as a moan; when they saw him lying on the ground, the assassins fled.

"For a long time the profoundest of silences reigned in that place, mute witness to the catastrophe. Francisca remained paralyzed with the double impression made by fright and horror. The Daughter of the Sun lay in a faint on the marble steps of the gallery; las Navas gave no sign of life! The moon shed a peaceful silver light on the scene, and the flowers perfumed it.

"After a time, the deep anguish that followed her panicked fright brings Francisca to her senses, she flies to her mistress, whom she now realizes has been dishonored and is lost; she takes her into her arms, brings her to, exhorts her.

"'My mistress! My mistress!' she exclaims. 'You are lost if they find this corpse here! My mistress, your honor and your destiny depend upon what we are able to do in the next few moments, and these are numbered! We must get rid of this corpse, for you are compromised by it. Courage, my mistress, courage! If you cannot do it for yourself, do it for your master! Let us take this corpse away to avoid scandal and offense. Help me to drag it to the *Albina*, as I cannot do it alone.'

"And the valiant Negress pulls her unfortunate mistress along, and forces her to help drag the cadaver to the *Albina*.

"'Enough! I can go on no longer!' her mistress whimpered.

"'You must go on, my lady!' replied the Negress in anguish. 'Do you want to appear before the tribunals?'

"And the two of them, overcoming their anguish, their terror, and their frailty, again took hold of the inert corpse to remove it to a point even more distant.

"Then Francisca, holding her lady up,

lo regular, no conocen al alba sino de oídas, el alba es triste. Cuando el día recae, todo se prepara al reposo; ¡al alba todo se prepara al trabajo y al sufrimiento! La luz del día alumbra a una ciudad muerta; ¡tanto brillo en el cielo y tanto silencio en la tierra contrastan penosamente! La Hija del Sol, bella y silenciosa, se parecía a esa madrugada sin vida.

Francisca la obligó a levantarse y a sentarse en su cierro de cristales, como tenía de costumbre, para evitar toda sospecha. Francisca entraba y salía en el gabinete.

—¿Qué se dice? —le preguntaba su señora a media voz.

—Todavía nada —respondía Francisca en el mismo tono.

—¡Dios Santo! ¡Ese cadáver abandonado! —gemía la infeliz.

Francisca cruzaba las manos y le hacía seña de que callase, señalándole a su madre, que rezaba tranquilamente sentada en el canapé.

De repente se oyeron los brillantes y animados sonidos de la música militar. Era la brigada de marina, que regresaba a Jerez.

Cada nota de la música, que tantas veces había oído cuando precedía a la brigada, y a su cabeza venía el hombre a quien amaba, y que ahora yace muerto y abandonado cadáver en la *Albina*; ¡cada una de estas notas es un puñal que se clava y destroza el corazón de la infeliz mujer, en la que hasta su dolor es un delito!

De repente, aquella mujer que gemía quédase muda, sus ojos se abren espantados y fijos, un temblor convulsivo se apodera de ella, y sólo tiene acción para extender el brazo con un ademán lleno de espanto hacia la calle. Francisca se arrojó al cierro, y sigue con la vista la dirección que indican el brazo y las miradas de su ama, y ve. . . ¡ve a las Navas a la cabeza de su brigada, que en aquel instante alza la

pulls her to her room, puts her to bed, returns to the garden, throws water on the blood stains, and causes every sign, every vestige of that lugubrious crime, to vanish, with that energy, born of affection, that gives rise to the greatest perseverance. She returns to her lady's side, and on seeing her lying like that, so white and so still, as though that bed were her coffin, falls to her knees, and bringing her trembling hands to her lady, bursts into tears, exclaiming:

"'My mistress, I am to blame for your perdition!'

"'No, Francisca, no,' her lady murmured, 'you have saved me!'

"And throwing one of her marble-white arms around the ebony neck of the slave, she pulled her to herself, bursting into tears.

"'The dawn is coming,' Francisca said a little later, and went to open the windows as if to bring that frightful night to an end as quickly as possible.

"No matter what the poets say, and they, in general, know nothing about the dawn except what they have heard, the dawn is sad. When the day ends, everything prepares for repose; at dawn everything prepares for work and suffering! The light of the day illuminates a dead city; so much brilliance in the sky and so much silence on earth form a painful contrast! The Daughter of the Sun, beautiful and silent, resembled that lifeless dawn.

"Francisca forced her to get up and to sit in her bay window, as was her habit, to avoid all suspicion. Francisca entered and left the chamber.

"'What are they saying?' her lady asked her in a low voice.

"'Nothing yet,' Francisca responded in the same tone.

"'Dear God! That cadaver abandoned there!' the miserable woman moaned.

cabeza, sonríe y saluda alegremente a su amada! Francisca da un grito y cae sin sentido: la Hija del Sol, fuera de sí, clama al cielo pidiendo misericordia. Refiere a voces lo acaecido aquella noche; la creen loca, y su madre manda llamar a un facultativo; pero Francisca, vuelta en sí, confirma la relación de su ama. Van a la *Albina*; pero allí no se halla cadáver alguno. Preguntan a las Navas; éste no ha faltado, no ha podido faltar de Jerez, lo que confirman unánimes sus compañeros.

La Hija del Sol, después de restablecida de una larga enfermedad, escribe a su marido, se confiesa culpable, le ruega que la perdone y le dé licencia para entrar en un convento a hacer penitencia. El marido le da esta licencia, la bula es otorgada, y la Hija del Sol entró y profesó en las Descalzas de Cádiz, en el que, después de una vida ejemplar, murió como una santa. Francisca la siguió al convento.

—¿Y cómo se explicó eso? —preguntó con profundo interés la marquesa a su amiga cuando ésta hubo concluido.

—Esto no se explicó *nunca* para los incrédulos; pero sí *muy luego* a las almas creyentes —respondió su amiga.

NOTA. Esta relación es verídica. La Hija del Sol nació en 1742 y murió monja descalza en Cádiz en 1801, a los cincuenta y ocho años de edad. El señor D. Francisco Micón, marqués del Mérito, compuso a la Hija del Sol, cuando profesó, el siguiente soneto, que si bien no tiene mucho del título de su autor, puede servir de comprobante a lo referido:

"Francisca crossed her hands and signaled to her to be quiet, pointing to her mother, who prayed peacefully, seated on the settee.

"Suddenly they heard the bright, animated sounds of military music. It was the marine brigade, returning from Jerez.

"Each note of the music, which she had heard so often when it preceded the brigade, and which brought to her thoughts the man she loved and who now lies dead, his cadaver abandoned in the *Albina*—each one of those notes is a dagger that wounds and shatters the heart of the unhappy woman, in whom even grief is a crime!

"Suddenly that woman who was moaning falls silent, her eyes open in fear and stare, she is gripped by a convulsive tremor, and she is able to do no more than stretch her arm toward the street in a gesture filled with fright. Francisca throws the window open and her eyes follow in the direction indicated by the arm and the look of her mistress, and she sees . . . she sees las Navas at the head of his brigade, and just then he raises his head, smiles, and gaily salutes his beloved! Francisca cries out and falls into a faint: the Daughter of the Sun, beside herself, cries out to the heavens begging for mercy. She shouts out what had happened the night before; they think her mad, and her mother sends for a doctor; but Francisca, now in control, confirms her mistress's story. They go to the *Albina*, but there is no trace of a corpse there. They question las Navas; he has not been missing, he was not able to leave Jerez, and his companions unanimously confirm his story.

"The Daughter of the Sun, after recovering from a long illness, writes to her husband, confesses her sin, begs his forgiveness and his permission for her to enter a

convent to do penance. Her husband accedes, the bull is granted, and the Daughter of the Sun entered and took the vows of the Discalced of Cádiz, and there, after an exemplary life, she died a saint. Francisca followed her to the convent."

"And how is this to be explained?" the marquise asked with deep interest when her friend had finished the story.

"It was *never* explained for the skeptical; but it was *immediately* clear to those souls who believe," her friend responded.

NOTE. This is a true story. The Daughter of the Sun was born in 1742 and died a Discalced nun in Cádiz in 1801, at fifty-eight years of age. Señor Don Francisco Micón, Marquis of Mérito, composed the following sonnet to the Daughter of the Sun when she took her vows, and though it does not do justice to the gifts of its author, it may serve as proof of the events related:

A la
Hija del Sol
Soneto

Ya en sacro velo esconde la hermosura;
en sayal tosco, garbo y gentileza
la Hija del Sol, a quien por su belleza
así llamó del mundo la locura.

Entra humilde y contenta en la
clausura;
huye la mundanal falaz grandeza:
triunfadora de sí, sube a la alteza
de la santa Sïon, mansión segura.

Nada pueden con ella el triste encanto
del siglo, la ilusión y la malicia;
antes los mira con horror y espanto.

Recibe el parabién, feliz novicia,
y recibe también el nombre santo
de hija amada del que es sol de justicia.

To the
Daughter of the Sun
Sonnet

Now with sacred veil she conceals her
loveliness;
With coarse woolen cloth, her elegance
and refinement,
The Daughter of the Sun, who for her
beauty
the world in its madness called so.

Humble and content, she enters the
cloister;
fleeing the false grandeur of the world:
triumphing over self, she ascends to the
heights
of holy Zion, a true mansion.

The sad enchantment of the century,
its illusions and malice can not touch her;

rather, she looks at them with horror and
　　fear.
　　Receive, happy novice, this blessing,
and receive, too, the holy name
of beloved Daughter of Him, who is the
　　Sun of Justice.

(Translated by Mary Ellen Fieweger)

Carolina Coronado

Carolina Coronado was born early in the second decade of the nineteenth century (dates given for her birth range from 1820 to 1823), in Almendralejo, a birthplace she shares with the poet José de Espronceda. She was ten when she wrote her first poem, and about thirteen when she published her ode "A la palma" (To the palm tree). Coronado was from a liberal aristocratic family — her father was persecuted by reactionary forces and even spent some time in prison when absolutism returned to Spain. Coronado received the traditional education of girls of her class: "I studied nothing but the sciences of needlepoint and embroidery and Extremaduran lace, which is certainly as complicated as Latin law, where there is no point that is not entangled."[1] She was not always so sanguine about her education, however. In 1842 she wrote to the poet Hartzenbusch:

> The town where I received my education is unrivaled in its opposition to literary education. The capital I live in is unsurpassed in its opposition to poetry. My town puts up vigorous resistance to all innovation in the occupation of young women, who after finishing their domestic chores ought to retire to gossip with their friends and not read books that *corrupt youth*. The capital has taken one step, but so timid and vacillating that it but concedes to women the reading of novels *as a distraction*; and mothers, instigated by their conscience, still reprimand girls for doing what they themselves were not permitted. The very men for whom the word *progress* generates enthusiasm when it is attached to politics, wrinkle their brows if they see their daughters drop their monotonous knitting for a moment to read the latest serial novel in the newspaper . . . Imagine the number of enemies a woman must have if she dare oppose these customs, and if such an unequal struggle would not, in the end, wear her out. Mr. Tejado gave me some classes in literature, but my domestic chores are many: to put them aside while I go for a walk, or to a party, is something the customs of Extremadura authorize; but to put them aside to study when a woman is not to be a *professor*, would be a ridiculously scandalous deed. A woman fears people's opinion because she was born always to fear: to avoid ridicule I put aside my lessons and gave my hours of sleep over to reading. But that weakened my health, and my family, worried about it, forbade me to continue. I decided, therefore, just to compose verses, not write them down but commit them to memory; but this *contemplation* interfered with the proper execution of my tasks and gave me a distracted air that made

strangers laugh and bothered my family . . . I resolved to *meditate* for just an hour a day, before getting out of bed. But thought cannot bear such slavery; the poet cannot live like this, and my meager talent is now half suffocated.[2]

The first edition of Coronado's poems came out in 1843, a year before her family moved to Madrid. The Lyceum Society (Sociedad El Liceo) celebrated the young poet's arrival in the capital by bestowing on her a crown of laurels.

In Madrid Coronado became a favorite of Queen Isabel, whose cause she supported when it was challenged by the conservative Carlists, who wanted to see a man on the throne. Coronado's marriage to Horace Perry, secretary of the U.S. delegation to Spain, was of use to her in her support of the queen. On one occasion, during the Revolution of 1866, Coronado opened the doors of her home to a group of liberals who had been sentenced to death. She protected them under the American flag until she was able to negotiate their safe-conduct to France. Coronado's literary and political activities often coincided. Although the novelist Juan Valera applauded her for "the artless vague and sweet melody of her songs"[3] and Gómez de la Serna remembers her "ineffable, amorous, young ladylike" romanticism,[4] Coronado also wrote poems expressing the other face of romanticism: the partisan politics of the Liberal party and the struggle for freedom and justice. In addition to her anti-Carlist poetry and her poems in praise of Liberal heroes, Coronado took on such themes as women's oppression, the loss of the Spanish empire, and slavery in Cuba. She was a member of the Abolitionist Society of Madrid; and in 1868, when writer, feminist, and social reformer Concepción Arenal was elected president of the society, Coronado became her vice president.

Although she is best known for her poetry, Coronado also wrote novels, essays, and plays. One of her dramatic pieces, *El cuadro de la esperanza* (The picture of hope), made its debut during a royal celebration. Coronado participated fully in Madrid literary society. She attended salons, wrote for journals, kept up friendships with the famous writers of the day. After her daughters were born (her only son died before he was a year old), she began to write less, and she all but stopped publishing her work. Many years later, Coronado's daughters encouraged her to edit a volume of poetry that would include poems scattered in various magazines as well as previously unpublished work, for they had heard that their mother had been a writer, but they could not find her books.

There was a strain of romantic extravagance in Carolina Coronado. Her very first poem, "A la muerte de una alondra" (On the death of a lark), served as a shroud for the poor little bird. She was extraordinarily sensitive: the German-American diplomat Carl Shurz marveled at her infallible ability to judge people's character, as well as her inclination to faint at the sight of her father's ghost. Among Coronado's eccentricities was her refusal to bury her dead. Her daughter, Carolinita, who died at the age of sixteen in 1873, was entombed in the back of a cupboard in the sacristy of a Madrid convent; and when Horace Perry died in 1891, Coronado kept his embalmed body in a

chapel alongside her bedroom, where she visited him daily until her own death twenty years later.

Coronado's abhorrence of burial might be traced to her own experience of apparent death. When she was still an adolescent, news of her death reached Madrid, triggering an outpouring of poetic lament. It may have been that an attack of catalepsy, from which Coronado suffered throughout her life, had been misrepresented as death. Despite this recurring illness, Coronado was a lively, decisive woman, with a striking amount of personal courage. One of her biographers tells of how one night she saved the life of the liberal politician Emilio Castelar. Seeing that he was about to be arrested, Coronado tossed her husband's overcoat over him and, covering his face with her fan in a gesture of marital intimacy, she walked the hunted man to saftey, under the nose of the police. A somewhat less heroic example of her strong character was her intransigence concerning the marriage of her daughter Matilde. According to the family legend recounted by Coronado's nephew, the writer Ramón Gómez de la Serna, Coronado consented to Matilde's marriage on the double condition that she would never have to see her son-in-law and that Matilde would continue to sleep in her—Coronado's—bedroom. Matilde agreed. Carolina Coronado's eccentricity is no doubt fascinating. More important to the history of women's writing, however, is the way in which she challenged the barriers set up against women writers.

Admired by the masculine literary world of her day, Coronado also sought a women's literary community. Romanticism facilitated this effort to a certain extent, with its glorification of certain characteristics traditionally considered feminine. Affective expression and passion were valued more that intellectual precision. Moreover, the romantic poet was associated with the elemental forces of nature, traditionally associated with the feminine. In a poem to her friend, the poet Gabriel García y Tassara, Coronado evokes attributes traditionally associated with women to prove women's superiority in dealing with emotion.

Coronado praised women's writing and strove to build a women's culture, looking both to her contemporaries and to history for a literary sisterhood. Even before moving to the capital she sustained herself poetically in a passionate correspondence with a young woman poet from Asturias, Robustiana Armiño. Coronado worked to establish a women's literary tradition in much of her writing. She wrote a historial novel, *La Sigea*, based very loosely on the life of the all-but-forgotten humanist poet Luisa Sigea. She also wrote a biography of the Cuban writer Gertrudis Gómez de Avellaneda, an essay on Spanish women poets ("Galería de poetisas españolas"), and an open letter to the novelist Emilia Pardo Bazán. In addition, Coronado used her influence to facilitate the publication of the work of other women.

In 1848, Coronado wrote an essay comparing Sappho and Saint Teresa, which was published two years later in the popular magazine *Semanario Pintoresco Español* (Spanish Picturesque Weekly). Writing first on Sappho, then on Saint Teresa, and finally, in the section of the essay reproduced here, on both together, Coronado overtly

highlights the similarities of these two aparently disparate women, and covertly includes herself in the women's literary history they represent. Coronado's Sappho will probably be unfamiliar to modern readers, who associate the poet of Lesbos with love and desire among women. The nineteenth century "regularized" Sappho's sexuality by attributing to her a heterosexual passion for a humble fisherman, Phaon, whose rejection precipitated her suicide. Yet to juxtapose Saint Teresa to even a heterosexualized Sappho, pagan and passionate, would have been a shocking gesture.

Coronado spent more than a third of her life in Portugal, where she moved after Carolinita's death. There her husband suffered financial ruin in his failed transatlantic cable venture, and there Matilde was married. Coronado lived her widowhood in Portugal, a quiet life, receiving old friends. She continued to write, in the company of her dead husband and her daughter, who was also a poet and who published her work under the pseudonym Luz. Carolina Coronado died in Portugal in 1911, but her body, together with the remains of her husband, were returned to her birthplace for burial. Her son-in-law took care of the funeral arrangements, and after he buried his mother-in-law, he had his sister-in-law interred as well.

1. "Nada estudié sino las ciencias del pespunte y el bordado y del encaje extremeño, que sin duda, es tan enredoso como el Código latino, donde no hay un punto que no ofrezca un enredo"; letter, 1909, cited in Ramón Gómez de la Serna, *Mi tía Carolina Coronado* (Buenos Aires: Emecé Editores, 1942), 63.

2. "Nada más opuesto a la educación literaria que el pueblo en donde yo recibí mi educación; nada más opuesto a la poesía que la capital en donde vivo. Mi pueblo opone una vigorosa resistencia a toda innovación en las ocupaciones de las jóvenes, que después de terminar sus labores domésticas, deben retirarse a murmurar con las amigas y no a leer libros que *corrompen la juventud*. La capital ha dado un paso más, pero tan tímido y vacilante que sólo concede a las mujeres la lectura de alguna novela *por distracción*, y todavía las madres, como instigadas por su conciencia, reprenden a las muchachas por entregarse a un ejercicio que a ellas no les fue permitido. Los hombres mismos a quienes la voz *progreso* entusiasma en política, arrugan el entrecejo si ven a sus hijas dejar un instante la monótona calceta para leer el folletín de un periódico... Calcule V. los enemigos que tendrá la mujer atrevida que se oponga a estas costumbres y si una lucha desigual y sostenida no debe al cabo fatigarla. El Sr. Tejado me dio algunas lecciones de literatura, pero mis labores domésticas son muchas: suspenderlas para concurrir a un paseo, a una sociedad, es cosa que autorizan las costumbres extremeñas; pero suspenderlas para estudiar cuando una mujer no ha de ser *catedrática*, sería un hecho ridículamente escandaloso. Una mujer teme de la opinión de cada uno porque ha nacido para temer siempre: por evitar el ridículo suspendí mis lecciones y concreté mi estudio a leer las horas dedicadas al sueño. Pero esto debilitó mi salud, y mi familia, celosa de ella, me prohibió continuar. Me decidí, pues, a hacer versos solamente, a no escribirlos y a conservarlos en la memoria; pero esta *contemplación* perjudicaba al buen desempeño de mis labores y me daba un aire distraído que hacía reír a los extraños y molestaba a mis parientes... Me resolví a *meditar* solamente una hora cada día antes de levantarme. Pero el pensamiento no puede sufrir tanta esclavitud; el poeta no puede vivir así y mi escaso numen está ya medio sofocado;" cited in Isabel Fonseca Ruiz, "Cartas de Carolina Coronado a Juan Eugenio Hartzenbusch," in *Homenaje a Guillermo Guastavino* (Madrid: Asociación Nacional de Bibliotecarios, 1974)," 178.

3. "la no aprendida vaga y dulce melodía de sus cantares", Juan Valera, "Carolina Coronado;" *Crítica literaria (1901-1905): La poesía lírica en la España del siglo XIX* (Madrid: Imprenta alemana, 1912), 241.

4. "inefable, amoroso, señoritil," Gómez de la Serna, 100.

1
¿A dónde estáis consuelos de mi alma?
(1848)

¿A dónde estáis consuelos de mi alma,
cantoras de esta edad, hermanas mías,
que os escucho sonar y nunca os veo,
que os llamo y no atendéis mi voz amiga?
¿A dónde estáis, risueñas y lozanas
juveniles imágenes queridas?...
Yo quiero veros, mi tristeza acrece
la soledad mi padecer irrita;
a darme aliento a mitigar mi pena
venid, cantoras, con las sacras liras.
He visto alguna vez que al cuerpo herido
flores que sanan con su jugo aplican,
de mi espíritu triste a la dolencia
yo le aplicara la amistad que alivia.
Flores, que la salud de pobre enferma
pudierais reanimar con vuestra vista,
¿por qué estáis de la tierra en el espacio,
colocadas tan lejos de mi vida?...
Ese es, cantoras, de infortunio el colmo,
ésa en el mundo la mayor desdicha;
sufrir el mal, adivinar remedio
y no lograrlo cuando el bien nos brinda.—
No he de lograrlo sola y olvidada,
como el espino en la ribera umbría,
de mi cariño las lozanas flores
lejos de la amistad caerán marchitas.
Nunca os veré; mi estrella indiferente
no marca en mi vivir grandes desdichas,
pero tampoco, ¡ay Dios! grandes placeres,
tampoco venturosas alegrías.
¿Qué valen las desgracias si a sus horas
de tormentoso afán sigue la dicha?
Es menos bella la existencia, hermanas,
pálida, melancólica, indecisa;
que no tenga un azar de los que rinden
ni una felicidad de las que animan.
    ¡A Dios, auras de abril, rosas de mayo,
cantoras bellas de la patria mía!
Yo no puedo estrecharos en mis brazos,
yo no puedo besar vuestras mejillas;

1
Where Have You Gone,
My Soul's Sweet Comforts?

Where have you gone, my soul's sweet
    comforts,
singers for these times, my sisters
whom I hear and never see,
whom I call yet never do you heed a
    friend's voice?
Where are you, my beloved youthful
images of laughter and freshness? ...
I long to see you, my sadness grows,
and solitude intensifies my grief;
come, singers of sacred songs,
bring me cheer and ease my pain.
I have seen once how flowers pressed to
a wounded body heal it with their fluids;
gladly would I apply friendship thus
to lift the sorrow from my sad spirit.
Flowers, who could restore to health
my poor, sick soul at just the sight of you,
why are you scattered from earth to sky
so far from me? ...
Such is, oh singers, the height of
    misfortune,
such the greatest misery;
to suffer an ill, know its remedy,
and not be able to take the good offered.
I cannot possess it alone and forgotten
like a hawthorn on a shady bank,
the luxuriant flowers of my love
will wither and fall if deprived of
    friendship.
I will never see you; my indifferent star
has neither destined me for great sorrows,
nor—Oh God!—for great pleasures,
or for consummate joys.
What care I for misfortune if at the
moment of greatest danger happiness
    prevails?
Oh, my sisters, a pallid, melancholic,
indecisive life lacks beauty
without the threat of calamity,

pero al ardiente sol mando un suspiro
y a la luna, al lucero y a la brisa
para que allá, donde en la tierra os hallen,
lo lleven en sus alas fugitivas.
¿Qué dais, hermanas, de mi amor en pago?
Dadme canciones tiernas y sencillas
reflejo puro de las almas vuestras,
consuelo activo de las ansias mías;
y así podré exclamar "¡nunca las veo,
sin verlas moriré, mas logro oírlas!"

or the promise of a happiness to make the
    spirit soar.
    Farewell, April mornings and May roses,
fair singers of my country!
I cannot embrace you in my arms,
I cannot kiss your cheeks;
but I send a sigh to the ardent sun
and to the moon, the morning star,
    and the breeze
so that there, wherever on this earth you are,
their swift wings will carry it to you.
How will you repay my love, my sisters?
With songs both sweet and simple,
pure reflection of your souls,
and welcome comfort for my cares;
so that I can exclaim, "I never see them,
I will die without seeing them,
but still can I hear them!"

(Translated by Lou Charnon Deutsch)

2
La poetisa en un pueblo
(1845)

¡Ya viene, mírala! ¿Quién?
—Esa que saca las coplas.
—Jesús que mujer tan rara.
Tiene los ojos de loca.
Diga Vd., don Marcelino,
¿será verdad que ella sola
hace versos sin maestro?
—¡Qué locura! No señora;
anoche nos convencimos
de que es mentira, en la boda:
si tiene esa habilidad
¿por qué no le hizo a la novia,
siendo tan amiga suya,
décimas o alguna cosa?
—Una décima, es preciso
dije— el novio está empeñado:
"Ustedes se han engañado
me respondió, no improviso."

2
A Woman Poet in the Village

Here she comes, look at her! Who?
"The one who writes poems."
"Gracious, what a queer woman.
Such wild eyes.
Tell me, Don Marcelino,
could it be that she writes
these verses without a teacher?"
"Absurd! No, madame,
last night at the wedding
we were convinced it is a lie:
for if she possesses such a gift
why did she not invent
a few strophes for the bride
who is such a dear friend of hers?"
"One strophe, at least,"
I clamored, "the groom is adamant:
'You are all mistaken,'
she responded, 'I do not improvise.'"

—Siendo la novia su amiga
vamos, ¿no ha de hacerlo usté?—
"Pero por Dios, si yo no sé,
¿no basta que yo los diga?"
La volvimos a rogar,
se levantó hecha una pólvora,
y en fin, de que vio el empeño
se fue huyendo de la boda.
Esos versos los compone
otra cualquier persona,
y ella luego, por lucirse
 sin duda se los apropia.
—Porque digan que es romántica.
—¡Qué mujer tan mentirosa!
—Dicen que siempre está echando
relaciones ella sola.
—Se enseñará a comedianta.
—Ya se ha sentado, ¡la mona!
Más valía que aprendiera
a barrer que a decir coplas.
—Vamos a echarla de aquí.
—¿Cómo? —Riéndonos todas.
—Dile a Paula que se ría.
—Y tú a Isabel, y tú a Antonia.
Ja ja ja ja ja ja.
¡Más fuerte, que no lo nota!
Ja ja ja ja ja ja.
Ya mira, ya se incomoda.
Ya se levanta y se va.
¡Vaya con Dios la gran loca!

"But the bride is such a dear friend.
Come, surely you'll do it for her?"
"But, dear sir, I cannot do it.
Is it not enough for me to read my
     poems?"
We persisted,
she rose in a fit,
and seeing everyone's resolve
fled from the wedding.
You can be sure
someone else writes those poems
and she, to put herself forward,
passes them off as her own.
"So that they will call her a romantic."
"What a deceitful woman!"
"They say she is always
going on to herself."
"She must be trying out to be an actress."
"Now she is sitting down, the silly imp.
Better she learn
to sweep than to recite verses."
"Let us be rid of her."
"How?" "By all laughing at her."
"Tell Paula to start laughing."
"And you tell Isabel, and you Antonia."
Ha ha ha ha ha ha ha.
Louder, she cannot hear you!
Ha ha ha ha ha ha ha.
Now she is looking, her discomfort grows.
She is getting up to leave, there she goes.
Farewell, madwoman.

(Translated by Lou Charnon Deutsch)

3
A España
(1846)

3
To Spain

¿Qué hace la negra esclava, canta o
     llora?
Tú, Europa, gran señora
que a tu servicio espléndido la tienes,

What is the Black slave woman doing,
is she singing or crying?
Oh, grand lady Europe,
who keeps her in your splendid service,

responde, ¡llora, canta,
o dormida a tu planta
apoya ora en tus pies sus tristes sienes?
    Yo que en su misma entraña me he
        nutrido
y en su pecho he bebido
su ardiente leche, con amor la adoro,
y por saber me afano
si al pie de su tirano
reposa, canta o se deshace en lloro.
    Venga el pueblo que a madre tan
        querida
debe también la vida,
las nuevas a escuchar, que de su suerte
por caridad nos diga
la señora enemiga
de quien vive amarrada al yugo fuerte.
    Oigan los hijos de la negra esclava
lo que orgullosa acaba
de trasmitir su dueña a las naciones,
para que mofa sea
del mundo que la vea
sufriendo eternamente humillaciones.
    Dice, que por nodriza solamente
al Norte y al Oriente
conducen a la madre, cuyo seno
a mucha boca hambrienta
sin cesar alimenta
con la abundancia que lo tiene lleno.
    Y nos dice también que latigazos
la dan con duros brazos
los hijos de Bretaña y del Pirene,
después de haber sacado
al seno regalado
el jugo que los nutre y los sostiene.
    Y se atreve a decir la fiera dueña
que en rendirla se empeña,
dejándola cansada, enferma y pobre,
para que no en la vida
emprendiendo la huida
su independencia y libertad recobre. . .

answer me, is she crying or singing?
Or, asleep before you,
does she rest her weary brow against your
    feet?
    I who was nourished in her very womb,
who suckled at her breast
her ardent milk, I lovingly revere her,
and I demand to know
if at the feet of her tyrant
the slave rests, sings, or weeps.
    Rise up, people who also owe
your life to this dear mother,
heed the story she tells of her sad lot;
have pity, fine lady,
and tell us, enemy,
whose yoke binds her fast.
    Listen, you children of the Black slave,
to what the proud lady her mistress
has just relayed to the nations
to make them mock her vassal,
and shower her with endless humiliations.
    She says that merely to be a wet nurse
do they take her to the North and East,
to be a mother whose breast
ceaselessly nurtures the hungry mouth
with the abundance of which she is full.
    And she tells us also of lashes
applied by the mighty arms
of the children of Britain and the
    Pyrenees
after she has generously emptied
her breast and provided
its nourishing liquid to sustain them.
    And the barbarous mistress dares to
      admit
that she is determined to break her slave,
leaving her tired, sick, and poor,
so that never in her life
even if she were to flee
would she recover her independence and
    freedom.

¿No tenemos un Cid? ¿No hay un
    Pelayo
que nos presten un rayo
de indignación, con que a librarla acuda
ese pueblo indolente,
esa cobarde gente
egoista, ambiciosa, sorda, muda?

¿Dónde está la bandera, caballeros,
que dos pueblos enteros
con su anchurosa pabellón cubría?
¿Dónde los castellanos
en cuyas fuertes manos
la enseña nacional se sostenía?

Ya no hay bandera; el pabellón lucido
en trozos dividido
como harapos levanta nuestra gente
sin escudo y sin nombre,
sirviendo cada hombre
de caudillo y de tropa juntamente.

Cual árabes errantes, cada uno
sin domicilio alguno
vagan los desdichados en la tierra
huyendo del vecino
que hallan en su camino
por no poder marchar juntos sin guerra.

Quién levanta su tienda de campaña
en un rincón de España
y por su rey a su persona elige,
y quien sobre la arena
traza, escribe y ordena
las leyes con que él solo se dirige.

Y quién burlando al Dios de sus
    abuelos
nombra para los cielos
otro señor que nos gobierne el alma,
juzgando la criatura
que siendo el Dios su hechura
más fácilmente alcanzará la palma.

Patria, leyes y Dios, siervo y monarca
el español abarca
refundiendo sus varias existencias
en el cerebro loco
para quien juzgo poco
de esa inmensa reunión, cinco potencias.

Have we no Cid? Is there no Pelayo who
can lend us a ray
of indignation to make her
indolent people rescue her?
That cowardly people,
vain, ambitious, deaf, and dumb!

Where is the flag, oh knights,
that with its ample banner
covered two entire peoples?
Where are the Castilians
whose mighty hands
proudly bore our nation's standard?

There is no more flag; our people
raise the once proud banner
now rent to pieces
like so many rags;
without coat of arms, without a name,
every man acting
as leader and soldier at the same time.

Like aimless Arabs, each one
without a hearth,
the unhappy of the land wander,
fleeing the companions
they encounter along the way,
unable to march together without strife.

One raises his battle tent
in a corner of Spain
and elects himself king,
and one traces in the sand,
writing and dispensing
the laws that he alone follows.

And one, mocking the God of his
    ancestors,
appoints a different lord of the heavens
to govern our souls,
calculating that since this God
was the creature of his own fantasy,
more easily will victory be his.

Nation, laws and God, servant and
    monarch
does the Spaniard monopolize,
recasting their various guises
in his demented brain,
for he judged too paltry

¡Soberbia, necia vanidad mezquina
que a padecer destina
la soledad, el duelo, el abandono
a esa España afligida
que siempre desvalida
se ve juguete de extranjero encono!

    Ha menester alzarse una cruzada,
ha menester la espada
blandir al aire la española tropa,
los reinos espantando
para salvar luchando
a esa que gime esclava de la Europa.

    Mas ¡dónde habéis de ir, tercios
        perdidos,
 de nadie dirigidos,
marchando sin compás por senda oscura
con rumbo diferente,
a dónde pobre gente,
a dónde habéis de ir a la ventura!

    ¿Resucitó Cortés, vive aún Pizarro,
o de encarnado barro
queréis poner vestido de amarillo
un busto en vuestro centro
por que al primer encuentro
vengan rodando huestes y caudillo?

    Nunca se lanza el águila a la esfera
sin medir su carrera;
nunca el toro acosado en la llanura
rompe en empuje fiero
sin pararse primero
a reforzar su aliento y su bravura.

    Unid el pabellón roto en pedazos,
enlazad vuestros brazos,
a un mismo nombre sea
el que invoquéis a un tiempo en
        vuestra ayuda.

    Así de negra esclava que es ahora
será España señora,
por vosotros el yugo rescatada,
y al abrigo del trono
con soberano tono
de los pueblos servida y respetada.

    Así ¡ay! de infeliz que hoy se presenta
será España opulenta,

the five powers of that immense
    assemblage.

    Arrogance, stupidity, and petty vanity
that destine the suffering Spain
to solitude, sorrow, and abandon,
and she, ever helpless,
remains a plaything to the greedy
    foreigner.

    What we need is a crusade,
a Spanish army to brandish its sword
in the air, and frighten the nations,
to rescue through its struggle
Europe's grieving slave.

    But where will you go, errant legions,
led by no one,
marching without compass on a dark
    road,
each in a different direction?
Where, my poor people,
where will your venture lead you?

    Has Cortés risen from the dead, does
        Pizarro live still,
or do you wish to place in your midst
a bust of lifelike clay, draped in yellow
so that when they see it
army and leader will rally around?

    The eagle never soars into the sky
without first measuring its flight,
nor does the bull, when attacked, explode
in fierce anger without stopping first
to garner its bravery and ferocity.

    Unite the pieces of your banner,
join your arms together,
let there be only one name
you all invoke to come to your aid.

    Thus the Black slave
that is our lady Spain today
will be rescued from her yoke by you
and protected by the throne
of noble sovereignty
and served and revered by all nations.

    Thus, oh! the poor wretch of today
will become tomorrow's opulent Spain
by you alone enriched,

por vosotros no más enriquecida,
bella y engalanada,
de laurel coronada,
respirando salud, contento y vida.

    ¡Veréis cómo ya entonces no la insultan
los que su diente ocultan
entre sus pechos, con hambrienta boca,
después de haber sacado,
su jugo regalado,
llamándola salvaje, necia y loca!

    Veréis ¡oh! cómo entonces las banderas
de aquellas extranjeras
que la trataron con tan dura saña,
inclinando su frente,
con voz muy reverente
la dicen al pasar—"Salud España."

beautified and adorned,
crowned with laurel wreath,
emitting health, happiness, and life.

    You will see then how they cease their
      insults,
those who today sink their teeth
into her breasts and with hungry mouths,
after having drunk
its bounteous liquid,
call her savage, stupid, and mad!

    Then you will see, oh! how the flags
of those foreign countries
who treated her so badly,
bow before her,
and how, with a reverent voice,
all will say as she passes, "Hail Spain."

(Translated by Lou Charnon Deutsch)

4
Libertad

    Risueños están los mozos,
gozosos están los viejos
porque dicen, compañeras,
que hay libertad para el pueblo.

    Todo es la turba cantares,
los campanarios estruendo,
los balcones luminarias,
y las plazuelas festejos.

    Gran novedad en las leyes,
que, os juro que no comprendo,
ocurre cuando a los hombres
en tal regocijo vemos.

    Muchos bienes se preparan,
dicen los doctos al reino,
si en ello los hombres ganan
yo, por los hombres, me alegro;

    mas, por nosotras, las hembras,
ni lo aplaudo, ni lo siento,
pues aunque leyes se muden
para nosotras no hay fueros.

4
Freedom

    The young men are smiling,
their elders are joyful
because they say, my sisters,
that they have gained freedom for the people.

    Everything is a frenzy of song,
the bells are ringing,
the balconies resplendent,
and the plazas festooned.

    The laws have been transformed,
but, I swear I do not understand
what it means to see men
in such a joyful state.

    Untold benefits await,
say the learned men of the kingdom,
and if by this men stand to gain,
I am pleased . . . for the men.

    But as for us, the women,
I applaud not, I feel nothing,
for even if the laws do change,
for us there are no statutes.

¡*Libertad!* ¿qué nos importa?	*Freedom!* What does it mean to us?
qué ganamos, qué tendremos?	What do we gain, what will we possess?
un encierro por *tribuna*	Imprisonment by *tribunal*
y una aguja por *derecho?*	and a needle by *right?*
¡*Libertad!* ¿pues no es sarcasmo	Freedom! what an irony to hear
el que nos hacen sangriento	them shout their
con repetir ese grito	bloody cry outside
delante de nuestros hierros?	the iron bars that confine us.
¡*Libertad!* ¡ay! para el llanto	Freedom! Oh! this cry
tuvímosla en todos tiempos;	is ever ours;
con los déspotas lloramos,	we pleaded before the despots,
con tribunos lloraremos;	and will plead before the courts.
que, humanos y generosos	Just as human and generous
estos hombres, como aquellos,	are these men as those who preceded
a sancionar nuestras penas	them,
en todo siglo están prestos.	as eager in every century
	to bless our pain.
Los mozos están ufanos,	The young men are joyful,
gozosos están viejos,	their elders are pleased,
igualdad hay en la patria,	there is equality in the land,
libertad hay en el reino.	freedom in the kingdom.
Pero, os digo, compañeras,	But I tell you, my comrades,
que la ley es sola de ellos,	that the law is but for them,
que las hembras no se cuentan	that women do not count,
ni hay Nación por este sexo.	nor is there a Nation for this sex.
Por eso aunque los escucho	Thus, though I do listen
ni me aplaudo ni lo siento;	I applaud not, nor feel emotion.
si pierden ¡Dios se lo pague!	If they lose, God bless them!
y si ganan, ¡buen provecho!	If they win, fare they well!

(Translated by Lou Charnon Deutsch)

5
A la abolición de la esclavitud en Cuba
(1863)

5
To the Abolition of Slavery in Cuba

Si libres hizo ya de su mancilla	If the immortal eagle has freed
el águila inmortal los africanos,	the Africans held in its mighty talons,
¿por qué han de ser esclavos los	why should their brothers,
hermanos,	their Antillean neighbors, remain
que vecinos tenéis en esa Antilla?	enslaved?
¿Qué derecho tendrás, noble Castilla,	What right have you, noble Castile,
para dejar cadenas en sus manos,	to leave their hands shackled

cuando rompes los cetros soberanos
al son de la libertad que te acaudilla?

    No, no es así: al mundo no se engaña.
Sonó la libertad, ¡bendita sea!
Pero después de la triunfal pelea,
no puede haber esclavos en España.

    O borras el baldón que horror inspira,
o esa tu libertad, pueblo, es mentira.

when you have broken the sovereign
    power
to the cry of liberty that led you forth to
    victory?

    No, it cannot be, the world is not
    deceived.
The cry of liberty has been heard, blessed
    be!
After the triumphant struggle,
there must not remain any slaves in Spain.

    If you abolish not this horrible shame,
such liberty as you possess, my people,
    is a lie.

(Translated by Lou Charnon Deutsch)

6
En el Castillo de Salvatierra
(1849)

    ¿Por qué vengo a estas torres olvidadas
a hollar de veinte siglos las ruinas,
espantando al subir con mis pisadas
las felices palomas campesinas?
    ¡Oh Walia![1] ¿No es verdad que
      prisioneras
la esclava del feudal y la del moro,
pobres mujeres de remotas eras,
regaron estas torres con su lloro?
    ¿Que perdido tu trono por Rodrigo[2]
y derrotado el moro por Fernando[3]
de tan largas batallas fue testigo
la misma torre donde estoy cantando?
    ¿Que inmóviles aquí tantas mujeres
tanto llanto vertieron de sus ojos
como sangre vertieron esos seres

6
In the Salvatierra Castle

    Why do I climb to these forgotten
    towers
to rummage through twenty centuries of
    ruins,
frightening with my footsteps
the carefree country doves?
    Oh, Walia,[1] is it not true that the
      imprisoned
slave of the feudal lord and the slave of
    the Moor,
those poor women of another era,
bathed these towers with their tears?
    And that when Rodrigo[2] lost his
      throne
and the Moor was vanquished by
    Fernando,[3]

---

  1. Walia fue rey de los visigodos en España y la Galia entre 415 y 420.
  2. Rodrigo, último rey godo de España, fue derrotado por los musulmanes en 711.
  3. Fernando V, que, junto con la reina Isabel I, derrotó a Boabdil, último rey musulmán de la península ibérica en 1492, unificando España bajo el signo del catolicismo.

  1. Walia was king of the Visigoths in Spain and Gaul between 415 and 420.
  2. Rodrigo, the last Gothic king of Spain, lost his throne to the Muslims in 711.
  3. Fernando V, who, together with Isabel I, in 1492 defeated Boabdil, the last Muslim king of Granada, to create a united, Christian Spain.

que arrastraron de Roma los despojos?

¿Y que tendiendo sus amantes brazos
al árabe y al godo que morían
y arrancando sus tocas a pedazos
en inútil dolor se consumían?

¿Y que tras tantos siglos de combate
que empedraron de fosiles la tierra,
subo a la misma torre de la Sierra
aún a pedir también nuestro rescate?

¡Ay! Que desde aquellas hembras que
cantaron
pidiéndolo, como yo, desde esta almena,
ni un eslabón los siglos quebrantaron
de nuestra anciana y bárbara cadena.

Y ya es preciso, para hacer patente
la eterna condición de nuestras vidas,
unir las quejas de la edad presente
a las de aquellas razas extinguidas.

¿Quién sabe si en la choza y el castillo,
contemplando estos bellos horizontes,
fuimos por estas sierras y estos montes,
más dichosas, en tiempo más sencillo?

¡Quién sabe si el fundar el ancho muro,
que libertad al pueblo asegura,
no nos trajo a nosotras más clausura
quitándonos el sol y el aire puro!

Palomas que habitáis la negra torre,
yo sé que es más risueña esta morada,
y ya podéis, bajando a la explanada,
decir al mundo que mi nombre borre.

Yo soy ave del tronco primitiva
que al pueblo se llevaron prisionera,
y que vuelvo a esconderme fugitiva
al mismo tronco de la edad primera.

No pudo el mundo sujetar mis alas,
he roto con el pico mis prisiones,
y para siempre abandoné sus salas
por vivir de la sierra en los peñones.

Yo libre y sola, cuando nadie intenta
salir de las moradas de la villa,
he subido a través de la tormenta
a este olvidado tronco de Castilla.

Yo, la gigante sierra traspasando,
lastimados mis pies de peña en peña

the very tower where I am singing
was witness to their lengthy battles?

And that confined here,
scores of women shed their tears,
just as those lost souls shed their blood
as they dragged their spoils from Rome?

And stretching their loving arms
toward the dying Arab or Goth,
renting their veils
they consumed themselves in senseless
suffering?

And after so many centuries of combat
that has filled this earth with bones,
do I not climb the same tower of the
Sierra
to plead our rescue still?

Oh! Since those women sang their
plaintive songs,
as I do from this battlement,
not one link has time chipped off
from our ancient and barbarous chains.

And thus must I come now to
denounce
the eternal condition of our lives,
to unite the complaints of a present era
with those of vanished races.

Who can say if in a simpler time,
contemplating from hut or castle this
beautiful horizon,
wandering about the hills and mountains,
we were more content?

Who can say if building this thick wall
to guarantee our people's liberty
did not bring us more confinement,
robbing us of sun and of fresh air!

You doves who inhabit this dark tower,
I know this is a sweeter home to me,
so along with you, down to the esplanade
below,
and tell the world to erase my name.

I am the songbird of this ancient wall
taken prisoner to the town,
but now I return, a fugitive, to hide myself
in these same walls of that early time.

vengo a juntarme al campesino bando
para vivir con vuestra libre enseña.

Comeré con vosotras las semillas,
beberé con vosotras en las fuentes,
mejor que entre las rejas amarillas
en las tablas y copas relucientes.

Iremos con el alba al alto cerro,
iremos con la siesta al hondo valle,
para que el sol al descender nos halle
cansadas de volar en nuestro encierro.

Nadie vendrá a decir qué fue de Roma,
ni llegará el francés a la montaña
y las nubes que bajan a esta loma
me ocultarán también la faz de España.

Aquí no han de encontrarme los
    amores,
aquí no han de afligirme las mujeres,
aquí no pueden los humanos seres
deshacer de estas nubes los vapores.

Es un nido que hallé dentro de una
    nube,
mis enemigos quedan en el llano
y miran hacia aquí: ¡Miran en vano,
porque ninguno entre la niebla sube!

Yo he triunfado del mundo en
    que gemía,
yo he venido a la altura a vivir sola,
yo he querido ceñir digna aureola
por cima de la atmósfera sombría.

Por cima de las nubes nos hallamos,
¡Libertad en el cielo proclamamos!
Las mismas nubes con los pies hollamos,
las alas en los aires extendemos.

Bajen hasta el profundo mis cadenas,
circule en el espacio el genio mío,
y haga sonar mi voz en alto brío
la libertad triunfante en las almenas!

Mas... ¿Por qué me dejáis sola en el
    cielo
huyendo del castillo a la techumbre?
¿Por qué se agolpa aquí la muchedumbre
de pájaros errantes en el suelo?

¡Oh! ¿Qué estrépito es ese que
    amedrenta?

The world could not hold my wings,
I have broken out of my prison with my
    beak,
and abandoned forever its walls
to live on the rocky mountain cliff.

I, alone and free, when no one dares
leave the walls of the village,
have climbed up here through the storm
to this forgotten ruin of Castile.

And crossing the majestic Sierra,
my feet torn, from boulder to boulder,
I come to join this rural band;
beneath your banner of freedom, I seek
    refuge.

I will eat the seeds with you,
I will drink with you from the mountain
    spring,
far better than from behind the gilded bars
at the tables with their crystal goblets.

We will soar at dawn to the highest
    peak,
and descend at noontime to the deep
    valley,
so that the setting sun will find us
safe in our nests, weary of flight.

No one will come to speak to us of
    Rome's glories,
nor will the French come to conquer our
    mountain,
and the clouds that descend this hillside
will also shade the face of Spain from me.

Here love will not find me,
here women will not torment me,
and mere human beings cannot
dispel the mist of these clouds.

I have found this nest inside a cloud,
while my enemies are left upon the plain
and they look up at me: they look in vain
because not one will rise above the mist!

I have triumphed over a world of grief,
I have come to the mountain to live alone,
I have chosen to crown my head with a
    worthy aureole
above the misty atmosphere.

La torre se estremece en el cimiento. . .
he perdido de vista el firmamento. . .
me envuelve en sus entrañas la tormenta.

    La torre estalla desprendida al
        trueno. . .
la sierra desparece de su planta. . .
la torre entre las nubes se levanta
llevando el rayo en su tonante seno.

    ¡El terrible fantasma hacia mí gira!. . .
¡tronando me amenaza con su boca!. . .
¡con ojos de relámpago me mira!. . .
y su luz me deslumbra y me sofoca!

    ¡El rayo está a mis pies y en mi cabeza!
¡¡ya me ciega su lumbre, ya no veo!!
¡Ay! ¡¡sálvame, Señor, porque ya creo
que le falta a mi orgullo fortaleza!!

    Bájame con tus brazos de la altura,
¡que yo las nubes resistir no puedo!
¡¡Sácame de esta torre tan oscura,
porque estoy aquí sola y. . . tengo miedo!!

    High above the clouds we go,
proclaiming freedom in the sky;
scattering the very clouds with our flight,
as we spread our wings into the air.

    Fall to the depths, my chains.
May my spirit circle in space
and my voice sound courageously
the triumphant cry of freedom from this
    battlement!

    But . . . Why do you leave me alone in
      the sky,
fleeing to the roof of the castle?
And why does this mass of fluttering birds
crowd the floor?

    Oh! What is that noise that startles me?
The tower shakes at its base . . .
I have lost sight of the firmament . . .
the storm envelops me in its fury.

    The tower explodes with thunder . . .
The mountains rise from their base . . .
The tower rises among the clouds
bearing a bolt in its thundering breast.

    The terrible phantasm races toward
      me . . .
thundering it threatens to engulf me . . .
with eyes of lightning it glares at me . . .
and its light blinds and suffocates me!

    The bolt strikes at my feet and pierces
      my head!
Its light blinds me, I can no longer see!
Oh, save me, Lord, because I believe
that my resolve lacks strength!

    Lower me in your arms from these
      heights;
I cannot endure these clouds!
Take me from this dark tower,
because I am here alone now, and I am
    afraid!!

(Translated by Lou Charnon Deutsch)

7
Quintillas
(1842)

Yo en tristísimo gemido
desahogara mi cuidado
si el temor de ver reído
por otros mi mal llorado
no acobardara el sentido.

　　Buen pueden ser los que un azar
sufrieron de la fortuna
sus desdichas lamentar
y sus lamentos alzar
sobre el cerco de la luna.

　　No haya miedo, ría el mundo
de su amarguísimo lloro,
que es un dolor sin segundo
el fiero dolor profundo
que al hombre le arranca el oro.

　　Los que en el mundo perdieron
riquezas, honores, poder,
ésos tan sólo sufrieron,
ésos solos consumieron
la fuente del padecer.

　　Ésos en el mundo son
no más los graves cuidados
que agitan el corazón,
sin ellos no hay aflicción,
desdichas ni desdichados.

　　Si llora joven doncella
es necia puerildad,
y al exhalar que querella
risas excita la bella
en la grave anciandad.

　　Que miden sus corazones
por la miseria las penas,
la dicha por los doblones,
y ellos no ven más cadenas
que el hierro de las prisiones.

　　Los hombres, libres azores,
la estrecha jaula no miran
do encerraron con rigores
sus egoístas amores,
las palomas que suspiran.

7
Poem

　　With heartsick lament,
I would unbosom my grief
if the fear of witnessing my pain
scorned by others
did not restrain me.

　　Well might those who have suffered
misfortune at the hands of fate
raise their cries
above the moon's aura.

　　Fear not, may the world laugh
at your bitter tears,
for no other pain can compare
with the deep, fierce pain
that gold produces in man.

　　Those who in this life have lost
riches, honors, power,
only they have suffered;
they alone have drunk
from the fountain of affliction.

　　In all the world are
those alone the solemn cares
that trouble the heart;
apart from them there is no pain,
nor sorrowers, nor sorrow.

　　When a young woman cries
it is some childish nonsense,
and when she sighs,
the young beauty only
inspires laughter in her grave elders.

　　Because they measure their hearts'
sorrows by want and poverty,
happiness by their gold,
and they see no other chains
than the irons of their prison walls.

　　Men, unfettered hawks,
do not see the narrow cage
where they have shut up tight
with their selfish love
the sighing doves.

　　From their sheltered strength

Que de su fuerza al abrigo
dieron al mundo esta ley,
como con genio enemigo
dieron el hambre al mendigo
y dieron la hartura al rey.

　　Diosecillos imprudentes
que alzando grandes ciudades,
fuertes muros, arcos, puentes,
legan a sus descendientes
miserias y calamidades.

　　¿Por qué necios trasplantaron
las rocas, por qué arrancaron
el oro de su manida,
y al fondo del mar bajaron
tras de la perla escondida?

　　¿Por qué, si no han de hallar
después de tanto afanar
entre ese rico montón
la piedra que te ha de dar
felicidad, corazón?

　　¡Ay! Si el oro ha de traer
sólo males, si han de ser
tiranos siempre los reyes,
valiera más no tener
reyes, tesoros ni leyes.

　　Fueran menos desdichados
en salvaje soledad
los hombres abandonados,
que no mal civilizados
en dañina sociedad.

　　Mas, al fin, pájaros son
que alas tienen, tienen viento,
la mujer en su aflicción,
¡ay!, no tiene ni un acento
para llorar un momento
los hierros de su prisión.

　　Que el temor de ver reído
por otros mi mal llorado
en el corazón herido
tiene el dolor comprimido,
tiene el llanto sofocado.

they rule their world,
as in their mean-spiritedness
they endowed the beggar with hunger
and the king with exhorbitant riches.

　　Imprudent little gods who,
while they build their great cities,
fortified walls, arches, and bridges,
bequeath to their descendants
only misery and calamity.

　　Why did these foolish men move
the rocks? Why did they wrest
the gold from its cave
and plumb the bottom of the sea
to search for the hidden pearl?

　　Why, if after all their trouble
they will not find
in that rich mountain
the one stone that would
gladden their hearts?

　　Ah! but if gold brings only
evil, if kings be always
tyrants, it were better
not to have kings, treasures, or laws.

　　Men would be less miserable
in savage isolation,
better abandoned
than so sadly civilized
in destructive society.

　　But, at least men are birds
with wings, and they can fly,
woman in her misery,
alas! does not even possess
a voice to bemoan for an instant
the irons of her prison.

　　Fearing that my lament will be
scorned by others
I bury my secret pain
in my wounded heart and stifle my cries.

(Translated by Lou Charnon Deutsch)

Los dos genios gemelos:
Safo y Santa Teresa de Jesús
(fragmento)

SAFO Y TERESA

¡Cuánta diferencia parece que existe entre estas dos mujeres, y a pesar de eso qué analogía, qué similitud, qué identidad hay en las dos!

Allí veo a Safo en medio de sus discípulas.

Allí veo a Teresa en medio de sus hermanas.

Ambas regalan generosamente a esta pobre mitad del género humano el caudal de sus lecciones, y ambas sienten un amor intenso hacia sus discípulas y sus hermanas.

La caridad se revela en Safo por la ardiente solicitud con que cultiva el talento de sus compañeras de gloria.

La caridad se revela en Teresa por la severa disciplina con que conserva la virtud de sus compañeras de martirio.

Ambas forman una escuela para elevar a la mujer.

Safo juzga que las eleva coronándolas de laureles.

Teresa vistiéndolas de silicios.

Safo las hace componer versos.

Teresa pronunciar oraciones.

Safo las habla de triunfos.

Teresa de penitencias.

Safo las lleva al Liceo.

Teresa las conduce al altar.

Y las dos creen trabajar por la virtud y la gloria.

Ambas luchan por el triunfo de sus doctrinas.

La hija de la república se emancipa del yugo que la sociedad ha impuesto a su sexo, y proclama en sus cantos la libertad.

La hija del absolutismo se encierra en el

The Twin Geniuses:
Sappho and Saint Teresa of Jesus
(excerpt)

SAPPHO AND TERESA

How vast the difference that seems to separate these two women, but in spite of that, what analogies, what similarities, what identity there is between the two!

There I see Sappho, surrounded by her disciples.

There I see Teresa, surrounded by her sisters.

Both generously give the wealth of their lessons to this poor half of the human race, and both feel an intense love for disciples and sisters.

Sappho's generosity is revealed in the burning solicitude with which she cultivates the talent of her companions in bliss.

Teresa's generosity is revealed in the severe discipline with which she preserves the virtue of her companions in martyrdom.

Both form schools for the betterment of women.

Sappho believes that she elevates them by crowning them with laurels.

Teresa, by dressing them in hair shirts.

Sappho has them compose verses.

Teresa has them say prayers.

Sappho speaks to them of triumphs.

Teresa, of penance.

Sappho takes them to the Lyceum.

Teresa leads them to the altar.

And both believe that they are working for virtue and glory.

Both struggle for the triumph of their beliefs.

The daughter of the republic frees herself from the yoke society has imposed on her sex and proclaims liberty in her poems.

The daughter of absolutism withdraws

claustro y abjura la independencia de la mujer.

La poetisa de Atenas quiere establecer liceos en todas partes.

La doctora de Ávila quiere fundar conventos.

Y ni a la una la contienen las calumnias de sus enemigos, ni a la otra las persecuciones de sus contrarios.

A las dos misioneras del bello sexo les faltó, para llevar a cabo su grande obra, a Safo la religión cristiana, a Teresa la libertad.

Safo vino al mundo demasiado temprano.

Teresa demasiado tarde.

Safo demasiado temprano, porque aún no se había destruido el gentilismo, ni había nacido la Virgen María, modelo de pureza, de castidad, de virtud.

Teresa demasiado tarde, porque ya los frailes habían falseado los principios del cristianismo y anulado los derechos de la mujer.

Los obstáculos que Safo halló en su siglo fueron Baco, Venus y toda la inmoral caterva de dioses fabulosos.

Los obstáculos que halló Teresa fueron los frailes.

El deseo de las reformas, la aspiración hacia un bien cuyo término era desconocido para ambas, agitaba sus cabezas y las hacía pensar en la regeneración.

Safo en España, nacida en el siglo de la tiranía, a la sombra de Felipe II, hubiera hecho refluir su poesía en la religión, y ceñiría su cabeza con el capelo de doctora.

Teresa bajo el cielo de Grecia, en el siglo de la libertad, iluminada por los rayos de Solón, hubiera espaciado su fantasía y ceñiría la corona de laurel.

La misma analogía, la misma similitud, la misma identidad hay en sus corazones.

Abrazadas ambas de un amor innato,

into the cloister and renounces woman's independence.

The Poet of Athens wishes to establish lyceums everywhere.

The Doctor of Ávila wants to found convents.

And the calumny of her enemies does not contain the one, nor the other the persecution of her opponents.

To bring to fruition her grand designs, each of these missionaries of the fair sex lacks something: Sappho, the Christian religion; Teresa, freedom.

Sappho came too soon to the world.

Teresa came too late.

Sappho, too soon because the sect of the Gentiles had not yet been destroyed, nor had the Virgin Mary, model of purity, of chastity, of virtue, been born.

Teresa, too late because by that time the friars had already distorted the principles of Christianity and abolished the rights of women.

The obstacles that Sappho encountered in her century were Bacchus, Venus, and the entire immoral horde of fantastic gods.

The obstacles that Teresa encountered were the friars.

The desire for reform, the longing for a good whose form was unknown to both, stimulated their minds and made them think of redemption.

Sappho in Spain, born in the century of tyranny, in the shadow of Philip II, would have written poetry influenced by religion, and she would have girded her head with the academic cap of doctor.

Teresa, under the Grecian sky, in the century of freedom, illuminated by the rays of Solon, would have rejoiced in her fantasies and encircled her head in a crown of laurels.

The same analogies, the similarities,

vivo, tierno, sublime, inapagable, ambas se enamoran en la juventud. Safo de Faon,[1] Teresa de Jesús.

Sus escritos revelarán su pasión mejor que sus palabras.

the same identity is to be found in the hearts of both.

The two of them, embracing a love innate, alive, tender, sublime, unquenchable, fell in love during their youth, Sappho with Phaon,[1] Teresa with Jesus.

Their writings will reveal their passions better than these words.

SAFO

"Feliz quien junto a ti, por ti suspira;
quien goza del placer de oír tu habla."

SAPPHO

"Happy the one who is at your side,
    who sighs for you,
who delights in the pleasure of hearing
    your words."

TERESA

"Mira que muero por verte,
y vivir sin ti no puedo."

TERESA

"See how I die to see you,
and am unable to live without you."

SAFO

"Siento de vena en vena, sutil fuego
discurrir por mi cuerpo al ver tu cara."

SAPPHO

"I feel a subtle flame from vein to vein
spread through my body when I see
    your face."

TERESA

"Todo es para más penar
por no verte como quiero."

TERESA

"Everything adds to my pain
because I do not see you as I would
    wish."

SAFO

"Extiéndese una nube por mis ojos,
pierdo el sentido, oprímenme las
    ansias."

SAPPHO

"A cloud moves before my eyes,
I take leave of my senses, anxiety
    weighs on me."

1. A Safo (siglo 7, A.E.C.) se le considera la inventora de la poesía lírica. Aunque el lesbianismo es uno de los marcos de Safo tal como la conocernos ahora, durante el siglo diecinueve la poeta Safo fue considerada mujer heterosexual, enamorada y no correspondida en su amor por el pescador, Faon, por lo cual se suicidó en un gesto también asociado con los ritos de Apolo.

1. Sappho (seventh century B.C.E.) is considered the inventor of lyric poetry. Although lesbianism is one of the marks of Sappho today, during the nineteenth century the legend that circulated about her held that she fell in love with a fisherman named Phaon, and when he spurned her she committed suicide by throwing herself into the sea from the Leucadian Rock (an act also associated with the rites of Apollo).

TERESA

"¡Ay! ¡qué larga es esta vida!
¡qué duros estos destierros!"

SAFO

"Y pálida, sin pulso, sin aliento,
me hielo, me estremezco, exhalo el
alma."

TERESA

"Y causa en mí tal pasión
ver a mi Dios prisionero,
que muero porque no muero."

Safo amaba a un hombre, y Teresa a un Dios; y a pesar de eso las emanaciones de su pasión son las mismas.

También Safo es epiritual cuando se contenta con el placer de una mirada.

También Teresa es voluptuosa cuando al tocar la sagrada hostia de la comunión, siente que su sangre hierve, que sus oídos zumban, que se turban sus ojos, y que su lengua se abrasa.

Y es porque Safo diviniza a su amante; y es porque Teresa personifica a su Dios.

Si os repito los coloquios de Safo con Faon, cuando está separada de él, cuando lo ve en su ideal, creeréis que es el arrobamiento divino de Teresa con Jesús.

Si os cuento los coloquios de Teresa, delante de Jesús, cuando sueña que le habla y le responde, que le escucha y le admira, creeréis que es Safo que habla con Faon.

Safo renuncia a la gloria.

Teresa al mundo.

Safo vaga por las noches, errante, trémula, desgreñada, en torno de la casa de Faon.

Teresa pasa las noches en el insomnio, en el llanto, al pie de la Cruz.

Safo arranca los cabellos llamando a Faon.

TERESA

"Ah, how long life is!
How hard these exiles!"

SAPPHO

"And pale, without heartbeat, without
breath,
I freeze, I shudder, I exhale my soul."

TERESA

"So great is the grief I feel
on seeing my God imprisoned,
that I die because I do not die."

Sappho loved a man, and Teresa a God; but in spite of that, the emanations of their passions are identical.

Sappho, too, is spiritual when she is satisfied with the pleasure a look brings.

Teresa, too, is voluptuous when, on taking the sacred communion host, she feels her blood stir, her ears buzz, her eyes glaze over, and her tongue burn.

And this is because Sappho deifies her lover, and because Teresa personifies her God.

If I repeat to you the dialogues of Sappho with Phaon when she is separated from him, when she sees in him her ideal, you would think they are the divine ecstasy of Teresa with Jesus.

If I recount to you the dialogues of Teresa before Jesus, when she dreams that he is speaking to her and she responds that she hears and adores him, you would believe that it is Sappho who is speaking to Phaon.

Sappho renounces heaven.

Teresa, the world.

Sappho wanders in the night, aimless, tremulous, disheveled, around Phaon's house.

Teresa spends the night sleepless, sobbing, at the foot of the cross.

Teresa macera sus carnes invocando a Jesús.

Safo acude en sus aflicciones a las pitonisas, y cumple sus presagios.

Teresa se postra ante los frailes, y cree en sus revelaciones.

Religiosas ambas, según sus creencias, llenas de unciones misteriosas, de aspiraciones sobrenaturales hacia la divinidad. Confiadas, crédulas, supersticiosas, son juguetes ambas de la malicia de sus falsos oráculos.

Las dos pasan su juventud en el éxtasis de la pasión, y las dos sucumben al vértigo que las domina.

Ambas desean morir.

Safo busca la muerte en los mares.

Teresa en la horrible penitencia que quebranta su cuerpo.

Safo en la agonía, aún clama por Faon.

Teresa vuelve su postrera mirada al Santo madero.

La división del amor profano y del amor divino es en cierto modo una división falsa de la metafísica.

Muchas veces el amor se hace profano por el objeto sensual que elige. Muchas veces se idealiza el amor porque se consagra a un objeto inmaterial.

Si Safo, comprimida por la rígida estrechez de las leyes monásticas, se hubiera fijado en el Dios del cristianismo, hubiera amado como Teresa y hubiera muerto al pie de la Cruz.

Si Teresa, libres los sentidos, y familiarizada con las licenciosas doctrinas de los dioses paganos, hubiera elegido por su amante a un hombre, hubiera amado como Safo, y hubiera muerto en los mares.

Todas las desemejanzas que existen entre estas dos mujeres, las crearon sus diferentes religiones, la educación, las costumbres de sus distintos países.

Dotadas ambas de un talento flexible y

Sappho tears at her hair, calling out to Phaon.

Teresa mortifies her flesh, invoking Jesus.

Sappho, in her afflicitions, turns to the soothsayers and fulfills their predictions.

Teresa prostrates herself before the friars and believes in their revelations.

Both religious, each according to her own beliefs, filled with mysterious fervors, with supernatural longing for the divine. Trusting, credulous, superstitious, both are toys of the cunning of their false oracles.

Both spend their youth in the ecstasy of passion, and both succumb to the vertigo that overwhelms them.

Both wish to die.

Sappho seeks out death in the sea.

Teresa, in the horrible penance that breaks her body.

Sappho, in agony, still calls out to Phaon.

Teresa turns her dying gaze to the holy cross.

The division of love into profane and divine is, in a way, a false metaphysical division.

Many times love becomes profane due to the sensual object it selects. Many times love is idealized because it is consecrated to an immaterial object.

If Sappho, constricted by the narrow rigidity of monastic laws, had fixed her gaze on the God of Christianity, she would have loved like Teresa and would have died at the foot of the cross.

If Teresa, her senses free, and familiar with the licentious doctrines of the pagan gods, were to have chosen a man as her lover, she would have loved like Sappho, and would have died in the seas.

All the dissimilarities that exist between these two women were created by

comunicativo, hubieran dado iguales re- sultados, colocadas en un mismo siglo y en una misma sociedad. Sus almas se tocan, sus ingenios fraternizan. ¡Safo! ¡Teresa! sois un engendro de la madre eternidad, para quien los siglos son minutos, que os dio a luz casi a un mismo tiempo. Sois dos gemelas que habéis recibido un mismo so- plo de vida, y la misma inspiración inmor- tal, que os hará marchar juntas en los si- glos.

El mundo antiguo tuvo para Safo una estatua.

El mundo moderno tiene para Teresa un altar.

their different religions, education, the customs of their respective countries.

Gifted with a flexible and communica- tive talent, had they been placed in the same century and the same society, the re- sults would have been the same. Their souls touch, their genius comes together. Sappho! Teresa! You are the children of mother eternity, for whom the centuries are minutes, who gave birth to you at nearly the same time. You are twins who have received the same breath of life, and the same immortal inspiration, and thus together you will march through the centuries.

The ancient world honored Sappho with a statue.

The modern world honors Teresa with an altar.

(Translated by Lou Charnon Deutsch)

Rosalía de Castro

Rosalía de Castro is one of the nineteenth century's most important poets writing in Castilian. Nevertheless, as a key participant in the collective effort to reestablish Galician as a literary language in the struggle against Castilian cultural and political hegemony, she wrote more than half of her poetry in the language of her native Galicia. Rosalía was born in the Galician provincial capital, Santiago de Compostela, February 24, 1837. She was baptized María Rosalía Rita, "daughter of unknown parents." These unknown parents were the seminarian (or perhaps already priest) José Martínez Viojo and Teresa de Castro, the unmarried daughter of an aristocratic family. Because of the clerical pretensions (or state) of the father, and the lineage of the mother, the child's birth was kept secret. María Francisca Martínez, who by one account was a confidante of the Viojos and by another a servant of the Castros, took the newborn baby to the town of Ortoño. Rosalía spent her early childhood there, first with María Francisca Martínez, and later with Teresa Martínez Viojo, her paternal aunt. It was several years — perhaps as late as 1850 — before Teresa de Castro took her daughter to live with her. The two probably lived together on the family estate in Padrón before they moved to the provincial capital, where Rosalía could study music and drawing. Rosalía and her mother had an affectionate relationship. When Doña Teresa died in 1862, Rosalía wrote a series of four poems, published in 1863 under the title *A mi madre* (To my mother), that express the love and tenderness she felt for her mother, and her sadness and sense of loneliness at her loss.

During the years she lived in Santiago, Rosalía attended the Liceo de la Juventud (Young People's Lyceum), which met in the same building where she and her mother lived. She participated in the Lyceum's literary and musical get-togethers, and there, with great success, she played the principal role in Gil de Zárate's drama *Rosamunda*. At the Lyceum she met Aurelio Aguirre, a poet who was part of an alliance of Galician students, workers, and intellectuals. Rosalía's first book, *La flor* (The flower, 1857), contains poems that some critics believe refer to her love for Aguirre, who drowned that same year. Manuel Murguía, whom Rosalía was to marry in 1858, was also a member of the Lyceum, but it is probable that they met later, in Madrid.

In 1856 Rosalía went to stay with her maternal aunt in Madrid while she saw to some legal matters concerning her mother's family. Although she probably did not participate in the capital's literary salons while she was there, her poetry was known;

and she did meet several noted literary figures, including Gustavo Adolfo Bécquer, who, like her, wrote for the magazine *El Museo Universal* (The universal museum) and who, together with her, is considered one of the two most important post-Romantic poets in Spain. While she was in Madrid, Rosalía married Manuel Murguía, but shortly thereafter she returned to Galicia to be with her mother and to give birth to her daughter Alejandra. Between 1858 and 1871, when she returned to Galicia for good, Rosalía frequently traveled back and forth between Madrid and Galicia. She lived apart from her husband for long periods of time, sometimes with her mother and sometimes alone with her children. She and Murguía also lived together in a number of places in Galicia — La Coruña, Santiago, Simancas, and perhaps Lugo — as well as in Madrid. Murguía encouraged his wife to write in Galician; and, according to the stories that have grown up around Rosalía de Castro, in 1863, without her knowledge, he published her second book of poetry, *Cantares gallegos* (Galician songs).

Rosalía wrote prose as well as poetry, and it appears that she was more willing to publish her novels, short stories, and essays than she was her poems. Still, she was bitter toward the male literary establishment. In the epilogue to her novel *La hija del mar* (The daughter of the sea, 1859), she writes that "women are still not permitted to write what they feel and what they know."[1] The two prose pieces included here, "Lieders" (1858) and "Las literatas" (The bluestockings, 1865), defend her right to freedom of the imagination and unequivocally denounce the oppression of women, particularly those who write. Rosalía admired other women writers. She praised George Sand and she dedicated her *Cantares gallegos* to Fernán Caballero.

We have just enough information about Rosalía de Castro to trace a schematic portrait of her. We know the date and place of birth, the names of her parents and of the women who raised her; we have evidence of her participation in the Lyceum, and of her meager education at the side of other rural girls. There are records of her moves between Castile, Extremadura, and Galicia, information about her husband and children, photographs of her family, indications of her financial problems and of her illness. We even have a report of her last words, pronounced on July 15, 1885. At the same time, there are many blank spaces. Was her father a seminarian or a priest when his lover became pregnant? The responsibilities of one would not be those of the other. Why did Doña Teresa wait so long before taking over the raising of her daughter? Was the woman who raised her her mother's family's servant or a friend of her father's family? Did Rosalía go to live with her mother at the age of eight or thirteen, or somewhere in between? She began to menstruate at the age of ten and to write poetry at eleven, so these were decisive years for her. Why, at the age of fourteen or fifteen, did she apparently undergo a change of personality, from being a happy child to a melancholy one? Did she ever meet her father, or even know who he was? When did she meet Murguía? Was she in love with Aguirre? Did he commit suicide? Did she love her husband? Was she pregnant before she married Murguía, and

was he Alejandra's father? Why were there ten years between her first and second pregnancies? Marina Mayoral, Rosalía's biographer, marks the riddle that is Rosalía:

> For many years critical silence surrounded the work of Rosalía de Castro . . . In the meantime, Rosalía had turned into something more than a literary and historical figure. She was turning into a symbol, an incarnation of the soul of Galicia. When criticism turned its eyes toward her, the process had reached its end: Rosalía was— is—a myth. Silence and mythification have made of her an ill-known figure. The complexity of her work and her biographical circumstances augmented the difficulties in knowing her.[2]

Rosalía de Castro is, in fact, not just one myth but the vehicle for many, sometimes contradictory, myths: the sickly heroine with a noble soul; the selfless mother; the happy wife, or the abused one, or simply the woman who foolishly married on the rebound; the abandoned child; the bastard rejected by conventional parents and conventional society; the beloved daughter of a father who entrusted his daughter to intimate friends to save her from the orphanage, or of a mother who suffered for years trying to reclaim her; she is the soul of Galicia; or she is the outcast, the suffering voice of woman, of the poor, of the Galician émigré.

Rosalía is sometimes portrayed as the victim of a mother who corseted her pregnant body and therefore gave birth to a weak and sickly child. (Shortly after Rosalía herself married, she went into a decline that was the first symptom of the uterine cancer that was to kill her years later.) For some, she is the vindicator of Galicia: a happy child who played with other children in the Galician countryside and who listened to the traditional tales from an old servant, and who, as an adult, always longed for Galicia when she was away, falling ill when she was gone and coming home to recover. She was, on this account, a lady who chatted with emigrant Galician peasants, denouncing their penury in her poetry, her writing a weapon hurled in defense of the language and culture of Galicia. For others, she is the woman who published her *Cantares gallegos* reluctantly, questioned the good of writing poetry, only kept writing at the insistence of her husband, and left orders that her daughters burn her unpublished work after her death. Still others remember her as the poet who, knowing her poetic power, refused to write in Galician any more after 1864, because she had been badly treated and neglected by Galician readers. And some know her as the recluse who never thought about any audience and who only wrote to alleviate her own distress, who needed the act of writing in order to survive.

All these one-dimensional images respond to the desire of the observer. The case of her husband is perhaps prototypical. The first time Murguía writes publicly of Rosalía, he twists the truth to respond to certain conventions, denying, against all logic, that they were even acquainted. His representation of Rosalía and of the life he lived with her always follows this pattern, adjusted first to the image he wants to present. By means of a verbal collage composed of letters, memoir, and his own book, *The Precursors*, Murguía creates a suffering, angelic, devout, sweet woman, within a

happy marriage. But a stain of ashes (Rosalía's letters, which he burned before his death) stand as an emblem of her silence — of her being silenced — calling into question the portrait he so carefully drew.

Murguía's static representation of his wife, and the other equally static ones of the mythmakers, reflect a desire to capture and know this paradoxical figure who does not conform to the norms of womanhood. Rosalía de Castro refuses to comply with expectations. She loved the mother who abandoned her, and she reclaimed her place in her mother's family through the Madrid suit that she fought and the biography she wrote — but then burned — of her maternal grandfather. She wrote tender poems and ferocious ones, poems of nostalgia and poems of anger, poems in Galician and poems in Castilian. Not even Rosalía's photographs look alike. The philosopher Miguel de Unamuno once commented that she was beautiful and ugly at the same time. As a mother she appears to have suffered in silence, or at least in privacy, when her son Adriano died before the age of two and her daughter Valentina died soon after birth; as a Galician she denounced social injustice with strength and power. She was poor and ill for many years, and at the same time she took care of the five children who depended on her.

It is impossible to reconcile the different faces of Rosalía de Castro in one smooth, familiar image of conventional femininity or conventional rebellion. Rosalía de Castro is a complex figure, a woman constrained by the circumstances of her life, who also molded the contours of her world. Without the missing historical evidence surrounding her life, it is impossible to reconstruct a "true" biography of Rosalía de Castro that takes into account not only the events of her life, but also the motives, the psychology, the creativity of this woman. Each fact we have is a fascinating piece of the complete figure, but the conjunction of these particulars is insufficient to compose a mosaic of her life. We may arrange and refract them in accordance with our knowledge of history to come up with a series of images that might approximate her lived reality. We are left, in the end, with a kaleidoscopic vision, a mix of colorful pieces that change form as they are rearranged and reflected in the mirrors that turn them into coherent and symmetrical and pleasing images, always related, but never identical to the formations that precede or follow them.

1. "todavía no les es permitido a las mujeres escribir lo que sienten y lo que saben."
2. Durante muchos años el silencio de la crítica envolvió la obra de Rosalía de Castro... Entretanto, Rosalía se iba convirtiendo en algo más que una figura histórica y literaria. Se iba haciendo un símbolo, una encarnación del alma de Galicia. Cuando la crítica volvió los ojos hacia ella, el proceso había llegado a su fin: Rosalía era —es— ya un mito. Silencio y mitificación han hecho de ella una figura mal conocida. La complejidad de su obra y sus circunstancias biográficas aumentaron las dificultades para su conocimiento" (Marina Mayoral, *La poesía de Rosalía de Castro* [Madrid: Gredos, 1974], 15).

En las orillas del Sar

1
Cenicientas las aguas

Cenicientas las aguas; los desnudos
árboles y los montes, cenicientos;
parda la bruma que los vela, y pardas
las nubes que atraviesan por el cielo:
triste, en la tierra, el color gris domina,
   ¡el color de los viejos!

De cuando en cuando de la lluvia el sordo
   rumor suena, y el viento
   al pasar por el bosque
   silba, o finge lamentos
tan extraños, tan hondos y dolientes,
que parece que llaman por los muertos.

Seguido del mastín que helado tiembla,
   el labrador, cubierto
con su capa de juncos, cruza el monte:
   el campo está desierto,
y tan solo en los charcos que negrean
del ancho prado entre el verdor intenso
posa el vuelo la blanca gaviota,
   mientras graznan los cuervos.

   Yo, desde mi ventana
que azotan los airados elementos,
regocijada y pensativa escucho
   el discorde concierto
   simpático a mi alma...

   ¡Oh mi amigo el invierno!,
mil y mil veces bien venido seas,
mi sombrío y adusto compañero;
¿no eres acaso el precursor dichoso
del tibio mayo y del abril risueño?

¡Ah, si el invierno triste de la vida,
como tú de las flores y los céfiros,
también precursor fuera de la hermosa
y eterna primavera de mis sueños!

On the Banks of the River Sar

1
Ashen Are the Waters

Ashen are the waters, the barren
trees and hills, all ashen;
a drab mist hovers over them,
and dark clouds cross the sky:
the color gray hangs over a dreary earth,
   the color of old men!

From time to time the rain's dull
   patter sounds, and the wind
   whistles through the trees,
   or feigns laments,
so strange, so deep and sorrowful,
they seem to summon the dead.

Flanked by his shivering mastiff
   and protected only by his
cape of reeds, a farmer climbs the hill:
   the fields are deserted,
a white gull circles down
to the dark pools scattered
amid the deep green of the broad meadow,
   while the ravens crow.

   From my window pelted by
the driving rain, I listen,
content and lost in thought,
   to the discordant concert
   that speaks my soul . . .

   Oh, winter, my friend!
welcome a thousand times;
for are you not, my somber and stern
   companion,
the happy precursor
of sweet May and smiling April?

Oh, if only my life's sad winter
were, like you of flowers and soft breezes,
a harbinger of the fair
and eternal springtime of my dreams!

(Translated by Lou Charnon Deutsch)

2
A la sombra te sientas
de las desnudas rocas

A la sombra te sientas de las desnudas
    rocas,
y en el rincón te ocultas donde zumba el
    insecto,
y allí donde las aguas estancadas dormitan
y no hay humanos seres que interrumpan
    tus sueños
¡quién supiera en qué piensas, amor de
    mis amores,
cuando con leve paso y contenido aliento,
temblando a que percibas mi agitación
    extrema
allí donde te escondes, ansiosa te sor-
    prendo!
    —¡Curiosidad maldita, frío aguijón
      que hieres
las femeninas almas, los varoniles pechos:
tu fuerza impele al hombre a que busque
    la hondura
del desencanto amargo y a que remueva el
    cieno
donde se forman siempre los mïasmas
    infectos.
    —¿Qué has dicho de amargura y cieno
      y desencanto?
¡Ah!, no pronuncies frases, mi bien, que
    no comprendo;
dime sólo en qué piensas cuando de mí te
    apartas
y huyendo de los hombres vas buscando
    el silencio.
    —Pienso en cosas tan tristes a veces y
      tan negras
y en otras tan extrañas y tan hermosas
    pienso,
que. . . no las sabrás nunca, porque lo que
    se ignora
no nos daña si es malo, ni perturba si es
    bueno.
Yo te lo digo, niña, a quien de veras amo;

2
You Hide Yourself
in the Shade of Some Barren Rock

You hide yourself in the shade of some
    barren rock,
or seek a corner where only the insects
    can be heard,
and there where the stagnant waters sleep
and where no human voices can
    disturb your dreams
who knows what thoughts are yours,
    then, my love of loves, when,
with soft trembling and bated breath,
and trembling lest you perceive my
    agitation,
I eagerly surprise you there in your
    retreat.
    "Cursed curiosity! cold needle that
      pierces
womanly souls and manly breasts:
you drive us to search the depths
of bitter deception, to stir the mire
where only fetid air can ever form."
    "What talk is this of bitterness and
      mire and disillusion?
Oh! Do not speak of this, my dear, I do
    not understand;
tell me instead of your thoughts when we
    are apart
and fleeing men you are off in search of
    silence."
    "Sometimes I think of things so sad
      and so bleak
and other times of things so strange and
    beautiful
that. . . but you will never know my
    thoughts, for what we do not know
will not harm us though it be evil, nor
    disturb our peace, if good.
I tell you, sweet girl whom I truly love,
that the human heart harbors such
    profound mysteries
that when our eyes are veiled from them,

encierra el alma humana tan profundos
    misterios,
que cuando a nuestros ojos un velo los
    oculta,
es temeraria enpresa descorrer ese velo:
no pienses, pues, bien mío, no pienses en
    qué pienso.
    —Pensaré noche y día, pues sin
        saberlo muero.
    Y cuenta que lo supo, y que la mató
        entonces la pena de saberlo.

it were truly rash to strip away that veil:
ponder not, then, my dear one, ponder
    not my thoughts."
    "This I do day and night, for it kills me
        not to know them."
The story goes she discovered what she
    sought to know,
and the pain of her knowledge was her
    deathblow.

(Translated by Lou Charnon Deutsch)

3
Cuido una planta bella

Cuido una planta bella
    que ama y busca la sombra,
    como la busca el alma
huérfana, triste, enamorada y sola,
y allí donde jamás la luz del día
llega sino a través de las umbrosas
ramas de un mirto y los cristales turbios
    de una ventana angosta,
ella vive tan fresca y perfumada,
y se torna más bella y más frondosa,
y languidece y se marchita y muere
cuando un rayo de sol besa sus hojas.

3
I Tend a Beautiful Plant

I tend a beautiful plant
    that loves and seeks the shade
    like the orphaned soul that searches
disheartened, lovesick and alone,
and there, where the light of day
never reaches except between shady
myrtle branches, or the dark pane
    of a narrow window,
she flourishes, so fresh and sweet-smelling,
and she becomes ever more radiant and
    luxuriant,
but when a ray of sun caresses her leaves
she languishes and withers and dies.

(Translated by Lou Charnon Deutsch)

4
Dicen que no hablan las plantas

Dicen que no hablan las plantas, ni las
    fuentes, ni los pájaros,
ni el onda con sus rumores, ni con su bri-
    llo los astros.
Lo dicen; pero no es cierto, pues siempre
    cuando yo paso,

4
It Is Said Plants Cannot Speak

It is said plants cannot speak, nor
    springs nor birds
nor the waves with their murmurs, nor
    the stars with light.
So they say, but it is not so, for whenever
    I pass by

de mí murmuran y exclaman:
           —Ahí va la
   loca, soñando
con la eterna primavera de la vida y de los
   campos,
y ya bien pronto, bien pronto, tendrá los
   cabellos canos,
y ve temblando, aterida, que cubre la
   escarcha el prado.
      —Hay canas en mi cabeza; hay en los
      prados escarcha;
mas yo prosigo soñando, pobre, incurable
   somnámbula,
con la eterna primavera de la vida que se
   apaga
y la perenne frescura de los campos y las
   almas,
aunque los unos se agostan y aunque las
   otras se abrasan.
      ¡Astros y fuentes y flores!, no murmu-
      réis de mis sueños;
sin ellos, ¿cómo admiraros ni cómo vivir
   sin ellos?

they whisper about me and exclaim:
             "There
   goes that madwoman, dreaming again
of her eternal springtime of life and of
   field;
she stares at the frost-covered fields with
   trembling and fear
knowing that soon, very soon, she will
   also be gray."
      "My hair is streaked with gray, like the
      frost on the meadows,
yet, incurable somnambulant, I continue
   to dream
of the eternal springtime of life, though I
   see it fading,
and the perennial freshness of the field
   and soul
though the field is already harvested,
and the soul reduced to ashes."
      Oh, stars and springs and flowers,
      mock not my dreams!
Without them, how could I admire you,
   nay, how could I live?"

(Translated by Lou Charnon Deutsch)

5
Recuerda el trinar
del ave

Recuerda el trinar del ave
y el chasquido de los besos;
los rumores de la selva
cuando en ella gime el viento,
   y del mar las tempestades,
y la bronca voz del trueno;
todo halla un eco en las cuerdas
del arpa que pulsa el genio.
   Pero aquel sordo latido
del corazón que está enfermo
de muerte, y que de amor muere
y que resuena en el pecho
como un bordón que se rompe

5
The Harp Touched Lightly
by Genius Recalls

The harp touched lightly by genius
   recalls
the sweet song of the wild bird,
the clap of kisses;
the murmur of the forest
as the wind whistles through its branches,
   the storm at sea,
and the roll of thunder;
all this echoes in the chords
of the harp touched by genius.
   But that dull beating
of the afflicted human heart
dying of love

dentro de un sepulcro hueco,
es tan triste y melancólico,
tan terrible y tan supremo,
que jamás el genio pudo
repetirlo con sus ecos.

that throbs in the breast
like a lute string that snaps
inside an empty crypt
is such a sad and melancholic sound,
so terrible, so supreme
that no genius could ever
capture it.

(Translated by Lou Charnon Deutsch)

6
Los que a través de sus lágrimas

6
Those Who Midst Their Tears

I

Los que a través de sus lágrimas
sin esfuerzo ni violencia,
abren paso en el alma afligida
al nuevo placer que llega;
    los que, tras de las fatigas
de una existencia azarosa,
al dar término al rudo combate
cogen larga cosecha de gloria;
    y, en fin, todos los dichosos
cuyo reino es de este mundo,
y, dudando o creyendo en el otro,
de la tierra se llevan los frutos,
    ¡con qué tedio oyen el grito
del que en vano ha querido y no pudo
arrojar de sus hombros la carga
            pesada del infortunio!
        —Cada cual en silencio devore
            sus penas y sus afanes
—dicen—, que es de animosos y fuertes
el callar, y es la queja cobarde.
    No el lúgubre vaticinio
que el espíritu turba y sorprende,
ni el inútil y eterno lamento
importuno en los aires resuene.
    ¡Poeta!, en fáciles versos,
y con esto que alienta los ánimos,
ven a hablarnos de esperanzas,
pero no de desengaños.

I

Those who midst their tears
without violence or force,
open a path in the afflicted soul
to any new pleasure that comes their way;
    or those who, after many trials
of a hapless existence,
at the end of their struggles
stop to gather a great harvest of glory;
    and, finally, those fortunate ones
whose reign is of this world,
and, whether doubting or believing in
    the next,
happily seize the fruits of the earth,
    with what tedium they hear the cries
of others who have wanted and not been
    able
to cast from their shoulders the heavy
        burden of their misfortune!
    "Let each man conceal his cares
        and suffer in silence,"
they say, "for the brave and strong
remain silent, and to complain is
    cowardly."
    Let not the gloomy prediction
that stirs up and surprises the soul,
nor the useless, endless
lament, disturb the air.
    Poet! With easy verse,

suffused with the soul's inspiration,
come speak to us of sweet hope,
but not of disillusion.

II

¡Atrás!, pues, mi dolor vano, con sus
  acerbos gemidos,
que en la inmensidad se pierde, como los
  sordos bramidos
del mar en las soledades que el líquido
  amargo llena. . .
¡Atrás!, y que el denso velo de los inútiles
  lutos,
rasgándose, libre paso deje al triunfo de
  los Brutos,
que, asesinados los Césares, ya ni dan
  premio ni pena. . .
  Pordiosero vergonzante, que en cada
    rincón desierto,
tendiendo la enjuta mano detiene su paso
  incierto
para entonar la salmodia, que nadie escucha ni entiende,
me pareces, dolor mío de quien reniego
  en buen hora.
¡Huye, pues, del alma enferma! Y tú,
  nueva y blanca aurora,
toda de promesas harta, sobre mí tus
  rayos tiende.

III

¡Pensamientos de alas negras!, huid,
  huid azorados,
como bandadas de cuervos por la tormenta acosados,
o como abejas salvajes en quien el fuego
  hizo presa;
dejad que amanezca el día de resplandores
  benditos,
en cuya luz se presienten los placeres infi-
  nitos. . .
¡Y huid con vuestra perenne sombra que
  en el alma pesa!
  ¡Pensamientos de alas blancas!, ni

II

Stand back! alas, my vain sorrow, with
  its bitter wail,
is lost in the immensity, like the deaf
  howls
of the sea in the loneliness with bitter
  water filled . . .
Stand back! so that the thick veil of useless mourning,
rent, may clear a way for the triumph of
  Brutuses,
who, the Caesars murdered, mete out neither penalty nor prize . . .
  A shameful beggar, there in some bleak
    corner,
extending a thin hand, his uncertain step
  detained
to intone a psalm that no one listens to or
  understands,
you, my cursèd sorrow, seem to me.
Flee, then, from this sick soul! and you,
  new, white dawn,
with promises all glutted, unfurl your rays
  above me.

III

Black-winged thoughts! flee, flee
  startled
like flocks of crows pursued by storm,
or like wild bees made prisoners by fire;
let dawn the day of blessed radiance,
whose light portends pleasures beyond
  number . . .
And flee, with your everlasting shadow
  that so weighs in the soul.
  White-winged thoughts, let us neither
    moan nor plead
again, but into luminous worlds let us
  delve,

gimamos ni roguemos
como un tiempo, y en los mundos lumi-
    nosos penetremos,
en donde nunca resuena la débil voz del
    caído,
en donde el dorado sueño para en reali-
    dad segura,
y de la humana flaqueza sobre la inmensa
    amargura,
y sobre el amor que mata, sus alas tiende
    el olvido.
        Ni el recuerdo que atormenta como
            horrible pesadilla,
ni la pobreza que abate, ni la miseria que
    humilla,
ni de la injusticia el látigo, que al herir
    mancha y condena;
ni la envidia y la calumnia, más que el
    fuego asoladoras,
existen para el que siente que se deslizan
    sus horas
del contento y la abundancia por la
    corriente serena.
        Allí donde nunca el llanto los párpa-
            dos enrojece,
donde, por dicha, se ignora que la Huma-
    nidad padece
y que hay seres que codician lo que, harto,
    el perro desdeña,
allí, buscando un asilo, ¡mis pensamientos
    dichosos!,
a todo pesar ajeno, lejos de los tenebrosos
antros del dolor, ¡cantemos a la esperanza
    risueña!
        Frescas voces juveniles, armoniosos
            instrumentos,
¡venid!, que a vuestros acordes yo quiero
    unir mis acentos
vigorosos y el espacio llenar de animadas
    notas;
y entre estatuas y entre flores, entrelazadas
    las manos,

where the feeble voice of the fallen ne'er
    resounds,
where the golden dream ends as sure
    reality,
and above the immense bitterness of
    human weakness
and above the love that kills, oblivion
    spreads its wings.
        Not the memory that torments like a
            fearful nightmare,
nor the poverty that beats one low, nor
    humiliating want,
nor the injustice of the whip that, as it
    wounds, bruises and condemns,
nor envy nor slander that burn more hot
    than fire
exist for those who feel upon the quiet
    current
their hours of contentment and abun-
    dance slip away.
        There, where weeping never reddens
            eyes,
the lucky place where no one knows of
    Humanity's pain
and that there are souls who covet what
    the sated dog disdains,
there, in search of refuge, my blissful
    thoughts!
from all sorrow remote, far from grief's
gloomy caverns, let us sing to smiling
    hope.
        Fresh young voices, melodious
            instruments,
come! To your harmony I wish to join my
    vigorous
tones and fill the space with spirited
    notes;
and among statues and among flowers,
    hands entwined,
dance in honor of all the happy people
of the present, of the future, and of ages
    past.

danzar en honor de todos los venturosos
    humanos
del presente, del futuro y las edades
    remotas.

IV

    Y mi voz, entre el concierto de las gra-
        ves sinfonías,
de las risas lisonjeras y las locas alegrías,
se alzó robusta y sonora con la inspiración
    ardiente
que enciende en el alma altiva del entu-
    siasmo la llama,
y hace creer al que espera y hace esperar al
    que ama,
que hay un cielo en donde vive el amor
    eternamente.
    Del labio amargado un día por lo
        acerbo de los males,
como de fuente abundosa, fluyó la miel a
    raudales,
vertiéndose en copas de oro que mi mano
    orló de rosas;
y bajo de los espléndidos y ricos artesona-
    dos,
en los palacios inmensos y los salones
    dorados,
fui como flor en quien beben perfumes las
    mariposas.
    Los aplausos resonaban con estruendo
        en torno mío,
como el vendaval resuena cuando se des-
    borda el río
por la lóbrega encañada que, adusto, el
    pinar sombrea;
genio supremo y sublime del porvenir me
    aclamaron,
y trofeos y coronas a mis plantas arroja-
    ron,
como a los pies del guerrero vencedor en
    la pelea.

IV

    And my voice, amid the concert of
        solemn symphonies,
of flattering laughter and mad joyousness,
rose robust and sonorous with the
    burning inspiration
that in the haughty soul ignites
    enthusiasm's flame,
and brings belief to him who hopes and
    hope to him who loves,
that there is a heaven where love eternal
    lives.
    One day, in torrents honey flowed as if
        from a copious spring,
from the bitter lip misfortune had once
    hardened,
emptying golden goblets that my hand
    edged with roses;
and beneath the rich and splendid cais-
    soned ceilings,
I, in vast palaces and gilt salons,
was like a flower from which butterflies
    drink perfumes.
    Clamorous applause resounded for me,
like gusty wind sounds when the river
    overflows
the melancholy vale that, austere, the pine
    grove shades;
they proclaimed me supreme, the future's
    sublime genius
and threw trophies and laurels at my feet,
as at the feet of the warrior who in battle
    was triumphant.

V

Mas un día, de aquel bello y encantado
   paraíso,
donde con tantas victorias la suerte brin-
   darme quiso,
volví al mundo desolado de mis antiguos
   amores,
cual mendigo que a su albergue torna de
   riquezas lleno;
pero al verme los que, ausente, me llora-
   ban, de su seno
me rechazaron cual suele rechazarse a los
   traidores.
   Y con agudos silbidos y entre sonrisas
   burlonas,
renegaron de mi numen y pisaron mis
   coronas,
de sus iras envolviéndome en la furiosa
   tormenta:
y sombrío y cabizbajo, como Caín el maldito,
el execrable anatema llevando en la frente
   escrito,
refugio busqué en la sombra para devorar
   mi afrenta.

VI

No hay mancha que siempre dure, ni
   culpa que perdonada
deje de ser, si con llanto de contrición fue
   regada;
así, cuando de la mía se borró el rastro
   infamante,
como en el cielo se borra el de la estrella
   que pasa,
pasé yo entre los mortales, como el pie
   sobre la brasa,
sin volver atrás los ojos ni mirar hacia
   adelante.
   Y a mi corazón le dije: "Si no es vano
   tu ardimiento
y en ti el manantial rebosa del amor y el
   sentimiento,
fuentes en donde el poeta apaga su sed

V

But one day, from that beautiful and
   enchanted paradise,
where fortune pleased to offer me so
   many victories,
I went back to the desolate world of my
   old loves,
like a beggar who returns, full of riches, to
   his hovel;
yet when those who, absent, wept for me
   beheld me
they turned me from their midst as one
   would spurn a traitor.
   And sharply whistling and amid
   derisive smiles,
they cursed my muse and trampled on my
   crowns,
by their wrath besieging me in the furious
   storm;
and somber and downcast like damned
   Cain,
with the dread anathema upon my
   forehead writ,
in the shadows I sought refuge to hide my
   shame.

VI

There is no stain that lasts forever, nor
   pardoned fault
that still exists if rinsed with tears contrite,
thus when the slanderous trace was
   blotted out from mine,
as that of a passing star in the heavens is
   erased,
I walked among mortals as a foot over
   coals,
neither turning my eyes behind nor looking on ahead.
   And to my heart I said: if your valor is
   not empty
and in you the spring of love and
   sentiment flows free,
fountains where the poet, his thirst divine
   may quench,

divina,
sé tú mi musa y cantemos sin preguntarle
    a las gentes
si aman las alegres trovas o los suspiros
    dolientes,
si gustan del sol que nace o buscan al que
    declina."

be my muse and let us sing and refrain
    from asking
if the people love happy songs or sighs of
    woe,
if they like the rising sun or seek it setting.

(Translated by Donna Lazarus
and Lou Charnon Deutsch)

Lieders
(1858)

Lieders

¡Oh, no no quiero ceñirme a las reglas del arte! Mis pensamientos son vagabundos, mi imaginación errante y mi alma sólo se satisface de impresiones.

Jamás ha dominado en mi alma la esperanza de la gloria, ni he soñado nunca con laureles que oprimiesen mi frente. Sólo cantos de independencia y libertad han balbucido mis labios, aunque alrededor hubiese sentido, desde la cuna ya, el ruido de las cadenas que debían aprisionarme para siempre, porque el patrimonio de la mujer son los grillos de la esclavitud.

Yo, sin embargo, soy libre, libre como los pájaros, como las brisas; como los árabes en el desierto y el pirata en el mar.

Libre es mi corazón, libre mi alma, y libre mi pensamiento, que alza hasta el cielo y desciende hasta la tierra, soberbio como Luzbel y dulce como una esperanza.

Cuando los señores de la tierra me amenanzan con una mirada, o quieren marcar mi frente con una mancha de oprobio, yo me río como ellos se ríen y hago, en apariencia, mi iniquidad más grande que su iniquidad. En el fondo, no obstante, mi corazón es bueno; pero no acato los mandatos de mis iguales y creo

No, I do not want to become a slave to the dictates of art. My thoughts are vagabond, my imagination errant, and only impressions satisfy my soul.

Never has the hope of fame blinded me, nor have I ever dreamed of laurel wreaths weighing upon my brow. My lips have babbled only songs of independence and freedom, though surely I heard, even from my cradle, the sound of the chains that would imprison me forever, because the shackles of slavery are a woman's patrimony.

And yet, I am free, as free as the birds, the breeze, the desert Arab, or the high seas pirate.

Free is my heart, free my soul, and free my thought, that reaches up to the sky and descends to the earth, proud as Lucifer and sweet as a hope.

When the masters of the earth threaten me with their looks, or try to mark my forehead with the stain of their disapproval, I laugh just as they laugh, and my iniquities seem to surpass even theirs. And yet my heart is good; though I heed not the commands of those who are my peers, because I believe their craft

que su hechura es igual a mi hechura, y que su carne es igual a mi mi carne.

Yo soy libre. Nada puede contener la marcha de mis pensamientos, y ellos son la ley que rige mi destino.

¡Oh mujer! ¿Por qué siendo tan pura vienen a proyectarse sobre los blancos rayos que despide tu frente las impías sombras de los vicios de la Tierra? ¿Por qué los hombres derraman sobre ti la inmundicia de sus excesos, despreciando y aborreciendo después en tu moribundo cansancio lo horrible de sus mismos desórdenes y de sus calenturientos delirios?

Todo lo que viene a formarse sombrío y macilento en tu mirada después del primer destello de tu juventud inocente, todo lo que viene a manchar de cieno los blancos ropajes con que te vistieron las primeras alboradas de tu infancia, y a extinguir tus olorosas esencias y borrar las imágenes de la virtud en tu pensamiento, todo te lo transmiten ellos, todo. . . y, sin embargo, te desprecian.

Los remordimientos son la herencia de las mujeres débiles. Ellos corroen su existencia con el recuerdo de unos placeres que hoy compraron a costa de su felicidad y que mañana pesarán sobre su alma como plomo candente.

Espectros dormidos que descansan impasibles en el regazo que se dispone a recibir otro objeto que el que ellos nos presentan, y abrazos que reciben otros abrazos que hemos jurado no admitir jamás.

Dolores punzantes y desgarradores por lo pasado, arrepentimientos vanos, enmiendas de un instante y reproducciones eternas en la culpa, y un deseo de virtud para lo futuro, un nombre honrado y sin mancillar que poder entregar al hombre que nos pide sinceramente una existencia desnuda de riquezas, mas

is equal to mine, my flesh the same as theirs.

I am free. Nothing can halt the steady march of my thoughts, which alone guide my existence.

Oh, woman! Why, being so pure, do they project upon the white rays emanating from your forehead the unholy shadows of earthly evil? Why do men shower you with the filth of their excesses, afterward despising and abhorring in your mortal weariness the horror of their own disorder and their feverish delirium?

All that comes to be shadowy and emaciated in your gaze, after the spark of your innocent youth fades, all that comes to mire the whiteness of your early youth, and extinguish your sweet essences, and erase the visions of virtue in your thoughts, all is transmitted by them, all of it, and still they despise you.

Regret is the inheritance of weak women. It corrodes their existence with the memory of pleasures bought today at the cost of their happiness, poised tomorrow to weigh on their souls like molten lead.

Sleeping specters that rest impassively in the lap that prepares itself to receive something other than what they present us, caresses that follow other caresses that we have sworn never to permit.

Sharp and shameless pain for what has gone before, vain regrets, reforms of an instant, and eternal reproduction of guilt; and a desire for a future virtue, an honorable, unsullied name to bestow on the man who asks sincerely for an existence more prodigious in goodness and chaste longings than in riches.

These are the struggles preceded ever

pródiga en bondades y sensaciones vírgenes.

He aquí las luchas precedidas siempre por los remordimientos que velan nuestro sueño, nuestras esperanzas, nuestras ambiciones.

¡Y todo esto por una debilidad!

by the regrets that hover over our sleep, our hopes, our ambitions.

And all this for weakness!

(Translated by Lou Charnon Deutsch)

Las literatas
(1865)

The Bluestockings

Mi querida Eduarda: ¿Seré demasiado cruel, al empezar esta carta, diciéndote que la tuya me ha puesto triste y malhumorada? ¿Iré a parecerte envidiosa de tus talentos, o brutalmente franca, cuando me atrevo a despojarte, sin rebozo ni compasión, de esas caras ilusiones que tan ardientemente acaricias? Pero tú sabes quién soy, conoces hasta lo íntimo mis sentimientos, las afecciones de mi corazón, y puedo hablarte.

No, mil veces no, Eduarda; aleja de ti tan fatal tentación, no publiques nada y guarda para ti sola tus versos y tu prosa, tus novelas y tus dramas: que ese sea un secreto entre el Cielo, tú y yo. ¿No ves que el mundo está lleno de esas cosas? Todos escriben y de todo. Las musas se han desencadenado. Hay más libros que arenas tiene el mar, más genios que estrellas tiene el cielo y más críticos que hierbas hay en los campos. Muchos han dado en tomar esto último por oficio; reciben por ello alabanzas de la patria, y aunque lo hacen lo peor que hubiera podido esperarse, prosiguen entusiasmados, riéndose, necios felices, de los otros necios, mientras los demás se ríen de ellos. Semejantes a una plaga asoladora, críticos y escritores han invadido la Tierra y la devoran como pueden. ¿Qué falta hacemos,

My dear Eduarda: Would I be too cruel if I were to begin this letter by telling you that yours has made me feel sad and bad tempered? Will I seem to you jealous of your talents, or brutally frank, when I dare to deprive you, without pretense or compassion, of those costly illusions you so ardently cherish? But you know who I am, you know my most intimate sentiments, all that my heart holds dear, and I can talk to you.

No, a thousand times no, Eduarda. Flee from that fatal temptation, publish nothing, and keep for yourself alone your verses and your prose, your novels and your plays, and let them be a secret known only to you, me, and the heavens. Can you not see that the world is filled with these *things*? Everybody writes, and about everything. The muses have been unleashed. There are more books than grains of sand in the sea, more geniuses than stars in the sky, and more critics than blades of grass in the fields. So many have chosen this as a trade; as a result they receive praise from the nation, and though they do it more poorly than one could possibly imagine, they go on encouraged, laughing, the happy fools, at other fools, while others laugh at them. Like a devastating plague, critics and writers have invaded the earth and they are

pues, tú y yo entre ese tumulto devastador? Ninguna, y lo que sobra siempre está demás. Dirás que trato esta cuestión como la del matrimonio, que hablamos mal de él después que nos hemos casado; mas puedo asegurarte, amiga mía, que si el matrimonio es casi para nosotras una necesidad impuesta por la sociedad y la misma Naturaleza, las musas son un escollo y nada más. Y, por otra parte, ¿merecen ellas que uno las ame? ¿No se han hecho acaso tan ramplonas y plebeyas que acuden al primero que las invoca, siquiera sea la cabeza más vacía? Juzga por lo que te voy a contar.

Hace algún tiempo, el barbero de mi marido se presentó circunspecto y orgullosamente grave. Habiendo tropezado al entrar con la cocinera, le alargó su mano y la saludó con la mayor cortesía, diciendo, "A los pies de usted, María: ¿qué tal de salud?" "Vamos andando —le contestó muy risueña—, y usted, Guanito?" "Bien, gracias, para servir a usted." "¡Qué fino es usted, amigo mío! —añadió ella, creyéndose elevada al quinto cielo porque el barberillo le había dado la mano al saludarla y se había puesto a sus pies—. ¡Cómo se conoce que ha pisado usted las calles de La Habana! Por aquí, apenas saben los mozos decir más que buenos días."

—¡Cómo se conoce que vienes de aquella tierra! —exclamé yo para mí—. Tú ya sabes, Eduarda, cuál es aquella tierra..., aquella feliz provincia en donde todos, todos (yo creo que hasta las arañas) descienden en línea recta de cierta antigua, ingeniosa y artística raza que ha dado al mundo lecciones de arte y sabiduría.

—¿Cómo no ha venido usted más antes? —le preguntó mi marido algo serio—. ¿No sabía usted que le esperaba desde las diez?

—Cada cual tienen sus ocupaciones

devouring it as fast as they can. What need have we, then, you and I, amid this ruinous tumult? None, for there is never any need for excess. You will say that I deal with this question as with that of marriage, that we speak ill of it after having married; but I assure you, my friend, that if marriage is for us almost a necessity imposed by society and Nature herself, the muses are a trap and nothing more. And, in any event, do they merit one's love? Indeed, have they not become so vulgar and plebeian that they rush to the first to invoke them, though it be the emptiest of heads? Judge by what I am about to tell you.

Some time ago, my husband's barber appeared with a circumspect and proud mien. Having bumped into the cook on entering, he extended his hand and greeted her with the utmost courtesy, saying, "Your wish is my command, María. How is your health?" "Go on," she answered him, smiling brightly, "and you, Guanito?" "Well, thank you, and at your service." "How refined you are, my friend!" she added, believing herself transported to the very heights because the silly barber had taken her hand in greeting and had put himself at her service. "How clear it is that you have walked the streets of Havana! Around here, young men can barely manage more than a 'good morning.'"

"How clear it is you come from that land!" I exclaimed to myself. You well know, Eduarda, to which land I refer, that happy province where everyone, everyone (even the spiders, I dare say) descends in a direct line from a certain ancient, ingenious, artistic race that has given the world lessons in art and wisdom.

"Why were you not here earlier?" my husband asked him, his tone a trifle annoyed. "Are you not aware that I have been waiting since ten?"

particulares —repuso el barbero con mucho tono y jugando con el bastón—. Tenía que concluir mi libro y llevarlo a casa del impresor, que ya era tiempo.

—¿Qué libro?— repuso mi marido lleno de asombro.

—Una novela moral, instructiva y científica que acabo de escribir, y en la cual demuestro palpablemente que el oficio de barbero es el más interesante entre todos los oficios que se llaman mecánicos y debe ser elevado al grado de profesión honorífica y titulada, y trascendental por añadidura.

Mi marido se levantó entonces de la silla en que se sentara para ser inmolado, y cogiendo algunas monedas, se las entregó al barbero, diciendo:

—Hombre que hace tales obras no es digno de afeitar mi cara— y se alejó riendo fuertemente; pero no así yo, que, irritada contra los necios y las musas, abrí mi papelera y rompí cuanto allí tenía escrito, con lo cual, a decir verdad, nada se ha perdido.

Porque tal es el mundo, Eduarda: cogerá el libro, o, más bien dicho, el aborto de ese barbero, a quien Dios hizo más estúpido que una marmota, y se atreverá a compararlo con una novela de Jorge Sand.

—Yo tengo leídas muchas preciosas obras— me decía un cierto joven que se tenía por instruido—. *Las tardes de la Granja* y el *Manfredo* de Byron; pero, sobre todo, *Las tardes de la Granja* me han hecho feliz.

—Lo creo— le contesté y mudé de conversación.

Esto es insoportable para una persona que tenga algún orgullo literario y algún sentimiento de poesía en el corazón; pero sobre todo, amiga mía, tú no sabes lo que es ser escritora. Serlo como Jorge Sand vale algo; pero de otro modo, ¡qué continuo

"Each of us has personal matters to deal with," the barber replied in grave tones while playing with his cane. "I had to finish my book and take it to the printer, as it was due."

"What book?" asked my husband, filled with astonishment.

"A moral, instructive, and scientific novel, which I have just finished writing, and in which I will demonstrate palpably that the barber's vocation is the most interesting of those vocations known as mechanical, and ought to be elevated to the level of honorific and titled, and, I might add, transcendental profession."

My husband then rose from the chair in which he had seated himself to be sacrificed, and picking up some coins, he gave them to the barber, saying:

"The man who produces such works is not fit to shave my face," and he walked away laughing loudly. But not I, who, irritated with the fools and the muses, opened my portfolio and tore up all that I had written there, and to tell the truth, nothing had been lost as a result.

Because such is the world, Eduarda: he, whom God has created more stupid than a marmot, will pick up the book, or, better yet, the stillborn creature of that barber, and he will dare to compare it to a novel by George Sand.

"I have read many exquisite works," a certain young man, who believed himself educated, said to me. "*Afternoons on the Farm* and *Manfred* by Byron. But, above all, *Afternoons on the Farm* has brought me happiness."

"No doubt," I said, and changed the subject.

This is unbearable for a person who has a degree of literary pride and some sense of poetry in her heart. But above all, my friend, you do not know what it means

tormento!; por la calle te señalan constantemente, y no para bien, y en todas partes murmuran de ti. Si vas a la tertulia y hablas de algo de lo que sabes, si te expresas siquiera en un lenguaje algo correcto, te llaman bachillera, dicen que te escuchas a ti misma, que lo quieres saber todo. Si guardas una prudente reserva, ¡qué fatua!, ¡qué orgullosa!; te desdeñas de hablar como no sea con literatos. Si te haces modesta y por no entrar en vanas disputas dejas pasar inadvertidas las cuestiones que te provocan, ¿en dónde está tu talento?; ni siquiera sabes entretener a la gente con una amena conversación. Si te agrada la sociedad, pretendes lucirte, quieres que se hable de ti, no hay función sin tarasca. Si vives apartada del trato de gentes es que te haces la interesante, estás loca, tu carácter es atrabiliario e insoportable; pasas el día en deliquios poéticos y la noche contemplando las estrellas, como don Quijote. Las mujeres ponen en relieve hasta el más escondido de tus defectos y los hombres no cesan de decirte siempre que pueden que una mujer de talento es una verdadera calamidad, que vale más casarse con la burra de Balaan, y que sólo una tonta puede hacer la felicidad de un mortal varón.[1]

Sobre todo los que escriben y se tienen por graciosos, no dejan pasar nunca la ocasión de decirte que las mujeres deben dejar la pluma y repasar los calcetines de sus maridos, si lo tienen, y si no, aunque sean los del criado. Cosa fácil era para algunas abrir el armario y plantarles delante de las narices los zurcidos pacientemente

to be a *writer*. To be one like George Sand is worth something; but otherwise, what a continuous torment! They constantly point you out on the street, and not for well-intentioned reasons, and everywhere they gossip about you. If you go to a social gathering and speak of something about which you know, if you so much as express yourself in language more or less correct, they will call you pedantic, say that you do it to hear yourself speak, that you think you know everything. If you maintain a prudent reserve, how fatuous! how vain! you will not stoop to speak except to the literati. If you assume a modest stance and, in order to avoid futile argument, allow to pass without comment questions that interest you, where is your talent?—you do not even know how to entertain people with pleasant conversation. If you enjoy social events, you are attempting to shine, you want to be talked about, you will find yourself booed off the stage. If you live in isolation from social intercourse, it is that you are trying to appear interesting, you are mad, your character is ill-tempered and unbearable; you spend your days in poetic swoons and your nights, like Don Quixote, contemplating the stars. Women emphasize your defects, including the best concealed of these, and men never tire of saying to you at every turn that a woman of talent is a veritable disaster, that one is better off marrying the ass of Balaan, and that only a silly little fool can make a mortal *male* happy.[1]

Above all, those who write and think themselves witty never miss an opportunity

---

1. En la historia bíblica, la burra de Balaan habló, milagrosamente, después de ser maltratado por no querer seguir caminando, habiendo visto el ángel de Dios. La referencia popular es a alguien que habla tonta o indiscretamente.

1. In the biblical story, Balaan's ass spoke, miraculously, after being beaten for refusing to move on once it had seen the angel of the Lord. The popular reference is to someone who speaks foolishly or indiscreetly.

trabajados, para probarles que el escribir algunas páginas no les hace a todas olvidarse de sus quehaceres domésticos, pudiendo añadir que los que tal murmuran saben olvidarse, en cambio, de que no han nacido más que para tragar el pan de cada día y vivir como los parásitos.

Pero es el caso, Eduarda, que los hombres miran a las literatas peor que mirarían al diablo, y este es un nuevo escollo que debes tener, tú, que no tienes dote. Únicamente alguno de verdadero talento pudiera, estimándote en lo que vales, despreciar necias y aun erradas preocupaciones; pero. . . ¡ay de ti entonces!, ya nada de cuanto escribes es tuyo, se acabó tu numen, tu marido es el que escribe y tú la que firmas.

Yo, a quien sin duda un mal genio ha querido llevar por el perverso camino de las musas, sé harto bien la senda que en tal peregrinación recorremos. Por lo que a mí respecta, se dice muy corrientemente que mi marido trabaja sin cesar para hacerme inmortal. Verso, prosa, bueno o malo, todo es suyo; pero sobre todo lo que les parece menos malo, y no hay principiante de poeta ni hombre sesudo que no lo afirme. ¡De tal modo le cargan pecados que no ha cometido! Enfadosa preocupación, penosa tarea, por cierto, la de mi marido, que costándole aún trabajo escribir para sí (porque la mayor parte de los poetas son perezosos), tiene que hacer además los libros de su mujer, sin duda con el objeto de que digan que tiene una esposa poetisa (esta palabra ya llegó a hacerme daño) o novelista, es decir, lo peor que puede ser hoy una mujer.

Ello es algo absurdo si bien se reflexiona, y hasta parece oponerse al buen gusto la delicadeza de un hombre y de una mujer que no sean absolutamente necios. . . Pero ¿cómo creer que ella pueda escribir tales

to tell you that women should leave off writing and darn their husbands' socks, if they have one, and if not, at least see to those of the serving boy. Some women find it easy to open the closet and stick the mending patiently worked under their noses to prove that in writing a few pages not all of them forget about their household tasks, managing to add that those who bring up this issue tend to forget, for their part, that they have not been born for nothing other than swallowing their daily bread and living like parasites.

But it happens, Eduarda, that men view women of letters in a light worse than they would view the devil, and this is a new trap that you will encounter, you, who have no dowry. Only someone of true talent could, considering what you are worth, discount silly and even mistaken worries; but then . . . woe is thee, since nothing of that which you write is yours, your muse has been used up, it is your husband who writes and you who signs her name to it.

I, who, evidently an evil spirit has hoped to lead down the perverse path of the muses, know all too well the road we tread in that pilgrimage. About me it is commonly said that my husband works tirelessly to make me immortal. Verse, prose, good or bad, all is his; but above all that which they judge less bad, and there is not a novice poet nor a prudent man who affirms otherwise. So they load him down with sins he has not committed. An irritating concern, a painful task, no doubt, that of my husband, that though simply writing for himself is an effort (because most poets are lazy), he also has to compose his wife's books, no doubt so that they will say that he has a poetess (that word has already been used to hurt me) for a spouse, or a novelist, that is, the worst that a woman can be these days.

cosas? Una mujer a quien ven todos los días, a quien conocen desde niña, a quien han oído hablar, y no andaluz, sino lisa y llanamente como cualquiera, ¿puede discurrir y escribir cosas que a ellos no se les han pasado nunca por las mentes, y eso que han estudiado y saben filosofía, leyes, retórica y poética, etc.?. . . Imposible; no puede creerse a no ser que viniese Dios a decirlo. ¡Si siquiera hubiese nacido en Francia o en Madrid! Pero ¿aquí mismo?. . . ¡Oh!. . .

Todo esto que por lo general me importa poco, Eduarda, hay veces, sin embargo, que me ofende y lastima mi amor propio, y he aquí otro nuevo tormento que debes añadir a los ya mencionados.

Pero no creas que pare aquí el mal, pues una poetisa o escritora no puede vivir humanamente en paz sobre la Tierra, puesto que, además de las agitaciones de su espíritu, tiene las que levantan en torno de ella cuantos la rodean.

Si te casas con un hombre vulgar, aun cuando él sea el que atormente y te oprima día y noche, sin dejarte respirar siquiera, tú eres para el mundo quien le maneja, quien le lleva y trae, tú quien le manda; él dice en la visita la lección que tú le has enseñado en casa, y no se atreve a levantar los ojos por miedo a que le riñas, y todo esto que redunda en menosprecio de tu marido no puede menos de herirte mortalmente si tienes sentimientos y dignidad, porque lo primero que debe cuidar una mujer es de que la honra y la dignidad de su esposo rayen siempre tan alto como sea posible. Toda mancha que llega a caer en él cunde hasta ti y hasta tus hijos, es la columna en que te apoyas y no puede vacilar sin que vaciles, ni ser derribada sin que te arrastre en su caída.

He aquí, bosquejada de prisa y a grandes rasgos, la vida de una mujer literata.

This is somewhat absurd, if one reflects on it well, and it even seems to set good taste at odds with the delicacy of a man and a woman who are not absolute fools . . . But how can one believe that *she* is capable of writing such things? A woman they see daily, whom they have known since she was a child, whom they have heard speak, and not wittily but purely and simply like anyone else, can she be reflecting on and writing about things that have never once passed through *their* minds, particularly since they have studied and are versed in philosophy, law, rhetoric, poetics, etc.? . . . Impossible, it is not to be believed unless God were to come to say so. If at least she had been born in France or Madrid! But right here? . . . Oh! . . .

Generally all of this matters little to me, Eduarda, but there are times, nevertheless, when it offends me and wounds my self-esteem, and this is another, new torment that you should add to those already mentioned.

But do not believe that the evil stops here, since a poetess or woman writer cannot humanly live in peace on this earth, given that, in addition to the anxieties of the spirit, she has those that are raised against her by all who surround her.

If you marry a common man, though it be he who torments and oppresses you day and night, without even letting you breathe, you are, for the world, the one who manages him, who drags him here and there, who orders him about; on visits he recites the lesson you have taught him at home, and he does not dare raise his eyes for fear you will scold him, and all that redounds in contempt for your husband will only wound you mortally if you have feelings and dignity, because the first thing a woman should see to is that the honor and dignity of her husband stand as

Lee y reflexiona; espero con ansia tu respuesta.

Tu amiga, Nicanora

Paseándome un día por las afueras de la ciudad hallé una pequeña cartera que contenía esta carta. Parecióme de mi gusto, no por su mérito literario, sino por la intención con que ha sido escrita, y por eso me animé a publicarla. Perdóneme la desconocida autora esta libertad, en virtud de la analogía que existe entre nuestros sentimientos.

tall as possible. Any stain that falls on him spreads to you and even to your children; he is the pillar on which you lean and he cannot waver without your wavering as well, nor be brought down without dragging you along in his fall.

I leave you here, hastily drawn in broad strokes, the life of a woman of letters. Read and reflect; I anxiously await your response.

Your friend, Nicanora

Strolling one day in the outskirts of the city I found a small purse that contained this letter. It appealed to me, not for its literary merit, but for the reason it had been written, and thus I decided to publish it. May the unknown writer forgive me for the liberty I have taken in view of the analogy that exists between our sentiments.

(Translated by Mary Ellen Fieweger)

Emilia Pardo Bazán

Emilia Pardo Bazán took advantage of her class privilege to devote herself to a literary and intellectual life, without giving up the pleasures that the world could offer her. The only child of a wealthy, aristocratic family, she learned from her father that "there could not be two sets of morals for the two sexes."[1] Her mother taught her to read, and Pardo Bazán spent many childhood hours with the books in her father's library. Later, at the elegant Parisian girls' school to which her parents sent her, she secretly devoured forbidden French novels.

Her marriage at the age of sixteen ("I put on a long skirt, got married, and the Revolution of 1868 broke out")[2] marked the beginning of a life of European travel, an intense social schedule in Madrid, and summers in Galicia. She filled the emptiness of this superficial life with study. She learned English reading Shakespeare, and German so she could translate Heine. Some friends of the family were Krausists, educational reformers, and her contact with them encouraged her to read the new scientific texts, as well as philosophers from Plato to Schopenhauer. Pardo Bazán studied even when she was convalescing from an illness. She read Zola and the brothers Goncourt in a sanatorium in the south of France, formulating ideas on the novel that would form the basis of her revolutionary and controversial defense of literary naturalism, *La cuestión palpitante* (The burning question, 1883).

Emilia Pardo Bazán was born in La Coruña, Galicia, on September 16, 1851. She made her literary debut at the age of nine, with a patriotic poem she declaimed from her balcony as soldiers returning from a successful war against Morocco passed by her home. She began her career by writing poetry, including a series of poems about her first child, Jaime; but she ultimately abandoned her career as a poet, declaring that prose was her true vocation.

In addition to nineteen novels and twenty-one novellas, Pardo Bazán contributed articles to numerous magazines, including the *Revista Compostelana, La Ciencia Cristiana, Revista de España, La España Moderna, El Imparcial, Blanco y Negro,* and *La Ilustración Artística.* In 1891 she founded her own magazine, *Nuevo Teatro Crítico* (New critical theater), which she wrote in its entirety. She was also the author of approximately six hundred short stories published between 1880 and 1919.

After 1885, Pardo Bazán lived apart from her husband. They had had three children, Jaime (b. 1876), Blanca (b. 1878), and Carmen (b. 1880). The year of their separation

coincided with that of Pardo's first public speech, in honor of the memory of Rosalía de Castro. She would give many speeches, on themes as diverse as Russian literature and politics, contemporary Spanish poets, and Spanish history. In 1906 she was named president of the literature section of the Madrid Athenaeum, and professor of neo-Latin languages at the Central University of Madrid in 1916. She was the first woman member of the Athenaeum and first woman professor at the university, but her university lectures went unattended and she never achieved the membership in the Royal Academy she so badly wanted.

Pardo Bazán's passion for literature and for new ideas, as well as her outspoken manner, brought her some detractors, among them the novelists Pereda and Palacio Valdés, as well as some problematic friends. Leopoldo Alas praised Pardo Bazán's early work, but he later attacked her viciously and ridiculed her attempts to enter the Royal Academy. Juan Valera admired Pardo Bazán's writing, but he disagreed with her literary philosophy and publicly made fun of her obesity. Like Clarín, he opposed her election to the Academy. Pardo Bazán did not always write favorably about the works of these writers, but she never answered their personal attacks on her. Pardo Bazán also had her admirers, among them the statesman Emilio Castelar, the writer Miguel de Unamuno, and the period's foremost realist novelist, Benito Peréz Galdós, with whom a literary correspondence evolved into a sexual relationship.

In 1876 Pardo Bazán won first prize in an important contest for her study of the works of the eighteenth-century essayist Benito Jerónimo Feijóo. Pardo's main competitor in the contest was Concepción Arenal, already well known, and several years Pardo's senior. Yet Arenal was neither a rival of nor a model for Pardo Bazán. The younger woman was not about to adopt Arenal's personal asceticism, nor would she have considered dressing as a man in order to attend the university, as Arenal did. But she did share the social reformer's interest in women's issues. Like Arenal, Pardo Bazán wrote many articles defending women's rights and exhorting Spanish women to claim them, and more than a few of her stories and novels question traditional gender relations. The story included here, "Los cirineos" (The Cyrenians), expresses a sophisticated and refreshing attitude toward sexuality, and a no less revolutionary view of women's friendship.

Pardo Bazán's book of psychological biographies, *Hombres y mujeres de antaño* (Men and women of yesteryear, 1896), is a series of feminist readings of figures from Spanish history, including the mad Queen Juana of Castile, the Nun of Ágreda, and Francisco de Quevedo. Juana la Loca was, for Pardo Bazán, the "Quixote of conjugal love," who tried to live by the ideals of married love with a tiresome husband who rejected her. Pardo explains Sor María de Ágreda's disappearance from the political and cultural history of Spain as a function of the inability of male arbiters of history and culture to reconcile their concept of weak, irrational woman with the strength, political acumen, and logic of this woman's theological vision. Quevedo's misogyny can be understood, according to Pardo, in the context of the writer's own social milieu.

In 1892 Pardo Bazán founded a publishing company, which she called Biblioteca de la Mujer (The Woman's Library). She published foreign books with feminist themes, including John Stuart Mill's *On the Subjection of Women* and August Bebel's *Women and Socialism*, as well as such Spanish works as María de Zayas's novellas and Sor María de Ágreda's autobiography. She was disillusioned by the lack of interest in these books, and the last volume published by Biblioteca de la Mujer was a cookbook, written by Pardo Bazán herself. Her loss of faith in the possibility of the development of a Spanish feminism can also be seen in her series of essays under the general title *La mujer española* (The Spanish woman, 1890). These articles comment disparagingly on the characteristics of middle-class Spanish women. Working-class and rural women fare somewhat better. Pardo Bazán considered herself a "feminist radical"[3] who believed that "the key to our [national] regeneration lies with women, in their education, their personality, their consciousness."[4] In a statement of extreme isolation from the two groups with which she identified herself, she confessed her lack of faith in the possibility of achieving such a regeneration because "all the writers and . . . all the women" are against it.[5]

Pardo Bazán's feminism coexisted with her conservative politics. She believed in the equality of rights for men and women, but not in democracy. Even so, her sympathetic depiction of the popular classes is manifest in her fiction. A complex and contradictory figure, Pardo Bazán could be both reactionary and forward-looking. She fought for and won the right to convert the papal title conferred on her father into a hereditary Spanish title that she could pass on to her own son during the same decade that she entered the age of technology with a typewriter and a car. Her polemical positions were a mixture of the radical and the traditional, most noticeably in her defense of literary naturalism. *La cuestión palpitante* aimed to reconcile the literary Darwinism of naturalism with Catholicism.

Pardo Bazán never lost her energy; she kept writing until the end of her life. Her last article, on Juan Valera, was published May 13, 1921, one day after her death.

1. "no puede haber dos morales para los dos sexos"; cited in Carmen Bravo Villasante, *Vida y obra de Emilia Pardo Bazán* (Madrid: Revista de Occidente, 1962), 15.
2. "Me puse de largo, me casé y estalló la Revolución del 68"; cited in Bravo Villasante, 30.
3. "una radical feminista"; cited in Bravo Villasante, 287.
4. "la clave de nuestra regeneración [nacional] está en la mujer, en su instrucción, en su personalidad, en su conciencia"; cited in Bravo Villasante, 287.
5. "todos los escritores y . . . todas las mujeres,"; cited in Bravo Villasante, 288.

Los cirineos[1]

Aquella cuitada de Romana Meléndez, tan mona, en lo mejor de la edad, los veinticinco; unida por su familia, sin previa consulta del gusto, al vejete socio de su padre, a don Laureano Calleja, pasó dos años medio secuestrada, recluída en su casa de Madrid, grande, cómoda, hasta lujosa, pero que trasudaba por las paredes murria y aburrimiento. El viejo marido, observando la perpetua melancolía de su esposa, a su vez se mostraba hosco y gruñón; los criados desempeñaban sus quehaceres de mal talante, recelosos; nunca llamaba a la puerta una visita, nunca se le ofrecía a Romana ningún honesto esparcimiento: a misa los domingos y fiestas de guardar, a "dar una vuelta" por Recoletos cuando hacía bueno, y el resto del tiempo sepultada en su butaca, peleándose con una eterna labor de gancho, una colcha, que no se acababa porque a la labrandera no le interesaba que se acabase, y en lugar de mover los dedos dejaba el hilo y las tiras sobre el regazo y se entregaba a una de esas meditaciones sin objeto, fatigosas como caminar sobre guijarros, entre polvo.

Tal género de vida y la pasión de ánimo que se originó de él, minaron la salud de Romana. Contrajo una de esas propensiones a languidecer que agotan y secan la vida en sus mismos manantiales y pueden dar origen a afecciones consuntivas. Tuvo una elevación diaria de temperatura, que en vano combatió con la quinina, y el médico, no sabiendo qué disponer, no teniendo remedios para aliviar, la envió a que pasase un mes respirando aire puro y saturado de emanaciones balsámicas en un

The Cyrenians[1]

Poor Romana Meléndez, that pretty little thing, was in the prime of her life, twenty-five years old. Married off by her family, without prior consultation as to her wishes, to her father's old-fogey business partner, Don Laureano Calleja, she spent two and a half years hidden away, a recluse in his house in Madrid, huge, comfortable, even luxurious, but whose walls oozed dreariness and boredom. The old husband, observing his wife's perpetual melancholy, acted sullen and grumpy in turn, and the servants went about their daily chores in a begrudging, distrustful manner. Not one visitor ever knocked at the door. Romana was never offered any real entertainment. She went to mass on Sundays and holy days, she took a stroll around Recoletos Park when the weather was nice, and the rest of the time she was buried in her armchair, struggling with an endless piece of needlework, a coverlet that never got done because she had no interest in its getting done. Instead of moving her fingers, she laid the yarn and crocheted strips in her lap and gave herself over to one of those purposeless meditations, tiresome as walking over stones in the dust.

That kind of life, and the suffering of spirit to which it gave rise, sapped Romana's health. She became afflicted with a sickly tendency, the sort that depletes life, drying it up at its very source, and that can give rise to symptoms of consumption. Every day she ran a fever, which she fought in vain with quinine; and the doctor, not knowing what to prescribe, not having any healing remedies, sent her to

---

1. San Simón Cirineo ayudó a Jesús a llevar la cruz. Los cirineos son, por extensión, personas que ayudan a otros en algún trabajo penoso.

1. Saint Simon Cyrenian helped Jesus carry the cross. A Cyrenian, by extension, is someone who helps another with an onerous task.

sanatorio del Mediodía, de esos en que la sobrealimentación y la suavidad del clima suelen proporcionar alivio; pero el tedio y la contemplación de tantas miserias fisiológicas abruman con la pesadumbre de la fatalidad que nos rodea. Para Romana el tedio era un compañero antiguo, y la variación, ya por sí sola, distracción segura y aprovechable. Además, la casualidad la deparó la adquisición de una amiga, una señora que ocupaba la habitación contigua: llamábase Ignacia López y era esposa de un modestísimo empleado en Hacienda.

Ignacia no padecía mal ninguno; se encontraba en el sanatorio acompañando y cuidando a una hermanita suya, criatura muy interesante, tísica confirmada. Simpatizaron Ignacia y Romana desde el primer momento; en el pinar allegaron las mecedoras y entre efluvios de resina y tibias caricias de sol, charlaron con alegrías y vivezas de pájaros. Eran casi de la misma edad; fuera de eso, en nada se parecían. La actividad de Ignacia contrastaba con la pasividad de Romana, siempre resignada y en brazos del destino, mientras su nueva amiga luchaba con él y aspiraba a vencerlo. Inteligente y jamás cansada, Ignacia, sin dejar de atender a la tísica, discurría diabluras, organizaba entre los pinos meriendas y paellas que galvanizaban hasta a los moribundos. Romana ponía el dinero, la empleadita el buen humor y la disposición. Pero la tísica empeoró y hubo que pensar en volverse al domicilio, que es al fin y al cabo donde mejor lo pasa un enfermo. La idea de quedarse sin su amiga achicó el corazón de Romana; en un santiamén hizo la maleta; reunidas se metieron en un departamento de segunda—no podía darse el lujo de primera Ignacia—y muy hermanadas llegaron a Madrid. Se despidieron en la estación, en la cual nadie las esperaba, con estrechos abrazos y

spend a month in a sanatorium in the south breathing air that was pure and saturated with restorative effluences, where excess nourishment and the gentleness of the climate often provide relief. But with the weight of fatality that surrounds us, the boredom and the contemplation of so much physiological wretchedness is overwhelming. For Romana, boredom was an old companion, and variation just by itself was a sure and profitable distraction. Besides, fate afforded her the acquisition of a friend, a married woman who occupied the adjacent room. Her name was Ignacia López, and she was the wife of a lowly clerk in the Treasury Department.

Ignacia was not suffering from any illness. She was in the sanatorium caring for a sister of hers, a very interesting creature who had been diagnosed as having tuberculosis. Ignacia and Romana got along well together from the first moment. Out in the pine grove they pulled their rocking chairs next to one another, and amid the rising sap and the sun's warm caresses, they chattered with the gaiety and liveliness of birds. They were almost the same age. Other than that, they did not resemble each other at all. Ignacia's active nature contrasted with Romana's passivity. Romana was always resigned and in destiny's embrace, while her new friend fought against it and aspired to prevail over it. Mentally active and never weary, Ignacia, without neglecting her consumptive sister, thought up amusing activities and organized picnics and cookouts among the pines that energized even the dying. Romana supplied the money, the clerk's little wife the good humor and the organization. But her patient got worse and Ignacia had to think about returning home, which is, after all, where a sick person gets along best. The idea of being left without her

letanías de promesas; Romana, al meterse en un coche, se sintió oprimida, como si le faltase de golpe aire blando y regenerador.

Desde entonces, su vida tuvo un objeto, una finalidad: escaparse a ver a la amiga, pasarse el tiempo en su casa, insensiblemente; aquel interés era vitalidad, era rayo de luz en el limbo. Hasta cuidar a la tísica le parecía género de diversión; y no digamos vestir y desnudar a los chiquitines —tres tenía Ignacia— porque eso sí envolvía inmenso placer. ¡Tan guapos, tan zalameros, tan rubios, tan ricos! ¡Si daban ganas de comérselos por pan! A la insípida existencia propia, Romana sustituyó la ajena; careciendo de afectos, recogió con avidez los que no la pertenecían; no padeciendo disgustos ni cuidados, adoptó los de Ignacia; la escasez de metálico, las inquietudes por la enferma, por el sarampión de los chiquillos, por la urgencia de vestirse de invierno—y se acostumbró a no entrar en casa de Ignacia sin un paquetito: ropa, artículos de consumo, medicamento caro, juguete. El momento de desenvolver el regalo proporcionaba a Romana gratísima emoción. Los chicos se agarraban a sus faldas, trepaban hasta su cuello, la asfixiaban a cariños.

—¡Hija, quién como tú! —exclamaba la empleadita. —¡Si estás mejor que quieres! ¡Encontrarte el primero del mes con mil pesetas que no sabes qué hacer de ellas! ¡Yo, que sólo me encuentro recibos atrasados de la tienda, del zapatero, del casero! ¡Tener un marido formal, que se babará por ti!

—Pues mira, yo —contestaba Romana, acariciando al angelito menor —te trocaba la suerte. Si me das este muñeco, ¡quieto, diabolico! te entrego las mil pesetas en un billete. Y ya que te gusta el marido viejo —te lo traspasaba, cediéndome tú, por supuesto, al joven.

friend shriveled Romana's heart, and in the blink of an eye she packed her suitcase. Reunited, they installed themselves in a second class compartment—Ignacia could not afford the luxury of first—and feeling like true sisters, they arrived in Madrid. They said farewell to one another in the station, where there was no one to meet them, hugging one another tightly and offering litanies of promises. When she stepped into the cab, Romana felt a crushing weight on her, as if she were suddenly left without soft, life-giving air.

From then on, her life had an objective, a goal: to escape to see her friend, to spend time in her house, carefree. That pastime meant vitality, a ray of light in limbo. Even nursing the ailing sister seemed to her a kind of diversion, not to mention dressing and undressing the little ones—Ignacia had three—because that really did involve immense pleasure. So attractive, so affectionate, so fair, so delightful. They made you want to eat them up, like bread! Romana replaced her own insipid existence with that of another. Lacking affection, she avidly gathered up someone else's. Suffering neither vexations nor worries, she adopted Ignacia's. The lack of spending money, anxiety over the ailing sister, the children's measles, the urgent need to get a winter wardrobe together . . . And it was her habit never to enter Ignacia's house without a little package—clothing, food items, expensive medicine, a toy . . . The moment the wrapping came off the gift provided Romana with a delectable feeling. The little ones clutched at her skirts, they climbed up to her neck, they smothered her with affection.

"Oh my, to be in your shoes," exclaimed the little clerk's wife. "Why, you're better off than you want to be! To get to the first of the month with a thousand pesetas and

Fue dicha esta enormidad como se dicen las frases humorísticas más gordas cuando hay confianza y ternura; las dos amigas rieron a carcajadas y se besaron. Es de advertir que por entonces, ninguna de las dos conocía al marido de la otra. El de Ignacia estaba en Zamora, con licencia de dos meses, ultimando asuntos de una testamentaría; el de Romana, envuelto también en negocios, y por contera, huraño y escamón, prevenido contra todo y todos, y en especial contra "los pobretes" y "los pegotes", no permitía ni oír nombrar a las recién adquiridas relaciones de su esposa. Mas sucedió que cierta mañana dominical, volviendo de las Calatravas el señor Callejas, en la acera de Alcalá le paró una señora. . . ¡Demontre! ¡Qué señora más despabilada! Aquello fue un acosón chancero, igual que si se hubiesen tratado tú por tú desde la cuna Ignacia y don Laureano. Hubo dichos graciosos, tiroteo de picantes frases.

—A mí ya sé que no me puede usted ver ni en pintura. . . —repetía Ignacia riendo, enseñando los dientes blancos, las bien frotadas encías.

Nadie gastaba bromas con el viejo; se le hablaba en tono grave, al diapasón de su cara seca y muerta como una hoja arrancada del árbol. La chistosa franqueza de Ignacia le hizo el efecto que hace al sobrio un vaso de vinillo puro.

—Pues quién la privó a usted de venir a mi casa. . ., digo, a la de usted? —barbotaba confusamente.

—Usted mismo, que es capaz de espantarme con un palo. . .

—Nada de eso.

—Pues si no me pega usted, cónstele que voy. . . a ver si me querrá usted tanto así, cuando vea que soy una buena persona, aunque me esté mal el decirlo. . .; y yo también me convenceré de que usted no es

not know what to do with the money! And there's me, who only finds overdue bills from the store, from the shoemaker, from the landlord. To have a proper husband who I bet drools over you!"

"But look," Romana answered, stroking the littlest angel, "I'd change places with you. If you give me this doll of yours—be still, you little rascal—I'll give you a thousand peseta note. And since you like my old husband, I'd hand him over to you, if you gave me your young one, of course.

This shocking remark was made the way the juiciest jokes are, when there is trust and tenderness. The two friends laughed uproariously and kissed one another. The reader should be warned that at that time, neither one knew the other's husband. Ignacia's was in Zamora, on leave for two months, finishing up business for an estate. Romana's husband was also involved in business affairs, and—to top things off—he was shy and distrustful, on guard against everything and everybody, and especially against "the poor folks" and "the spongers." He did not even allow his wife's newly acquired friendship to be mentioned. But it so happened that on a certain Sunday morning, as Mr. Calleja was returning from Calatravas, a woman stopped him on the sidewalk. Unbelievable! What a lively lady! That was quite a merry sparring match, as if Ignacia and Don Laureano had been on familiar terms since the cradle. There were witty comments, a battery of spicy phrases.

"I already know you can't stand to look at me," Ignacia said laughing, showing her white teeth, her well-massaged gums.

No one ever wasted any jokes on the old man. People addressed him in a serious tone of voice, attuned to his face, dry and dead as a leaf ripped from its tree. Ignacia's witty frankness had the effect

un tirano, sino un barbián simpático y amable. . .

A la hora de comer, don Laureano rezongó entre los vapores de la sopa:

—No sé por qué has de andar corriendo la fama de que soy raro. . . ¿Te quito yo ningún gusto? Hoy mismo vendrá aquí esa amigota que te echaste en el Sanatorio.

Y vino "la amigota", y de un modo gradual fue repitiendo las visitas, diciendo a Romana:

—Hija, no te celes si atiendo más a tu esposo que a ti, si le llevo las manías al buen señor. Nos conviene conquistarle. . . Que crea que me tiene prendada... Tú hazte la sueca. . .

¡Ya lo creo que se haría la sueca, y loca de contento! Y el viejo se acostumbró a la presencia de Ignacia a la hora del café, a su pico fresco y vivaz, a sus entrometimientos de mal tono, pero chuscos y divertidos. Había aquello de —¡Jesús, y qué hombre tan tacaño! ¿Por qué no hace usted así. . . o asado?. . . ¡Si yo fuese su mujer de usted!. . .

Y la respuesta: —Pues como yo fuese su marido. . . la encerraba, por aturdida, por liosa. . .

Transcurrido un mes, Calleja se corrió e invitó a "esa golfa" a cenar los domingos. Romana notó, con agradable admiración, que ese día su marido se mudaba, se acicalaba, se afeitaba cuidadosamente, recortándose los cuatro pelitos de la calva, y se ponía la levita, anticuada por desuso; y colmó su satisfacción el anuncio de que tenían palco en Lara, donde acabaron la noche divertidísimos, riendo como tontos con las ocurrencias y los gestos de Rodríguez. . .

Poco después llegó a Madrid el esposo de Ignacia, y fue presentado a Romana. Como sucede siempre que se ha hablado mucho de una persona antes de conocerla, hubo cortedad, al pronto, en las relaciones. Miguel—así se llamaba el consorte—

that a glass of pure wine has on a teetotaler.

"Well, who kept you from coming to my house . . . ? My house is your house, you know," he mumbled in confusion.

"You did yourself; I thought you'd chase me off with a stick."

"Not at all."

"Well, if you promise not to hit me, you can count on me to come. We'll see how much you like me, when you find out what a good person I am, though it may be wrong for me to say so . . . ; and I'll also convince myself that you're not a tyrant, but just a sweet old libertine."

At mealtime, Don Laureano grumbled into the steam rising from his soup: "I don't know why you have to go around spreading the word that I'm odd. . . Have I ever denied you any pleasure? This very day that much-prized friend you made in the sanatorium is coming over."

And "the much-prized friend" came over, and ever so gradually she began visiting again and again, saying to Romana:

"My dear, don't get jealous if I pay more attention to your husband than to you, if I cater to the good gentleman's whims. It's to our advantage to conquer him. Let him think he's got me under his spell. You act dumb."

Of course she would act dumb, and she would be delighted to do so! And the old man became accustomed to Ignacia's presence at coffeetime, to her fresh and vivacious loquacity, to her meddling comments, impertinent but witty and entertaining. There were those remarks, "Jesus, what a stingy man! Why don't you do it this way? . . . or thataway? If I were your wife! . . ."

And the answer: "Well, if I were your husband I'd lock you up, as a mental case, as a troublemaker . . ."

frisaría en los treinta; el rubio bigotillo, la boca roja, le daban aspecto más juvenil aún: su cara era adamada, su piel fina, pero sólido su tronco y sus piernas ágiles y nerviosas. A la segunda entrevista, confesó a Romana su única debilidad, su único vicio: la afición a la fotografía. A la sordina, el entretenimiento es caro; nadie sabe lo que se gasta, amén de los aparatos, en placas, películas, reactivos, cartones, mil accesorios. Eso sí: con Huertas y Franzén se las tenía él. . .

—Anda, enseña tus monos —exclamó Ignacia, como quien se aviene al capricho de un niño. —Hija, ya verás. . . Yo le digo que se establezca; al menos nos valdría guita la manía de las instantáneas. . .

Romana y Miguel se instalaron cerca de la ventana, con un velador delante, y el fotógrafo de afición fue trayendo álbumes, cartera, envoltorios de papel —su tesoro. Los niños jugaban en la antesala; se oían sus voces, sus chillidos, su batalla con las cuatro sillas que les servían para improvisar un coche: allá, muy abajo, en la calle, poco transitada, rodaba algún simón, se alzaba algún pregón; el sol se ponía; un frío suave, ligero, cruzaba los vidrios, y las cabezas de Miguel y Romana se aproximaban involuntariamente, al inclinarse para mejor ver las pruebas.

—Mañana haré una instantánea de usted —declaró el aficionado.

—¿Dónde?

—¡Bah! En cualquier parte. . . En la calle. . . Cuando vaya usted a misa, a tiendas. . . Los mejores clichés son esos que se obtienen así, cogiendo al modelo descuidado. . .

Ignacia, que entraba en aquel momento, intervino:

—En la calle, no. ¡Qué tontería! Cruza un perro, cruza un golfo. . . ¡echa a perder la placa! Es más bonito en el Retiro, con el

After a month had passed, Calleja outdid himself and invited "that scamp" to come to dinner on Sundays. Romana noted, with cheerful admiration, that on that day her husband was transformed; he primped, he shaved carefully, clipping the four little hairs on his bald spot, and he put on his frock coat, an out-of-style antique. He topped off his satisfaction with the announcement that they had seats at the Lara Theater, where they finished up the evening marvelously entertained, laughing like fools at the wit and antics of Rodríguez.

Not long after, Ignacia's husband arrived in Madrid, and he was introduced to Romana. As always happens when a person has been talked about a great deal before the first meeting, their initial interaction was a bashful one. Miguel—that was the spouse's name—was around thirty. His little blond mustache and his red mouth gave him an even more youthful appearance. His face was soft, his skin fine, but his torso was solid and his legs agile and tense. On the second meeting, he confessed to Romana his only weakness, his only vice: a fondness for photography. Having a hobby on the side is expensive. No one knows what it costs—aside from the equipment—for plates, film, reagents, photographic papers, a thousand accessories. One thing was certain: he had run up quite a bill with Huertas and Franzen . . .

"Go on, show her your tricks," Ignacia exclaimed, like a person giving in to the whim of a child. "My dear, you'll soon see . . . I keep telling him to set up shop. At least his mania for taking pictures would earn us some cash."

Romana and Miguel set everything up near the window, with a pedestal table in front of them, and the amateur

fondo de los árboles sin hojas, que dices tú que hace tan fino... ¿No sabes? Como la que sacaste cuando éramos novios...

Se convino el sitio, la hora, todos los detalles. La mañana de aquél día Romana se levantó agitada, cual si esperase que algo extraordinario, algo desconocido, iba a aparecerse en su horizonte. Desde temprano se lavó, se peinó, se rizó, se acicaló, se puso su mejor traje, su sombrero más de moda. Luego, sin saber en qué invertir el tiempo que faltaba, dio por la casa mil vueltas; y de pronto, pensando que ya era tardísimo, descendió las escaleras precipitada y tomó un coche de punto. A la entrada del Retiro la esperaba, solo, el marido de su amiga. Ésta no había podido venir por no sé qué pupa del menor de los pequeños...

Era la mañanita una de las que el calumniado clima de Madrid ofrece como regalo divino: bañada de luz, de una luz rubia, vibrante, reanimadora, una luz que parecía que nunca iba a acabarse, que nunca transigiría con la noche. Las calles enarenadas y los arriates del Retiro convidaban a ejercitarse en pasear; las estatuas blancas, sin pedestal, destacándose de su alfombra de césped, parecían sugerir cosas recónditamente dulces, un misterio gozoso de la vida. La ramazón rojiza del arbolado desnudo de hoja formaba un fondo como de viejo guipur, y la masa sombría, intensamente verde, de las coníferas, realzaba aquellas delicadezas otoñales, contrastando con ellas de un modo brusco y vigoroso. De los macizos de arbustos ascendían perfumes de violetas tardías, y azules estrellitas de agerato miraban a Romana y Miguel, como miran las cándidas pupilas de los niños. No había un alma en el parque; la gloria matinal, la hermosura de un día tan radioso, pertenecía únicamente a la pareja, la cual podía creer que el

photographer began bringing albums, portfolios, paper envelopes—his treasure. The children were playing in the foyer. Their voices could be heard, their shrieks, their battle with the four chairs that served as a makeshift coach. There, way down below, in the sparsely traveled street, an occasional carriage rolled by and a street vendor cried out his wares. The sun was setting, a gentle light chill cut through the windowpanes, and Miguel's and Romana's heads were drawing closer, involuntarily, as they leaned over to get a better view of the proofs.

"Tomorrow I'll take a snapshot of you," the amateur photographer declared.

"Where?"

"Bah! Anywhere . . . In the street . . . When you go to mass, to the store . . . The best photos are those that you get just like that, catching the model unawares."

Ignacia, who was coming in at that moment, interjected: "Not in the street. What a foolish idea! A dog will walk through, a vagrant will pass by . . . it will spoil the plate! It's prettier in Retiro Park, with the bare trees as background, that you say make it so delicate . . . You know, like the one you took when we were engaged.

The place was agreed upon, the time, all the details. On the morning of that day Romana got up feeling agitated, as if she expected that something extraordinary, something unknown, was going to appear on her horizon. Beginning early she bathed, she combed her hair, she curled it, she primped, she put on her best outfit, her most fashionable hat. Then, without knowing how to spend the time she still had to wait; she took a thousand turns around the house. And suddenly, thinking that it was already terribly late, she rushed down the stairs in a great flurry and took a carriage for hire. At the entrance to the

cielo celebraba fiesta en su honor. Se sentaron en un banco. No sabían qué decirse. Al fin, Miguel, bromeando, entabló la conversación lírica, la que naturalmente fluye en la soledad, cuando escucha una mujer. Habló de amores, de cosas pasadas; disertó sobre lo que forma el único atractivo real y poderoso de la existencia. Aquello no era ofender a Romana, pues no era cortejarla. Un palique dulce, entretejido de recuerdos, una página de subjetivismo, la lectura en alta voz de una novela vivida. . . Miguel había querido mucho a una mujer; obstáculos invencibles le habían separado de ella, después de aventuras románticas, bonitas. . . y raras. . . Ya las referiría, ya. . . En una crisis de desaliento, para olvidar, fue cuando se casó con Ignacia.

—A usted se lo puedo contar, a usted, su mejor amiga. . . pero guárdeme el secreto. . . Esto entre los dos. . .

Romana prometía discreción, reserva absoluta. ¡El primer secretillo de amor que la fiaban! Un cosquilleo delicioso activaba en sus venas el curso de la sangre. . .

Al preguntar por la tarde Ignacia ¿qué tal el Retiro? Romana respondió, titubeando un poco:

—Divinamente. . . ¡Qué mañana! ¡Parecía de primavera! Sólo faltabas tú. . .

—Pues, serrana. . . yo a cada paso más sujeta. Entre los muñecos de carne y la enfermita. . . Pero me encanta que os hayáis divertido la mar. . . Paseítos así te convenien, hija; tienes hoy una cara que te la han hecho de nuevo. Hay que mirar por la salud. Cuando quieras, Miguel te acompañará. Me lo cuidas, ¿eh? Porque él es de la piel de Barrabás, y si no hay quien le llame al orden. . .

Y como el empleado protestase sonriendo, Ignacia insistió:

—Nada, nada, que te pongo a Romita de guardia civil. . .

Retiro, her friend's husband was waiting for her, alone. Ignacia had not been able to come on account of the youngest of the little ones, who was complaining of a tummyache or who knows what.

The early morning was one of those that the much-reviled climate of Madrid offers as a divine gift: bathed in light, in a golden, vibrant, exhilarating light, a light that seemed forever inexhaustible, that would never yield to the night. The Retiro's walkways and gravel-covered paths invited one to walk about for exercise. The white statues, without pedestals, standing out from their carpet of grass, seemed to suggest secretly sweet things, a joyful mystery of life. The reddish branchwork of the leafless trees formed a background that seemed to be made of old lace, and the shadowy mass, intensely green, of the conifers, heightened those fall delights, contrasting with them in a brusque and vigorous way. From the clusters of shrubs arose the fragrance of violet dahlias, and little blue stars of yarrow stared at Romana and Miguel, the way the guileless pupils of children stare. There wasn't a soul in the park. The glory of morning, the beauty of a day so radiant, belonged only to the couple, who might think the sky was celebrating a feast day in their honor. They sat down on a bench. They did not know what to say. Finally, Miguel, teasing, began the conversation, a lyrical exchange, the kind that flows naturally in an intimate setting when a woman is listening. He spoke of old loves, of things of the past. He waxed eloquent on what constitutes the only real and powerful enticement to existence. It was not offensive to Romana, since he was not courting her. A gentle bit of chatter, interwoven with memories, a page of subjectivity, the reading aloud of a novel that he had lived. Miguel had loved a woman very

Establecido así el *modus vivendi*, fue la existencia fácil y suave como el curso de un arroyo, y crecieron en sus márgenes florecillas y plantas frescas, tersas, lozaneadoras, cuyo color regocija el espíritu. Romana, poco a poco, recobró la salud, se puso inmejorable; una de esas curaciones que hacen decir a los doctores: "El efecto de la aeroterapia no se nota hasta el invierno". Lo extraño es que don Laureano, sin tomar más aires que los que descienden armados de navaja barbera de las altitudes del Guadarrama, también se mostró remozado, al menos en el genio y condición; volvióse expansivo y casi galante; su dinero, oculto por la parsimonia, sudoroso de fatiga al multiplicarse en negocios sórdidos, empezó a ostentarse, a relucir, a correr con argentinos choques, sonoros y limpios como una explosión de risa. El viejo, ¡qué maravilla! se abonó a landó y palco, señaló cantidades para trapos y moños, despidió a la cocinera por guisar mal—Ignacia solía dejar en el plato la blanqueta de gallina— y declaró a voces:

—¡Para el tiempo que hemos de vivir! Pasémoslo bien, ¿verdad, Romana?

Romana lo aprobaba todo. Por las tardes, largas ya, los dos matrimonios paseaban en coche descubierto; y si la esposa de Calleja tenía algún capricho especial y necesitaba cuartos, decía a su amiga:

—Mujer, Nacita, tú que entiendes mejor el carácter de Laureano, ¿eh?

Hacia mediados de abril espiró la tísica, cuya vida se prolongaba a fuerza de cuidados y de alimentos exquisitos. Ignacia se mudó a un piso mejor, que no le recordase tristezas, y llevó un luto elegante; primero crespón inglés, luego ríos de azabache y oleadas de encaje negro. Romita no manifestó extrañeza ante la prosperidad de su amiga; pero ésta la hizo confidencias en tono chancero...:

much. Invincible obstacles had separated him from her, after romantic adventures, lovely . . . and rare . . . In time he would relate them to her, in time . . . In a crisis of disheartenment, in order to forget, he married Ignacia.

"I can tell you, you, her best friend . . . but keep the secret for me. This is between the two of us."

Romana promised discretion, absolute reserve. The first little love secret that she had been entrusted with. A delicious tickling sensation sent her blood coursing through her veins.

When Ignacia asked in the afternoon, "How was Retiro Park?" Romana responded, stammering a bit: "Superb. What a morning. It seemed like spring! Only you were missing . . ."

"Well, my dear funny girl . . . with every step I'm more tied down. Between my little darlings and my poor ailing sister . . . But I'm delighted that you had such a wonderful time. Little excursions like that are good for you, my dear. Your face looks like it's been made anew. You have to look after your health. Whenever you wish, Miguel will accompany you. You'll keep an eye on him, won't you? Because he's a regular devil, and if there's no one to make him mind . . ."

And should the clerk offer any resistance, Ignacia, smiling, insisted: "It's nothing, nothing; I'm just assigning Romita to you as a Civil Guard . . ."

With the modus vivendi thus established, life was smooth and easy as the current of a stream, and on its banks grew little flowers and fresh plants, resplendent, luxuriant, whose color brought joy to the spirit. Little by little, Romana regained her health. She could not have been better. It was one of those miraculous recoveries that causes doctors to

—¿No te enteraste? Pues en la lotería de febrero me ha caído un premio regular. . . ¡Qué suertaza! Sí, serranita, unos cuantos miles de pesetas. . . Y yo pensé: ¿por qué no he de disfrutar algo? Bastantes privaciones he aguantado. . . El dinero es redondo. . .

—Has hecho perfectamente, —contestó Romana, acariciando a la empleadita.

Sin embargo, hacia el mes de julio, cuando empezaba a agitarse la cuestión de veraneo y a discutirse las ventajas de San Sebastián comparadas a las de Santander, Romana, a solas con su marido, sacando los pies del plato, indicó que debía preferirse una playa modesta.

—Si han de acompañarnos Ignacia y Miguel. . . —advirtió.— Ellos no son ricos. . . El gasto de dos matrimonios, uno de ellos con niños. . .

—¿Qué importa? —exclamó enfurruñado don Laureano. —Les ayudaremos. . ., al fin nosotros no tenemos hijos. . . ni esperanzas. . .

Romana se turbó, bajó los ojos y murmuró, sobando el lindo broche de strass de su cinturón grana:

—¿Quién sabe?

El viejo, inmóvil de sorpresa, la miraba de hito en hito. Al fin, halagado, envanecido, tendió las manos, atrajo hacia sí a su mujer, y la abrazó despacio, de un modo lento y profundo, mientras ella se ponía toda del color de su cinturón. Y ambos, al darse aquel abrazo, se sintieron dichosos, libres un instante del peso de la cruz.

declare: "No one notices the effect of fresh air therapy until winter." The strange thing is that Don Laureano, without taking any more fresh air than that which descends from the heights of the Guadarrama armed with its straight-edged razor, also appeared rejuvenated, at least in his mood and general state. He became expansive and almost gallant. His money, once hidden away by miserliness, sweaty with exhaustion from being multiplied in sordid business deals, began to make a show of itself, to shine, to flow with a silvery jingle-jangle, resonant as an explosion of laughter. The old man, what a marvel! He fortified himself with rides in the convertible carriage and box seats at the theater, he devoted large sums to fancy clothes and hairpieces, he dismissed the cook for preparing the food badly—Ignacia was in the habit of leaving the chicken stew on her plate—and he declared in a loud voice: "Here's to the time that we have to live! Let's spend it well, isn't that right, Romana?"

Romana approved of everything. In the afternoons, which were getting long now, the two couples went riding about in the carriage with the top down. And if Calleja's wife had some special fancy and needed spending money, she would say to her friend: "Hey, Nacita, you're the one who understands Laureano's character best . . . ?"

Toward the middle of April the ailing sister breathed her last. Her life had been prolonged by special attention and delicate food. Ignacia moved to a better apartment, so as not to be reminded of sad things, and she observed the period of mourning with elegance: first English crepe, then rivers of jet and waves of black lace. Romita did not exhibit any surprise in the face of her friend's prosperity. But

the latter confided in her in a playful tone: "You didn't hear about it? Well, I won a fairly decent prize in the February lottery . . . What a piece of luck! Yes, my friend, a few thousand pesetas . . . And I thought about it: Why shouldn't I have a little enjoyment? I've had my fill of hardship. Money is meant to be spent."

"You've done just fine," Romana answered, giving the clerk's wife an affectionate pat.

Nevertheless, toward the month of July, when the issue of summer vacation was beginning to be tossed around and the advantages of San Sebastián compared to those of Santander were in the initial stages of discussion, Romana, alone with her husband, getting up her courage, indicated that a simple beach resort should be given preference: "If Ignacia and Miguel are to accompany us . . . ," she warned. "They aren't rich. The cost of two couples, one of them with children . . ."

"What does it matter?" Don Laureano exclaimed grumpily. "We'll help them; after all, we don't have children . . . or any prospects."

Romana became flustered, lowered her eyes, and murmured, stroking the pretty rhinestone clasp on her scarlet red belt: "Who knows?"

The old man, frozen with surprise, stared at her from head to toe. Finally, feeling flattered and flushed with pride, he stretched out his hands, and pulled his wife toward him, embracing her leisurely, in a slow and poignant manner, while she turned the color of her belt. And both of them, sharing that embrace, felt blessed, free for a moment from the weight of the cross.

(Translated by Elaine Dorough Johnson)

Sources

Leonor López de Córdoba
Ayerbe-Chaux, Reinaldo. "Las memorias de doña Leonor López de Córdoba," *Journal of Hispanic Philology* 2 (1977): 11-33.

Florencia Pinar
Cancionero general de Hernando del Castillo from the 1511 edition. 2 vols. Madrid: Sociedad de Bibliófilos Españoles, 1882.

Teresa de Cartagena
Arboleda de los enfermos. Admiración operum Dey, ed. Lewis J. Hutton. *Boletín de la Real Academia Española,* suplemento 16. Madrid: Real Academia Española, 1967.

Saint Teresa de Ávila
Libro de la Vida, vol. 1 in *Obras,* ed. P. Siverio de Santa Teresa. Burgos: Biblioteca Mística Carmelita, 1915.

Luisa Sigea
Antología de poetisas líricas, vol. 1, ed. Manuel de Serrano y Sanz. Madrid: Real Academia Española, 1915.

Beatriz Bernal
Don Cristalián de España. Alcalá de Henares: Casa de Juan Íñiguez de Lequerica, Impresor de Libros, 1587.

Sor María de la Antigua
Antología de poetisas líricas, vol. 1, ed. Manuel de Serrano y Sanz. Madrid: Real Academia Española, 1915.

Leonor de la Cueva y Silva
Antología de poetisas líricas, vol. 1, ed. Manuel de Serrano y Sanz. Madrid: Real Academia Española, 1915.

María de Zayas y Sotomayor
Desengaños amorosos. Parte segunda del sarao y entretenimiento honesto, ed. Agustín G. de Amezúa. Madrid: Aldus, 1950.

Ana Caro Mallén de Soto
"Ana Caro Mallén de Soto, *Valor, agravio y mujer,*" ed. Luisa F. Foley. M.A. thesis, Temple University, 1977. Serrano y Sanz, Manuel. *Apuntes para una biblioteca de escritoras españolas desde el año 1401 al 1833,* vol. 1. Madrid: Real Academia Española, 1903; repr. 1975.

Sor Marcela de San Félix
Serrano y Sanz, Manuel. *Apuntes para una biblioteca de escritoras españolas desde el año 1401 al 1833,* vol. 1. Madrid: Real Academia Española, 1903; repr. 1975.

Sor María de Santa Isabel
Antología de poetisas líricas, vol. 1, ed. Manuel de Serrano y Sanz. Madrid: Real Academia Española, 1915 (poems).
Serrano y Sanz, Manuel. *Apuntes para una biblioteca de escritoras españolas desde el año 1401 al 1833,* vol. 2. Madrid: Real Academia Española, 1905; repr. 1975 ("A quien leyere estos versos").

Catalina Clara de Guzmán
Antología de poetisas líricas, vol. 1, ed. Manuel de Serrano y Sanz. Madrid: Real Academia Española, 1915 ("Romance pintando el invierno").
Serrano y Sanz, Manuel. *Apuntes para una biblioteca de escritoras españolas desde el año 1401 al 1833,* vol 1. Madrid: Real Academia Española, 1903; repr. 1975 (other poems).

María Gertrudis Hore
Poetas líricos del siglo XVIII, ed. M. Rivadeneyra. *Biblioteca de autores españoles,* vol. 3. Madrid, 1875.

Margarita Hicky y Pellizoni

Antología de poetisas líricas, vol. 2, ed. Manuel de Serrano y Sanz. Madrid: Real Academia Española, 1915.

Fernán Caballero

Caballero, Fernán. *Relaciones,* Madrid: A. Romero, 1907.

Carolina Coronado

Coronado, Carolina. *Poesías,* 1852 ("¿A dónde estáis consuelos de mi alma?" "La poetisa en un pueblo," "A España," "Libertad").

Fonseca Ruiz, Isabel. "Cartas de Carolina Coronado a Hartzenbusch," *Homenaje a Guillermo Gustavino*: 179-80 ("Quintillas").

Sandoval, Adolfo de. *Carolina Coronado y su época.* Zaragoza: Librería General, 1944 ("A la abolición de la esclavitud en Cuba").

Semanario Pintoresco Español 12 (March 24, 1850): 89-94 ("Los genios gemelos: Safo y Santa Teresa de Jesús").

Semanario Pintoresco Español 46 (November 17, 1850): 367-368 ("En el Castillo de Salvatierra").

Rosalía de Castro

Obras completas, ed. Xesús Alonso Montero, vol. 2, Biblioteca de Autores Gallegos. Santiago de Compostela: Ediciones Sálvora, 1983.

Emilia Pardo Bazán

Pardo Bazán, Emilia. *Sud-expres.* Madrid: Pueyo, 1909.

Amy Katz Kaminsky is professor of women's studies at the University of Minnesota. She is the author of *Reading the Body Politic: Latin American Women Writers and Feminist Criticism* (Minnesota, 1993).